The publisher and the University of California Press Foundation
gratefully acknowledge the generous support of the
Joan Palevsky Imprint in Classical Literature.

The Rich and the Pure

TRANSFORMATION OF THE CLASSICAL HERITAGE
Peter Brown, General Editor

The Rich and the Pure

*Philanthropy and the Making of Christian
Society in Early Byzantium*

———

Daniel Caner

UNIVERSITY OF CALIFORNIA PRESS

University of California Press
Oakland, California

© 2021 by Daniel Caner

Library of Congress Cataloging-in-Publication Data

Names: Caner, Daniel, author.
The rich and the pure : philanthropy and the making of Christian society
    in early Byzantium / Daniel Caner.
Other titles: Transformation of the classical heritage ; 62.
Description: Oakland, California : University of California Press, [2021] |
    Series: Transformation of the classical heritage ; LXII | Includes
    bibliographical references and index.
Identifiers: LCCN 2020046809 (print) | LCCN 2020046810 (ebook) |
    ISBN 9780520381582 (cloth) | ISBN 9780520381599 (ebook)
Subjects: LCSH: Charity—Religious aspects—Christianity. | Byzantine
    Empire—Social aspects—To 527. | Byzantine Empire—Social
    aspects—527–1081.
Classification: LCC BV4639 .C2625 2021 (print) | LCC BV4639 (ebook) |
    DDC 261.8/32094950902—dc23
LC record available at https://lccn.loc.gov/2020046809
LC ebook record available at https://lccn.loc.gov/2020046810

Manufactured in the United States of America

25   24   23   22   21
10   9   8   7   6   5   4   3   2   1

For Emma

CONTENTS

ACKNOWLEDGMENTS

This book is a product of slow scholarship. The idea for it came to me in 2008, but the core research goes back to 2003. Much has happened since then that prevented me from finishing it more quickly, but I found the work so absorbing that I also prolonged it as long as possible.

I am indebted to several institutions for time and support. First and foremost, this is a Dumbarton Oaks book, since it was born out of use of the Dumbarton Oaks Research Library in 2004–2005 and was finished there in 2018–2019. I thank all of my fellow Fellows for their collegiality and humor in both years. I subsequently benefited greatly from an invitation to join Miriam Fraenkel and Jacob Lev's Research Group on Charitable Giving in the Monotheistic Religions at Hebrew University's Institute for Advanced Study in Jerusalem in spring of 2007. A visiting position during 2011–2012 at New York University's Institute for the Study of the Ancient World resulted in an unforeseen chapter on charity. A sabbatical at Monash University's School of Political and Social Inquiry in 2014 prompted me to recast the whole project more broadly as a study of early Christian philanthropy. A National Endowment for the Humanities fellowship funded a crucial period of writing in 2015–2016.

I am grateful to the directors, trustees, and senior scholars at these institutions who gave me those opportunities, to the mentors and colleagues who wrote so many letters of recommendation, and to American taxpayers who unwittingly footed part of the bill. Anthony Kaldellis and Reyhan Durmaz each commented on chapters, while Dina Boero read a draft of the whole manuscript—an exemplary gesture of collegiality that greatly improved it. Janet Timbie, Reyhan Durmaz, and Erin Walsh helped with Coptic and Syriac matters. Hal Drake, Susanna

Elm, and Claudia Rapp provided generous review comments, and Peter Brown and Eric Schmidt helped me reformulate the introductory parts. For all its errors and shortcomings, I am of course alone responsible.

Two scholars I want to thank in particular. Susan Ashbrook Harvey not only provided me with an intellectual community in southeastern New England for over fifteen years through her Providence Patristics Group and our annual summertime lunches, but she also prompted me to write the book in the first place with a casual observation made in February 2008. Ilana Friedrich Silber, whom I met at Hebrew University's Institute for Advanced Study in 2007, challenged me to think about gift giving with greater sophistication than I ever would have done otherwise, raising questions I have tried to answer here. The attention and encouragement that both gave me I consider tantamount to a godsend.

WHAT IS A CHRISTIAN GIFT?

Studying gift giving is perennially fascinating. It not only reveals a society's ethical priorities and valued relationships, but also invites us to contemplate the possibility of human kindness and the wellsprings of generosity or gratitude more generally. Not all cultures promote the same gift ideals, customs, or instincts. Today we tend to speak of "gifts" in generic fashion, without using more specific terms, as if our main concern were to differentiate things or favors given as such from those used to make purchases or advance our careers. The people we will meet in this book were similarly concerned to distinguish genuine gift giving from "worldly" exchanges, favors, or transactions. Yet, as inhabitants of a premodern world in which basic economic activities were closely intertwined with social interactions, and as adherents of a religion that was novel in its espousal of self-sacrificial ideals, Christians of the late Roman world recognized a variety of gifts and gift-giving relationships, all of which supported, directly or indirectly, a new, religious conception of philanthropy. This book studies these ancient Christian gift ideals and the relationships they were meant to foster. It seeks to understand not only the religious and social ideals they were meant to support, but also the society in which they evolved—namely, Early Byzantium, the late Roman Empire of the East, the first truly affluent, complex Christian society.

Following an introduction to themes, sources, and methods, we will survey, in chapter 1, historical developments particular to the Roman East that I deem important for understanding the social and cultural circumstances in which Christian philanthropy took shape and evolved. Thereafter, in chapters 2 through 7, we will turn to the meaning and practice of early Christian philanthropy itself, its roots in classical culture, and its articulation through five different Christian gift ideals. Each of these chapters is devoted to a particular ideal. Central to the book, both conceptually and organizationally, is a gift known as a "blessing." Because this is the least familiar of all the gift ideals studied here, and in order to describe the conceptual lineage of the book as a whole, let me explain how I came upon this topic and thus to gift giving as a means of studying early Christian philanthropy more generally. Anyone not interested in such discussions should feel free to skip directly to the introduction.

While writing *Wandering Begging Monks*, a book about radical notions of apostolic poverty in the late Roman Empire, I repeatedly found the Greek word *eulogia*, "blessing," used to describe material gifts given to monastery visitors. Following previous scholarship, I understood this as a synonym for "alms" (i.e., *eleēmosynē*). That translation never seemed correct, however, since such "blessings" included many objects, such as pieces of scripture given as parting gifts, that are not usually associated with almsgiving. A survey I subsequently made of all references to *eulogiai* in Greek hagiography written between the fourth and seventh centuries confirmed my doubts. My survey revealed not only that the settings, purposes, and resources associated with Christian blessings consistently differed from those associated with Christian alms, but also that references to material blessings far outnumbered references to alms, especially in hagiography written in the Holy Land between the sixth and seventh centuries.[1] Furthermore, it showed that hagiographers repeatedly depicted such blessings as a means of fulfilling one of the most demanding challenges associated with ancient Christian philanthropy: namely, Jesus's command to "give to all who ask" (Mt 5:42, Lk 6:30). What, then, was the origin and significance of such gifts? And why did they become so prominent in church and monastic literature written from the fifth century onward, especially in the Holy Land?

Because at the time I was reading Leslie Kurke's *Coins, Bodies, Games, and Gold: The Politics of Meaning in Archaic Greece*, which deals in part with competing types of valuation and currencies during a transitional phase of ancient Greek history, my research turned, as had hers, to anthropological work on the emergence of pure gift ideals in developing countries. Foremost among these was Jonathan Parry's well-known article "*The Gift*, the Indian Gift, and the 'Indian Gift,'" on unreciprocated gifts used to support holy people among Hindus in southern India. Noting that Marcel Mauss's seminal 1924 study, "Essai sur le don," had often been misunderstood to mean that there could be no such thing as a nonreciprocal or disinterested gift, Parry sought to account for the existence of such ideals in the donative customs practiced by Brahman holy people and their supporters. He concluded that the otherworldly aspirations of these ascetics, together with their concern for purity and dependence on lay supporters for sustenance, resulted in the emergence of a concept of a pure gift—a category of religious gift called *dāna*—

that was considered distinct from, while remaining dependent upon, more mundane modes of commerce and exchange. Conceived as a means by which Hindu laypeople could divest themselves of sins while feeding their spiritual exemplars, such *dāna* and related practices evolved in dialectical contrast to other gifts (such as those given as dowries) or currencies that explicitly betokened some sort of transaction, those for which some sort of return was expected. Parry concluded that a similar phenomenon might be found in other religious cultures featuring a comparable ascetic emphasis and "other-worldly orientation." "The more radical the opposition between this world and a world free from suffering to come," he wrote, "the more inevitable is the development of a contemptus mundi which culminates in the institution of renunciation but of which the charitable gift—as a kind of lay exercise in asceticism—is also often an expression."[2]

Parry's insight that "pure" gift ideals are often by-products of religious asceticism has been corroborated by James Laidlaw's studies of gift giving among the Jains.[3] Such ideals, it has been emphasized, "have nothing to do with ordinary social relationships."[4] Parry presumed that the closest equivalent in Christian culture to the Hindu *dāna* was a gift of alms, at least until Christian almsgiving became identified as a "purchase price of salvation"—a historical development he placed in the third century.[5] My research, however, revealed that the Christian blessing provided a closer parallel. At the same time I found that certain facets of this Christian ideal made it a symbol of sacred wealth, providing a key to studying positive notions of material wealth in ancient Christianity more generally.[6]

One reason for writing the present book was my need to understand how such blessings fit in with other Christian gifts of the era. The very existence of this unfamiliar Christian gift ideal raised questions about how it differed from more familiar ideals like alms and offerings. It also forced me to refine my vague understanding of those gifts themselves. At this point I happened to meet Ilana Silber, whose brilliant 1995 article "Gift-Giving in the Great Traditions: The Case of Donations to Monasteries in the Medieval West" examined the shifting nature of religious gift categories in Western medieval monasteries. Building on Parry, Annette Weiner, and others, she pointed out the inherent instability of all such categories, and stressed the need to understand them as a "total social fact."[7] Derived from Mauss, this sociological approach posits that no gift phenomenon can be properly understood apart from the social and ideological web that contextualizes and supports it, any change of which might cause the gift ideal itself to change, or to fall into abeyance. Inspired by Natalie Zemon Davis's *The Gift in Sixteenth-Century France,* Silber went on to study how religious gifts differed in purpose and properties depending on their intended recipients. Regarding monotheist traditions, she proposed that we distinguish "sacrificial" gifts given to gods from "sacerdotal" gifts given to religious leaders or their institutions, and both of these from "caritative" gifts given to the poor or needy.[8] I follow that scheme here roughly in reverse order, exploring the articulation of Christian philanthropy first through the caritative (but also sacrificial) gifts of alms and charity, then through the sacerdotal (but also caritative) gift of blessings, then through two types of sacrificial (but also caritative and sacerdotal) gifts known as fruitbearings and liturgical offerings.

"Alms," "charity," "blessings," "fruitbearings," and "offerings" are the English words I have found convenient to translate the Greek words *eleēmosynē, agapē, eulogiai, karpophoriai,* and *prosphorai* throughout this book. Each designates a category of Christian gift. I have chosen to study these gift categories both because they are the ones most frequently attested in Early Byzantine literary and documentary sources (Greek being the dominant language of the Christian elite in the late Roman East) and because they have consistent counterparts, if not equivalents, in Syriac (*zedqē, rhem, burktā, y(h)ab pērē,* and *qurbānē*) and Coptic (*mntna, me, smou, tikarpos/tioutah,* and *prosphora*).[9] Others might have chosen to focus on different gifts, and I have deliberately chosen not to discuss *charis,* "favor" or "grace," an essential but still rather vague notion that seems to have referred in Early Byzantium to a divine gift that underlies and energizes everything else.[10] Apart from alms and offerings, scholars have usually treated the categories I have chosen (especially alms and charity) either synonymously or without differentiation.[11] To be sure, each ideal shares caritative, sacerdotal, or sacrificial aspects of at least one of the others in the spectrum. This is not surprising: as Silber and others maintain, gift ideals are inherently unstable,[12] and we will see that "offerings" could be turned into "alms" or "blessings," or "alms" into "charity," depending on how they were given or handled. Yet as noted above, each category was associated with a distinct set of goals, responsibilities, relationships, and material resources.

The book is grounded in what might be called philological research. The data-mining capacities of the Thesaurus linguae graecae online search engine enabled me to collect all passages in Early Byzantine literature that contained one or more of the Greek terms under discussion and generate a distinct profile of each. While doing this, I especially sought to ascertain which term was or was not being used in a particular genre (e.g., homiletic, hagiographical, epistolary) as well as what types of donors or recipients (e.g., rich, poor, laypeople, holy people) were usually associated with each. This laid the foundation for my historical approach. Although I have not conceived this book as a word study, each chapter focuses on the discourses and dynamics related to a specific term and its related concerns. I have sought to reproduce the terminological consistency of the Early Byzantine sources by consistently using throughout the book the same English word (*philanthropy, alms, charity, blessing, fruitbearing,* or *offering*) when referring to a particular term and idea, and by using only that particular word when its corresponding term is used in the original. In this way I hope to make clear what specific terms and ideals were under discussion in any particular ancient instance or context.

Of course, Early Byzantine literature does not always allow me to discern or draw sharp distinctions. Christian authors in this era often used more generic words to describe gifts more broadly (e.g., δῶρα, *dona, mawhabta, ntaeio*) or had legal terms for formal acts of donation (δωρεά, *donatio*).[13] Context sometimes enables us to infer that a more specific gift ideal was probably meant, but in many cases that remains unclear. Nor can we know how far the distinctions drawn by elite authors would have been meaningful to casual Christians "on the street." Yet it is important to recognize when Early Byzantine writers were being specific, especially since their choice of language is, indeed, remarkably consistent.[14] Like the classical Greeks, the Old Testament Jews, and the later rabbis with their rich vocabularies for sacrifices and good works,[15] or like the proverbial Eskimos with their multiple words for snow, Christian authorities of this era developed a fairly broad but specific repertoire of words to distinguish their gift ideals, practices, and concerns.

Finally, it is in the nature of the subject that, while some will look at depictions of gift giving and think of generosity, others will think of manipulation, exploitation, obfuscation, or deceit.[16] This was as true in Early Byzantium as it is today, and in the following pages I try to take all possibilities into account. Yet my primary interest is to understand the positive significance of these ideals, some of which, like charity and philanthropy, are still espoused today. Again, one goal of this book—albeit at risk of historical essentialism—is to clarify what these ideals actually meant to people living in this first complex and affluent Christian society.

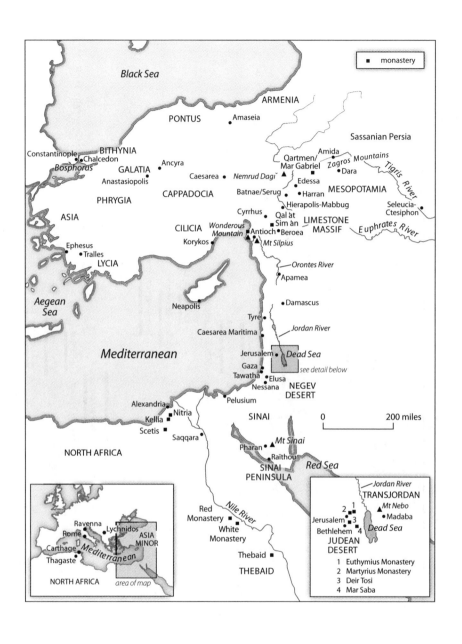

Black Sea

ARMENIA

PONTUS • Amaseia

Sassanian Persia

Constantinople • BITHYNIA • Chalcedon
Bosphorus GALATIA • Ancyra
Anastasiopolis

Amida
Qartmen/ *Zagros Mountains*
Mar Gabriel • Dara
Tigris River

Caesarea • Nemrud Daği ▲
Edessa

PHRYGIA CAPPADOCIA
Batnae/Serug • Harran
MESOPOTAMIA
Hierapolis-Mabbug
Seleucia-Ctesiphon •

ASIA
Cyrrhus • Qal'at
Sim'an LIMESTONE
Euphrates River

CILICIA Wonderous
Mountain ▲ Antioch • Beroea MASSIF
Korykos • ▲ Mt Silpius

Ephesus
• Tralles
LYCIA

• Orontes River

Neapolis • Apamea

*Aegean
Sea*

• Damascus

Tyre •
Caesarea Maritima • *Jordan River*

Mediterranean

Jerusalem • □ *Dead Sea*
Gaza • *see detail below*
Tawatha • Elusa
Nessana • NEGEV
DESERT

Alexandria • Pelusium

Kellia • ■ Nitria SINAI

Scetis ■
Saqqara •
NORTH AFRICA

0   200 miles

Pharan • ▲ *Mt Sinai*
Raïthou •
SINAI *Red Sea*
PENINSULA

■ monastery

■ (legend box)

Inset (lower left):
Ravenna •
Rome • Lychnidos • ASIA
MINOR
Carthage • *Mediterranean*
Thagaste •
NORTH AFRICA   *area of map*

Red
Monastery ■ *Nile River*
White
Monastery ■

Thebaid ■
THEBAID

Inset (lower right):
Jordan River
TRANSJORDAN
2 ■ 1 ▲ *Mt Nebo*
Jerusalem ■ ■ 3 • Madaba
Bethlehem • 4 *Dead Sea*
JUDEAN
DESERT
1 Euthymius Monastery
2 Martyrius Monastery
3 Deir Tosi
4 Mar Saba

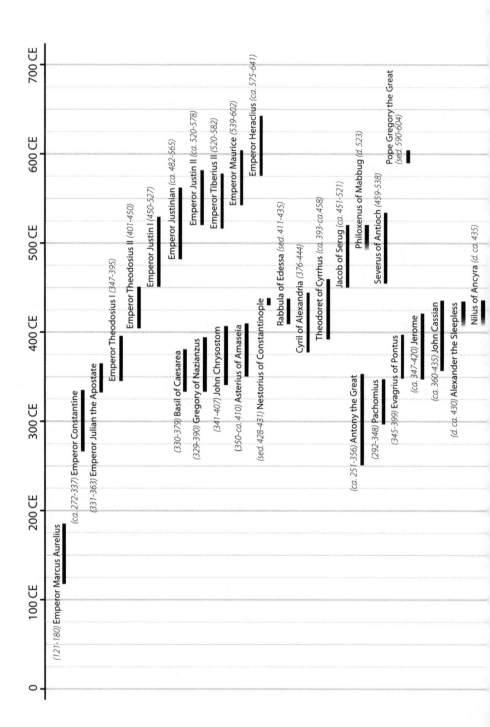

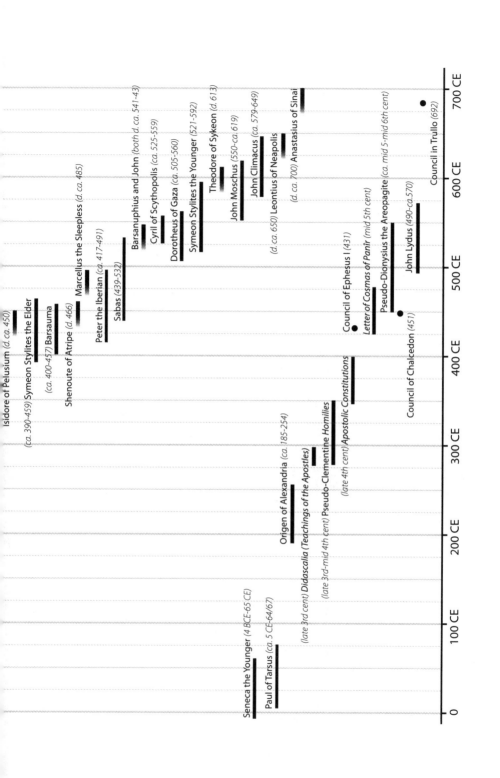

Seneca the Younger (4 BCE–65 CE)

Paul of Tarsus (ca. 5 CE–64/67)

(late 3rd cent) Didascalia (Teachings of the Apostles)

(late 3rd–mid 4th cent) Pseudo-Clementine Homilies

Origen of Alexandria (ca. 185–254)

(late 4th cent) Apostolic Constitutions

Isidore of Pelusium (d. ca. 450)

(ca. 390–459) Symeon Stylites the Elder

(ca. 400–457) Barsauma

Shenoute of Atripe (d. 466)

Marcellus the Sleepless (d. ca. 485)

Peter the Iberian (ca. 417–491)

Sabas (439–532)

Barsanuphius and John (both d. ca. 541–43)

Cyril of Scythopolis (ca. 525–559)

Dorotheus of Gaza (ca. 505–560)

Symeon Stylites the Younger (521–592)

Theodore of Sykeon (d. 613)

John Moschus (550–ca. 619)

John Climacus (ca. 579–649)

(d. ca. 650) Leontius of Neapolis

(d. ca. 700) Anastasius of Sinai

Council of Ephesus I (431)

Letter of Cosmas of Panir (mid 5th cent)

Pseudo-Dionysius the Areopagite (ca. mid 5–mid 6th cent)

John Lydus (490–ca.570)

Council of Chalcedon (451)

Council in Trullo (692)

0   100 CE   200 CE   300 CE   400 CE   500 CE   600 CE   700 CE

Introduction

This book is a social and cultural history about the evolution of Christian philanthropy, the rise of sacred wealth, and the motives for religious giving in the late Roman Empire of the East, circa 350–650 CE. Also known as Early Byzantium, this time and place produced history's first truly affluent, multifaceted Christian society. As the Pax Romana broke down in Western Europe during the fifth century, the core of long-term stability and prosperity moved decisively eastward: in years traditionally known for "decline and fall," the Mediterranean Near East rose to unprecedented heights under the aegis of New Rome. By the sixth century it was the biggest polity in western Eurasia. Centered in Constantinople (a.k.a. ancient Byzantium or modern Istanbul), its administrative and ecclesiastical superstructures connected cities and countrysides ranging from Greece and the Balkans to Mesopotamia, Egypt, and Libya. The approximately twenty-four million people living in this vast expanse, now all ruled as Roman citizens, were as diverse as the landscape itself. One way that imperial and church leaders sought to unify them from the fourth century onward was under a Christianized ideology of *philanthrōpia*, "love of humanity."

The monotheist version of that ancient ideal espoused the extension of at least some form of aid to all human beings, no matter what their origin, status or lack of demonstrable merit. It therefore provided an unusually inclusive basis for promoting what might be called the Common Good. Yet it arose in a society marked by sharp gradations of aristocratic rank and privilege, which, following the conversion of Constantine, the first Christian emperor (r. 306–337), were gradually extended to professional Christians—that is, clerics and monks. The latter also enjoyed unprecedented prosperity in this period, thanks to their perceived

1

sanctity, subsidies from the state, and a surge of lay gifts. This raises intriguing historical and ethical questions: How did church and monastic leaders propose to put a universal extension of philanthropy into practice? How did they reconcile their newfound wealth with an older ideology of Christian leadership and holiness based on material renunciations? How, in particular, did they negotiate the potentially corrupting influence of gifts in the "oily, present-giving world" of Early Byzantium?[1]

I argue that the idea of universal philanthropy was taken seriously enough in Early Byzantium to force Christian authorities—not only, but especially monastic authorities—to think hard about the manner, methods, and materials by which they gave, as well as about their relationships and responsibilities toward other people. One result was that, by the sixth century, philanthropy came to be articulated in the Roman East by five distinct modes of religious giving: alms, charity, blessings, fruitbearing offerings (e.g., firstfruits), and liturgical offerings. Each of these gift ideals reflected different purposes, practices, resources, and relationships; the last three also came to be identified with the creation of sacred wealth. By exploring how each was promoted and depicted in contemporary sermons, letters, and literature, my purpose is to clarify what each meant and how each differed from the others. I also seek to explain how these ideals evolved in relation to concerns of holy people or laypeople and shaped their interactions. If a basic purpose of any gift is to establish or symbolize a relationship, what relationships were established, symbolized, or transcended by these different modes of gift giving? How, in other words, were religious gifts used to shape an ideal social order in a newly Christian world?

We will see that all these gifts were interrelated. Indeed, inasmuch as offerings could be used to generate blessings, and blessings could provide resources to give alms, all facilitated the practice of universal philanthropy espoused by Christian professionals. Nonetheless, we will see that each came to be identified with different types of material resources (e.g., superfluous resources, essential resources, justly or unjustly acquired resources) and was thought to foster a different relationship—different in terms of duration, or giver or recipient involved, or type of services and responsibilities implied. We will furthermore find that these ideals, like that of Christian philanthropy itself, were shaped not only by religious concerns but by imperial and secular norms. Studying them therefore enables us to explore how people interacted and how ideas were generated at different levels: from top to bottom, bottom to top, and among peers. I aim to provide a composite description of how the "macro" and "micro" layers of this society were linked, and how these social linkages influenced the formation of some of its ethics and ideals.

One purpose of this project is to raise the visibility of an ideologically important, if numerically marginal, new social layer within the Roman Empire—namely, its monastic population. Because most of my sources originated in monasteries and were written about monks or related Christian "holy people,"[2] it is crucial that my readers know about them and what was expected of them. But I have also chosen to focus on this group because their contribution to Early Byzantine society and Christian ideas is largely absent from modern histories of this era. "A cruel unfeeling temper has distinguished the monks of every age," Edward Gibbon opined, to quote just one of the many caricatures he used to introduce the phenomenon of Christian monasticism in his *Decline and Fall of the Roman Empire*.[3] Few would express such contempt today, yet monasticism, despite being the last great social experiment in the ancient world (as well as the most successful, and the one we know most about), still remains largely neglected in modern explorations of the challenges that accompanied the promotion of Christian ideals in the Roman Empire, even as a foil. This neglect is detrimental not only to understanding this Christian society itself but also to appreciating a key aspect of the transformation of the classical heritage. For, as Judith Herrin observes, "The gradual establishment of a social order devoted to those who pray . . . completed the Christianisation of the ancient world."[4]

In the Roman East, this new social order became especially focused on monks—considered "those who pray" par excellence—and gained great momentum in the fifth and sixth centuries. During this period Christian monasticism became a recognized lifestyle and viable professional choice, with accompanying rewards and demands. It also grew alongside mainstream society and responded to some of its basic concerns, if often in new and unusual ways. Following the lead of Évelyne Patlagean and her landmark 1977 study, *Pauvreté économique et pauvreté sociale à Byzance, 4ᵉ–7ᵉ siècles*, I hope to make particularly clear the importance of monasteries (as opposed to churches) as nodes for the circulation of material and spiritual wealth from the fifth century onward. This offers a counterpoint to the emphasis that is often placed exclusively on urban bishops as inventors of a Christian response to the civic traditions of public benefactions that had been such a hallmark of the classical age. Regrettably, I have not been able to give ancient Jewish traditions the attention they deserve, although it is clear that rabbinic notions of almsgiving and "righteousness" provide parallels or antecedents to certain early Christian traditions, and that Jewish authorities were equally concerned to find alternatives to the civic traditions of patronal gift giving found in Greek and Roman societies.[5] Nonetheless, my aim is to look as broadly as possible beyond the usual urban aristocrats, toward more "middling" Christian sites and actors—including those people who, in this era for the first time, started to adopt monasticism, fire imaginations, and attract aristocratic patronage in sizeable numbers. Ultimately, this book is about people and their religious aspirations as much as about philanthropic gifts and their religious meanings.

Finally, it is crucial to understand the imperial ecology and environment that nurtured the Christian ideals studied here. "Early Byzantium" is a convenient modern shorthand for describing both the territorial polity established in the Mediterranean Near East by the division of the Roman Empire into eastern and western halves at the death of Emperor Theodosius in 395 (a polity that would survive, in various forms, well into the medieval "Byzantine" period) and the cultural synthesis of Roman imperial government, classical forms, and Christian ideals that arose within it from the fourth to the seventh centuries. One of its defining, underlying features was a new emphasis on religion as a basis for social unity. This was rooted in the Antonine Constitution of 212, when Emperor Caracalla bestowed citizenship on all the empire's free provincial subjects, extending it to virtually everyone, well beyond the army veterans and urban elites previously favored. The consequences of this decision can be hard to detect outside the religious and legal spheres. Nonetheless, it appears that rulers increasingly recognized their responsibility to explain how their policies benefitted all the empire's free population, most of whom now lived outside the traditional centers of imperial benefactions.[6] Constantine's adoption of monotheism aside, this need to universalize the benefits of Roman rule was arguably a factor behind the Early Byzantine promotion of philanthropy as a unifying imperial ideal.

But it was the imperial adoption and promotion of Christian monotheism that most clearly defined the distinctive political and cultural entity we call Early Byzantium. One of its hallmarks was an increasingly close integration of church and state. The resulting mixture of sacred and profane was often problematic and never complete. I call Early Byzantium history's first complex Christian society, not because other early Christian communities existed without complications (one only need look at the situation of Christians at the time in the "pagan" Persian Empire next door),[7] nor because it sought to promote Christianity among all its citizens, from top to bottom (the late Roman Empire of the West and its successor kingdoms did so too). I call it "complex" because throughout this period it featured an imperial superstructure that existed on top of traditional aristocracies, urban councils, and provincial governorships, as well as the new ecclesiastical and monastic institutions. This overarching superstructure and its attendant aristocracy had its own patterns of public giving that weighed on Christian imaginations and stimulated notions of religious gift giving. It is true that Early Byzantium changed over time—some would say that it became simpler due to Justinianic administrative streamlining and other factors during the sixth century. Yet, because no major political crisis interrupted its development until the seventh century, we can trace the evolution of Christian ideals within this imperial framework for some three hundred and fifty years, from the conversion of Constantine to the Arab Conquests. Of course, no attempt to explore any complex society can hope to be comprehensive, especially one marked by competing Christianities as well as lingering Jewish and pagan ideals. Nonetheless, I have sought to portray Early Byzantine society as much as possible "in the round." Apart from being necessary for the subject, I hope to set this distant era, its people, and utility for historical inquiry more fully in the minds of modern readers.

SURVIVING SOURCES AND HISTORICAL DISCOURSES

Who were those people? We get a glimpse of the social and economic complexity that could be found even in minor Early Byzantine towns from the fifth- and sixth-century tombstones at Korykos, an unspectacular fishing port along the coast of southern Asia Minor. Besides the imperial, civic, and ecclesiastical officials who make up a quarter of the total (church clerics comprise 16.8 percent), their epitaphs mention sailmakers, netmakers, shipwrights, assorted traders, bootmakers, tailors, granary guards, doctors, bakers, tavern keepers, singers, bankers, money changers (these had their own cemetery), potters, machinists, gem engravers, glaziers, and many more.[8] Numbering 456 in all, these inscriptions offer the kind of raw demographic sampling that modern historians might expect to find serving as the basis of a social history. But rarely do we find anything else like it, especially in our literary sources. Compare a description written by John Moschus early in the seventh century. For him, a typical Christian community consisted of

> city and country folk, natives, migrants; all who travel by land or sail the sea; men, women, the elderly and infants, youths and adults; masters and slaves; rich people and poor people; rulers and ruled; wise and simpletons; clergy, virgins, ascetics, widows, and the honorably married; magistrates and landlords.[9]

It might be said that Moschus was just trying to be comprehensive. Yet his sketch reveals a social vision limited not merely to generic categories but to a binary way of thinking whereby mentioning one group immediately brought to mind its opposite. This is the mentality, and the imagined components of Early Byzantine society, with which we will be mainly dealing here.

As historians of Byzantium know, our sources are largely limited to the range preserved by medieval Orthodox monastic scribes after the sack of Constantinople in 1204. These selected a few ancient authors to reproduce and discarded the rest. As a result, we have hundreds of homilies by Greek preachers of the late fourth and early fifth century who were later considered "Hierarchs" of Byzantine Orthodoxy (Basil of Caesarea, Gregory of Nazianzus, and John Chrysostom), but little else written on ethical subjects unless saved under their names.[10] Treatises on ascetic and theological subjects abound, but there are few on church administration, and none on any gift category discussed in this book. Few letter collections survive, and those that do rarely preserve two sides of an exchange. It is therefore impossible to follow the flow of ideas among high-profile personalities over successive generations as Peter Brown has masterfully done for Western Europe in his *Through the Eye of a Needle: Wealth, the Fall of Rome, and the Making of Christianity in the West, 350–550 AD.*[11] By contrast, historians of Early Byzantium must pick through a scattering of monoliths, archetypes, and sherds.

But all is not lost. Besides imperial laws, church manuals, and monastic rules addressing conditions and explaining expected norms and concerns, we have papyri and inscriptions from church and monastic sites that surpass any documentary evidence available for the West. We have secular and church histories written in Greek and Syriac from the fifth to the seventh centuries, the likes of which have not survived in Latin. Moreover, in addition to Greek preaching, we have homilies and sermons written in Syriac by Jacob of Serug and in Coptic by Shenoute of Atripe.[12] We also have the fifth-century letters of the priest-monk Isidore of Pelusium and the sixth-century letters of the ascetic recluses Barsanuphius and John. The latter were written on a variety of issues to monks, clerics, and laypeople in southern Palestine, and, for my purposes, have truly been a gift that keeps on giving.

Above all there is Christian hagiography. By this I mean narratives meant to depict, define, and commemorate human holiness. It is true that hagiography is a normative genre that presents an idealized world in which prayer made everything possible, and it is true that hagiographers depicted gift giving to cast their Christian exemplars and pious supporters in the best possible light. It is also true that hagiography tends to be stereotyped and prone to describe its subjects in terms of scriptural models. Usually, such schematic features would make the genre highly problematic as historical evidence.[13] Yet in our case, these features can be particularly illuminating. In the first place, when read side by side, hagiography's stock episodes create semantic fields in which certain words predictably appear in certain contexts, enabling us to reconstruct a series of discourses connecting specific gifts to particular contexts and purposes.[14] In the second place, hagiography was still an innovative genre in Early Byzantium. Schematic features notwithstanding, its variations depict situations from different angles, often revealing unexpected layers of issues and concerns. Of course, it is frustrating that hagiographers rarely present their subjects in terms of development or change, and we can never know how faithfully their depictions reflect actual circumstances or common understandings. Yet they also highlight "divine" dimensions of mundane interactions that would have otherwise been lost. Indeed, Early Byzantine hagiographers sometimes make a point of criticizing people for thinking "like a human" (*anthrōpinon*), especially when it came to generosity.[15] This was a basic lesson they wished to convey to their readers. Ignoring it would make us miss important facets of certain gift ideals.

To relate this hagiographical evidence to that of sermons and other genres, I treat all such depictions and discussions as expressions of an Early Byzantine discourse particular to each gift. Each chapter seeks to delineate and explain the discourse that arose around a particular gift ideal and gift-giving practice in this era, tracing relevant concerns from the fourth to the seventh century.[16] I am not always as regionally specific as I would have liked: each chapter gravitates towards a particular area or context, but my sources have often forced me to weave together material from multiple Near Eastern locations. Nonetheless, I am confident that the discourses I trace reflect suppositions held by most church and monastic authorities and their Early Byzantine followers—whether partially or in whole, consciously or not. My confidence is partly based on documentary evidence. Excavations of the Early Byzantine town of Nessana in southern Palestine (Auja el-Hafir/Nitzana in Israel's Negev desert) in the 1930s uncovered nearly two hundred papyri, including records related to an early seventh-century monastery dedicated to the saints Sergius and Bacchus on top of a hill in the center of town. One of these papyri, *P. Ness.* III 79, called by its editor "An Account of Offerings to the Church of St Sergius," reflects a major distinction discussed in this book. It contains a series of registers listing gifts that the monastery received over a two-year period. Most of these were registered as *prosphorai* offerings, but some were not: two of the registers were entirely devoted to gifts called *eulogiai*, (blessings), instead. The papyrus shows that the monastery's stewards carefully distinguished between the *prosphorai* and *eulogiai* they received, just as we might expect from the Early Byzantine discourses on liturgical offerings and blessings. In other words, *P. Ness.* III 79 proves that contemporaries drew distinctions along the categorical lines indicated by hagiography and other types of literature examined here.[17]

Nonetheless, we are dealing with ideals and practices whose roots in the social complexity of Early Byzantium are largely obscured by normative literature. For context we must consider how late Roman social and administrative structures shaped Christian notions of generosity, piety, and holiness. We must apply anthropological insights about the tendency of gift ideals to develop in contrast to other gifts or preexisting modes of exchange (see my prologue), requiring us to think of their dynamic relation to each other. And we must recognize that the discourses we are discussing were, for the most part, ascetic discourses.

By ascetic discourses, I mean those produced by monks and their lay admirers, or by ascetically minded preachers like Basil of Caesarea, Gregory of Nazianzus, and John Chrysostom. We are examining the implications of an ancient Christianity that affirmed stark differences in spiritual attainments and measured "righteousness" (i.e., holiness) not only by degrees of abstinence from carnal distractions like sex, wealth, and consumption but by relative capacities for sacrificing oneself or one's possessions for others. Indeed, a distinction between monastic and lay (or "worldly," *kosmikos*; cf. John 18:36) society was one of the binary structures that shaped Early Byzantine religious thought and culture.

Because of the process by which our sources were preserved in the Middle Ages, we cannot be certain how far this ascetic outlook actually prevailed in Early Byzantium. It certainly pervades Early Byzantine Christian literature, however, and it was not just a monastic outlook. Several sources confirm that ascetic aspirations and practices also inspired laypeople. Some of these founded confraternities and called themselves "Zealous Ones" (*spoudaioi*), "Lovers of Labor" (or "Fellow Workers," *philoponoi*), and "Sons [or Daughters] of the Covenant" (*bnay, bnāt qyāmā*).[18] Monastic authorities knew them more generally as "Christlovers" (*Philochristoi*)— that is, committed laypeople who took their religion seriously. Attested mainly in hagiography but also in historical narratives and letters of Barsanuphius and John, these Christians could be found at all levels of late Roman society. They ranged from fictional characters like Eucharistius the Secular, a peasant who reportedly reserved two-thirds of his earnings to entertain monks and feed the poor, to historical figures like John Vincomalus, a fifth-century consul who changed clothes each day to work in a monastery kitchen after attending his senate meetings; Gratissimus, a palace eunuch who entered a monastery after retirement; and Christopher, a sixth-century palace guard who wore a hair shirt beneath his uniform and spent winter nights passing out coins in the streets of Constantinople.[19] They also came from informal bible study groups, such as those attested in cities like Edessa, Gaza, and Alexandria that included people like the classically trained orator named Aeneas, who participated in sessions with an Egyptian monk in suburban Gaza, and the numerous lay theologians mentioned in the sixth-century writings of Cosmas Indicopleustes and John Philoponus.[20] Amateurs in the truest sense of the word, these groups met to discuss finer points of Christian exegesis and evidently took great satisfaction from interacting with spiritual experts. Some of them became even more closely connected to local holy people through the rituals of baptism and rigors of penance found in ancient Christian culture.[21]

Such Christlovers formed supportive relationships with clerics and monks, attending their services, asking their advice, and providing accommodations and other forms of hospitality during their travels. Undoubtedly, they represented a valued pool of reliable contributors to church and monastic finances; sometimes they put church or monastic leaders on the spot, asking them to explain their colleagues' actions, pressuring them to maintain standards.[22] They also would have been reliable consumers of the ascetic discourses examined here. As a hagiographer remarked about the lay *spoudaioi* attending a monastic lecture outside Constantinople, "Even in the world, there are many who are spiritually ardent and thirst for some charismatic pious person to convert their souls to a fear of God."[23]

But even casual Christians had impact on the ascetic discourses examined here. Unexpected needs prompted people of all sorts to seek out the services of religious professionals, and one reason authorities sought to define different types of gifts was to clarify what expectations each type established between such lay patrons, church leaders, or ascetic exemplars. In other words, the Early Byzantine repertoire of religious gifts was meant not just to provide Christians with the means to meet various obligations of their religion, ranging from philanthropy to expressions of gratitude for divine benefits. It was also meant to foster transparent, "righteous" interactions between secular and religious ranks.

Only in the sixth century do references to gifts called "charity" and "blessings" become commonplace alongside alms, fruitbearings, and offerings in hagiography and ascetic literature; we may therefore assume that only then did this repertoire and the relevant Christian discourses become fully formed.[24] Although we cannot trace the evolution of these discourses with chronological precision, we can distinguish between an incipient phase (late fourth and early fifth centuries) and an established phase (late fifth to the early seventh centuries). This roughly corresponds to the progression of evidence for church and monastic wealth in the Roman East. This evidence only begins to grow during the Theodosian age (379–457), when personalities and institutions associated with Nicene Orthodoxy became fashionable subjects of imperial and aristocratic patronage. It is during this era that the lay foundation or financing of monasteries became viewed as laudable expressions of aristocratic Christian piety, on par with giving to the poor or founding martyr shrines, hospitals, and poorhouses.[25] Michel Kaplan maintains that Early Byzantine monks lived partly off lay gifts, even concluding that "outside of Egypt, work as a source of revenues for the monasteries of the Roman East . . . occupied a secondary place after alms and donations." Historians have often pointed out examples of such "alms and donations," usually without further comment.[26] Unfortunately, we do not have enough documentary information to assess how much lay gifts contributed to the overall wealth of any particular monastery in this period, let alone how much wealth any possessed, or the impact such wealth had on the economy as a whole. I therefore seek to determine instead what such "alms and donations" and the resulting wealth—whatever its amount—was supposed to mean for the Christians both giving and receiving them.

PHILANTHROPY AND ASCETICISM AS COMPLEMENTARY VIRTUES

Readers may nonetheless suspect that the ascetic discourses discussed here would not have had much impact on mainstream philanthropy. To be sure, in our day, *philanthropy* usually connotes a secular practice carried out through impersonal foundations by the superrich to gain tax benefits and advance a particular cause, while religious self-denial is usually preached only on certain occasions, when almsgiving might be recommended (as it was in antiquity) to complement individual fasting. In Early Byzantium, however, these two ideals, philanthropy and asceticism—one essentially about giving, the other about not taking—were closely related and, indeed, came to mind as complementary virtues. This is illustrated in a chance remark that Emperor Justinian (r. 527–565) made in the preface to one of his laws. Issued at Constantinople in 531, this law barred any municipal councilor or governor's staff member from ever entering the church clergy, on the grounds that these secular occupations would have rendered them permanently unfit for the

Christian priesthood. "For it would not be right," Justinian remarks, for one "brought up to indulge in extortion with violence . . . suddenly to take holy orders, and to admonish and instruct about philanthropy and freedom from possessions."[27]

Described as "the most extraordinary of all the constitutions ever promulgated by the Roman emperors" due to its recognition of the habitual brutality that landowners and government officials inflicted on the Roman peasantry,[28] Justinian's law is also notable for referring to *philanthrōpia* and *aktēmosynē* ("freedom from possessions," a technical ascetic term often translated as "voluntary poverty") together in conjunction as matters of sixth-century preaching. No doubt Justinian mentioned the two in this law not because they dominated Christian preaching, but because both conjured clear antitheses to behavior he wished to contain. Nonetheless, his remark indicates that philanthropy and some form of material self-denial for the sake of a higher good could be seen as related in Christian preaching and discussions of lay civility. This is confirmed by a contemporary description of an aristocrat named Phocas, who served as Praetorian Prefect of the East in 532, just a year after Justinian's law was issued. According to our informant, John Lydus, Phocas had been selected for this post precisely because he combined public generosity with personal austerity:

> Solicitous about the needy, he used to exercise thrift solely when it came to himself. Such was his mode of life . . . that he might be counted among frugal people who have very limited livelihoods. Moreover, he used to distribute possessions from his hearth to his friends in a manner worthy of his fortune's abundance, while feeding himself only on his guests' cheerful spirits.[29]

So excessive was Phocas's *philanthrōpia*, Lydus adds, that he had been known to sell some of his wardrobe to raise funds to release captives of brigand raids—a practice not unlike what contemporary hagiographers were ascribing to Christian saints.[30] Lydus himself was not a hagiographer. His portrait of Phocas, however, shows how philanthropy toward others combined with austerity toward oneself had become touchstones of aristocratic virtue in the sixth-century Roman East. In sociological terms, these two ideals had become social facts, shaping discourses and practices. This book studies how such discourses and practices reinforced each other in Early Byzantium, especially where lay and monastic concerns overlapped. And by studying those concerns, it provides an opportunity to view this complex Christian society as a whole, as seen from the inside.

The Present-Giving World of Early Byzantium

One place where lay and monastic concerns frequently overlapped in Early Byzantium was the late Roman Holy Land. To introduce the lay customs and structures supporting early Christian philanthropy, as well as the prominence of Christianity in a region now mainly identified with the modern state of Israel and Islam, it is worth surveying this microcosm of Early Byzantine piety when the Christian development of the Holy Land was first at its height. That was in the sixth century, during the so-called Justinianic Age. Named after the long-lived and unusually ambitious Roman emperor Justinian (r. 527–565), this era lasted roughly from the accession of his uncle, Emperor Justin I, in 518 until the execution of Emperor Maurice in 602. Due to Justinian's reconquest of North Africa, Italy, and other western regions, as well as to his systematic codification of Roman law and the high quality of art produced during his reign, this has often been called the "golden age" of Early Byzantium. That description is grossly misleading for a time that also witnessed the arrival of the bubonic plague (endemic after 541); catastrophic earthquakes; systematic persecutions of Jews, Samaritans, pagans, heretics, and homosexuals; violent regional insurrections; and the exhaustion of lives, resources, cities, and countrysides on wars of dubious merit.[1] But it certainly was a golden age for state-sponsored Christianity and monasticism, as becomes evident from contemporary descriptions of the Holy Land.

CHRISTIAN GIFTS IN THE LATE ROMAN HOLY LAND

We could find no more engaging guide for this time and place than a visitor from northern Italy known as the Piacenza Pilgrim. His roughly ten-page *Travelogue* has received relatively little attention compared to the much longer pilgrim account written by the fourth-century Spanish aristocrat Egeria. Yet it offers a firsthand layperson's description of a world that we otherwise see mainly through hagiography or monastic letters—a world that took special interest in religious gifts. The Pilgrim set out from his native city of Placentia (modern Piacenza, Italy) with an unknown number of fellow pilgrims early one winter at the start of the reign of Justin II (r. 565–574). Their tour, like Egeria's, encompassed Palestine, Egypt, and Mesopotamia, a much larger region than most modern Christians identify as the Holy Land today. After sailing to Constantinople and landing in the Levant near Tripoli, they travelled down the Mediterranean coastline to Ptolemais (modern Acre, Israel), where they entered Palestine to begin their pilgrimage proper. Having reached Nazareth, they toured the Galilee, where one of them died. After following the Jordan River to the Dead Sea, they went up to Jerusalem, where, the Pilgrim reports, "we prostrated ourselves, kissed the ground, and entered the Holy City." After an unspecified time visiting sites there and at Bethlehem and Mamre, they returned to the Mediterranean coast, headed south to Gaza and turned inland to Elusa (Halutza, Israel), "at the head of the desert that leads to Sinai." Here they joined a caravan to Mount Sinai, where a week later they were welcomed by a procession of psalm-singing monks. After touring the mountain, his group left the caravan and went west to Egypt to see Pharaoh's residence and Joseph's granaries (i.e., the pyramids) on the Nile before returning to Jerusalem via Alexandria. Then, after being waylaid by an illness (relieved, he says, through the visit of saints in a dream), the Pilgrim set out again, now to see martyr shrines in northern Mesopotamia. Passing through Damascus, Larissa, Aristosa, Epiphania, Apamea, and Antioch in Syria, he turned east to Chalcis, Harran, Barbalissus, and Sura on the Euphrates. That may be as far as he got: his account ends by observing that the shrine of St. Sergius lay twelve miles further "into the desert, among the Saracens," along the Roman-Persian frontier.[2]

This *Travelogue,* written ca. 570, is a precious document. While Egeria's account two centuries earlier shows that she was of high enough rank to ride along on the *cursus publicus* and stay in its station houses at night, the Pilgrim seems to have traveled by foot on a budget (perhaps subsidized by "Lord Paterius the Patrician," mentioned as recipient of some large dates he brought back from Jericho),[3] lodging at inns and taking the shortest routes. Such travel explains not only his careful counting of milestones but the details that make his pilgrim account so revealing about this area in the second half of the sixth century. To start just with the facts: his ability to travel unimpeded from the southern Sinai peninsula to northern Mesopotamia (it is 1,023 kilometers, or 635 miles, from Jerusalem to the city of Harran/Carrhae in modern Turkey alone) indicates the level of unity and safety that prevailed, while the sheer number of cities he visited (he names fifty-two, not counting all the unnamed cities, villages, strongholds, and encampments he mentions passing on the way) shows the high level of urbanization and social complexity still found there.[4] Nor did these cities lack luster. Due to its silk factories, Tyre was rich, he writes, and its people indulged in luxuries; Ptolemais was a decent city; Apamea a "most splendid home to the Syrian nobility"; Alexandria "splendid and easy-going"; and Gaza "splendid, charming, and filled with very decent people distinguished by their great liberality and fondness for pilgrims."[5]

It is not surprising that someone leaving war-torn Italy in winter should warm to life in the eastern Mediterranean. But the Pilgrim was not blind to blemishes. Besides the destruction caused in the Levant by the earthquake of 557, he noticed religious divisions throughout Palestine. Sycamina was a "city of Jews," and Sarepta "very Christian"; Jews in general had no affection for Christians, but Jewish women in Nazareth loved them because Jesus's mother, Mary, had come from there; and Samaritans hated both Jews and Christians so much that they cursed them as they approached, burned off their footprints from the ground with straw, washed immediately after contact, accepted their coins only if first soaked in water, and posted guards outside their cities to warn them against spitting or touching anything without buying it.[6] He notes that Alexandria was "full of heretics" (i.e., Anti-Chalcedonians), and that pagan Bedouins posed a serious danger to Christians living or travelling in the Sinai peninsula.[7] A cavalry unit of eighty horsemen provisioned by the Duke of Egypt was stationed in its central oasis to protect monks and monasteries from attacks. Each day a contingent left town to patrol the desert, bolting the gates behind, but, the Pilgrim remarks, "the Saracens do not tremble in fear of them."[8] That was a prescient assessment of the limits of Roman power in a region that would prove the empire's Achilles' heel in the next century.

Yet, the Arab conquests were still a long way off. At this point no major challenge was conceivable to Christian hegemony in the Mediterranean Near East, which had been in Roman hands for over half a millennium. It is true that archaeologists have found signs of economic recession in the late sixth century. We know that Elusa, a city mentioned in the *Travelogue,* stopped collecting trash in the 550s, perhaps evincing impact of the plague; Justinian's western reconquests also severely taxed eastern resources just as a little ice age was setting in that challenged the capacity of the Near East to produce more.[9] Yet the Pilgrim gives a general impression of prosperous stability, despite underlying tensions and events he does not mention, like the plague itself, or the war with Sassanian Persia that had devastated Mesopotamia in the 540s and would break out again soon after the Pilgrim left. Churches and synagogues built in this period present a similar picture. Even towns isolated deep in the Negev desert had five or more churches each; many Egyptian villages had more than ten; some towns along the Nile, over twenty-five.[10] This exceeded communal needs. It has long been surmised that such building should be linked to the pilgrim trade: certainly inscriptions on Sinai pilgrimage routes attest how many people came from abroad to visit this difficult terrain simply for the sake of piety.[11] But these religious buildings also reflected the agrarian prosperity discussed in chapter 6, while the Pilgrim's reference to military patrols in the Sinai and their ties to the Duke of Egypt alerts us to another factor so important for the economic prosperity of the late Roman East that it can go unappreciated: namely, the persistence of an overarching imperial superstructure, the likes of which had ceased to exist in western Europe.

Created to restore stability and extract resources after a series of crises nearly destroyed the Roman Empire in the third century, this imperial superstructure in the East was centered on the Praetorian Prefecture of the Orient. This provided the financial and judicial administration for five different territorial sectors called dioceses, each governed by a deputy, each encompassing several provinces that had their own military commands and governorships. With this restructuring, the government of the earlier empire, a more or less decentralized experiment that had relied heavily on local city councils to collect taxes and keep the peace, was replaced by the "elaborate centralized machine" of the later empire.[12] Employing thousands, it created a professional service aristocracy paid in annual salaries of gold coins (solidi/*nomismata*), which, when invested in land, could turn low-level bureaucrats into estate-owning lords and influential local patrons of the new Christian culture.[13] We know something about their esprit de corps thanks to John Lydus, a bureaucrat who retired on April 1, 552, after working forty years in a judicial branch of the Prefecture within the offices of its headquarters in Constantinople.[14] At the end of his *On the Magistracies of Rome,* a singular work of antiquarian history and autobiographical reflection, he recalls how his favorite supervisor, the praetorian prefect Phocas, in addition to displaying the civic philanthropy, which is described in the introduction,[15] bestowed largesse on a church outside the city of Pessinus in rural Asia Minor. Having heard that someone had already given it twenty pounds of gold in a lump sum, Phocas decided to furnish an endowment for its priests, "for the sake of providing hospitality." This resulted in their receiving an income of eighty solidi, apparently each year, which was a huge sum for a provincial church at a time when a builder might hope to earn half a solidus a month and two solidi fed a person for a year.[16] Whatever motivated Phocas—he later committed suicide after being accused, for a second time, of paganism—the episode illustrates how such civil servants made a point of supporting the Christian establishment with their philanthropy.

Long disparaged as oppressively burdensome and hopelessly corrupt, the late Roman superstructure is now recognized, for all its flaws, as an effective innovation that revived the fortunes of the Eastern empire repeatedly in the fifth and sixth centuries.[17] It enabled Emperor Anastasius (r. 491–518) to leave nearly 320,000 pounds of gold at his death (though partly by selling offices), thereby creating the reserves that enabled Justinian to launch his invasions of the West twelve years later. It created the military and logistical capacity that managed to maintain stability despite constant external threats and internal brigandage. Furthermore, through its annual collections of grain (*annonae*) that supplied both the frontier troops and privileged residents of Constantinople—a city that had over half a million people before the plague, more than anywhere else in the Western world—it stimulated agriculture and trade networks that made even far-flung provinces profit from the hungry vortex on the Bosporus. Of courses, much of this productivity was siphoned off by tax officials and landowners like those denounced in Justinian's law of 531. Yet this elaborate superstructure ensured that there was ample work to be had, coins to be circulated, resources to be taxed, and material wealth on hand to attract luxury trade from afar, as the Piacenza Pilgrim attests when mentioning ships arriving on both sides of the Sinai peninsula, laden with aromatics from India.[18]

Though largely invisible in his *Travelogue,* this superstructure also sustained the Christian culture and population that the Pilgrim found in the Holy Land. Two things especially caught his attention while there, besides all of its relics of ancient Christianity on display (these included the couch that Jesus had purportedly used during the wedding at Cana, on which the Pilgrim says he carved his parents' names, and a writing tablet in the synagogue where Jesus had learned his ABCs). First, there were the many monks and monasteries to be seen in the Holy Land; second, there was its sheer material bounty, made freely available to visitors. To begin with monasticism: along with lepers, monks were the group of people he most regularly mentions in his account; evidently, he considered them a feature worth noting to folks back home. Besides large monasteries attached to churches in Jerusalem, he saw many "servants of God" living in tombs and a "multitude of cloistered males and females" in various structures on the Mount of Olives. "Huge" monasteries and "multitudes" of monks and hermits could be seen in the Jordan River valley, as well as in the Judean desert and the environs of Bethlehem and Sinai. Not only does he mention imperial cavalry assigned to protect monks on the Sinai, but he also notes a fortress that dispensed rations to hermits, revealing how the empire employed its logistical and military strengths to support and protect this Christian lifestyle.[19]

Let us take this opportunity to survey the state of Christian monasticism in the Roman East more broadly. By the late sixth century, it was hardly a new phenomenon. Over two hundred years had passed since the death of Antony the Great (ca. 251–356), traditionally regarded as the first monk. For various reasons, ascetic rigorism had always been an important part of ancient Christianity, and different forms of what would become defined as "monasticism" began to emerge in the third and fourth century. Readers will note, however, that most of the monastic personalities discussed in this book lived during the fifth century. This was the crucial century for the development of their profession. For it was during the fifth century that earlier regional monastic experiments coalesced into a pan-Roman movement with increasingly distinct and readily identifiable institutions.

To summarize a complicated history, this more standardized monasticism was closely tied to the founding of the Theodosian dynasty (379–457), its rejection of

"Arian" Orthodoxy (reversing forty years of imperial favor), its espousal of "Nicene" Orthodoxy, its embrace of ascetic heroes like Antony identified with the cause, and its patronage of ascetic theorists like Evagrius of Pontus (d. 399), Jerome (d. 420), and John Cassian (d. 435). It was no coincidence that these masterly writers were all connected to influential bishops. Promoted as Christian counterparts to the pagan Neoplatonic philosophers of the day, they promoted an elite form of contemplative monasticism that emphasized physical isolation, transformation through prayer, and deference to the powers that be. This form of monasticism, closely associated with Egyptian desert practices, became the recognized norm. By the middle of the fifth century, contentions regarding the relation of monks to church clergy that had marked the fourth century had largely been put to rest, thanks in part to the appointment of abbots to serve as "exarchs" in Constantinople and Palestine, where monks tended to concentrate. These monastic officials were tasked with keeping order, upholding standards, and providing liaisons with the episcopal palace.[20]

The gradual standardization of monastic practices culminated with Justinian's sixth-century laws formally requiring all monasteries to be surrounded by walls and ruled by an abbot.[21] The Pilgrim shows his familiarity with the basic taxonomies of his day by distinguishing between "cenobites," who lived together in communal houses (*cenobia*), and solitaries (*eremitae*), who withdrew (*anachorēsis*— hence, also called anchorites) to live alone or in groups in remoter "desert" places. He visited two of the major areas of Eastern anchoretic practice, namely the Judean and the Sinai deserts, where hermits (desert anchorites) tended to live in semi-communal clusters of cells joined by paths (an arrangement called a *lavra*). More extreme isolation, or enclosure, was considered a mark of elite monasticism, pursued for the sake of transformative tranquility or penance: on Olivet the Pilgrim notes seeing many "enclosed" monks, as well as the cell in which a legendary fourth-century prostitute named Pelagia had reportedly sealed herself until she turned into a male monk. Cenobitic and anchoretic practices were of course often integrated, with elders living outside larger institutions. Had the Pilgrim gone south of Gaza, he could have seen the cell outside the Seridos cenobium where the anchorite Barsanuphius had resided, and which he is said to have left only once, to prove to the monastery's junior members that he actually existed. Such elders lived as dependencies on the cenobium proper.[22]

There were never any monastic "orders" in Early Byzantium. Some communities produced confederations, but most remained unconnected to others, forming around ascetic teachers known for their charismatic attainments.[23] Even when founded by wealthy patrons (an important development discussed in chapter 7), monasteries never became aristocratic preserves, as often in the West. Nor were they filled with peasants and unlettered rustics, as once presumed. The profession perhaps drew many from the middling, functionally literate classes whose excess children could be spared for such religious pursuits.[24] Early Byzantine monks came from all walks of life, especially, it seems, the military. The late-sixth-century *Life of Dositheus* profiles one such recruit. An attendant on a general's staff in Palestine, Dositheus "knew nothing about God" but wanted to see the sites at Jerusalem. His commander gave him leave, and while visiting the city, Dositheus saw a painting of Judgment Day. Later that night he had a vision of the Mother of God warning him that to avoid damnation, he must renounce meat and start praying. When his comrades saw his sudden change of behavior after his return, they suggested he join a monastery. So he left and presented himself at the Seridos Monastery outside Gaza, still dressed in his uniform, "talking like a Goth."[25] Dositheus proved a model disciple, but he soon died of tuberculosis. He was probably a teenager; some recruits were as young as five years old, but perhaps many more adopted monasticism in old age, viewing it a safe form of retirement and prudent preparation for death.[26]

An estimated 50,000 monks inhabited the Eastern empire by the late sixth century. Our best clues come from conciliar documents. Sixty-eight monasteries existed in Constantinople, and forty in Chalcedon across the Bosphorus in 536; some housed 300 to 1,000 monks in three-story buildings, suggesting a population of 10,000 to 15,000 for the city or suburbs as a whole. In the provinces, Shenoute's confederation in Egypt is the largest on record, with about 4,000 males and females in his White and Red Monasteries combined. Alexandria reportedly had six hundred monasteries; according to the sixth-century hagiographer Cyril of Scythopolis, the monastic population of Jerusalem by the year 516 totaled 10,000, and it is estimated that there were sixty-five monasteries in the Judean desert alone, with one of them, the Great Lavra founded by Saba, having 250–300 residents. The city of Amida (Diyarbakir, Turkey) in northern Mesopotamia had fifteen, including one with 750 to 1,000 monks (the same author gives both figures). A doctrinal letter written in 569 lists signatories from 137 monasteries, most of which were situated in villages stretching from the outskirts of Damascus to the Transjordan. Three monks, apparently solitaries, are mentioned on tombstones from the Cilician town of Korykos. Otherwise the number of residents recorded in cenobitic monasteries in Syria and Asia Minor range from 12 to 120 members; the first figure, considered by the author to be unusually small, tallies with what that the Piacenza Pilgrim found in a poor monastery in the Negev.[27] Monks thus represented a tiny, yet noticeable presence in the Roman East at this time, comparable to the numbers of imperial bureaucrats in the eastern Prefecture. Most important, they were highly visible in key areas such as the suburbs of large cities, outskirts of villages, or easily accessible countrysides in Syria, Palestine and Egypt.

The other feature the Pilgrim noticed in the Holy Land was its material bounty. Indeed, it is not surprising that he assumed that the pyramids at Giza, which Egeria had similarly identified as Joseph's granaries, were still filled with the grain that Joseph had collected to distribute in Old Testament times (Gn 41:48–49).[28]

The Pilgrim had seen several examples of scripturally based abundance elsewhere in the Holy Land. He notes that Jesus's homeland in the Galilee was a "paradise" that produced wine and oil better than Egypt's, and that its wheat was extraordinarily tall, up to human height.[29] Jericho was another "paradise": it had a field that yielded grain twice a year by itself, without human cultivation (Jesus had reportedly seeded it), as well as a spring associated with Elisha (2 Kgs 2:21) that caused massive dates to grow, each weighing a pound.[30] Such fecundity was directly connected to holy people, but the Holy Land had *virtutes* of its own that produced salubrious gifts, there for the taking. A stone off the coast of Sinai excreted oil so powerful in driving out demons that locals did not let it be taken away undiluted. Dew wafting up from Jericho was gathered wherever it fell in Jerusalem in order to cure diseases, while dew that fell between the peaks of Sinai and Horeb and then solidified into manna (probably an insect secretion on tamarisk trees) was collected to ferment in the Sinai monastery, making a liqueur dispensed to visitors. The Piacenza Pilgrim left with five flasks filled with this particular "blessing."[31]

The Samaritan warning that anyone entering their towns had to buy what they touched indicates that such pilgrims were sometimes viewed simply as customers. Yet the Pilgrim makes clear that the items he valued most in the Holy Land, like Sinai's manna liqueur, were obtained *pro benedictione*, "as a blessing."[32] We cannot presume that such items were directly sold: he mentions taking or being given them, but never purchasing them.[33] Sometimes he simply consumed them on the spot, as when he drank water from the bejeweled skull of a deceased saint in Jerusalem; other times he used strips of ribbon to absorb places where Jesus had stepped, or took away what he could in pint flasks. All these items he called *benedictiones*, "blessings."[34] He was also impressed by offerings he saw, especially gold bracelets, necklaces, crowns, and other valuables hung over Christ's Tomb. The Pilgrim himself offered a pitcher of wine at an altar in Cana.[35]

These two features of the Pilgrim's Holy Land—monasticism and religious giving—come together in an enigmatic passage of his *Travelogue*. As his Sinai caravan entered the Negev desert, it came upon a monastery housing about a dozen young female monks. Besides an ass that turned a millstone, they had a lion that would lead the ass out to pasture; as the caravan approached, its roar made all the caravan's pack animals piss. The monastery seems to have been quite poor. It was supported by outside donations—"Christians habitually provide them with sustenance," the Pilgrim observes. Another member of his group, only described as "that most Christian man [*ille Christianissimus*] who was with me," asked the Pilgrim to offer them a hundred gold coins. When the monks declined his offer, this companion arranged to have thirty tunics, a supply of beans, and oil for their lamps delivered to their monastery from Jerusalem. Then, having been told that a hermit named Mary lived far off in the marshes of the Dead Sea, he set out to find her, carrying clothes, dates, and baskets of chickpeas.

Two days later he came back weeping, no longer carrying the food: "He just kept saying, 'Alas, how wretched I am! What right do I have to call myself a Christian?'"[36] It is unclear whether this *Christianissimus* was lamenting his failure to find the legendary Mary, reflecting on his own inadequacies in comparison to the saint, or rebuking himself for consuming all the supplies he had meant to give to her. Hagiography describes similar scenarios in which pilgrims dispensed food and gold coins to Holy Land monks, however.[37] If the Pilgrim did not intend to parody such literature or ridicule his companion (neither of which seem likely), his account shows that unprompted generosity towards ascetics had become a gesture of pilgrim piety that could qualify someone as "most Christian."[38] Of course the Holy Land, located at the symbolic heart of the Christian empire, was an unusual setting that inspired unusual behavior. How, then, did such generosity correspond to norms elsewhere?

SECULAR GIFTS AND THE LATE ROMAN IMPERIAL ORDER

If the Piacenza Pilgrim set out from Italy in the middle of the 560s, then his sojourn in Constantinople, the first stop mentioned in his *Travelogue*, could have coincided with two important ceremonies described by the North African poet Fl. Cresconius Corippus. One of these marked the accession of Emperor Justin II on November 14, 565, and the other his inauguration as consul on January 1, 566. Both were orchestrated for maximum effect. After thirty-eight years of rule, Justinian had finally died, and a new purple day had dawned. The Pilgrim, if he had arrived at this time, would have entered a city locked in a cycle of rituals meant to establish Justin in his place. In addition to hastily arranged processions and the usual pompous speeches, these rituals included the ostentatious outlays of largesse that new emperors traditionally made to secure their futures.

These were technically known as the *augustaticum* (formal gifts to chief officers and high-ranking civilians), *donativum* (moneys distributed equally to all soldiers in the armed forces), and *sparsio* (coins dispensed to crowds). In Justin's case, such outlays began the morning after Justinian's death with "solemn gifts" to guards, chamberlains and officers in the palace. This was followed by an elaborate performance in the hippodrome involving dispersals of cash to representatives of the *populus Romanus,* payments of Justinian's imperial debts, amnesty for prisoners taken under Justinian's reign, and assurances of more benefactions to come at the consular inauguration on the Kalends—that is, on New Year's Day.[39] Over the next month a four-story grandstand festooned with palm leaves and laurels was constructed in downtown Constantinople. This was set for the tossing of coins that traditionally expressed a new consul's munificence toward his Roman citizenry. The Kalends was always celebrated throughout the empire with public gift giving at all levels, but never so extravagantly as in the capital, and rarely so theatrically as it was in this year. That morning, after giving silver plates to senators and lumps of cash to high-ranking officials inside the palace, Justin emerged to scoop and toss handfuls of solidi up to a wall of citizens amassed in the grandstand. Here they stood in long rows, marshaled

> so that they could thrust out and extend their hands for the gifts . . . make the folds of their garments ready for the gifts which the consul was about to throw to the people in vast amounts, and stretch out their palms to receive them, so that the golden rain might flow far and wide.[40]

After exhausting this glittering largesse, "scattering it like snow," the emperor proceeded to Justinian's magnificent cathedral of Hagia Sophia, where he "dedicated many gifts for his vows, and enriched the pious temple with a vast donation" before riding off in a golden chariot.[41]

This illustrates the enduring importance of dramatic gestures of public giving in the world the Piacenza Pilgrim knew. The consular inauguration on New Year's Day was the closest the Romans ever came to a potlatch. So expensive had it become that Justinian had suspended it in 542, meaning that by Justin's day, a whole generation had come and gone without seeing the storied spectacle for the first time since the era of the Republic. Corippus does not record exactly how much the new emperor spent on the occasion, but chroniclers remembered it as the year when he "enriched many."[42] This was a calculated expense, meant to create a lasting impression of the emperor as an unparalleled source of bounty and instill gratitude among those who mattered most.

Ostentatious public giving had always been a distinct part of Greco-Roman civilization, beyond anything known today. Most emblematic were the civic benefactions that aristocrats bestowed on fellow citizens in a practice that scholars call euergetism (a modern coinage derived from the Greek word for civic benefactions, *euergesiai*). Better known as "Bread and Circuses" and associated with the spectacular entertainments or bread dole that emperors funded in Rome (and later in Constantinople), such gift giving also accounts for most of the porticoes, baths, stadiums, libraries, and other structures that give classical ruins their striking appearance of civic vitality and secular affluence. Bestowed in pursuit of honor or public acclaim (*philotimia*—never *philanthrōpia*), it was exclusively meant for enrolled citizens (never "the poor") and was the price of a social contract by which local aristocrats furnished a range of amenities to fellow citizens "for free," in return for their acquiescence to increasing disparities of wealth and privilege.

But Bread and Circuses were just the most memorable expressions of a donative culture that shaped religious life as well as social relations in the Greco-Roman world. Besides the religious vows and sacrifices that worshippers offered to gods or items that neighbors exchanged at the Brumalia, Saturnalia, and Kalends festivals, there were more or less private, secular gift-giving customs that united people across social lines. These ranged from prenuptial gifts between prospective spouses to the gifts of introduction or friendship (*xenia*) that aristocrats gave each other throughout the year, to the baskets of food or cash (e.g., *sportulae*) that patrons gave to their clients to maintain their loyalty and services, to the fruits, produce, handcrafts, or services that workers offered out of their own labors or earnings as expressions of respect (e.g., *dasmata, 'iqāre, honoraria*) to their employers, lords, and patrons. Such gifts bound the social fabric. There were additionally all sorts of bribes and sweeteners that everyone had to give (on top of bureaucratic fees and government taxes) to live and get things done in this "present-giving world."[43]

Civic euergetism reached its height in the second century. The emperors' third-century seizure of municipal revenues and eventual promotion of Christianity as a new collective identity reduced the capacity and incentive for the traditional pursuit of *philotimia*. While private patterns of social giving continued,[44] civic benefactions gave way to imperial and Christian benefactions. This change, which Judith Herrin describes as a shift from "Bread and Circuses" to "Soup and Salvation," is one of the great topics of late antique social history.[45] It transformed urban landscapes around the Mediterranean, as notions of Church and Empire replaced the classical *polis* as the basis of political and cultural identities. The drive for *philotimia* was never extinguished ("Many rush to build most sacred churches for the sake of a name," complained Justinian in 538), and elite Christian donors often wanted their church benefactions commemorated according to classical conventions.[46] But such benefactions, communal though they were, served a nonclassical conception of society, one composed not so much of fellow citizens as of fellow Christians, including two new, ideologically important groups of constituents conceived along scriptural lines as "the poor" and the "poor in spirit."[47] Meanwhile, statues and inscriptions honoring local benefactors gradually disappeared, as civic spaces became filled with private homes and imperial placards. John Lydus (d. ca. 570) notes the withdrawal of aristocrats from civic life. Romans of old used to welcome all strangers into their city, he claims; their houses had "always remained open to all for the granting of every abundance, no guard or doorkeeper barring entry to the needy." But this did not continue in Constantinople. "Such philanthropy also reached our Rome," he explains, "although . . . it did not become established, for the illustrious men among us display the superiority of their fortune to themselves, and to themselves alone."[48]

Lydus was referring to a classical mode of *philanthrōpia* described in his Greco-Roman texts. If it failed to take hold in Constantine's Rome, this was because, on the one hand, it was subsumed by Christian modes of philanthropy discussed in chapter 2, and because, on the other, it was stifled by the overwhelming presence of governors, emperors, and imperial benefactions in late Roman cities. Such benefactions tended to favor religious (i.e., Christian) or utilitarian structures over monuments "on which labor was expended for useless show."[49] But Bread and Circuses continued through chariot races and other shows, and, at Constantinople, by the imperial provision of the *annona civica*. Constantine had attached eighty thousand rights for a bread dole to parcels of real estate in order to attract wealthy residents to his new city. These rights could be inherited, bought, or sold; they entitled their possessors to receive free loaves of bread dispensed each week from various locations that were set up by state bakeries on urban steps. John of Ephesus, a resident of Constantinople with rights to the dole in the late sixth century, reports receiving five loaves at each distribution. Serving symbolic purposes as much as anything else, the dole gave emperors a mechanism to display their civic concern on a massive scale. By the sixth century Constantinople was importing over 175,000 tons (1,600,000 kilograms) of wheat, transported each year from Egypt to be stored along the Golden Horn or dumped into an enormous granary that Justinian built on the island of Tenedos. After the last shipment had arrived at the end of summer, the emperor would ceremoniously descend to inspect the stores, consult with magistrates, and publicly assure the surrounding populace that they had a full supply. This remained the most traditional and paternalistic form of imperial benefactions in Early Byzantium.[50] But equally significant were the gifts discharged at ceremonies like those described by Corippus, which overtly rewarded support for the imperial hierarchy.

We know this thanks to Corippus. He first highlights the theme of hierarchical order in the accession speech put in the mouth of Justin II. This compares the empire to a body whose head (the emperor) must impose its councils on its shoulders (the senate), which must uphold its arms, legs, hands, and feet (the lower orders) without unjust seizures or contempt, since these must feed the stomach (the treasury) to energize the body (the empire) as a whole.[51] The theme recurs when Corippus describes how Justin's ceremonial gifts were carefully graded according to rank. "The state enriches with gifts those who have served it well," he observes, describing how Justin summoned each senator individually to receive "silver vessels full of yellow gold" from his hand, before turning to palace guards and chamberlains, receiving these "faithful friends" collectively in descending groups: "he joyfully offered them pious gifts ... according to their deserts and their rank."[52] Even those in the grandstands were ordered according to their guilds.

Repeated each New Year's Day and on comparable occasions, such gift giving had long provided an opportunity to affirm the Roman political hierarchy in a visible, tangible way.[53] Had any of the vessels Justin dispensed to his senators been preserved, we might have seen this hierarchical order commemorated on its very surface. An extant example is the so-called Missorium of Emperor Theodosius I (r. 378–395). Unearthed in Spain in the nineteenth century and now displayed at the Real Academia de la Historia in Madrid, this massive silver dish, measuring 74 centimeters in diameter, was issued in 388 to celebrate the tenth anniversary of the emperor's accession. Both of its silver sides are engraved: one records its original weight—"50 lbs."—while the other shows an enthroned Theodosius looking impassively out at the viewer, seated between two junior co-emperors and their armed guards beneath a classical entablature, dropping a codicil of office into the hands of a smaller magistrate. Thus the Missorium depicted the ceremonial act of imperial gift giving that produced the Missorium itself. Beneath the giver and recipient lies a personification of Tellus (Earth) herself, reclining amid a swirl of grain, symbolizing the agricultural bounty that sustained the regime through taxation. Thus, the use of gifts to celebrate allegiance to the imperial order had, by Justin's day, had a long history.[54] It reminded recipients of an emperor's unique ability to tap into and distribute great stores of temporal bounty. As Justinian remarked when discussing his responsibility to replenish any funds borrowed from Christian churches, "How could a sovereign object to giving ... seeing that God has given him much to possess ... and no difficulty in giving?"[55]

Founded partly on the government's need to keep its taxpayers predictably fixed in place, ideals of hierarchical regimentation pervaded this society. The sixth-century *Dialogue on Political Science* assumed that in a well-run state, the best people would "harmoniously regulate everything of all kinds, while all the other classes ... would be aware of the close and present oversight of superiors appropriate to each of them."[56] Papyri show that Egyptian villagers by the sixth century were claiming elevated titles for themselves, assuming aristocratic postures in the countryside that mirrored those of the big city ("It looks as if the central authorities had lost control of the hierarchy of imperial rank," Wolf Liebeschuetz remarks).[57] It has been argued that the vertical emphasis of this late Roman ideal ultimately resulted in fragmentation rather than unity.[58] But contemporaries assumed it was essential to stability, believing that good order (*eutaxia, eunomia*) was achieved by promoting concord (*harmonia, symphonia*) between clear, because more or less fixed, ranks.[59]

Such assumptions informed Christian gift giving. Except for Justin's donations at Hagia Sophia, Corippus does not mention any inaugural gifts to the ecclesiastical orders. Yet the most renowned Chalcedonian monk of the day, Symeon Stylites the Younger (521–597), issued a prophesy supporting Justin's accession, and soon afterward the new emperor supplied all of Justinian's churches and monasteries with expensive liturgical wares, exemplifying again the imperial use of gifts to garner and reward allegiance, this time among the religious elite.[60] As Justinian declared in 534, "all affluence and subsistence of the most holy churches is forever bestowed ... by acts of sovereign munificence."[61]

Justinian viewed clerics and monks as virtual servants of the state. Their job was intercession, using their expertise in prayer to secure God's favor for the realm. As he put it in the preface to a law,

Nothing could have as great a claim on the attention of sovereigns as the honor of the clergy, seeing that they are the ones who constantly offer prayers to God on the sovereign's behalf. Hence, should the one be above reproach in every respect . . . while the other keeps in correct and proper order the realm entrusted to it, there will be satisfactory harmony, conferring every conceivable benefit on the human race.[62]

Regarding monks, the emperor similarly explained his need to legislate their lifestyle:

This is because, should it be with clean hands and bared souls that monks address their prayers to God for the state, surely all will be well with the armies, there will be stability in the cities, the earth will bear us harvests and the sea will yield its own. Because their prayer brings God's favor upon the whole realm . . . how shall it not be that all things abound in perfect peace and good order?[63]

As this shows, Justinian considered monks as important as priests for securing imperial prosperity, their prayers raising bounty from the earth and sea while blocking the inroads of the heathen Persians and Huns menacing from outside.[64] But such powers depended on maintaining their integrity—hence, Justinian's demand that monks live in buildings surrounded by walls outside and none inside, to ensure that all remained closely watched, vigilant, and pure.

To support and sponsor their intercessory services, Justinian provided clerics and monks with patronal gifts and encouraged others to do the same. Early in his rule he more than doubled the sum that donors could give to religious institutions without reporting it to the government, raising it from two hundred to five hundred solidi, while removing the need to register anything given for philanthropic ends; he subsequently declared any gift a member of the senatorial class donated to a religious institution to be immune from taxation.[65] Of course, Christian emperors had supported Christian institutions financially from the start. Constantine had subsidized the clergy by making metropolitan churches recipients of state grain. We know far less about the church *annona* than about the *annona civica* from which it derived.[66] Nonetheless, it is clear that major bishoprics benefitted from it: Justinian mentions Constantinople, Alexandria, and Antioch as receiving it in a law of 535, noting that other bishoprics might be receiving it as well.[67] Thus, the empire bestowed part of its state *annona* on at least three patriarchal churches, effectively giving their patriarchs a fungible resource they could use not only to feed clerics and poor people in their cities but also to furnish subsidies to affiliated churches and monasteries farther afield. This systematic flow of resources from emperors through patriarchal churches into the hands of influential abbots and monks is indicated through an allusion to an "annual stipend" that the ecclesiastical historian Evagrius says a sixth-century monastery collected each year from the church of Antioch "from which it was allocated"; it is also implied by the Piacenza Pilgrim's reference to *stipendia* being issued to monks from a fortress in the Negev desert at about the same time.[68]

Such episcopal subsidizations of monks and monasteries may have become a regular, systematic practice only after 451, when the Council of Chalcedon instructed bishops to assume oversight (*pronoia*) for monasteries within their jurisdiction.[69] Such benefits would not have been extended if monks just represented "idle mouths," whose vocal support for their benefactors did not matter.[70] What must be added is that this imperial subsidy was intended only for the imperially aligned "orthodox" churches.[71] Using gifts to sway doctrinal allegiances was a practice already known in the fourth century, when John Chrysostom castigated Christians for being influenced by such measures ("Shame on whoever should participate in other dogmas motivated by human patronage!").[72] It becomes more evident, however, in the fifth century, after the Council of Chalcedon. From then onward, eastern Christendom became riven by Christological divisions, primarily between Chalcedonian "dyophysites" and anti-Chalcedonian "miaphysites" (proponents, respectively, of a double-nature, and a single-nature understanding of the relationship between the human and divine in Christ), but also between these and older confessional camps. These divisions were a serious impediment to imperial unity.[73] When dialogue failed, emperors and bishops resorted to other methods to draw opponents into their camp, including the time-tested diplomatic practice of providing material gifts and subsidies. Early in Justinian's rule, Severus of Antioch (sed. 512–538), an anti-Chalcedonian bishop, observed that his Chalcedonian counterparts exerted "all energy and watchfulness in making presents to their opponents and endeavoring to bring them over to them by a gift. For . . . nothing persuades unlearned persons so effectually as a present and a gift."[74] Everyone seems to have adopted this approach: Emperor Anastasius, a miaphysite sympathizer, reportedly offered thirty pounds of gold as a "gift for the poor" to a Palestinian abbot in hope of winning his support for Severus's single-nature doctrine.[75] But we mainly hear about such initiatives under Justinian, when authors variously praised their anti-Chalcedonian comrades for resisting—or castigated them for betraying Christ, not unlike Judas, for just a few loaves of bread.[76] Evidently the church *annona* gave imperial bishops a persuasive tool. It was part of a strategy to induce religious uniformity that might otherwise take the form of exile, imprisonment, or extortion.[77]

Aristocrats adopted similar practices: the ascetic heiress Melania the Younger (d. 439) reportedly used gifts not only to fund churches and monasteries but also to convert pagans, Samaritans, and heretics. Such was the culture in which Christian philanthropy evolved.[78] What remains to be stressed is that the imperial superstructure and practices described here, especially the systematic provision of imperial subsidies to affiliated institutions, supported further religious gift-giving and enabled even modest Christian institutions to thrive on a scale beyond anything possible in the Christian West at the time. It did so, moreover, without greatly burdening the state: even under Constantine, the portions of the *annona civica* earmarked for ecclesiastical recipients—such as the 36,000 *modii* (about 214 tons) that the church of Antioch received in 331—were a tiny part of the imperial budget compared to what soldiers and privileged civilians received. Like the coins scattered on New Year's Day, it was a calculated expense. Peter Brown observes, "The purpose of such doles was to define an obligation,"[79] making churches and monasteries grateful to the imperial order and mindful of responsibilities that came with it. This was not very different from how they were taught to respond to material blessings obtained from God. Let us therefore consider how Christian professionals themselves envisioned their place within the late Roman state.

PROVIDENTIAL ORDER AND THE RISE
OF A RELIGIOUS ARISTOCRACY

The late seventh-century *Chronicle* of Bishop John of Nikiû helps put church and state relations in Early Byzantium in a broader perspective. According to his fanciful account, Justinian early in his reign was induced by two Roman patricians to hold an audience with a magician named Masides. Masides offered to use his demons not only to attack the emperor's foes in Persia but to administer nations and ensure an excellent collection of taxes on Justinian's behalf. The emperor was not persuaded: after affirming his allegiance to "Christ, Creator of the heavens and the earth," he ordered that Masides be burned at the stake. We might think this a story about the Early Byzantine suppression of sorcery. But in this case it is probable that "Masides the magician" was a garbled reference to a Zoroastrian magus named Mazdak, whose teachings rocked Sassanian Persia next door in the 520s.[80] Initially backed by Shah Khavad I (r. 488–531), Mazdak allegedly called for a redistribution of all private property on the grounds that the Zoroastrian deity Ahura Mazda wanted the world's material bounty to be inherited equally by all. His teachings ignited a rebellion that was suppressed by the future shah Khosrow I Anushiruwan (r. 531–579), but not before it had forced government officials to open state grain silos to feed the poor in southern Mesopotamia.

By all accounts Mazdak was a genuine radical. Like the Persian prophet Mani (d. 277) two and a half centuries before him, he exploited the dualist aspects of Zoroastrian teaching to pose challenging questions about humanity's spiritual relation to the material world. John of Nikiû's account may not be credible, but his attribution of tax reforms to Masides aligns with modern speculations that Mazdakism responded to Sassanian efforts to impose on the peasantry a more exacting tax structure like the one that the Romans had implemented for centuries.[81] In any case his example underscores the fact that, by contrast, as far as we know, no such radicalism was ever espoused by Christian leaders in Early Byzantium.[82] The authorities whose writings survive from this era were almost all children of imperial bureaucrats or landowning families. Though not members of the highest aristocracy—

which perhaps explains the blistering criticisms they sometimes launched against those they called "the rich"—they nonetheless received the best educations and benefitted from the status quo. Accordingly, they sought to fix its abuses rather than to advocate its overhaul.[83] Even John Chrysostom, whom nineteenth-century scholars regarded as a socialist, believed that the Roman hierarchy was providentially ordained, so that humans might live peacefully together until Judgment Day. God had created monarchy, not democracy, he assured his congregations, placing husbands over wives, masters over slaves, and rulers over subjects "so that all might exist in *harmonia* and *eutaxia.*" Otherwise, all would perish in anarchy.[84] Acceptance of this arrangement was inculcated among monks as well. When Antony the Great asked how unrighteous people could prosper while the righteous were starving, a voice reportedly replied, "Look to yourself: these are God's judgments, and it does not behoove you to understand them."[85]

Indeed, we owe the very notion of *hierarchia* to Early Byzantine Christianity. A mysterious author known as Pseudo-Dionysius the Areopagite coined the Greek word in the fifth century to describe a proper ecclesiastical order, whereby bishops, priests, and deacons presided over monks, ordinary churchgoers, and penitents without dissension. In fact he used the term to convey how such ideal church governance reflected the triune deity's governance over a three-tiered angelic host.[86] Consonant with the Council of Chalcedon, he was expressly concerned to subordinate the occasionally insubordinate monastic population to the institutional church. He conceded that monks, due to their exemplary piety, deserved to stand at the threshold of the inner sanctuary of a church, but since they were still technically just members of the laity, they could go no farther.

This hierarchical outlook only solidified during the fifth century and is never contested in the literature discussed in this book.[87] Indeed, late Roman preachers openly acknowledged that not all members of a church were "of equal honor."[88] Monks never gave up the conviction that they merited greatest esteem, however. "There is no nation under heaven like that of the Christians," went a monastic saying, "and of that nation, nothing like the order of monks."[89] We may smile at their self-regard, but it was shaped by the aristocratic ideology that pervaded this society, and monks clearly believed that their austerities, discipline, and humiliations made them religious aristocrats in the true sense of the word. Unlike worldly aristocrats, they could count on being accompanied up to heaven by the highest-ranking angels when they died; and as angels illuminated their way, so monks believed they had to shine for all humanity. As John Climacus wrote in his seventh-century handbook, *The Ladder of Divine Ascent,* "Monks must set good examples in all things, giving no occasion for scandal in anything they do or say. For if the light becomes dark, imagine how dark it will become for those living in the world?"[90]

Climacus voiced such caution partly because he knew that many of those "living in the world" held their profession in contempt. We glimpse this only occasionally in our surviving sources, but it was a fact of monastic existence. The anonymous author of the *Dialogue on Political Science* opined that the emperor should allow fewer monasteries to exist, arguing that most monks would better serve the state if they were forced to farm the fields or fight in the army. Elders warned novices to anticipate becoming objects of "jest and mockery in the eyes of men who do not even merit speaking with them." Mimes publicly lampooned monks on stage, and people dressed up in cowls to ridicule their exorcisms or posed as demoniacs to expose them as frauds.[91] Perhaps most predictable were allegations about monks accumulating heaps of wealth. Charges of hypocrisy are heard from the fifth century onward. A hostile historian writing during Anastasius's reign, probably paraphrasing an earlier source, wrote that monks "claimed most of the earth as their own," and that, "under a pretext of sharing everything with the destitute, they have ruined practically everyone."[92]

It is impossible to assess these allegations or to estimate how much any Early Byzantine monastery possessed on average. Wealth is a relative concept, and there were clearly as many poor monasteries as there were rich ones, with much depending on their location or connections to the lay aristocracy. We may safely assume that few enjoyed anything like the level of resources attributed to metropolitan churches. These not only collected produce and rents from shops and villages they owned, but they also sometimes exacted "tribute" from monasteries in their dioceses. Bishops in wealthier regions could live like lords of secular estates, and we know that some of them tried: a sixth-century bishop of Tralles (Aydin, Turkey) in a hot valley of southern Asia Minor got into trouble with Justinian when he took over an imperial monastery high up in the mountains in hope of turning it into a summer retreat.[93]

Nonetheless, it is also clear from archaeology and papyri that monasteries were becoming landowners during our period.[94] Our only statistic comes from an early sixth-century papyrus tax register that shows eight or nine monasteries owning about five percent of the land around the Egyptian town of Aphrodito.[95] That is not much, but critics could point to some obvious examples of monastic wealth from the fifth century onward. The ruins of Deir Turmanin in northern Syria, Qartmin/ Mar Gabriel in northern Mesopotamia, the exquisite Martyrius Monastery outside Jerusalem (Ma'ale Adummim, West Bank; see the figure), and the hulking White Monastery at Sohag in the central Nile valley, to just name fifth-century foundations, still look impressive today.[96] Like the metropolitan churches described above, some had dozens of village or monastic dependencies working for them, or became villages unto themselves. Shenoute's two thousand or so male monks worked as cobblers, weavers, carpenters, potters, scribes, bookmakers, and the like, enabling him to raise more than 5,635 solidi to care for refugees for three months during a nomadic incursion in 441. The enclosed space in which they lived was, as befits the land of the Pharaohs, the size of a small city; the White

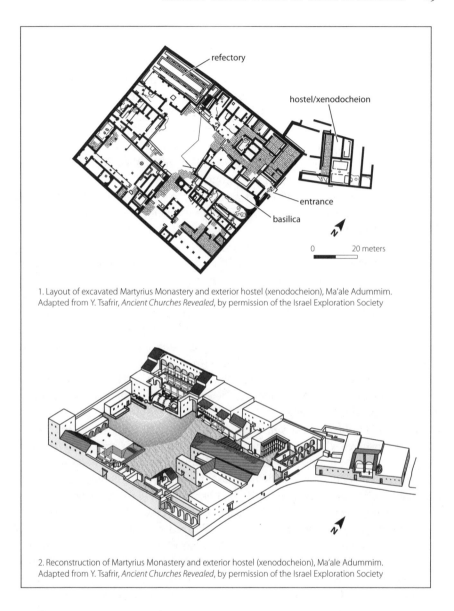

1. Layout of excavated Martyrius Monastery and exterior hostel (xenodocheion), Ma'ale Adummim. Adapted from Y. Tsafrir, *Ancient Churches Revealed*, by permission of the Israel Exploration Society

2. Reconstruction of Martyrius Monastery and exterior hostel (xenodocheion), Ma'ale Adummim. Adapted from Y. Tsafrir, *Ancient Churches Revealed*, by permission of the Israel Exploration Society

Monastery's church alone is one of the largest structures known from Christian antiquity, covering an area of 2,700 sq. meters (the size of half an American football field). The Duke of Egypt, a patron, was said to have once "taken his ease in the abundance of the monastery" for three days.[97] Thanks to the recent restoration of the paintings in the neighboring Red Monastery church, we now have some inkling of how exuberantly colorful the interior walls of the White Monastery would have been.[98] From hagiographers we also get an idea about the smaller adornments and moveable assets of other monasteries that are now lost: Cyril of Scythopolis mentions a monastery outside Jerusalem that kept six hundred solidi on hand in three purses in its main office, and John of Ephesus "admires explicitly the fine craftsmanship in monastic buildings, and the sumptuousness of their church furniture."[99] Given these examples it is not surprising that even Symeon Stylites, the great Syrian pillar saint (ca. 390–457) discussed in chapter 6, could be suspected of possessing gold. According to his hagiographers, when a priest visited Symeon's pillar, a deacon in his entourage jested that the saint should drop down something from his purse as a gift. This caused Symeon to retort, "Did someone tell you I have money, or have you yourself noticed this?" Before the deacon had time to reply, the joke redounded on him: his pants exploded with diarrhea, everyone laughed, and two days later, he died.[100]

Clearly these were sensitive matters. Ewa Wipszycka believes that ideological reservations silenced discussion of the topic in our sources.[101] But contemporary authors were not as reticent about the monastic acquisition of wealth as we might suppose, and ascetic attitudes toward voluntary poverty were not as inflexible than we might think. Of course, Jesus's admonition, "If you would be perfect, go, sell your possessions, give to the poor . . . and come, follow me" (Mt 19:21; cf. Mk 10:21, Lk 18:22), meant that a noticeable level of *aktēmosynē* was always expected of such Christians: hence admirers sometimes described monasticism simply as "the life without possessions."[102] What, however, determined appropriate levels of material poverty or personal property?

Criteria of utility and need guided most orthodox discussions, but only Basil of Caesarea specified what this should mean in practice ("on the subject of *aktēmosynē* . . . this should be the measure, that each should limit his possession to the last tunic"), and it is not clear that he intended this comment to be taken seriously.[103] By the fifth century such authorities had generally adopted the compromise of distinguishing the poverty of individual monks from the corporate wealth of their monasteries: while individuals were expected to reduce their personal possessions to a bare minimum, no limit was placed on what a community might possess as a whole, and wealthier monasteries were simply expected to share with those that were poorer.[104] This was based on the scriptural example of the original apostolic community, in which "none . . . claimed any of his possessions as his own, but everything was held in common among them" (Acts 4: 34). The rule of thumb formally became law in 535, when Justinian required those who joined a cenobium to formally transfer all of their individual property into its corporate legal possession, and prohibited them from privately possessing or controlling any property thereafter.[105] This law gave monastic communities an incentive to recruit people of means. It may account for the enticements of daily sustenance we hear were promised to attract novices in sixth-century Jerusalem, and for the minimum contribution reportedly required to join a female monastery in seventh-century Alexandria.[106]

It was therefore perfectly plausible for hard-core ascetics like Symeon Stylites to live amid opulence without contradiction. Accumulating corporate resources was not considered antithetical to monasticism if the resulting surplus was justly obtained and put to proper use. After all, Abraham, Joseph, and other biblical exemplars had possessed cattle and hundreds of slaves, yet they were prompt to spend their riches on pious acts. As Philoxenus of Mabbug (d. 523) pointed out, "These all were owners of great possessions and wealth, but they were masters of their riches, and their riches were not masters of them."[107] In his opinion, because Jesus had possessed nothing, neither should monks. But the Old Testament forced him and other rigorists to acknowledge the possibility of possessing righteous material wealth. An entire hagiographical tradition arose around the notion that God would enrich anyone who used such wealth to give to people in need.[108]

Indeed, ascetic wealth could itself be construed as a godsend. Monks identified their community's enrichment as a sign of God's blessing, and corporate poverty a sign of divine disfavor. Traveling outside Jerusalem, the anti-Chalcedonian hagiographer John Rufus saw a dilapidated cenobium covered with brambles; upon asking about it, he was simply told that its occupants had embraced the accursed Chalcedonian creed.[109] The founder of what later would be the biggest Chalcedonian monastery in Palestine said on his deathbed that if his monks saw their monastery expand after he died, it meant that his teachings had met divine approval—but if it did not, they should infer the opposite.[110] Increased patronage indicated the same thing. It was fondly recalled that when Symeon Stylites was expelled from a cenobium because of his extreme mortifications, its abbot kindly gave him four darics upon his departure, saying, "These will be for your food and clothing, until men appreciate you."[111]

Much of this might seem to anticipate modern Christian notions about God-given wealth enshrined in the so-called Prosperity Gospel. But there were major differences between the Early Byzantine outlook and that product of twentieth-century capitalism. The ancient outlook was grounded in an optimism that there would always be enough for all, if people just resisted all unnecessary consumption and left whatever they did not need for others. Like their Hebrew and Greco-Roman predecessors, Christian authorities held a positive view of the potential for material abundance that might surprise us, given modern economic theories and our general impression of premodern hardships. To explain why ancient authors frequently give glowing descriptions for what must have been low yields of grain, Gildas Hamel notes a difference between ancient and modern expectations:

In modern parlance, one considers the finiteness of resources and the unlimited nature of human needs as solid facts. This point of departure allows one to set off dwindling or finite resources against a background of rapidly growing needs and consequently establish a theory of prices. The ancients did exactly the opposite: they were inclined to consider resources as infinite, or at least very adequate, but needs as limited in number and intent, at least among proper people.

Scarcity was not an economic problem but a moral problem, caused by people taking more than they needed. Hamel believes this ancient outlook stemmed from a preference to focus on what was manageable rather than confront the inevitability of dearth "straight in the eye."[112] But for orthodox Christians, it was also the only acceptable outlook, given their precapitalist understanding of economics and providential view of material creation.

THE CHRISTIAN IDEAL OF STEWARDSHIP

We must remember that neither classical nor Early Byzantine authorities ever developed anything like the subject or way of thinking we call "economics." Their reasoning was especially unsophisticated regarding the generation of wealth. Since land was the only predictably safe and productive asset in this nonindustrial, agrarian economy, Greco-Roman elites made it the basis of honorable wealth and noble status. Most wealthy families just followed the same plan, amassing as much land as possible, working it as cheaply as possible, releasing as little as possible to drive up prices, then reinvesting as much as possible back into more land or loans that might yield land on default.[113] Taking risks to pursue wealth directly through commerce was disparaged as a sign of vulgarity and greed. It is true that an alternative view was sometimes aired, proposing that wealth must be self-generated to qualify as either noble or just. In a provocative moment, John Chrysostom even told his elite churchgoers that all the wealth they had inherited must have originated in some act of seizure or exploitation and so must be considered unjust, even if those injustices had occurred generations ago. For him, good, clean wealth had to be generated either through one's own "just toil and sweat" or from what one already had, as was the case with Abraham's slaves, "all born into his household" (Gn 17: 23).[114] This expressed an ideal of self-sufficiency known as *autarkeia*. Though romanticized by Stoic philosophers and advocated by later Byzantine authorities (guided partly by scripture, as for example, Mi 4:4: "They shall sit every man under his vine and under his fig tree"), this ideal may bring us to the outlook of ordinary farmers. But it was not a sophisticated view, and in Early Byzantium it was mainly attributed to monastic solitaries as a means of "turning economic behavior into non-economic behavior."[115] While preaching against excesses, church authorities in the Roman East generally acquiesced to strategies of wealth accumulation based on land acquisition, forced labor, hoarding, and lending at interest.[116] Indeed, elite prejudices against trade and other commercial activities often colored their thinking. John of Ephesus writes that two ascetic Christian traders "resolved to abstain entirely from the evil practices which traders of the world are wont to follow," such as lying and using false weights or measures. For him, they represented two saintly exceptions to a very common rule.[117]

If early Christians contributed anything to economic thought, then, as with classical philosophers, it was in the area of domestic wealth management. In patristic tradition, this meant a stewardship (*oikonomia*) that was supposed to serve the aims of the divine dispensation (also *oikonomia*).[118] Orthodox authorities agreed not only that God had created the world to support humanity, but that everything in the world ultimately belonged to God. In this view, landowners who thought they had exclusive rights were deceiving themselves. At most they were earthly wardens of the divine domain, whose job was to make God's land as productive as possible. God had provided everything needed to cultivate it, from seeds to sunshine to muscles to rain. But the point of such production was not to enrich the wardens but humanity as a whole. In fact, the material world could itself be seen an expression of divine *philanthrōpia*—a gift showing God's merciful desire to benefit human creation.[119] Scholars have observed that this argument justified the enrichment of Christian leaders, inasmuch as it implied that they would be most knowledgeable about the best uses of God-given resources.[120] Be that as it may, this Christian ideal of stewardship may be summarized as one of taking no more than needed and leaving the rest for others in need. We will see in more detail what this meant in chapters 4 and 5, but let me conclude by noting certain theological presumptions that are applicable throughout the book.

First, the church and monastic authorities under discussion conceived of their deity as a supreme gift giver. Like a Roman emperor, the Christian god was imagined to be the source of all earthly bounty, capable of showering inexhaustible gifts of grace (literally "favors," *charis*) generated from inexhaustible stores. As Chrysostom put it,

> Even if the whole world should come [seeking succor], His *charis* is not spent nor His power exhausted, but it remains equally great. And just as beams of the sun shed light each day but are not exhausted, nor is their light diminished by giving so great a supply; so . . . the power of the Spirit is in no way diminished by the number of those who enjoy it.[121]

In addition, this deity reveled in reciprocity, rewarding those who imitated His generosity. Inscriptions called Him a "god who gives back what he owes" (*misthapodotēs theos*), a divine characteristic sometimes expounded upon at length.[122] Christians were advised to regard this as a means to right wrongs between them and God. "We should love the Lord as we do our friends," remarked John Climacus, "[some of whom] I have seen resort to . . . every gift, simply to restore an old relationship upset by some minor grievance."[123]

Second, this tradition rarely demanded or expected complete altruism. After all, the New Testament made clear that perfect gifts came only from heaven ("every generous act of giving, with every perfect gift, is from above," Jas 1:17). Although Christians were encouraged to emulate God's generosity by deliberately giving to those who could not repay them (cf. Lk 14:13), it was understood that they might do so to obtain their own salvation.[124] Truly selfless giving could be expected only of advanced ascetics. As a result, altruism was not as great a concern in Early Byzantine valuations of religious giving as it is in modern anthropology and popular culture; it was regarded as essential only to charity and blessings (especially the latter), without tarnishing the other gifts.

Finally, despite this divinity's delight in his debtor status, authorities reminded audiences that they owed Him whatever they had, thanks entirely to His "love of humanity"—that is, His divine philanthropy that had created so many material goods for their use. The best way to acknowledge this was by releasing these goods as often as possible to circulate as usefully as possible to as many as possible. Basil of Caesarea pictured a mighty river growing out of many small streams: "As water becomes more abundant in sluices where it is held but stagnates . . . so too immobilized wealth is useless, but if put in movement and circulation, becomes fruitful and conductive to the common good." Such *oikonomia* increased the wealth of all. Basil proclaimed that whoever dispensed his material surplus in this manner—rather than locking it up in a granary or wasting it on public entertainments for the sake of *philotimia*—would be acclaimed as "nourisher, benefactor, and all the names of *philanthrōpia*" on Judgment Day.[125] Philanthropy was thus an essential part of Christian stewardship. As Basil's friend and episcopal colleague Gregory of Nazianzus explained in his own torrent of words:

> Who has given to you to see the beauty of the heavens, the course of the sun, the moon's orb . . . the growing things of the earth, the pouring forth of air, the depth and vastness of the sea, ever flowing, ever held in check, the depths of rivers, the ceaseless flow of the winds?
>
> Who gives you the rains, the tilling of the earth, the arts, homes, lands, laws, manner of life, and love of our kindred? From where have you received the living creatures that serve you, and those given for your food? Who has made humanity the master and ruler of all on the earth? And so that I need not speak of each single thing—who has bestowed all the things by which humanity is placed over all things? Is it not He who now for all this, and in return for all this, asks for philanthropy?
>
> Let us not shame ourselves, receiving so much from Him, and hoping for more, by refusing God this one thing: philanthropy.[126]

We will examine the exact terms of this proposition in the following chapters.

"Give to All Who Ask of You"

The Challenge of Early Byzantine Philanthropy

The greatest goods known to humanity are Justice and Philanthropy. The first ensures equitable distribution to each person without encroaching on what belongs to another; the second inclines towards mercy and liberates the needy from harsh wants. These adorn our reign, make government safe and secure, and set human life on a good course. For this reason we, who have received our scepter from God, must be prompt to manifest them through good deeds.

—EMPEROR TIBERIUS II, PREAMBLE, NOVEL 163, ISSUED 575 CE[1]

No Roman emperors expressed such concern for philanthropy as the emperors of the Justinianic age. Forty years before Tiberius II (r. 574–582) formulated the statement above, Justinian had referred to his reign as "these philanthropic times," and he repeatedly invoked *philanthrōpia* as a guiding principle of his legislation.[2] Usually this signaled an emperor's willingness to hear legal petitions or mitigate sentences,[3] but anyone struck down by the multiple calamities that plagued his reign would have appreciated the steps he took to express it through material welfare. All around the eastern empire, but especially in Constantinople after the Nika uprising of 532, Justinian built, refounded, or repaired an unprecedented array of hospitals, hostels, poorhouses, and related facilities.[4] That one of these, the Sampson Hospital, was grandly restored with two new infirmaries next to Hagia Sophia in the ceremonial heart of the capital indicates their centrality to Justinianic propaganda. If a fourth-century priest could be credited with "extraordinary philanthropy" for building a hospice (*xenodocheion*) for sick monks and strangers at a monastic settlement in the Egyptian desert, then Justinian's philanthropic foundations—which probably offered services on a sliding scale, if not for free— showed how far a Christian emperor could fulfill that ideal.[5] These were not the type of amenities formerly associated with classical euergetism, meant to enhance the civic experience of citizens in their cities. More than any other innovation of Early Byzantium, hospitals and poorhouses reflected a religious ethic aimed at alleviating the most basic needs of an anonymous mass of humanity.[6] Such monotheist Christian philanthropy drew on the Greco-Roman concept of *philanthrōpia*, but pressed it farther than ever before.

This chapter will explain how this happened, first by examining what early Christian philanthropy meant as a concept, and then by exploring how it was supposed to be put into practice in Early Byzantium. The Justinianic age is often seen as one in which two traditions of ancient philanthropy—classical and Christian, imperial and church—reached full synthesis.[7] In fact, these traditions never greatly differed from each other, since the ancient Christian ideal was an extension of the older classical ideal. Indeed, before the reign of Constantine, Greco-Roman philanthropy was never as restricted in theory and Christian philanthropy never as expansive in practice as often assumed. It must therefore be clarified how Christian authorities adapted this Greco-Roman ideal to extend aid universally, not only by establishing institutions like those described above, but by asking individuals to live up to Jesus's command, "Give to all who ask of you" (Mt 5:42). How was classical philanthropy adapted to support such universal policies and practices?

To begin, we must recognize that in neither classical nor early Christian tradition did the Greek word *philanthrōpia* usually just mean "love for one's fellow human beings, expressed in kindness and benevolent action."[8] The ideal had a concessive dimension that emphasized clemency. In both traditions, *philanthrōpia* more precisely meant "being benevolent to others, even if doing so goes against one's natural inclination" or "showing kindness to fellow humans, despite full knowledge that they do not deserve it." This dimension gave ancient philanthropy its hard, distinctive edge, turning a lofty ideal into a provocative (and potentially burdensome) challenge.

This observation, though nothing new as far as classical tradition is concerned, has not informed scholarship on early Christian philanthropy. We shall see, however, that it was an early Christian author who most emphatically insisted on restricting the word *philanthrōpia* to describe acts of benevolence done despite knowing full well that its beneficiaries were one's enemies or adversaries. His view conformed both to New Testament usage and to secular notions of philanthropy that prevailed in the Roman Empire at the time. In fact it was probably imperial propaganda that introduced the Greek word *philanthrōpia* as a term for clemency among the early empire's eastern subjects, including New Testament authors. Greek and Roman officials had long used the term to describe actions that mitigated whatever harsh consequences a strict application of law might entail. This secular usage persisted to the end of antiquity. "No transgression of any of our subjects is so great as not to merit our philanthropy," Emperor Justinian affirmed when restoring rights to recalcitrant Samaritans after their uprising in 529, "even if our hatred of their acts should rouse our vengeance against them."[9]

Justinian's understanding of *philanthrōpia*, it must be emphasized, conformed not just to ancient imperial conventions but to the thinking of contemporary Christians. Of the seventy-two precepts that an ambitious deacon of Hagia Sophia named Agapetus sent to the emperor early in his reign, three of them pertain to *philanthrōpia* or acts of mercy. Agapetus did not list his precepts systematically, but ordered them alphabetically, so that their initial letters would form an acrostic spelling out his own name and rank (an artifice that suggests the underlying purpose of his gift). Nonetheless, Agapetus consistently presents philanthropy as something to adopt concessively, despite an emperor's possible inclination not to do so:

> *Precept 6:* Nothing produces higher esteem than when a person both wants and does what is philanthropic, despite being able to do whatever he wants.[10]

> *Precept 40:* Most honorable of all things is to rule. This is especially true when he who holds power inclines not towards obstinacy but towards mildness. Rejecting what is inhumane as bestial, he exhibits philanthropy as something divine.[11]

> *Precept 63.* God needs nothing, and rulers only need God. Therefore, imitate Him who needs nothing and be generous to those who petition for mercy [*eleos*]. Do not examine Your servants strictly. . . . For the sake of the worthy, it is far better to show mercy even to those who are unworthy, than to deprive those who are worthy on account of the unworthy.[12]

It might be argued that, because these precepts were written for an emperor, they reflect imperial conventions rather than Christian sentiments. Yet we shall see that Gregory of Nazianzus (329–390) similarly emphasizes philanthropy's concessive dimension in his fourth-century sermon *On Loving the Poor,* the most extensive treatment of Christian philanthropy to survive from Early Byzantium. For him, *philanthrōpia* meant extending kindness even to lepers—people whom both Christians and pagans alike believed were divinely accursed, and so deserving of their suffering.

As Gregory demonstrates, this concessive facet helped preachers justify the universal extension of mercy (*eleos*) to all humanity, beyond one's own circle or tribe. It also helped them expound Jesus's command, "give to all who ask of you" (Mt 5:42; Lk 6:30). However skeptical we might be that people took this imperative seriously, Early Byzantine authorities grappled with how to put it into practice. Their solution was universality through prioritization. Such prioritization, already sanctioned by Paul's recommendation that Christians "do good to all, but especially to those who belong to the family of the faith" (Gal 6:10), was scripturally justified by the apostolic principle of giving "to each, as any had need" (Acts 4:35; cf. 2:45). According to this principle, aid was to be extended to all, but not necessarily to all in the same degree. This approach made Christian philanthropy institutionally feasible on a universal scale.

Fundamental was an understanding that some people deserved more mercy than others. Like their counterparts in the West, Christians in the Roman East devised a notion of "the deserving poor." But while Western authorities like Ambrose of Milan (sed. 374–397) defined this category primarily in terms of kinship (a rule of thumb that went back to the Stoics),[13] Eastern authorities based theirs on the implications of the Greek word most frequently used to designate poor people in the New Testament: *ptōchoi*. Historians have tended to identify these *ptōchoi* as "destitute poor people," distinguishing their absolute poverty from that of a *penēs,* meaning a laborer born to a life of toil (*ponos*) and penury, equivalent to the modern "working poor." When pressed, however, Early Byzantine authorities, following classical precedents, defined the state of *ptōcheia* not so much as extreme poverty as a loss of prosperity.[14] Origen of Alexandria (ca.185–254), for example, observed that "the *ptōchos* . . . is someone who has fallen from wealth, while the *penēs* earns his livelihood from toil." Likewise Basil of Caesarea (330–379), when explaining what the designations meant in Scripture, states:

> Remembering that [Paul] said of the Lord, "For your sake he became a *ptōchos,* though he was rich" [2 Cor 8:9], I reckon a *ptōchos* to be someone who has come down from wealth into neediness, but a *penēs* to be someone who existed in need from the start and conducts himself in that circumstance pleasingly to the Lord.[15]

Thus, not all *ptōchoi* were destitute; the term encompassed anyone who had experienced a decline in worldly fortune. Furthermore, because of Jesus's praise of the "*ptōchoi* in spirit" (Mt 5:3) and Paul's description of Christ as one who "became a *ptōchos,* although he was rich" (2 Cor 8:9, quoted by Basil above), this designation had ideological significance, so that all clerics and monks who voluntarily renounced worldly prosperity for Christ's sake deserved special consideration as Christian *ptōchoi.*[16] In theory, however, anyone who had "fallen" from former prosperity represented a priority for Christian aid. That point is made in a papyrus written on behalf of a fourth-century wine merchant who, though not poor, was suffering at the hands of creditors and magistrates: "Regarding those who have fallen into misfortune," his letter begins, "the divine word exhorts us to help them all, especially our brethren."[17]

Unless we recognize this ideological privileging of "the fallen," we will not see and appreciate the institutional priorities of Early Byzantine philanthropy. It explains the difficulty of finding references to the working poor—in contrast to widows, orphans, the sick, the aged, invalids, and distressed gentlefolk—in connection to the church dole and other philanthropic institutions of the day; it perhaps also explains why an emperor as vocally philanthropic as Justinian could build so many institutions to aid the afflicted in Constantinople while simultaneously establishing a magistracy to evict able-bodied beggars from the city.[18] Such priorities were based, however, on a presumption that individuals would provide alms on the micro level to those who did not have access to the institutional system or if it ran out on the macro level. This individual responsibility was supposed to make up for institutional shortcomings and ensure that Christian philanthropy attained universality. It weighed especially heavily on monks, who were supposed to "give to all who ask" without favoritism while striving to recognize and respect the needs of each. They met this challenge partly by following the institutional priorities noted above, but also (as we shall later see), by reconceptualizing Christian gift giving itself.

THE CLASSICAL ROOTS OF CHRISTIAN
PHILANTHRŌPIA

A highly tendentious but customary place to start discussing the relation of Christian philanthropy to Greco-Roman tradition is a letter that Emperor Julian "the Apostate" (r. 361–363), Constantine's grandson, sent in the last months of his life to Arsacius, his newly appointed high priest of Galatia in Asia Minor. One ambition of this emperor's short reign was to reverse his grandfather's Christian revolution and revive traditional pagan cults by enhancing them with philanthropic services.[19] Christianity provided an obvious blueprint: "Do we not notice," Julian asks, "how philanthropy towards strangers, care for burial of the dead, and an affected loftiness of lifestyle, has advanced impiety?" He requests that Arsacius build hostels (or hospitals, *xenodocheia*) in Galatian cities so that "strangers may enjoy our philanthropy—not only those of our own faith, but whoever should ask." He reveals a plan, surely inspired by the church *annona*, to supply pagan temples with provisions to distribute to the needy, explaining that it was shameful that the "impious Galileans feed both theirs and ours, while ours appear to lack aid from us."[20]

Called "one of the greatest tributes paid to Christian charity by one of Christianity's most resolute imperial opponents,"[21] Julian's *Letter to Arsacius* shows that, by the second half of the fourth century, Christian philanthropy had become sufficiently institutionalized with facilities called *xenodocheia* to provide models for imitation. It also implies that Christians had much to teach staunch traditionalists like Julian about extending philanthropy to the anonymous poor. Yet this letter, if authentic,[22] should be read in light of an earlier, more extensive discussion Julian had already sent to a high priest named Theodore. When explaining his expectations for Theodore's pagan priesthood, Julian insisted that they "above all practice *philanthrōpia*."

> We ought to share our resources with each and every human being—more generously with those who are respectable, but also with those who are helpless and poor, as much as suffices for their need. And I will assert (even if it is paradoxical to say so) that it would be a sacred act to share our clothes and food even with the wicked. For we are giving to a person's humanity, not to his character.[23]

In this discussion, Julian advocates giving universally to all prisoners, even if presumed guilty, lest any innocent person be neglected. Philanthropy comes in many forms, he notes, and can be expressed not only by punishing leniently but by supplying material needs. He assures Theodore that such generosity would not bankrupt him ("For whoever became poor by giving to his neighbors?"), observing that it would not befit a priest of Zeus, the old god of strangers and kinship, to treat other people as if they came from a different race—for "like it or not," he adds, each human being is akin by their common divine descent.[24]

Of these two pastoral letters, Julian's *Letter to Theodore* is arguably the more instructive about his outlook on philanthropy and its appropriation by Christian leaders.[25] Toward its end, he concludes,

> I think that it was when the impious Galileans saw that the poor were being neglected and overlooked by our priests that they devoted themselves to *philanthrōpia*. . . . Through their "charity-feasts," "receptions" or "table-ministrations" (they call it by many names, since they have many ways of carrying it out), they have led many into atheism.[26]

Undoubtedly, Julian had Christian models in mind when discussing philanthropy with his priests. Having spent the two past years in Constantinople and Antioch, he could have seen for himself the *xenodocheia* his grandfather and uncle, the emperors Constantine (306–337) and Constantius (337–361), had put to Christian use in both cities; these may have been the facilities he had in mind when writing to Arsacius. In his *Letter to Theodore,* however, he neither mentions those facilities nor gives the impression that the institutionalization of Christian philanthropy had advanced beyond "charity-feasts, receptions, or table-ministrations." Nor, furthermore, does he claim that Christians were the first to extend philanthropy to the poor. Instead, his main point is that they had turned it into a religious practice, making giving aid to the poor a "sacred act" for their priests.[27] Julian wanted his pagan priests to see it as such too. Otherwise, his proposals for their practice of *philanthrōpia* —in particular, the extension of aid to all humans whether deserving or not—were deeply rooted in classical precedents.

It is now recognized that ancient Mediterranean cultures were not unusually callous or ungenerous toward sick or poor strangers.[28] The dominant ethics, however, remained tribal, aristocratic, or citizen-based. This tended to keep moral obligations limited to one's own kin, class, civic, or religious group.[29] Justification was rarely made at the level of principle to help people outside those groups. In classical tradition, however, one such principle did exist: *philanthrōpia.* This ideal already had a long history before the dawn of Christianity.

That history began in archaic Greece.[30] The Greek word *philanthrōpia* was apparently first coined to describe the propensity of certain entities to treat humans kindly, even though this went against behavior normally associated with their nonhuman kind. Hence, it was originally used to describe a few select deities (Prometheus, Hermes, Asclepius), animals (dogs, dolphins, horses) and climates

(Asia). Only in the fourth century BCE do we find it connected to humans, first to quasi-divine figures like Cyrus the Great, then to aristocrats who deigned to give gifts to their city-states or to individuals within them. Then, with the rise of Hellenistic kingdoms, it came to also designate royal acts of pardon or indulgence ranging from release from prison to hearing petitions or dismissing tax obligations. This usage influenced subsequent Jewish (in the Greek writings of Philo and the Septuagint), Roman, and New Testament conventions. Greek translators, for example, regularly used *philanthrōpia* to convey the *clementia* (clemency, reconciliation) a Roman emperor might bestow on his subjects or political opponents. The shift of imperial power to the Greek East made this usage all the more familiar from the fourth century CE onward, when courtiers began to represent even barbarians outside the empire as potential beneficiaries of Roman indulgence. This helped save face for an empire held at bay. Alluding to the embarrassing concessions that Emperor Theodosius I was forced to make to stop the Goths from pillaging Balkan lands in 382, his spokesman presented them as imperial acts of *philanthrōpia*, pointing out that any ruler who had this virtue need learn only if the one needing philanthropy "is human—not if he is Scythian or Massagetic . . . or did the first wrong."[31]

Two facets of classical philanthropy remained constant: first, a concessive force that justified extending clemency despite the evident inferiority or lack of merit of its beneficiaries; second, a tendency to extend such clemency to ever more distant groups of outsiders, including not just barbarians but people at the bottom of the social spectrum who were poorer than the rest. Indeed, these two facets complemented each other.[32] Scholars, however, have often insisted that "royal *philanthropia*, the exercise of clemency towards the defeated and guilty [was] . . . far removed from the care of beggars."[33] To be sure, classical discourse nowhere explicitly mentions beggars or anyone outside a citizen body as potential beneficiaries, and most surviving examples have a juridical or political emphasis. Yet this alleged classical neglect of anonymous beggars, if it truly existed, had little to do with the Greco-Roman concept itself; what mattered instead was the size or scope of the community being imagined. The Aristotelian *Constitution of Athens*, written in the fourth century BCE, illustrates the tyrant Peisistratus's philanthropy by stating that "he was not only gentle and forgiving even to those who had committed an offense" (i.e., he treated criminals with clemency), "but he also advanced money even to those without means, so that they could make a living as farmers."[34] This passage, like Julian's *Letter to Theodore* seven hundred years later, cites both judicial leniency and material giving to poor people as apparently equivalent expressions of philanthropy (a point that needs to be borne in mind in Christian contexts as well). If it differs from later Christian descriptions, the difference lies in the scope of the imagined community in which acts of *philanthrōpia* were being envisioned—a small, agrarian polis community of rich and poor farmers, not a universalizing, monotheistic empire filled with rich and poor people—rather than in any limitation in the classical conception of philanthropy itself.

To put it differently, anonymous poor citizens "without means" (*aporoi*, also Julian's term) in classical civic discourse were the counterparts of anonymous poor people in early Christian discourse. Both represented poor inferiors and relative outsiders, the helping of whom constituted an act of philanthropic mercy and indulgence.

Indeed, other, less overtly political examples from Greco-Roman literature confirm that the classical ideal implied acts of generosity across socioeconomic boundaries, and not just by monarchs. Diogenes Laertius (d. 240), for example, recognizes that "greeting all" and "helping everyone who suffers misfortune" were two of its basic manifestations, expected of anyone; a satire by Lucian of Samosata (d. 192) explains that the legendary curmudgeon of Periclean Athens, Timon, became a misanthrope after ruining himself by showing "philanthropy and pity toward each and every one in need"; and Aelius Aristides (d. 181) argues that it was "far more philanthropic" to honor people who did not merit it than to risk depriving those who did.[35] Of course, in casual usage, classical *philanthrōpia* might lose its concessive edge, and, like modern philanthropy, it was mainly considered a patrician virtue. "It is ridiculous," Theodosius's spokesman Themistius wrote, "to ascribe philanthropy to a weaver or builder who has a squalid little dwelling and rarely goes out of his house due to weariness and lack of leisure."[36] Note, however, that Themistius saw that it was a lowly artisan's restricted circumstances and inability to either circulate in or interact with the broader world that impeded his ability to show *philanthrōpia*. Otherwise, philanthropy was a virtue that everyone who was able was expected to display toward all, despite obvious differences in social origins, civic status, or economic circumstances.

If such philanthropy appears detached, it was often explicitly promoted as such. When explaining in his *Letter to Theodore* that it was acceptable to help even a wicked person because "we are giving to [that] person's humanity, not to his character," Julian was voicing an old Stoic view. There was no simple equivalence between *philanthrōpia* and the Stoic notion of *humanitas,* but both principles justified extending benevolence to unknown people based on the impersonal, abstract fact of their humanity. This provided Roman aristocrats like Seneca (d. 62 CE) and Marcus Aurelius (d. 180) with a rationale for transcending aristocratic prejudices when making universal benefactions: "We give not to the man but to his humanity" (a distinction ultimately attributed to Aristotle).[37] This did not rule out prioritization: while insisting on giving to anyone who was poor and needy (*pauper* and *egens,* Latin equivalents to Julian's *penēs* and *aporos*), Seneca, like Julian, recommends preferring people who might reciprocate with gratitude.[38] Seneca, however, also advised not giving out of feelings of pity or mercy (*misercordia*), lest such feelings disturb the tranquility of one's soul.[39] This was not just a Stoic stance. Aristotle distinguishes *to philanthrōpon* from *to eleos* (pity or mercy), reserving the latter emotion for members of one's group who had suffered a tragic reversal of fortune—"undeserved evil of the sort that one might expect oneself, or . . . one's own, to suffer." In contrast, *to philanthrōpon* denoted an impulse to alleviate suffering "irrespective of merit," without entailing strong emotional involvement.[40]

Classical philosophers thus regarded *philanthrōpia* as a generous impulse or principle that, unlike pity or mercy, could be extended to unfamiliar groups. It was never considered a religious obligation, despite its associations with certain gods and occasional mention as means of emulating the divine.[41] Moreover, it never seems to have been connected to civic euergetism, remaining a matter of private gifts and gestures. Yet its force as a principle justifying kindness to all, especially the unworthy, must not be underrated, for this was precisely the universalizing, concessive force that became prevalent in Christian discourse on the subject.

CHRISTIAN PHILANTHROPY BEFORE CONSTANTINE

It might be thought that early Christians, armed with their "gospel of love and charity" (to use Adolf Harnack's phrase), would not have needed such a concessive force. After all, the Sermon on the Mount (Mt 5:42–48; cf. Lk 6:27–36) makes its own concessive argument for giving to all:

> Give to everyone who asks of you, and do not refuse anyone who wants to borrow from you. You have heard that it was said, "You shall love your neighbor and hate your enemy." But I say to you, Love your enemies and pray for those who persecute you, so that you may be children of your Father in heaven; for he makes his sun rise on the wicked and on the good, and sends rain on the righteous and the unrighteous. . . . Be perfect, therefore, as your heavenly Father is perfect.[42]

Elsewhere Jesus requests that his followers be especially solicitous about the anonymous poor, promising to save on Judgment Day those who helped his "lowliest brothers," imagining himself as the recipient of all kindnesses done for them, listing activities that would later become canonical in Christian preaching on almsgiving: "for I was hungry and you gave me food, I was thirsty and you gave me something to drink, I was a stranger and you welcomed me, I was naked and you gave me clothing, I was sick and you took care of me, I was in prison and you visited me" (Mt 25:35–36). Furthermore, the parable of the Good Samaritan (Lk 10:25–37) indicated that such kindness should extend beyond coreligionists. Second-century literature like the *Didache* and the *Shepherd of Hermas* enjoined Christians to "give to all in want, without hesitating as to whom to give," while apologists depicted them as sharing with "each in need," and bringing together at the same table people who had formerly despised each other.[43]

Normative and apologetic writings rarely reflect actual practice, however. By most assessments, the generosity of Christian communities in pre-Constantinian times was "limited, discriminating in its reach, and introverted."[44] Such communal insularity is displayed in the writings of a relatively cosmopolitan author, Clement of Alexandria (ca. 150–215). His treatise *On the Rich Man's Salvation* is the most extensive Christian treatment of wealth to survive from the pre-Constantinian era. Clement wrote it for a group of Alexandrian Christians who were educated people of means.[45] Among the questions it addresses is who should benefit from their disposable income. Because theirs was the largest Christian community of the day outside Rome, we might expect to find in this treatise, if anywhere, indications that such beneficiaries included outsiders. But while Clement agreed with earlier authorities that donors should give whenever possible to whoever asked ("for such a love of gift giving is truly divine),"[46] he clearly assumed all potential recipients would be members of his church:

> Do not judge who is worthy or unworthy. . . . By going in turn to all in need you will necessarily find one of those empowered by God to save. "Judge not, then, that ye be not judged . . ." [Mt 7:1–3]. Open your tenderness to all enrolled as disciples of God, without contemptuously looking down on their physical appearance, without carelessly reckoning their age, without feeling irritation or turning away if any appears to be without means, badly dressed, deformed, or infirm.[47]

"All believers," wrote Clement, deserved generosity, but some were more deserving than others. In recommending that affluent Christians give to all in the community, he sought to ensure that they would not overlook those members who were "even more elect than the elect,"[48] whom God had endowed with special charisms to edify others. Because these "zealous ones" hid their holiness, donors had to either seek them out individually and risk missing one, or else give indiscriminately to all to ensure that each of the "more elect" been included, unremarkable though they might appear.

Clement may have been alluding here to church ascetics he elsewhere calls "true gnostics," people wholly committed to controlling their passions in pursuit of Christian wisdom. If true, then by prioritizing these before other "enrolled" disciples of God (as he calls widows, orphans, old people, and "men adorned with piety"), Clement anticipates later Christian customs privileging monks.[49] In any case his treatise envisions that Christian generosity in his Alexandrian church stayed within it. When he does allude to outside beggars "scattered along the roads," he does not depict them as either proper or potential recipients of Christian mercy or aid; instead, he characterizes them as "counterfeit *ptōchoi*," who had adopted begging as a profession.[50] Clement's preference for poor people attached to a Christian community is corroborated by a third-century text preserved in Syriac known as the *Teachings of the Apostles* (hereafter the *Didascalia*), a church manual that addressed a seemingly large community somewhere in western Syria. Written for bishops and laypeople alike, it specifies what groups were eligible to receive the church dole: orphans, widows, "the afflicted," and strangers. The last two groups might sound as if they included non-Christian outsiders, but when the manual refers to "strangers" elsewhere, it seems to mean visitors from another Christian community.[51]

It is perhaps relevant that the *Didascalia* nowhere mentions *philanthrōpia* (in Syriac, *mraḥmānutā*) and that Clement does so only twice, once to describe God's willingness to extend salvation to rich believers and once to describe his own willingness to help them secure it.[52] Indeed, references to philanthropy as a human (rather than a divine) trait are rare in Christian literature before the fourth century.[53] This makes all the more startling its extensive discussion in the Pseudo-Clementine *Homilies*. This collection is a series of commentaries or amplifications based on the better-known Pseudo-Clementine *Recognitions,* a Christian novel about the adventures of an early bishop of Rome named Clement (ca. 92–99). Its discussion of philanthropy is cast as a diatribe delivered by the Apostle Peter to his protégé one evening as the two were relaxing on the deck of a boat sailing up the Levant. Having mentioned to Peter that his mother had arranged the charismatic healing of a widow who had sheltered her after a shipwreck, Clement referred to his mother's gesture as an act of *philanthrōpia*. Hearing this, however, the apostle objected and spent the rest of the evening lecturing Clement on how gifts and acts of philanthropy differed from those of friendship, mercy, or charity.

According to Peter, Clement's comment showed that he had "no idea whatsoever about the greatness of *philanthrōpia*." Neither what the widow had done for his mother nor what his mother had done for her afterward counted as such. Instead, the hospitality that the widow had shown after his mother's shipwreck was an act of mercy (*eleos*) prompted by pity, since the widow had once been shipwrecked herself and recognized her own sufferings in his mother's plight; in fact, Peter adds, even an "impious" person would have been moved to pity after hearing all his mother's tragic reversals.[54] As for the help his mother arranged for the widow, this was not philanthropy either, but merely a friendly gesture of reciprocity (*philia*) to repay her kindness: "There is much difference," Peter explained, "between friendship and philanthropy, because friendship arises out of reciprocity."[55] Only if the widow or his mother had bestowed such kindnesses on people who had actually caused them harm, he insists, would it have qualified as *philanthrōpia*. For "a philanthropic person is one who benefits even his enemies."[56]

Their discussion continued. Surely, said Clement, the widow's hospitality counted as philanthropy, since she had offered it despite not previously knowing his mother. No, Peter maintains, "I still would not call her philanthropic." True, she had shown herself to be merciful (*eleēmōn*), but to qualify as philanthropic, a person must act with—and despite—full knowledge that her beneficiaries are in some way inimical to her interests. Acts of mercy or almsgiving (*eleēmosynē*), though akin to philanthropy, are not the same. "Listen how this is so," he says.

> Philanthropy is androgynous, part male and part female. Its feminine side is called "almsgiving" (*eleēmosynē*), its masculine side "charity [*agapē*] to our neighbor." Now, each human is a "neighbor" to every other human, not just a particular one, and humanity includes both the good and the bad, people friendly and people hostile. Therefore, anyone who strives to imitate God's philanthropy must benefit both the righteous and the unrighteous alike, as God Himself bestows his sun and rain upon all in the present world [cf. Mt 5:42]. But if you want to benefit [only] good people and not bad people—or if you even want to punish the bad—you are then undertaking the work of a judge, not striving for philanthropy.[57]

Charity (*agapē*), he explains, inclines a person toward extreme forgiveness, because anyone who "loves his neighbor as himself" will want that neighbor to receive as much forgiveness as he would want for himself. When extended to all humanity, such charity becomes perfect. Indeed, Peter adds, it may be considered philanthropy's masculine aspect. "But its feminine aspect is to show mercy (*to eleein*). This is done by feeding the hungry, giving drink to the thirsty, clothing the naked, visiting the sick, receiving strangers, and going as often as possible to help someone in prison [cf. Mt 25:35–36]: in short, to show mercy to whoever is in misfortune."[58]

If only we knew more about this remarkable text. Believed to have originated in third-century Syria (possibly Edessa), the *Homilies* in their present form represent a redaction made in the fourth century before Julian's reign; we can say only that this homily represents a pre-Julianic discussion of Christian philanthropy.[59] It has received little attention from historians.[60] It reflects rigorous thinking on the subject, exemplified by a syllogistic clarity not found elsewhere. It should not be dismissed as an anomaly or mere academic exercise, however. It is highly illuminating on each of the Christian gift ideals it names, especially on differences between almsgiving and charity (*eleēmosynē* and *agapē*), a distinction discussed in chapter 4. It is important for our present discussion not only because it makes the concessive dimension of Christian *philanthrōpia* its essential feature—indeed, its sine qua non. It also recognizes categorical differences between *to philanthrōpon* and *to eleos* while attempting to harmonize the two, positing mercy/almsgiving as an aspect, however limited (hence imperfect and feminine, according to classical notions of gender), of philanthropy. This is the only extant text in classical or Christian tradition where a complementary relationship between philanthropy and mercy is philosophically argued and explained. What inspired its author?

If we cannot assume he was acquainted with the Greco-Roman distinctions described above,[61] we may be confident that he would have known the relation between *philanthrōpia* and *eleos* set forth in Christian scriptures. New Testament literature refers to *philanthrōpia* only three times. In the Book of Acts the word is used twice, both times referring to kindnesses unexpectedly shown to Paul by outsiders: in the first instance, his prison guard, a Roman centurion, "philanthropically" grants him permission to leave his cell to receive private care from local friends (Acts 27:3); in the second, barbarians offer him "unusual philanthropy" after his shipwreck on Malta (Acts 28:2).[62] Both instances presume that philanthropy meant helping someone outside one's group against expected inclinations. More influential for Christian tradition, however, is the appearance of the concept in the Pauline Letter to Titus (Ti 3:4). To persuade readers to show "every courtesy to every person," the letter explains how *philanthrōpia* made God merciful toward humanity in general, despite their sins:

> For we were once foolish, led astray, slaves to various passions and pleasures, passing our days in malice and envy, despicable, hating one another. But when the kindness and philanthropy of God our Savior appeared, He saved us, not because of works of righteousness we had done, but according to His mercy [*to eleos*].[63]

This letter presents clemency as an intrinsic element of divine philanthropy, and divine philanthropy as a lofty indulgence expressed toward humans in the manner of certain pagan gods, Hellenistic kings, and Roman emperors. Like the passages from Acts, it suggests the impact of classical tradition on Christian tradition, probably mediated by the Septuagint, whose Deuterocanonical books use *philanthrōpia* almost exclusively to designate acts of clemency bestowed by kings.[64] Thus a concessive understanding of philanthropy was held by pagans and Christian authors alike. Yet the Pauline letter also presents divine philanthropy as akin to—but not identical with—mercy. Considering that classical authorities tended to keep these two ideals separate, their close, if subordinate, association in this letter is arguably Christian scripture's most seminal contribution to the expansion of the ancient ideal. In any case it helps explain why later Christian tradition, unlike classical tradition, closely associates philanthropy with mercy (*eleos*), especially as expressed through gifts or acts of alms (*eleēmosynē*). What must be emphasized is that, according to this letter, such mercy was to be extended to humans despite the fact that they had done nothing to deserve it.

To return to the Clementine *Homily*: if a late-third-century date for its origin is accepted, then we might regard it as an attempt to conceptualize Christian obligations to outsiders during the "Little Peace of the Church," an era of relative acceptance that Christianity enjoyed before the Tetrarchic persecutions of the early fourth century. In any case, its author makes clear that universal *philanthrōpia* was exceptional. There were of course practical reasons why church authorities would have been reluctant to extend communal resources to non-Christians in pre-Constantinian times: besides exposing themselves to scrutiny, it is unlikely that most would have had enough resources to expend beyond their own needs, whatever existed was already being heavily taxed by their own claimants.[65] The *Didascalia* admonishes readers to distinguish "the trusted poor" from scroungers in their communities who wanted bread but refused to work. Origen notes the skill needed to discern legitimate claims from false ones in his church—this at a time when the church at Rome, the closest to what Origen knew in Alexandria, was supporting more than fifteen hundred "widows and afflicted persons" in addition to its clergy.[66] No doubt such numbers caused priorities to be formulated within each church. In any case, the only evidence we have for the extension of Christian resources to anyone outside an established community comes during large-scale upheavals like war, famines, or mass conscriptions in the late third century.[67] Such humanitarian outreaches no doubt won converts to the Christian cause. One only needs think of the story of Pachomius, the future Egyptian abbot (d. 348), and his conversion after some Christians brought food when he was being held in an Egyptian stockade along with other forced conscripts during the civil war between Constantine and Licinius (r. 308–324): "When [Pachomius] asked about this, he was told that Christians were merciful to everyone. He asked again what [a Christian was] and they said, 'They are people who bear the name of Christ . . . they do every good to everyone.'"[68] But this incident, if historical, happened ca. 323–324, more than a decade after Christianity had received legal sanction in 313; there is no evidence of systematic philanthropic outreach (or its use to win converts) before that.

CONSTANTINE AND THE EXTENSION
OF CHRISTIAN PHILANTHROPY

It is clear, however, that this situation began to change once Constantine vanquished Licinius in 324. Constantine's court historian, Eusebius of Caesarea (d. 339), later represented their entire conflict as a confrontation between philanthropy and misanthropy. So inhumane was Licinius, claims Eusebius, that he even imprisoned Christians who brought "humanitarian aid" (*philanthrōpa*, a rare Christian use of the technical term for imperial indulgences) to prisoners in jail. Conversely, Constantine was philanthropic to a fault. Once victorious, he "tempered with philanthropy the rigidity of justice . . . hasting to save the bulk of humanity by putting a few malefactors away." He proceeded to make his reign "agreeable to each and every one of his subjects, being guided by principles of philanthropy"; he exemplified this "devotion to philanthropy" by refusing to permit executions, even if this made him look soft. He showed philanthropy even to heretics, saying they should be pitied instead of punished. He was not affected by their follies, we are assured, "except insofar as he showed them compassion due to his excessive philanthropy."[69]

Such rhetoric might be expected from a classically trained propagandist. More revealing of Eusebius's own understanding of *philanthrōpia* may be his account of the benefactions that Constantine had earlier made in Rome after defeating Maxentius at the Milvian Bridge (312). In his *Life of Constantine* Eusebius describes how, after enriching churches with gifts and subsidies, the emperor

> showed himself a philanthropic benefactor even to non-Christians who approached him. On the one hand, he provided money and necessary food as well as decent clothes for the bodies of pitiful outcasts who went begging in the Forum, while on the other hand, he bestowed more lavish resources on those who had formerly been prosperous but had suffered a reversal of fortune. To these he made magnificent benefactions with regal spirit, granting land to some and honor to others [by granting them] various positions of dignity. To orphans . . . he stood in place of a father, and to such an extent did he make the destitution of widows his special concern, that he married them off to wealthy members of his entourage.[70]

This is actually the earliest description we have of any philanthropic initiative undertaken by a Christian layperson. Three points must be emphasized: First, Eusebius specifically invokes the concept of *philanthrōpia* to characterize Constantine's extension of benefactions to people outside the Christian community, including members of his enemy's camp. Second, these people spanned the entire spectrum of society, ranging from indigent beggars to distressed gentlefolk. And third—anticipating Christian policy after Constantine—"those who had formerly been prosperous but had suffered a reversal of fortune" were privileged to receive more aid than ordinary indigents, reflecting a graded approach that Eusebius evidently considered exemplary.

Although the idea of indulging all humans despite their flaws or suspected faults was intrinsic to early Christian and classical philanthropic traditions alike, there is no evidence that either tradition envisioned dispensing aid to the poor on a systematic basis before Constantine's conversion. No doubt once his imperial attitude and favor toward Christians became known, churches here and there would have continued or expanded the outreach they had begun during the civil war, sensing its proselytizing potential: as John Chrysostom later observed in fourth-century Antioch, "our secret consists of the extent of our philanthropy and mercy."[71] To facilitate this extension of philanthropic aid, Christians began to make use of commercial inns called *pandocheia* and *xenodocheia* (anyone-receivers and stranger-receivers) that had long existed in classical cities of the Roman East. During the fourth century some of these inns were repurposed to serve as hospices or food banks. As institutional consciousness developed over the later fourth and fifth centuries, these generic terms gave way to the more technical designations *xenones* or *nosokomeia* (and *xenodocheion* reverted to its original meaning of "inn or hostel"), while other facilities appeared, specializing in long-term care for lepers, cripples, and other invalids (*ptōchotropheia, ptōchia*), orphans and foundlings (*orphanotropheia, blephotropheia*), and the elderly (*gerokomeia*). Unlike churches, these institutions were often named after their lay founders (e.g., the Sampson Hospital), a convention that perhaps encouraged their proliferation.[72] Some were monumental and built to last (Empress Eudocia founded a hospital with four hundred beds in Jerusalem), but many would have been cheap, makeshift structures like those that John the Almsgiver set up along the harbor for the poor to use as shelters during winter in Alexandria; these sound like wooden quonset huts furnished with nothing but rugs on the floors.[73] In any case such Christian *xenodocheia* (and imperial subsidies that occasionally supported them) are first attested in Constantinople and Antioch,[74] where Julian, among others, could have seen them at first hand.

It must be reiterated, however, that these facilities did not proliferate overnight. There is no decisive evidence that any church community outside of Constantinople and Antioch undertook philanthropic outreach beyond the "charity-feasts, receptions, and table-ministrations" that Julian described in his *Letter to Theodore* in 362–363. Nor do we hear of individuals following Constantine's example of providing for anonymous outcasts. When a severe famine struck the Cappadocian highlands of central Asia Minor between 368 and 370, Basil of Caesarea (Kayseri, Turkey) complained that wealthy members of his church were doing nothing to help. Less than a decade after Julian had represented Christian philanthropy as an embarrassment to his pagan priesthood, Basil similarly remarked, "descriptions of philanthropy among the Hellenes [i.e., the pagans] put us to shame!"[75] During the famine, Basil himself took action in precisely the manner Julian had described, setting out vats of soup and directing his slaves to feed the people streaming in from the countryside. "Of this philanthropy," his brother Gregory of Nyssa later recalled, "he extended a share even to children of the Jews."[76]

But that humanitarian crisis, like those of the third century, soon came to an end. As we have seen, a universalizing Christian philanthropy was still an emerging ideal and practice in the second half of the fourth century during the lifetimes of Basil and Julian the Apostate. Before then, inspired by their scriptures (and no doubt also by teachings and practices in Jewish synagogues, although a direct connection is hard to make except in the early fourth-century writings of Aphrahat "the Persian Sage," a Christian authority living outside the Roman Empire), church communities became known for supporting their enrolled members, especially their widows and orphans.[77] But there is no certainty or even probability that they reached out beyond these members until after Constantine's conversion, when ambitions for universality became a major facet of Christian ideology. Till then, the concept of *philanthrōpia* was rooted in relatively small communities, not yet tested within a universalizing empire.

In the second half of the fourth century, however, preachers reared in classical rhetoric began to press this ancient concept to its logical extreme, invoking it to persuade congregations to help all sorts of people they previously felt able to ignore. Indeed, it was against a singularly callous case of scornful neglect that Basil's Cappadocian colleague Gregory of Nazianzus wrote his sermon *On Loving the Poor*. As the most comprehensive exposition of philanthropy to survive from either classical or Christian antiquity, this sermon provides a useful starting point for studying challenges raised by the Christian universalization of *philanthrōpia* in the Roman East.

PREACHING PHILANTHROPY IN CHRISTIAN CAPPADOCIA

Peri Philoptōchia (literally, *On Loving Ptōchoi* or *Ptōcheia*) is not only the most sustained treatment of Christian philanthropy to survive from Early Byzantium but also the most widely disseminated, having been translated into Coptic, Armenian, and Syriac by the sixth century and Georgian by the seventh. Conventionally listed as Gregory's fourteenth "oration,"[78] it was originally composed sometime between 365 and 374, although its length has made some scholars surmise that it was later revised and extended for circulation as a treatise.[79] By any measure it is a tour de force. After presenting "love of the poor" as a chief Christian virtue, Gregory quickly focuses on one distinct group of poor people—lepers—who especially needed such love. Here we will examine how he invoked the notion of *philanthrōpia* to persuade audiences to show mercy to lepers,[80] and then why he chose to focus on them in particular in a treatise nominally about loving the poor (or the state of *ptōcheia*) in general. This leads to an exploration of Christian philanthropic priorities in fourth-century Asia Minor, one of the earliest regions to show institutional innovation in this area.

It is a mark of his classical training that Gregory starts his sermon by imagining all Christian virtues competing for first prize, surveying all possible shining contenders (including *philanthrōpia*) before declaring Charity the champion and *philoptōchia* its best supportive part. Then he reviews the range of people who needed it most:

> We must open our hearts to all *ptōchoi* who suffer distress for whatever reason . . . whether on account of being widows or orphans, or by being exiled from their fatherland, or through the cruelty of their masters, abuses of magistrates, inhumanity of tax collectors, depredations of brigands, greed of robbers, confiscations, or shipwrecks. All are similarly to be pitied, looking to our hands as we do to God's for what we ourselves need. And among these, those who suffer distress contrary to their dignity are to be pitied more than those who are habituated to misfortune—but especially those who waste away with the sacred disease.[81]

Gregory thus surveys various examples of *ptōchoi* and the circumstances that reduced them to that state before settling on those who deserved pity most:

victims of "the sacred disease"—that is, lepers.[82] What follows is a vivid description of their plight. Lepers require special attention, he says, because unlike everyone else brought down by misfortune, they are thoroughly ostracized, not even inspiring pity: "We flee them with all our might—oh the inhumanity!—hardly able to share the same air with them."[83] They themselves recoiled at the sight of their own putrefying flesh. But their plight went beyond that. Banished from all public venues ("even from the springs available to everyone else"), they were shunned by their own families and forced to live in the wild, bereft of any hope. Nor was that all: their inability to use their hands or feet forced many to repeatedly return with great shame to plead for mercy from the same people who had ostracized them. Hence, they gathered at martyr festivals, and could even now (a clue to the original setting of this sermon) be seen outside the church writhing in the dust and begging for food, with their "strange songs" of lamentation, caused by collapsed nasal passages, heard in the background during the liturgy. Such degradations beset them every day despite their possession, like every other human, of the divine image (Gn 1:27). This underlying connection made them "our own brothers in God," Gregory affirms, "even if you might wish that they were not."[84]

We may wonder what Gregory's congregation made of his mixture of social, medical, and theological descriptions. The next third of his sermon builds on his reference to the divine image to discuss social justice and Christian stewardship more generally.[85] Gregory reminds his audience that social and economic inequities were neither natural nor ordained by God, but had arisen after the Fall due to human lust for domination and immoderate acquisition (*pleonexia*).[86] The purpose of all creation, however, had been to sustain the divine image that God had implanted in all humans. Christians must therefore share whatever surplus they had with others in need, in order to achieve the "equitable distribution of gifts" God had originally intended.[87] But most people—including Gregory's audience—did the opposite: "Shame on you for holding back what belongs to others," he says. "Imitate God's equity. . . . Imitate the first and highest law of God, 'Who rains on the righteous and sinful, and makes His sun rise on all alike'" (cf. Mt 5:45).[88] Lepers represented a singular case of need due to their bodily decay. Their loss of flesh and limbs deprived them of the most basic resources everyone else enjoyed; hence, the extreme merit of their claim to a share of God's material benefits. But responding to this claim would require his congregation to transcend their disgust and practice indulgence towards those whom they most reviled.

Gregory had already mentioned *philanthrōpia* in his preamble,[89] but only at this point does it become pervasive in his sermon, when he reminds listeners of their stewardship responsibilities and God's expectation that they would share His bounties with fellow bearers of His image.[90] Philanthropy is incumbent on all, Gregory argues, both because God wanted it and because it provided a way of imitating Him; and lepers offered opportunities for everyone to do so, since their needs lay so immediately at hand.

> Never refuse to do good for anyone in need, but first and foremost give to each who asks of you. . . . But if you cannot manage that, then help as you can in lesser ways: give aid, give food, give rags, bring medicine, bandage their wounds, ask about their misfortunes, philosophize with them about fortitude, encourage and come close to them—for nothing very bad will happen to you because of this.[91]

"See only to this," he reiterates near his conclusion, "that your philanthropy finds no delay!"[92]

Material benefactions aside, Gregory was first and foremost challenging his listeners to adopt a kindly disposition (*to philanthrōpon*) toward lepers despite the revulsion and fear they provoked. Lepers were the most abused of all humanity. "To them," Gregory observes, "a person is philanthropic not so much when he attends to their needs as when he does not angrily shove them away."[93] Worse still, virtually everyone considered such cruelty acceptable: in only their case, "we embrace inhumanity as the mark of a gentleman, denigrating compassion as shameful. . . . Toward them, even the most kindly, philanthropic people become exceedingly callous."[94]

It was against this ingrained hardness that Gregory invokes the concessive force of *philanthrōpia.* He addresses his audience as "philanthropic slaves of Christ," enjoining them not to ignore their leprous brothers in the road: "Before you lies the challenge of philanthropy, even if the devil should try to divert you."[95] Gregory knew he had to overcome objections. One was that lepers were not mentioned among the afflicted described in the Psalms or Proverbs (cf. Ps 9:18, 22:26, 40:18, 74:2, 82:3, 140:12; Prv 22:22–23). That did not excuse their harsh treatment—instead, "Let it incite you to be all the more philanthropic," he proposes, especially considering the gratitude that would greet such unexpected kindness.[96] Nor, Gregory insists, is there any evidence to support the assumption that lepers deserve their fate, thinking that God had imposed it to punish them for past wickedness. Comparing this to pagan superstitions that excuse human sacrifice, Gregory laments that it has caused "even some of our own"—that is, fellow Christians—not merely to neglect lepers but to actively insult them. He warns listeners that if they do not set a different example, such superstitions might be turned against them someday.[97]

What Gregory believed was this: lepers were simply ordinary people who had been "betrayed by their lowly, mischievous, untrustworthy body."[98] Neither was their awful plight divine punishment, nor had they been born into their state of need. On the contrary, these "wretched remnants of former human beings" were *ptōchoi,* who, like all the others listed at the start of the sermon, had once known more prosperous conditions before being struck down by misfortune. Indeed some, says Gregory, could still recall who they had once been and how they had lived before being stripped of their money, family, faces, and friends.[99] Instead of exemplifying something accursed, they deserved compassion as testimony to the inconstancy of human prosperity. Lepers, in other words, were vivid exemplars of people who had suffered a tragic reversal of fortune and fallen from a former state of prosperity—that is, vivid exemplars of *ptōchoi*.

Thus, Gregory was not just challenging ancient superstitions about the causes of leprosy. He was establishing a premise of "fallenness" (*ptōcheia*) to convince Christian listeners that lepers deserved their *philoptōchia*. Indeed, though he admits that the cause of their disorder was mysterious, he points out that such a fate could potentially befall anyone, since it was rooted in the weakness and inconstancy of flesh itself. In a personal aside, he confesses his own ambivalence toward the body that enmeshed his soul: this "well-meaning enemy and treacherous friend" crippled him as often as it bore him aloft. God must have bestowed such physical frames on humans, he suggests, so that they would not become too conceited by the "dignity" they had received as spiritual bearers of the divine image.[100] "We have been so composed for this reason, that as often as we might become inflated by this image, we will be brought down again by our clay." Lepers epitomized the paradox that humans were both the most exalted and most lowly of God's creations, illustrating how far an individual might change due to unforeseen infirmities.[101] This "common weakness" provided the fundamental rationale for compassion between humans, following the example of Christ:

> We call ourselves disciples of Christ who is gentle and philanthropic, who embraced our weaknesses by lowering himself into our humble clay, turning himself into a *ptōchos* in this fleshly, earth-bound veil, experiencing pain and vulnerability on our behalf. With such an exemplar of sympathy and compassion, what will we do? Look the other way? Just pass by? ... Let that not be attributed to human nature. ... Mutual weakness teaches us to be pious and philanthropic.[102]

Healthy or not, each human represented a limb attached to another (cf. Gal 3:28; 1 Cor 12:12). "So we must never neglect those who, through this common weakness, have fallen. ... Instead we should think our very own flesh and soul depend on this alone: showing them philanthropy."[103]

Gregory does two things that deserve emphasis. First, he repeatedly invokes the ideal of *philanthrōpia* to convince Christians to extend mercy to people whom they normally feel justified to revile. That is precisely what makes his speech the longest and clearest articulation of the ideal to survive from antiquity. Second, he manages to turn lepers into dramatic symbols of the plight of all *ptōchoi*, meaning all whose loss of former prosperity caused them to "suffer distress contrary to their dignity."[104] "We are all *ptōchoi*," observes Gregory in the sermon's opening, "in need of divine favor, even if one may seem to possess [it] more than another." This broader symbolism may account for the sermon's appeal and dissemination in later Byzantine periods.[105] But what had prompted Gregory to devote a sermon to lepers in the first place? It has been surmised that he did so to support Basil's efforts to build a philanthropic institution outside the Cappadocian city of Caesarea. Eventually called the Basilias (Basil's Place), this facility has attracted considerable attention from modern historians, because it is one of the earliest examples of an institution technically called a *ptōchotropheion* ("place that sustains *ptōchoi*," as Basil himself called it), and the only one described in any detail. Modern reconstructions of it have been uniformly expansive, ranging from a general hospital to a "whole range of buildings for the care of the sick and the destitute, and for distribution of surplus food for those in need," to a "charitable multiplex . . . nothing if not ambitious."[106] But how ambitious was Basil's Basilias?

That question requires some discussion here, being important not only for understanding Gregory's focus on lepers but for anticipating the ambitions of early Byzantine philanthropic institutions more generally. The truth is that historians have let their imaginations run riot regarding the Basilias. It was neither a hospital in a general sense nor a place to dispense food to the poor in a general way. No evidence supports such expansive interpretations.[107] Furthermore, despite what is usually assumed, there is no evidence that Basil built his Basilias in response to the famine that struck Cappadocia circa 368–370. No ancient author links it with that crisis. Indeed, it is not even certain that the year conventionally assigned for its completion, 372, is accurate. That dating is entirely modern and is based primarily on a belief that the facility was conceived in response to a famine and on Theodoret of Cyrrhus's description of a visit made by Emperor Valens (r. 364–378) to Caesarea in 372. Theodoret reports that, at the end of that visit, Valens gave Basil land "as a gift for the paupers under his care, who needed utmost attendance because they were mutilated [*lelōbēmenoi*] all over their bodies."[108] This has usually been taken to mean that Valens saw a completed Basilias and decided to help finance it with a grant of revenue-producing imperial land. But it could equally mean that he saw Basil's work with people "mutilated all over their bodies" (which is all Theodoret actually says) and was so impressed that he gave him land outside Caesarea on which to build a permanent institution, not to serve people suffering from famine, but to house the group whom Theodoret describes as *lelōbēmenoi*. These are the only people Theodoret identifies as benefitting from Basil's institution. That is important, because *lelōbēmenoi* was the most common euphemism used in Early Byzantium for lepers.[109] His description thus implies that the Basilias was not a general hospital, but a leprosarium—nothing more, but also nothing less.

This inference is in fact consonant with all the other ancient evidence we have regarding this institution, ranging from Gregory of Nazianzus's fourth-century funeral oration for Basil (which describes only Basil's care for lepers and not for any other group) to the little-known description in Gregory the Presbyter's sixth- or seventh-century *Life of Gregory of Nazianzus*. The latter deserves to be quoted in full:

> When Basil the Great saw that his mutilated [*lōboumenous*] brothers were much in need of mercy and worthy of compassion but received the least possible pity due to the stupid inhumanity of most people, who treated them as a kind of polluted, repellant abomination, [Basil], as he came to know their nature, formed a pious plan worthy of his brotherly love. After erecting immense houses and assigning to them annual incomes, which he procured from well-to-do persons whom his wise words had persuaded to make donations, he gathered all the infirm into this same place, calling its buildings "school-houses for *ptōchoi*."[110]

Although we know nothing about the author of this *Life*, its manuscripts identify him as a priest of Cappadocian Caesarea, so we may assume that he could have been familiar with the Basilias and local traditions about it, perhaps preserved in church records. Several features indicate that his description represents independent testimony, not lifted from any known source: first, he states that Basil furnished his facility with buildings both separate and "immense"; second, he explains that Basil arranged for (each of?) these to be funded through annual pledges from local donors; third, he states that he "collected" all lepers from the area to live in them; and fourth, he reports that he called them by a distinct name: "school-houses for *ptōchoi*." His description is also notable for what he does not mention but could have lifted from other sources, had he sought to construct a fiction: no famine, no Emperor Valens, no treatment of sick or poor people generally—just lepers constituting, it seems, the only *ptōchoi* he had in mind.

Why did Basil build a facility focused on lepers? Some have presumed that he and other bishops (e.g., John Chrysostom and Rabbula of Edessa) who founded leprosaria in Asia Minor and northern Syria in this era were responding to a sudden, rapidly expanding epidemic. But leprosy, whether identified as Hansen's disease or some other skin deformity with which leprosy was associated in antiquity, is not prone to such sudden outbreaks, and in any case we know it was already pervasive in Asia Minor and Syria long before the fourth century. Aretaeus of Cappadocia, a doctor who probably lived in the second century, describes the sad fate of "many" of its victims, abandoned on distant mountainsides by their families due to fear of contagion: "While some assist them in their hunger for a time, others help as little as possible because they want them to perish."[111] Thus, there was no need to posit a novel outbreak or fourth-century crisis: leprosy was already endemic in Cappadocia, and Basil was providing a philanthropic alternative to the traditional method of handling it. Moreover, we know that the term Basil himself uses to refer to the facility, *ptōchotropheion*, was already being used during his lifetime to describe facilities established by Bishop Eustathius (d. 377) of Sebaste (Sivas, Turkey) to sequester lepers in western Armenia. Sebaste lay just two days north of Caesarea; it would be no stretch to suppose that Eustathius himself, Basil's former ascetic mentor, inspired Basil's initiative.[112]

If the Basilias had any dimension beyond a leprosarium, it was a pronounced monastic element. The facility was designed so that part of it could house "attendants of the divine," as Basil reports in a letter to an imperial governor, using a florid locution sometimes used in this era to refer to monks.[113] Elsewhere he identifies monks as those whom Jesus had meant when saying, "Blessed are the *ptōchoi* in spirit" (Mt 5:3), calling monasticism the *"ptōcheia* made blessed by Christ."[114] This is important, because it suggests another way of conceptualizing the Basilias. As we have seen, Gregory the Presbyter reports that Basil had called its buildings "school houses for *ptōchoi."* This unexplained, highly unusual, and probably authentic appellation recalls a remark that another Cappadocian Gregory, Basil's own brother Gregory of Nyssa (335–394), made in a funeral oration he composed after Basil died. Basil constructed the Basilias, he says, as a place for teaching lesser *ptōchoi* to learn higher forms of *ptōcheia*: it was "a place constructed in the suburb [of Caesarea] where, through good instruction, [Basil] taught those who were *ptōchoi* in body to become *ptōchoi* in spirit."[115]

A picture emerges of Basil's *ptōchotropheion* as a facility intended to ameliorate the state of *ptōcheia* in both a physical and ideological sense. Staffed by doctors and orderlies, featuring workhouses and a martyr church, but set apart like a monastery (though also equipped with guesthouses for "travelers," probably meant for visiting relatives),[116] Basil's Place was not just a leprosarium but a place where monks and lepers—the spiritual and the physical *ptōchoi* par excellence—could live together in seclusion for their own mutual edification and support.

My reason for establishing this relatively limited purpose of the Basilias is to set a touchstone for assessing the philanthropic ambitions of other institutions founded in this era for which we have less information. The length of Gregory's *On Loving the Poor* and its focus on lepers suggest it was composed for some central (perhaps inaugural?) event at the Basilias.[117] Gregory took the opportunity not only to emphasize philanthropy's universal aspect but to articulate the corollary that, while Christians must pity "all *ptōchoi* who suffer distress," they should prioritize those who are suffering "contrary to dignity" over those who are "habituated to misfortune."[118] He was expressing a rule of thumb adopted in later Christian institutions. Before considering examples in the next section, let us see how this rule probably played out at the Basilias.

As the Basilias exemplifies, one approach to universalizing philanthropy was to offer specialized care to all claimants of a certain type. While it hard to believe that his facility would have turned away people with dire infirmities or anyone starving, any general openhandedness would have been contrary to Basil's well-attested emphasis on discriminating when managing institutional resources, especially when dealing with beggars. In their case, he advised vigilant restraint. In response to his monks' inquiries "Shall we send away those who come to beg at the gate?" and "Must the steward . . . fulfill the command, 'Give to all who ask of you' [Mt 5:42]?" he quotes Jesus, answering, "It is not fair to take children's food, and throw it to the dogs." Only after careful scrutiny should any be given institutional resources. As for non-Christians, stewards must consult their superiors to determine if they had enough "to make the sun 'rise on both the wicked and the good,' as it is written."[119]

Basil was no soft touch. Nor were his episcopal counterparts in other Cappadocian cities. In the sermon *On Lazarus and the Rich Man*, Asterius (ca. 330–410), Bishop of Amasea in northern Pontus (Amasya, Turkey), expresses deep distrust of people who "lacked possessions involuntarily." A former lawyer, Asterius notes that if you looked at those being arraigned for burglary, human trafficking, murder, and the like, you would see that all were paupers, "unknown, homeless, and hearthless." In his view, the only commendable group among the involuntary poor were *ptōchoi* who, like Lazarus (Lk 16:19–31), endured their hardships philosophically, without using them as excuses for various types of wickedness.[120] Basil expressed a similar regard for philosophically tempered *ptōchoi*.[121] We find more nuance, however, in a homily in which Basil sought to clarify what Jesus meant by "Give to all who ask of you" (Mt 5:42). This commandment, he argues, had to be understood in light of the approach to stewardship adopted by the apostles:

> For the sake of charity, [Jesus] wants you to be generous toward those who ask, but at the same time to discern, with reason, the needs of those who beg. And this we have learned from Acts:
>
> > "As many owned lands or houses sold them, brought the proceeds of what was sold, and laid it at the apostles' feet, and it was distributed to each according to the need of each" [Acts 4: 34–35].
>
> Since [therefore] many go beyond what is necessary for their need, and make begging an opportunity for commerce and pretext for harmful extravagance, those entrusted with care of the *ptōchoi* must collect money from which to distribute with managerial expertise what is necessary for the needs of each.[122]

Basil's reference to collections and distributions of money by people "entrusted" with care for *ptōchoi* suggests he was delivering this homily in a philanthropic institution, perhaps within the Basilias itself (as his remarks below also imply). Discernment and discrimination were essential for such caregivers: just as the sick needed doctors who knew how to measure and administer proper amounts of wine for their condition, so too needy people needed experts who knew what was good for them. "For liberality in this ministry," he continues, "is in no way helpful to those who clearly compose songs of lamentation to deceive women, or who wound and maim their bodies as an opportunity for commerce. Provisioning them will only provide occasions for wickedness." Instead, he advises, "discourage their wailing with a small dose, saving your compassion and brotherly love for those who have learned to bear their affliction patiently."[123]

For all his emphasis on discrimination, it is crucial to see that Basil does not insist that dubious claimants be given nothing at all. Instead, he advises giving them a discouragingly "small dose" (*mikra dosis*), not in the same measure or with the same degree of compassion given to virtuous claimants. This approach was both concessive and discriminating, combining universality with prioritization in adherence with the apostolic principle "To each, according to need of each" (Acts 4:35).

Other authorities took a similar tack regarding Jesus's command, "Give to all who ask of you," as we will see in the rest of this book. Throughout his career, Basil devised ways to put Christian ideals into practice.[124] His Basilias was another instance of this; when introducing it in his funeral oration for Basil, Gregory of Nazianzus observes that "*philanthrōpia, ptōchotrophia,* and supporting human frailty, are good things." Banal though that sounds, it summarizes the principles that Basil's Basilias (and Gregory's *On Loving the Poor*) sought to enshrine.[125] Significantly, Gregory chose to mention and describe Basil's treatment of lepers in his funeral oration at precisely that point where he wanted to highlight Basil's episcopal philanthropy. This may have set a precedent for honoring deceased bishops in the decades that followed. When panegyrists in the early fifth century wished to acclaim the extraordinary *philanthrōpia* of the deceased bishops John Chrysostom (d. 407) and Rabbula of Edessa (d. 435), they did so by describing their construction of leprosaria—indeed, leper care in both cases is the only example given to illustrate the philanthropy in question.[126] Thus institutionalized leper care became iconic of episcopal philanthropy in action, perhaps because it most convincingly bespoke a bishop's concern for the plight of even the most repellent of "the fallen."

"TO EACH ACCORDING TO NEED":
PHILANTHROPIC PRIORITIES IN
CHURCH INSTITUTIONS

Because of its proximity to the imperial court, the Church of Constantinople was well placed to aid parishes in its diocese when it wanted. On one such occasion its bishop, Atticus (sed. 406–425), sent three hundred solidi to help Nicaea (Iznik, Turkey) recover from an earthquake. We have a letter that Atticus dispatched to a priest there, which a church historian preserved to show how generously this bishop cared for the *ptōchoi* even from afar:

> Atticus to Calliopus, Greetings in the Lord. I have learned that thousands in your city are hungry and in need of mercy from the pious. . . . Therefore take, my dear friend, these three hundred gold coins and dispense them as you wish. No doubt you will want [to bestow them on] people who are ashamed to beg, not on those who have made a life-long business of their bellies.

Moreover, Atticus adds, "when you give, do not take religion into account. Make it your sole purpose to feed the hungry, not considering whether they are religious in our own way."[127]

Perhaps reflecting policies in place at Constantinople itself, Atticus presented a discretionary rule of thumb that is reminiscent of what the Cappadocians advised and that sheds light on how Christian philanthropic institutions managed their resources in this era. To guide hard choices, stewards required consistent but flexible principles. As noted above, one striking development in the history of Christian *xenodocheia* is how diversified they eventually became, so by the sixth century there were not only short-term hospitals or infirmaries for temporarily sick people (*xenones*) and poorhouses for permanently disabled people (*ptōchotropheia* and *ptōchia*), but also an array of orphanages, foundling homes, geriatric or nursing facilities, and so on.[128] While we do not know what decisions led to such specialization (much probably depended on the concerns of lay donors), we may assume that it helped reduce claimants to a manageable number, so that an institution could maximize its limited resources to aid every claimant from a certain group.

The most basic Christian welfare institution of the day was, however, the church dole—that is, the regular distribution of bread, grain, or cash by local churches to people in need. Information about it is rudimentary: we have several references to people enrolled on church lists, but no actual lists or administrative documents (not even among Egyptian papyri) that might enable us to discern who was considered eligible for it and why. Of course, that lists were kept at all meant that beneficiaries were limited to a select group of people (just as the civic *annona* was restricted to certain privileged citizens).[129] Like Basil, church manuals of the era advised discrimination when distributing resources: qualifying Jesus's commandment that Christians "give to all who ask" (Mt 5:42), for example, the late fourth-century *Apostolic Constitutions* explains that this "clearly means someone truly in need."[130] We know that deacons were supposed to consult with their bishops before issuing letters certifying that claimants were eligible, indicating a two-level screening process. Yet we do not know if such deacons, stewards, or bishops employed objective measures (such as the medical examinations performed for this purpose in medieval hospitals) to evaluate either claimants or their needs.[131] Anecdotes discussed below suggest that much depended on subjective perceptions and instincts, with clerics evaluating claims on the basis of appearance.[132] What, therefore, made claimants seem sufficiently "needy" to qualify for the church dole? And how was such selectivity justified, given Christian philanthropy's universal aspirations?

It becomes apparent that the church dole was no less specialized than any other philanthropic institution in Early Byzantium. As signaled by the name of the church fund behind the dole, *ta ptōchika* (things of the *ptōchoi*), this was meant not for poor people in general, but for those suffering from a state of *ptōcheia*.[133] In other words, it was meant not for people born into poverty or lifelong beggars, but for those who had come down into reduced circumstances of health or wealth. This had been true from the start, as indicated by third-century references to widows, orphans, elderly and "afflicted persons" (*thlibomenoi*), as well as church clerics, who had given up worldly prosperity for the sake of Christ.[134] Institutional privileges always remained primarily focused on these. But "afflicted persons" was a vague category, susceptible to expansion. John Chrysostom, while preaching in Antioch during the 380s and 390s, surveyed the range of claimants who taxed his church: "Consider," he asked his audience, "how many widows and virgins the church aids every day, for the number on the list amounts to three thousand. Besides these, there are those languishing in prison and suffering in the hospital, as well as people who are healthy, or dying, or mutilated in their bodies; also those who serve the altar, and those who simply come around each day for food and clothing."[135]

This survey, though somewhat puzzling (by "healthy people," did Chrysostom mean orphans and old people whom he does not mention?), suggests a list of categorical priorities, possibly mentioned out of habit in descending order: first, widows and virgins permanently enrolled for the dole; second, people in prison, hospitals, and leprosaria; third, church clerics; last, whoever showed up as casual claimants. A description ascribed to Edessa's famous deacon Ephraim (ca. 306–373) lists "widows, orphans, the disabled, the incapacitated, the maimed, the crippled, the blind, the leprous, and all the paupers [*penētes*] who sit by the doors of the churches," all of whom it collectively identifies as *ptōchoi*.[136] Again, the impression is one of descending priorities, moving from widows and orphans to the sick or disabled and ending with able-bodied paupers. Together with the reference to their "able bodies," the placement of this last group by church doors suggests people who had fallen into debt, *penētes* who had become *ptōchoi*, seeking sanctuary until they managed to have their loans paid, since the area within fifty feet of the front of a church was legally recognized as a place of asylum from creditors (a sixth-century letter describes farmers seeking asylum from tax collectors "within the boundaries of the holy churches," as if this were a widespread practice).[137] Putting speculation aside, we may at least say Ephraim's list corresponds closely enough to Chrysostom's to suggest a recognized gradation of claimants to church philanthropy, one that prioritized enrolled members while allowing for an incidence of casual claimants.

Confirmation that such gradations existed as a matter of policy comes from a manual known as the *Canons of Athanasius*. Probably written in Alexandria in the fifth century, it offers rare details about the administration of a large church community. After identifying the church steward as a "father of orphans and widows" alongside the bishop, it sets out his responsibilities:

All them that have need, he shall write down their names and give them unto the bishop. And if the bishop bid him give ten *artabs*, or less, or more, he shall give them unto each one of those written down, and shall not add thereto. But from the summer onward, when anyone begs him for a half [*artab*] of corn, he hath authority up to five *oipe*.[138]

Setting aside its fractions and figures (an *artab* constituted roughly 30 kgs, an *oipe* 3 kg), this passage differentiates two groups of claimants: one registered to regularly receive sizeable amounts of assistance, and another whose members turned up unpredictably, seeking smaller, occasional handouts. It attests that all decisions about enrolling the first group of claimants were supposed to be left to the bishop, but that stewards could dispense smaller sums at their own discretion to the latter group during summer months. These months, not coincidentally, fell after the grain harvest, when church supplies would have been at their peak. This suggests that casual claimants could be processed without special authorization only at times of maximum abundance. Elsewhere the manual refers to sick claimants, instructing stewards to check if these had the means to survive without taxing the church—claimants were to receive food and shelter only if they were poor.[139] Otherwise, it authorizes bishops, once they had taken care of their clergy and the sick, to give whatever was left to the poor, broadly conceived. "For God saith," it adds, "give to him that asketh of thee" (Mt 5:42).[140]

As appropriate for the wealthiest church in the Roman East—one that had the inexhaustible bounty of the Nile flowing through its backyard—the Alexandrian system of institutionalized philanthropy was designed to fulfill its mandate to "give to all who ask." At the same time, it envisioned a two-track system of enrolled and incidental claimants, with handouts carefully controlled in such a way as not to guarantee anything to anyone who was not a widow, orphan, or poor person who was sick. That this policy normally excluded ordinary beggars is apparent from the seventh-century hagiography of the Alexandrian Patriarch John the Almsgiver. Upon arriving in the city in 610, John is said to have convened a meeting of his church administrators and stewards, as well as Alexandria's "Keeper of the Peace," its city police chief. Explaining, "it is not right for us to prefer anyone before Christ," the bishop instructed them to enroll all the city's beggars for the daily handout. This resulted in 7,500 claimants being added to the church list.[141] Modern historians have frequently cited this figure to illustrate the ambitious scale of church philanthropy in Early Byzantium. But the hagiographical point is that this registration of extra claimants was an unprecedented departure from the norm, that it was carried out at John's personal expense, and that it would not have happened at all if not for his saintly disposition, wealth and initiative. What the figure actually illustrates is an estimate of how many of Alexandria's poor would normally have been left off the list and excluded from the dole.

If this exclusion of ordinary beggars from the dole was true for the wealthiest church in the empire, it is no surprising to find it in less affluent communities. By strictly restricting expenses in other areas, Bishop Rabbula reportedly found seven thousand darics to bestow on poor people who were not enrolled on Edessa's church list, indicating a comparable departure from the norm (even though Edessa, located off a silk road, was itself a wealthy city).[142] Even at Constantinople we learn that, in the late fourth century, "among [its] paupers, some were maintained by church funds, while others had no share in this assistance because they had other opportunities for earning income"—a policy remarkable only because lepers were counted among the latter, since their bodily decay was thought to enable them to attract alms and thus provide an opportunity for an income.[143] But our fullest information comes from Antioch. Chrysostom concedes that its church, because of all its land and rental properties, could compete with the city's richest landowners in affluence. He also knew that many in his congregation considered philanthropy to be a responsibility of the church ("What is your usual saying? 'He has the common stores of the church.' . . . Is this why you refuse to give, because the church already gives to the needy?").[144] But he insisted that the church's outlays exceeded its income,[145] making it hard to help all claimants. It therefore needed individuals to step up and make up the difference by privately providing relief. In his view, the main obstacle to their doing so was "cruel inhumanity," which made them dismiss beggars as frauds and deny them mercy.

It was precisely this need to handle casual claimants—especially ordinary beggars not guaranteed anything by the church—that prompted him to invoke *philanthrōpia* as an ideal for individuals in his audience.

> The pauper has one plea—his want and his standing in need. Do not demand from him anything more. Even if he be the most wicked man of all, if he lacks his necessary food, let us free him from hunger. Christ commanded us to do this in saying, "Be like your Father in Heaven, for He makes His sun rise on the wicked and on the good, and sends rain on the just and on the unjust" (Mt 5:45).[146]

While preaching on the story of Lazarus (Lk 16:19–31), Chrysostom repeatedly urged listeners to give alms despite their distrust of beggars, advising them not to repeat the error of the Rich Man, who failed to realize that God had deliberately placed Lazarus, "who was more a *ptōchos* than anyone else in the whole world," at the gate of his house to test his *philanthrōpia*.[147] "A gift of mercy [i.e., alms] is called such," Chrysostom argues, "because we give it even to the unworthy." Moreover, if we give to all, then those who are truly worthy will also fall into our hands.

> Need alone is the pauper's merit; whoever comes to us with this recommendation, let us not meddle further. We provide not to his character but to his humanity, and show mercy not because of his virtue but because of his misfortune. . . . If we start investigating and scrutinizing the merit of our fellow slaves, God will do the same for us. If we seek to demand an accounting from our fellow slaves, we ourselves will fall away from the philanthropy that comes from above.[148]

We have heard these arguments before, articulated by Julian the Apostate, Clement of Alexandria, and earlier Stoic philosophers. But Chrysostom adds a rationale from the New Testament, presenting acts of *eleēmosynē* (mercy, almsgiving) as expressions of philanthropy, tantamount to God's pardoning of sinners: "'Give to all who ask of you,' [Jesus] requests. You ask God to forget your own sins; so even if [a beggar] is exceedingly sinful, do not dwell on his. This is the time for *philanthrōpia*, not for close examinations; this the time for mercy, not for reckoning."[149]

When it came to mercy, beggars found no better advocate in Early Byzantium than John Chrysostom. As we shall see in chapters 3 and 4, he had spiritual reasons for encouraging personal almsgiving. What must be emphasized here, however, is that his promotion of indiscriminate philanthropy was also calculated to make up for the inability of church institutions to provide for all. Cooperation between individuals and institutions seems to have been built into this approach, local churches being responsible for the privileged claimants, and individual almsgivers for everyone else. Chrysostom once even affirmed that if the richest ten percent in Antioch provided for the poorest ten percent, there would be no poverty left in the city at all.[150] That required, however, the rich to indulge able-bodied beggars, even if they suspected that they did not deserve it. It also required them to stop wasting wealth on the vanity projects typical of civic euergetism, building sumptuous public baths or funding theater performances in their vain pursuit of popular acclaim. God needed no grand buildings either, Chrysostom professed: all He wanted from Christians was mercy.[151] Unlike Basil of Caesarea and Asterius of Amasea, who upheld classical paradigms by occasionally representing almsgiving as a Christian form of *philotimia*, Chrysostom espoused it solely as an expression of Christian *philanthrōpia*, modeled on divine indulgence toward all.

Chrysostom may have been exceptional.[152] As with Julian's pagan priesthood, it probably took considerable time, instruction, and experience to inculcate philanthropy as a "sacred" responsibility among those entering the Christian priesthood. No doubt most would have assumed that they had fulfilled their obligations for universal giving if they simply prioritized qualified claimants at distributions and gave casual claimants anything leftover. Such prioritization was absolutely necessary, given the limited resources and poor fiscal understanding that afflicted most church dioceses even at the height of prosperity (the Antiochene church was deeply in debt by the end of the fifth century).[153] What is interesting is that church ministers were repeatedly instructed to be as inclusive as possible, despite the potential burden. Practical uncertainties about how much should be given, or to whom, were secondary to fulfilling the universal imperatives of Christian philanthropy in theory. As Chrysostom insisted, Paul's exhortation to "do good to all, but especially to those in the house of the faith" (Gal 6:10) meant extending mercy even to Jews and Greeks, "in graded measures, but showing mercy nonetheless."[154] Being able to demonstrate such universal giving must have been advantageous in an era of religious competition, while the hierarchical approach taken to do so made it ideologically coherent to people who were already members of the faith, since it privileged those who had gone down in worldly prosperity for religious reasons. Just as Clement of Alexandria exhorted donors to seek out the "elite of the elite" in his third-century church, the fourth-century *Apostolic Constitutions* maintained that "holy people must be preferred."[155] But what philanthropic priorities guided such holy people themselves?

"TO EACH ACCORDING TO RANK":
PHILANTHROPIC PRIORITIES IN
SIXTH-CENTURY MONASTERIES

About six miles south of Jerusalem, on a flat hill overlooking the Kidron valley to the east of Bethlehem, is a forlorn site known as Dayr Tosi. Apart from a dilapidated wall, a massive reservoir, part of a church apse, and heaps of weathered blocks strewn about everywhere, nothing stands of the Theodosius Monastery, once the largest coenobium in Roman Palestine. Fortunately, a learned resident named Theodore of Petra described it in detail in the year 530. By then it had become well equipped to provide hospitality and medical services— extraordinarily well, even for a monastery located just over the hills from the pilgrim traffic at Bethlehem. Besides dormitories for four hundred monks and three separate churches for conducting liturgies in three different languages, it featured three separate quarters for visitors, each furnished with its own lodge (*katagōgion*) and infirmary (*nosokomeion*). Each was designed to accommodate a different type of guest: one for visiting monks and clergy, another for lay visitors, and the third for visitors in need, or rather, "those who are called *ptōchoi,* but have the same form as us . . . for whom [Jesus], having become a *ptōchos* for our sake, took special foresight." These Theodore describes as people who were blind, lame, leprous, or otherwise "humbled by *ptōcheia* and sickness."[156] In addition, there was a geriatric home for elderly monks as well as a "monastery inside the monastery" for monks who had gone insane, with various workshops to supply their needs. All these facilities, Theodore says, enabled the monastery's founder, known to tradition as Theodosius the Cenobiarch (fl. 479–529), to "extend a philanthropic hand."[157]

Truly a charitable multiplex, the Theodosius Monastery is the only institution in Early Byzantium that seems to have come close to modern imaginings of Basil's earlier Basilias. Indeed, the Basilias probably inspired it. Theodosius grew up just two days away from Cappadocian Caesarea; Theodore depicts him as exhorting monks with citations taken from Basil's ascetic writings and as kissing resident lepers on the lips, just as Gregory of Nazianzus claims that Basil did at the Basilias.[158] But the Theodosius Monastery was not Basil's Place. Besides being located near the greatest pilgrim centers in the empire, it was endowed by members of the imperial court—it is the only monastery in the Judean desert known to have possessed agricultural estates, as well as a pig farm, all given by a Comes Orientis (the Praetorian Prefect's deputy in charge of the Diocese of the East) to whom

Theodosius had given his cowl to wear into battle. It was also inhabited by retired dignitaries and favored by the Patriarch of Jerusalem, who made Theodosius responsible, as "exarch," for all cenobitic monasteries in Palestine.[159] This not only enabled Theodosius to extend his "philanthropic hand" farther than Basil could have ever done in Cappadocia, but also forced him to accommodate a much larger range of claimants at his gate.

The later hagiographer Cyril of Scythopolis (d. ca. 559) also thought it worth remembering the extent to which Theodosius excelled in the scale of his generosity, "showing no partiality for persons," welcoming "each person who came to him."[160] But it took Theodore of Petra, an eyewitness, to explain in detail how this was done. First, Theodosius had his monks set out one hundred tables each day, stacking them with free bread for anyone who came. Thus, he provided for strangers in a manner identified with Job in apocryphal literature, who reportedly ministered to the poor each day by setting thirty tables with food inside his house and leaving all the doors open on all of its sides so that anyone could quietly slip in and eat unnoticed without feeling shame. (Due to this practice and the access to material abundance it created, Theodosius's monastery was rumored to have been built on the very site of Jesus's miraculous Feeding of the Five Thousand.)[161] In addition, Theodore explains that the monastery's quarters had been deliberately arranged to accommodate its guests according to their type: religious, lay, and poor. Theodore uses a remarkable formulation to describe Theodosius's aim:

> Accommodating one person this way and another that way, [Theodosius] cared similarly for all; by preserving the equity of equality for all, he fulfilled the ancient teaching of the Apostles, that distribution was to be made to "each, as he had need" (Acts 4:35).[162]

Thus, according to Theodore, Theodosius adhered to apostolic example by providing something different to each, yet "similarly" to all, following the broad categorical distinctions (holy, lay, poor) that defined Christian society at large in Early Byzantium.

This "separate but universal" approach may look dubious to modern eyes, but it probably would have seemed equitable to sixth-century audiences. A similar arrangement of guest quarters has been detected in the ruins of the famous Egyptian martyr-shrine at Abu Mina west of Alexandria, which seems to have provided an open-air dormitory for poorer guests and several colonnaded *xenodocheia* of various sizes for the rest.[163] Indeed, we find parallels to Theodosius's approach attributed to Pachomius (ca. 292–348), the fourth-century founder of cenobitic communities along the Nile. According to his hagiographers, Pachomius, like Theodosius, used the apostolic principle of "each according to need" when organizing his monasteries. This was done internally and externally: internally, by appointing stewards to provide food "according to the differences" of each monk;

externally, by appointing guest masters to receive all who came "according to the rank [*axia*] of each."[164] Thus, while distributions of food inside a Pachomian monastery were based on a monk's individual physique, health, or ascetic regimen, the handling of visitors and the distributions made at its gate were based on the rank or status assigned to visitors and claimants by the outside world.

The propriety of this approach is affirmed in a vignette set in Egypt about a monk who possessed a charismatic ability to sense how much should be given to each of those who came to him, "according to their need."

> Once he was dispensing charity in a village, when behold! a woman came to him wearing old clothing. Seeing she wore old things, he moved his hand to give her much, but his hand closed and dispensed little. Then behold! another came wearing good clothing. Seeing her clothes he intended to give her only a little, but his hand opened and dispensed much. Inquiring about both, he afterwards learned that the woman who wore good clothes was from illustrious origins but, having become a *ptōchos,* had put on good clothes in concern for her reputation. The other one, however, had put on old clothes in order to receive [even] more.[165]

As the earliest version of this story specifies, both of the claimants in question were originally imagined to be indigent.[166] Its monastic protagonist therefore faced two simultaneous cases of deception: on the one hand, a member of the ordinary poor was attempting to look less prosperous for the sake of gain; on the other, a member of the "fallen" poor was attempting to look more prosperous for the sake of honor. Only the protagonist's God-given instinct enabled him to sense the true need in each case, so that he discharged the amount of aid appropriate to each. The story attests that making the distributions properly "according to need" required special sensitivity to social backgrounds,[167] partly to shield any "fallen" recipient of high rank from feeling unnecessary shame.

Confirmation that this was considered appropriate policy comes from letters written by the reclusive John of Gaza (d. ca. 542). We will meet John and his colleague Barsanuphius more fully in later chapters; what matters here is the advice John gave to lay correspondents about dispensing alms and hospitality. Besides answering questions about the location where alms should be distributed (answer: wherever needy people are) and how much should be given at a time (answer: nothing beyond one's means),[168] he fielded questions about almsgiving priorities. Some of these were relatively simple—when asked, "If there are two paupers and I can't give to both, whom should I prefer?" John answered, "the one more infirm"— but others were more complex. To the question,

> Since there are some who openly receive in public at the distribution, but others are embarrassed to receive openly because of their noble birth and others stay lying infirm at their homes—should these be treated differently, or should they all be given the same amount?

John replied, "All who receive in the open are in one class, unless any is weak and suffering, in which case give a bit more. But those who are embarrassed to receive openly in public or lie infirm are in a different class. Give them extra, according to their need and what you happen to have in your hand."[169] As for beggars who roved from door to door, John pronounced that one should give them at least something ("a bit of bread, two coins, a penny") as long it caused no strain, "for in this way," he concludes, "our philanthropic God is glorified."[170]

Consciously or not, John of Gaza was advising individuals to follow the church's philanthropic policy of universal giving through prioritization: give something to all, he affirmed, but invalids and distressed gentlefolk should receive more. John shows the same preferential regard for the "shame-faced poor" that was found in Atticus's letter to officials at Nicaea and in Gregory of Nazianzus's remark that those suffering "contrary to dignity" should be pitied more than people "habituated to misfortune."[171] Indeed, the fall of elites from prosperity into the depths of shameful impoverishment was a stock theme of contemporary sermons.[172] Likewise, hagiography of the era is populated by patricians reduced to beggary by brigands, wealthy merchants brought down by creditors, and well-born youths forced to wear "sordid clothing and downcast looks, the utter marks of *ptōcheia*," as John Moschus describes an Alexandrian shipowner's son who had "fallen from being one of the great to become one of the small." This youth, though "raised up high in riches," Moschus explains, "was brought low" not by dissolute living, but by a series of shipwrecks. Like other Christian gentlefolk, he is depicted as receiving several pounds of gold as aid from his bishop to relieve his distress.[173]

It is easy to explain this focus on downfallen elites in terms of aristocratic prejudice. "Do not scorn those who approach you in cheap clothing," Isidore of Pelusium felt compelled to advise one of his episcopal correspondents. "Even if they are undistinguished and from undistinguished lineage, do not turn them away, but extend a hand however you can, reflecting that an appearance of low birth is neither chosen nor an object of reproach."[174] Yet there was more to such concerns than mere snobbery. Christian and pagan orators alike expected audiences to be riveted by tales of sudden impoverishment. Its drama fell close to home. It is hard for us to imagine the fragility of a society where so many depended on so few for job security. Many subordinates hung on the fate of each aristocrat, and the fall of any great house was disastrous to all involved: the steward of a Georgian prince who wished to renounce all his worldly inheritance is said to have exclaimed, "He will make all of us, who count on him, wretched!"[175] Justinian reportedly sent a lump of gold to prop up another household that was on the verge of collapse due to the asceticism of its master, an imperial court chamberlain.[176]

At the same time, this society held different assumptions than our own about what constitutes "the equity of equality" (to use Theodore of Petra's phrase). The aristocratic cultures of Greco-Roman civilization had always embraced notions of proportional equality and distributive justice, according to which differences of rank and status had to be taken into account when assessing how people should be treated or what quantity or quality of benefits they should receive. Otherwise, as Pliny the Younger remarked, "Nothing is more unequal than equality."[177] Such reasoning is often found in societies that take the concept of honor seriously. Its influence is found not only in Roman law but in philosophical deliberations on equality ranging from Aristotle to various rabbis.[178] It is therefore not surprising to also find it voiced by Christian authorities. Indeed, as Douglas Rae observes, it is epitomized by the phrase, "to each according to his or her deserts."[179]

Thus, the priorities proposed by John of Gaza reflected standard assumptions of what constituted fair and equitable treatment in Early Byzantium. But John recognized another level of elite status that needed to be considered when distributing aid. Because monks were also considered *ptōchoi* who had suffered a decline in worldly wealth and prestige for the sake of humanity and religion, they deserved the preferential treatment given to distressed gentlefolk. John told a layperson who asked if it was permissible to give poor people inferior wine and save the good stuff for monks,

> Concerning *ptōchoi*, until we reach the point of holding them as equals and loving them as ourselves . . . do what you can and give them the inferior. But concerning the Fathers, you must honor them first, as slaves of God. For it is written: "Give honor to whom honor is due" [Rom 13:7], and the Lord has honored them first.[180]

Pachomius similarly ordained that those who visited his monasteries should be received "with greater honor if they are clerics or monks."[181] Such religious déclassés recalled the condition Paul attributed to Jesus, who, "though rich, became a *ptōchos*" for humanity's sake (2 Cor 8:9), a description of profound significance for the self-understanding of this Christian religious elite.

We might consider such discriminatory conventions as unbecoming for people who were regarded as saints, but contemporaries believed it enabled them to extend a "philanthropic hand" to the "dignified and undignified" alike,[182] producing a capacity to give universally to all precisely because they enabled these saints to do so differently in each case. By the sixth century, the ideal of *philanthrōpia* had been pressed beyond anything attested in pre-Constantinian times. Its concessive force could still be invoked to broaden a Christian's outlook on what constituted generosity, as when John sought to encourage a landowner to allow some neighboring Jews to use his wine vats. If, John proposed, when God made it rain,

> He rained on your land but ignored the Jews' land, then don't press wine with them. But if He is philanthropic towards all, and "rains on the righteous and unrighteous alike" [cf. Mt 5:42], why would you want to be inhumane rather than pitying like Him Who says, "be pitying like our Father in heaven" [Lk 6:36].[183]

Occasionally, we hear of mercy being extended even to slaves and heretics: one landowner in Asia Minor reportedly shared his grain with the latter during a famine, "even though it went against his gut instincts," taking consolation that it might convert them to orthodoxy. Otherwise, however, these two groups have left remarkably little trace as beneficiaries of Early Byzantine philanthropy.[184]

In this chapter I have sought to explain the facets and emergence of a Christian discourse on philanthropy that not only emphasized the extension of mercy to an ever-broadening circle of recipients but also sought to remove any excuses for not giving aid to claimants, even when reluctance seemed justified. My focus has been on institutional strategies for extending mercy to "all who ask" and privileging of a core constituency known as *ptōchoi*. Institutional limitations, however, placed responsibilities on individual Christians to give, and as will be seen in the following chapters, this contributed to the elaboration of religious gift-giving ideals and practices. We will now examine individual almsgiving practices, starting with ministries that taught compassion by directly exposing privileged people to the misfortunes of the sick, downfallen, or poor. Indeed, it was only by promoting such acts of individual almsgiving that Christian philanthropy could begin to fulfill its aspirations of universal giving and, ultimately, universal salvation.

"Bend Your Heart to Mercy"

Almsgiving and the Christian Advocacy of Social Compassion

"In the great imperial city, it is possible to see various ministries of men and women that wash the sick who lie in the neighborhoods." So reports John of Ephesus (ca. 507–588), describing the lay "deaconries" that provided informal outreach to sick and homeless people in sixth-century Constantinople.[1] John attributes the origin of these ministries, which existed alongside philanthropic institutions affiliated with the imperial church, to an anti-Chalcedonian layman named Paul. According to John, religious zeal had prompted Paul to carry the sick, poor, and old to his home each night in Antioch. There he would bathe them, mend their clothes, and give them something to drink before sending them off with coins, given "to all as suited each." Soon, other people secretly joined in: "Even many of the great and eminent men of the city," writes John, "having clothed themselves in poor men's apparel and hoods . . . put straps on their necks and carried chairs for the sick and poor . . . performing this ministration for them, while with earnest zeal gladly they spent money to provide for each, according to his state in life."[2] Paul planted similar ministries in other cities up the Aegean coast, eventually reaching Constantinople, where more "great and eminent men" participated. It was to one of its "ministries that bathe the sick at night" that a layman named Ishāq repaired to pursue a religious life. Formerly a leading citizen of Dara, the great Roman citadel on the Persian frontier, Ishāq served in a Constantinopolitan deaconry until his aristocratic appearance began to attract attention, prompting him to sell his clothes, put on sackcloth, and work in a suburban hospital. There he served till he died, when his wife affirmed that it was "out of humility for God's sake, and not as a man in need, that he had submitted to minister to the sick."[3]

These passages offer precious details about lay-organized philanthropic ministries that have been called one of the "distinctive features of Byzantine worship."[4] Unlike church-affiliated institutions run by professional doctors, orderlies, clerics, and monks,[5] these organizations (known as *diakoniai*, based on the Greek term for ministration or service, *diakonia*, whence "deacon" and "deaconry") gave lay volunteers a chance to practice benevolence on a regular, short-term basis. John presents them as a sectarian innovation (Paul only allowed fellow Anti-Chalcedonians to participate), but by the end of the century, Roman emperors were endowing similar ministries.[6] Those who served in Paul's, John emphasizes, included the rich. Elsewhere we learn about a prominent Christian couple at Antioch, a pious moneylender named Lord Andronicus and his wife, Anastasia, who decided to seal their pact of sexual renunciation by spending four nights a week washing men and women in separate deaconries "out of love of *ptōchoi*."[7] Staffed and supported by enthusiasts like these, such ministries "expanded everywhere,"[8] offering grassroots relief amid the crumbling cities of the late Justinianic empire.

We are fortunate that contemporary writers took notice, because otherwise, information about non-imperial lay philanthropy in the Roman East becomes sparse after the fourth century. As John of Ephesus observes, what made such deaconries remarkable was their promotion of direct interactions, even physical contact, between groups that ordinarily had none: namely, the healthy and the sick, and the rich and the poor. His account is illuminating because, in addition to describing their activities, he reveals his own sense of their religious significance. He notes that they sought to assist people "as suited each" "according to his state in life," taking inspiration from Jesus's words, "Come to me all you who are weary, that I may give you rest" (Mt 11:28).[9] But more specifically, in his view such ministries provided opportunities for direct interactions that not only connected high to low but even turned high into low, at least temporarily, "for God's sake."

This chapter explores objectives and dynamics associated with regular acts of merciful giving in Early Byzantium. More than any other expression of Christian philanthropy, a gift of alms denoted an indulgent action as much as an item, its mercy signaled not by what was given but how it was given. Learning how to give properly was a prerequisite for making such a gift. Essential was a respectful attitude toward its recipient, partly because almsgiving by definition implied asymmetries of need, exemplified most often by vertical giving by the rich to the poor. My aim here is to highlight two aspects of almsgiving discourse that, if not unique to Early Byzantium, were especially pronounced in this hierarchical, aristocratic society: first, an awareness of the sheer challenge of promoting positive interactions between individuals of markedly different status or rank, and second, a conviction about the transformative power of giving alms on a direct and regular basis, especially for individual almsgivers. First, I examine how John Chrysostom promoted direct almsgiving as a means of fostering compassion (or empathy, shared-suffering, *sympatheia*) between different social ranks in late fourth- and early fifth-century Antioch and Constantinople; then I examine analogous rationales for practicing direct ministrations within monastic institutions; then I return to urban contexts to explain the emergent depiction of monks as expert mediators between rich and poor both outside and inside eastern cities in the later fifth and sixth centuries.

By focusing on these aspects of Early Byzantine almsgiving, I do not mean to imply that it had no other significance or purpose.[10] Almsgiving in the later Roman Empire is a multifaceted topic and was articulated somewhat differently by Greek and Syriac-speaking authorities. As noted above, Greek authorities spoke in terms of *eleēmosynē*, acts of mercy. Syriac-speaking authorities did so in terms of *zedqē*, derived from the Hebrew word for gifts or acts of righteousness, *tzedakah*. These underlying concepts often overlapped. The former (*eleēmosynē*), however, tended to emphasize an almsgiver's emotional involvement or response, while the latter (*zedqē*) tended to emphasize a poor person's God-given entitlement to (and a rich person's duty to provide) a share of Creation's material bounties.[11] The next chapter will discuss "redemptive" purposes of Christian almsgiving, by which alms provided recompense for injustices caused by greed and improper acquisitions. Here we focus instead on the positive transformation that Christian authorities believed took place whenever people of superior wealth or status deigned to interact directly and respectfully with their inferiors.

In modern society, idealizing such interactions de haute en bas has fallen out of favor as degrading to recipients. As Marcel Mauss observed, "The whole tendency of our [egalitarian social] morality is to strive to do away with the unconscious and injurious patronage of the rich almsgiver" by replacing it with state welfare systems that mediate between society's wealthy and non-wealthy.[12] Church institutions likewise provided a more professional and efficient conduit for dispensing alms in late antiquity, at least in theory. The *Apostolic Constitutions* recommends that laypeople give alms through their clergy, since only these "clearly know who the afflicted are."[13] But the preachers who promoted direct, personal almsgiving in Early Byzantium did so with a conviction that they were introducing something new, if not revolutionary, and positively transformative. Chrysostom, its most famous Eastern exponent, declared, "Nothing is so characteristic of a Christian as mercy, and nothing do all so much admire—even unbelievers—as when we show mercy."[14] Such preaching gave fresh life to an old Roman aspiration, occasionally aired by philosophically minded writers, of making society more humane.[15] But what made a Christian gift of alms identifiable as a gift of mercy?

As John of Ephesus attests, one key term for understanding Early Byzantine almsgiving ideals was *diakonia*, "ministration." Originally referring to any delicate task that a high-level slave might perform for a master, in the New Testament it usually refers to respectful gestures such as foot washing performed for a guest (e.g., 1 Tim 5:10). Paul, however, applied it more narrowly to distributions to the poor (Rom 15:25; 1 Cor 16:5; 2 Cor 9:1; cf. Acts 11:29, 12:25), and Acts 6:2 uses it to describe the daily distributions of food and waiting at tables that took place in the original apostolic community. In Early Byzantium it became a semi-technical term for deliberate and respectful almsgiving. Authorities in the seventh century interpreted the *diakonia* depicted in the Book of Acts as an "archetype of zealous philanthropy toward the needy," while Chrysostom claimed that such activities were deliberately described in Acts as a *diakonia* instead of a distribution of alms in order to dignify all involved, "both givers and receivers."[16]

That it was Chrysostom who made this point is not surprising. Known to later Byzantine tradition as "John of Alms,"[17] he stands out among Christian preachers for his emphatic promotion of direct, personal, respectful almsgiving. Like John of Ephesus, he was especially interested in how such engagement instilled humility and improved the disposition of the almsgivers themselves. His major scriptural inspirations for this were, on the one hand, the Old Testament depiction of Abraham's solicitude for the strangers who passed his house at Mambre, whom the patriarch served "with his own hand" (Gn 18:1–18); and on the other, Paul's description of Christ as one who, "though he was rich, made himself poor" for the sake of humanity (2 Cor 8:9, cf. Phil 2:7–8). Both offered precedents for a salvific act of condescension (*synkatabasis*) that Chrysostom hoped to promote among wealthy Christians both for their own good and for that of society at large. He noted how contemporary Christians lacked the social cohesion of the original apostolic community. There, he observed, all Christians had shared the same table, "the rich bringing provisions, the poor and possessionless being invited by them," all dining together. But later, "this custom became corrupted." He imagined that Christian society would recover its lost apostolic cohesion if its wealthier members would only resume such interactions with its poorer.[18]

This solution for alleviating the asymmetries of aristocratic society eventually became axiomatic in Eastern Christendom. Chrysostom's notion of practicing condescension for the sake of acquiring humility was not shared by all, however.[19] Asterius of Amasea, for example, explicitly proposed just the opposite: "Let us imitate the joy and philanthropy of our Master by condescending to the lowly," he preached to congregations in Cappadocia, "not so that we might humble ourselves to their level, but that we might elevate them as well."[20] No doubt Chrysostom's outlook was influenced by the fact that he was preaching in two of the most densely populated cities of the day, Antioch (386–398) and Constantinople (398–404), where it was hard to ignore social asymmetries or the reluctance of rich Christians to rub shoulders with the poor. For Chrysostom, however, exposing the upper crust to lower society had another rationale: it offered a chance to encounter the voluntary lowliness of Christ himself in the abject guise of the poor. Behind this was a scriptural refrain he cited more than any other known preacher: "Come, you who are blessed by my Father, inherit the kingdom prepared for you . . . for I was hungry and you gave me food, I was thirsty and you gave me drink, I was a stranger and you welcomed me, I was naked and you gave me clothing, I was sick and you took care of me, I was in prison and you visited me. . . . as you did it to one of the least of my family, so you did it to me" (Mt 25:31–36).

This passage, which Chrysostom called the "sweetest" in the New Testament,[21] presents direct almsgiving as a consummate act of Christian worship and right- eousness. All depends, however, on treating "the least" of humanity with the same indulgence that one might extend to Christ. John Moschus illustrated this in the seventh century with a story about a layman tasked with dispensing underwear in a deaconry at Antioch. Seeing a beggar repeatedly sneak back to get more, the lay- man rebuked him and sent him off "deeply ashamed." The next night, gazing on an icon set into a street-corner wall, he imagined Christ himself was stepping out of it, wearing the extra pairs of underwear the *ptōchos* had taken. Collapsing in con- trition, he tearfully apologized for having been so petty and "human" in his rea- soning, and resolved to be more generous in the future.[22]

Of course, *petty* and *human* describes most people. It was partly because so few were prepared to voluntarily lower themselves that direct almsgiving became pre- scribed as a humiliating act of redemptive penance, as discussed in the next chap- ter. Yet, while Chrysostom may have been unusual in emphasizing almsgiving as a means of attaining humility, compassion, and spiritual change (indeed, later tradi- tion also called him "John of Repentance"),[23] he was not the only exponent of this idea. Describing a deaconry that "perfected every ministry to the poor," John of Ephesus explains that its practices were deliberately modeled on monastic conven- tions, "ministering to and washing the poor according to a monastic rule."[24] In fact, monastic literature offers the closest parallels to what Chrysostom proposed and John of Ephesus described.[25] The *Life of Symeon Stylites the Younger* shows how intertwined the notions of almsgiving and *diakoniai* had become with acquir- ing humility and encountering Christ in sixth-century monastic discourse:

A monk's boast is to make alms by any means possible. A monk's boast is to not mock but to feel compassion for brothers in affliction. A monk's boast is to wash their feet and say, "bless you." A monk's boast is to conquer arrogance and make no one ashamed. A monk's boast is to humble himself and believe himself to be least of all. . . . It is pure brotherhood, hospitality and unfeigned *diakonia* toward all—young and old, poor and rich—as to Christ the Savior Himself.[26]

If monks could actually boast of such virtues, it was because monasteries had trained them to attain them. Most required novices to spend several years per- forming a series of ministrations within the community itself. Such training aimed to foster the humility needed to see the divinity latent in each fellow monk, as well as compassion between lower and higher ranks. And it prepared some to serve not just as expert almsgivers but as zealous exponents of righteous relations between rich and poor in society at large.

PREACHING DIRECT ALMSGIVING IN CHRISTIAN ANTIOCH

Rising up the slopes of Mount Silpius in northwestern Syria, the city of Antioch looked out on the Mediterranean yet remained closely bound by trade, provincial administration, and military affairs to central Anatolia and the eastern frontier. By all accounts it was a charming place. Ever since its foundation in the Hellenistic age, people had come from as far as Egypt to build summer retreats on its terraced mountainside or the posh suburb of Daphne. By the fifth century CE, it stretched four miles along the Orontes River, boasted over 150,000 residents, and rivaled Alexandria as second city of the Eastern empire. Local leaders continued to meet, as they had for centuries, at the municipal hall in the city's eastern quarter; but as metropolis of Roman Syria Prima, Antioch was now the seat of the imperial governor and other high officials, including, for part of the fourth century, emperors as well. This imperial presence added new luster to the old urban grid. Its centerpiece was an island in the Orontes that featured a palace, a hippodrome, and a gleaming cathedral known as the Golden House, a Constantinian construction encircled by a marble portico. Bridges connected these to fora on higher elevations; oil lamps lit the way at the night, making the city's central boulevard "bright as day." Two coastal harbors, a fertile hinterland, and nearby Lake Amik kept markets open well into the evening; cool breezes wafted up the Orontes, while fresh water gushed down the mountain to fill fountains and bathhouses below. To contemporaries, Antioch was "the beauteous crown of the East"; in the words of Libanius (314–394), its chief civic spokesman and pagan traditionalist, "This I can say of my native city: it is the fairest thing in the finest land under heaven."[27]

At the same time the city produced some of the starkest descriptions of urban poverty and neglect known from antiquity. Even Libanius decried the fact that, while "these poor wretches groan and cry, people rush past under lamplight from the baths to banquets laden with everything but ambrosia and nectar."[28] But the most vivid testimony comes from his former pupil, John Chrysostom. As Chrysostom announced one winter Sunday to an audience perhaps gathered in the Golden House itself,

> I rise before you today on a righteous embassy.... For as I was hastening to this congregation through the market and alleys I saw many sprawled in the middle of the street, some missing hands or eyes, others covered with tumors and incurable wounds with parts of their body completely exposed which, because of their advanced putrefaction, should have been covered up. I thought it inhumane not to address you about them.[29]

Chrysostom presents this population as if they inhabited a foreign city, but he could have also described them as populating a different church. Patterns of social segregation were heightened in ceremonial church centers like the Golden House.[30] Equipped with a soup kitchen and hostel like an ancient synagogue or medieval Ottoman mosque,[31] this urban cathedral became a magnet for the city's burgeoning homeless population. Chrysostom sought to give those that lingered at the doors a liturgical function, urging congregants to hand them alms to cleanse their souls before the service just as they did by washing their hands in the church plaza fountains before entering.[32] Otherwise, they were avoided. If the working poor attended, they also received little attention: "With [them] we approach this holy table, but when we go outside we seem not to have seen them at all."[33]

Chrysostom belonged to a remarkable generation of Christian preachers who raised a "call to alms" against poverty and neglect all around the Mediterranean during the fourth and early fifth centuries.[34] In him, however, wealthy congregations faced a relentless provocateur. Only after Chrysostom died was he remembered for his "golden mouth" (*chryson stōma*). While alive, he plainly enjoyed discomfiting his elite audiences with challenging propositions. "Every day you lecture us on alms and philanthropy," he imagined them complaining. "When will you stop bringing the poor into your sermons, prophetically portending misfortune and penury for us, eager to make us beggars?"[35] It was not just that he denounced inherited wealth as evidence of sin and injustice, as discussed in the next chapter. Also unsettling was his insistence that they take remedy by giving alms directly themselves, with their own hands, and not through their church:

> Do not give to those presiding in church to distribute. Minister yourselves . . . so that you might have the reward not [merely] of spending but of serving. Give with your own hands. . . . Give through yourself, for great is the profit if through yourself you give. . . . Do not treat [the poor] with contempt because they loiter outside houses or amble around the marketplace. . . . If we must wash their feet, so much the more must we give them money with our own hands.[36]

> You will not be saved if it is I who does the giving, nor will you be wiping out your own sins if the church should provide. If you are not giving because [you think] the church ought to give to the needy, [consider:] since priests pray, will you never pray? Since others fast, will you be continually drunk? Don't you know that God ordained almsgiving not so much for sake of the poor, as for the sake of those who give them? Do these things yourself, so that you will reap a double reward. For I do not talk about almsgiving so that you might bring [alms] to us, but that you might minister them yourself through yourself.[37]

"Even if you are giving to poor people," Chrysostom adds, "don't think it undignified to give through yourself; for it is not to a poor man that will you be giving, but to Christ."[38]

These passages show that Chrysostom conceptualized direct almsgiving as a lay ministration (*diakonia*). To persuade elite listeners that such involvement befitted any Christian patriarch, he often referred, as had rabbis before him,[39] to the hospitality that Abraham bestowed on the mysterious three strangers who passed his house at Mambre (Gn 18:1–18):

> When Abraham received those who came past as travelers (for so he thought them to be), he did not let his servants take up preparations for their welcome, but carried out the greater part of the *diakonia* himself . . . though he had 318 slaves born in his house. . . . He wanted himself and his wife to be rewarded not just for the outlay but for the ministration. So we too must show "love of strangers" by doing everything ourselves, that we may be sanctified and so that our hands be blessed.[40]

Abraham was the foremost biblical exemplar of the righteous rich man. What Chrysostom wanted listeners to especially notice was his zeal and humility in serving such strangers himself, despite all the slaves he had on call. The patriarch had "adopted the guise of a suppliant and domestic servant, even though he did not know who it was who was receiving," Chrysostom observed. "Instead of deeming himself worthy to sit with them, he stood under a tree while they were eating . . . taking the role of a servant. . . . What surpassing humility!"[41]

Like other preachers, Chrysostom believed Abraham illustrated almsgiving at its best.[42] His recurring interest in this Old Testament episode is, however, striking. Since it highlighted generosity toward anonymous strangers, it provided Chrysostom with a scriptural basis to encourage elite Christians to give "without respect of persons," like Abraham, who gave "even though he did not know whom he was receiving," rather than giving to people they already knew.[43] But above all, he emphasized the patriarch's direct, personal involvement because he knew that, if his listeners ever gave alms on the street, they usually did so through the mediation of their slaves. "When we see a stranger or a poor man, we knit our brows and think them not worth a word; but if we've been softened by a thousand supplications, we order our servants to give them a little silver, and think we have done it all,"[44] he observed.

> Many have come to such a level of cruelty as to ignore starving people with the slightest excuse, saying these words: "I have no servant with me now." . . . We admire the patriarch because he himself ran to his cows and grabbed a calf even though he had 318 domestics. But some are so arrogant now as to do these things through slaves, yet not feel ashamed.[45]

Slaves thus mediated between the rich and poor where the church did not. In fourth-century cities, the practice of slavery was still a thriving institution, "the water in which everything else floats."[46] Aristocrats found it fashionable to adorn their houses with images of domestic slaves serving at banquets and other high-end ministrations; Chrysostom notes that domestics were ostentatiously used to clear a path in the street for their master's litter or carry his purse to dispense largesse where directed.[47] Uncertainty about urban beggars, as well as their stench, made distancing desirable, but Chrysostom considered such excuses utterly specious. In his view, these practices stemmed from an aristocratic fear of being seen among poor people. "One of you might say, 'If I personally myself do the giving, will I not seem vain?'" No, he responds; by refusing to give on that pretext, "you will [reveal] another kind of vainglory—that of feeling ashamed to be seen talking with someone who is poor. . . . You think it undignified to be seen giving or talking to poor people. Blast your haughty conceit!"[48]

Chrysostom was clearly aware of Jesus's prohibition against giving alms ostentatiously in public (Mt 6:2–4). In his view, however, direct almsgiving was worth the risk if done appropriately, without exacerbating the plight of the recipient: "Vainglory is bad in every matter, but especially when it comes to philanthropy, for it is the ultimate cruelty to parade the misfortunes of others, all but insulting their *ptōcheia.*"[49] A gift of alms, he stressed, was a gift not of money but of mercy. It must never increase a recipient's shame or grief.[50] Almsgivers had to show extra goodwill, lest they "cast down rather than raise up" their recipient.[51] Chrysostom believed Abraham taught this. "You see how he used various means to importune those transients, seeking to win them over by his posture, words, and everything?" he asked. "According to scripture, [Abraham] first 'bowed down low,' then called them 'Lords' and himself a 'slave'; then told them what he was going to bring them, minimizing and showing it to be no great thing."[52] Abraham's behavior was calculated to put needy strangers at ease, claimed Chrysostom, marking a clear contrast with current practices. "Consider how much honor, how much humility he displayed . . . unlike most people who, should they ever do something similar, become fat-headed toward their recipients and even scorn them for all the care being showered on them."[53]

Such sensitivities developed only through repeated practice. Above all, giving alms had to communicate a merciful intention, both because this is what infused the alms with its essential quality, and because it was often impossible to ever give a sufficient quantity of alms to anyone (a practical consideration that we will see repeatedly). One of Chrysostom's concerns was to make audiences understand that a giver's intention—signaled by a person's degree of engagement—was as important as anything else in turning any object or gesture into a gift of mercy. This criterion of quality over quantity tended to make poor people better almsgivers, in his view, since the poor knew from experience what the unfortunate needed. "We ought not consider ourselves forsaken due to our penury," he observes, "for it makes giving alms even easier for us."

> While one who has acquired many things is consumed by haughtiness and an even greater desire for material possessions, he who has little is free from these tyrannical

passions and therefore finds more opportunities to do it well. He will go easily into a prison, visit the sick, and give a cold drink, while a person who is inflated by wealth will do none of these things.[54]

"If your soul has nothing else but a capacity to commiserate," he continues, "for this you will be rewarded."[55] Abraham illustrated how displaying humility and zest could augment a gift. In fact, giving with such a spirit could double the substance of the gift—Chrysostom compares it to amassing a fortune and gleefully giving it all away at once.[56]

To give with a shared sense of suffering (*sympatheia*) to someone in need: this was the essential spirit of Christian almsgiving. People brought down by loss of health or wealth could readily appreciate this, but rich Christians often needed more help. Here it is important to remember that compassion is an emotive, empathetic trait that usually needs to be learned through experience.[57] In Chrysostom's view, privileges tended to make rich Antiochenes fat-headed (*megalophrōn*, a favorite description) and unable to see that "we are all each other's limbs—not just the inferior to the superior, but the superior to the inferior."[58] Because of this, they especially needed to engage in personal ministrations such as Abraham had practiced: for giving with one's own hands "dispels vanity . . . and deflates pride."[59] Almsgiving had been ordained to instill wisdom. "One who regularly gives to the poor," Chrysostom explains, "will never be fat-headed," having been humbled "by realizing humanity's condition in the misfortunes of others."[60] Cripples lying before the church teach how worldly prosperity can vanish like smoke. God put them there, Chrysostom told audiences, to "move us to pity with great compassion and fear, lest one day we might suffer the same."[61] Nothing induces compassion like seeing the potential for one's own downfall in the tragic cases of others,[62] or direct contact with the afflicted. "Not just to give generously, yet without compassion, but to make oneself bend down in mercy, grieving and commiserating with the needy—this is why God has ordained almsgiving. He could have nourished the poor without this, but He commanded us to feed them to bind us together . . . and make us fervent for each other."[63]

Thus, for Chrysostom, almsgiving was not simply a means to express mercy and compassion but a method of humbling oneself to obtain those virtues. This was why in his view it especially had to be practiced out of public sight whenever possible, "for what profit is it . . . to gain esteem from onlookers or give scrupulously and according to God's pleasure, but to become elevated by this and fat-headed?"[64] This focus on obtaining personal humility seems to have made Chrysostom's preaching different from that of his predecessors. While the Cappadocians stressed giving out of compassion, they did not advocate it as a means of inducing compassion within givers themselves. Nor do we find this purpose in Aphrahat's sermon *On the Care of the Poor*. Known as the "Persian Sage," Aphrahat (d. 345) wrote in eastern Mesopotamia to encourage his audience to perform personal ministrations (*tešmešta*) to poor people, using several tropes that Chrysostom would later use in Antioch, including the example of Hebrew patriarchs.[65] But Aphrahat does not relate this to acquiring humility or compassion. His immediate concern seems to have been to persuade wealthy Christians to give, so that their neglected fellow Christians might not drift into neighboring Jewish communities for aid.[66] Aphrahat treats giving alms in terms of *zaddiqā*—that is, as an act of righteousness that corrected a communal imbalance, rather than an act of mercy that improved the emotive capacity and spiritual state of individual almsgivers.

Indeed, Chrysostom's approach was informed by his reflections on religious condescension (*synkatabasis*). This was a loaded theological concept in Antiochene Christian circles; Chrysostom refers to it so often that he has been called "le docteur de la condescendance."[67] In theology, it described all the shapes and guises that God has assumed throughout history to make his infinite majesty accessible to humanity, whether in the guise of a whirlwind, a burning bush, or a human body—emptying and lowering himself to assume a "shape of a slave" in order to make salvation comprehensible to the full range of humanity (Phil 2:7; cf. 2 Cor 8:9). Such self-effacing condescension was crucial for giving philanthropically to all, despite all possible reservations, and for becoming compassionate. As Chrysostom concluded, "Whoever wants to become rich, let him become poor, that he might become rich."[68]

This was the almsgiving discourse that Chrysostom developed in Antioch and brought with him later to Constantinople. There as bishop, he similarly advised audiences to "become humble through almsgiving."[69] It is easy to see how such gift giving became closely associated with penance, as discussed in the next chapter. It was considered sufficiently challenging to be frequently identified with Christian saints. John of Ephesus, for example, illustrates the "humility and compassion" of a sixth-century abbot by describing how, like Abraham, this abbot would "with his own hands make himself into an attendant" to serve the poor at tables set out at his monastery.[70] Chrysostom himself had no illusions that his lay listeners would imitate such exemplars. Ultimately, he simply called for restraint: "I ask only that you give, whether through yourself or through another; and that you do not insult, strike, or denigrate anyone."[71]

The challenge of Chrysostom's Christian ideal becomes most apparent when viewed against the hierarchical notion of good order (*eutaxia*) pervading Roman society at the time. This made social segregation seem an appropriate, countervailing ideal. We find this outlook vividly articulated by the sixth-century historian Agathias. Recounting the effects of the earthquake at Constantinople in 557, he describes how chaos ensued when "all order, respect, and recognition of rank" were thrown into "confusion." Not only did women mingle with men, he reports, but "inferiors were put at equal honor with men of stature." Suddenly, "things praised in word but rarely put into practice were most eagerly pursued. . . . Prominent citizens walked the avenues at night giving food and blankets to the helpless and pitiful people lying maimed and mutilated on the ground." But these ministrations subsided along with the tremors, causing Agathias to reflect that only amid fear "do we get any taste of good works."[72] Chrysostom would have agreed: short of confronting elite Christians with the spectacle of a tragic collapse, little could compel them to practice compassionate condescension. To find that, one had to enter a monastery.

THE MONASTIC MIDDLE WAY OF
COMMUNAL MINISTRATIONS

Congregations often suspected Chrysostom of foisting monastic practices on them, and they had good grounds when he presented almsgiving as a method of inculcating humility and compassion. If ever they took the time to visit a monastery, he said, they would see "humility at its height." For there they would find

> people formerly illustrious in worldly rank or wealth, putting themselves down in every way through their clothes, dwellings, and those whom they serve. . . . Gone are the fancy apparel, splendid houses, and innumerable slaves that make men arrogant. . . . They light their own fires, chop their own wood, do their own cooking, and minister to all who come. Nowhere can you hear anyone giving or receiving insults and being bossed around. All are devoted to those to whom they minister, each washing the feet of strangers and vying to do this.

In such settings all people shared the same table, servers and served alike, including sick and leprous strangers. Hence, there was not only "much equality" there, but also "much opportunity for virtue." Did this mean that "confusion" reigned as a result? Far from it, listeners were assured: only "first-rate *eutaxia*—for whoever is superior does not notice that another is inferior, but considers himself even lowlier than the other, and thereby becomes all the more superior."[73]

Thus, Chrysostom presents monasteries as places committed to an alternative *eutaxia* in which equality prevailed, except to the extent that advancements in humility made one superior to another. This depiction seems to have been calculated to appeal to late Roman sensibilities. No other author describes monasteries in such paradoxical terms, but it was precisely this conception of a monastery as a hierarchical inversion of worldly norms that made it admirable to contemporary observers. Because Eastern monasteries accepted, as far as we know, people from all walks of life (even slaves, with permission of their masters), each potentially included a variety of backgrounds. Here Christians might forge a religious aristocracy upheld by firm distinctions of superiority and inferiority, albeit based on humility, asceticism, and spiritual attainments rather than birth, rank, and material wealth.

At least that was the ideal. In reality worldly distinctions crept into monasteries, no doubt especially in those that required minimum contributions in order to join.[74] We get a different picture from what Chrysostom described when we turn to the fifth-century treatise *On Repentance* by a certain Mark the Monk:

> It is obvious that we behave arrogantly with those who are beneath our notice or are poorer than we, as if wishing to exert authority over hirelings or slaves, or claiming that nobility is no longer defined by being "in Christ" but defined rather by physical appearance and wealth. When we find some small cause for complaint about those who are less well off, immediately we ostentatiously go on the attack. . . . This, then, is how we treat inferiors. With regard to those of the same social standing as ourselves, at the smallest sort of pretext we immediately turn our backs on them. . . . As for our wickedness toward those more powerful than ourselves, it is so varied and well-hidden that it is difficult to speak or conceive of it. . . . We flatter those whom we cannot harm and with a jealous eye we bitterly look on their prosperity. . . . By outward show and irenic speech we flatter such persons as these, but our thoughts are disposed against them.[75]

Mark may have written this sketch for lay readers,[76] but there is no reason to believe it did not reflect his monastic experience as well. A sixth-century hagiographer refers to a new recruit being hazed by his brethren for simply wearing "humble, contemptible clothing" in their cenobium: "Some bit him, others beat him, while others rained down insults upon him."[77] This is presented as nothing unusual. Shenoute threatened to expel any monk from his monastery who called another a "stupid or good-for-nothing slave."[78] For both good and ill, conformity was the rule. A monastic saying went, "He who lives with brothers should not be square but round."[79]

Those entering monasticism needed as much training in communal compassion as outside laypeople did. For reasons discussed in the next chapters, almsgiving in material form was never encouraged as a practice within cenobitic institutions. Instead, humility, mercy, and compassion were instilled by a series of obligatory communal ministrations called *diakoniai*. Conceived as acts of mercy performed by one resident for another, this was, in effect, training in almsgiving in immaterial form. Beyond imposing self-effacing condescension to nurture humility and compassion, its goal was to train monks to become sensitive to each other's needs and, as Mark the Monk put it, aware of their shared "nobility in Christ." The following reconstruction is not meant to describe any particular system in detail but to indicate the role of ministrations in social and spiritual formation of a monastic community from the fourth to the seventh century.

By the seventh century, a monastery's entire system of initiation and philanthropic work (as well as the monastic space dedicated to this) could be known as its *diakonia*.[80] Participation was required for two to ten years after entry as a novice. According to John Cassian (ca. 360–435), those joining Egyptian communities began with a year's service in the outside reception room. Candidates in this liminal position served visitors under the supervision of a guest master adept at treating guests "diligently and humanely." Cassian notes that this was considered basic training in humility and patience; here they would learn to greet strangers with appropriate respect, acknowledging that they, like Abraham, were no more than dust and ash (Gn 18:27).[81] Only if they served "without complaint," he reports, could they join the rest of the community, advancing thereafter in a series of ministrations now directed mainly toward other monks. This began with routine duties, working in teams in alternating weekly shifts to cook, clean, wait tables, make beds, wash the floors, and so on. Monks who did so "with utmost humility and eagerness" were noted.[82] *Diakonia* duties thereafter became increasingly longer, individualized and refined, beginning with annual positions such a chief gardener, carpenter, gatekeeper, or baker, rising to offices of infirmarian and guest master, culminating with that of steward.[83] According to the fifth-century *Canons of Marutha*, the last three positions were to be reserved for monks whose zeal demonstrated that their brothers' needs "lay on their hearts" and that they could care for "each in his place."[84] Bénédicte Lesieur observes that such offices "allow us to discern a sort of *cursus honorum* for a monk of a coenobium."[85] An abbot was expected to make appointments without preferring freeborn monks over former slaves; moreover, he would ideally continue to participate in the most lowly ministrations himself, lest "the server of all be served."[86]

Even if we cannot examine any particular instance of this monastic system, it is clear that the concept of *diakonia* shaped the structures of early Byzantine monasteries. Neighboring laity must have come to know local monks partly through their ministrations, given the apparent openness of early monastic guesthouses. An estimated 70 percent of references to *xenodocheia* from this period refer to monastic-run facilities; seven hostels and infirmaries are attributed to the Saba monastery in Palestine alone (several were in Jerusalem, perhaps meant only for Saba's monks visiting the city).[87] As far as we know, all offered free room and board and were staffed by monks, who were required to attend to strangers in addition to performing their liturgical duties: Dorotheus of Gaza (d. ca. 560) recalls the exhaustion he suffered as a guest master, being regularly awoken to receive travelers and their camels at night.[88]

We can see what a high-end guesthouse was like from one built beside the gates of the Martyrius Monastery near Jerusalem in the sixth century. This facility, measuring nearly 150 feet (43 m) long, is the only Early Byzantine monastic hostel that has been completely excavated. Its six or seven white-tiled rooms could accommodate 60–70 people; there was also an attached stable for pack animals and a chapel. Guests may have also been allowed to use the bathhouse and two-story refectory built at the same time within the monastery. The bathhouse had a steam room and a cold pool, while the refectory consisted of a colonnaded hall capable of seating 200 people around semicircular marble tables, set into colorful tiled floors; hundreds of utensils and wine cups have been found beneath the ruins of its upper-story kitchen.[89] Perhaps more typical was a *xenodocheion* recently excavated south of Gaza, about half the size of the one at the Martyrius Monastery.[90] For our purposes, however, it is not the size of these structures that are important but the opportunities they presented for monastic *diakoniai*. Rules attributed to Saba's Great Lavra in Palestine stated that monks coming from Syria, because they were naturally diligent and dutiful, should be preferred for positions of steward, guest master, and other high *diakoniai,* short of abbot. Evidently, it was assumed that recruits from everywhere else needed institutional training to acquire such virtues.[91]

What must be emphasized is that these ministrations were devised not just to run a monastery but to provide a mechanism for socialization. Their purpose, Cassian reports, was to ensure that no member of the community would "blush to be on an equal level with the poor, meaning the monastic brotherhood."[92] Training that began in the guesthouse carried over to the kitchen, refectory, and latrines. Often done in the lay world by slaves, such drudgework was potentially degrading for anyone, but especially for monks from privileged backgrounds. When Emperor Justin II wanted to punish highborn heretics in Constantinople, he condemned them to perform "all the ignominious work of monastic life," including serving tables, sweeping hallways, and cleaning latrines at local monasteries.[93] Not surprisingly, we hear of resistance. It is said that the Egyptian abbot Pachomius initially had to set all the tables and care for the sick in his monastery by himself, because his recruits had not yet "attained such a disposition as to serve like a slave for others."[94] John Moschus tells of a novice who began to grumble about the *diakoniai* assigned to him after joining a cenobium near Jerusalem, thinking he had already contributed enough gold to the community upon entry to entitle him to leisure. This offended others, "especially those from less affluent backgrounds." So the abbot issued a stern reprimand:

> I will not break the rule of the community, offend the brothers or anger God for the sake of your coins. As for your ministrations, I took you in to be one who would do them just like the other brothers and just as I did in my youth, and still do now.... Strive with your brothers in every ministration assigned to you, performing them without shame, for Christ's sake, remembering the Lord's words: "The Son of Man came not to be served, but to serve" (Mk 10:45).

Agreeing to do as he was told, the monk thereafter "acquired great humility ... toward all."[95]

Precisely because it was considered degrading, this system produced saints known for serving with "utmost humility and alacrity." John the Hesychast and George of Choziba in Palestine both came from aristocratic families close to the imperial court. John's family was "plumed in wealth"; nevertheless in the monastery he "cared for all the fathers with his services, slavishly submitting to each with utmost humility and respect." George proved his humility at Choziba by scrubbing the communal cistern, cooking over the blazing furnace, and serving tables in the refectory; later, after becoming abbot, he "eagerly participated in every ministration out of zeal and desire to set an example for others."[96] Located near the steep road leading up from Jericho to Jerusalem, his Choziba monastery may have especially prized this type of zeal (another elder is remembered for demonstrating his unusual capacity for *sympatheia* by offering travelers bread and water and by carrying their luggage and children for miles up hill on his back).[97]

Similar enthusiasts could be found in other institutions. At a monastery outside Amida in northern Mesopotamia, John of Ephesus met the monk Ḥala, known as the Zealous. "During the days of my association with him I was thoroughly amazed at . . . his humility and zeal, which imitated the High One who taught this type of humility to His disciples," writes John.

> From the very beginning of his training, [he] chose for himself to perform all the menial tasks required for the needs of his monastery, and resolved not to see a stranger enter the convent without associating himself in careful attention to his wants. . . . He never saw a poor person come to the monastery gate without imparting some small thing to his necessity, or saw a sick man without associating himself in careful attention to his wants.

"Constant in washing" the building and its latrines, Ḥala would also scour refectory pots after dinner to find scraps for people outside the monastery gate. Because he continually pestered fellow monks to give him their leftovers ("Does anyone have anything to give my Lord Jesus? Does anyone have a morsel for the children of my Lord Jesus?"), they accused him of vainglory. Nonetheless Ḥala persisted in "all ministrations to the needy, washing away the excrement of that community and carrying water, even though he held the rank of a priest."[98]

Admittedly, monastic exemplars of such active outreach are relatively rare. As John's account shows, vainglory was considered an ever-present problem among those who insisted on collecting materials to give as alms to outsiders, making such zeal potentially unsettling. If a monk could avoid vainglory, John Climacus allowed, he should perform acts of mercy everywhere, "without ceasing."[99] Yet vainglory was always a risk when giving alms. Here, aside from Jesus's criticism of the Pharisees (Mt 6:2–4), one might recall Jacques Derrida's "tragic" view of altruism, which maintains that it is impossible to give a gift altruistically without taking pride and congratulating oneself for having done a good deed.[100] To free novices from such impulses upon entering a monastery, they were advised to entrust the dispersal of their property to their abbot. Just as the earliest Christians, after selling their possessions, left the proceeds at the feet of the apostles (Acts 4:34), so too should they give the proceeds to their abbot to distribute as alms; he would do so on their behalf, but "not according to their will."[101] Even monks living in more independent lavra arrangements were instructed never to give alms without consulting an elder, and "certainly not" in secret.[102] John of Gaza advised a young monk not to dispense alms for others, since "not all are sufficiently advanced to carry out this *diakonia*, but only those who have attained tranquility and mourned for their sins."[103]

Access to material resources aside, these concerns may explain why we find relatively few descriptions of monks (apart from abbots of wealthy monasteries) as giving alms to the poor in normative ascetic literature. Ascetic theory was distinctly ambivalent toward the practice. Indeed, there was disagreement about whether monks should devote themselves to such material deeds at all. From the fifth century onward, most of the surviving literature prioritizes the isolated pursuit of prayerful serenity (*hesychia*) as the most appropriate means for the spiritually advanced to serve God, relegating material works or physical activities to low-level monks (or better yet, the laity). According to their hagiographer, when the aristocratic couple Melania and Pinian first adopted a religious life, they expressed their zeal by dressing in cheap clothing and by "making the rounds of all the sick and poor people without exception, visiting them and giving them treatment," as Paul of Antioch later would do. They adopted these practices because they feared monastic life would require "asceticism beyond their strength."[104] Another aristocrat, having been discovered serving tables "in Abrahamic manner" for pilgrims at Jerusalem, was advised to leave such work to others and join a monastery, "for this," he was told, "is more profitable."[105] One ascetic authority explained that a monk who "constantly trained himself in the world" by giving alms or succoring the sick should be viewed as a good person. "But he is occupied with earthly things. Better . . . is a contemplative who has risen from active work to the mental sphere and has left it to others to be anxious about earthly things."[106]

These spiritual priorities shaped monastic institutional hierarchies, releasing elders from physical ministrations so that they could dedicate themselves to ministering to all through prayer, leaving all other ministrations mainly to novices and their supervisors working in the monastery's reception room or at the gate. Yet some senior monks remained torn. Theodosius the Cenobiarch was distressed when pressed by his disciples to build their great monastery east of Bethlehem. On the one hand, he loved the desert's tranquility; on the other, he wanted to extend his "philanthropic hand" to all. Finally, he decided he could do both, realizing that "tranquility is not a matter of physical isolation but of disposition."[107] Others proposed an alternative *via media* that allowed those serving in the highest ministrations to pursue tranquility while helping others. We learn of this "middle way" of humility and compassion from letters that John of Gaza sent to his disciple Dorotheus while the latter was infirmarian at the Seridos monastery in the early sixth century. Dorotheus had asked if he should divide his time between ministering in the infirmary and pursuing *hesychia* alone in his cell. John responded that rather than separating these activities, he could combine them:

This is the middle way that does not fail, that maintains humility in tranquility and innocence amid distractions. . . . One must share the sufferings of all who live in the cenobium, for this fulfills the Apostle's command that if one is afflicted, each should share in the affliction [1 Cor 12:26]. This means consoling and comforting—this is compassion. It is good to share the sufferings of the infirm and collaborate in nursing them. For if a doctor is paid for caring for the sick and infirm, how much more will a person [be paid in heavenly rewards] who feels compassion for this neighbor in everything as far as he can?[108]

John reminded Dorotheus that above all God wanted mercy, not *hesychia,* which in any case required practitioners to realize their lowliness by "suffering the evils of those who are suffering . . . 'as if inhabiting a single body' [cf. Heb 13:3]."[109] "Therefore, bend your heart to mercy," he urged, adding that Dorotheus would lose all the benefits of works of mercy if others served in his place while he sat praying alone in his cell.[110]

That this exchange arose over tending the sick in a monastery infirmary is not surprising. By the sixth century, monasteries often had their own infirmaries. One late fifth-century example, identified by an inscription in the Jeremias Monastery south of Cairo, was nearly as large as the monastery's refectory. Some had baths that could be used for washing the sick.[111] Whether they accepted non-monastic patients is unclear, but the level of care could be remarkably professional: Dorotheus had studied medicine, and other infirmary wardens were trained surgeons. As Andrew Crislip observes, one result of such investment and care was the destigmatization of illness in Early Byzantine monasteries.[112] At the same time, ministering to the sick ideally forced monks to face their own infirmities. This was recognized by the anchoretic theorist Evagrius of Pontus (d. 399). His explanation of why desert solitaries were susceptible to vainglory was not unlike Chrysostom's reasoning about the fat-headed urban rich:

This demon [i.e., vainglory] vanishes when faced with the misfortunes of those oppressed by illnesses or who suffer in prison or who meet with sudden death. Then, pricked with compunction, the soul gradually becomes compassionate as its demonic blindness dissipates. We lack these opportunities because of the rarity of sick people among us in the desert. It was in fact to put this demon to flight that the Lord commanded us in the Gospel to go visit the sick and those in prison, saying, "I was sick and you visited me, in prison and you came to see me" (Mt 25: 36).[113]

Cenobitic infirmaries offered the opportunities lacking in Evagrius's desert settlements. It seems that junior monks served on rotations in them just as they did in monastery kitchens, refectories, and latrines.[114] Besides changing beds and cleaning clothes, their duties involved washing and handling sick people's diseased bodies— challenging work even for saints, causing one to be reprimanded, "Aren't you ashamed to be so harsh to your brother? Don't you know he is Christ, and that you are afflicting

Christ?"[115] This was the crucible of the monastic novitiate, considered the most effective means of fostering mercy, compassion, and later, charity; hence, when asked how best to balance their spiritual and communal pursuits, Dorotheus advised monks that they first "take care of the sick, primarily so as to gain compassion."[116]

Once infirmary training was over, monks were deemed to have become "perfected." They were allowed to live alone as solitary anchorites without participating in further communal *diakoniai* if they wished. Yet, even outside their cenobium they were expected to keep the door to their cells open to all who came. (This "open-door" rule was evidently meant to prevent any from practicing favoritism as much as to enforce an ethic of hospitality itself; one anchorite reportedly said it was better to keep his door closed to all, because the only alternative was to open it to everyone!)[117] Of course, not every monk attained the same level of humility or compassion, even after years of training. Hence, important positions in the institutional *diakonia* were reserved for those like Theodosius the Cenobiarch who continued working in his monastery's infirmaries as abbot "because he burned with loving compassion."[118] It is also true that, although we sometimes hear of Early Byzantine monasteries possessing external hostels or hospitals in suburban areas, none is depicted as organizing or pursuing active outreach to sick and needy strangers outside its walls in the manner of Paul of Antioch. To that extent, their philanthropic practices seem to have been limited. Yet, thanks to the internal practices reviewed here, at least some capacity for humility and compassion was theoretically ingrained within every member of a cenobitic institution. John of Ephesus describes a community outside Amida that was unusually devoted to hospitality: "They did not in the case of anyone who came to them hold him to be a mere man of flesh, but though a mean and poor body, he appeared in their eyes as God who became flesh. And so they were eager to serve, refresh, wash, and honor him as if he were Christ."[119]

MONASTIC MEDIATION BETWEEN THE RICH, THE CLERGY, AND THE POOR

By the time John of Ephesus had written that description of the monastic community at Amida, "Merciful and Compassionate" had become a common description of high-ranking Christians, whose combined almsgiving and willingness to interact with mainstream society seemed to fulfill Chrysostom's ideal of vertical solidarity. Besides certain court officials, those to whom it was applied included patriarchs of Antioch and Alexandria.[120] The best known is John of Cyprus, also called John the Merciful and known to posterity as John the Almsgiver. This urbane aristocrat served as Chalcedonian Patriarch of Alexandria (sed. 610—ca. 620) during the first decade of Emperor Heraclius's reign. He inspired a series of seventh-century hagiographies, including one by a fellow Cypriote and bishop named Leontius of Neapolis (d. 668; Limassol, Cyprus). So extensively does Leontius's account focus on John's almsgiving that it constitutes a virtual treatise on the practice itself.[121] Leontius says that John as a boy once dreamt that the emperor's favorite daughter, an unusually beautiful woman, had slipped into his bed at night to caress him. Imagining her later to be Compassion or Almsgiving personified, he devoted the rest of his life to pursuing her by displaying "surpassing generosity and compassion, by virtue of which he certainly deserved to be called 'the Merciful.'" As bishop, his "hand was open unsparingly, providing for all as from an ever-flowing spring."[122]

Leontius turned John of Cyprus into an archetype of episcopal compassion. In reality, he was a patrician landowner closely involved in the military coup that brought the usurper Heraclius into power. Having been "parachuted onto the patriarchal throne" without any prior ecclesiastical experience, his task was to keep peace between Chalcedonian and anti-Chalcedonian factions within this strategically crucial city.[123] Nonetheless, thanks to Leontius, we now mainly know stories about his almsgiving. Underlying many of them is an important point already noted in the previous two sections: mercy and compassion were uncommon virtues that usually had to be learned. Hence, according to Leontius, if John ever heard that someone was merciful, "he would send for him and playfully ask, 'How is it that you are this way, Lord so-and-so? How did you become merciful? Is it by nature, or due to reflection?' For the saint used to say that those who are merciful by nature will not receive so great a reward . . . as those who must compel their own inclination and heart, achieving this virtue by laborious force."[124] Leontius says John was especially attentive to tales of ascetic saints, including one named Sarapion Sindonites, a fourth-century Egyptian monk who, "moved by compassion," sold himself into slavery to generate alms for a widow in need. John was so moved by this story that he summoned all his church administrators to hear it as well.[125]

Thus, a monk became an exemplar to an archetype of episcopal compassion. That hagiographical conceit may reflect a historical development. With few exceptions, after Chrysostom's death in the early fifth century, little of the preaching on almsgiving that survives from Early Byzantium is attributed to church preachers. Monastic authorities emerge as the most vocal exponents of the practice. This may be more than a coincidence. In a recent study, Ariel López argues that monastic leaders during the fifth century deliberately began to appropriate for themselves the Christian discourse on almsgiving and advocacy for the poor that had earlier been associated with bishops and priests. According to López, monastic leaders adopted this discourse for much the same social reason that had motivated church leaders in the fourth and early fifth century: namely, to legitimize their involvement in public life. "Together with defense of orthodoxy, the care of the poor became the primary argument for a Christian monk to justify his actions in the world."[126] López substantiates his thesis by studying the fifth-century homilies of

Shenoute of Atripe (d. 466), the imperious abbot of the White Monastery in Egypt. Before both lay and monastic audiences in his enormous monastic church, Shenoute denounced rich "pagans" for oppressing the poor in nearby Panopolis as stridently as Chrysostom ever did at Antioch. His sermons give the best evidence of this phenomenon, but as López points out, contemporary hagiographers portrayed other cenobitic leaders—"forceful fifth-century abbots of large eastern communities," like Alexander the Sleepless (d. ca. 430), Hypatius of Chalcedon (d. ca. 444), and Marcellus the Sleepless (d. ca. 485)—in a similar mode. For example, Callinicus says that his abbot, Hypatius, due to his prodigious almsgiving, became known as a "consul of Christ." This title (*hypatos*) obviously played on Hypatius's name, yet it would have also conjured acts of public munificence in imaginations of late Roman readers.[127] Significantly, Callinicus chose to insert his description of Hypatius's generosity to the poor between his accounts of his campaigns against pagans and opposition to abusive civic magistrates and their clerical supporters.[128] Such descriptions cast monastic leaders as conscientious new players in urban society, celebrating them as defenders of Christian righteousness, speaking out from the margins not only against the abuses of powerful laypeople but against the negligence of bishops and subordinate clerics within the church hierarchy.

The *Life of Symeon Stylites the Elder,* a Syriac hagiography completed in 473, suggests that this development was closely connected to the collection and redistribution of alms to the poor. We will discuss its subject, the ascetic superstar Symeon (d. 459), at length in chapter 6. Early in his *Life,* Symeon's hagiographers describe how vexed he became when he learned that his interventions on behalf of Antioch's poor (including his defense of Antioch's dye workers, after the city council had tripled its tax on their work) were making people grumble. Feeling unappreciated, he went on strike, ordering that the collection and distribution of donations at his enclosure be suspended. "Do not send word to anyone, do not accept anything from anyone," he instructed.

> Sufficient for me is God who charged me in soul and mind both to advise them for their own lives . . . and to persuade them to benefit and be merciful to the poor. As for the poor, I was to exhort them to live uprightly and to fear God. But since this annoys them, I place the affair in God's hands.

A whole month passed, during which "the oppressed came, but no one answered them, while people brought gifts . . . but no one accepted them, so both sides went away distressed." These ministrations only resumed when an angel descended to reproach Symeon for lacking patience and for stopping the flow of gifts, assuring him, "Your task is to speak out, and our Lord knows how to arrange the affairs. You do what is yours, and your Lord will do his part."[129]

Miraculous elements aside, this scenario suggests that Symeon had become an outside mediator between Antioch's rich and poor, advocating and providing for the latter in a manner that might have been expected of an Antiochene bishop. To explain such monastic mediation, we should consider the case of another fifth-century monk, Isidore of Pelusium (d. ca. 450). Formerly a priest in Pelusium, Isidore decided to retire partly because of what he saw happening under Eusebius (sed. ca. 415–435), the new bishop of this prosperous port city at the eastern mouth of the Nile Delta (Tell Farama, Egypt). Like other bishops of his generation, Eusebius wanted to adorn his bishopric with a sumptuous cathedral. What alarmed Isidore were not his episcopal priorities so much as his means of funding them, because to raise cash he put priesthoods up for sale, attracting clerics who then used their positions to embezzle from the church poor fund. At the request of concerned lay donors, Isidore wrote a series of letters, some addressed to Bishop Eusebius himself: "They say you are building a church in Pelusium that gleams with ingenuities but also with wicked materials like the sale of ordinations and injustices and threats, pressuring the poor and wasting the funds set aside for them. This is nothing short of building Sion in blood," he wrote.[130] We do not know how the story ended, but Isidore took it to the highest level, asking his patriarch, Cyril of Alexandria (sed. 412–444), to intervene.

To be sure, complaints about clerical abuse of the poor fund and the poor had circulated since the third century.[131] Part of the problem was that church moneys tended to be pooled together, with clerics having first claim to anything that came in.[132] Without close surveillance by a conscientious bishop, little might be left for other *ptōchoi*. After being exiled from Constantinople, Chrysostom had to write to one of his lay supporters, asking him to save the city's widows and virgins whom clerics had cut off from the dole in his absence.[133] Patriarch Severus of Antioch (sed. 512–518), upon returning from a tour of his diocese a century later, complained that some of his congregation wanted to be repaid with interest for coins they had given to people enrolled on the dole. The problem was "that the poor, having no one else from whom to receive their livelihood, would bitterly complain of our prolonged [absence], if they did not get their usual ten bits." In other words, the dole had broken down in his absence so that those who usually received it had resorted to members of the laity for handouts.[134] Clerics were similarly called out for negligence in sixth-century Amida, where it took an outspoken holy woman to shame clerics into admitting poor people into the local hospitals.[135]

In light of such problems, it is not surprising that many saw monks and their institutions as more trustworthy conduits for alms. Barsanuphius and John of Gaza wrote letters instructing monks how to act if asked to carry out the laity's almsgiving, as if this were not unusual.[136] Yet the emergence of monks as intermediaries was related not just to their receipt of resources but to their liminal position between lay Christians and church officials. The fifth century saw a certain secularization of ecclesiastical culture. By the Justinianic age, bishops and patriarchs of major sees were often imperial appointees tasked with enforcing doctrinal unity, while many clerics followed their fathers into office or purchased their positions for the sake of status and protection from governmental impositions.[137] Whereas some metropolitans became as wealthy as secular magnates (from whose ranks they were often drawn), rural clerics often barely differed from other peasants.[138] Without further study, it would be premature to assume that the consequences of this for the poor were entirely negative. Nonetheless, it seems that the laity would have likely faced an increasingly complacent or formidable ecclesiastical hierarchy, focused on its own needs: it is noticeable that John Moschus's stories about "merciful and compassionate" patriarchs mention only how they helped other bishops or rich people fallen on hard times.[139] Even Severus, who claimed to always be surrounded by Antioch's poor, was considered so formidable a patriarch that a provincial deacon, fearing "the grandeur of such a bishop," hid his face behind a woman's veil before pressing a petition into Severus's hands as he passed in a procession.[140]

Leontius's hagiography illustrates the scale of the problem. He reports that when John of Cyprus arrived in Alexandria, he soon learned that petitioners feared approaching him in his patriarchal court on account of all the ushers and secretaries who blocked their way. Therefore, "concerned to grant free access to those who wanted to approach him," he set out stools in the cathedral square each Wednesday and Friday afternoon to hold the episcopal court where all could approach him in the open, making sure that just a single officer attended him.[141] He also made a practice of visiting twice a week the sick people in the infirmaries he had built.[142] But Leontius's other stories remind us that John was a Roman aristocrat with late Roman habits. When it came to material almsgiving, only once is he depicted as doing so directly himself, when a fellow cleric had fallen into *ptōcheia*.[143] Otherwise he is depicted as dispensing all his largesse through secretaries and the "distributers" that followed him around Alexandria. The latter officers (*diadotes*, a term also used for municipal financial officers) are particularly prominent in Leontius's account: entrusted with the patriarchal purse, they awaited John's order to hand out coins and were ready to thrash anyone who brazenly sought more.[144]

So whether it was dispensed in material or immaterial form, seeking mercy from such bishops could be a potentially humiliating task, even if they were saints. Added to this was the fact that bishops now had their own ecclesiastical police (John reportedly ordered his officers to whip a male monk he saw begging with a young girl) and worked closely with the equivalent of their city's secular police chief. "It is the duty of bishops like you," Severus reminded an episcopal colleague, "to cut short and restrain any unregulated movements of the mob . . . and to set themselves to maintain all good order in the cities, and to keep watch over the peaceful manners and customs of those they feed."[145] Just such a mob once blocked Severus's own congregation as it travelled out to a martyr shrine on the road between Antioch and Daphne to celebrate the feast of St. Leontius. Severus recalled afterward, "The poor [had] assembled in great numbers and barred the road, refusing to yield until they [had] received some part of the outlay you [had] come here to make." In retrospect, Severus tried to make light of the situation—"What price would you not pay to feed Christ through the mediation of the hungry?"[146]— but it must have been unsettling when it happened, and it helps contextualize an incident that took place outside Antioch about thirty years later.

When the Patriarch of Antioch died in 545, he was succeeded by another imperial appointee named Domninus (sed. 545–559). Domninus was not inexperienced with poor people—he had supervised a *ptōchion* at Lychnidos (Ohrid, Northern Macedonia), a Balkan city on the Via Egnatia. But according to a local hagiographer, things went wrong as soon as he approached Antioch to assume his patriarchal post. Drawing near, he saw "the *ptōchoi* attached to St. Job" standing before the city's gate. "Disgusted by the sight" (perhaps St. Job was a leprosarium, and its *ptōchoi* were lepers), he sent orders to have them removed. When the poor in question caught wind of this, they turned to a local abbot, who denounced Domninus's callous plan. "Cease crying, brothers," he reportedly replied. "In the next few days the Lord will let this man be felled with suffering, so that he will learn by experience to be compassionate, which he has not learned by nature." Domninus soon suffered such a terrible palsy in his feet that he had to be carried everywhere: "For this reason he lived thereafter as the object of deep contempt."[147]

The local abbot in this case was Symeon Stylites the Younger (ca. 521–592). This notable imitator of the original pillar monk, the elder Symeon Stylites, set up a column of his own on a high hill (Sem'ān Daği, Turkey) overlooking the Mediterranean near the port of Seleucia Pieria, some eighteen miles (29 km) west of Antioch. Thanks to Symeon, his pillar, and the cures dispensed at the church and monastic complex built around it, this hill came to be known as the Marvelous Mountain (Mons Mirabilis). We know about the regional importance of Symeon and his monastery partly through his hagiography, the *Life of Symeon Stylites the Younger*. Compiled soon after his death, it reports that people began to flock from the city and surrounding villages to see Symeon and receive healings from him after he had cured a beggar of blindness. Despite suspicions voiced by some clerics about the efficacy of his cures, Symeon remained a reassuring beacon of stability and charismatic light for the local laity over the next half century.[148] Indeed, about this Symeon we are unusually well informed. Besides his hagiography (the longest to survive from Early Byzantium) and the ruins of his monastery (preserved amid the pylons of a modern Turkish wind farm),[149] we have sermons he apparently delivered while standing on his column. Most of these forty sermons are about monastic virtues, but some address broader socio-ethical issues.[150] One rebukes an Antiochene landowner (*krētor*) for seizing houses, flocks, and fields of peasants and using his bailiffs to "menace the poor like a lion in the road."[151] Another scolds listeners for welcoming visitors of high rank while "despising everyone else as beggars."[152] Tables will turn on Judgment Day, Symeon warns: "The rich man says, 'My alms will save me.'" True, but only if it did not come from wealth stolen from others. "If you want to be merciful," he advises, "dispense to the poor from your own substance, clothing one, feeding another, releasing the imprisoned, pitying widows, and doing good to orphans."[153]

These brief sermons show that Symeon assumed an authority that stretched beyond his rural confines to situations within Antioch itself. They offer nothing new as far as their ethical content is concerned: Symeon certainly says little about almsgiving not already said by John Chrysostom or Severus of Antioch. Yet they remain noteworthy because they were delivered by an abbot to a laity gathered in his own monastery. The behavior he proposes for the laity was consonant with the practices he propounded to his monks, as remembered by the *Life of Symeon Stylites the Younger*: "Do not prefer demons who come deceitfully cloaked in golden finery," his hagiographer quotes him as exhorting his monastic community. "Let not worldly delusion make you insult Christ when he comes round in a poor man's penury. . . . Seek God in both the rich and the poor. . . . Joyfully receive the rich as the poor, the poor as the rich, regarding all people as one, fulfilling the needs of each out of whatever comes to you."[154] Symeon preached an ethic of open access to rich and poor alike, without "respect of persons" (cf. Rom 2:11). His Marvelous Mountain was to be a place where worldly differences were to be replaced with ascetic compassion and Christian solidarity.

It is notable that Symeon delivered his sermons in the same years that Paul of Antioch was organizing lay deaconries in downtown Antioch. Did Paul's efforts in active outreach respond to a breakdown in church services there? We do not know, but it is clear that late-sixth-century Antioch was no longer the charming place that Chrysostom and Severus had known. A catastrophic earthquake had buried much of its population in 526, destroying the Golden House and leaving only buildings with the thickest walls standing. Following another local holy man's advice, a cross was placed on top of Mt. Silpius and the city was renamed Theopolis, "God's City," in hope of preventing further destruction. But in 540 a Sassanian army obliterated the rest, carting off whatever citizens and classical treasures remained to Persian territory.[155] Justinian rebuilt the city and it gradually revived, but the "increasingly shoddy state of repairs" in the hinterland suggests a permanent decline in regional wealth and investments.[156]

Symeon could have watched all this unfold from his perch on the Marvelous Mountain. His sanctuary must have received refugees from all walks of life. Indeed, it survived unscathed, we are told, "due to its almsgiving and agreeable *diakonia* to the poor."[157] Amid this general leveling, Symeon's hagiographer positioned his subject as a pillar of the rural Christian community and moral counterweight to urban bishops like Domninus who came in the aftermath. Besides dispensing medical care and food, Symeon reportedly attracted influential visitors, making his monastery a new point of access, creating opportunities for interactions between government officials and the local peasantry. A similar development is attested at a monastery in northwest Asia Minor, where an imperial officer, "out of regard for the saint," regularly deigned to hear petitioners during his visits.[158]

To maintain this mediating position, Symeon reiterated that his monastery had to maintain its "fraternal *diakonia*," providing alms and access without bringing "shame to a beggar's face ... while anointing the rich man's corrupt flesh for the sake of money."[159] The same warning was repeated elsewhere in the early seventh century. One evening, when George of Choziba was negotiating with a lender so that his monastery could purchase grain, he failed to meet a poor widow who had come to visit him at the gate. Before turning away and disappearing down the road, she dropped a bag in the hand of the gatekeeper, remarking, "Why do you care only for the rich and disregard the poor? For this reason rightly you need gold. ... This holy place is supposed to be a rest house for *ptōchoi* and strangers, not just a meeting house for the rich."[160] As it turned out, the poor widow was the monastery's divine patron, the Mother of God, and the bag she left contained a blessing (*eulogia*) of sixty solidi, which George subsequently used to give alms. We shall examine the relation of such blessings to almsgiving after we explore the Early Byzantine notion of charity, but the story shows how sensitive monastic authorities were to any perception that they lacked compassion for the poor, and how easily it might lapse, even where expected most.

"Give It With Your Whole Soul"

From Alms to Charity in Early Byzantine Monasticism

Sometime in the mid-sixth century, in a monastery outside Gaza—then still a gem of the ancient Mediterranean, thriving on its wine industry—a monk we met in the last chapter, Dorotheus (d. ca. 560), now an abbot, wrote an essay, "On the Structure and Harmony of the Soul's Virtues," that included a digression on almsgiving. Little did he know he was writing the last extended analysis of Christian almsgiving to survive from Early Byzantium. Times had certainly changed since the fourth century. Rather than lament, as Chrysostom did, a reluctance among Christians to give alms, Dorotheus could survey a practice that had become almost too routine. This gave him numerous examples of how it was possible to do good without pleasing God. To see this, readers need only consider why most people gave alms.

"If you want to know the goodness and grace of almsgiving [*eleēmosynē*], how great it is," Dorotheus began, "note that it can even obtain forgiveness for sins." Yet most people gave for alms for reasons that did not truly please God. "There are many different motives for almsgiving. One gives so that his land might be blessed, and God blesses his land; another to save his ship, and God saves his ship; another for his children, and God protects them; another for his reputation, and God glorifies him."[1] Then there were those who gave to escape punishment in Hell or gain rewards in Heaven. Insofar as these gave to benefit their souls, they were better than those who were giving for worldly gains. Yet they too failed to please God, for anyone who gave alms to avoid punishment was acting like a slave out of fear instead of desire, while anyone who gave for the sake of rewards was like a worker laboring for future pay. Only one motive truly pleased God: when alms were given because it was good to give them. "We too," Dorotheus concludes, "ought to give alms for goodness itself, acting compassionately toward each other as if to our own selves, nursing each other as if each were nursing us, giving as if receiving." This was giving alms "with knowledge"—that is, with a reason and manner that pleased God.[2]

With this survey of examples, Dorotheus wanted his monastic readers to start thinking of almsgiving as a practice that admitted increasing levels of refinement. To be sure, he considered all almsgiving good, even if its motives were crass. Yet he clearly believed that some motives were better than others, and that the best alms were those given "not out of any human calculation, but out of compassionate goodness itself."[3] It was incumbent on everyone to practice almsgiving—after all, it could be done through a merciful act instead of a material item, and even a *ptōchos* could minister in an infirmary or utter a kind word.[4] But Dorotheus had more in mind. His ultimate aim, which had prompted him to discuss the scale of almsgiving in the first place, was to teach monks how to fulfill Jesus's command "Love your neighbor as your self" (Mt 22:39). Fulfilling this lofty goal was difficult, he acknowledged, and he advised monks to approach it like a ladder, climbed alms by alms. Starting at the bottom, they should first just try to refrain from insulting each other; then they should start adding merciful words of forgiveness:

> In this way you begin to benefit your brother by nursing him verbally, by being compassionate to him, by giving what he needs. Gradually . . . you reach the top of the ladder; by helping your neighbor little by little, you come to want what is beneficial for him as if it were beneficial for yourself, making his interests your own. This is what is meant by the saying "Love your neighbor as your self."[5]

Dorotheus sought to encourage small, repeated gestures of mercy that would eventually unite a monastery in mutual affection. This started by forgiving perceived slights, an act tantamount to immaterial almsgiving: "God has given each a capacity to forgive another's sins against us. . . . So if you have no means to show mercy physically, do so emotionally—for what mercy is greater than mercy shown to a soul?" Only once this became habitual could one begin to love another as oneself; only this way, when repeatedly practiced for the sake of good, could such small acts of mercy or almsgiving (*eleēmosynē*) lead to mutual exchanges of charity (*agapē*).

In this chapter we explore how Early Byzantine authorities distinguished a gift of alms from a gift of charity, and why they thought that good almsgiving eventually led to feelings and expressions of charity. Dorotheus's conceptualization of almsgiving as a handmaiden to charity may come as a surprise. Today we tend to treat giving alms and giving charity as more or less identical caritative practices. Early Byzantine authorities, however, did not. The ascetic theorist Isaiah of Scetis (d. 489) anticipates Dorotheus by maintaining that "almsgiving with knowledge begets foresight, and leads to charity."[6] Chrysostom also repeatedly depicted almsgiving as a means of fostering a capacity for charity, explaining that if alms "gushed forth from just gains," it would become "the fount by which charity is watered, for nothing so nourishes charity, as when a person is merciful."[7]

> Hence God enacted almsgiving. He might have nourished the poor without it, but he commended them to be nourished by us, so that he might bind us together in charity and that we might become fervent toward each other.[8]

"For almsgiving is the mother of that charity," he maintained, "which is characteristic of Christianity, which is greater than all the [other] wonders by which Christ's disciples are made manifest."[9] Chrysostom and Isaiah both believed that alms and charity were conceptually akin yet qualitatively different, charity being the more advanced practice, ideal, and goal. According to this view, every gift of charity was a gift of alms, but not every alms qualified as charity; charity presumed a capacity for mercy and forgiveness, but mercy and forgiveness did not necessarily mean that a person possessed a capacity for charity.

This is consistent with the views of Pseudo-Clement, whose gendered analysis of philanthropy we saw in chapter 2. To recall, Pseudo-Clement thought alms and charity to be akin, yet different. Specifically, he claimed that almsgiving, defined as helping someone in misfortune, represented the female side of philanthropy, while charity, defined as extending as much forgiveness to another as one might desire for oneself, represented its male side.[10] If we consider that Greco-Roman and Jewish societies tended to consider what was female to be an incomplete complement of what was male, then this may explain what Pseudo-Clement meant to convey by feminizing alms/mercy in relation to gifts and acts of charity: he regarded the former as an incomplete, lesser version of the latter. Indeed, we shall find that Early Byzantine authorities distinguished these two gifts largely in terms of degree. While giving alms came to be associated with giving surplus resources to procure a benefit primarily for oneself (like redemption or salvation, "out of human calculation," as Dorotheus puts it), giving charity became identified with giving one's most essential resources—even one's own life—for the benefit of all involved.

Charity, in other words, represented a selfless, or rather, a self-sacrificing version of almsgiving. Its scriptural exemplar was the poor widow who, by giving up her last two "mites" (the King James Bible's description for her smallest denomination of coin) surpassed all the almsgiving of the rich, even though they had quantitatively given far more (Mk 12:41–44; Lk 21:1–4). Most Early Byzantine examples, however, relate to gift giving by Christian ascetics living in desert cells. Indeed, charity is primarily a topic of anchoretic discourse in Early Byzantium. It is the most prominent type of religious gift found in the Christian ascetic wisdom literature known as the *Sayings of the Desert Fathers* (*apophthegmata patrum*). These short stories and sayings constitute what I call the Egyptian desert tradition. Of the thousand or more included in their Greek collections, only thirteen refer to alms (*eleēmosynē*) at all, while references to gifts of charity (*agapē*) abound. This was not accidental. Anchorites were imagined to value "giving more than receiving,"[11] yet were also expected to practice *aktēmosynē*, "freedom from possessions," more than any other type of monk. Accordingly, almost by definition, anything that anchorites gave to others had to derive from essential resources. Moreover, "in most sayings about charity," observes Graham Gould, "the emphasis lies on a desire . . . to push oneself to the limit of self-sacrifice . . . in the service of someone else."[12] As noted above, it was precisely this merciful spirit of self-sacrifice on behalf of others that distinguished gifts of charity from all other categories of Christian gifts.

We will therefore start by examining the role of charity portrayed in the *Sayings of the Desert Fathers*. It is important to emphasize that the world conjured in the *Sayings* is largely an imaginary construct. Thanks to Evagrius of Pontus (346–399), who lived in the desert southwest of Alexandria for seventeen years, we know that the settlements of Nitria, Kellia, and Scetis pictured in this literature were populated by a cosmopolitan range of monks and frequented by all sorts of visitors selling goods, bringing supplies, or looking for spiritual healings or handouts.[13] But the *Sayings* portray an isolated world of stark self-sufficiency and reduced material need, positing it as a theoretical background to pose and work out basic ethical problems. Its depictions of Christian charity take place almost exclusively within highly insular, anchoretic communities; as one elder allegedly remarked when bringing money back from work at the harvest, "My widows and orphans are at Scetis."[14] The imagined restrictions and deprivations of this anchoretic world shaped the Egyptian desert tradition on Christian charity, emphasizing extreme situations that resulted in memorably dramatic gestures of charitable self-sacrifice.

By the sixth century, these *Sayings* had become basic inspirational reading in monasteries like the one Dorotheus ran. Indeed, they probably tell us more about the logic and fantasies of monks in his cenobitic milieu than about the outlook of any early Egyptian solitary.[15] Monasticism in sixth-century Gaza involved close cooperation between cenobites and anchorites, as well as frequent contact with laypeople. Solitaries in the region earned their keep by mentoring both the less spiritually advanced residents of cenobitic institutions and members of the lay world at large.[16] Fortunately, we possess a sizeable collection of letters from two such solitaries, John of Gaza and his elder colleague Barsanuphius (d. ca. 543). Here, "what the *Sayings of the Desert Fathers* let us glimpse only in the form of transitory flashes, is . . . played out before our eyes in a film."[17] In particular, these letters describe episodes in which Barsanuphius and John, like the fictional monks of desert mythology, pledge their own souls to secure God's pardon for sinners in their community. The letters help us understand these gestures of voluntary self-sacrifice as Barsanuphius and John did—namely, as gifts of charity.

The Egyptian desert tradition and the letters of Barsanuphius and John enable us to see an ascetic discourse on charity that was evolving just as almsgiving was becoming more narrowly identified as a means for ordinary lay Christians to expiate sins of greed, unjust wealth and excessive self-interest. The development of these two Christian gift ideals were closely related (one emphasizing self-sacrifice, the other self-interest), and it is convenient to treat them together in the same chapter. Therefore, after examining the discourse on charity preserved in the Egyptian desert tradition and the writings of Barsanuphius, John, and their protégé Dorotheus, we will contrast it with the discourse on "redemptive" almsgiving that John Chrysostom and others propagated among the laity at large. We will see that the gift ideals of alms and charity each gained definition in light of the other. Besides explaining what these two ideals meant for contemporary authorities, my aim is to show how each evolved in contrast to one another in the ascetic and lay milieus of Early Byzantium.

DEFINING CHARITY IN EGYPTIAN
DESERT TRADITION

As noted above, the *Sayings of the Desert Fathers* treat Christian charity (*agapē*) as an ascetic virtue. In monastic imaginations, it had flourished among the early solitaries of the Egyptian desert, monks who had renounced all worldly comforts to unite with God in the barren wastelands above the Nile Valley.[18] Set for the most part at desert settlements like Nitria, Kellia, and Scetis southwest of Alexandria (al-Barnuji, al-Muna, and Wadi al Natrûn, Egypt), this was a perfectionist's milieu, premised on rigorous self-sufficiency. Although most anchorites were thought to have survived by weaving palm leaves and selling baskets or laboring at harvests along the Nile, all were imagined to have fulfilled, before arriving, Jesus's admonition "If you would be perfect, go sell what you have, give to the poor . . . and come follow me" (Mt 19:21). Utility was the sole criterion of value here; any hint of luxury (novices were told never to wear shirts that would be picked up if discarded) was scorned as a violation of *aktēmosynē*, "freedom from possessions."[19] Unless sick, no one was supposed to keep anything beyond basic needs, and fasting might diminish that even more (while eating two or three loaves of bread a day was considered acceptable, many reportedly reduced their consumption further to minimize their need for provisioning or outside contact). It was said that Emperor Theodosius II (r. 408–450) once asked how those at the settlement of Scetis survived. On being told that they "ate each other"—that is, that they scavenged and reused whatever was left in the cell after one of them had died—the emperor pronounced them all blessed and free from care.[20]

Such stories must be understood as thought experiments that later monks constructed to envision what might happen if Christian perfectionists pressed scriptural ideals to extremes.[21] Material self-denial was the premise on which the practice of charity, among other communal ideals, was conceived by ascetic theorists.

Indeed, Christian charity was a central monastic concern. Despite their anchoretic emphasis on physical isolation, no Egyptian hermit was imagined to have lived completely alone. Each was expected to fulfill the commandments attributed to Jesus in the Gospels: "Love your Lord God with all your heart, soul, and mind—that is the first great commandment. The second is similar to it—love your neighbor as yourself. In these two commandments reside all the Law and the Prophets" (Mt 22:37–40; cf. Mk 12:29–31, Lk 10:27, Jn 13:34). As Douglas Burton-Christie remarks, "It would not be an exaggeration to say that the biblical commandment to love, more than any other, defined and gave shape to the world in which the desert fathers lived."[22] Yet the desert problematized the fulfillment of this command: how could one possibly love another while maintaining solitude? How could ascetics who truly pursued freedom from possessions possibly give anything? The means by which desert fathers were imagined to live up to Jesus's command provided guidance for the practice of "perfect" charity among the monks of Dorotheus's day.

"Do we really know what charity is?" Abba Joseph reportedly asked his fellow elders. Answering his own question, Joseph told them about a solitary named Agathon, who, when he heard another praise the knife he used to make baskets, "did not let him go until him took the knife," although it was the sole basis of his livelihood.[23] To count as charity, this implied, giving something not only had to be hard but had to pose a loss for the giver. Furthermore, as others pointed out, such a giver had to prioritize a recipient's benefit over his own: "One elder said, 'If someone asks for something and it is a struggle to provide it, your thoughts must be well disposed toward what you are giving, for it is written, 'If someone should force you to go one mile, go with him two' [Mt 5:41]—that is, if someone asks you for something, give it with your whole soul."[24] This intensity of effort, verging on self-sacrifice, for another person could transform virtually any act or item into something that would fulfill the commandment of charity. Yet such effort could also make recipients reluctant to accept. One elder, for example, refused to take the bread a disciple had gone to great lengths to procure because he viewed it as representing the brother's own blood, and acquiesced only after others urged him to "eat [his] brother's sacrifice."[25] It was therefore important for givers to hide the fact that they were making a sacrifice, as when another elder, seeing a monk unable to weave handles to put on his baskets in time before their sale, gave him the handles off his own baskets, claiming they were extras: "And so he worked to advance the work of his brother, letting his own come to nothing."[26]

Of course, if pressed to its logical extreme, this approach could annihilate a monk's material resources and yet still not go far enough. Commenting on Agathon's affirmation "If I could find a leper, I would gladly give him my own body, while I took his," the tradition remarks, "This indeed is perfect charity." Another vignette presents a solitary stripping himself bare to obtain something for the poor, only to realize afterward that, being alive, he had still not fulfilled the commandment.[27] Therefore, the tradition recognized less physical but equally dramatic modes of charitable giving. One story tells how a hermit discovered that his neighbor was possessed by a demon; therefore, "seeking his brother's advantage and not his own," he asked God to give him the demon instead. Now "burdened with that brother's demon," he forced himself to both pray and fast with redoubled intensity, until "on account of his charity," God released them together.[28] Another story tells of two elders who became separated in a village. When they met up again, one refused to return to the desert because he had succumbed to fornication. But the other, "wanting to gain" his brother, falsely claimed that he himself had fallen into the same sin and proposed that they both seek God's forgiveness together. So they applied themselves to fasting, "the one doing penance for the other as if he had sinned too." Seeing this "toil of charity," God pardoned the lapsed elder "on account of the great charity of the brother who had not sinned." The story concludes, "Behold, this is to 'lay down his soul on behalf of his brother.'"[29]

Rarely does the Egyptian desert tradition provide such helpful explanations for its stories. Indeed, the scripture quoted at the end of this story—Jesus's remark that "one can have no greater charity than this, that one lay down one's soul for one's brothers" (Jn 15:13)—is the key to understanding what Christian charity meant not only in monastic culture but in Early Byzantine tradition generally. Indeed, this emphasis on self-sacrificial love helps explain why ascetic discourse focuses on one expression of charitable giving in particular. In the narratives above, supreme charity is illustrated by a monk's willingness to risk eternal perdition by taking responsibility for his neighbor's sin and performing penance for that sin, without knowing whether God would forgive him or condemn them both; thus, a willingness to sacrifice one's very soul for another person constituted the most advanced gesture of Christian ascetic charity. How relevant were such stories to monastic realities? And what would monastic readers have made of their language of "gaining" a brother and assuming his "burden"? Were they mere metaphors?

At the most basic level, these stories dramatized the challenge of loving anyone who was sinful, negligent or different. This is a prominent theme in the tradition. When someone asked, "If I give charity to my sister, who is a *ptōchos*, is it the same as giving to one of the [other] *ptōchoi*?" the reply was no, it was not, because "kinship inclines you a little toward her."[30] Basic charity, in other words, required generosity even toward those to whom one was not naturally disposed to be generous—it required that one be philanthropic. In this desert milieu, however, the main challenge was imagined to be one's fellow anchorites. Toward them, forbearance itself was considered a form of charitable self-sacrifice, based on Paul's words, "Charity suffers long, and is kind" (1 Cor 13:4). To handle perceived slights, stories advocated that monks "die" to their neighbors and focus on their own faults instead. "If one feels . . . belittled and endures it without retaliating, then he is giving his soul for his neighbor."[31]

This passive approach was considered especially appropriate for novices who needed to face up to their own faults.[32] Spiritual advancement required, however, that they eventually practice forgiveness toward each other more actively, even if doing so was initially premised on self-interest: "He who prays on behalf of his brother shares in the benefit before his brother, on account of his charitable purpose; so, let us pray for one another."[33] Acknowledgment of shared sins was considered the wellspring of such forgiveness, and the practice of mutually sharing the hardships of atonement was known as "burden bearing." It is most clearly illustrated in stories about relationships between masters and disciples. When, for example, a distressed monk confided that he had committed such a great sin that he could not reveal it to his own elder (he had sacrificed to demons to obtain their help in seducing a virgin), Abba Lot agreed to share the burden of the monk's sin himself, saying, "Take courage, for penance is possible. Sit in the cave, fast for two weeks, and I will bear half the sin with you." After three weeks, Lot received assurance that God had pardoned the sin, and the two lived together permanently thereafter.[34]

Inspired by Paul's exhortation to "bear each other's burdens and thereby fulfill the law of Christ" (Gal 6:5), Lot's story highlights the penitential and cooperative aspects of such burden bearing.[35] What must be emphasized is that the desert tradition imagined this as a supreme expression of charity, premised on the real danger that staking one's own soul on a sinner's reform entailed. Nonetheless, as Lot's story shows, taking such risks also provided a basis for building reciprocal, long-term relationships. Other stories present an elder's willingness to spiritually assume his disciple's sins as a prerequisite for their cohabitation and counterpoint to a disciple's willingness to physically support the elder's material needs.[36] But these relationships were also supposed to progress beyond such master-disciple distinctions. The ideal was to reduce all differences over time, so that "if affliction ever arose for one, it would be suffered by the other as if for himself, just as it is written, 'We are one body in Christ'" (Rom 12:5).[37]

> The elders said that each should inhabit his neighbor's condition whatever it might be; that he should, as it were, dress himself in his neighbor's body and wear his whole humanity, compassionately suffering with him, sharing all his joys and tears, being so disposed that he wears the same body, face, and soul, so that if affliction ever befell his neighbor, he will be afflicted as if for himself.[38]

Such willingness to "empty" one's self in order to merge with a neighbor (cf. Phil 2:7) was considered the supreme gift and ultimate goal of anchoretic charity.

We may see this as a mystical conception of charity, since the tradition also presents praying for a neighbor as a way of learning "how one must love God."[39] Yet the logic of these stories was not dictated by piety or scripture alone. Throughout the desert tradition, there runs an ascetic calculus that reckoned any unnecessary material gain as a spiritual loss. This limited the scope for charitable giving in material form, as illustrated by the problem that arose when one ascetic neighbor tried to relieve the poverty of another who wanted to live on a bare minimum:

> One of them used to hide whatever he might have, be it a piece of money or crust of bread, and toss it into his neighbor's things. The neighbor was unaware, and amazed to see that his things kept increasing. Then one day he unexpectedly arrived while the other was doing it. He began to take issue with him, saying, "Your physical things have made a mockery of my spiritual things!" The other gave him his word that he would no longer do it, and so was forgiven.[40]

Material gifts brought into anchoretic settlements were imagined to be passed from cell to cell and returned to their donors untouched, having found no one anywhere in need.[41]

The dilemma posed by reconciling strict *aktēmosynē* with the commandment of love is especially apparent in connection to the "*Agapē*," or Charity Feasts. The desert tradition includes many depictions of this ancient Christian custom carried out in an anchoretic setting. Held in solitary cells or in a settlement's church after the weekly liturgy (as well as after commemorations for deceased saints, elders, or donors), such collective meals were one of three communal practices (besides attending the liturgy and washing a visitor's feet) that were supposed to be observed with "fear, trembling, and spiritual joy."[42] From a practical perspective, they provided opportunities to give away superfluous resources accumulated from one's gainful employment or lay admirers. Yet the desert tradition depicts them with marked ambivalence, highlighting aspects antithetical to anchoretic existence such as crowds, gossip, and the consumption of extravagances, like vegetables served cooked instead of raw, or wine instead of water. Such circumstances were especially imagined to challenge elders to square their individual regimens of fasting with the communal imperative of charity.

> A brother asked Abba Sisoes, saying, "What should I do? When I go to church, there is often an *Agapē* after the service and they make me stay for it. The old man said to him, "That is a vexing question."

Elsewhere, it is recommended to view such occasions as opportunities for even more self-denial: "Instead of fasting, focus on praying without limit."[43] This was a consummately perfectionist approach, one that prioritized the fulfillment of charity by acknowledging that "fasting has its reward, but whoever eats for the sake of charity fulfills two commands, because he sets aside his own will, and fulfills the commandment by refreshing his brothers."[44]

By depicting such feasts as opportunities for ascetic forbearance and self-sacrifice, "setting aside" one's own hard-won discipline for the benefit of others, these stories captured the essence of anchoretic charity.[45] Whether expressed by dying to a neighbor or pledging one's own soul for his salvation, such gestures ideally provided unproblematic gains for all involved in the form of saved, reformed, cheered, or otherwise improved colleagues. Hence the theme of "gaining one's brother" in the desert tradition on charity. Some stories present this as the main objective of charitable self-sacrifice. According to John the Dwarf, "The foundation [of anchoretic life] is your neighbor, whom you must gain. That is the place to begin. For 'in this reside all' the commandments of Christ" (cf. Mt 22:40).[46] This might mean helping a sinful neighbor transform into something else. "Wanting to fulfill God's commandment and to gain" a brigand chief, Abba Paphnutius acquiesced to drink a cup of wine that the chief had mockingly forced on him. "Thanks to this cup," Paphnutius predicted, "God will show you mercy now and forever"—a remark that struck the brigand chief as so generous and forgiving that it converted him and his whole brigand band.[47] Such spiritual gains posed no ascetic dilemmas. As Agathon reportedly remarked, "I have never given a Charity Feast, but for me giving and receiving is an act of charity, for I consider my brother's gain to be [my] contribution."[48]

In the early seventh century, the level of *aktēmosynē* at Scetis was still said to be so great that not a drop of vinegar could be found there.[49] Eventually, these settlements would undergo extensive development. In one part of Kellia alone, archaeologists have counted over fifteen hundred professionally built dwellings, clustered in blocks of mud-brick cells, all in rows with their courtyards uniformly facing east, giving the impression of a carefully planned suburban grid.[50] Most of these postdate the Arab conquest, however, when the patriarch himself was living in the region; before that, nomadic raids made the anchoretic life portrayed in the *Sayings* largely untenable during the fifth and sixth centuries. Egyptian desert tradition was fundamentally a nostalgic tradition, read by monks living under later conditions, imagining a lost paradise: "Then there was charity, and each pulled his neighbor up. But now 'charity has grown cold' [Mt 24:12] and each pulls his neighbor down," one saying concluded.[51] Yet monks of the sixth-century Seridos monastery in Palestine could have seen a real resemblance between the mythic elders of the desert tradition and their own resident recluses. The letters of Barsanuphius and John show how ascetic notions of Christian charity came to life in an actual monastery.

GIFTS OF CHARITY IN THE SERIDOS MONASTERY

Located on the highway connecting Egypt to Palestine, the region of Gaza served as a gateway for the northward spread of Egyptian anchoretic monasticism. Its hinterland included a village called Tawatha (Umm al-Tut in the Gaza Strip), located about five miles (8 km) southwest of the city. This was the birthplace of Hilarion (d. 371), the reputed founder of Palestinian monasticism. During the fifth century, it became a mecca for solitaries who wished to follow in his footsteps and obtain contemplative serenity (*hesychia*).[52] One such recluse, Isaiah of Scetis

(d. 489, a.k.a. Isaiah of Gaza), wrote an influential anchoretic manual, the *Asceticon*, while living in seclusion at a place called Beit Daltha, slightly south of Tawatha. Isaiah reportedly never left his cell and relied on a nearby cenobium to bring him food and deliver mail between him and his admirers, including students from Gaza's famous school of rhetoric. This was an affluent circle: some of Isaiah's disciples are said to have given him "thousands of coins" to distribute upon joining.[53]

A slightly later eminence, also of Egyptian extraction, was Barsanuphius. Invited by an elder already living in the area, he soon became mentor to Seridos (d. ca. 541), the leader of another cenobium. Like Isaiah, Barsanuphius opened his cell door only to take the food or correspondence that Seridos brought him. He is said to have emerged from his enclosure only once, to wash the feet of Seridos's monks and prove that he actually existed. Not long after his arrival, he invited a former protégé named John (d. ca. 541, a.k.a. John of Gaza or John the Prophet, probably to also be identified with John of Beersheba) to take up residence in a cell nearby. Informally known as the "Great Old Man" and "the Other Old Man,"[54] these two anchorites became the monastery's leading *hesychasts*. Working out of separate but seemingly close cells, they dispensed prayers and consultations to a wide range of clients, with John mainly handling questions about practice, and Barsanuphius about theory. Their partnership as spiritual consultants thrived for about twenty years. Then, ca. 541, Seridos and John suddenly died in rapid succession, and Barsanuphius fell silent, his time of death unknown—possibly all victims of the Justinianic plague.

We know little about the size and wealth of Seridos's community except that it had connections with a military commander's staff, was able to recruit a member of the educated elite (Dorotheus), and seems to have included about forty to fifty monks.[55] The ruins of a "large and splendid" monastery recently discovered elsewhere in the Gaza Strip may help us envision its layout. Now identified with followers of Hilarion (possibly built over his tomb), this monastery resembled the Martyrius Monastery outside Jerusalem, with a central courtyard surrounded by a ramble of cells and hallways, a church with stuccoed walls and polychrome floors, a refectory, a modest hostel, and a bathhouse.[56] Otherwise, all we know about the Seridos monastery we owe to Dorotheus. As a favored disciple of both Barsanuphius and John, he seems to have been responsible for collecting and editing their letters, resulting in the 854 examples we possess today. Divided into sets addressed to hesychasts (i.e., anchorites), to cenobites, and to laypeople and clerics, this represents the richest archive available for reconstructing any Christian community in the late Roman East. The letters do not come to us untouched, but include editorial comments explaining situations that had prompted them.[57] While they leave much unknown—there are no dates, and few preserve details about their lay, clerical, or monastic recipients—they nevertheless offer unique access inside the walls of an Early Byzantine monastery. Among other things (including a high level of literacy among the monastic rank and file), they reveal how charitable giving through burden bearing was used to forge cooperative, long-term bonds between mentors, disciples, and peers.

Dorotheus alludes to this setting and its challenges in his own writings. As noted in the last chapter, social relations in Early Byzantine monasteries could be difficult, and Dorotheus's early years at the Seridos monastery were not easy. Born into a noble family and educated in rhetoric and medical theory at Antioch, he must have seemed a stellar catch for the institution. He rapidly advanced to serve in its highest *diakoniai,* including the offices of guest master and infirmarian (his brother, who remained a layman, funded the monastery's infirmary). But this did not help him get along with the monastery's rank and file. They already suspected their abbot of picking favorites, and it could not have helped that Dorotheus and his brother were promised that Barsanuphius would be Dorotheus's personal intercessor if he stayed at the monastery (evidently a deal made in advance between the Seridos monastery and Dorotheus's family, perhaps reflecting a common way of attracting wealthy recruits to monasteries at the time).[58]

Dorotheus vividly describes the resentment he suffered. One day, after John of Gaza's disciple fell ill, he was selected to replace him, stirring up indignation among those who wanted the prestigious discipleship themselves. "Believe me, brothers," Dorotheus later recalls, "one brother followed me all the way from the infirmary to the church, casting insults at my back." Worse still,

> another brother, whether to provoke me or out of simplicity, made water all over my head and soaked my bed. Similarly, some of the other brethren began, during the day, to shake their rush-mats in front of my cell, and I saw such a horde of flies and stinging insects coming into my cell that I could not kill them all. They were in such great numbers because of the heat. When I came back to lie down they all settled on me. Sleep came upon me, I was so tired from my labor, but when I woke up I found my body bitten all over.[59]

Having invested considerable time (and perhaps property) in their monastic careers, these monks vied for attention from their institution's "fathers" and "saints"—that is, from its elite hesychasts who held spiritual authority even over the abbot.[60] They could have applied to the monastery's two other hesychasts, Paul or Euthymius, but the most prized discipleships were with Barsanuphius and John ("How many have desired to acquire us as elders, and strove to achieve this purpose, but were not successful?" remarked one to the other). Dorotheus served John for nine years, during which he "would kiss the outside door of [John's] cell with as much devotion as one might [use to] reverence the precious Cross."[61]

Such rivalries, however, seem to have left Barsanuphius and John unscathed. Their letters exhibit genuine concern for all the members of the community.[62] This was partly out of self-interest. A distinct feature of Gazan monasticism was its notion that forging master-disciple relationships was as crucial for a master as it was for his disciple. Guy Stroumsa put this outlook into the broader history of late antique religious change:

> Almost unknown in the ancient world, [in this Christian setting] there is no salvation except through an intermediary, a *mesitēs*, a master at once human and divine. . . . Obedience to the spiritual father, however, does not simply mean submission to authority, but is established upon faith, trust, and love. This explains why the pagan teacher of wisdom has absolutely no need of a disciple; he can return any time to his personal reflection and abandon humanity to its fate. The Christian spiritual master, on the other hand, is closely tied to his disciples from an existential point of view. He is worth as much, or as little, as they are, and his own salvation depends on theirs. Abba Isaiah [of Scetis] explains to his disciples that if they practice his precepts, he will speak to God on their behalf. If they do not, however, God will not only ask them to account for their negligence, but will also accuse Isaiah of being useless. . . . Each was about transforming the self—its goal was not knowledge, but salvation.[63]

Except for Barsanuphius, every elder at the Seridos monastery combined roles of mentorship and discipleship, serving as masters to less advanced monks while receiving instruction as disciples from others still more advanced. One gets an impression of relationships being regularly renegotiated according to a disciple's time and perceived spiritual progress at the monastery.

Suffusing this entire system, indeed the monastery itself, was an ideology of charitable giving.[64] At the most basic, material level, all corporate items that the institution issued to its residents, such as their uniforms, were identified as "charity."[65] Otherwise, its leaders sought to promote "the 'greater love' of Christ" through burden bearing.[66] Even members of lower ranks were asked to bear each other's burdens with compassion.[67] That said, the practice of burden bearing could differ greatly, depending on who was involved. Among novices, charity mainly meant just showing patience to one another. Among advanced monks, it meant taking active responsibility for each other's sins, requiring advanced capacities for intercessory prayer and self-sacrifice.

The result was a cautiously scaled approach to charitable giving. Barsanuphius and John explained its premises to a monk who had asked how anyone committed to voluntary poverty could fulfill Jesus's command to love his neighbor as himself, as well as what "degree of charity" should exist between any two monks. John reassured this correspondent, evidently a cenobite, that charity could be expressed in any number of ways aside from giving a material object; for, in fact, "if we wished to fulfill the scriptural commandment that way, we could surely not be able." Indeed, he reasons, if Jesus had proclaimed all humans to be one another's neighbors (cf. Lk 10:36–37), then how could anyone treat so many people charitably in a material manner? True, monks must share whatever resources they had, even if they only had enough for themselves. Among the less advanced, however, "loving one's neighbor as oneself" mainly meant just not rejoicing at another's loss or withholding any wisdom an elder might have imparted about the ways of God.[68] In another letter to this same monk, John warns against even praying for an ailing brother out of compassion, explaining that demons often tempted novices to do this to make them think themselves better than their peers. Praying for a sick brother was only for those who had attained perfection through training: "As for showing someone compassion out of charity, you have not yet reached that level."[69]

"The charity of the Fathers for their children is one thing," Barsanuphius himself explained; "the charity of the Brothers for each other is another."

> Each loves his neighbor according to his level. The measure of perfect charity is when a person loves his neighbor as himself in accordance with his love for God. But youth requires caution in everything. The Devil causes younger people to stumble. . . . The level of their charity toward each other ought to be this: to not malign, hate, or despise each other; to not seek one's own interest, or seek to love someone out of corporeal beauty, benefit them, or sit side by side without great compulsion, lest this induce such familiarity as to destroy their fruits and leave them dead wood.

"Only so far," Barsanuphius repeats, "should be the level of charity between the young."[70]

Thus Barsanuphius reinforced John's position. Neither of them explained, however, what "perfect charity" itself meant or how it was expressed, in actual practice. Fortunately, this can be gleaned from letters Barsanuphius issued to his disciples as their spiritual master. These reveal the terms by which various burden-bearing relationships were undertaken.[71] Note the formality with which Dorotheus requested, and Barsanuphius laid out, their burden-bearing arrangement:

> *Letter 270:* Request from [Dorotheus] to the same Great Old Man to bear his sins.

> *Response:* Brother, although you are asking of me something that is beyond me, nevertheless I shall show you the limits of charity: namely, that it forces itself to exceed even its own limits. Behold, I admire you as a person, and I will assume responsibility for you and support you. But on one condition: that you endure keeping my words and commandments; for these will bring you salvation.[72]

Barsanuphius agrees to pledge his soul for Dorotheus and to keep him under his protection for all eternity, as long as Dorotheus obeys his commands. Elsewhere, he refers to this agreement as their "covenant" (*diathēkē*).[73] Barsanuphius similarly agreed to pray for another disciple as long as he followed everything prescribed for him. "Brother, learn this too," Barsanuphius added in closing, "I would gladly sacrifice my very life for you, and my prayer for you is unceasing."[74]

The quasi-contractual nature of these arrangements may surprise us. Barsanuphius seems not to have known a notion of unconditional love: for him, "perfect" charity by definition went beyond any one-sided sacrifice; it required a reciprocal relationship founded on Jesus's remark "If you love me, you will keep my commands" (Jn 14:15).[75] The emphasis was not so much on obedience as on close cooperation. As Barsanuphius remarked, it was natural for any worldly petitioner to help his patron in any way possible to reach the imperial court to plead on the petitioner's behalf before the emperor; accordingly, a disciple should contribute at least a little of his own "sweat and toil" to help his master plead his case before God.[76] Barsanuphius specified that any disciple wanting his intercessory prayers must perform a set of prostrations three times daily, saying "Forgive me" each time, for forty days. Due to the prayers of their elders, all residents of the Seridos monastery could be assured of receiving at least some mercy on Judgment Day, he explained. But whether that divine mercy would be great or small depended entirely on how much humility and penance each of them had individually contributed beforehand.[77]

But none of this compared to what Barsanuphius himself was ready to put into someone's salvation. He told a monk who ran the monastery's kitchen that he was prepared to do "even ten times more than you are able to do" to release the monk from sin, proposing that "to your 100 denarii, I will add my 10,000,000 talents" (cf. Dn 1:20; Mt 18:24–28), before further offering to regard all the monk's sins as his own, if necessary.[78] Barsanuphius admitted that it was madness to think himself capable of carrying the full weight of anyone's sins. Accordingly, it was better, he told a senior monk, Andrew, to assume just half of Andrew's sins—neither a third nor two-thirds, Barsanuphius specifies—to ensure that neither of them would succumb to idleness or vainglory. Nevertheless, Barsanuphius also offered to assume all of his sins if Andrew wished to "cast the whole burden" upon him.[79]

Besides conveying the magnitude of Barsanuphius's capacity for charity, such numerical negotiations offered a certain semblance of precision to communicate where a monk stood in the monastic hierarchy and how far he needed to progress before he could assume spiritual burdens equal to those of a mentor. They also provided mentors with excuses to cut their losses if a disciple proved recalcitrant. Barsanuphius warned that the devil, knowing that burden bearing was the "sole basis for our salvation," was always trying to lead disciples astray. Such seems to have been the case with the kitchen monk, who was evidently a constant disappointment. "To this day," Barsanuphius complained,

> I have extended my wings over you; I have borne your burdens and transgressions, as well as your contempt for my words and your negligence. . . . But I need a little cooperation from you. In the name of God, behold, I am giving you a commandment for salvation. If you keep it, I shall bear the indictment against you. . . . Do not be discontent, thinking this commandment is heavy. For it is not possible for anyone to be saved without labor and keeping the commandment. So then, I have assumed the weight, the charge, and the obligation. Behold, you have become new, free from guilt, and purified. Therefore, stay in this purity.[80]

With resignation, Barsanuphius later wrote, "Either ask me questions and reject your own will . . . or I shall stay away from you."[81] Repeated failure to cooperate was considered sufficient reason to terminate a master-disciple relationship before investing any more in the hope of future reciprocity.

Inconstancy was expected of novices and so was relatively easy to forgive. When advanced hesychasts let each other down, however, the consequences were potentially more dire.[82] Charity at this level was based on a proven record of mutual commitment, with each now bearing the others' sins, burdens, and risks nearly equally. Barsanuphius's decision to assume exactly half of Andrew's sins acknowledged that, as a fledgling hesychast, Andrew was almost his peer. Barsanuphius made this explicit: "What I have said to you—that 'I will bear half your sins'—[means] 'I have made you my partner.'"[83] Having become one of the monastery's anchoretic "saints," Andrew was now expected to atone not only for his own sins but for those of the rest of the community, including those of its spiritual elite. Hence, Barsanuphius frequently asked him to pray for himself as well, just as he asked his fellow hesychasts John, Euthymius, and Paul.

These three were Barsanuphius's closest protégés. While remaining their superior, he regarded them as "true brothers" and "same-soul mates" (homopsychoi).[84] The aim of charitable reciprocity among such peers was to become "a single heart in Christ's kind yoke."[85] This was not just sentiment. Their letters show a sense of having achieved a fusion of souls: when writing to Euthymius, Barsanuphius remarked that he felt he was addressing his own soul, while John affirmed that he could read Barsanuphius's mind.[86] Such compassionate bonding was based on years of reciprocal confession, each assuring the other that he recognized and appreciated the risks that the other was taking for him. "To say, 'I offer my soul for you,'" Barsanuphius told Paul, "may be interpreted as, 'I am accountable for your charity.'"[87] Barsanuphius relied on their prayers as well. As he asked Euthymius, "Out of charity, give me your hand and draw me up toward [God], so that through you, He will save me, who needs mercy."[88]

In such exchanges, charitable self-sacrifice and merciful acts of condescension seem virtually identical. When extended to monks at lower levels, the two became more distinct, the master's willingness to atone for his disciples' sins representing more plainly a gift of charity, his prayers constituting more clearly a ministration providing immaterial alms or mercy ("To find mercy," advised Barsanuphius, "find the saints' prayers"), which might diminish if a disciple was not ready for a lasting relationship. Yet it was incumbent on this elite to provide at least something for all who asked. Barsanuphius told Andrew that he should continue to engage a negligent disciple, "for your brother believes he is finding mercy through you."[89] To ensure that all might get access to their prayers, monks were told to address their elders with a simple formula: "Abba, I am not well. I beseech you to pray for me as you know how, for I need God's mercies."[90] Twenty petitions of this sort have survived, ranging from routine requests to urgent appeals at approach of death. One dying elder told Barsanuphius,

> I am in your hands—God's and yours. Show me your mercy to the end and quickly release me, entrusting me to your Master Christ, guiding me with your holy prayers and accompanying me on the road in the air, whither I know not.[91]

Barsanuphius assured his correspondents that God's "ineffable philanthropy" would grant them all pardon.[92] Yet most seemed content with simply receiving the prayers given to them by this spiritual elite. Dorotheus remarks that merely writing to Barsanuphius or John gave him a profound sense of peace,[93] while the dying elder quoted above evidently saw little difference between petitioning Barsanuphius and petitioning God himself.

These letters reveal the Christian culture of charity that a single monastery in southwestern Palestine sought to promote within its walls. We do not know if others promoted a similar culture, but Symeon Stylites the Younger reportedly offered exuberant charity during the same years to the lay public at large. It is easy to forget that Barsanuphius, John, Dorotheus, and Symeon were all more or less contemporaries, the enclosed and the exposed. Symeon says nothing about charity in his sermons, but his hagiographer presents *agapē* as the primary impulse behind his tearful petitions to obtain mercy for the Antiochenes amid their many afflictions. His supplications on their behalf reportedly prompted even God to protest, "Are not the sins of worldly people many? Do not love them more than me."[94] Christians increasingly relied on the charity of such public penitents to collectively secure mercy for their sins, as discussed in chapter 6. The next section examines how individual lay sinners were taught to obtain mercy for themselves through redemptive almsgiving, an explicitly self-serving practice that did not necessarily demand any burdensome self-sacrifice.

SINS OF EXCESS AND REDEMPTIVE ALMSGIVING

One of the strangest remnants of early Egyptian monasticism is the fifth- or sixth-century *Life of Syncletica*.[95] Ascribed to a famous bishop, Athanasius of Alexandria (d. 373), its author uses Syncletica, one of the very few females mentioned in the *Sayings of the Desert Fathers*, as a mouthpiece to explain various virtues, including the interrelation between charity and freedom from possessions, or *aktēmosynē*. According to Syncletica, only those who embraced complete poverty without any possessions could be considered "guardians of genuine charity." This, she reasons, is because Jesus obliged Christians to love all their neighbors, and "no one could possibly possess enough" resources to give to all if Jesus had meant charity to be expressed in material form. But should monks nonetheless acquire possessions so as to give alms? her disciples ask. No, she explains, almsgiving is incumbent only on worldly people:

Almsgiving has been ordained not so much for the sake of feeding poor people as for the sake of charity, since God, who supplies the rich, also feeds the poor [cf. Ps. 9:9]. Does this mean that almsgiving was ordained for no purpose? By no means! It provides a starting point for people who are unfamiliar with charity. Just as physical circumcision [in the Old Testament] provided a preliminary sketch of circumcision of the heart [in the New Testament], so too almsgiving was established to teach charity. But for those already given charity by grace, almsgiving is superfluous.

"I say these things," she explains, "to emphasize the purity of aktēmosynē, lest the inferior goal [of almsgiving] become an impediment to the superior goal [of charity]. Since you recently have accomplished the inferior goal by giving away all that you had in a single act [of almsgiving], from now on look to the higher goal of charity."[96]

Syncletica's diatribe makes clear that material almsgiving was considered more appropriate for propertied Christians than for monks. It agrees with the Gazan School in viewing almsgiving as a handmaiden to charity and affirming that charity, unlike alms, could not be adequately expressed through material gifts. But it adds something new by explaining how both types of giving fit into the providential structure of human society, each gift being appropriate to a certain type of human in the created establishment. God, Syncletica observes, had established among humans a "twofold order of people who are capable of pity." One had been created to cultivate the earth and was allowed to acquire and possess material resources. The other, consisting of people "equal to angels," was not. While the former were expected to give alms from their material resources, the latter could bestow mercy only spiritually—but therefore their resources were potentially inexhaustible, making them capable of bestowing mercy on all. "Therefore let us have merciful intentions," Syncletica exhorts her disciples, "for 'blessed are the merciful in soul.'"[97]

Such strict segregation of material and spiritual responsibilities is usually found only in early Syrian ascetic tradition. Yet Syncletica's presumption that almsgiving is more appropriate for laypeople than for monks is found in the letters of Barsanuphius and John, as well as in Egyptian desert tradition, which mainly depicts almsgiving as a lay activity.[98] In one of its stories, for example, a monk tried to support his lay brother with alms. Seeing that this only made his brother poorer, the monk taught him to work instead. Soon the lay brother began to generate a surplus. At first, he gave this to his monastic brother to distribute as alms to strangers, but soon he began dispensing them himself and prospered all the more. An elder observed, "This is more advantageous for him, that he make alms from his toil and receives a prayer from the holy ones, and thus is blessed."[99] The story gives an anchoretic perspective on the proper distribution of labor in Christian society: laypeople should physically toil to generate material wealth, which monks should either help distribute or augment through their prayers. More specifically, it identifies alms as a product of surplus resources: "I have achieved superfluity" (perisseuō), the brother observes when ready to give alms. Barsanuphius likewise identified an ability and an obligation to give alms with the possession of material wealth: "Do you not discern, my beloved, from whom God demands almsgiving, the poor or the rich man?"[100]

By the time Barsanuphius had posed that question, its answer no longer rested on the obvious response that God required the rich to give alms because, like the propertied cultivators in Syncletica's diatribe, they simply had more to give. By the sixth century, almsgiving was being specifically promoted to atone for two sins closely identified with material affluence itself: namely, greed and plunder, *pleonexia* and *harpagē*, the desire for, and unjust seizure of, more than one needed. We find Basil of Caesarea expounding this rationale for almsgiving already in the fourth century. Having been asked, "Since the Lord says, 'Give as alms the things that are within' [Lk 11:41], can a person be purified for all sins through almsgiving?" Basil replied,

> The meaning of this saying is clear from the context. For after [Jesus told the Pharisees], "You cleanse the outside of the cup and the dish, but inside you are full of plunder and wickedness," He added, "But give as alms the things that are within; and behold, all things are clean for you" [Lk 11:39–41]. By "all things," He meant as many sins and wicked deeds as we commit through plunder and avarice. Zacchaeus also declares this when he says, "Behold, I give half my possessions to the poor, and if I have wrongfully exacted anything from someone, I restore it fourfold" [Lk 19:8]. So in this way we can purify ourselves from as many sins of this sort as can be absolved and repaid many times over.[101]

Inspired, it seems, by the Old Testament notion of almsgiving as righteousness, giving gifts had long been advocated as a sacrificial means by which Jews or Christians might redress wrongs and expiate low-level sins (Dn 4:27; Tb 12:9).[102] When writing this explanation for his monastic audience, however, Basil provided much greater precision, associating the practice with the sins of *pleonexia* and *harpagē* in particular. He presents it as a means of offsetting the possession of any excess goods obtained through those sins by repaying them "many times over" in alms. This made almsgiving an act of penance or atonement. Usually called "redemptive" almsgiving today, Early Byzantine discourse came to identify such alms not so much as a gift, as a voluntary reparation made to those people from whom a surplus had been unjustly extracted—that is, the poor. These associations with sinful surplus and unjust material gains made alms very different from charity, especially for ascetic authorities.

It was primarily John Chrysostom, in his guise as "John of Repentance," who advanced the Christian concept of redemptive almsgiving as we know it in Eastern tradition. Chrysostom detected *pleonexia* behind nearly all social injustices. Once, while preaching on the Gospel of Matthew, he asked listeners to reflect on standard sources of income of the day and identify which, if any, produced wealth in a just manner. Of the military profession he refused to speak, so obvious was its lust for plunder. So he turned to artisans and craftsmen, since "these especially seem to earn a living from their own righteous toil and sweat." But on closer inspection these too committed great injustices, "heaping oaths and false claims on their avarice" because they "always want to increase what they have."[103] So he turned to landowners and proprietors of great estates. These, not surprisingly, proved to be most unjust of all, due to the ferocity with which they pressed laborers to reap a surplus, "filling their wine vats with toil and sweat" while hardly giving them a share.[104] This propensity to desire more than needed pervaded society from bottom to top; in Chrysostom's view, not even the poor were free from *pleonexia*, "for they rob those who are poorer than they."[105] "Perhaps you are saying, 'Every day you talk about greed,'" he imagines his audiences complaining. "I wish I could talk about it day and night," Chrysostom lamented, "for this disease has seized the whole world and occupies the souls of all."[106]

Indeed, Chrysostom made *pleonexia* the "beginning, middle, and end of all evils."[107] This is partly explained by his understanding of the Fall. Like Origen and the Cappadocians, he believed that God had originally given the world a precise structure, setting borders and limits on everything so that each had its own place, purpose, and specific resources to sustain it. As explained in his *Homilies on Genesis,* Adam and Eve, as bearers of God's image, enjoyed the most privileged place in this scheme, so that all their needs were supplied in Paradise. Only the Tree of Knowledge was off limits. Original sin lay in the desire to transgress those limits, inspired by Satan, who, "having ideas above his station, became carried away to a degree beyond what was granted to him, and so fell from heaven."[108] Similarly "not content to remain within her own proper limits," Eve seized its fruit and offered it to Adam, who negligently followed.[109] Eve's primordial act of greed and plunder thus caused the first fall from high prosperity in human history (making Adam and Eve, by implication, history's first *ptōchoi*).[110]

Although Chrysostom did not explicitly posit greed itself as the original human sin, he clearly thought it the principle cause of the Fall.[111] Neither greed nor avarice adequately conveys what *pleonexia* meant to him. It was a desire "to have more than allotted;" its essence was to transgress whatever limits God had imposed. This not only made it a sin by itself but also the impulse driving all other sins, prompting humans "to go beyond what is necessary" in whatever they did,[112] creating an excessive state of interior drives that rendered a soul impure.[113] Envy spread *pleonexia* even farther through the world: "Like fire catching wood," it enflamed everyone—"some more, some less, but all nonetheless," catching men, women, and children equally in its grip. God had tried to loosen its hold by expanding the limits of creation, but to no avail—people just kept grasping for more.[114] Hence, the need for the countervailing force of almsgiving. Besides making people realize their relative lowliness and the true limits of human nature, it relieved them of impure excrescences.[115] But only if these alms derived from "just profit or labor, pure of all greed, plunder or violence"—that is, from one's original, essential resources and not those added by unjust seizures—could they restore proper limits and regain the purity enjoyed in Paradise.[116]

This must have left listeners wondering how they could give anything sufficiently pure. An ascetic at heart, Chrysostom at one point conceptualizes purity itself simply as the state of having no more than one ought.[117] Only monks, he believed, managed to become entirely free of *pleonexia*. Monks, he claimed, "do not even know what avarice is," earning what sufficed for each day through their daily toils.[118] Yet even among them, just gain was a complicated issue: how could material earnings be received at all, without creating a dangerous surplus or impulse for more? Ascetic economics was ideally a noneconomic discipline. Evagrius of Pontus wrote in a guidebook, "In the giving and receiving of payment, you cannot avoid sin." He advised readers to find some trustworthy junior monk or layperson to do the buying or selling for them, but if that were impossible, they should deliberately seek a material loss: "When selling or buying, take a small loss on the just price, lest you succumb to splitting hairs or other profit-loving ways."[119] Barsanuphius recommended taking something off the price when selling, "like a penny—nothing burdensome," to offset unnecessary gains, while John of Gaza advised taking no more than exactly what a thing was worth.[120] Egyptian desert tradition imagines similar strategies for minimizing profits, balancing each gain with a commensurate loss.[121] But challenges remained. It was said that a young monk of the Pachomian confederation was sent to sell sandals for his monastery's cobbler. He tried to sell them for as little as they were worth, but nobody bought them, thinking they must have been stolen. So he took whatever price they chose to pay and returned to the monastery with three times what it had cost to make the shoes. The cobbler alerted the abbot that the monk had a "worldly mind." So, despite his protests that he had only taken what his customers had wanted to give, the monk was forced to return the excess and do penance for having "greatly sinned in his love for more."[122]

It was thus nearly impossible in theory or practice to avoid contracting some taint of *pleonexia* in market exchanges. Demanding such ungainful purity from congregations had been standard in the pre-Constantinian era, which may have influenced Chrysostom. We get a sense of the instruction he might have received early in his career from the church manual known as the *Apostolic Constitutions.* Compiled at Antioch in the 380s, it prohibited bishops, deacons, and stewards from accepting from the laity anything that had come from unjust seizures or was given by people known to covet goods of others. Gifts from such sources were "abominable to God," and could not be used to supply the needs of the poor. Instead of accepting them, they should make collections for the poor from members of their community known to "walk in a holy manner."[123] Such was the written guidance that Chrysostom would have received. But these passages from the *Apostolic Constitutions* would have been woefully out of date for the situation Chrysostom faced in the late fourth century, since they had been lifted from the third-century *Didascalia*, a document written for smaller communities that would not have included many casual Christians from privileged ranks. How, then, did church authorities handle the fact that most lay alms were not going to come entirely free of "greed, plunder, or violence"?

One way was to recognize a scale of almsgiving that could accommodate the pure and tainted together at once. Dorotheus, as we saw, evaluated alms by motive, ascribing value even to those motivated exclusively by hopes of material gain. Others ranked them according to the circumstances or materials from which they derived. To explain whether giving alms erased every sin, a later compilation known as *Answers to Questions of Duke Antiochus* responded: "There is sin, and then there is sin; there is almsgiving, and then there is almsgiving. . . . The reward of a farm hand who shows compassion from his own sweat is one thing, that of a magistrate who offers it out of bribes and [unjust] revenues is another." The *Answers* distinguished between alms given while atoning for sin or while still living in sin, between those given in times of scarcity or of plenty, and between those given directly or through an agent.[124] Similar distinctions were drawn by Anastasius of Sinai after the Arab conquests. Asked if stolen money was acceptable to God, Anastasius differentiates between a variety of thefts and injustices:

> It is one thing to steal from a church, another from revenues that infidels extract from the earth or sea. It is one thing to be unjust toward farmers and poor people, another to steal from rich people who are wicked and love money. Note that God does not seek quantity, only the intention; if, however, you cannot altogether avoid acting unjustly, it behooves you to spend money from evil things on good things, instead of on bad things.

Only one source of alms did Anastasius absolutely condemn: "Money derived from injustices toward *ptōchoi* and farmers is unacceptable to God, and accursed."[125] Such resources could never convincingly be used to demonstrate a merciful change of heart.

A more common solution, however, was to require that alms be given in greater proportions than whatever had been unjustly taken in the first place. This approach was inspired by the publican Zacchaeus's explanation to Jesus that he was accustomed to give back four times whatever he seized from his victims, as depicted in Gospel of Luke (Lk 19:1–10). Even Chrysostom embraced his example: "Have you vexed God by seizing money?" he asked listeners. "Then reconcile Him through money. Give back what you seized and then still more; say, like Zacchaeus, 'I am giving back all that I seized fourfold.'"[126] But to be redemptive, such almsgiving had to entail some personal expense as well, coming not only from the resources a sinner had seized but from his own reserves as well.[127] Alternatively, they could be augmented by rich gestures of humility. Chrysostom proposed that sinners imitate Ahab (1 Kgs 21:27) in putting on sackcloth and pouring forth tears: "If we do this and mourn as he did, then like Zacchaeus we shall shed the charges against us and gain some pardon."[128]

ALMSGIVING AS PURIFICATION
IN EASTERN HAGIOGRAPHY

This discourse left a mark on monastic imaginations. Most depictions of almsgiving in Early Byzantine hagiography present it as a form of lay purification. Before embracing monasticism, for example, the fabulously wealthy heiress Melania the Younger is said to have dispensed alms "as if by this alone she hoped to receive mercy."[129] The sister, aunt, and grandmother of Theodore of Sykeon, all former prostitutes, "purified and ennobled themselves" by giving alms before entering a convent, while Theodore himself advised other lay folk fast, pray, and give alms as a fixed program of penance.[130] In *Ladder of Divine Ascent,* John Climacus presents almsgiving as the primary means by which laypeople might emulate the penitential practices monks undertook to obtain salvation. After describing the exertions by which monks humbled themselves, he adds that even if ordinary Christians did not have such ascetic strategies, "some of them, through almsgiving, know what they will gain at the end."[131]

Yet it is John of Ephesus, writing in Syriac about alms as expressions of *zaddiqā,* "righteousness," who makes its connection with expiation most explicit and palpable. One of his hagiographical portraits is of a sixth-century layman named Thomas, who inherited a huge amount of gold, slaves, and estates from his father, a rapacious imperial officer in Syria and Armenia. "What will come of it for me," he laments, "except hell and eternal torment, since none of this has been amassed by justice or righteousness, but by plundering and cheating the poor?" According to John, Thomas resolved to make copious alms in hope of securing "at least a little mercy" on Judgment Day. When dispensing them, he would tearfully ask his recipients for their prayers in return: "Since you have not provoked God by robbery and injustice, entreat Him . . . that He may be reconciled to us and have mercy on us on that great day, since even this which we are giving comes from the blood of the souls of the poor, of the indigent, of orphans, and of widows." In this way, Thomas laid "a sound foundation for penance," soon adding fasts and prayers to his alms. Eventually, his "thoughts progressed" to the point that he decided to sell the rest of his inheritance, give the proceeds away, and become a monk.[132]

John's narrative follows a common hagiographical trajectory: Thomas, seeking redemption, gave alms in such quantity and contrition that he began thinking with the penitential fervor of a monk; eventually he joined a monastery, and his material almsgiving gave way to more spiritual forms of purification. But John's portrait contains other features that suggest why monks would have been reluctant to receive such alms themselves. In his narrative, John identifies the materials that Thomas was distributing not merely with his father's ill-gotten gains but with the very "blood of the poor" his father had plundered. Elsewhere, John describes unjust wealth as tainted with the blood, sweat, and sins that had originally produced it: thus Mare the Solitary refuses to live "on the labor and sweat—that is, on the sins—of others," for which reason he rejects all the riches his lay admirers wished to bestow on him.[133] Likewise, an ascetic named Tribunus declines all such material support on the grounds that "my sins are enough for me, and to share in other men's sins or to refresh myself by the sweat of others I shall never consent,"[134] while Euphemia of Amida accepts nothing from her admirers for fear that she might receive in her hands "the stains of their sins." When they continue to press her, she replies, "A truce to this kindness of yours, since you wish to pollute me with the mire of your sins; my own blots are sufficient for me."[135]

Blots, stains, pollutants: John depicts material alms as if they were tainted by sin and served as vectors of sin itself. We must not discount this as mere metaphor, despite the tendency of Syrian hagiography to "literalize symbols."[136] John's imagery of toil and sweat seems to have been inspired by Genesis's depiction of humanity's accursed state after the Fall ("Through painful toil you will eat food from it all the days of your life. . . . By the sweat of your brow you will eat your food," Gn 3:17–19). Its elaboration here suggests, however, that an object might transmit the spirit, or "curse," of whatever action or resources produced it, contaminating its recipient in turn. Anthropologists have documented similar beliefs in other cultures, noting that gifts tend to create bonds of complicity (whether positive or negative) between donors and recipients: "In accepting the gift, the recipient cannot strip it of its connection with . . . the donor's reason(s) for giving it. To accept the gift is on some level to consent to that total complex reality, and to consent to become part of it."[137]

This was a recurring problem with suspicious gifts in general, as shown in the next chapter. But due to its explicit entanglement with sinful actions and sinful resources, alms given for the sake of redemption were especially problematic: how to divest such gifts from the sinful act, material, or spirit that originally produced them? An early attempt to solve this in the *Didascalia* advises that if impoverished communities felt obliged or forced by necessity to accept money from sinners to support widows and orphans, they should not spend it on food or clothing, but on coal or firewood instead, because only this way a sinner's gift might be safely consumed.[138] This advice was copied into the later *Apostolic Constitutions,* whose compilers added a caveat against accepting anything from sinners who showed no sign of remorse: "for the items offered are not defective by their nature, but by the mindset of those who supplied them."[139]

Similar concerns are illustrated in the fifth-century *Life of Pelagia the Harlot*. Here a bishop forbids his church steward from accepting anything the reformed prostitute Pelagia had amassed through sin: "I adjure you by the exalted Trinity, let nothing out of all these belongings enter the church of God, or be given to any of the bishops; let none of it enter the house of any of the clergy, or even your own house; do not let anything be defiled by it, whether through your agency or through the agency of anyone else . . . even though it might seem desirable and good." All of it was to be given to widows, orphans, and the poor instead. "This way," the bishop explained, "just as it was amassed in a wicked and wrong manner, so shall it now be administered in upright and just fashion."[140] What made the consumption of such tainted wealth by the poor now acceptable, contrary to the earlier ruling of the *Didascalia*? The answer, it seems, was that the gift was accompanied by demonstrative acts of humble, penitential contrition. So remorseful was Pelagia, we are told, that her subsequent asceticism turned her into an emaciated male monk. Such a penitential spirit of contrition apparently cleansed her wealth, making it sufficiently clean for the poor, if still too tainted for holy people.

The *Didascalia*, the *Apostolic Constitutions*, and the *Life of Pelagia* were all written in Syria, but this concern about alms as a vector of sin was not just a Syrian concern. Indeed, Anastasius of Sinai's seventh-century *Questions and Answers* provides the closest parallel. To explain how alms can atone for sins, he introduces an anecdote set in Raïthou, a Red Sea port on the Sinai peninsula that featured a monastic colony often visited by pilgrims headed up to Mt. Sinai.

> Once a Christlover visiting Raïthou was dispensing coins to the brothers. He also gave one to a recluse living in the area. That night the recluse had a vision of a field filled with thorns. Monks were harvesting them and one said to him, "Get into the field! You too must reap the thorns of the one who gave the coin, for you took his pay." The next morning the recluse sent for the person and gave back his coin, saying, "Take what you have given me, brother. It is not my work to harvest the thorns of another person's sins. Would that I might cleanse myself of my own sins."

Written to illustrate how "a soul is purged through almsgiving," Anastasius's story implies that giving alms achieved this by transferring some of a donor's sins into the hands of his receiver.[141]

This returns us to the problem of complicity, which earlier Christian authorities had perceived in relation to gifts given to widows in return for their prayers. According to the *Didascalia*, widows who prayed for unrepentant sinners would be required to answer for those sinners on Judgment Day, "as partakers in their works."[142] Such widows effectively risked eternal perdition by bearing their donor's sins, without being able to demand penitential practices from their donor. Indeed, according to the *Apostolic Constitutions*, their willingness to take unworthy gifts made them complicit in "saddening Christ" and thus "defiled" them. These manuals therefore forbid widows from receiving anything directly themselves, requiring all gifts to be screened by the clergy.[143]

That approach was no longer an option for the later clergy of major churches. As emphasized in the last chapter, Chrysostom wanted to promote direct almsgiving, and he left it to individual almsgivers to decide the purity of the resources from which they gave their alms. He envisions the poor accepting whatever was offered to them with the humility of a Lazarus, calling down "countless goods" on their donors while thanking God for supplying their needs. He remarks that the poor served almsgivers better than slaves when they "disrobed" them of their sins.[144] He wanted, of course, to convince elite congregations that the prayers of even a lowly beggar were worthy of their gifts. Yet the imagery he used to promote such redemptive almsgiving also shows the subservience it implied for those who voluntarily received it.

All of this suggests why Early Byzantine hagiographers rarely identify monks or other Christian holy people as recipients of alms.[145] Alms giving might relieve sinners of some of their unjust surplus by putting it into the hands of the poor—thereby restoring a certain harmony between traditional ranks of oppressors and oppressed. But even if given in great quantities, such alms could never be mistaken for charity. Hence, Euphemia's criticism of rich Christians who gave to the poor on the streets of Amida: "A mighty matter it is that you do toward Christ . . . smearing off your superfluities on him, [you] think your charity is great."[146] Charity required more than simply giving away excess resources that should never have been accumulated in the first place. It required, above all, a sacrifice.

"GIVE AS YOUR ALMS FROM THE THINGS WITHIN": ALMS, CHARITY, AND CHRISTIAN ALTRUISM

Having begun this chapter with the scale of almsgiving described in Dorotheus's treatise, let us conclude with a comparable description from fifth- or sixth-century hagiography.

The voluminous Syriac *Life of Barsauma of the North* refers to alms only once, in a passage about sin, repentance, and redemptive almsgiving. Having been exiled to Jerusalem on suspicions of adultery, Empress Eudocia (d. 460) met with the formidable archimandrite Barsauma (d. 457) to seek advice on how to be saved. Barsauma quoted the Book of Daniel: "Absolve your sins with almsgiving and your wickedness with mercy for the weak" (Dn 4:27). This did not comfort the empress, however, for how could she ever sufficiently atone by giving alms? "After all," she explained, "it is not from the work of my hands that alms will be given."

> The martyrs offered their bodies as a sacrifice to God and reconciled him by their physical sufferings. Those who hold vigils and keep fasts give glory to God from the labor of their bodies; indeed, the labor of their bodies is considered equivalent to the

agonies of the martyrs. All the poor, the orphans, and the widows offer the abasement and distress of their bodies to God as a sacrifice; when they give a morsel of bread to others in faith, the sacrifice of their hands is acceptable in heaven, because they give it from the labor of their bodies.

As for me, however much I want to give, my alms shall not be given at the cost of my body's discomfort, but at the cost of the labor and the exhaustion of the poor. My alms will not come out of what I myself need, like those of a pauper, but out of an excess of wealth.

"If a poor man gives a little of what he needs, he will go short," Eudocia pointed out. But "I, even when I have given much, shall lack for nothing. In what way does my almsgiving resemble that of a distressed widow, who has earned a loaf of bread with the labor of her hands and gives half to one poorer than herself?" Barsauma reminded her that Jesus's promise to whoever gave food or clothes to the poor (Mt 25:24–30) had not been addressed to martyrs, monks, or poor people, but to wealthy almsgivers: "If the rich act mercifully toward the poor, they will be spared the misfortune which had been prepared for them." Upon hearing this, Eudocia groveled at his feet: "My lord ... now that I have it on your unerring authority that there is indeed hope for sinners such as me, I shall practice this virtue with all my strength." And so, we are told, she gave copious alms the rest of her life.[147]

Comforting though Barsauma's words might have been, this hagiographer directly correlated the redemption that a gift of alms obtained for its giver with the degree of effort that went into it. Like Dorotheus, the hagiographer clearly believed that all alms were good, but that some were better than others. In addition, since he focused on alms as *zedqē* (that is, as a form of *zaddiqā*, righteousness), his Syriac hagiography envisioned a scale of almsgiving aimed not so much at acquiring a merciful or charitable disposition as at reconciling oneself with God. On his scale, martyrdom, asceticism, and material items offered by poor people held more or less the same weight, having all been given through "dislocation and distress of their bodies." By contrast, anything an empress or rich man offered seemed insufficient. What finally tips the scale in Eudocia's favor, it seems, is her tearful avowal to give alms "with all my strength." Only if augmented with intense humility, the hagiographer implies, could the copious alms of a sinful empress even begin to resemble those of a distressed widow.

Although Barsauma's hagiographer no doubt was influenced by Old Testament notions of righteous reconciliation, he must have also had in mind the New Testament widow whose almsgiving put rich donors to shame by dropping her last two coins into the temple coffers (Mt 12:41–44; Lk 21:1–4). For Chrysostom, such almsgiving qualified as "great" because it derived from essential rather than surplus resources. He and other preachers regularly invoked the widow's example to chide less generous Christians:

Almsgiving is that of the widow who emptied out "all her living." If you cannot contribute as much as the widow, at least contribute your entire surplus: keep what is sufficient, not superfluous. But no one contributes even his surplus.[148]

The theological dimension behind such remarks is indicated when Chrysostom reminds listeners of Christ's generosity: "What charity did he show us? . . . He poured forth his blood—but we not even our money."[149] Exemplary almsgiving—that is, charity—required "emptying out" all that one had to benefit others. Thus, despite the effort of Christian authorities to promote almsgiving by minimizing the effort involved (as when Barsanuphius advised that alms should be given only from "what is at hand"),[150] when it came to redemptive almsgiving there was a tendency to veer toward the standard signaled by Jesus's rebuke to the Pharisees: "Give as your alms from the things that are within, and behold! all will be pure for you" (Lk 11:41).[151]

Such almsgiving was recognized as being too exhaustive for most people, and unnecessary if not performed for the sake of redemption. For the well-meaning laity, it was enough that they should regularly give enough alms to keep their possessions and consumption within healthy limits. The Coptic *Life of Macarius of Scetis* describes how an Egyptian monk taught a widow to give alms to reduce the amount of food she was feeding her son (ten pounds of bread a day!), realizing that a demon had fostered an excessive appetite in the boy that would eventually reduce them both to starvation.[152] More was expected of saintly ascetics. Hence the emphasis in hagiography on monks giving "more than you could possibly imagine," leaving nothing for themselves, their families, or their monasteries. Such selfsacrificial effort made almsgiving tantamount to an expression of charity and was mutually beneficial—that is, redemptive—to givers and receivers alike. "I beg you," Symeon of Emesa reportedly asked a friend in preparation for Judgment Day, "with all your power—and if possible, beyond your power—love your neighbor with almsgiving. For this virtue, above all, will help us then."[153]

With its emphasis on self-denial and self-sacrifice, this higher, charitable standard of almsgiving might seem close to modern notions of a "pure," altruistic, disinterested gift. Dorotheus conceptualized almsgiving motivated "by goodness itself" in comparable terms. Yet as noted above, authorities often discussed even gifts of charity not as purely altruistic gestures, but as gifts that secured salvation for both givers and receivers.[154] What mattered was how much self-interest was directed toward another's benefit. While ordinary almsgiving might be aimed at securing benefits exclusively for its giver, charity was thought to produce gains for its giver and its recipient alike, on the belief that another person's salvation resulted in one's own. One might say that this was the self-interested nature of Christian self-sacrifice. When affirming his intention to plead for mercy for all within his monastery, Barsanuphius explained that he considered "the gain and the advantage of every human, every soul to be my own." For this reason, he added, "I would gladly burn as a sacrifice for the sake of your souls."[155]

Such charitable exchanges may have been conceivable only in small, intentional communities like the Seridos monastery, focused on fostering a fusion of souls. Barsanuphius and John both indicated that a capacity to give "for the sake of goodness itself," as Dorotheus described, was attained only by suppressing all worldly inclinations toward "giving and receiving, people-pleasing and the like." This rendered a monk's heart pure enough to receive God's love alone.[156] Years of self-denial had reduced these two anchorites and their possessions to practically nothing, so that all they had left to give had to come from deep within themselves, and therefore came out purely as charity.

Of course, Barsanuphius's and John's ability to dispense prayers continuously from within their cells was sustained by their monastery's ability to secure surplus material resources from the outside. Although we know nothing about the finances of the Seridos monastery, the "thousands of coins" that Isaiah of Scetis received from monks entering his community may indicate how much other monasteries in Gaza might receive. This returns us to an interesting dilemma: how could any monastic community reconcile such material infusions with an ascetic calculus that reckoned most material gains a spiritual loss? "Just as life and death cannot coincide in the same person at the same time," wrote Evagrius of Pontus, "so too is it impossible for charity to coexist in a person along with money. For charity is destructive not only of money, but of our transitory life itself."[157] It is true that Evagrius, like Barsanuphius, was an anchorite, and that their ascetic calculus was largely a feature of anchoretic rather than cenobitic discourse. Yet how did cenobitic authorities view their institutions' capacity for charity in light of their acquisition of wealth?

This question is central to the next chapter, but two solutions immediately appear. First, the charitable culture of the Seridos monastery envisioned manual labor itself as an expression of "laying down one's soul" for a brother—that is, a charitable gift of burden bearing.[158] In that case, the physical exertion and generous intention that junior monks displayed through such activities could offset whatever material gains they produced. Second, the practice of fasting could always generate an untainted surplus, when needed. Such charitable self-denial had long been recommended as a means by which Christians could acquire enough resources to give to others.[159]

Monastic authorities, however, conceived of a third source of surplus resources that required neither labor nor self-sacrifice but remained nonetheless "pure" by definition. These were material gains that came from God. Egyptian desert tradition includes a story about an anchorite and his disciple that may have been known to Dorotheus and his cenobitic disciples:

> The elder was merciful [eleēmōn], and when a famine arose people came to his gate to receive charity. He provided small loaves of bread to all. . . . Seeing his intention,

God blessed his bread so it did not run out. . . . But prosperity returned and the needy kept coming to receive charity. One day the brother saw their supply had run out. A *ptōchos* came and the elder [told him] to give the bread. The brother said, "There is none, Father." But the elder replied, "Go look." The brother went and found their basket filled with bread. Seeing this he was afraid; he took and gave to the *ptōchos*. Learning the elder's faithful virtue, he praised God.[160]

As might be expected, this story presents an elder's effort to give away all he possessed for the sake of others as an exemplary expression of mercy, resulting in material gifts of charity. Yet it also presents those possessions as material products of God's blessing. As we shall see in the next chapter, such material "blessings" were not just figments of hagiographical imaginations but important facets of monastic economies and a pivotal feature of the Early Byzantine repertoire of Christian gifts.

"What God Has Put in Your Heart to Give"

Divine Patronage, Sacred Wealth, and Material Blessings

Early in the fifth century, decades before Theodosius the Cenobiarch built his cenobium southeast of Jerusalem, another Cappadocian monk formed a small monastery on an arid ridge overlooking the desert northeast of Jerusalem, not too far from the main road.

Initially known only to nomads and goatherds, this community seemed unlikely to last, but for its chance discovery by a group of hungry pilgrims traveling between Jericho and Jerusalem. As the hagiographer Cyril of Scythopolis (d. ca. 559) explained a century later, one day four hundred Armenian pilgrims veered off the road and headed for the monastery searching for food. Seeing them approach, the monastery's abbot and founder, Euthymius (377–473), told his steward to prepare something to eat. When this steward, named Domitian, responded that there was barely enough for themselves, let alone all these unexpected guests, Euthymius simply replied, "They shall eat and have something left over" (cf. 2 Kgs 4:44). Cyril explains what happened next:

> Going to the small cell called by some the pantry, where a few loaves were lying, Domitian was unable to open the door, for God's blessing had filled it right to the top. So calling some of the men, he took the door off its hinges, and out poured loaves from the cell. The same blessing occurred likewise with the wine and the oil. All ate and were satisfied [cf. Mt 15:37; Mk 8:8], and for three months they were unable to reattach the door of the cell. Just as God through the Prophet's voice made the jar of meal and cruse of oil well up for the hospitable widow [1 Kgs 17:14], so too He granted this godly elder a supply of blessings equal to his zeal for hospitality.

After Domitian apologized for having been so "human" in his way of thinking, Euthymius pointed out that their future depended on receiving all strangers honorably, reminding him of the Apostle Paul's remark "He who sows in blessings will also reap in blessings" (2 Cor 9:6).[1] And so it turned out: thereafter their monastery "began to be blessed in both income and expenditures," eventually rivaling even Theodosius's grand cenobium in size.[2] Today its ruins, precariously preserved in a busy industrial zone (Mishor Adummim, Israel), attest the wealth that an Early Byzantine monastery could amass by receiving a steady supply of material blessings.

Blessing is indeed the operative word (*eulogia* in Greek, *burktā* in Syriac, *smou* in Coptic, *benedictio* in Latin), and not just in Cyril's hagiography, but in nearly all descriptions of God-given wealth in this era. As Cyril's narrative illustrates, it denoted not only the divine force that made something increase ("for God's blessing . . . filled it") and the material results of that increase ("He granted . . . a supply of blessings") but also the material resources from which those increases were made ("he who sows in blessings will also reap in blessings"). Such stories were patently inspired by Old and New Testament miracles like Elisha's multiplication of the twenty loaves (2 Kgs 4:42–44) and Jesus's feeding of the multitudes with a few loaves and fishes (Mt 14:13–21; Mk 6:30–44, 8:1–10; Lk 9:10–17; Jn 6:1–13). Due to their miraculous, scriptural, and seemingly stereotypical features, they have rarely been taken seriously in relation to reality.[3] Yet the fact that Cyril concludes his narrative with a description of material growth presented in plain economic jargon ("blessed in both income and expenditures") indicates that he was not just repeating a topos but employing a discourse on sacred wealth characterized by references to material gifts called blessings.

This chapter explores what such "blessings" meant, how they functioned, what their sources were, what concerns and relationships they did (or did not) imply, and how they differed from other gifts, religious and secular, in the late Roman East. Although certain examples, like those that the Piacenza Pilgrim collected, have been extensively studied in isolation—especially the clay and lead ampullas now displayed in museums, which once were filled with oil, dust, or other materials and given to pilgrims at sacred sites and healing shrines—there remains a tendency to understand this gift phenomenon solely on the basis of those examples.[4] As Cyril's account indicates, however, such flasks were only a small part of a much broader church and monastic gift economy based on the receipt, distribution, and consumption of a wide variety of material blessings. Indeed, though often discussed in the context of miracle stories like the one Cyril tells, these Early Byzantine blessings were not magic gifts. They were manifestations of a distinct category grounded in Paul's explanation in Second Corinthians of the type of donation he wanted his followers to provide—a gift he called a *eulogia*, a blessing—in support of "holy people" in Jerusalem (2 Cor 9:5–12). In this passage, Paul provided details that later authorities used to conceptualize a gift that theoretically could not only support Christian holy people but also generate pure, sacred wealth, untainted by greed and other forms of worldly *pleonexia*.

We are arguably dealing here with the earliest evidence of a "pure," disinterested gift, deliberately invented and defined as such, in Western civilization. This ideal only becomes fully manifest as such, however, from the fifth century onward.[5] According to John Chrysostom, when Paul used the word *eulogia* in Second Corinthians, he had meant a gift of alms, which he had called a blessing only because "it was ancient custom to call it so."[6] Even if Chrysostom was correct in this supposition that this is what Paul meant (no earlier evidence supports it), his explanation implies that alms and blessings were no longer considered identical gift ideals in his own day, and certainly no authority suggests an easy equivalence between the two. This does not mean that blessings were not akin to alms or other gifts. It is clear that they were often derived from lay offerings and could be used in turn to produce alms for the poor. Yet, certain features distinguished blessings not only from alms and charity (both always given to people in need, while blessings often were not) but also from offerings (all ultimately given to God, while blessings never were). As mentioned in the introduction to this book, a papyrus found in the ruins of a seventh-century monastery in southern Palestine preserves lists that carefully distinguish the *eulogiai* the monastery received from the *prosphorai* (offerings) it received. These lists not only confirm that these two types of gifts were considered conceptually different, but they also indicate that patrons who gave offerings expected them to be used according to their requests, while those who gave blessings did not.[7]

As that papyrus document attests, the significance of Christian blessings becomes most apparent when viewed in a framework of religious patronage and patronal gifts. Ideally, anything given as a blessing liberated church or monastic recipients from the demands that patronal donations in Early Byzantium (or any era) usually imposed. Its most obvious secular counterparts were traditional Greco-Roman gifts known as *xenia*. Theoretically "hospitality" gifts, these were often less gracious than that name suggests, being frequently (if not always) used to confirm unequal patron-client relationships, implying expectations that recipients would return favors at a later date.[8] Church and monastic writers sometimes make the correspondence between *xenia* and blessings explicit.[9] Nonetheless, we shall see that most authors of this period represented Christian blessings as intrinsically different from all other gifts and, indeed, divine. As we shall see, their emergence from the fifth century onward can be partly explained as a response to the problems that arose from potentially compromising interactions between religious and secular concerns in general, and between religious professionals and lay patrons in particular. In other words, this Christian pure gift ideal gained definition over time in contrast to the worldly gifts that usually attended patronage in the Early Byzantine secular sphere.[10]

Essential to this ideal was the notion that God was the ultimate patron of any Christian institution and that donors who gave blessings were merely acting as his agents, transmitting his divinely created material goods to their deserving recipients.

This religious conviction, along with other related conceits and practices, helped Christian professionals reconcile their general dependence on the gifts of lay donors with their need to maintain a sense of purity, integrity, and detachment from worldly concerns. According to this view, all that God demanded of recipients of his blessings was that they be shared with anyone who asked. This closely connected them with the fulfillment of Jesus's command to "give to all who ask of thee" (Mt 5:42; cf. Lk 6:30) and, thus, the fulfillment of the universal aspirations of Early Byzantine philanthropy.

The following pages therefore examine the invention and nature of a new Christian ideal: a material gift that theoretically originated from God, that imposed no obligation on its human givers or recipients, and that passed on a vital spirit of increase and healing whenever properly given. Largely a fixture of cenobitic discourse, this gift ideal helps explain how Christian authorities sought to promote generosity without demanding a depletion or sacrifice of essential goods. At the same time, it provided a symbol signaling the favored status of "holy people" within God's providential order, while presenting a key for understanding ascetic Christian notions of sacred wealth.

THE PAULINE CONCEPT OF A CHRISTIAN BLESSING

The variety of material items designated as blessings in this period has not gone unnoticed. Besides flasks of oil, dirt or dust received at Holy Land sites or shrines,[11] they include bits of skin, hair, or fingernails dispensed by Christian holy people, often compounded with oil as healing talismans or medicaments (e.g., ḥnāna),[12] as well as sanctified relics or objects placed in contact with them;[13] bread prepared for, but not used in, a liturgy;[14] bread, fruit, and other victuals given to visitors as hospitality by solitaries or at monasteries;[15] and various tokens of communion that churches, bishops, and abbots sent one another—usually loaves of bread, but also figs, shoes, and clothing (Gregory the Great once gave another bishop a horse).[16] At the same time, the word was applied to gifts in cash or kind that laypeople gave to church leaders, monasteries, or solitaries, sometimes on occasion of a festival, but not always.[17] This range is more diverse than what we find for other religious gifts. So was *blessing* just a term that Early Byzantine Christians used to describe any religious gift? Or were there specific ideals, expectations, or uses that made a blessing different from others?

Of course, for readers of the Old and New Testaments, the word *blessing* had rich connotations. It was through God's *beraka* that the world was created and could be again revived; by blessing just five loaves and two fish, Jesus fed multitudes in the desert (Mt 14:19; Lk 9:16). The word conjured fields made fertile and offspring plentiful, with the promise of more to come: Isaac says of his preferred son, Jacob, "The smell of my son is like the smell of a field that the Lord has blessed" (Gn 27:27).[18] This meant that anything called a blessing in this period was in some way associated with divine favor and benevolence. Yet the question remains how to account for the application of the word *blessing* to material gifts, since such a usage is rarely attested in the Old Testament (only five times in the Septuagint, without discernable consistency),[19] not attested at all in rabbinic literature or Gospel narratives,[20] and appears rather late in Christian sources, where, as seen above, it is often exemplified by objects so banal or profane (e.g., a horse) that scholars have regarded it simply as a casual Christian word for a gift, without bearing any special connotation or sense.

Those who have tried to trace the origin of this Christian usage have naturally focused on its earliest non-scriptural example, which is found in the regulations for *Agapē* (i.e., Charity) Feasts preserved in a third-century church manual known as the *Apostolic Tradition*. This states that participants should "take a little bread from the bishop's hand before they break their own bread, because this [bread from the bishop's hand] is a *eulogia*, not a *eucharistia*, that is, a [symbol of the] Body of the Lord." It further states that if their bishop were absent, participants should receive their *eulogia* from a priest, since "laypeople are not allowed to give *eulogia*."[21] This passage, despite the many obscurities surrounding it, has given rise to what might be called a "liturgico-historical" theory about the origin of material gifts called blessings in Christian tradition. According to this theory, the earliest Christians had used the terms *eulogia* and *eucharistia* interchangeably to refer to the bread and wine they brought to a communal feast. But as the eucharist evolved into a formal ritual detached from communal Charity Feasts, technical language also evolved: *eucharistia* remained a designation for liturgical gifts of gratitude that were consecrated by a bishop at an altar (a.k.a. *prosphorai*, which we discuss in chapter 7), while *eulogiai* became reserved for communal gifts that were verbally blessed (thereby becoming "blessings") but not consecrated or used during the liturgy. Usually consisting of loaves of bread, these *eulogiai* were distributed at the Charity Feasts held after a liturgy, dispensed to catechumens not yet allowed to receive the *eucharistia*, or sent to other church communities as tokens of solidarity. From these precedents, it is argued, the word gradually became applied to Christian gifts in general, no matter how remote from a liturgical context.

This remains the consensus explanation for the origin of this phenomenon.[22] Certain evidence would seem to support it. Besides the *Apostolic Tradition*, Paul refers to eucharist wine as a "cup of blessing that we bless" (1 Cor 10:16), thereby connecting a verbal blessing to the creation of a material blessing in a liturgical context; hagiography sometimes refers to Christian leaders exchanging "bread of blessing," making plain that these were liturgical remnants,[23] and there are other reasons to associate bread *eulogiai* with church liturgies, as we shall see. But this liturgico-historical theory is, for the most part, wrong. Indeed, by presuming that a verbal blessing was necessary to create a material blessing, the theory implies that only gifts created that way represent genuine blessings, suggesting that all other examples not created in that way represent an inferior or corrupt version of such gifts and practices. That hardly explains either the range or the high regard ascribed to non-liturgical blessings in Early Byzantine literature.

The correct and more comprehensive explanation is found in Second Corinthians (9:5–12). Invoked by Cyril of Scythopolis to contextualize the blessings that Euthymius's monastery received, this passage provides the scriptural key for understanding the origin, range, and significance of such Christian gifts. Paul wrote it in advance of the emissaries he was sending to collect funds from the Christian community at Corinth to support the apostolic leadership (whom he simply calls "the holy ones") in Jerusalem. To this end, he repeatedly uses the word *eulogia* to describe the resources he wanted the Corinthians to donate. Since modern translations tend to obscure Paul's distinctive Greek phrasing (for example, the Revised Standard Version renders *eulogia* variously as a "bountiful gift," a "voluntary gift," and so on, but never as a "blessing"), it is important to restate more literally what he wrote in this passage:

> I thought it necessary to ask the brothers to go on ahead to you and arrange in advance this blessing [*eulogian*] that you have promised, so that it may be ready as a blessing [*eulogian*] and not as an extortion [*pleonexian*]. [6] The point is this: he who sows sparingly will also reap sparingly [cf. Prv 22:8], but he who sows in blessings [*ep' eulogiais*] will also reap in blessings [*ep' eulogiais*]. [7] So let each give as intended in his heart, not with grief or under compulsion, for God loves a cheerful giver [cf. Prv 22:8a]. [8] And God is able to make every grace [*charin*] abound in excess [*perisseusai*] for you, so that by having enough of everything, you may abound with excess [*perisseuēte*] for every good work, [9] as it is written,
> "He scatters abroad, He gives to the poor,
>   His righteousness endures forever [Ps 112:9]."
> [10] Indeed, He who supplies seeds to the sower and bread for food will supply and multiply your seed for sowing and make the harvest of your righteousness increase. [11] In every way you will be enriched for every generosity [*en panti ploutizomenoi eis pasan haplotēta*], which will produce thanksgiving [*eucharistia*] to God through us; [12] for rendering this ministration not only relieves the wants of the holy people, but also makes abundant excess [*perisseuousa*] through many thanksgivings [*eucharistiai*] to God.[24]

This passage has never been cited to explain the use and concept of material blessings (or their relation to the Eucharist) in early Christianity or Early Byzantium. Whatever Jewish precedents or rabbinic practices might have inspired Paul,[25] his presentation of this gift ideal provided a rich semantic field for later development. Indeed, it clarifies the Early Byzantine blessings phenomenon and related discourse in at least four ways.

In the first place, it explains the universal application of the word *blessing* in different regions and languages to a wide variety of material Christian gifts, ranging from Gregory's horse to liturgical supplies, to cash donations and other provisions given by laypeople to the acknowledged "holy people" of Early Byzantium—namely, clerics and monks (especially, but not only, those living around Jerusalem). Furthermore, it demonstrates that we need not seek the origin of such gifts in a verbal blessing, liturgy, or contact with items already blessed, as previously supposed.[26] Those circumstances might be involved as well, as often in the case of *ḥnāna*. But they are rarely mentioned or even implied in our descriptions, because they were not, in fact, needed to create a genuine blessing.[27] As Paul himself explains (2 Cor 9:7), the essential spirit creating such a gift arose from each donor's heart—a point recognized by later authorities, as we shall see.

Second, Paul in this passage forcefully articulates what blessings were not supposed to be. He explicitly contrasts a *eulogia* against any item associated with *pleonexia*. We have seen this word before. Usually translated in this passage as "an extortion," Paul probably meant gifts of deference that powerful people typically exacted from peasants and other dependents (cf. the Syriac word *'iqārē*, "gifts of honor"). Here the contrast between a blessing and a gift of *pleonexia* may recall the contrast between a gift of alms and *pleonexia* discussed in the last chapter. But that does not make a blessing the equivalent of an alms. Although anything that is kindly given might be called an alms, Paul specifically presents blessings as the products of divinely sanctioned wealth rooted in both God's foundational gift of grace (*charis*) and a material surplus amassed through generosity (*haplotēs*), not plunder or greed. Moreover, he also contrasts it with anything given involuntarily, or otherwise associated with any sense of compulsion or grief. Altogether, this made blessings not only qualitatively different from gifts of alms, but also a convenient symbol of clean wealth, fit for anyone to either give or receive, but especially for relieving "the wants of holy ones." Indeed, although Paul refers to these Christians elsewhere as "the holy *ptōchoi*" (Rom 15:25), it is perhaps significant that he does not mention poor people as intended recipients of Christian blessings. At any rate the Early Byzantine discourse on blessings is mainly concerned with interactions between lay and holy people, not between rich and poor.

Third, Paul articulates here what gifts called blessings were themselves ideally supposed to be. In terms of spirit or intent, they were things given freely and cheerfully, without any sense of compulsion or grief. But equally essential was his repeated use of the verb *perisseuō*—variously meaning "to be abundant," "to possess in excess," or "to be left over"—to describe the state of both giver and gift. According to Paul, blessings were to derive from whatever surplus resources or superfluity (*perisseia*) God had granted beyond what Christians needed for their own consumption or use. Therefore, the gifts that were derived from such divinely given, excess resources represented something not just divine, but something extra, left over, or supplemental (*perisseuma*)—in other words, something that could be easily given away freely and cheerfully, as would please God ("for God loves a cheerful giver"). Ideally, a blessing provided its recipient with something extra to pass on to others, initiating a generous flow of God-given surplus.[28]

Finally, Paul emphasizes throughout the passage the potential of such gifts to multiply, employing agrarian imagery to conjure spontaneous growth sprung from a generous scattering of seeds. In particular, his remark that whoever sows "in blessings" would also reap "in blessings," as well as his promise that such donors would be "enriched in every way" for their generosity, provided the terminology and logic behind Cyril's hagiographical account of Euthymius's material prosperity and other depictions of monastic wealth. As we shall see, such hagiography was not altogether fanciful. Rather, it reflected a contemporary ascetic concern to handle surplus material goods with sufficient spiritual detachment to encourage their circulation and flow rather than their hoarding.

Thus, distinctive features of the Early Byzantine discourse on material blessings were established by Paul. Here as elsewhere he provided the language and logic that helped Christian institutions function on their own terms in the Roman world. Preaching outside Carthage, Augustine of Hippo (354–430) invoked this passage to expound the right of clerics to live on whatever Christians brought to church, while Chrysostom used it to convince audiences to give from their superfluous material resources, since "no one who gives a blessing feels any grief."[29] Most striking, however, is how this Pauline gift ideal inspired the provisioning of rations called blessings in church and monastic settings, an institutional development well attested in the late Roman East.

THE INSTITUTIONAL AND LAY PROVISION OF MATERIAL BLESSINGS

Undoubtedly, the most common source of material blessings was the liturgy. As discussed in chapter 7, it remained customary in late antiquity for lay Christians to contribute their own bread offerings to a communal eucharist service.[30] Although bringing such offerings (*prosphorai* in Greek, *qurbānē* in Syriac, *oblationes* in Latin) was encouraged and perhaps even expected, they were technically not required—certainly, lay participants were not supposed to feel compelled to offer them. Usually consisting of small round loaves, sometimes marked with a cross and stamped EULOGIA THEOU or EULOGIA KYRIOU in advance, these were added to and supplemented those which the church or monastery conducting the service prepared from its own reserves.[31] All received a verbal blessing, but only the institution's oblation, it seems, was consecrated and used at the altar. One result of this process was a potential superfluity of leftover blessed bread.

What happened to these excess blessings? It is usually presumed that they were distributed to the laity after the service like the *antidora* and *pains bénits* of medieval times. Yet there is no clear evidence that this regularly happened in our period.[32] In fact, just the opposite: according to a fourth-century section of the *Apostolic Constitutions* entitled "Concerning Leftovers," superfluous *eulogiai* were to be divided among the clergy after the service, and no distribution to the laity is mentioned at all:

> By consent of the bishop or priests, let the deacons distribute to the clergy blessings [*eulogiai*] that are superfluous at the mysteries: let four portions go to the bishop, three to priests, two to deacons, and one to the others, the subdeacons, readers, psalm-singers, and deaconesses. For it is good and agreeable to God to honor each according to rank, since the Church is not a school of disorder but of good order.[33]

Practices probably differed from place to place. Yet this pronouncement by the fourth-century compilers of the *Apostolic Constitutions*, which became the definitive ruling on the subject for churches in the Roman and Sassanian (later, Arab) Near East,[34] indicates that the distribution of leftover liturgical blessings in Early Byzantium was normally restricted to the clergy.

To summarize, church clerics could regularly count on receiving surplus blessings based on the loaves of bread that laypeople brought to church each week as offerings for God.[35] This helps explain how such blessings could become more narrowly identified as a source of supplemental income for church clerics, as well as a symbol of church wealth more generally, in the Eastern empire.

There was a difference in the way church personnel were paid in Western and Eastern Christendom. Even before the Western empire's collapse, church clergy there received no salaries or fixed income, but were paid instead through a dividend system whereby all proceeds of a diocese (ranging from lay offerings and contributions to rents or the sale of produce from church domains) were pooled together each month and divided among the clerical staff. In the East, however, church clerics received a fixed monthly salary like other state employees, graded according to rank.[36] Stable though such salaries were, they were never high, partly because it was expected that clerics would supplement them by dividing up (among other things) any blessings generated by a liturgy. This feature of Eastern church finance is illustrated by a letter that Severus of Antioch wrote ca. 519–525 to a fellow bishop, advising on whether priests who had retired should continue to receive a portion of the residual blessings:

> As to the question you ask about priests who have grown old, I mean whether their share in the customary distribution of the blessings [*būrkāthā*] ought to be cut off from them on the grounds that they cannot perform the sacred ministry, and others introduced in their place who ought to be supported, and receive the portion cut off from these, know that such a thing is not legal, nor otherwise holy.[37]

Evidently there were not always enough blessings to go around: we hear of priests in rural Syria overstocking altars with bread to ensure they would have more to take home afterward.[38] That does not seem to have been a regular problem in urban churches, however. As noted in the first chapter of this book, certain major bishoprics were issued a supply of grain each year by the Roman state, to be delivered by governors and used at a bishop's discretion.[39] Presumably some of this was used to provide liturgical bread that might go to the clergy after a service. This would have been especially true at metropolitan churches. As Pope Leo reminded Bishop Dioscorus of Alexandria in the fifth century, it was supposed to be policy for metropolitan bishops to perform a eucharist each week in their central churches for the entire Christian population of their city. Logistically, that required preparing large quantities of liturgical loaves for the church service in advance. This institutional provisioning, when combined with supplemental loaves brought by the laity, would have predictably generated many leftover bread blessings.[40] According to the church historian Socrates, it was a praiseworthy habit of a wealthy Novatian bishop in Constantinople not to take anything from his church except for the "two loaves of the *eulogiai*" he took every Sunday.[41] That was an exquisitely small amount—but Socrates's point was both that this bishop was so wealthy that he needed nothing more, and that more was always available.

Such examples make clear that leftover bread blessings represented a significant element of clerical support in Early Byzantine churches. No author directly relates this to what Paul wrote in Second Corinthians, but there are interesting parallels. As already mentioned, the liturgical offerings from which such blessings derived were supposed to be voluntary. Not only that: the bread loaves used for such offerings were apparently made readily available so that laypeople could both purchase it and give it away easily, for cheap. The fact that John Moschus, writing in the early seventh century, equates a bread *eulogia* with a "twenty-bit offering" indicates that such loaves were known to be regularly sold (bakers are said to have set out tables in front of the metropolitan church at Emesa, evidently to sell bread) at a low, standard price.[42] Thus, nearly anyone might have enough resources to contribute something at church. In turn, the resulting leftovers helped supply the wants of needy holy people. These residual blessings, however small, had great symbolic value as a God-given windfall, adding a little extra to the meager salary Christian clerics otherwise received. Ideally, the loaves provided just enough to enable them to bestow blessings on others if occasion arose. Augustine mentions sending "*eulogiae* of bread, generously and cheerfully given" to a layperson.[43] His words, lifted from Second Corinthians (9:7, 11), attest not only his awareness of Paul's teachings on generosity but perhaps also his use of leftover liturgical blessings to carry them out.

Thus, from blessings might come blessings indeed, as Paul had promised. Occurring every week at churches large and small, this liturgical process probably generated the most recognizable examples of such gifts in Early Byzantium. Yet also significant was the role of material blessings in monastic life. Already in the fourth century, the Spanish pilgrim Egeria reports regularly receiving *eulogiai* of fruit or bread from various monastic communities she visited in Palestine and the Sinai: "It is customary for monks to give them to those they welcome in their monasteries."[44] We similarly hear of desert solitaries in Egypt or monasteries in Constantinople giving *eulogiai* to guests on their departure.[45] Although this custom of giving gifts upon departure had Old Testament and classical precedents (cf. the *xenia*, discussed below), its monastic practice was facilitated by an institutional policy of issuing supplemental rations, as can be inferred from oblique references in our sources. Hagiography from the fifth to seventh centuries frequently depicts monks dispensing edible blessings, otherwise undescribed, in quantities of three.[46] There are also multiple references to loaves of bread being eaten by monks or given to guests to eat in quantities of three.[47] We are told that monks travelling in the Palestinian desert took with them "small blessings of bread," and that one of these, the legendary hermit Mary, on deciding to become an anchorite, made it her first act to buy three loaves of bread "as a ration [*ephodion*] of blessing."[48] At first we might think this "three loaves" motif derives from the Gospel of Luke (Lk 11:5–6), where Jesus urges disciples to pray as if asking a neighbor for "three loaves of bread" to feed a guest who suddenly arrived at midnight. Yet nothing in hagiography suggests that this detail had such a scriptural origin, nor does it appear in Western hagiography as we might expect if it were scripturally inspired. How then, should we account for so many references to bread blessings being given or received by monks in quantities of three?

It appears they reflect a system of bread rationing in Early Byzantine monasteries: a supplemental three-loaf ration of blessings, perhaps modeled on the three-loaf ration of bread that landowners of this era issued to workers laboring in their fields during harvest time.[49] There is considerable evidence for such a monastic ration in non-hagiographical sources. In his study of dietary rules at Shenoute's White Monastery in Upper Egypt, Bentley Layton notes that Shenoute allowed his monks to receive an extra supply of bread beyond what they otherwise received at a daily meal. Shenoute permitted them to keep this supplemental bread in their cells, "provided they never accumulate more than three loaves at a time." Layton calls this three-loaf allowance "an explicit feature" of Shenoute's monastic system.[50] Shenoute himself attributed it to the good will of his monastic forebears, perhaps referring to Pachomius's fourth-century monasteries where flat bread cakes (*korsenēlia*) were handed out directly to monks or through their leaders after a meal, in quantities "enough for three days."[51] That such an allowance was also standard in Syrian monasteries is suggested by a monastic rule: "No one can give anything without [permission of] the abbot, except for three loaves of bread."[52] None of these rules refer to such loaves as blessings. Yet a letter written by Barsanuphius indicates that this was what they were commonly called in the sixth century. Barsanuphius was responding to another anchorite, who had requested that the Old Man send him a *eulogia* because visitors had unexpectedly arrived at his cell. Barsanuphius understood what his colleague meant, but replied that he was unable to send such a loaf because he had no more than "the three loaves of bread assigned per week."[53]

For recluses like Barsanuphius, such rations may indeed have represented the only bread their cenobium issued to them each week; Mary the hermit is said to have subsisted on her three small loaves for seventeen years.[54] The bread in question was probably dry hardtack of the sort commonly used in the late Roman army. Typically, this came in flat, thick, unleavened discs (*paxamatia*) that could be stored indefinitely and made edible by sprinkling with water.[55] What must be emphasized is that for most monks, this ration of bread blessings (known to John Moschus and monks of Gaza as "the *eulogia* of the Fathers") was a supplementary allowance, provided in addition to whatever else cenobites received at refectory meals or anchorites procured through manual labor or foraging.[56] Analogous to the bread supplied to clerics by their church, this was an integral feature of monastic life, furnishing monks with a small supply of extra resources they could consume as needed or use to provide as alms or blessings for others.

To be sure, rationing procedures must have differed from place to place, and restrictions sometimes applied. Pachomius forbad any solitary in his confederation from giving his "small loaves" to anyone "as a favor, not even to someone going away";[57] other controls on their circulation within monasteries will be discussed below. It must be emphasized, however, that no prohibitions are attested preventing cenobitic monks from giving their blessings to outsiders (as noted above, Syrian monks were explicitly allowed to give up to three loaves without permission from their abbot). Indeed, this supplemental allowance may have originated as a means of preventing monks from pilfering their monastery's communal supplies, whether to satisfy their own hunger or that of their relatives. That problem is attested in numerous sources, and indicates the pressure some felt to share their institution's goods with family or strangers beyond its gates.[58] Barsanuphius and John advised that cenobitic readers give a "small *eulogia*" to whatever beggar came by.[59] Anything could be given as such, but perhaps nothing as easily as the extra bread blessings those readers regularly received from their monastery for free.

Thus, like churches, monasteries had systems for providing supplemental resources called blessings built into their institutional structures. For dependent hermits residing deep in the desert, these life-saving rations could easily be imagined to have been sent down by God when delivered each week on the back of a monastery mule.[60] Similarly, cenobitic monks were supposed to consider the supplies that generated them to be blessings that God bestowed on their community in recognition of their generosity, to help them do even more good works, as Cyril of Scythopolis and other hagiographers explain. But how did these monasteries actually obtain such surplus material resources?

Sometimes they must have derived from monastic labor and thrift, as the Egyptian desert tradition suggests. Industrious solitaries at Scetis were said to have pooled together enough resources from their labor each week to enable them to indulge in a blessing of bread and wine before departing to their individual cells after the Sunday service.[61] But the most attested source of such surplus resources was the ad hoc donations and permanent endowments that monks received from admiring outsiders, especially from pious laypeople. That seems to have been true everywhere, but is best documented in Palestine and Egypt.[62] This was not simply because the Holy Land attracted so many pilgrims like the Piacenza Pilgrim's *Christianissimus* who were eager to support local ascetics, or because the Bishop of Jerusalem subsidized Chalcedonian monasteries and solitaries in his diocese (as suggested by John Moschus's reference to a Chalcedonian monk who subsisted only on the "*eulogia* of the church" he received each week from his church in Palestine).[63] This was also because distant communities of lay Christians in both West and East (perhaps including the Persian Empire) frequently sent contributions to supply the wants of their "Jerusalem saints." In making and collecting such donations, such communities were self-consciously fulfilling the precepts that Paul had set down for the Corinthians. Jerome (d. 420), a Western monk living in Bethlehem, praised his patron Lucinus in Spain for "sustaining with [his] abundance the needs of many" living in Palestine and Egypt, selecting his words from Second Corinthians 8:14 for that purpose.[64]

The result was a Holy Land enriched by a generous flow of material blessings. This was openly celebrated. Pilgrims who wished to dispense coins as blessings could find monks lined up around Jerusalem, ready to receive. John Moschus tells of a dog that alerted various abbots when a visitor wanting to distribute such gifts had arrived in the Jordan valley; Theodore of Petra describes how Theodosius's monks urged him to attend a distribution near Bethlehem where donors were giving a third of a solidus to each who showed up, enough for a person to live on for months.[65] But not all distributions were so random. We hear of several aristocratic patrons dispensing their blessings from afar on a predictable, annual basis. Cyril of Scythopolis refers to large sums being provided each year as blessings for Euthymius and other Palestinian abbots, noting, for example, the *eulogia* that Euthymius received each year from a magistrate of Antioch and the fixed sum of gold that a senator at Constantinople sent each year as a blessing to Theodosius.[66] He makes clear that both abbots depended on such annuities to dispense blessings of their own to visitors on a major scale. He reports that Euthymius even sent a monastic priest to collect the sum a patron had promised to send each year—an indication of how reliant some monasteries became on the predictable receipt of such supplemental blessings.[67]

It is important to recognize that Cyril's use of the word *eulogia* to describe such annual benefactions reflected actual monastic parlance of the day. As already noted, archaeologists excavating Nessana in southern Palestine in the 1930s discovered an invaluable cache of papyri related to a local monastic church of Sergius and Bacchus. Besides the registers of offerings and blessings preserved in *P. Ness. III* 79, another document in this archive (*P. Ness. III* 80) preserves a list of *eulogiai* given to the monastery ca. 685 by nine lay donors in varying quantities of wheat, adding up to nearly a thousand pounds.[68] We do not know if such *eulogiai* were akin to the annuities mentioned by Cyril of Scythopolis, or how they were used after their receipt. The list shows, however, that even a small monastery (the Nessana monastery could have housed only a handful of monks) might gain enough in lay donations of grain to provide bread blessings of its own.[69] The Nessana list also reflects a concern to record benefactors' names—perhaps to confirm that someone had fulfilled a promise, or perhaps to note those who might be counted on to provide such donations again in the future.

Thus, lay blessings represented a crucial source of the surplus material resources that Christian clerics, monks, and monasteries received in Early Byzantium (a closely related source, a type of thank-offering called a *karpophoria*, will be discussed in the next chapter). Rarely do we learn how donors themselves regarded or spoke about these gifts, but it is important to see how holy people were taught to think about them. Already in the fourth century, Basil of Caesarea had instructed monks to regard their lay benefactors as agents of God, whom God had inspired to deliver his benefits.[70] During the fifth, sixth, and seventh centuries, Isaiah of Scetis, Barsanuphius, and Leontius of Neapolis all attest a comparable way of thinking: when someone gave a blessing, it was because God had "put it in [their] heart" to give.[71] Antony of Choziba remarks that the blessings his abbot regularly received from his divine patron, the Theotokos, enabled him to give alms in her name even beyond his ability.[72] Similarly, John Moschus presents a Jerusalem priest who gave food to beggars as explaining, "It is not I who provides this, but my Mistress, the Mother of God, who feeds both them and me."[73] Such imagined cooperation between human and divine agents ascribed all such blessings to Providence. In turn, it made any lay gift potentially acceptable as a blessing. "If God knows that I need something, and plants in someone [the impulse] to offer it," Barsanuphius remarked, "I welcome it."[74]

This Early Byzantine conceit recalls how Paul himself had explained the origin of a material blessing: it was specifically a gift that Christians "intended in their hearts" to give out of the surplus God had given them (2 Cor 9:7). Having established the use and importance of such gifts in church and monastic institutions of the era, we may turn to their symbolic significance. But first I should clarify how and why they were thought to differ from other types of patronal gifts in the late Roman East. Paul aside, what need was there for religious authorities to idealize a Christian blessing in Early Byzantium?

HUMAN AVARICE AND DIVINE PATRONAGE

Since no Early Byzantine authority explains outright what Christian blessings were supposed to signify to their givers or recipients, it is instructive to note a story preserved in the ninth-century *Chronicle* of Theophanes the Confessor:

> In this year [447/8 CE] Chrysaphius, a eunuch who exercised power over the palace . . . suggested to the emperor, who was quite innocent and staying in Chalcedon, that he should instruct the patriarch [of Constantinople] to send him *eulogiai* on the occasion of his appointment. So Flavian sent him pure loaves as *eulogiai*. But Chrysaphius sent these back, declaring that the emperor wanted *eulogiai* of gold.[75]

This story recalls an era of church and state politics in which material blessings played a notorious role. Fifteen years earlier, during the tumultuous Council of Ephesus (431), Bishop Cyril of Alexandria (d. 444) had sought to influence decisions made at Constantinople by arranging for copious blessings to be dispensed to monks in the street and to members of the court. Nestorius, his episcopal rival at Constantinople, later complained that the monks were issued foodstuffs as "wages of fervor." Cyril ordered his agents to stock the city's monasteries with bread, wine, and vegetables for monks to take, "paying them with things called 'blessings'" to agitate on his behalf.[76] Members of the court later received far more sumptuous gifts. A letter records, in minute detail, all the "humble *eulogiai*" that Cyril authorized his archdeacon to send to chamberlains and other courtiers so as to "satisfy their avarice" and maintain their favor years after the council had ended. Besides 1,080 pounds of gold, these included luxurious silks, tapestries, ivory chairs, ostrich eggs, and other "worthy blessings."[77]

In light of Cyril's gifts, it is not surprising that modern scholars have regarded the word *blessing* as an ecclesiastical euphemism for a bribe,[78] or that a medieval chronicler like Theophanes could find an anecdote in which church *eulogiai* were being demanded by an imperial eunuch in the form of gold. Indeed, Theophanes's narrative demonstrates that even in later Byzantium this word remained far from banal, for it presumes that his contemporaries would have known that *eulogiai* could signify church gifts, bread and wealth all at once. But to take his story as confirmation that blessing was commonly used as a euphemism for a bribe is to miss its point entirely. Theophanes's story is about a worldly eunuch's avarice, not a bishop's bribery. It is about the pressure exerted on a church leader to comply with a secular custom—the giving of gifts upon assumption of office—and the cynical contempt with which his humble gifts were received. It is also about a gift extorted through compulsion—something a blessing was never supposed to be.[79]

Factual or not, Theophanes's story is illuminating precisely because it places this gift ideal at the center of a conflict between two very different spheres of valuation and exchange: church and court, sacred and profane. In this case, the main root of the conflict is the notorious venality of Chrysaphius (d. 450), a high-ranking member of the imperial court. Yet Theophanes's story suggests that friction was always possible between these two spheres in times of gift giving, if simply because gift giving brought them into close contact. To understand how such friction contributed to the development of the concept of a Christian blessing in Early Byzantium, it is helpful to review how anthropologists have explained the emergence of disinterested gift ideals in modern developing societies. Especially helpful in this regard is work done by Maurice Bloch, Jonathan Parry, and others during the 1980s in India, Fiji, and Peru, each of which was experiencing a rapid expansion in their market economies.

What Bloch, Parry, and other researchers repeatedly found is that the advent of new markets and commercial systems prompted the creation of tokens or gifts that were not meant to make purchases, that did not demand something in return, and that were not supposed to be used to advance an individual's interests over those of the greater good. Bloch and Parry explain this by positing in each community the perception of different transactional orders or spheres of exchange, one being short-term, profit-driven, and profane, the other being long-term, communally beneficial, and sacred. These two orders differ markedly in motivation and purpose, yet remain intertwined and interdependent, either by economic or social necessity. In each case, the long-term transactional order is always more positively valued, because it is believed to reflect and sustain the traditional values and prosperity of the general community. According to Bloch and Parry, the notion of a pure gift tends to arise in these societies from a perceived need to shield participants in the long-term order from the short-term's "selfish" motives of individual advancement and gain. What needs to be emphasized is that these different orders and their respective currencies or gifts, though defined against each other, nonetheless remain interdependent, the one often relying on and benefitting from the other. For this reason, members of long-term communal orders occasionally develop procedures to convert wealth derived from profit-driven, self-interested motives, so that it can be "purified" for their use.[80]

There was a similar sense that Christian communities and their leaders in Early Byzantium should be insulated from the short-term interests of the world that surrounded and supported them. As in modern developing societies, Christian authorities in antiquity viewed commercial marketplaces as the locus of base self-interest and human greed par excellence. Church officials of the third and fourth centuries were instructed to inspect lay contributions to ensure that they did not come from marketplace hucksters (or other purveyors of deceitful or degrading trades).[81] But a more insidious threat to church and monastic integrity emerged from the fourth century onward. This came from secular gift practices by which career advancements and gain were often achieved. On the one hand, there were all the *munuscula* ("little gifts")—tips, fees, sweeteners, bribes—that one had to give to obtain signatures, gain access to courts, or simply maneuver through the state bureaucracy.[82] But equally onerous and occasionally more sinister were the gifts that aristocrats exchanged to confirm solidarity and social standing, and which superiors also issued to their inferiors to maintain bonds of loyalty and *obsequium* in patron-client relationships. Usually presented as gifts of hospitality (*xenia*), these might range from costly wardrobes and gold coins to little baskets of bread and other foodstuffs. Tenants and clients were also expected to give their patrons and landlords annual gifts. Though often referred to as *xenia, honoraria, gebyātā, or 'iqārē,* they were sometimes more plainly just called "tribute" (*dasmos, madatā*).[83]

This is the social and cultural background against which we must appreciate Paul's idealization of a *eulogia* and its subsequent development in Early Byzantium. In spirit and intent, Christian blessings were supposed to be different. The need for an alternative to secular gift-giving practices was made all the more necessary by the patronal relationships that developed between lay aristocrats and Christian leaders in the post-Constantinian era. Such relationships were to some extent desirable, but they raised ethical questions. After all, the position and authority of Christian leaders in this period—not only as judges in episcopal courts but as champions of doctrinal orthodoxy and advocates for the community's poor—depended in no small part on their perceived ability to remain independent and speak truth to power (*parrhēsia*). Such authority derived from their avowed detachment from worldly affairs and avoidance of favoritism; like God, they were expected to be "no respecters of persons" (Acts 10:34; Rom 2:11; Col 3:25; Jas 2:1–9). Nothing threatened that more than the preferential treatment and implied obligations that came with aristocratic patronage,[84] yet it was hard to avoid patronal interactions (or dealings with the imperial court) altogether. Chrysostom in the fourth century noted how some provided hospitality to certain distinguished Christian saints—that is, church leaders—solely to make them "more useful" to their family, spoiling their hospitality by asking favors in return, such as help in gaining access to court officials.[85]

Nestorius came under similar pressure as Bishop of Constantinople (sed. 428–431) thirty years later. To defend his integrity against insinuations made by Cyril of Alexandria, he wrote:

> Was I, while bishop, devoted to luxuries and sensual pleasures as you claim? On the contrary, some thought me to be mean and disdainful, because I didn't accept anything sent to me beyond what I needed. Did I take on airs in palaces or country estates, while away from the church? Far from it. . . . So how can anyone say I cared for offerings and favors or sought to hoard them for myself? Never did I let myself get misled by such things. For I know that they oblige whomever they snare to act like a slave and do what they're told, whatever it might be.[86]

As this letter attests, a real challenge faced by church and monastic leaders was how to exchange gifts, receive support, or interact with benefactors without becoming beholden to them or accused of some form of self-promotion or avarice. This situation gave Paul's description of a *eulogia* special significance in the Early Byzantine era: blessings were gifts that, by definition, were supposed to be innocent of all such *pleonexia*, free of any compulsion, obligation, or human self-interest—a pure, disinterested Christian gift.

That significance was not lost on hagiographers. Once when Empress Verina (d. 484) visited an abbess named Matrona in late fifth-century Constantinople, Matrona reportedly served her some moistened bread *eulogiai*. In secular circles, such a gesture of hospitality would have usually served as a means of softening the empress before importuning her for favors. "But [Matrona] asked for nothing whatsoever in return, although the empress quite expected to be petitioned by her for something, seeing that the blessed one . . . was in no way prosperous." Indeed Verina, we are emphatically told, "derived extraordinary benefit by her neither asking for anything nor being ashamed to give such *eulogiai* to an empress."[87] As this indicates, such humble blessings served the needs of hospitality but, unlike traditional *xenia*, conveyed no obligation or pressure to reciprocate, seeking nothing in return—except, perhaps, a verbal blessing. A Syrian solitary reportedly set a roadside table with bread and wine, leaving a sign inviting whoever passed to "take a blessing . . . from the gifts of our Lord," asking only that they leave behind "the blessing of [their] prayers."[88]

Such hagiographical vignettes again make clear that blessings were supposed to differ from other gifts by being considered "gifts from our Lord." Indeed, the fact that they were imagined to ultimately come from God and not from their immediate donors helped make them a somewhat impersonal, alienable, and disposable type of gift. They were not infused, as anthropologists might say, with the spirit of their human giver.[89] Its nature and value derived solely from the selfless spirit of generosity that was believed to flow through it. This may help explain why the Early Byzantine discourse on blessings, alone of all Christian gifts, never alludes to any sort of reciprocity or receipt of reward. The non-transactional aspect of this gift reflected its divine origin and recognized that no human gift or service could ever repay a gift from God.

It is in this light that we must understand Nestorius's outrage at his colleague's use of "things called blessings" against him during the Council of Ephesus, as well as the hubris implicit in Theophanes's account of Chrysaphius's contempt for Flavian's loaves and demand for "*eulogiai* of gold." Both represented abuses of a sacred ideal. At the same time we must appreciate the difficulty of maintaining that ideal's purity in a world awash with shady gifts. When defending some colleagues accused of simony, Severus of Antioch explained, "The bribe [*šuḥdā*] had been concealed under the name of a blessing [*burktā*] by those gain-hunters, and it deceived them."[90] Obviously, much depended on recognizing a Christian blessing for what it was and what it was not. So we may ask, Were there special signs or properties that made a blessing not only easy to give, but easily identifiable as such?

Virtually anything, it seems, could be given as a blessing. It was therefore perfectly acceptable that aristocratic churchmen or ascetics of the time should offer,
as "small *eulogiai*," items that might otherwise seem extravagant, like the horse
that Pope Gregory sent a bishop in sixth-century Italy or the "precious ornaments
of great value" that Melania the Younger gave to imperial dignitaries in fifth-
century Rome. For churchmen and saints like these, such gifts were trifles. What
mattered was the spirit with which they were given. Hence, Melania's hagiographer
crucially adds that, when giving such blessings, she likened herself to the Gospel
widow who gave her two mites (Mk 12:41–44, Lk 21:1–4).[91] Nonetheless, to avoid
any confusion, it was helpful for a blessing to signal by its very appearance the
sacred origin and selfless nature of its intent. Hence, the properties in most examples found by archaeologists or described in our sources: small, cheaply made, and
therefore easily given away without implying any need for repayment or return,
like the bread Flavian brought the emperor or the moist loaves Matrona served
Verina—these were the standard visible signs of a Christian blessing.

Indeed, these are the characteristics of most of the ampullae, or *eulogia* flasks,
visible in museums today. Such vessels originally contained oil, dirt, or sweat
skimmed off the soil of some Early Byzantine sanctuary or the skin of a holy person.[92] Scholars have noted the unprepossessing appearance of such flasks. Usually
fashioned out of lead or clay, "the humblest of substances," and sometimes stamped
EULOGIA but often bearing no marks at all,[93] their value was derived entirely from
the trust people put in the holiness they held inside.

No hagiography or papyrus document records any monk or shrine selling such
eulogiai. Indeed, we have only descriptions of them being dispensed, apparently for
free, as when all participants at the festival of St. Lawrence at Constantinople
reportedly took home "a share of" the myrrh dispensed from his relics.[94] We should
not presume that such descriptions concealed commercial transactions. Describing
visitors to her shrine in Seleucia, the fifth-century *Life of Thecla* differentiates
between people who came to obtain healings and people who came to honor the
saint by leaving offerings. It discusses each type of visitor and associated action of
giving or receiving in separate categories (not unlike the depiction of donors and
the poor coming separately to take or leave gifts at the column of Symeon Stylites,
described in chapter 3). It is therefore possible that flasks filled with blessings were
given to one group in the belief that any cost would be recouped through offerings
received from the other.[95] Of course, from a purely economic perspective, such gifts
would have been easy to give for free because the materials used to produce them
(dirt, clay) were so easily obtained. A monk living southeast of Chalcedon is said to
have carved little wooden crosses out of sticks he collected from a nearby forest to
give as *eulogiai* to visitors.[96] The Holy Land abounded with blessings just for the
taking, as the Piacenza Pilgrim discovered to his delight: water gushing from a
spring, petroleum oozing from caves, manna hanging from trees.[97]

But the most readily identifiable type of material blessings must have always been the small loaves of stamped liturgical bread that Christian professionals received from their institutions. These needed no packaging at all, since anyone who had gone to church and seen their markings would have immediately recognized their significance.[98] Only in light of Theophanes's story, however, can we truly appreciate the social value of this religious resource. Lowly by any worldly standard yet considered "full of grace,"[99] such loaves provided clerics and monks with tokens they could use to offer hospitality at any level, but especially to social superiors, without worrying about the expense, preparation, or potential embarrassment (note Matrona's lack of shame in giving moist bread to an empress) normally involved. As Theophanes implies, only a eunuch as avaricious as Chrysaphius would have spurned a bishop's "pure loaves" for *eulogiai* made of gold.[100]

CONVERTING LAY OFFERINGS INTO BLESSINGS

Yet the question remains: What about gifts given to churchmen and monks by pious admirers? Their danger was proverbial. According to Ecclesiasticus, "Gifts and presents [*xenia kai dōra*] blind the eyes of the wise" (Sir 20:29). Chrysostom interpreted this to mean that they "muzzled the mouths" of their recipients.[101] Of course, one solution was to decline them altogether, a policy ascribed to numerous church leaders and ascetics. An anti-Chalcedonian activist named Mare reportedly practiced manual labor so as not to need the money being offered to silence his criticisms of Justinian and his dyophysite policies. When Empress Theodora handed him a bag containing a hundred pounds of gold, he astonished everyone by hurling it across the room "as if it were filled with light apples," saying, "To hell with you and your money, because through this you wish to tempt me and mock me."[102] Yet, as Nestorius's letter to Cyril shows, such policies were not always easy to adopt. In the first place, as discussed in chapter 7, churches and monasteries from the fifth century onward were frequently being founded as patronal institutions, intended to serve their lay founders. As a result, the monks or clerics recruited to serve in them were tied to the gifts and interests of their patrons from the very start. Moreover, rejecting a gift might aggrieve its giver. According to desert tradition, the hermit Zeno, though "from the outset he had never wanted to receive anything from anyone at all," nevertheless changed his mind when he saw that all who brought him something "went away sad because he did not accept it," and others were disappointed when they saw he had nothing to give them. So he came up with a different plan: take what was given and pass it on. "And so he did, and was at peace, and satisfied everyone."[103]

Simplistic though it sounds, Zeno's policy resembles a procedure frequently ascribed to abbots of large monasteries for converting gifts into divine blessings. It was, after all, one thing to affirm that all blessings came from God, or to keep them separated from offerings given to fund commemorations or some other service, as was done in the monastery at Nessana. But to ascertain that something was a blessing and "not a curse," as church canons warned, was another matter. When in doubt, what really ensured that a gift would be a blessing was how it was handled after its receipt. The solution was either to take no more than needed (as Nestorius did) or nothing at all (as Zeno did) and give the rest away, putting it back into circulation for those in need.

Such stewardship was patently different from conventional approaches to managing surplus resources in antiquity. In the Mediterranean imagination, this was typified by locking up food in strongholds in hope of getting the highest price while others starved (cf. Prv 11:26, "People curse the man who hoards grain"). Christian stewardship was supposed to do just the opposite: to save lives by dispensing God-given superfluities whenever anyone had need.[104] The same practice could be used to turn suspect offerings into blessings. We see this in an account of how Dalmatius (d. 436), the abbot of a monastery in Constantinople known as the Dalmation, processed the lay gifts he received from local dignitaries.

> All who came . . . would bring offerings [*prosphorai*] and put them into saintly Dalmatius's hands. The offerings brought at that time were considerable, and [Dalmatius and his mentor, Isaac] would give them to prisoners and whoever came to the holy monastery, making a distribution every day without exception. . . . Lord Dalmatius's name is attached to the monastery to this day, because whenever the brothers went to the gate to ask to receive the *eulogia* from them, they would mention his name, saying to each other, "Let's go to Lord Dalmatius, for he has provisions from God with which to feed us."

In this way, we are told, "God supplied the holy ones with many things in accordance with their intentions, for they would distribute them with great generosity, giving thanks to . . . Christ."[105]

This fifth- or sixth-century *Life of Dalmatius*, more than any other text, reveals the intricate connections that Early Byzantine authorities drew between lay patronage, saintly abbots, and the generation of sacred wealth, or *eulogiai*.[106] It shows precisely how offerings provided by lay patrons could become identified with wealth supplied by God when properly handled by a holy person. Comparable scenarios are found in other hagiographies about cenobitic saints. According to the early eighth-century *Life of Theoduta of Amid*, for example, this abbot of Amida, after being pressured by his fellow elders, relented to accept the gift a rich layman had wanted to offer him for healing his daughter. After receiving it, however, Theoduta immediately told his steward to distribute it to local orphans, at which point the hagiographer describes the rich man's gift as a "*burktā* from the Lord."[107] This hagiographical pattern suggests that a rule of thumb had arisen for handling inappropriate and/or suspect patronal gifts. But the *Life of Dalmatius* further indicates that such lay offerings often stemmed from the perception of a holy person's generous intentions (*proairēseis*), evinced by his regular distribution of whatever offerings he received. It thus indicates that both attracting patronal wealth and converting it into sacred wealth depended on demonstrating a willingness to give it away to whoever came by. Any lay gift could be turned into a God-given blessing if handled with such openhanded generosity.

Indeed, by focusing on Dalmatius's personal receipt of these offerings (we hear that his patrons "put them into saintly Dalmatius's hand"), the hagiographer alerts us to a sensitive situation. Nestorius implies that he was presented with offerings (*qurbānē*) while visiting people's estates, a situation where it would have also been awkward to simply reject the gesture. Anthropologists agree that gifts tend to exert their hold over their recipients by reminding them of their givers. In Early Byzantium, a similar effect was associated with both alms and offerings. As seen in the next two chapters, the latter were not only often highly personalized gifts (sometimes inscribed with a donor's name), but they also explicitly imposed obligations on Christian professionals to perform religious services on their donor's behalf.[108] This was not problematic when their purposes were recorded and set forth in writing. Difficulties were more likely when they were handed over directly and informally, especially in an imperial court or stately home.

One approach to handling such offerings was to insist on putting distance between their givers and their recipients. This was explicitly attributed as a policy to Rabbula of Edessa (sed. 411–435). Edessa (Şanlıurfa, southeastern Turkey) was an affluent city, and Rabbula, who was not merely an ascetic but also a member of the regional aristocracy, must have frequently found himself in situations like those that Nestorius encountered. So, according to his hagiography, he adopted the following policy, for similar reasons:

> Now, he . . . gladly received gold sent to him from afar. But when emperors and honorees in person brought him a great deal of gold, with ornaments and clothing . . . and asked him to receive their offerings [*qurbānē*], he was fearful and said, "Although truly the actions that forced me to come [into their presence] are evident, perhaps it might seem to them that I sought for myself a false pretext by which I could . . . take gifts from them." Thus, because he . . . would not pawn his freedom for anything, he [became] more precious in their eyes, and was believed.[109]

Barsauma, a contemporary archimandrite from the same region, likewise reportedly accepted anything sent to him from afar, but forbad anything offered directly while he was traveling on the road.[110] Another strategy Barsauma adopted was to deflect whatever was offered away from himself and toward his institution as a whole. Thus he rejected the many great "gifts of honor" (*'iqārē*) Theodosius II offered him, but accepted a small veil that the emperor sent as a "blessing" and "first fruit of the harvest" (*rišitē*) for his monastery instead.[111] This institutionalization of the gift effectively depersonalized it. But the ultimate solution for handling items meant to flatter, ingratiate, or manipulate a holy person was to pass them on to the poor, thereby repurposing them to serve God's purpose rather than the donor's.[112] A similar safeguard can be seen in the procedure for processing lay offerings during a church liturgy, inasmuch as pooling them together before and after the service detached them from their individual lay patrons and rendered them anonymous before ever passing into clerical hands.

Otherwise, much depended on a saint's capacity for self-restraint or self-denial to ensure that anything he or she received might be used in a philanthropic manner pleasing to a celestial patron who made "His sun rise over both the wicked and the good" (Mt 5:45). Hence, it was seen as a chief virtue of Theodosius the Cenobiarch that he provided indiscriminately, "without respect of persons," to all poor strangers. Likewise, Euthymius on his deathbed reminded his monks to keep their gate open to "all humanity," without favoritism, if they wished God to continue supplying them with blessings.[113]

Of course, it was precisely because such stewardship went against all human instinct that it was considered a sign of sanctity. The *Life of Shenoute* mentions a patron who decided to give "alms [only] for his salvation" (probably a *mortis causa* arrangement is envisioned, such as discussed in chapter 7) to Shenoute's monastery after he had seen the abbot distributing a preliminary gift of 120 gold coins to the poor.[114] Evidently, this donor wanted to test Shenoute before giving more, suggesting how others might have waited for clear demonstrations of altruism before committing goods to a monastery.[115] Handling lay donations thus involved ethical questions and decisions, best left to trained, ascetic stewards. Yet even ordinary clerics and monks might practice a degree of divine philanthropy, if they simply gave the rations they received from their institutions away with indiscriminate generosity. Thus, John of Gaza encouraged monks to give a "*eulogia* of the Fathers" not just to random beggars but to non-Christians as well: "For he who is of another religion can in no way harm the *eulogia*, but in fact it will bless him and make even him recognize the truth, since the *eulogia* holds the power of God."[116]

ASCETIC STEWARDSHIP AND THE MULTIPLICATION OF MONASTIC BLESSINGS

John of Gaza leaves no doubt that monastic authorities like himself ascribed a divine force to such gifts. Early Byzantine hagiographers attributed to them an ability not just to revitalize and heal but to expand and increase. Hagiographies about cenobitic abbots abound with stories in which bread supplies miraculously multiply through an abbot's generosity, especially in times of scarcity.[117] A vivid example is set in Shenoute's White Monastery in Upper Egypt. One night when people came streaming into his monastery seeking relief from a famine, a shining

figure appeared to him in a dream. "I am Paul, the Apostle of Christ," the appari-
tion announced. "Because you love charity and give alms to anyone that asks . . .
behold! the Lord has sent me . . . to comfort you." Then he placed in Shenoute's
hand a loaf of bread that Jesus had blessed, instructing him to put it in the storeroom of the monastery "from which the brothers distribute the bread." As soon as
this was done, "an abundance of bread" arose, feeding the monastery and its refugees for the next six months. And so, the story concludes, "to this very day, that
bread-store is called 'the Storeroom of the Blessing.'"[118]

Like Cyril of Scythopolis's account of the blessings that multiplied at Euthymius's
monastery, this story is modeled on Jesus's Feeding of the Multitudes. Yet its reference to Shenoute's receipt of a blessed loaf of bread from Paul also strongly suggests
that it was inspired by Second Corinthians and the monastic practice of using
reserves of bread as gifts for visitors and rations for monks. Such stories were a
reminder that it was in such humble treasuries that the sacred wealth of a monastery
was supposed to be most manifest. Later, monks in the White Monastery would have
grasped this point: for the storeroom in which that divine "abundance" (smou in
Coptic) reportedly appeared was no doubt the same room in which they actually did
store their smou (also "blessing" in Coptic)—that is, their extra eulogia bread.[119]

Such hagiography, Vincent Déroche observes, envisions the operation of a
"miraculous economy" in the Christian world, whereby God bestowed ever-
increasing amounts of material resources on those who spent whatever they
received on good works.[120] We are in fact dealing with a perception that material
blessings could be stretched out and even increased so as to be given away as philanthropically as possible (we are told that Shenoute was rewarded for "giving alms
to anyone who asked"). This was not as unrealistic as it might first sound. John of
Gaza wrote three letters to members of the Seridos monastery answering whether
they were obliged to give to all who came by. His first letter addresses whether it
was necessary to give to people who came without apparent need or who wanted
more than they were given; his second addresses whether anything had to be given
to wandering monks (i.e., gyrovagues); and his third addresses whether such
monks should allowed to enter the monastery (perhaps to receive greater hospitality). He answers these questions with slightly different but revealing detail. Yes, he
says, the monastery should prioritize whoever was ashamed to ask, especially if
they were suffering because of aktēmosynē and "not out of prodigal living"; moreover, it should reserve any demonstrative display of compassion for the latter, "lest
anyone develop a habit of continually asking on the pretext of poverty." Nonetheless, he affirms that everyone must be given something, "even if he be a thief."[121]
This policy, which John attributes to "the Fathers," recalls Basil's advice that stewards give everyone at least a "small gift," while reserving compassion for those truly
known to be afflicted.[122] John makes the same point about giving to all twice, both
times using the phrase "Give [the claimant] a eulogia and send [him] off."[123] In his

third letter, however, he slightly alters this formulation, writing instead, "If you need to give a *mikron perisson,* give it and send [him] off."[124] This effectively offers a gloss on what he meant when recommending that monks give a *eulogia:* such gifts represented a "little extra," or a "small superfluity."

This recalls Paul's emphasis on the verb *perisseuō* when describing the material resources from which a blessing should ideally come. Translators of Second Corinthians have usually emphasized only one aspect of this verb's meaning—namely, "to be abundant." The New Revised Standard Version, for example, translates Second Corinthians 9:8 as "God is able to provide you with every grace in abundance [*charin perisseusai*], so that by always having enough of everything, you may share abundantly [*perisseuēte*] in every good work." Yet *perisseuō* and its cognates can also mean "to have something left over" or "to be a leftover." Accordingly, Dieter Georgi translates the same sentence, "God is able to grant you every grace in excess [*charin perisseusai*], so that you ... have plenty left over [*perisseuēte*] for much good works."[125] Whatever Paul meant by these words, they helped later authorities develop a highly flexible notion of what constituted the material resources from which gifts called blessings might derive. By insisting that monks give a *eulogia* to anyone who came by, John of Gaza was insisting that they give out a *mikron perisson*: a "little leftover"— something small and superfluous that they did not need themselves.[126]

To some extent this resembles what other authorities recommended. Isaiah of Scetis, for instance, advised that monks never possess anything of such value or quality that they might refrain from giving it away to someone who asked, thereby causing them to fail to observe Jesus's command to "love thy brother."[127] But by a *mikron perisson,* John clearly had in mind a question of quantity—that is, how much was to be given—and his advice more closely recalls ascetic teachings found elsewhere about the productive use of leftovers. Pachomius, for example, instructed his stewards to collect whatever remained of their monks' rations after a three-day period and mix them up in a common pool for later use.[128] As a solitary, George of Choziba was said to have lived on whatever scraps ("whether vegetables, beans, or bones") he could scrape off of tables from a nearby cenobium; these he rolled into balls and dried in the sun for his own reuse.[129] Theodore of Petra reports that his monastery provided for all who attended a feast one year by collecting the "superabundance of leftovers" of bread from each table, reheating them in the sun, and redistributing the supply produced thereby.[130] Such practices reflected a concern not to waste anything God had provided. Yet they also represented an ascetic strategy of recycling leftovers, by revitalizing scraps to generate more.

What must be emphasized is that the extra supply generated by these leftovers was imagined in terms of blessings. We see this in an episode told about Nicholas, abbot of a cenobium called Sion located high in the mountains of Lycia in southwestern Asia Minor. One year, when famine struck the villages below, Nicholas responded by taking wine, grain, and oxen from his monastery and traveling from martyr shrine to martyr shrine, performing a liturgy and feeding the villagers in each, visiting ten in all. This lasted for three weeks, during which the hagiographer insists that Nicholas received no additional supplies. He was able to manage with what he had, we are told, because "many *eulogiai* were left over" from each liturgical feast, leaving a "superfluity of *eulogiai*"—that is, leftover grain, wine, and oxen—that he reused at the next feast. In this way, "his provisions kept multiplying."[131] John of Ephesus describes a similar dynamic, explaining how a monastery denied itself food during a famine to feed the poor who came to its gate. After the bread was served and only a "little remained over," the abbot addressed the monks in the refectory, saying, "Let each of us receive a little blessing with thanksgiving, and continue without murmuring, for thus we will have recompense from God." Because they so selflessly fasted on these leftovers, "the tables were found to be full of bread in abundance."[132]

Thus, monks extracted blessings from blessings, as Paul himself might have foretold. These stories illustrate how the term *eulogiai* could imply both abundant and leftover material resources at once. They also indicate that a monastery could fulfill its philanthropic mandate by dispensing whatever low-quality leftovers it saved. This held true even in times of plenty. A sixth-century monastic rule from Italy permitted monks to sell "anything superfluous that might be leftover" from the produce of their labors if it seemed useless either for their monastery, or "for sending out as *eulogiae*." In other words, the resource from which a blessing derived was supposed to be useful as such, yet nonetheless was supposed to derive from a "superfluous . . . leftover" all the same.[133]

Finally, these teachings implied that whatever was given as a blessing, even if given from resources of low quality, would usually be appreciated by their recipients due to their need,[134] and that such gifts could be given without establishing lasting bonds or implying further obligations, such as might be suggested by a "bigger" gift, derived from resources of high quality. Theodore of Sykeon, while passing winter outside his seventh-century monastery in northwestern Anatolia, reportedly kept a basket of bread and apples on hand "from which he was accustomed to give *eulogiai* to visitors." So philanthropic was Theodore that he dispensed these not only to human visitors but to visiting animals as well, "in order to fulfill the commandment of God that says, 'Give to all who ask of thee'" (Mt 5:42). Three years in a row, an enormous bear arrived, took a *eulogia* out of Theodore's hand, then went away. But the next year a wolf came and refused to leave until he had been given, in addition to a slice of apple, a piece of bread as well. As if following John's advice that the Seridos monastery cope with undesirable interlopers by giving them a *mikron perisson* before sending them off, Theodore's solution was to give this "impudent" beast an extra *eulogia*, and then send him off.[135] The wolf did not come back. Thus the saint's gifts fulfilled God's philanthropic imperative without encouraging his unwanted visitor to return, not unlike, mutatis mutandis, the proverbial cold shoulder of meat served up as hospitality to an unwelcome guest.

GIFTS OF A SACRED ORDER

Such stories make it easy to romanticize a Christian blessing. As Bloch and Parry point out, however, "pure" gifts invented to support traditional orders have often been used to define status and enforce obligations within those orders themselves.[136] Church leaders continued sending each other *eulogiai* as tokens of communion and affection throughout antiquity, having done so since at least the third century. Yet the fact that church councils prohibited them from receiving these gifts from heretics ("for they are full of curses") alerts us that the circulation of blessings could be used to mark inclusion and exclusion in a Christian community.[137] When a solitary named Arsenius was left out of a distribution of dried-fruit blessings one day at Scetis, he reportedly exclaimed, "You cast me out by not giving me the *eulogia* that God sent the brothers, which I was not worthy [*axios*] to receive."[138] Egyptian desert tradition presents this as a lesson on humility (Arsenius had formerly been a tutor to the imperial family), but it reveals the sensitivity with which *eulogiai* distributions could be viewed, for giving or receiving them signaled not only one's inclusion but also one's status or worth (*axia*) within the religious community.

This function was intrinsic to the church and monastic rationing systems described above. Indeed, the indiscriminate manner with which *eulogiai* were dispensed to lay visitors contrasts markedly with the way they were issued inside church and monastic institutions. As we saw, the apportionment of liturgical blessings according to clerical rank was explicitly affirmed as a means of instantiating proper ecclesiastical order: "For the church is not a teacher of disorder but of good order [*eutaxia*]."[139] Monasteries do not seem to have apportioned rations in such hierarchical fashion (three loaves was standard for all), but it is evident nonetheless that their flow was supposed to be exclusively under the abbot's control. Monastic rules indicate that rations might be withheld as punishment for minor infractions,[140] and it appears that once given, a blessing could not be given to another resident (as opposed to an outside visitor) without permission.[141] Thus, the rationing system provided a means of symbolizing and enforcing hierarchical relationships in monasteries as well. Indeed, contemporaries recognized that to receive a material blessing from an abbot was to acknowledge one's subordination. We hear how the pride of a desert solitary finally broke when God stopped feeding him and a monastery began bringing him bread blessings,[142] and how an arrogant anchorite spurned the figs an elder dispensed to him at Scetis, declaring, "I am not inferior to you, that you should send me a *eulogia!*"[143]

To some extent this approach to issuing blessings in Christian institutions was necessary to prevent indiscretions or insubordinations. That problem is illustrated by a remarkable episode in Gerontius's *Life of Melania the Younger*. After founding her convent in Jerusalem, Melania, "due to her superlative humility," ceded its leadership to another woman. Thinking the abbess too hard on the other residents, however, she started secretly slipping refreshments into their cells without the abbess knowing it. Once her fellow nuns realized that it was Melania who was doing it, "they began to cling to her and became excessively keen to obey her in all matters, recognizing that her compassion had no bounds."[144] The story shows how unsanctioned gift giving might undermine a leader's position. Rabbula of Edessa was praised for punishing any outside priest who dared give a member of his staff any gift at all. He supposedly explained,

> If they bring us presents [or bribes, *šuḥdē*] calling it a blessing, [they should not, since] we, who are held in honor by them, rightly should give [blessings]. In the case of an honorarium [*'iqārā*], this is a mockery as we, who possess authority, appropriately confer honor. But in the case of a gift from compulsion, we, who should be supported by them, should take no part. Therefore on every count it is we who ought to give and not to receive.[145]

Thus Rabbula sought to prevent improprieties from arising through gift giving between clerics in his diocese. The passage also reveals, however, Rabbula's concern to maintain his own supremacy as the leading patron and dispenser of gifts within his church.

Rabbula's position on clerical gift giving may have been exceptional, but his understanding of its symbolism was not. No one disputed the notion that bishops were supposed to be chief mediators of God's gifts to His people. As we have seen, the third-century *Apostolic Tradition* had already required that participants at communal Charity Feasts receive bread *eulogiai* from their bishop's own hand (in his absence, a priest's).[146] Distributing blessings provided an inexpensive yet effective means for such leaders to symbolize their superior position. Hence, all members of the Sons and Daughters of the Covenant, a Syrian corps of acolytes and clerics-in-training, were required to assemble twice a year to receive *būrkāthā* in front of their bishop,[147] while Italian monks were told to rise whenever their monastery received a *eulogia* sent by a bishop or priests "next in rank." Their abbot was supposed to kiss this gift; then all would say, "We are receiving Your mercies, God, in the midst of Your temple" (Ps 48:9).[148] By periodically dispensing blessings to monasteries (as Severus of Antioch and Gregory the Great frequently mention doing),[149] a bishop could foster bonds of loyalty and deference from his top-ranking clergy on down to local monks—all the while ensuring that a blessing would remain regarded as something rare and precious.

When used this way, there is no question that *eulogiai* resembled the *xenia* that patrons traditionally gave to promote loyalty among peers and subservience among subordinates in the secular sphere.[150] Yet there was nothing controversial about this institutional use of blessings. Bishops expected clerics and monks to "honor order,"[151] and the *Apostolic Constitutions* stated in regard to the distribution of *eulogiai* portions, "It is good and agreeable to God to honor each according to rank [*axia*]."[152] Such giving reflected the more general Christian embrace of hierarchical order in Early Byzantium. As Theodoret of Cyrrhus (ca. 393–458) explained in his treatise *On Divine Providence*, God had deliberately divided humanity into rich and poor, masters and slaves, and rulers and subjects to foster the most stable existence possible for humans after the Fall. According to this view, people were to be honored for using their God-given resources not to change society or anyone's status in it, but to help out each in his place.[153]

Nothing more dramatically illustrates that static social outlook, or the role of a blessing in it, than the cautionary tale of Eulogius the Stonecutter. Preserved in a sixth-century collection of edifying tales attributed to monk named Daniel of Scetis, this story shows the dangers of not recognizing a blessing for what it was and of tampering with God's providential apportionment of status and gifts. Eulogius was a hundred-year-old Egyptian stonecutter who used part of his daily salary—a small bronze *keration*, worth either 1/24 or 1/48 of a solidus—to feed strangers and monks he found sitting in his village square at night. Having often benefited from his hospitality, Daniel, the narrator, prayed and fasted for three days that God might give Eulogius extra wages as a *eulogia*, so that he could "benefit even more people." Despite an angel's repeated warnings that the stonecutter was fine as he was, Daniel kept praying, till one day Eulogius discovered a large sum of money in a cave. Fearing that his village headman might seize it, Eulogius sailed to Constantinople, where he arrived during the reign of Justinian's uncle, Justin I (r. 518–527). In return for giving the emperor part of the blessing, Eulogius was rewarded with a large estate and patrician rank. But with this worldly elevation came his downfall: having turned pompous and merciless towards monks, Eulogius became implicated in a plot against Justin's successor, Justinian. Fearing for his life, he fled back to his village, where Daniel helped "establish him in his former station." After Eulogius apologized, Daniel assured him, "Brother, don't expect to be entrusted by God with anything in this world again but that one *keration*." The story ends, "How wondrous is God's goodness, that in a little time He both elevated Eulogius and humbled him so, to his advantage."[154]

In many respects, this story resembles the treasure stories often told in peasant societies where upward mobility seems impossible except through a chance discovery or windfall.[155] But its lesson for Early Byzantine readers is that no such mobility should ever be wished for or pursued—and certainly not by means of a God-given blessing. The story implies that, when put in the hands of a layperson (even a demonstrably scrupulous layperson like Eulogius), a *eulogia* of massive size would not be put to its proper use of benefitting others. In any case, it makes clear that Eulogius himself did not need such a blessing: for as his name reveals,

God had already given him a *eulogia* by "supplying him with strength to earn his *keration* from his manual labor"[156]—namely, such robust health that even at a hundred years of age, he could still earn the wage that had sufficed till then to provide both for himself and his accustomed hospitality.

We may suspect that, while lay folk like Eulogius could have learned about the concept of material blessings through local liturgies, festivals, or visits to monasteries, it was mainly among clerics and monks that *eulogiai* were consciously identified or valued as such. Except for the papyri from southern Palestine,[157] there is little documentary evidence that this type of gift was widely known outside of professional circles. There are, however, references to them in papyrus letters addressed to or by churchmen and monks. Most refer to gifts of food that arrived with a letter; since the correspondents needed no explanation of what a *eulogia* (or *smou*) was, they cast little light on the subject. But we do have a letter written in Coptic by an Egyptian nun named Maria to a hermit named Cyriacus. Of unknown date, it confirms that this type of gift could forge positive relationships between those who appreciated it, and it was believed to be something truly special: "Send thy blessing to me that I may have it in my house, for it brings fragrance to my soul, and I may see it in my house, for it urges me to do good."[158]

SACRED WEALTH AND MONASTIC CULTURE

A memorable episode in the Bohairic *Life of Pachomius,* set in late fourth-century Egypt, describes how distressed Abba Theodore, third leader of the Pachomian confederation of monasteries, became when he saw all the fields, boats, and animals his monasteries had accumulated, remembering that in the days of their founder, they had had so few. "What am I to do with this great wealth and these numerous possessions which have increased so?" he asked the confederation's second leader, Horsiesius, who was now living as a recluse in retirement. Theodore expressed his readiness to get rid of all these material possessions, knowing them to be no true source of profit. But Horsiesius had a different way of seeing it. Worry not, he replied: "For it is the Lord who has blessed [*petaphsmou*] the community and expanded it, [and] He also has the power to diminish it again according to . . . His righteous judgment."[159]

Probably written before the sixth century, this story indicates how monks of a later generation were taught to think about the material wealth that their monasteries had acquired over time. While acknowledging that they had a burden to bear that their saintly predecessors had studiously avoided, it also asserts, more positively, that this was no cause for dismay. Theodore's monks had God's blessing; their wealth was God's wealth, which would wax or wane as God judged fit. A similar outlook is expressed in other cenobitic literature. According to the *Regulations of Horsiesius,* Theodore's predecessor had declared that as long as Pachomian monks displayed their accustomed fear of God, then "in this age too He will give us the blessings of all the saints for everything that we shall undertake, either in the village or in the field. And he will bless our bread and water; and the rest of the blessings."[160] This is possibly the first time in antiquity that moralists talked about the acquisition and possession of material surplus in such positive terms—and, paradoxically, it took Christian ascetics to do it. Conversely, tales were also told about communities that lost their wealth for failing to open their storerooms for hungry orphans and the poor.[161]

It is no coincidence that this discourse arose in the fifth and sixth centuries. As noted at the beginning of this book, monasteries in this era attained, for the first time, not only increasing wealth but also integration into the economic life of the mainstream empire.[162] Monks regularly bought and sold huts, leased land, formed corporations, and sometimes overspent, falling into debt.[163] No doubt the gold that Palestinian abbots annually received as *eulogiai* from Constantinopolitan patrons helped them not only issue rations and hospitality but also pay taxes, purchase grain, or use other funds for these purposes.[164] But such mundane concerns were not central to the Early Byzantine discourse on blessings. This focused instead on explaining and preserving the privileged status of Christian holy people within the divine *oikonomia*, God's dispensation. Above all, it sought to help ascetics reconcile their newfound wealth with an older tradition of Christian holiness based on material renunciations. It did so by inculcating new ways of conceptualizing such wealth, its origins, and the responsibilities that came with it.

Basil of Caesarea in the fourth century had already formulated the orthodox view: "A person will not be condemned because he has [possessions], but because he cared for them wrongly, or used them badly." He was untroubled by monks possessing property, as long as they cultivated a detached (*aprospathēs*) attitude, using it to help others.[165] Yet it remained challenging to think about property in terms other than personal possession. The problem, Basil observed, was the propensity for *prospatheia,* an emotional attachment that, when left unremedied, could engender not only possessiveness but a desire for compensation for anything taken or given away. Considered basic to laypeople and novice monks, this weakened all but the most advanced: "A pious person will give to anyone who asks, and the more pious . . . even when not asked," observes John Climacus. "But to be able to ask for nothing back from the recipient is perhaps characteristic only of those who are entirely free of emotional attachments."[166] When his steward became angry with monks who failed to return their monastery's goods, Dorotheus reminded him to regard these "not as things of his own, but as things dedicated to God," in order to diminish his personal attachment (*prospatheia*) to them. The steward replied that he liked the advice but found it hard to put into practice.[167]

That attests both the spiritual goal and the difficulty of attaining it: how to achieve sufficient detachment to appreciate resources in terms of divine providence rather than possession or gain? According to John of Gaza, one way was to thank God for anything one received while judging oneself unworthy to receive it. Doing so, he explained, not only kept one from becoming unduly attached to whatever was offered, but also, as a result, "God will make it something sacred, and a blessing."[168] Thus, one way to turn something into a blessing was to have the humility not to take it for granted.

Otherwise, attaining such a perspective required "migrating," as Basil put it, "to another world in our habit of mind."[169] Karl Heussi once observed that a basic purpose of a monastery was to create a *Sonderwelt* in which monks could learn to see their existence in a divine light.[170] As far as material circumstances were concerned, this was primarily achieved by disassociating all they received from its original human origin by redirecting gifts sent by outside donors away from their intended recipients and toward the abbot or steward, who kept them for distribution later as gifts "from our Lord."[171] Some institutions went to great lengths to instill a sense of wonder in this regard. Stewards of a monastery in Italy were instructed to suspend the daily bread in a basket above the abbot's refectory table. At each meal, after the abbot had said grace, the basket would be lowered by a pulley, so that the "rations for God's workmen might seem to be coming down from heaven."[172]

Metaphorical language offered a subtler means of shaping monastic perceptions. As Bentley Layton notes, learning the vocabulary that monasteries applied to food was a way by which new recruits "internalized monastic reality" and became monks.[173] By the sixth century, "blessing" was a basic element of that initiatory vocabulary, as seen in the *Life of Matrona of Perge*. When Matrona joined a male and female confederation in Constantinople, the first things that its leader issued to her, besides a monastic gown, were three *eulogiai*. Others were similarly inducted: "When they came, he blessed them, and [after] admonishing them with many passages from the Holy Scriptures . . . he gave them *eulogiai* and sent them off to their mother superior." Later, when a highborn woman sought to join, she asked to be given "some of the *eulogiai* of which the sisters partook." The steward refused, warning that, as an aristocrat, she would not be able to stomach such frugal fare.

Receiving such basic blessings from an abbot served not only to mark initiation into a monastic hierarchy but to raise awareness of the divine hand at work behind their material existence. When asked how she and her ascetics could afford their apartments, Matrona reportedly responded, "God and our abbot provide them for us."[174] Thus, the very language of blessings helped explain and mystify at once the origins of church and monastic wealth. Ideally, it inculcated a religious outlook that appreciated the divine agency behind one's provisions, so that whatever was received, no matter how slight, was perceived as a gift from God.

Of course, upholding this outlook in Early Byzantium was the solid structure of lay benefaction and imperial subsidies that sustained it. As noted in chapter 1, the East Roman imperial superstructure supplied churches and, by extension, affiliated monasteries with a portion of the state *annona*. These subsidies suggest why gifts called blessings became so prominent in early Byzantine hagiography, yet left no comparable trace in Western hagiography.[175] But also important was the steady stream of religious offerings that laypeople bestowed in quantities great and small. Whether designated as fruitbearings (*karpophoriai*) or liturgical oblations (*prosphorai, oblationes, qurbānē*), these offerings paved "the road to riches" for most Christian institutions of the day.[176] Such gifts were believed to merit something in return, however. "Truly, people who give fruitbearings to a monastery are making offerings to God, from whom they receive their reward," writes Cyril of Scythopolis.[177] It was precisely because lay donors expected something in return for their offerings that they had to be handled with such care. But what did donors want in return? And what made them think that any particular church, monk, or monastery could obtain it for them?

"You Are the Firstfruits of the World"

Monasticism, Fruitbearings, and Prosperity
in the Countryside

One day in the fourth century some pious laymen arrived at the desert settlement of Scetis, home to the greatest Christian ascetics of late Roman Egypt. These were not the usual pilgrims who came to get prayers and blessings throughout the year. As explained by John Cassian (ca. 360–435), they were landowners (*possessores*) and farmers of means, who had banded together to cross the desert, travelling sixty miles in the stifling heat of a late Egyptian spring. They had come to deliver "religious gifts" from the Nile valley on occasion of Pentecost. We do not know how many there were, but their group would have travelled overnight with a train of pack animals, since they were bringing "tithes and firstfruits produced from their properties," apparently all agricultural goods.[1]

Upon reaching the settlement, they immediately went to meet its communal guest master, named Abba John. Seeing their gifts, John reportedly exclaimed, "I am delighted, my sons, at the kind generosity of your donations, and gratefully accept the devotion that is part of this offering."

> By offering these things, you believe that your entire harvest and all your property, from which you have given this for the Lord's sake, will be abundantly blessed and that you yourselves will be heaped high with a vast abundance of every good thing even in this world, in keeping with his trustworthy command: "Honor the Lord from your righteous labors, and give him the fruits of your righteousness, so that your barns may be full of an abundance of wheat and your winepresses may be overflowing with wine" [Prv 3: 9–10].[2]

John commended them for observing Old Testament standards of righteousness. Then he took the opportunity to suggest an even higher standard. If they wished to be perfect, he observed, Jesus had proposed that they sell whatever they had and follow him (Mt 19:21). This meant offering their souls by becoming monks. Such a sacrifice was not obligatory, he conceded, but Christians who continued to offer just firstfruits and tithes from their possessions would miss out on the great treasures Jesus had promised for the perfect who reached heaven. What such landowners would have made of Abba John's proposal, we do not know, but Cassian says that one of them, named Theonas, took his words to heart. Upon returning home, he sold all his property, abandoned his wife, and returned to Scetis to become a monk.

Later in life, this same Theonas, now a venerable elder, related his story to Cassian, who then used it to open his chapter "On Pentecost" in his *Conferences,* the great compendium of anchoretic dialogues Cassian wrote in the 430s for monks who wished to imitate the desert fathers in southern Gaul. For all Cassian's artifice there is no reason to doubt its plausibility. It presumes that long before the end of the fourth century, landowning Christians in Egypt had become accustomed to bringing non-liturgical offerings to rural monasteries at Pentecost. In this case the tithes (*dekatai, decimae*—theoretically, a tenth of one's profits or produce, an amount scripturally justified by Abraham's gift of gratitude to the priest-king Melchizedek, "one tenth of everything," Gn 14:20) and firstfruits (*aparchai, primitiae, rēšyātā, nišorp*—theoretically, the best portion of one's profits or produce) probably consisted of wheat, corn, or barley, because Cassian points out that they had come from the landowners' harvests, and these were the harvests that took place in Egypt before and during the season of Pentecost (late May–late June).

Indeed, this lay practice was not just restricted to Egypt. What Cassian describes could have been found in most of the Near East, where a similar Christian custom of giving firstfruits from grain harvests at Pentecost had taken hold by the fifth century.[3] In Syria, Theodoret of Cyrrhus interpreted the Old Testament command "Observe the festival of the harvest, of the firstfruits of your labor" (Ex 23:16) as an anticipation of the Christian celebration of Pentecost.[4] Barsauma is said to have returned from the wilds of Armenia to his monastery in northern Mesopotamia each year at the beginning of Pentecost so as to keep the feast with villagers who had come bearing gifts like Cassian's farmers: "At such times Barsauma would take all the grace that God sent him," writes his hagiographer, "and distribute it to the poor and to the brethren wherever they were."[5]

Such descriptions alert us to a fact that contemporary readers would have taken for granted: namely, that prestigious church and monastic institutions would have been able to anticipate receiving deliveries of non-liturgical offerings each year on a regular schedule, tied to the agricultural cycle on which the rest of the late Roman economy and tax structure depended. For most people living in the Roman Empire, life revolved around these annual exactions and deliveries. This itself helps explain the prevalence in hagiography of the timely delivery of "blessings" of grain and other foodstuffs to monasteries at the end of a lean period.[6] A fifth-century example expects readers to see the temporal connection. When, toward the end of Lent, the Apollo monastery in upper Egypt discovered its food supplies had almost run out, we are told that its monks prayed so hard that a company of laymen suddenly arrived delivering bread and fruits, "all remarkably out of season"—that is, fresher than they should have been that time of year, before the new harvest. The monks subsisted on these donations "till Pentecost," when they could expect their stores to be replenished in the usual fashion.[7] There are signs that such firstfruits were given in substantial amounts. Seventh-century papyri from perhaps the same Apollo monastery show that it annually used the *aparches* it collected from local villagers during the grain harvest to cover taxes it owed to the government, which also came due at that time.[8] Thus, some institutions received firstfruits not only on a predictable yearly basis but in sufficient quantities to pay off consequential annual debts.

This chapter focuses on how authorities justified and encouraged Christian laypeople to furnish churches, monasteries, and ascetics with gifts of gratitude in Early Byzantium. Firstfruits and tithes were qualitative and quantitative descriptors of a general category of religious gift called a "fruitbearing" (*karpophoria*).[9] Of all the religious gifts discussed so far, this may seem the most commonplace. The Greek term *karpophoria* had been in use since classical times, and parallels to its Christian usage can be found in Greco-Roman cults and Hebrew traditions.[10] In all three traditions, such gifts were meant to be given to express gratitude for divine benefits bestowed, both commercial and agricultural (*karpos*, "fruit," being a standard word for profit), as well as corporeal and spiritual. In Christian tradition, they were given in gratitude for material profits as much as for physical healings.[11] In return, donors received assurance that they would continue receiving such blessings in the future. As a fourth-century preacher informed his audience at Alexandria, "If you have given the firstfruits of your threshing floors and wine presses to the house of God just as it was commanded to us, 'Honor God, give him your firstfruits' [Prv 3:19,] . . . your storehouses will be filled and your wine overflow."[12] Likewise, the monk Isidore assured a landowner named Count Herminus in Pelusium, "You honor God well by sending us firstfruits of your profits and a tithe to Him Who gave your land its bounty. You will enjoy it for many seasons, preserving whatever is needed for your self-sufficiency for now, and providing eternal joy in the future."[13]

As these examples show, this type of religious gift giving was explicitly self-interested. It was not, however, simply a calculated, "I-give-that-you-might-give" (*do-ut-des*) religious transaction. As Theodora Jim has argued regarding firstfruits in classical Greece, they represented a post-factum acknowledgment of divine favors already received: "It was their backwards-looking character that made them akin to thank-offerings."[14] Likewise, the very essence of a Christian fruitbearing was its expression of gratitude for divine benefits already bestowed.

If such offerings remained constant throughout Mediterranean antiquity, it was partly because farmers had few other options for hedging against their fickle agricultural environment. But Jewish and Christian farmers had further considerations. Monotheism taught them that their deity controlled the natural elements, that humans were there to manage his creation, and that fruitbearings represented his due of what was rightfully his. An inscription found on several ancient synagogue and church floors neatly conveys the circularity of this religious reasoning in psalmist terms: "Your things, from Your things" (*ta sa, ek tōn sōn*).[15] The piety that caused people to provide such religious offerings may be compared to that of tenants living on an estate who felt entitled to reap the benefits of a harvest as long as they delivered a cut of the crop to the lord of their domain. Climacus says that farmers sometimes chose to sow a special type of seed to have enough to honor their lord with gifts.[16] He was writing about ascetics, but the basis of his analogy is clear.

To complete this analogy, however, we must consider this particular landlord's stewards and bailiffs, his religious intermediaries on the ground. Jewish and Christian traditions both held that, since God had no use for material profits himself, he ordained that his representatives on earth should receive them instead.[17] Whether delivered to a bishop's palace during the harvest, deposited in a collection box before a church service, or contributed during special church fundraisers (sometimes a good translation for *karpophoria* is just "vow" or "contribution"), such gifts provided a pool of resources that church and monastic leaders could divide among themselves, ransom prisoners or use to support needy members of their community, following the example of the prophet Elisha, who bestowed on his village all the "firstlings" of corn and barley that a donor had given him (2 Kgs 4:42).[18] Epiphanius of Salamis (d. 403) notes that some priests worked solely to provide *karpophoriai* "for the needy brethren with their own hands"; likewise, monks who worked the harvests in the Nile valley reportedly sent a portion of their earnings to Alexandria each year for dispersal to the poor.[19] But we mainly hear about fruitbearings being given directly to clerics and monks themselves. Indeed, thanks to hagiography, we especially hear about them being given to monks. Cyril of Scythopolis notes that citizens of the town of Madaba in Transjordan regularly visited the anchorite Sabas in the Judean desert "in order to draw on his many spiritual benefits and give his monasteries and lavras *karpophoriai* of beans and grain." Like Cassian, Cyril presents this as a routine expression of Christian lay piety, one that needed little explanation or defense.[20]

It is clear that such fruitbearings bore close resemblance to the material blessings discussed in the last chapter, which were themselves often given in the form of grain or other foodstuffs. Leontius of Neapolis virtually equates the two in his *Life of John the Almsgiver* in an episode where the bishop receives a large *karpophoria* of cash from a widow and then identifies it as a *eulogia* God had placed in the widow's heart to give.[21] Evidently, the two types of gifts could become identical when given with the right spirit. Other similarities and differences will be noted below. Here it should be pointed out that unlike blessings, however, there is no record of clerics or monks ever similarly offering fruitbearings directly to laypeople (as opposed to sending them to a church, in support of its institutional almsgiving). But many laypeople may have considered a fruitbearing to be simply the dark side of a blessing. No other Christian gift in this period is so strongly associated with allegations of compulsion and even extortion. A law of the fifth century reports that bishops and priests were punishing communities that did not provide such gifts in the Constantinopolitan hinterland. "None of the most God-beloved bishops or clerics," the law decrees, "should constrain laypeople unwillingly to payment of *karpophoriai*, which in the provinces are called firstfruits or offerings, exacting these as if a kind of tax." "We have learned," it says, "that entire villages and agricultural regions have come under excommunications and anathemas," their sacraments being withheld, including baptism. The practice violated Christian principle, "for it is obvious that it is proper for each to contribute to God and to those who serve him from his own labors whatever he himself should think right voluntarily, and not be forced or compelled to do this."[22]

Voluntary or involuntary—that was the question. While an emperor might have thought it "obvious" that no one was obliged to give church leaders such fruitbearings "as if a kind of tax," this may have been far less clear to the ordinary laity. Early Byzantine church authorities remained studiously ambiguous on the matter (unlike their counterparts in sixth-century Gaul, who officially pronounced tithes obligatory).[23] Typical are the contradictory pronouncements of the third-century *Didascalia*, which first demands that congregations provide clergy with firstfruits and tithes, then in the same chapter states that Christians were released from all such Old Testament obligations; typical too were the *a fortiori* arguments of Chrysostom and Jerome, who maintained that firstfruits and tithes were not obligatory for Christians, but if Jews had given them, so should Christians all the more.[24] Such authorities were trying to tread a line between obligation and discretion. It took a real radical to cross that line and say what others preferred to leave implicit. In the 420s a monk named Alexander allegedly did just that:

> You seem to me to have an outlandish practice, using insults and rage to compel people to furnish you with *karpophoriai*. These are not fruitbearings. Rather, they are ... inappropriate to the extreme and harsher than the most oppressive public taxation and impositions. Please stop this improper behavior and devote yourself instead to prayer and spiritual tranquility. Then God will rouse worthy people of good character to offer to you everything sufficient for your needs.[25]

Written by Nilus of Ancyra (d. ca. 435), this letter presents a monk trying to police his profession.[26] Significantly, he was not challenging Alexander's right to receive and live on *karpophoriai*, but the overbearing means by which he was extracting them from the laity. His observation that Alexander's demands resembled a form of taxation anticipates the language of the imperial law, and indicates that a discourse was developing in the fifth century around the abuse of such offerings, a discourse that pertained not only to clerics but also to monks.

Such tensions frame the questions explored in this chapter. How did monks justify their receipt of lay fruitbearings? Their claim initially did not go uncontested. Bishops at Gangra in Asia Minor (Çankırı, Turkey) in the 340s or 350s condemned a group of monks for claiming an exclusive right to church *karpophoriai* on the grounds that they (alone, it seems) were "holy people."[27] No subsequent contestation is recorded, but this incident should prompt us to ask what rationales were used to persuade laypeople to give monks such gifts or to believe that they would be "abundantly blessed" (to quote Abba John of Scetis) as a result.

Here the rationale that the *Apostolic Constitutions* added to the third-century *Didascalia* is illuminating: to its exhortation "Give to your priest the things owed to him," its fourth-century redactors added the justification "as to one who provides mediation with God for people in need of purification and intercession."[28] Hagiography promoted a similar notion that monks served as mediators between God and sinners, providing expert prayers and purifications needed to coax God's blessings down from heaven. It almost went without saying that their efforts merited honor and expressions of gratitude through fruitbearings. Peter Brown notes that hagiographers tended to gloss over the gifts expected from the laity, preferring to focus instead on a saint's asceticism and "the seemingly effortless, gravity-free flow of divine favors that stemmed from his person in the form of acts of success-ful . . . intercession," rather than discussing the economic aspects of the relationship.[29] This hagiography did, however, propagate novel ideas about the power of ascetic prayer and penance to protect or transform the natural environment, and it occasionally mentions how these efforts garnered gifts of gratitude.

To put this into historical perspective, we must set these Christian penitential practices against the kind of aid that other religious experts had been providing in the countryside throughout antiquity. Indeed, the discourse that developed around monastic fruitbearings must be understood in relation to three concurrent trends found in the fifth-century Mediterranean Near East: first, the expansion of agriculture into previously uncultivated regions; second, the simultaneous proliferation of monasteries within those same regions; and third, the emergence of a penitential form of Christian asceticism that combined the public performance of intercessory prayers with spectacular feats of self-mortification. Exemplified above all by pillar saints like Symeon Stylites (d. 459), such asceticism differed markedly from the contemplative pursuit of tranquility promoted by recluses like Barsanuphius, inasmuch as it emphasized an extraordinary level of physical suffering aimed at purifying its practitioners and making God sympathetic to their requests. While it would be wrong to distinguish too strongly between penitential and philosophical forms of monasticism in Early Byzantium (Isaiah of Scetis's *Asceticon* incorporates elements of both),[30] hagiographers drew a direct connection between the afflictions endured by monks like Symeon and their capacity to persuade God to bless creation as a whole. The result was a very public class of penitential "holy men," a religious resource that promised to bear fruit even in the most unforgiving countryside.

AGRARIAN AND MONASTIC EXPANSION
ON THE RURAL MARGINS

One of the remarkable achievements of archaeology in the past quarter century has been to demonstrate that, with few exceptions and contrary to prior assumptions, the Early Byzantine period was one of the greatest eras of agricultural expansion the Near East has ever seen. New surveys and excavations have revealed a rural world that was almost lost to history. Far from the deteriorating or deserted conditions that economic historians who only knew the Roman legal sources envisioned in the 1960s and 1970s, archaeologists have uncovered a countryside that was "busy" with production and development. Evidence for this phenomenon used to be restricted to the seven hundred or so separate ghost towns of the Limestone Massif, the plateau of rolling hills located east of Antioch in northwestern Syria above the Orontes River, and the six so-called dead cities of the Negev desert southeast of the Gaza Strip in southern Israel. The carefully constructed stone houses, churches, towers, grain silos, and hydraulic installations found in these locations have never failed to impress (villages on the Massif contained between twenty and fifty stone houses, usually consisting of two stories, with verandas overlooking inner courtyards), but until recently they stood as anomalies in a landscape otherwise imagined as critically depressed. Now instead, they represent the best-preserved examples of a proliferation of settlements on marginal land that had never been exploited before and, in the case of northwest Syria and the Negev, never since. Surface finds indicates that this efflorescence lasted between the third and seventh centuries, reflecting roughly four hundred years of prosperity, "a period of material abundance sharply defined by periods of material absence."[31] Terraces, dams, and cisterns in hard-to-access terrain from the upper reaches of Cilicia to the arid plateaus of Anatolia and Transjordan attest the sheer exertion of labor invested to maximize its potential for cultivation. Decorative masonry, coin hoards, and church treasures, as well as the founding of whole new "agro-towns" in these regions, attest the resulting boom in agricultural productivity.[32]

It is hard not to be exuberant over these discoveries. "Rarely, if ever, in the history of the pre-industrial Mediterranean," remarks Michael Decker, "have levels of agrarian development, intensity of settlement, and a combination of security, easy communication and monetization coalesced than they do in the late antique East."[33] Evidently, the demand for food in Constantinople and the concentration of fortresses on the eastern frontier stimulated new markets and trade networks that encouraged rural development, making Early Byzantium one of the economic high points of Near Eastern history. Moreover, large aristocratic estates do not seem to have predominated or directed this development, as once believed. Except in the Nile valley, most big estates were located along the Mediterranean coastland or in the suburbs of major cities. Of course, powerful landlords continued to operate in absentia, owning entire villages and demanding various forms of corvées and tribute from their serfs on top of rents.[34] But unlike Western Europe, where castellated manors dominated the countryside from the fifth century onward, the Roman Empire of the East tended to feature small estates and a freer peasantry.[35] There was also a general leveling, or greater diffusion, of monuments of "civilization," as cities began to shrink and villages began grow, with multiple churches being built in the latter. Most intriguing is the emergence of the "urban villages," or agro-towns (kōmopoleis, metrocomiae) mentioned above. Run by local headmen, these agglomerations of rustic homes, churches, and workhouses tended to produce a single commodity.[36] These provided a new basis for communal solidarity in the countryside. Epigraphy and hagiography from Asia Minor show villagers banding together to act against distant dynasts in the sixth and seventh centuries, suggesting the growth of a "rustic audacity" similar to what Ariel López and others have found in Early Byzantine Egypt.[37]

Most important for our purposes, the archaeological evidence from Asia Minor, Syria, and the Negev suggests the growth of independent farmsteads, built on a small or medium scale in previously unexploited areas.[38] As seen below, the *Life of Symeon Stylites* refers to plots on the Limestone Massif that were independently owned and worked by local priests and headmen alike. Indeed, the houses constructed in this area display a modest grandeur, reflecting the pride derived from hard-earned agricultural or pastoral wealth. Michael Decker and Peter Brown have drawn attention to a series of inscriptions that give poetic voice to such rural pride. These epigrams, written in Greek in southwest Syria, once adorned the stone houses that stood in the area. What is striking is their allusions not only to the fortunes that built the houses but also to the personal labor that built the fortunes: made "out of my own toils" says one; "from farming," "from farm work," "from noble farming" say the others.[39] Dated to the late fourth century, these inscriptions, besides celebrating an owner's acquisition of material wealth, capture a brief moment in antiquity when toiling in the fields could be presented as a point of personal pride and boasting.

At the same time this rural setting also saw a boom in Christian monasteries and ascetic culture. Thanks to hagiography, it has long been known that communities with hundreds of monks run by powerful abbots began to proliferate in the fifth century. Yet, except for the Pachomian confederation along the Nile, most of these were suburban foundations, located just outside cities like Constantinople, Jerusalem, and Amida. They were prestige institutions, built in affluent neighborhoods alongside large secular estates. Only recently have archaeological surveys revealed a simultaneous proliferation of much smaller communities in rural regions ranging from Lycia to northern Mesopotamia, western Galilee, and the Negev. Accommodating thirty monks or fewer, their ruins include storage tanks, silos, and equipment to process grain, grapes, or olives. They are nearly indistinguishable from ordinary farmsteads, except for consistently being surrounded by walls, situated near churches, and set apart from other houses.[40]

Such rural monasticism mapped onto the agricultural expansion described above. Most striking is the proximity between these monasteries and the local villages. That they existed as such close quarters in these regions had already been inferred from anti-Chalcedonian letters written in the 560s. The archimandrites, anchorites, and stylites who signed these letters (137 monastic signatories in all) also recorded the connection of their monastery to one of fourteen villages. Sometimes four or five monasteries are identified with a single village; as many as ten were attributed to a village outside of Damascus.[41] Fieldwork has made plain that these monasteries were indeed built very close to, if not actually ensconced within, such villages. In the Galilee, most of them were "integrated into fringes of villages or connected by a short path."[42] Monks and villagers lived virtually side by side; monks may have kept their distance, but there was no isolation. Indeed, it is estimated that half of the 120 known monastic sites on the Limestone Massif—a strip of land consisting of about 30,400 acres (12,290 hectares)—were built within half a mile of a village, and more than three-quarters of them placed within eyesight.[43] Thus, monasteries and stylites became a distinct and integral feature of the Early Byzantine landscape, so that inhabitants of these areas would have undoubtably known about and frequently encountered local Christian holy people.[44] Indeed, by the seventh century, "a traveller on the Roman road from Antioch to Dana and Chalcis/Beroea would have found himself, whether willing or not, within the visual range of a holy man for over 10 km, or 2 to 3 hours of travel, and never more than 2.4 km distant from the next pillar ascetic."[45] This makes all the more plausible the report that villagers sleeping in their fields on the Limestone Massif could hear angels singing around Symeon Stylites's pillar at night, so close were they to his hilltop enclosure.[46]

What was the economic relationship between these rural monasteries and the surrounding villages? This is a perennial question. For the Limestone Massif, Lukas Schachner has simply proposed "a framework of mutual dependence whose details presumably are still buried in the ground."[47] One reason for his caution is the rhetoric of Syrian monastic literature itself. Syrian authorities of the third, fourth, and fifth centuries not only identified manual labor with Adam's Fall, but also promoted the notion that to regain his prelapsarian, paradisal condition, monks must abstain from all such labor, devoting themselves totally to spiritual work instead. We know some monks embraced this ideal, including the stylites who stood on pillars over the Limestone Massif from the fifth century onward, high on prayer. In Peter Brown's view, "These work-free avatars of [prelapsarian] Adam were not rejected as layabouts. . . . In a society caught in a frenzy of labor, they had opened a window onto another, more ancient, more free world."[48]

With these comments, Brown is challenging entrenched prejudices. Modern historians have been quick to assume that the relationship between rural monks and local laypeople was parasitic. But the ascetic perfectionism that Syrian authorities prescribed seems to have been adopted by a highly ascetic, stellar few. Fifth-century sources betray a different norm. Nilus of Ancyra and Rabbula of Edessa both inveigh against monks for spending their days pursuing material wealth by tending fields and raising livestock; Ishāq of Antioch urges them to put down their ploughs, complaining that the sun blushed at seeing them stuffing their silos with grain and storing so much wine in their cellars.[49] Archaeology supports this story. Oil presses, millstones, and storage spaces found at monastic "industrial facilities" on the Massif seem to have accommodated a surplus exceeding the needs of their residents.[50] No doubt some operated like manorial estates, using slaves, serfs, or hired laymen to work the land; some were also funded by bishops precisely so that they could devote themselves to prayer and doctrinal vigilance.[51]

We may get an accurate picture of what such prestige monasteries looked like from a later source that lists the possessions of the Qartmin/Mar Gabriel monastery in northern Mesopotamia before 580:

> The monastery had camels and mules and horses on which they brought flour from the mills which they possessed in Mt. Singara and the Valley of Henehna . . . and in the city of Sarwan and in the city of Nisibis and in Harmoso. In Mt. Singara was another monastery called after Mar Gabriel and monks who lived there by ploughs. Serfs who belonged to this monastery could collect the food and the seed and everything and would grind the flour and sent it with [other] serfs to the monastery. They would also tend the vineyards that the monastery possessed there. Peasants and hired men worked [here] too. The monastery also possessed parks and lands and gardens in the city of Nisibis and in Sarwan and in the region of Hezu, and in all the region of Hesno and indeed in every region and village.[52]

This describes (seemingly one) full-fledged monastic estate, with holdings of land, vineyards, pack animals, and free and unfree laborers as well as other assets on par with those of great secular domains. This account claims that Qartmin/Mar Gabriel had been given seven villages by Emperor Anastasius (r. 491–518) in addition to "vows" from many other admirers. Yet elsewhere in Syria, monasticism was far more humble, like that of rural Palestine. Here, archaeologists have detected the presence of "tiller monks" who toiled in the fields to generate an agricultural surplus like ordinary farmers.[53] It has even been speculated that most of the agricultural work outside Jerusalem should be attributed to small rural monasteries, which may have been satellites of much larger suburban institutions.[54]

Thus, archaeology suggests a different picture than what we find in ascetic literature. What should we make of this discrepancy? Rather than presuming a sharp disagreement among Syrian monks on the issue of manual labor, we should probably assume that most, at least by the mid-fifth century, regarded it like other ministrations, with physical labors assigned to more "corporeal" novices so that advanced monks could attend to administrative duties, scribal work, or hagiographical compositions (Symeon Stylites's hagiographers affirm that they wrote his *Life* "by the toil of their hand and the sweat of their brows"), as well as spiritual labors.[55] Such a division is implied by John of Ephesus's description of an elderly rich layman's hesitation to retire to a Syrian monastery. "What should I do?" he reflected. "If I go to a monastery, I cannot work and they will say, 'This man has come upon us in order to receive a gift of honor.'"[56] Indeed, we may speculate that assignments of labor for monastic residents depended on how much money each of them had donated upon joining. But we also know that some monasteries in Syria required labor from all as a matter of policy. Symeon Stylites the Younger insisted that his disciples should never touch any of the fruitbearings people sent; he demanded instead that they obtain their food entirely by "toiling at manual labor" in the orchards and fields below the Marvelous Mountain, so that all else could be given over for the poor. Seeing all the lay offerings piling up, some of his monks grumbled, but Symeon held firm to this "sage *oikonomia*," claiming it had been ordained from the start by an angel, "both so you will not burden people, and so your monastery will always have what it needs."[57]

I therefore propose that regimens of monastic labor were far more variegated in rural Syria than has usually been imagined. Of course, the fact that the *Life of Symeon Stylites the Younger* mentions Symeon's imposition of physical labor on everyone in his monastery suggests that it was unusual to demand it of all. Theodoret of Cyrrhus depicts a fifth-century abbot in rural Cilicia instructing his monks to "add to their labors of the soul the sweat of bodily exertions," as the Apostle Paul had done (1 Thes 2:9; Acts 20:4). The abbot explained,

> While those engaged in life toil and labor to support their children and wives, and in addition pay taxes, and are dunned for tribute, and also offer firstfruits to God, and supply the needs of beggars as far as they can, it would be absurd for us not to supply our essential needs from labor . . . but to sit indoors with our hands folded, reaping the work of other hands.[58]

The speech shows sensitivity, at least on Theodoret's part, to the possible awkward differences between monks and peasants in the countryside. A century later Cyril of Scythopolis copied it almost verbatim to explain why Palestinian monks, "especially novices," should work and not "reap the toils of others."[59] This advocacy of productive labor for cenobitic monks was more in keeping with the secular spirit of the day than were the complaints of Nilus and Ishāq mentioned above. But we should not assume that its intention was merely to deflect criticism from outside detractors of monasticism. It may have been meant to forestall criticisms arising within monasteries themselves. John of Ephesus recalls meeting a monk visiting his monastery near Amida who refused to eat anything without mumbling many words of grace at every bite. When asked about this practice, the monk replied that he was afraid of consuming anything without first praying "for those who labor and sweat and toil to supply my need." For how, he reasoned, can it be that God would not be angry that "instead of pray[ing] for the men whose sweat and labor we eat, we sit and enjoy ourselves in idle talk?"[60] Sharp words—but this criticism was directed against other monks in the monastery who forgot to say grace at all, while sitting talking about business. In the same story, John mentions monks who "attended to the plots of land" after the liturgy.[61] Rather than attesting sensitivity to the exploitation of outside laborers, his story may recall grumblings against monastic elites who were not sufficiently grateful of how hard the junior members were working to supply their needs.

In any case, such stories may explain the emphasis placed by Syrian monastic literature on the sheer *ponos*—physical labor or toil—that elite asceticism entailed. References to the "toil of asceticism" and to various monks' "love of toil" abound in descriptions of their rigors.[62] Theodoret, for example, to explain the aforementioned abbot's decision to include manual labor in his own ascetic regimen before imposing it on his monastery as a whole, writes that the abbot was deliberately "augmenting his *ponoi* with *ponoi*"—heaping toils on his toils.[63] Even if this motif originated in classical athletic parlance, by the fifth century it had become basic to the way monks were taught to think about the physical aspects of their profession. Indeed, advanced regimens of ascetic prayer were nothing if not demanding, including multiple upward stretches and downward prostrations conducted in repeated cycles over long periods of time, often carried out amid rigorous fasting. Theodoret recalls that one of his attendants once tried to count all the head-to-toe movements that he saw Symeon Stylites the Elder perform one day: he managed to count 1,244 genuflections before giving up.[64] Thus, at least in theory, elite monks were all toiling, all the time; even if not visibly in motion, each was "tilling the earth of his heart."[65] Such ascetic imagery was patently inspired by the agrarian setting and culture. But were such monastic labors actually valued by rural populations?

A SYRIAN VILLAGE PERSPECTIVE:
THE *LETTER OF COSMAS OF PANÎR*

There is considerable evidence that they were. In a letter to a local cenobium, Severus of Antioch wrote that a monk's footsteps could make a barren desert "spring to life."[66] He wrote this to ingratiate himself to a community that supported his doctrinal initiatives, but he was drawing on an old hagiographical conceit.

Egyptian and Palestinian hagiographers had already been depicting monks as having the power to bring fertility upon marginal landscapes since the late fourth century. We are told that farmers came to Abba Copres's Egyptian monastery each year
carrying shovels. When asked why, Copres explained that after he had converted
them, these farmers asked him and his monks to pray for their harvest. He
responded that if they truly believed in God, even the desert would bear fruit.
"Without a moment's hesitation," Copres said, "they filled the folds of their tunics
with the sand . . . trodden by us, and bringing it to me, asked me to bless it." Since
this resulted in a bountiful crop, "it is now their custom to do this, and every year
they trouble us for sand."[67] John Rufus, a sixth-century hagiographer, claims that an
imperial officer in Cilicia once chased down Peter the Iberian and his monastic
companion, asking them to live on his land if he gave them a monastery with an
endowment. Rufus later says that another layman in Gaza spent large sums to build
a place for Peter beside his vineyards near the sea to the south of the city. The vineyards had produced low-quality wine due to the sandy soil. After persuading Peter
to stay, the landowner took him around each of his vineyards so that he could bless
them all. Thereafter, the grapes began to abound in great quality and quantity,
"something that no one from among the workers of that soil [could] ever remember
happening."[68] Such miracles might induce any farmer to put a monk on his land.
We are told that villagers near a monastery outside Alexandria "kept constant watch
so they would not be deprived of their blessing and . . . presence among them."[69]

Fortunately, we also have evidence that this was not just a hagiographical conceit. The so-called *Letter of Cosmas of Panîr* is preserved as an attachment to the
earliest version of the Syriac life of Symeon Stylites the Elder. This *Life*, discussed
below, is one of the very few Early Byzantine hagiographies whose provenance and
date of completion are known with precision: its colophon records that it was completed by two authors, Symeon Bar-Eupolemus and Bar-Ḥaṭar, son of Aden, "on
the seventeenth of the month Nisan, on the fourth day of the week, in the year 521
according to the Antiochene reckoning."[70] In other words, on April 17, 473 CE,
fourteen years after Symeon Stylites had died in 459. The colophon also states that
it was finished in the time of a priest named Symeon and his archdeacon, Cyrus.
Dina Boero argues that these are the same Symeon of Marimîn and Cyrus mentioned by inscriptions as the founders of a hostel built on the road leading up to
the stylite's enclosure at Telneshe (Telanissos in Greek; modern Dayr Simʿān,
Syria), a village on the Limestone Massif, just off the highway that connected Antioch to Beroea (Aleppo, Syria).[71]

This hostel, to judge from its ample ruins, was built with big ambitions. It consisted of three limestone dormitories, each fitted out with arched windows, a stable,
courtyard, and refectory. Its construction took place between 471 and 479 and enabled Telneshe to become a major pilgrim site. Indeed, it was probably built in anticipation of the cross-shaped martyrium eventually built around Symeon's column

on top of the hill in the 490s, creating the cult center that, thanks to its magnitude, would later become known as Qal'at Sim'ān ("Symeon's Castle").[72] If so, Symeon the Priest and Cyrus appear to have been farsighted entrepreneurs, instrumental in helping Telneshe capitalize on its deceased saint's reputation for dispensing blessings and cures. A Greek inscription found at their hostel can be read either as "Health is gain to its guests" or "Health to its guests is gain," displaying an ambiguity perhaps emblematic of the aims of the project as a whole.[73] An account of Symeon's ascetic deeds would have been central to this project, and Boero proposes that the clerics commissioned the hagiographers Bar-Eupolemus and Bar-Ḥaṭar to produce it, which they completed three years into the construction of the hostel.[74]

The result was a masterpiece of early Syriac hagiography, one unusual feature of which is the non-hagiographical document attached to its end as supporting testimony. Introduced as the *Letter of Cosmas of Panîr*, it takes up nearly three columns of Assemani's editio princeps. There is no reason to doubt its authenticity.[75] Since we now know that Bar-Eupolemus and Bar-Ḥaṭar were working at the behest of local clerics, we can assume that they had access to, and obtained the document from, local church records. Its Cosmas identifies himself as a priest of a village called Panîr, and says he is writing on behalf of "deacons and readers and all the congregation, and from the procurator and the veterans and all the village."[76] It records their collective pledge to adhere to rules that Symeon had issued to them. Besides maintaining liturgical observances on Fridays and Sundays, these include not moving each other's boundary stones, not charging high interest on loans, not showing favoritism in legal disputes, not cheating laborers or stealing from the poor, not raping women, nor associating with sorcerers or brigands. "Pray . . . that we be established and confirmed in what you have commanded us," Cosmas concludes. "Pray for us, my lord, that we may always be held by your prayers and that there may be upon the world mercy and hope and redemption by your prayers for ever. Amen."[77]

Few documents are more precious for the social history of rural Syria in this era. Besides shedding light on the social composition (including army veterans) and troubles that could be found in villages of the Limestone Massif during its agricultural boom, Cosmas's letter substantiates Peter Brown's thesis that ascetics like Symeon came to wield significant authority in recently Christianized, isolated communities. As Brown famously put it, "Symeon, the model holy man of the early Byzantine world, was the 'good patron' writ large."[78] But most important for us are the reasons the Panîrians gave for showing Symeon such deference. In his opening salutation, Cosmas praises him not only as a companion of the prophets and a colleague of the apostles, but as a "herald of life who stood between God and His creation," who "effected reconciliation between God and His creation [*briteh*]," and "petitioned his God by the pain of his limbs [*b-ḥašā d-hadāmeh*] and rejoiced his Maker by his ascetic practices."[79] Thus, Symeon was praised for his ability to reconcile the created world with God through his prayers, which were deemed effective because they were viscerally voiced through "the pain of his limbs" and his dedication to physical asceticism.

This documentary evidence is just what we need to verify that Early Byzantine villagers actually did value such ascetic toils. Elsewhere in the *Life* itself, Bar-Eupolemus and Bar-Ḥaṭar allude to "written covenants" (*qyāmā b-ktibāyā*) that Symeon had made with other villages of the region, including one that forbad a village to break the Sabbath by irrigating its fields on Sundays.[80] The *Letter of Cosmas* may represent another such covenant; for reasons discussed below, these should be seen as akin to the "covenants" that Barsanuphius set down in writing before bearing the burden of his disciples' sins, as discussed in chapter 4. The *Letter of Cosmas*, however, may have responded to a letter that at some point Symeon issued to all Christians of the region, castigating them for oppressing the poor, practicing usury, and failing to go to church or obey its laws. Preserved in a single sixth-century manuscript of the *Life*, this missive commanded its recipients to placate God by following a series of rules reminiscent of those mentioned in Cosmas's letter. It has been suggested that Symeon issued this letter after experiencing some regional catastrophe, such as an earthquake, that was believed to express God's wrath.[81] In any case, the *Letter of Cosmas* was not a result of hagiography but attests instead the "unanimous" (so Cosmas claims) sentiments of actual rural Christians regarding Symeon's practices. Furthermore—and this must be stressed—it was written while Symeon was still alive. It therefore provides solid historical background for understanding the attitudes and claims later depicted in Bar-Eupolemus and Bar-Ḥaṭar's hagiography. In particular, it shows that contemporary villagers respected Symeon because his stellar feats of physical asceticism inspired confidence in his ability to sway God on their behalf. Before examining examples from the *Life* itself, let us consider why farmers might have been prepared to put their trust in such a person.

AGRICULTURE AND RELIGIOUS SCIENCE IN THE ROMAN NEAR EAST

"Temples are the soul of the countryside," Libanius, the famous orator of Antioch, reminded Emperor Theodosius I in the late fourth century. "In them the farming communities rest their hopes for husbands, wives, children, for their oxen and the soil they sow and plant." Libanius was hoping to stop the wholesale destruction of ancient shrines that was happening outside Antioch in the 380s. Driven by Christian zeal and a pressing need to raise funds for the army after the military disaster at Adrianople in 378, Theodosius's Praetorian Prefect of the East had already looted the great temple of Baal at Apamea, as well as several other smaller temples on private estates in the countryside. It is unlikely that he was acting on orders from Theodosius himself, but he found plenty of monks in the area ready to help. Some of this "black-robed tribe," as Libanius calls them, not only joined the demolition crews, but also seized temple lands, allegedly encouraged by their Christian priests. In this way, those who claimed to "worship their god by fasting," Libanius says, had "grown fat on the misfortunes of other folk."[82]

This usurpation of sacred treasures and spaces only gained momentum in the last years of Theodosius's reign. Baptismal fonts have been found in significant quantities at rural monastic sites, suggesting that monks were drawn there partly by fervor to colonize and convert the countryside.[83] Monasteries never completely replaced ancient temples or synagogues as religious centers in the Near East. Churches did that, with several being built in most villages, sometimes directly over temple foundations.[84] Agricultural profits that formerly would have financed temples and synagogues now went to these. Palladius of Helenopolis praises one Christian landowner for choosing to give a portion of the fruits he reaped from his country estates in Asia Minor to local churches rather than share them with his own children.[85] It was considered prudent to use some of these profits to propitiate the divine force that had bestowed them. A Christian villa outside the coastal city of Caesarea Maritima in Palestine featured mosaics framed by crosses and inscribed "The Lord God will bless your grain and your wine and your oil, and He will multiply [them]" and "From their fruit, grain, wine, and olive oil, they were multiplied." Set into the middle of the floor of its dining room where they could be read by all who consumed its bounty, these paraphrases of the Old Testament (cf. Dt 7:12–13; Ps 4:8) spelled out the religious ideas that had long been associated with the acquisition of agrarian wealth in this region.[86]

The *karpophoriai* that individuals or communities gave out of such wealth to build, adorn, or repair churches in the countryside are commemorated in numerous inscriptions.[87] But there had always been more to religion in the rural Near East than buildings and sanctuaries. Here as elsewhere locals cultivated unusually tall trees, cold springs, and strangely shaped rocks, whose "accidents of geomorphology, like other kinds of contradiction, portent, paradox, and departure from normality . . . were readily assimilable to the world of the divine."[88] They also put up talismans shaped like animals and other predators around fields to ward off birds, rodents, and beasts, or placed statues of gods or heroic figures on borderlands to deflect rivers, locusts and other pests, or planted freestanding columns to contend against the elements themselves, such as the "enchanted pillars" that protected Syrian Tripoli from encroaching sand dunes, and the expensive porphyry post that the citizens of Antioch set up in a downtown square, inscribed "unshakeable, immovable," to prevent earthquakes. Many of these talismans were attributed to a first-century CE "philosopher" known as Apollonius of Tyana.[89] The Near Eastern countryside once teemed with such roving consultants. Whatever we might think of their methods, they offered a semblance of control over environmental conditions that otherwise allowed none. Some of these experts were hired to lay down protective circles around fields using apotropaic rites and leading processions along boundaries. Others, especially among Jews in Palestine, specialized in summoning down rain.[90] Others were credited with securing regional prosperity more generally. During the second century, the shrine at Hierapolis-Mabbug in northern Syria (Manbij, Syria) featured men who scaled massive stone penises within the sacred precinct. Twice a year one of these "phallus-climbers" would sit for a week on top of one of the two that had been erected in front of the temple of the goddess Atargatis, uttering blessings for whoever left coins at its base. "The populace believes he communes with the gods on high and asks for good things for all Syria," wrote a local contemporary.[91]

Monks gradually supplanted local anomalies and filled the shoes of such experts. This transition took time. Symeon Stylites warned villagers against seeking help from sorcerers in the middle of the fifth century, but Christian authorities were still denouncing those who consulted rainmakers at the end of the seventh.[92] If we cannot see the situation in detail, we can at least appreciate the needs behind it. Ancient farmers lived from year to year on the brink of disaster. Inscriptions confirm that mice and vermin posed perennial threats, and swarms of locusts brought terror.[93] So much depended on a change in the weather. Asia Minor and northern Mesopotamia were reliably watered by high mountain runoffs during the summer, but few springs exist in northern Syria, and almost none at all are found on the sunbaked Limestone Massif, the surface of which still remains riddled today with ancient shallow cisterns.[94] Nor did agricultural science change as farmers pressed into even more sketchy margins. Most of the techniques discussed in Early Byzantine farming manuals were hundreds of years old, and none of the additions found in them showed any significant advance. To avert hail, farmers were instructed to place mirrors in their fields, post dead vipers on sticks, and then, accompanied by menstruating women, walk three times around their fields' borders at noon, carrying tortoise shells or crocodile skins. If that were not possible, they were advised to hire people who were trained in chasing away clouds.[95]

It did not take much for Christian professionals to compete with advice of their own. As an Alexandrian preacher boasted in fourth-century Egypt, the ancient ritual of loading gifts onto the wagon of a god called Buchis and pulling it around fields of the Nile Delta at sowing time ("The pagans used to give great gifts to him, that he might bless them") had in his day been supplanted by giving gifts to the archangel Michael, who would intercede "for the growth of the fruits of the entire land."[96] It has often been noted that the advice dispensed by Christian holy men to farmers from the fourth century onward resembles the advice found in ancient agricultural manuals. Symeon Stylites frequently recommended that villagers protect their fields by carrying some of his ḥnāna around them (see the next section, "The Intercessory Powers of Simon Stylites the Elder"), posting crosses on their perimeters, and casting holy water into them. When Barsanuphius was asked how to protect fields from locusts, he similarly advised sprinkling them with holy water.

But he also suggested just chasing the locusts away—as long as this could be done without angering one's immediate neighbors.[97]

Such continuity, argue Peregrine Horden and Nicholas Purcell, reflects the fact that Near Eastern farming presented similar challenges under any religion.[98] It is misleading, however, to identify monks like Symeon simply as Christian "shamans," or to think of their techniques in terms of pagan survivals, as is still occasionally done.[99] These ascetics brought new insights to the field about what God wanted, informed by the latest theology and penitential methods. They arrived with detailed knowledge about an unseen and previously unknown demon world lurking below. And they claimed to have influence with divine forces that could benefit not just separate fields but "the entire land." This was the rationale which the Alexandrian preacher mentioned above suggests had persuaded his Egyptian congregation to give up bestowing gifts on their old country god Buchis in favor of the archangel Michael: the latter deity promised universal results. That was a benefit of using religious techniques based on an all-embracing monotheism, instead of archaic rites focused on localized gods. But what really made the new Christian specialists credible was their demonstrable application of an all-embracing physical penance. Aside from the *Letter of Cosmas* discussed above, this is apparent in hagiographies written about rural ascetics in the Roman Near East from the fifth to the seventh centuries. After examining miracles ascribed to Symeon in the *Life of Symeon Stylites,* we shall briefly inspect the *Life of Barsauma of the North* and the *Life of Theodore of Sykeon.*

THE INTERCESSORY POWERS OF SYMEON
STYLITES THE ELDER

Born ca. 386 at Sis in eastern Cilicia (Kozan, Turkey), Symeon Stylites is possibly the only Early Byzantine saint who needs no introduction. Though little remains of the sixty-foot column on which he stood for the last thirty-seven years of his life, its stump and surrounding ruins attest the monumental status he achieved before and after his death. During his life, he received letters from heads of state and admirers as far away as Gaul and Spain. Craftsmen hung his image over the entryways to their workshops for security in the center of metropolitan Rome.[100] All this was unprecedented for a fourth-century shepherd boy from rural Cilicia, but it was allegedly heralded by a vision he once had while tending sheep. "Only gain patience and endurance, let there be love in you toward everyone," it said, and "there will be no one, either among the ancients or the moderns, greater than you."[101]

Those words accurately foretold the subsequent trajectory of Symeon's career. Kicked out of a cenobium as a teenager for excessive fasting and other forms of self-abuse, Symeon made his way east to the Limestone Massif, and by 412 had joined a monastery occupied only by an old monk and his son outside Telneshe, nineteen miles (30 km) west of Beroea. A local headman named Maris bar Barathon had built this small monastery on his land for the old monk to use. Initially, the three lived in it together (one might imagine what that was like), but after Symeon managed to survive the following Lent without touching any of the bread or water left outside his room, a village priest named Daniel asked him to move onto land he owned at the top of a hill overlooking the village. Having moved into an enclosure there, Symeon replicated the same feat the next year. When he opened the door of his enclosure at the end of Lent, villagers brought him a sample of olive oil to bless. Oil started gushing out of its container. This, we are told, "was the first sign wrought by the blessed Mar Symeon in public."[102]

Such details about Symeon's first years at Telneshe show that, like the old monk before him, Symeon had been invited to settle with special accommodations on a landowner's private property, apparently for the specific purpose of obtaining blessings for the owner's fields and produce. His repeated feats of physical fasting established his credentials to such an extent that he was soon pursued by a growing number of sick or curious fans. According to Theodoret, who visited sometime before 444, their repeated jostling to touch or snatch a piece of his tunic first inspired him to stand on a column so he could keep safely out of reach (elsewhere we learn that Symeon was "quite strong, but on the short side").[103] Bar Eupolemus and Bar-Ḥaṭar record sixteen different healings he effected, first by using the oil generated by his first miracle, then by dispensing a cure-all known as ḥnāna (Syriac for "pity"; here, dirt mixed in with the blessed oil) from atop his perch. Otherwise, the miracles attributed to him are almost all acts that made life safer or more profitable for the region's villagers, such as purifying their springs, doubling their crops, driving off vermin and beasts, and preventing a landside from burying a village. In each instance, Symeon instructed villagers first to sprinkle some of his ḥnāna on the problematic area, and then to plant three or four crosses around it.[104]

But when it came to the weather—which universally affected everything and everyone in the region—Symeon became more directly involved. His hagiographers give special attention to one instance in particular. One year, winter had passed without bringing a drop of water. The drought conditions became increasingly serious, until "the whole creation was prostrating in the saint's enclosure." Eventually, after hearing someone murmur that no one could bring down rain like the Old Testament prophets (1 Sm 12:14–18; 1 Kgs 17–18), Symeon commanded everyone in the region to gather before him. "When the saint saw all this—the priests with their heads covered in dust standing in sorrow and distress, men and women . . . raising their voices on high, those children like little lambs . . . he was deeply distressed and his merciful heart opened." Then he prayed with tearful genuflections and it began to rain. After finishing, Symeon told the people that if they obeyed God's commands, their crops would double, but he confided to his disciples that he had offered God his own life so that, if God intended to show no mercy, he would at least die before seeing any more suffering. At that point an angel had appeared, announcing that his petition had been accepted. And so, the hagiographers explain, "the year was blessed."[105]

This dramatic episode showcased how Symeon's tearful penance and self-sacrificial intent enabled him to successfully intercede for God's creation. Symeon's hagiographers acknowledge that the saint's approach was not entirely new. The Ninevites' sackcloth and ashes (Jon 3:6) and Elijah's prostrations for rain (1 Kgs 18:42) provided Old Testament models for assuaging God either collectively or individually. Indeed, if Christian tradition added anything new, it was an emphasis on collective confession. As the New Testament's *Letter of James* explains, "Confess your sins to one another and pray for one another, that you may be healed. The prayer of the righteous is powerful and effective" (Jas 5:16). The early fifth century seems to have seen the birth of the Christian phenomenon of communal confession and penance, and certainly its growing practice. Rogation ceremonies organized by local bishops or priests to circle around towns and fields with hymns and processions became common during Symeon's lifetime. Public displays of mass contrition led by the emperor himself, standing with his head bare in the hippodrome, were introduced to assuage divine wrath and improve crops.[106] Litanies ascribed to Severus of Antioch survive with notes explaining what crises they had been composed to address. Besides expressing contrition, these often reminded God that he had been willing to take pity when faced with similar remorse on previous occasions: for example, "Lord, when calling us to penance . . . You did say, 'If you shall turn and groan, you shalt live' [Is 30:15]." Thus sang the people of Antioch in January 515, at the end of a long drought.[107]

While technically such rites did not require monastic participation to be effective, the contribution of serious ascetics like Symeon certainly was believed to help. The sixth-century *Chronicle* attributed to Pseudo-Joshua the Stylite points this out when explaining why God allowed life to return to normal in Edessa after a solar eclipse in 499. Pseudo-Joshua, apparently an eyewitness, writes,

> By the order of our father the bishop Mâr Peter, public prayers were offered, and everyone besought mercy from God. He took all his clergy and all the members of religious orders, both men and women, and all the lay members of the holy Church, both rich and poor, men, women, and children, and they traversed all the streets of the city, carrying crosses, with psalms and hymns, clad in black garments of humiliation. All the convents too in our district kept up continual services with great diligence; and so, by the prayers of all the holy ones, the light of the sun was restored to its place, and we were a little cheered.[108]

Pseudo-Joshua makes clear his belief that it was the additional prayers and "diligence" (*ḥpiṭutā*) of the local monks that had tipped the balance in securing God's mercy. This was partly because, as his *Chronicle* shows, ecclesiastically organized penance required the participation of an entire community—clerics and laity with rich and poor, old and young at once—over long periods of time.[109] Mass cooperation was difficult to sustain. Accordingly, while monks might encourage communities themselves to carry out such penitential procedures, their monastic discipline and relative freedom from distractions made it convenient for everyone if they took responsibility for performing the penance on their own. Elite monks were theoretically always praying for humanity anyway. Symeon refused to be distracted by a visiting official on the eve of his annual forty-day fast. "That idiot!" he reportedly exclaimed. "He wants us to worry about him all during Lent, and to abandon petitioning God for our own sins and [for] those of the whole world!"[110]

That of course was just what was needed: someone able to shoulder the sins of the whole world. Symeon exemplified burden bearing on the grandest scale. "By his intercessions he carried the weight of creation," wrote his hagiographers. "His prayers, just like the beams in a building, held up creation."[111] Indeed, Bar-Eupolemus and Bar-Ḥaṭar, like Cosmas of Panîr, linked the success of Symeon's intercessory petitions to his voluntary physical suffering. This attracted divine sympathy. As with the monks Pseudo-Joshua describes, after Symeon began to demonstrate his penitential "diligence" (ḥpiṭuṭā) in "purifying his limbs," God "granted whatever his soul desired."[112] The prophet Elijah was said to have encouraged this form of monasticism, instructing Symeon early in his career "not to neglect to afflict the body"; thereafter, his afflictions (ʾulṣānē) astonished all of his onlookers and captured imaginations from rural Syria to central Rome. According to Bar-Eupolemus and Bar-Ḥaṭar, Symeon "chose such affliction that was not seen either among the ancients or in middle or modern times." Even before ascending his pillar, he had mastered "fasting without limit" and broken his body with genuflections: "The vertebrae of his spine were dislocated through constant supplications, but he was fastened and held together by love of Christ. . . . These [were] the sufferings and bitter afflictions, and many more than these, that the saint endured."[113]

Pillar-standing and fasting aside, it was Symeon's apparent ability to endure a severe case of gangrene that most excited contemporaries. One afternoon a pain shot up Symeon's left leg. By evening, boils began to appear on his foot; by morning, these had burst open, creating an open wound that swarmed with maggots. So foul was the stench that no one could approach him; attendants had to pack perfumed resin in their nostrils before climbing up to feed him. For eight months, worms and pus fell down like rain on the base of the pillar. Bishops and the imperial family wrote imploring him to relent, but Symeon held forth. Finally, two days before Easter, he appeared "visibly restored, glad and merry and asking mercy from God." This feat was considered to have been pivotal in universalizing his powers: "Because of this, God, who saw his endurance, exalted him and magnified his victory from one end of creation to the other."[114] So famous was the episode that it inspired three different Syriac homilies, one written by Severus of Antioch and two by a preacher named Jacob of Serug (451–521). Jacob focuses on Symeon's detachment from pain, even fantasizing that he had cut off his foot and soothingly spoken to it before discarding it:

> Who would not weep at having his foot cut off at its joint? But he looked on it as something foreign, and was not even sad. And as Satan was allowing blood sprinkled with pus and covered in mucus, and the rocks were spattered, the just man nevertheless sang. While a branch of his body was cut off from its tree, his face was exuding delightful dew and comely glory. And he said to it, "Peace until the resurrection. And do not grieve, for your hope will be kept in the kingdom." And even though all of him lived, his limb died and was cast before him.

Despite these physical sufferings and loss, Symeon maintained his spiritual composure. According to Jacob of Serug, this turned him into a "pledge to God for all of creation," to which he brought healing; when Symeon died, "creation stood still and groaned in pain in response."[115]

This reflected concurrent Christian teachings about the possibility of making the created world a Paradise again by restoring the proper harmony between its physical and spiritual elements. Sebastian Brock notes that the Syrian authors Ephrem of Edessa (ca. 306–373) and Ishāq of Nineveh (ca. 613–ca. 700) posit an "inherent interconnectedness between everyone and everything." Hymns ascribed to them assume that balance and harmony had originally prevailed within three different dimensions of God's creation: first, between the physical and spiritual elements existing within human beings; second, between humans and their physical surroundings; and third, between that circumscribed physical world and the infinite spiritual world. Adam and Eve's initial purity had let them enjoy unimpeded interaction with God, whose divine image in them provided a point of contact for all three dimensions of creation. Once that image became tarnished through sin, however, only renewed obedience and good works could restore it, and with it, the harmonious connections it had originally sustained. In one hymn, Ephrem wrote,

> One person falls sick—and so another
> can visit and help him;
> one person starves—and so another
> can provide him with food and
> give him life . . .
> In this way the world can recover:
> tens of thousands of hidden ways
> are to be found
> ready to assist us.

That there could be a restoration of creation's prelapsarian state was ensured by Christ's incarnation and the actions of saints whose "cooperation with God has brought about the restoration of the image within themselves."[116]

Similar ideas about the role of asceticism in restoring a proper balance between spirit and matter were articulated by Isaiah of Scetis (d. 489). His *Asceticon* affirms that God became incarnate to "transform that which is contrary to nature to the state that is according to nature."[117] To regain Adam's pristine condition, ascetics must subordinate their corporeal impulses to God's spiritual priorities. "Take control of all our [bodily] members until they are established in the state that is according to nature," advised Isaiah.[118] This required a penitential regimen: "God has given us transformation through repentance, through [which] we become completely new."[119] Physical asceticism was thought to make God sympathetic: "Think to yourself, 'It is because of the mortification of my body that God hears my misery.'"[120] As Dorotheus later taught, "Afflictions move God's mercy to a soul, as winds blow the rain."[121]

It is important to emphasize that none of this was seen as sorcery. Bernard Flusin explains that monks were credited with influencing nature because they knew from experience what was congruent with God's will, and therefore they knew how to make their petitions "acceptable."[122] Cyril of Scythopolis illustrates this when explaining how Abbot Euthymius helped save Palestine from a drought in the fifth century. After no rain had fallen all winter, the Patriarch of Jerusalem formed a procession and headed out to Euthymius's monastery, begging for help. Euthymius agreed to try, but first seized the opportunity to explain the laws that governed the situation:

> Our sins stand in the way between Him and us. . . . We have obscured His image and defiled His temple by being slaves to a variety of lusts and pleasures. . . . This is why in His anger He has brought this correction on us, so that, sobered by it and improved by repentance, we might approach Him in fear and He accordingly may hear us.[123]

Most Christians, of course, were hardly aware of their need for self-reform. After all, there was run-of-the-mill conversion and baptism, and then there was real change, *metanoia*. Such "repentance" had been the goal of Christian conversion since the days of John the Baptist (Mt 3:2; Mk 1:4).[124] Yet few ever achieved this degree of conversion, for which reason God, out of divine philanthropy, allowed terrible calamities to occur, to awaken people to their sins and save them from having to suffer far harsher punishments in the afterlife.[125] Monasticism, on the other hand, made a thorough-going repentance its abiding concern. Its purpose was nothing less than "to engrave on us the life of penance as on a tablet."[126] Monasteries sought to effect this through rites of confession devised to instill constant contrition and awareness of sin. This routine fostered in some monks a capacity to shed tears easily, an attainment deemed so cleansing it was called a second baptism.[127] Regarded as the ultimate proof of inner reform, weeping for humanity was also believed to secure divine sympathy. And so, while the anxious laity cooperated with their prayers outside, Euthymius tearfully petitioned God in his cell to "have mercy on his creation." Then rain fell, indicating that God had heard and granted these petitions. But before letting them go, Euthymius implored the people henceforth to be more "exacting" in their behavior (tantamount to the Syrian emphasis on "diligence," *ḥpiṭutā*) and to honor God with good works.[128]

Such was the new religious science being propagated in the late Roman Near East. Rousing creation from its "heavy torpor," Symeon's physical asceticism alerted all to the need for diligent repentance. At the same time he provided a singular example of a Christian's ability to put mind over matter and bring one's physical existence into proper alignment with the spiritual. As Bar-Eupolemus and Bar-Ḥaṭar explained, even in the depths of his agony, Symeon's "body was with human beings, but his mind with spiritual beings."[129] Meanwhile, his shrine helped more ordinary Christians put the spiritual and material elements of their lives into proper alignment by giving it their gifts.

Over the following centuries, Symeon's achievements gave rise to emulators all around the eastern Mediterranean from Constantinople to Egypt. The Limestone Massif gradually became studded with stylites. At least eighty-seven have been counted between the fifth and the ninth century; some of their pillars can still be seen half standing amid the ruins of ancient monastic courtyards.[130] Stalwart novices were chosen to train and replace resident stylites when they died. Some became famous: Symeon's namesake may have built his sanctuary on the Marvelous Mountain to resemble the cruciform enclosure at Telneshe, albeit on a smaller scale.[131] But the toils attributed to these later imitators pertain mostly to individual exorcisms and healings.[132] For closer parallels to the elder Symeon, we must turn to the monks Barsauma and Theodore of Sykeon. Although neither were pillar saints, their hagiographers celebrated both their penitential asceticism and the impact of their intercessions on countrysides far and wide.

ASCETIC PENANCE AND LAY PROSPERITY IN
THE *LIVES* OF BARSAUMA AND THEODORE

Born near Samosata in northwestern Mesopotamia, Barsauma (ca. 400–457) could have been another Symeon Stylites. They were almost exact contemporaries; like Symeon, Barsauma grew up in the foothills of the upper Euphrates before entering a Syrian cenobium at a young age, which he subsequently left in order to pursue greater rigors on his own. But their careers took different paths. While Symeon settled permanently at Telneshe, Barsauma never stayed more than part of the year in the monastery that villagers built for him on the "Mountain of the North" (Nemrud Dağı, Turkey). Otherwise, he constantly kept on the move, traversing between Mesopotamia, Syria, Armenia, Palestine, and eventually, Constantinople. By all accounts, Barsauma was the rogue monk writ large, credited with razing temples, torching synagogues, terrorizing Samaritans, and after the Council of Chalcedon, harassing heretics until the day he died. Indeed, his life ended just ahead of the law; he reportedly expired just as government troops were massing below, preparing to storm his monastery and arrest him.

Some of this we know from conciliar records, but most of our information comes from a fifth or sixth-century hagiography whose author, Samuel the Priest, claims to have been one of Barsauma's disciples. Written in Syriac, this hagiography is a sectarian tour de force, meant to craft a superhero who could rally the anti-Chalcedonian communities of the Near East.[133] Samuel bluntly claims that Barsauma surpassed all other Christian holy men of his generation. He depicts an angel informing Symeon Stylites, "There is no other Righteous Man in this generation on the face of the earth who can compete with the blessed Barsauma." Upon hearing this, Symeon told the people at his pillar to prepare for "the Chosen One of God," who would appear at three o'clock that afternoon. Just at that moment, Barsauma passed through the gate, making Symeon his prophetic forerunner.[134] The two may never have actually met, but it would be surprising if they were unaware of each other. Besides operating in the same general area and time, both were credited with highly physical regimens of penitential prayer that brought God's blessings down on the landscape.

An emphasis on self-imposed physical afflictions ('ulṣānē) pervades and unifies Barsauma's Life from his initial attempt to perish by fasting at Lent to his final exertions against the Chalcedonian regime. As with Symeon, his survival of a Lenten fast precipitated harder afflictions. These included his refusal to ever sit or lie down (explained by the belief that no slave should lie down in front of his master); complete abstinence from bread, wine, water, and oil (an "extreme hardship"); self-immolation by wearing an iron chest plate, apparently a kind of cuirass, over his hair shirt, always kept turned towards the sun ("How much hardship he was able manfully to bear!"); as well as multiple genuflections, performed punctually each day with "great groaning and weeping and astonishing tears" ("every day . . . he would subject himself to this"). Samuel compares these to the corporeal sufferings that martyrs had offered to appease God.[135] What did not kill Barsauma only made him stronger: winter cold may turn stones into dust, observes Samuel, but it made Barsauma's body "firm and enduring by the power of God, who gives power to the weak."[136] Angels constantly descended to wipe away his tears.[137]

Samuel depicts Barsauma as resuming these physical afflictions each year after completing annual forays to the world below his mountain monastery, as if the saint's penitential regimen were necessary to recharge his spiritual powers. He also depicts Barsauma's endurance of sufferings as closely connected to his ability to channel and transmit divine blessings. According to Samuel, his very first miracle was contingent on his youthful endurance of ascetic 'ulṣānē, following his decision to never sit down. "When the blessed Barsauma first bound himself to this hardship," writes Samuel, "God gave him the following sign," referring to his miraculous revival of a stale loaf of bread.[138] Thereafter, Barsauma "grew greener from day to day and blossomed and flourished in the Holy Spirit," while his prayers made sour grapes sweet, barren fields fertile, and diseased bodies sound.[139] "Those who loved the earthly [i.e., the laity] were blessed by his prayers," the hagiographer affirms.[140]

Indeed, Samuel highlights what villagers of the region wanted from this saint. Whenever Barsauma traversed Mesopotamia, they invited him to purify their springs, avert hail, and stop whatever plague was assailing their livestock ("To him alone . . . God has given authority to stop the disease which kills animals, domestic and wild, and even people").[141] Success meant increased demand: "Soon villagers from the surrounding countries began to invite Barsauma to bless their infertile lands and render them productive."[142] Such was his reputation that even the most lax laity performed penance in his absence. Samuel reports a case in which a village with poor soil was located too far away for Barsauma to help out in person. So a boy carved a message onto a stone and put it in his family's field for his parents to discover when they came out to farm. It read:

> I, Barsauma, head of the mourners, have left these written instructions. If the owners of this land wish to eat of its produce let them perform a rogation here, then fast and pray for seven days and finish by holding a commemoration of the martyrs at which the oblation is offered. Then our Lord will show mercy and the land will produce enough for all to eat and praise God for it.

Finding this forgery and believing Barsauma had prescribed the procedure himself, the villagers followed it. As a result, their land became productive, and "still the blessing rests on it today."[143]

The tone of this inscription is reminiscent of the covenants that Symeon Stylites the Elder created for villagers on the Limestone Massif. Indeed, the title it ascribes to Barsauma—"Head of the Mourners"—is otherwise attested only in connection to Symeon.[144] But the monastic classification to which it refers—ʾabilā, "mourner"—is known from numerous other Syrian sources. Derived, it seems, from the beatitude "Blessed are those who mourn [ṭubayhon la-ʾbilē], for they shall be comforted" (Mt 5:4; cf. Lk 6:20–21), this form of Christian asceticism, "mourning" (ʾabilutā), was penitential in focus. Some practitioners wore heavy chains and long hair to heighten their penitential fervor; others devised contraptions to exert stress on their bodies, such as the metal jacket Barsauma wore while praying in the summer sun; all punctuated their supplications with copious prostrations and audible lamentations.[145]

Another monk who fit this profile was Theodore of Sykeon (d. 613). Theodore's hagiography was written or revised after 641 by a protégé named George of Sykeon. Historians prize it for its "village perspective."[146] Although George says that Theodore visited Constantinople and Jerusalem, he mostly operated in the rural environs of northwestern Asia Minor; though he briefly served as bishop of the small city of Anastasiopolis (Dikman Höyük, Turkey), his fame derived from his activities as abbot around Sykeon, a Galatian village 56 miles (90 km) west of modern Ankara along the ancient Constantinople-Ancyra highway. Theodore grew up just off this military road. His home was partly an inn and partly a brothel, his mother both an innkeeper and a prostitute, and his father a former circus rider who slept there one night and was never heard from again. George says that Theodore's asceticism blossomed out of the "thistles of harlotry";[147] but he also attributes it to the visits Theodore regularly made as a youth to the many martyr shrines surrounding his village.

Modern historians have never regarded Theodore as an avatar of either Symeon Stylites or Barsauma the Mourner, but his hagiography portrays his penitential activities along similar lines. One day as a teenager, Theodore ran off to imitate John the Baptist by fasting in a cave. When he finally came out, two years later, his face was so disfigured, hair so rank, and body so emaciated that a local bishop, seeing such sanctity, reportedly ordained him on the spot. Later, Theodore had blacksmiths fabricate a penitential outfit to wear during Lent. According to George, this consisted of two pairs of iron shackles for his wrists and ankles weighing fifteen pounds each; a thirty-five-pound iron belt for his waist; a fifty-pound breastplate, worn over his hair shirt; and an eighteen-pound collar for his neck, from which hung an iron cross. Demons reportedly called him "iron eater."[148] But that was not all. Theodore had his smiths forge a cage and hang it near his monastery so he could spend the weeks of Christmas and Lent standing in it, suspended in the cold winter air. As trees groaned and cracked with frost, Theodore's disciples poured hot water on his feet to keep them thawed. Meanwhile, the saint sang psalms and "did not touch any bread at all nor even any pulse from Christmas day to Psalm Sunday, his sole food an apple or a mix of vegetables, and this only on Saturdays and Sundays."[149]

Like Symeon and Barsauma over a century earlier, Theodore proved himself an asset to surrounding villagers by orchestrating processions, defending against hail and locusts, driving out vermin, curing livestock of diseases, and deflecting encroaching riverbanks. He was especially known for bringing down rain. George claims that villagers who went to Jerusalem boasted to other pilgrims that Theodore could fill the whole earth with rain with just a single prayer.[150] Such intercessory prowess, George indicates, originated in the fasts and vigils Theodore had been practicing since his youth.[151] Just as Theodore emphasized his monks' need for repentance while serving as their abbot, so too he prescribed prayer, fasting, and almsgiving to purify his lay congregations while serving as their bishop.[152] Like Symeon Stylites the Elder, Theodore also had imitators after he died. George reports that some of his disciples sought out villages in which they could pass Lent suspended in cages of their own. One eventually became a stylite.[153]

We may think such behavior so eccentric as to be meaningless. Perhaps the most striking aspect of George's seventh-century account, however, is how unremarkable this asceticism seems to have become by then. Unlike Bar-Eupolemus and Bar-Ḥaṭar, George evidently felt no need to explain his subject's practices, assign them Old Testament precedents, or justify them by allusions to angelic directives. Readers of his day must have been sufficiently familiar with such penitential monasticism to regard it as both beneficial and exemplary.[154] Nor was it known only in northern Syria and Asia Minor.

An inscription found in excavations of the Jeremiah monastery at Saqqara in Egypt marked the spot "on which our lord and father Apa Jeremias bowed himself until he removed the sins of the people of the whole world."[155] Even Egyptian desert tradition eventually found a complement to Symeon Stylites. In the Coptic version of the *Sayings of the Desert Fathers* there are several entries—immediately following an anecdote in which Symeon preaches on penance—about a monk of Middle Egypt named Banes. He had been so committed to fasting as a boy that authorities asked him to distribute alms to the poor. Eventually he tired of this and withdrew to a cell, where, after closing the door, he stood for fifteen years in the dark, all the while praying without moving. So boney did his feet become, we are told, that they resembled those of a gazelle. Later it was said that Banes considered all his prior almsgiving worthless in comparison to this penitential effort. When visitors asked why he held this opinion, another elder explained, "When Apa Banes distributed alms, did he nourish a village, a city, a country? Now, Banes is able to raise both hands to make sure that barley comes to the whole world in abundance. He is also able to ask God to forgive the sins of this entire generation." The visitors left happy, "knowing that they had such a suppliant to intercede for them."[156]

FRUITBEARINGS, GRATITUDE, AND SACRED VESSELS

Who in the outside world has worked wonders, raised the dead, expelled demons? No one. Such deeds are done by monks. It is their reward. People in secular life cannot do these things, for if they could, what would be the point of ascetic practice and the solitary life?

—JOHN CLIMACUS, *LADDER OF PARADISE*[157]

As John Chrysostom reminded his congregations in the early fifth century, "Great is the gift given in return for taking care of the slaves of God, and they give their fruits back to us."[158] Authorities like him propagated an understanding that reciprocity between the Christian laity and their religious leaders was proper, following prayers and profit with expressions of gratitude. While Early Byzantine hagiographers do not dwell upon the lay provision of fruitbearings to holy people in great detail, they do not neglect it either. George of Sykeon specifies that Theodore variously received, as gifts of *karpophoriai*, a horse from an innkeeper, fishing tackle from a sailor, and, from a military commander, a liturgical cross and a lump of cash. Each was given after their donor had received a healing or some other blessing thanks to Theodore's prayers.[159] Elsewhere, we hear of parents bringing a *karpophoria* to Daniel the Stylite after the birth of their child and a farmer who brought firstfruits to George of Choziba in a basket after a harvest.[160] So consistent is this identification of fruitbearings with gratitude that we are warranted in identifying all gifts given to acknowledge the receipt of divine benefits through holy people as *karpophoriai,* even when the word is not specifically used. Hagiography is full of such undesignated thank-offerings. George of Sykeon, for example, reports that Theodore's monastery received a supply of wine each year from a village which he had saved from hail, and a vineyard from another for the same reason.[161] Each of these gifts represents an expression of gratitude for a divine benefit secured through a holy person.

Such fruitbearings contributed to the sacred wealth of churches and monasteries, enabling them to provide blessings or alms to those who came by. As seen in chapter 3, the gifts that people placed at the foot of Symeon Stylites's pillar were taken by the poor as needed; otherwise, they remained in the sanctuary to honor both God and his ascetic representative. To thank him for healing his children, a Persian shah is said to have sent Symeon a silk veil covered with gold crosses and fringed with golden bells. From local rustics, he received animal hides skinned off wild beasts that had been subdued according to the saint's instructions. Besides a lion's skin, these included three hides that were "not like those of leopards or bears, but the colors varied and were different from anything seen in these times." They had been skinned off predators resembling wild women with shaven heads, who snatched babies and ate them before their parents' eyes. The villagers trapped these by planting crosses around their land; "after howling so loud it carried over the mountain," three were thus captured and died. According to Bar-Eupolemus and Bar-Ḥaṭar, their hides were hung over the entry to Symeon's enclosure, revealing the original, "shamanic" appearance of this hilltop sanctuary before it became the monumental Qalʿat Simʿān.[162]

Hagiographers naturally wanted to celebrate and make known such gifts of gratitude. But the nature of a Christian fruitbearing was complex: Did it actually express gratitude, or was it an investment calculated to obtain further profits? Did it represent a conscious payment for a blessing? Was a fruitbearing, as I suggested at the start of this chapter, the compulsory side of a *eulogia?* In asking such questions, we should not forget that many would have enjoyed giving such gifts, since they provided even humble people a chance to make magnanimous gestures toward someone who had seemed to help them. Hagiography aside, this impulse is attested in letters of Barsanuphius and John.[163] At the same time, like the contractual gifts described by Marcel Mauss, such gifts of gratitude almost always implied expectations that their givers would continue to receive benefits from their recipients in the future. And finally, the ambiguity regarding the voluntary or involuntary nature of fruitbearings was also inherent in the very nature of gratitude itself. As studies of gift giving point out, gratitude must be freely expressed for it to be recognized as genuine, yet no other type of gift is more intensely desired or even pressured, partly because it tends to be so infrequently or inadequately expressed.[164]

Theodora Jim notes that in classical Greece, "it [was] the mixture of different elements which makes it difficult to see first-offerings as *intrinsically* thank-offerings. . . . The coexistence of several seemingly contradictory motivations was not perceived by the Greeks as inconsistent."[165] Yet, the situation surrounding Early Byzantine *karpophoriai* was also complicated by the secular convention of honoring powerful people with gifts of gratitude and deference (*xenia, 'iqārē*). Libanius, for example, refers to an army officer who had received "barley, corn, ducks, and fodder" as gifts from villagers in Syria after helping them in a court case.[166] This clearly shaped Christian imaginations. Although John Chrysostom insisted that God had no need for any material offerings, he nonetheless maintained that God had instituted firstfruits so that humans could show him gratitude, and at one point explained that God had accepted Abel's firstfruit of a sheep (Gn 4:3–5) because Abel had offered it "as to a master," in acknowledgement of his need for divine philanthropy.[167] Thus, giving these gifts may have been voluntary, but to neglect to give them risked losing essential future blessings. When drought struck Cappadocia, Gregory of Nazianzus instinctively suggested that it was because someone in his congregation had "robbed God, the giver of all, of the firstfruits of his barn floor and winepress, showing himself at once thankless and senseless, in neither giving thanks for what he has had, nor prudently providing, at least, for the future."[168] Pseudo-Joshua reasoned that God had deliberately withheld his blessings after a fine harvest in 499 because the people of Edessa had carelessly withheld their gratitude: "They did not even send up thanks for the gifts of God, but were neglectful."[169] At least one eighth-century monk was wont to demand bread offerings in return for his verbal blessings, as we know from papyri.[170]

In any case, the failure of ordinary people to adequately feel or sufficiently express religious gratitude helped explain the need for religious professionals who could devote themselves to honoring and thanking God full time. "You are the firstfruits of the world," Hypatius informed novices entering his monastery, adopting a phrase used to describe the earliest Christians in the New Testament (Jas 1:18). "Just as a farmer grinds grain and offers it as a firstfruit to God, and thanks to this small thing the Lord blesses all his grain," Hypatius continued, "so too does God show mercy to the world through his holy people."[171] Monks were laypeople who had been set apart from the rest of the world, sometimes by their own parents,[172] to honor God alongside other dedications put up in a shrine. Often a monastery, including its buildings and liturgical vessels, was the product of a single lay *karpophoria*, or was built and maintained through fruitbearings that a local community collectively contributed.[173] The total ensemble was held to be sacrosanct: "Do you not know that all things in monasteries are sacred, inasmuch as they come from *karpophoriai?*" Abbot Euthymius reportedly asked a thieving steward.[174] To safeguard their sanctity, monks were to observe certain rules in handling of fruitbearings, as seen in the previous chapter. One obvious danger was that, in giving such thank-offerings, people might be seeking, consciously or not, to reward God's servants rather than God himself for a blessing received. Hypatius reportedly refused to accept a *karpophoria* that an imperial chamberlain named Urbinus had wanted to give him in thanks for a healing, but relented once Urbinus proposed instead to refurbish the monastery with a sumptuous church "in order to glorify God."[175] This may explain why so many *karpophoriai* were given in the form of crosses and other instruments for the altar. Such liturgical gifts more patently glorified God, rather than his human representatives.[176]

Indeed, God's representatives were expected to be productive of fruitbearings like everyone else. As affirmed in a homily composed in seventh-century Palestine, "monks especially must offer God firstfruits and tithes—not only visible proceeds from what they administer for others and the work of their hands, but also spiritual sacrifices, which please God even more."[177] Such differentiation between "visible" and "spiritual" recalls the scale of firstfruits that John Cassian attributed to the monastic steward at Scetis in his *Conferences,* as discussed at the beginning of this chapter. There, it will be recalled, Cassian had Abba John explain that giving firstfruits taken from the earth was fine, but what God really wanted were spiritual fruits. Indeed, monastic literature rarely refers to monks as offering material fruitbearings themselves;[178] it mainly describes them as giving *karpophoriai* in the form of virtues and prayers. Melania the Younger reportedly told her monastery that they should render prayers up to God more promptly than farmers delivered firstfruits to their earthly lords.[179]

Thus, authorities recognized material and spiritual gradations of offerings just as they recognized material and spiritual gradations of alms. This chapter has focused on non-liturgical offerings intended to thank God for material profits or benefits conferred; the next chapter will focus on liturgical offerings intended to thank God for life itself. Like more routine almsgiving, fruitbearings were never supposed to be holocausts, and monastic givers not expected to sacrifice themselves in order to produce them. Like the laity, they were only expected to offer from their spiritual labor what best expressed gratitude to God (cf. 2 Cor 9:12). But some hammered out their flesh with penitential fervor and self-sacrificial refinement for years on end. As a result, they were imagined to become liturgical instruments themselves, able to glorify God and contain his grace in their own persons. Thus, Symeon Stylites the Younger was said to have been picked up and carried into church "like a sacred vessel" while other monks chanted the liturgy.[180] This instrumental value might outlast such ascetics themselves, as was the case with a mourner named Paul who once lived in a cave above the Tigris River. According to John of Ephesus, Paul's "asceticism and labors and humility were beyond description." After twenty-five years, he finally died, but that did not stop villagers from using his body to benefit their land: "Taking his skull, men went around the districts; wherever . . . came locusts, hail, scorching wind, or bubonic plague [and] his right hand or his head went, God straightway made deliverance."[181]

"Imperishable Remembrance in Heaven and Earth"

Liturgical Offerings and the Rise of Patronal Monasteries

In 410, just as Symeon Stylites was setting up practice in northern Syria, a young and unusually glamorous ascetic couple landed on the coast of Roman North Africa.

Valeria Melania (ca. 383–439) and her husband, Valerius Pinianus, were retreating from Alaric's descent on Rome to an estate they owned near the inland city of Thagaste (Souk Ahras, Algeria). Equipped with a bathhouse, two churches, and craftsmen trained in gold, silver, and copper work, the estate was said to be "bigger than the city itself." Melania and Pinian came from two of the richest families of the Roman Empire. Theirs was an arranged marriage, imposed on them as teenagers, but after losing two children in infancy, they swore themselves to a celibate life and began doing things their own way. At a time when most other aristocrats in Italy would have been trying to secure whatever wealth they could, Melania and Pinian reportedly used Alaric's invasion to do just the opposite. After liquidating holdings in Gaul and Spain, freeing hundreds of slaves, and sending thousands of coins to churches and monasteries in the secure Roman East, they came to Africa intending to do the same. According to Melania's hagiographer, Gerontius, they rejoiced in thinking such dispersals enacted biblical descriptions of the blessed rich: "They distributed freely, they have given to the poor, their righteousness endures forever" (Ps 112 [111]:9). But before they carried out their plan, three major bishops intervened: Alypius of Thagaste, Aurelian of Carthage, and Augustine of Hippo. "Whatever coins you are now providing to the monasteries will soon be gone," they explained. "But if you want to have imperishable remembrance in heaven and on earth, grant to each monastery a house and an income." Following this "excellent advice," Melania and Pinian built two large monasteries, filled them with freed slaves (one male, one female), and provided a "self-sufficient income" for each through endowments of "houses, revenues and lands."[1]

Written in Jerusalem perhaps thirty years later (ca. 452), this episode in the *Life of Melania the Younger* recaptures a watershed moment in monastic and Early Byzantine cultural history. It describes a moment when an elite Roman family decided to found a monastic institution for the express (and perhaps sole) purpose of commemorating themselves. It presents this not merely as a concession to episcopal prudence but as a superior practice to the casual dispersals that Melania and Pinian had previously made in their hope of gaining a reputation for righteousness that would "endure forever." It is hard not to see their initial practice of open-handed almsgiving (as Gerontius describes these dispersals) as a continuation of the old Roman aristocratic practice of showering coins on one's fellow citizens to garner their goodwill and a reputation for "greatness of soul."[2] But the proposed alternative—creating whole new communities of their own and filling them with ascetic freedmen in order to secure eternal remembrance—that was truly new and significant. So too was the rationale of founding such communities to perpetuate memory in heaven as well as earth. As the bishops in the story point out, endowments were crucial to this long-term goal because they provided monasteries with incomes that were theoretically permanent—that is, eternal. The connection that Christian authorities drew between founding monasteries, endowing them with offerings, and achieving "imperishable remembrance in heaven and earth" is the subject of this final chapter.

Patronal monasteries, material offerings, and liturgical commemoration: this is a distinctly medieval triad, one that has been extensively studied for Western Europe due to the preservation of numerous church and monastic records from the Carolingian and Ottonian periods. Often called *Libri vitae* (Books of Life; cf. Rv 20:12, 15), these necrological records listed, beside each donor's name, the degree of commemoration that was owed to each based on offerings he or she had made to the institution. Patrons whose offerings were small had their names mentioned either collectively in prayers or written in a list placed on the altar during the service (lists at Cluny included up to forty thousand names). Patrons who provided for the liturgical offering itself—that is, the bread and wine of the Eucharist—had their names uttered aloud while the Eucharist oblation was being presented. But those who had founded the institution in which the liturgy was being held received constant attention. Their names, together with those of their family and descendants, were mentioned not only at weekly liturgies and feast days but also at annual services held specifically in their memory. This arrangement, whereby patrons provided offerings in return for commemoration, helps account for the proliferation of church and monasteries—especially private ones—during the Middle Ages.

On the face of it, this arrangement was beneficial for all involved. For clerics and monks, it provided work directly related to their area of professional expertise—

lengthy liturgical rituals and repetitious prayers—that gave them a sense of importance and attracted long-term endowments for their institutions. For patrons, it gave a sense of prestige and provided the highest possible assurance that one's name would be presented positively forever to God and not forgotten or damned after death. An eleventh-century monastic *Liber vitae* stated that the purpose of the commemorative book was to ensure that the names in it "might be present to the divine gaze forever."[3] Getting one's name into such institutional books so it would be repeatedly chanted before God was probably the closest a medieval Christian could ever come to assurance of eternal remembrance and, thus, eternal salvation.

A similar nexus between monastic patronage, offerings, and commemoration appears in medieval Byzantium. It has even been said that "the central motivating factor for every Byzantine [was] that they be remembered by God himself for eternity, and it goes far to explain why it was so important to leave others behind to remember and pray for salvation."[4] Indeed, so prominent is the emphasis on commemorative activity in both Eastern and Western monasteries of the medieval era that it tends to be taken for granted. Its roots in the Western the Eastern Roman empires have received little attention. For Early Byzantium, John Philip Thomas's *Private Religious Foundations in the Byzantine Empire* and Ewa Wipszycka's *Les ressources et les activités économiques des églises en Égypte du Ve au VIIIe siècle* are indispensable. Both discuss the numerous papyri, mainly dated from the sixth century onward, that record quid pro quo, postmortem arrangements in which individual Egyptian donors make bequests of wine, grain, and other resources to monasteries in return for liturgical commemorations. These documents are the closest we come in Early Byzantium to the later Western "Books of Life." Yet no one has explained the striking fact that all of those discovered so far attest arrangements between donors and monasteries, and none between donors and local churches. Wipszycka believes this reflects just an accident of survival: "For my part," she declares, "I cannot see why churches were not as well placed as monasteries to celebrate the masses for the soul of the dead."[5]

The Justinian Code confirms that churches and clerics also received bequests in this era, and I will be discussing arrangements made between donors and local churches here, as well as between donors and monasteries. References to bequests to monasteries, however, greatly exceed those made to churches in the voluminous papal letter collection of Pope Gregory the Great (sed. 590–604), and, as we shall see, there were reasons why monks and monastic institutions might have been considered better suited to serve as long-term stewards of a patron's memory. On this, Gerontius offers unique insight. He explains that Melania, in the last decade of her life, now living in the Holy Land, poured her remaining wealth into a new cluster of religious foundations on the Mount of Olives outside Jerusalem. These consisted not only of a church called the Aposteleion dedicated to Peter and Paul and a martyr shrine dedicated to St. Stephen, but two monasteries—one female,

one male—built nearby. According to Gerontius, Melania intended the Aposteleion and the St. Stephen shrine to serve as her family's burial chapels, the first
for her mother and husband, the second for herself. Liturgies at the two shrines
would be provided by the male monastery, which Melania founded, Gerontius
reports, so that the Aposteleion would resound with psalmody all day and night. It
was her wish "to see the church liturgy being performed incessantly and the bones
of [her] mother and husband finding rest in their singing of psalms."[6] Gerontius
also reports that she chose to build the St. Stephen shrine on the site where Jesus
ascended after the resurrection (Acts 1:9–11) so that, after her death, "in this place
too a *prosphora* on behalf of my soul and those of my [mother and husband] can
be incessantly offered."[7] She filled her male monastery with "God-loving holy men
who brightly performed the liturgy" to perform these sepulchral serenades. She
asked that its monks be assembled at the hour of her death, "for that had always
been her vow, to deliver up her spirit among holy men."[8]

Thus, Melania founded a male monastic community in Jerusalem for the same
reason that she had founded monasteries in North Africa: namely, commemoration,
or more specifically, to staff her burial churches and to provide liturgies "incessantly"
over her family's tombs. Although Gerontius does not say that she chose monks over
church clerics to serve in these foundations, he indicates that it was her priority to
staff them with those on whom she could rely to chant not only "brightly" but "incessantly," using the adverb *adialeptōs* three times to describe what she wanted. Here we
may be confident that Gerontius was accurately reporting Melania's intentions,
because she had chosen none other than Gerontius himself to construct her male
monastery, recruit its residents, and supervise their liturgical activities. How Melania
and her husband made acquaintance with Gerontius is unknown, but he was a native
of Jerusalem and had already served them earlier in some capacity as a page or custodian.[9] Eventually, they "took him from the world" and made him a monk, after
which he remained Melania's personal factotum and priest ("I spent not a little time
with her," he remarks).[10] Toward the end of her life Melania entrusted him with safeguarding all her institutions. He did not let her down.

As a memorial, the hagiographical portrait Gerontius crafted for Melania has
proved more enduring than the institutions or liturgies he supervised. His *Life of
Melania* manages to capture her idiosyncratic voice without divulging her hereti-
cal sympathies, thereby helping it find future audiences.[11] But Melania might have
been more pleased to learn how Gerontius carried out her liturgical commemorations. The sixth-century writer John Rufus describes the impact of his performances on others attending the services:

> Appointed simultaneously as priest and as abbot of the holy Mount of Olives and of
> the monasteries on it, often he [Gerontius] would celebrate three gatherings of the
> divine service in a single day, and especially on the holy Sunday: one on the holy

mountain, and one in the monastery for men, and again one in the monastery for women. On the remaining days, he celebrated daily a gathering and a private service for the blessed Melania according to the custom of the Church of Rome. In each liturgy, when he had begun the holy service, he shed tears ceaselessly until the end with grief and anguish of heart such that no one of those assembled could control himself, while all [the members of] the congregation were in penitence and impassioned with gasping and groans were shedding tears like him.[12]

Such devotion was what all patrons would have wanted from stewards of their memory.

In this chapter we shall put such Christian patronal concerns into a broader framework. One point must be stressed from the start. As Julia Hillner observes, the advice that Gerontius attributes to the three African bishops about providing institutional endowments was in fact something new. Generally speaking, before the fifth century, Roman benefactors tended to prefer financing the final touches that made public projects noticeable (the "icing on the cake") rather than furnishing the endowments needed for salaries and maintenance.[13] The nature and form of Christian endowments will need some discussion here. Melania gave her North African monasteries real estate, but other patrons preferred to retain ownership of such assets for themselves and merely sign over the income (*prosodon*) they produced to the religious institution. This latter arrangement created a relationship of economic dependency between monks and their patrons, as well as other consequences discussed below. But the historical point to be first grasped here is that long-term institutional endowments were a late antique Christian innovation, encouraged by church and monastic authorities and bolstered by imperial laws meant to ensure that patronal bequests would last "forever."

A remark by John Rufus shows that Melania endowed her Jerusalem monasteries too.[14] It may be tempting to interpret this as a consequence of the advice of the African bishops, and an example of Western pragmatism influencing Eastern practices. None of Augustine's writings, however, voice the advice Gerontius attributes to him and the other bishops. It is therefore equally possible that Gerontius was ascribing to their authority the wisdom that he himself had gained by running his patron's monasteries after her death. At any rate, the Greek phrase Gerontius ascribes to these Western bishops, *alēston mnēma* ("imperishable memory," also "memorial" or "remembrance"),[15] was commonly being used at the time by Christian authorities in the East to describe not only the purpose of traditional Roman aristocratic mausoleums ("People frequently toil to build ostentatious tombs to make their memory imperishable," said Chrysostom)[16] but also the kind of honors that Christians owed God and his saints ("Carry with you imperishable remembrance of God's martyrs," others advised).[17] Significantly, it was also used to describe the state of God's memory itself. As Gerontius's contemporary, Theodoret, explained, "God holds in imperishable memory" everything a righteous man does.[18]

This chapter explores the implications of that usage, examining how ideas concerning divine memory, eternal salvation, and liturgical commemoration became intertwined in Early Byzantine imaginations, and how *prosphorai* offerings, monastic endowments, and "incessant" prayer were imagined to contribute to the creation and perpetuation of Christian memory. This constitutes, in effect, an investigation of the long-term material underpinnings of monasticism itself. For the future of the monastic movement lay not with public penitents like Symeon Stylites, but with the nameless mass of chanting monks whom aristocratic patrons like Melania installed in their private monastic foundations to service their family tombs. Before considering these monastic issues, we must familiarize ourselves with the *prosphorai* and commemorative services that were routinely offered in an Early Byzantine church.

LAY OFFERINGS AND CHURCH COMMEMORATIONS

As statues for local benefactors in public venues gave way to imperial imagery from the fourth century onward, churches became the new monumental centers of communal benefaction and commemoration in the Roman East. Even routine fundraisers offered opportunities to gain public acclaim. Writing in Bethlehem, Jerome complains that whoever promised offerings—probably referring to lay *karpophoriai* contributions—had their names proclaimed during the service: "This one has offered so much, that one has vowed so much," church deacons announced to congregations that applauded in response.[19] Everyone was invited to join in: "Be that which he offereth small, yet shall it be a remembrance of himself," states the *Canons of Athanasius*.[20] Inscriptions in Syrian and Palestinian churches show the results. While some ask God to remember groups of donors anonymously described as "those whose names you know,"[21] most record their individual names (occasionally citing the exact number of coins that each one donated, down to the last fraction), sometimes portraying the donors themselves, their faces prominently displayed, requesting that God "remember" them, perhaps inspired by the Penitent Thief's appeal to Jesus on the cross, "Remember me when you enter your kingdom" (Lk 23:42).[22] Had the ceilings and walls of these Early Byzantine churches survived, many more such portraits undoubtedly would have survived. Choricius describes how a local magnate who paid for the Church of St. Sergius in sixth-century Gaza was depicted up in its apse, forever memorialized alongside images of the saint and Emperor Justinian for his contribution to his Christian city. Seeing the crowd that had assembled to hear recitations of St. Sergius's deeds at the inauguration, Choricius remarks that if "erecting churches renews this kind of memory, then the single cause of these good memories is inferred to be the person who builds churches."[23]

Thus, as in the late Roman West, churches became "sites for the production of a particular shared memory" in the recently Christianized communities of the Near

East.[24] While we might see in their patronal inscriptions and imagery the old com-memorative customs of a classical forum, a more useful analogy might be that of a memory palace, designed to make Christians remember their benefactors amid saints and other members of the divine hierarchy. Such memory palaces were two-sided in purpose, however, for their decor and furnishings explicitly addressed themselves to God and sought to make an impression on God's own memory.

Essential to facilitating such divine remembrance was the weekly liturgy per-formed around the Eucharist. Technically known in Early Byzantium as "the holy *prosphora*," this liturgical type of offering was conceived as categorically different from a fruitbearing offering. The late seventh-century Council in Trullo, for example, identified a firstfruit as "an act of thanksgiving . . . [to] the giver of the fruits by which our bodies are increased and fed," but defined the Eucharist *prosphora* as a gift "for the quickening of souls and release from sins"—that is, a gift to God for life and salvation itself.[25] Today, the liturgy of processions and prayers that once attended such offerings is the least visible feature of ancient Christian experience, but in antiquity it was the most elaborate. Liturgical history is a technical field where only the most confident specialists dare tread. Nonetheless, it is clear that by the fourth century, commemora-tive prayers were a central part of the portion of the liturgy known as the *anaphora* (literally, prayers "raised up" during the Eucharist offering).

After catechumens had been dismissed from church and the deacons had placed the sacrificial bread and wine of the Eucharist on the altar, a priest or bishop would ask God to collectively remember various groups within the community in categorical order, starting with clerics, ascetics, apostles, and martyrs and then moving to emperors and laypeople in general, including even the poor. Separate remembrances were then made for whoever had contributed the bread and wine offered at the service, as well as for those who had died. If reconstructions of the so-called *Byzantine Liturgy of St. Basil* reflect sixth-century practices, these last two categories gained commemorative importance over the fifth century. No longer do we find them listed in sixth and eighth place among the groups being remembered (as found, for example, in the earlier *Egyptian Anaphora of St. Basil*), but we find them listed first and third: "Remember all those who have fallen asleep in hope of resurrection to eternal life," the celebrant was supposed to intone. "And remember, Lord, those who presented these gifts, and those for whom, and through whom, and account of whom, they presented them."[26]

Performed every Sunday around altars at theoretically the same time all across the Roman East, this communal liturgy provided the basic mechanism by which the empire's entire Christian population was thought to be regularly remembered and briefly reunited, the living and deceased together.[27] Such remembrances were prob-ably not as impersonal as the categorical prayers cited above make them seem. Whereas modern Christians tend to think of their communion services as occasions for receiving liturgical bread and wine provided by their church and clergy, Early

Byzantine Christians were taught to view them as occasions for giving such offerings themselves. Families were encouraged to bring "oblations" (simply Latin for *prosphorai*) to church in order to commemorate deceased parents, spouses, children, and other relatives during the liturgy. As explained in chapter 5, these liturgical lay offerings usually consisting of small, round, inexpensive loaves of bread; after being blessed along with the bread and wine that the church had prepared in advance for the Eucharist, these extra loaves were collected for later distribution among clerics as leftover "blessings." But an important additional facet of this ancient practice was the recording of individual names associated with such offerings.

A Syrian document called the *Testament of Our Lord Jesus Christ* states how this was supposed to be done in the fifth century. It envisions donors arriving before the service with their loaves, presumably like the twenty-cent bread *prosphorai* sold outside churches in Syria and Palestine.[28] They would hand these over to a priest waiting to receive them near the church entrance, attended by a deacon and reader. "Let the priest write down the names of those who offer oblations or of those for whom they have been offered," prescribes the *Testament*, "so that, when the bishop offers the holy things, the reader or chief deacon may name in commemoration those for whom the priest and congregation are making their supplications."[29]

According to this document, clerics were to give personalized attention to individual names connected to lay offerings, while the celebrant issued the more categorical, communal commemorations during the anaphora. This procedure suggests that at least some of the clergy were expected to utter aloud each name entrusted to their care.[30] Gerontius tells how Melania confronted him during a Eucharist in Jerusalem, threatening never to return if he ever mentioned again at the altar the name of a deceased aristocrat suspected of being a heretic. His anecdote presumes that she had overheard him uttering that individual's name aloud, and surely illustrates what every patron would have wanted (or as in this case, not wanted) to happen during a service.[31] Gerontius explains, "I had uttered her name in the holy anaphora along with those of saints who have already died, for it is our custom to do this, so that they may intercede on our behalf."[32]

No doubt customs varied, depending on logistical constraints such as the size of a congregation. By the late fourth century, some churches had begun posting names of living and dead Christians that needed inclusion at an anaphora on placards known as diptychs, also called Books of Life. We do not know how inclusive this commemorative practice was—although we do know that diptychs in the main Chalcedonian church in Constantinople included the names of aristocratic laymen, we do not know whether such diptychs existed outside of metropolitan churches, or whether they included the names of ordinary Christian layfolk.[33] But another custom was introduced in this era that may have been intended to handle an increasing number of commemorations. According to the *Apostolic Constitutions,* all Christians were to receive individual "remembrances" on the third, ninth, and thirtieth day after their death. These would be annually followed by liturgies and meals held once a year "as a memorial" for them, accompanied by distributions made to the poor from property of the deceased, also to "remember" them.[34]

Thus all the elements of the commemorative rites that we will find requested of Early Byzantine monastic institutions—annual liturgies, Charity (*agapē*) Feasts,[35] dispersal of alms—were already being proposed in late fourth-century churches. The *Apostolic Constitutions* preserve some of the intercessory prayers to be spoken at these events, asking God to overlook a dead person's sins and admit them into the land of the blessed; the manual also bars clerics from commemorating unrepentant sinners and exhorts them to not get drunk at commemorative meals.[36] Their inclusion in the eighth book of the *Apostolic Constitutions* indicate that these rituals were post-Constantinian innovations. Yet Early Byzantine authorities insisted they had authentic apostolic origins. This was not simply because these later authorities regarded the *Apostolic Constitutions* to be a document handed down from the original Christian community, but also because they believed the sanction of the apostles themselves was necessary to provide assurance that the rites actually helped the dead obtain intercession and salvation.

As John Chrysostom reiterated to his congregations on several occasions,

> Not in vain did the apostles legislate that we should make remembrance of the departed at the awesome mysteries, for they knew that it was much to their profit and much to their advantage.[37]

> Not in vain are offerings made for the departed, or supplications, or alms. All these things hath the Spirit ordered. . . . It is not just the deacon who cries, "For those who have fallen asleep in Christ, and for those who perform memorials on their behalf." It is not the deacon who utters this, but the Holy Spirit.[38]

> Not for nothing have these things been devised, nor do we make mention of the departed at the divine mysteries in vain. . . . These things have been ordained by the [Holy] Spirit.

"So let us help them by performing memorials on their behalf," Chrysostom concludes. "For if the children of Job were purified by the sacrifice [offered by] their father, why doubt that when we ourselves make offering on behalf of the departed, they receive some consolation?"[39]

A century later, Severus of Antioch used the same argument in a letter written to assure a noblewoman that the deceased took "some consolation" from the offerings, prayers, and alms made for them at a commemorative service. Severus concludes by adding, "It is not lawful for us to say that any of the things enjoined in the churches is useless or vain."[40] Skepticism had evidently arisen (or had always existed) about the utility of these practices. But before considering the causes of that skepticism, we should consider how authorities like Chrysostom and Severus imagined church commemorations to influence divine Judgment and help someone after death.

CHURCH APOLOGETICS FOR COMMEMORATIVE RITES

How could any prayers, offerings, or alms save the deceased, especially if they had not been particularly virtuous while still alive? Fear not, Chrysostom assured his audiences. There was no good reason to doubt their efficacy. Convinced that God was "wont to favor" those who made petitions on others' behalf, he insisted that God would heed prayers made even for people who had lived unrighteous lives.[41] Evidence of God's acceptance of vicarious atonements included not only the burnt sacrifices that Job had regularly made to assuage God for his children's possible sins (Job 1:5, mentioned by Chrysostom above), but also the posthumous propitiations made by the Maccabean soldiers, who managed to "blot out the sins" of their comrades by supplicating God and sending an offering to Jerusalem (2 Mc 12:38–46).[42] Chrysostom claimed that Eucharist services offered occasions for Christians to do the same as these Old Testament forebears, for it was then that Christ himself descended with his heavenly host, making the moment opportune for petitioners to make themselves known. He invited listeners to recall what happened when a Roman emperor descended with his court on Antioch:

> Just as it is then, when the emperor sits down, that a petitioner should hasten to say whatever he wishes—for when the emperor has risen, whatever is said might be said in vain—so too, while the mysteries are being celebrated, all have the greatest honor to be deigned worthy of remembrance. . . . And just as it is when emperors celebrate their victories that all those who joined in the victory receive positive mention and all who are bound in chains are freed—but when the moment is past, whoever did not try to obtain anything no longer gets the chance—so too it is here now: for this moment is a victory celebration.[43]

"Knowing this," Chrysostom concludes, "let us arrange as many consolations we can for the departed, and instead of tears, lamentations, and monuments, [give them] alms, prayers, and offerings, so that together we and they may attain the promised goods."[44]

It is not surprising that Chrysostom used the analogy of petitioning the imperial court to address the intercessory and commemorative concerns of his audiences. Late Roman emperors at this time had a court official called the Magister Memoriae, "a sort of imperial remembrancer," whose function was (among other things) to remind emperors of the names of civil servants awaiting promotion. Church priests might be considered to have performed a similar service for the heavenly court.[45] Likewise his allusion to prisoners being liberated by the emperor on special occasions, meant to conjure God's pardoning of condemned sinners, reflects an actual imperial custom of pardoning prisoners during Easter and other celebrations.[46] Leontius of Neapolis developed a similar analogy in his seventh-century *Life of John the Almsgiver* to encourage the performance of posthumous liturgies. His story told how a Christian soldier from Cyprus was captured and incarcerated by the Persians in a remote Persian stronghold called Oblivion. Thinking their son dead, his parents arranged for commemorative liturgies to be performed for him three times a year. Eventually, the prisoner escaped and came home; after speaking to his parents, he realized that the same days on which an angel had appeared in his cell and released him from his chains had corresponded to exactly the same days on which his parents had made the memorials each year.

Leontius says that John the Almsgiver told this story to persuade Alexandrians to provide commemorative liturgies "ceaselessly and without reservation" for their departed.[47] It is clear, however, that Leontius has rewritten an earlier Latin anecdote transmitted in the sixth-century *Dialogues* of Gregory the Great about a Roman soldier who was released from Lombard chains whenever commemorative liturgies were performed for him in northern Italy. Gregory's *Dialogues* circulated widely in the Roman East. What is significant is that Leontius completely altered the details of Gregory's story to set it in "Oblivion," an actual detention center in southwestern Iran well known to Early Byzantine authors, where the Sassanian state sent political prisoners whom they wanted to permanently disappear.[48] Surely, Leontius exploited the allegorical potential of this Persian prison's name to suggest that church memorials not only saved the dead, but did so by overcoming oblivion itself.

Chrysostom similarly suggests that Christians could help the dead by making "continual prayers" on their behalf.[49] Indeed, at one point he observes that some attended church for no other reason than to commemorate a wife, mother, or child, paying no attention to his sermons.[50] The emphasis that Chrysostom places on the necessity for these prayers to be "continual" anticipates a basic rationale for entrusting it to monks. We have seen, however, that Chrysostom and others could be quite defensive in advocating such rites. Indeed, authorities were increasingly pressured to explain how posthumous offerings and prayers could improve the condition of the dead and other questions related to the afterlife, such as, What happens to people's souls in the period between death and Judgment Day? What can be done for them? How can we know? A spectrum of views arose to answer these questions,[51] voiced by a variety of people whose concerns sound similar but seem to have been only tangentially connected.

First, there were recent converts for whom communal commemorations through church offerings and priestly intercessions were something novel. Greco-Roman pagan memorials for the dead had featured annual sacrifices followed by picnics or banquets held each year in local cemeteries or, in the case of aristocrats, ancestral mausoleums. Such meals served both to commemorate and to "refresh" the deceased.[52] As Éric Rebillard emphasizes, they were largely private affairs conducted by families or funeral clubs.[53] Wealthier families often employed professional mourners to supply elaborate dirges, tears, and histrionics. Christian leaders exhorted congregants to give up such "vain" traditions in favor of more sober ceremonies offered by the church, and it has been proposed that the rites prescribed by the *Apostolic Constitutions* were devised to provide appropriate substitutes. Churchmen tended to condemn the persistence of such practices as unreformed paganism.[54] Rebillard and others point out, however, that equally at issue was the church's desire to coopt, if not suppress, ancient methods of mourning.[55]

Thus, the defensiveness of preachers like Chrysostom may have been in response to a reluctance to abandon time-honored family conventions, as much as to doubts about the efficacy of the new communal rites themselves. Eventually, however, Christian intellectuals began asking deeper questions: Did souls of the dead remain active or asleep until Judgment Day? How could vicarious prayers and material sacrifices help them in either case? Such difficult questions vexed church authorities. In Rome, Gregory the Great chose to respond with the series of edifying tales he included in his sixth-century *Dialogues*. At about the same time in Constantinople, a priest responded with a treatise called *On the State of Souls after Death*. The fact that his treatise almost entirely consists of quotations lifted from earlier authorities indicates the difficulty he had in proving his case any other way.[56] Yet these literary and theoretical efforts should not mislead us. Neither the perceived persistence of "pagan" practices nor the doubts of a few Christian intellectuals ever seriously jeopardized church rites, as is made plain by Chrysostom's complaint that some came to church only to offer commemorations. To the extent that there was any real challenge, it came mainly from critics concerned about the emphasis placed on obtaining intercession through the cult of the martyrs,[57] or about "the (often very lucrative) economy of the afterlife" that grew up around church practices.[58] A fifth-century sermon roundly scorned the idea that priests performed commemorative services "out of love of gain." The fact that this idea arose, however, or that bishops like Rabbula of Edessa needed to prohibit priests from demanding honoraria for attending memorial banquets, suggests how profitable they could be.[59] In any case, the allegations show that Christian commemorative liturgies for the dead had, by the fifth century, become routine.

JACOB OF SERUG'S *ON THE LOAF FOR THE DEPARTED*

It is in this light that we must approach a homily composed on the subject in Syriac by Jacob of Serug (449–521). Jacob spent his career travelling as a circuit priest around villages and monasteries of northern Mesopotamia before serving, in the last years of his life, as bishop of Batnae-Serug (Sürüç, Turkey), a prosperous city near a silk route southwest of Edessa. Jacob stands out for having mastered the Syriac homiletic form known as *mimre*. These were twelve-syllable verse sermons performed before congregations in a kind of rhythmic chant. Hundreds of Jacob's *mimre* have survived on topics ranging from biblical stories and church festivals to mundane aspects of everyday life, making them invaluable for learning about was going on in the minds of Christians east of Antioch at the time. Several castigate the "liturgical laxity" of his flock,[60] including one preserved under the title, *On the Commemoration of the Departed, and on the Oblation, and That the Departed Benefit from the Offerings and Alms Made in Their Behalf.*

Probably originally just called *On the Loaf for the Departed,*[61] this sermon addressed a church audience that included poor widows and female slaves as well as rich men. This diversity suggests that Jacob wrote it after he had become ordained bishop of Serug. In any case, he makes clear in the sermon which of these groups he felt could be trusted to fulfill their commemorative responsibilities and which could not. Because the sermon has never been discussed in detail before, I examine it closely here. It especially illustrates the challenge of persuading certain types of laypeople to carry out their commemorative responsibilities for the dead, and this will help us understand in turn the attraction of alternatively enlisting monks to serve this purpose.

Running nearly three hundred lines of verse, Jacob's sermon focuses on the expectation that laypeople would bring bread to church to offer as liturgical oblations in memory of dead relatives during a service. It includes the longest description of this ancient Christian custom to survive anywhere:

> On behalf of the souls of the dead the priest goes in and stands,
> And he sets the Bread and Wine of sanctification on the altar,
> And there commemorates the death of Jesus and His Resurrection,
> And calls to the sacrifice everyone that has departed, to receive forgiveness.
> And all that have set apart a loaf and brought it, he commemorates with love,
> And inscribes the mystery with the commemoration of the departed.
> He sends up sacrifices for all the dead that have slept,
> And calleth on the Father while putting Him in mind of the death of His Son.
> And the Spirit stirs forth and descends, and dwells on the oblation. . . .
> With this sacrifice the priest bestows forgiveness on all the dead,
> For in it there is power to vanquish death and waste his realm.
> Unto the fragrance of salvation that has welled forth from this great sacrifice,
> All souls gather and come, to receive absolution.[62]

It is striking that this homily presents the Eucharist as if its sole purpose were to secure intercession for the dead. Jacob was almost certainly talking about the regular procedure at a weekly service rather than a special commemorative liturgy.[63] His discussion focuses on the extra offerings that members of his congregation added to the church's "Bread and Wine of sanctification." These lay offerings were loaves of bread taken from household supplies that individuals were supposed to have "set apart" in advance before a Sunday service.[64]

Jacob conceptualized each of these offerings as an instrument whose purpose was to convey the name associated with it to God's attention at the altar during the liturgy:

> On the stones of the ephod Moses engraved the names of the tribes [Ex 28:11–12],
> So that the priest should bring the remembrances of them into the Holy of holies.
> And thou, inscribe on the loaf the commemoration of thee and of thy departed,
>
> And give it to the priest to offer up before God.
> His name and commemoration give to God with thy oblation,
> And thy faith shall not be disappointed by justice.
> Set his memorial on the altar of the sanctuary,
> In the Bread and Wine that are the Mystery of the Body and the Blood.
>
> This, O men of discernment, is the faith of the Church:
> That [the Church] is able to make the bread and wine to be the Body and Blood.
> . . .
> Over the oblation [the Church] reads the names of all her dead,
> And mingles them with herself in the spiritual sacrifices.[65]

Once conveyed to the altar, each bread offering would be mixed with the other oblations, while the name associated with it would be "read" during the anaphora. In this way, the identity as well as the substance of each gift would be presented before God.

We must linger over the attention given to the names attached to these offerings. While Jacob does not explicitly state that it was customary for each name to be read *aloud* during the service, some sort of vocalization was imagined to take place. Jacob remarks that, when the names of the dead were mentioned at the altar, their souls would join in the celebration, taking refreshment in the Eucharist itself:

> Over the oblation [the Church] reads the names of all her dead,
> And mingles them with herself in the spiritual sacrifices.
> She gathers them together for the feast of the Body and the Blood,
> And in spiritual wise they make merry with her.[66]

Possibly his church registered individual names on lists before the service, as prescribed by the *Testament of the Lord*. At one point, Jacob insists that his fellow Christians should commemorate the dead in church because it was there that "their commemorations and their names are written, in the great book of the Godhead, wherein each one is."[67]

In any case, his exposition shows that liturgical commemoration hinged not only on giving God a liturgical gift but on maintaining a close identification between that gift and a person's name. This was likewise true of all the "paraliturgical" offerings used at a Eucharist service, including those labeled as *karpophoriai*. Hoards of inscribed liturgical instruments, such as silver chalices, patens, censers, and spoons, dating from the sixth to the seventh century have been discovered in southern Turkey (e.g., the so-called Sion Treasure, including over fifty objects) and northern Syria (e.g., the Kaper Koraon Treasure, with over fifty-five). Some have copper interiors, and all were manufactured for dedication and use in relatively minor village churches, but each of these items contains at least a pound of silver, "comparable to the price of a floor mosaic panel, a complete New Testament, or a camel."[68] Several of them bear inscriptions explicitly asking God to remember their donor.[69] As that indicates, such "paraliturgical" gifts to a church, like a liturgical offering itself, were meant to keep a person's name placed before God during the Eucharist. Possibly, they represent gifts offered on approach of death. John of Ephesus tell us about an elderly ascetic couple named John and Sosiana who worked in the palace in sixth-century Constantinople and lived together as celibates like Melania and Pinian, sleeping on separate goat-hair mats. When Sosiana sensed their approaching death, she collected all their silver, ceremonial silk clothing, and other valuables and sent them to their bishop, requesting that he use them to fashion altar cloths, chalices, patens, and other liturgical instruments to be used in his church and affiliated monasteries. She also arranged to have their names inscribed on each, asking the bishop, "And for God's sake remember me, the wretched one, in your acceptable prayers to God."[70] Jacob of Serug presents his laity's weekly liturgical offerings as serving the same purpose as such paraliturgical offerings. What made their humble loaves of bread as effective in securing God's remembrance as those more permanent, high-end gifts was the direct contribution they made as liturgical offerings to the Eucharist itself, as well as the frequency and diligence with which they were brought. "Wherefore be ye diligent over the commemoration of your beloved ones," he advises, "and over the oblation that is able to pardon your departed."[71]

Yet Jacob was discussing this custom precisely because so many in his church were failing to participate in it. "Little by little the world has let go customs that are good," he laments. "Today it hath fallen to thee to offer a loaf, and thou scorneth and neglecteth the oblation that profits thee."[72] Repeated throughout the sermon, Jacob's complaint leaves an impression of apathy and neglect. The more closely we examine it, however, the more varied the situation appears. Some of his laity's behavior stemmed from instincts we discussed in the previous section. Jacob devotes several verses, for example, to the persistence of "graveside lamentations." While complaining that men were guilty of this too, he directly addresses the women in the audience for neglecting church rites to go mourn instead "like a madwoman among the graves."[73] He also sought to dispel doubts we have already seen about postmortem intercession. Besides invoking precedents like Second Maccabees (2 Mc 12:43–45),[74] he makes an argument that was possibly his own invention: Anyone who was willing to think that baptisms could purify uncomprehending babies, he argues, should logically also think that Eucharists could purify the uncomprehending dead too. Otherwise, they might as well consider all church sacraments vain.[75]

If this were all Jacob had to say on the matter, his *memra* would offer nothing new to explain the apparent lapse he perceived in commemorative offerings at church. But later in the sermon, he reveals further grounds for his frustration. In other sermons, he often complained that members of his congregation were wont to leave church halfway through a service, slipping out at the dismissal of the catechumens before the anaphora began.[76] On this occasion, however, he focused on two groups in particular that did not even deign to appear at church at all. One group was wealthy men who declined to attend, yet sent their slaves to bring offerings in their place; the other was the heirs of a deceased person who not only declined to come to church but also neglected to send any offering to commemorate their dead at all. By focusing on these two groups, Jacob adds social dimensions to his complaint that are absent from other testimony on the subject.

The problem comes to view only toward the sermon's conclusion, where Jacob begins contrasting the indiscretions of the rich man with the piety of a humble widow. The latter, in her bereavement, could be counted on to come to church bringing her loaf with faith and love: "The *prosphora* is in her hands, tears are in her eyes, and praise is in her mouth." She brings it "in her own hands," he emphasizes, offering it herself.[77] Not so the rich man: "What rich man brings the *prosphora* to the house of God, bearing it in his own hands as he brings it in to the sanctuary?"

> Many there be that have left off altogether and never bring it,
> And some that, while they bring it, bring it without discretion.
> This sort sends the sacrifice to the house of God by the hands of his maidservant,
> And deems it a dishonor to bring his sacrifice to the Lord in his own hands.
> Such despised servants of his house as are put to the basest tasks,
> He charges to bring his sacrifice, while he remains aloof.

Either the rich man brings nothing at all, Jacob remarks, or he does so after ordering "the most scorned of his house to bring the sacrifice, while he never comes near." Unlike the widow—but also, he notes, unlike Abraham, who brought food to visiting angels with his own hands—these wealthy members of his congregation practice righteousness "only by the hands of others," and more specifically indeed, by using their household slaves.[78]

By referring to both Abraham and the use of domestic slaves to deliver offerings, Jacob recalls Chrysostom's fourth-century complaints regarding aristocratic almsgiving. "It is with scorn, and disregard, and as something mean, that the loaf is brought to the House of God to be presented,"[79] Jacob remarks. They send bread "as to a man in need," he adds, implying that this was tantamount to treating God like a beggar. This crescendo of indignation brings Jacob's sermon abruptly to an end, leaving the impression that he found such behavior personally offensive—perhaps because it was to himself that the rich man's offerings were actually being delivered, "as to a man in need."

Yet the rich man was not the only one whose absence caught Jacob's attention. Others had inherited someone's property but refused to come or send commemorations afterward. Instead, they had "taken his property and forgotten his love."

> They take pains to divide up the inheritance of the dead man,
> But it is not their custom to offer a commemoration of him.
> They make commemoration for him neither out of their own substance nor of his;
> The wicked heirs have taken his property and forgotten his love.
> Like thieves, they have divided the good garments that he had,
> And cast lots for his finest belongings.
> In peace do all thieves divide the booty they have plundered,
> But heirs [do so] with anger and quarrels and contentions.
> Heirs, then, are worse than thieves,
> For in all things they wrong the dead man's love at all times.[80]

Failing to set aside even a small portion of a deceased person's property "for his commemoration and his oblation after him," these "wicked heirs" took everything for themselves. As a result, "the departed is cheated out of the oblation that would succor him."[81]

Rather than revealing a decline in commemorative offerings, Jacob's sermon shows that the church custom had become predictable enough to allow him to typecast his congregation into groups according to his perception of their likelihood to carry out or deviate from their responsibilities. Some preferred to grieve at tombs, others doubted that offerings would make a difference, others sent them through their slaves, while others had forsaken both their offerings and their dead completely, allegedly out of greed. All such family and friends could be predicted to fail to uphold their commemorative duties, quite unlike the humble widows of the congregation—these being the only ones, it seems, whom Jacob trusted to regularly show up with a loaf in hand. But the worst offenders in his view were a dead person's heirs. Jacob depicts this group as being entirely indifferent to these basic rites of Christian commemoration.

There were other reasons, however, why wealthy families and their heirs may have been less inclined to bring commemorative offerings to communal churches of the fifth and sixth centuries than they had done in the past. Certainly, the way that local clergy were sometimes known to handle lay offerings did not help: families protested Rabbula's melting down of silver and gold vessels they had offered for deceased relatives in order to raise alms in fifth-century Edessa, and Anne Marie Yasin has detected efforts to cover over old donor inscriptions with new ones in Early Byzantine church mosaics. This is reminiscent of the kind of behavior that had formerly made Greco-Roman donors reluctant to provide endowments to maintain amenities in their cities, lest the councilors entrusted with them end up using them for different purposes than their donors desired.[82] But such priestly behavior was just part of the reason that churches like the one Jacob presided over could no longer rely on receiving liturgical offerings from all members of a local congregation. The fact is that wealthy Christians of the fifth and sixth centuries were increasingly creating private churches and monasteries of their own to serve as settings for their family's commemorations.

PATRONAL PRAISE AND THE PROLIFERATION
OF PRIVATE MONASTERIES

Sometime in the 380s or 390s, John Chrysostom digressed from a homily to encourage landowners in his congregation to consider building churches on their country estates. They had already built marketplaces, bathhouses, and taverns for their laborers—why not churches as well? They already were using their land to harvest grapes—why not, like the apostles, harvest souls? A church on a country estate would make it a paradise. Besides bringing blessings to the winepress, it would bring them peace and order like nothing else, as well as prestige. Others erected mausoleums just to hear themselves proclaimed builders. Be outstanding for erecting a church, Chrysostom exhorted. Give it a priest and a deacon; let them have the firstfruits and a cut of the crops. Then there will be "continual prayers through you, liturgical hymns through you, and a *prosphora* every Sunday." If the cost caused concern, start small; descendants could add later refinements and you will still get credit. "Tell me, is it of no consequence to have your name always included in the holy anaphoras, as well as prayers addressed every day to God for your village?" Such gains were worth any investment.[83]

Chrysostom did not need to press the point. Christians had already begun building churches and oratories on their properties during the fourth century, and this practice only accelerated during the fifth.[84] John Philip Thomas has studied the proliferation of such private foundations and the legislation around them in the Roman East.[85] Known in the later medieval West as proprietary churches (*Eigenkirchen*), these were patronal institutions, built on private properties with the rights of their founders protected by Roman law. This made them different from the communal churches considered so far, whose upkeep, staffing, and finances were controlled by ecclesiastical administrators. "Until the mid-fifth century," Thomas observes, "private benefactors enjoyed nearly complete liberty in the construction, endowment, and management of their foundations."[86] Restrictions eventually were applied. The Council of Chalcedon passed canons in 451 requiring episcopal approval and forbidding the alienation of consecrated properties; these canons were confirmed and expanded over the next century by secular laws that gave bishops broad authority to intervene. What never changed, however, was a founder's right to appoint whomever he or she wanted to serve in them, a legal right that could be ceded but otherwise theoretically remained in the founder's family forever.[87]

Though well attested in the written record, the remains of such foundations can be difficult to distinguish from those of communal churches, and archaeologists are only beginning to identify examples in the Mediterranean Near East.[88] One of the best known is the martyr shrine of St. Polyeuctus that Anicia Juliana (462–528), an immensely wealth scion of the Theodosian dynasty, built toward the end of her life on the central heights of Constantinople adjacent to her palace, replacing a church that her great grandmother had built on the same location. Juliana's church was excavated in the 1960s. Except for its foundations, little remains to impress us today (although one of its carved marble pillars can be seen in Venice's Piazzetta San Marco, taken during the Crusaders' sack of Constantinople in 1204). But her massive church—said to have been modeled on Solomon's Temple—rivaled Constantine's Church of the Holy Sepulcher at Jerusalem in the amount of gold (an estimated 331 pounds) expended on its ceiling alone. It was easily the most sumptuous Christian structure to ever grace the imperial city before Emperor Justinian lavished even more gold on Hagia Sophia in the 530s.[89]

Its interior must have positively shimmered when light from the ceiling hit the tens of thousands of glass gold and silver tesserae embedded in its walls. Lower down, the interplay of carved marble polychrome paneling, and geometric mosaics exemplified the "jeweled style" of Early Byzantine ornamentation, designed to delight and bedazzle the eye. Green peacocks and purple pomegranates set against gold backgrounds enlivened the entablatures, which were held up by columns inlaid with pieces of glass or semiprecious stones; grapevines swirled all over these surfaces, connecting disparate parts and framing the inscriptions. On the outside, above the entrance, people on the street would have seen a monumental epigram, now preserved in the *Greek Anthology:*

> What choir suffices to sing the labors of Juliana,
> Who, after the adorner of his Rome, Constantine, and
> After the all-golden sacred brilliance of Theodosius,
> Built in a few years, after so many imperial ancestors,
> A work so worthy and even more of her lineage?. . . .
> Such is this, after countless labors, that Juliana
> Accomplished for the souls of her progenitors,
> And [for the souls] of her own living self, and of those who are, and who are to come.[90]

Otherwise, testimony for patronal churches comes mainly from references scattered in chronicles, histories, hagiographies, and documentary evidence. Most of these refer to memorial chapels (*mnēmata*) built in Constantinople by imperial officials, aristocratic landowners, or their descendants; many were located on suburban estates and were designed to achieve optimal conditions for an enduring repose. One was surrounded by a series of parks, a fishpond, and a reception hall used only for emperors.[91] Most were dedicated either to the Theotokos, to a martyr, or to a group of martyrs—these being also the principle agents of heavenly intercession. Such memorial churches tended to share two other features as well. First, they were built so that their founders could be buried in them;[92] and second, in every case for which we have clear evidence, the founders either staffed them with monks or placed their tombs within monasteries that they had already established in advance (alternatively, some founded a monastery next to a preexisting ancestral tomb).[93] The martyr shrine and monastery complex that Melania built in fifth-century Jerusalem is a good example. Closer to the capital itself and slightly earlier in date is the Apostoleion that Emperor Theodosius's Praetorian Prefect of the East, Flavius Rufinus (d. 395), built on his estate three miles outside Chalcedon in the early 390s. Like Melania's Apostoleion, Rufinus built his church not only to house the relics of Peter and Paul but his own remains as well; like her, he founded a monastery beside it and filled it with select recruits, all brought in from Egypt. Justinian's minister, Narses, similarly brought in seventy Cappadocian monks, called the *Katharoi* (Pure Ones), to serve in a burial complex he built on his Bithynian estate outside Constantinople in the 550s.[94]

Thus, a distinct trend was underway from the fourth century onward that had little to do with Chrysostom's ambition to spread Christianity and much to do with the ancient desire of Christians to be buried among holy people or their relics (so-called burial *ad sanctos*).[95] Whether built on suburban properties or in more central urban locations, these foundations were part of the broader trend in the privatization of aristocratic life found in late antiquity. Yet it must be emphasized that Christian aristocrats wanted their institutions to be appreciated by the public as commemorative offerings. Some of them had their buildings inscribed and explicitly labeled as *prosphorai,* and some of these continued to be identified by their lay founders' names long after their deaths. Rufinus's church and monastic burial complex, for example, was collectively known to posterity as the *Rufinianae*; John of Ephesus mentions a monastery that an aristocrat named Caesaria founded and endowed with a working gold mine in Alexandria, noting that it contained her tomb and continued to be called "the Monastery of Caesaria the Patrician" many years after her death.[96] As with smaller liturgical offerings, the aim was to present one's name to God as prominently and persistently as possible, in order to achieve maximum remembrance and intercession.

Essential to this purpose was the recruitment and maintenance of liturgically trained monks. This feature turned such Early Byzantine foundations into "power-houses of prayer," to use the phrase Mayke de Jong coined to describe medieval

monasteries in Carolingian Europe.[97] In addition to performing the "holy prosphora"—possibly every day, as indicated by John Rufus's description of Gerontius's
schedule—such monks might conduct other sequences of psalms and prayers
designed to glorify God and make supplications for their patronal founders and
their families. The hopes that lay founders staked on these liturgical arrangements
are expressed at the entrance of a monastery in Scythopolis (Beit She'an/Baysān,
Israel). Originally built to hold the bones of a certain Lady Maria and her son in its
chapel, the monastery was expanded by their sixth-century descendants, who
explained their aspirations in a mosaic inscription that would have been visible on
the floor to anyone coming through the entry door:

> + *Prosphora* for the memory and perfect rest in Christ of the *Illustris* Zosimus, and
> for the preservation and succor of John, the most glorious ex-prefect, and of Peter
> and Anastasius, Christ-loving counts, and of all of their blessed household, through
> the prayers of the holy ones, Amen. +[98]

None of the inscriptions in this monastery refer to any martyr or group of martyrs, so we may infer that the "holy ones" mentioned in this one referred to resident monks.[99] From the oldest of the inscriptions, we know that Maria originally
built the monastery to accommodate just a single hermit named Elijah. After its
renovations, it remained relatively small, having room for only a few (living)
inhabitants.[100] Nonetheless, its principle refounder, Zosimus, clearly trusted that,
through their prayers, this *prosphora* (as he explicitly calls the monastery) would
secure both commemoration and "perfect" repose for him. These were the same
objectives that Gerontius attributed to Melania when he explained her patronal
recruitment of "God-loving holy men who brightly performed the liturgy" at her
family's tombs in her churches. We find no comparable references to local clergy
being recruited for these commemorative purposes. However, rather than simply
assume that this was due to shortcomings within the clerical class, it is better to ask
what so many lay founders would have seen in monks that made them stake their
hopes for remembrance on the monastic profession, going so far as to build monasteries and import foreign monks for this purpose.

The answer is rooted in these founders' belief that monks could be trusted to
remember them constantly in their prayers. Christians had traditionally sought
this from their holy people: Paul regularly affirmed that he was constantly providing prayerful commemoration for the recipients of his letters ("Without ceasing, I
make remembrance of you always in my prayers," Rom 1:9–10).[101] Requests for
similar remembrance by monks are found in papyrus letters as well as graffiti
scratched into monastery walls from the fourth century onward. These show what
pious lay folk hoped to obtain from local monks.[102] Most are both brief and insist-
ent ("Abba, remember me"). Although such requests are often put at the closing of
a letter, we should not infer that they represent mere formulaic conventions

(although they were this too).[103] Beyond appealing for intercession, they expressed a person's desire to remain present in a monk's mind long after an exchange had ended.[104] Often they ask for not just remembrance, but constant remembrance.

Barsanuphius's correspondents asked him to remember them "always" and, like Paul, he affirmed that he was doing so "unceasingly," "night and day."[105] When pressed for further assurance, he would elaborate, as illustrated by these different responses:

> Do not believe, my beloved, that my delay in writing you means that I have wiped your memory from my heart and consigned it to oblivion. . . . Be assured of this, that just as God does not forget us in being merciful to the world, so too I shall not forget your beloved self while I beseech God night and day for the salvation of your soul.[106]

> As God Himself knows, there is not a moment or blink of the eye in which I do not have you in my mind or in my prayer.[107]

> Your memory is fixed in my heart. I believe that it will never be effaced from there in all eternity.[108]

Such phrasing shows how closely entwined the notions of memory and eternal salvation had become in Barsanuphius's milieu. The more one became fixed in a monk's memory, the more assurance one could have of obtaining salvation. "I know that as long as you remember me in your prayers," an Alexandrian layman explained to an Egyptian abbot in the fourth century, "the Lord will not abandon me."[109]

Barsanuphius warned that agreeing to remember people "always" in prayer was something only perfect monks should do. This, however, was not the only opinion,[110] and monks who came to Constantinople in the fifth century soon discovered that the lay demand for perpetual prayers created ample opportunities for their professional services. While Hypatius (d. ca. 444) was abbot of the reconstituted monastery at the Rufinianae, wealthy Christians reportedly used to ask him to give some of his disciples (having seen that "they really crucify themselves") to serve as priests in *martyria* they were building in the vicinity. Hypatius did not readily comply, we are told,[111] but by the end of his life, a more enterprising generation of monks had arrived on the scene to answer the call.

Among these were the so-called Acoemete monks, "the Sleepless Ones." Theirs is the greatest comeback story recorded in all early monastic history. Their original leader, Alexander, was almost certainly the recipient of the angry letter sent by Nilus of Ancyra discussed at the start of the last chapter. Alexander had become notorious in the early fifth century for his uncompromising ascetic poverty as well as for the protests he raised against the failings of church clerics, imperial officials, and lay aristocrats he encountered during his travels around the Roman East. A strict literalist when it came to interpreting scripture, while living in Syria he devised a twenty-four-hour cycle of continuous, "sleepless" liturgical prayer and doxology to fulfill the

Psalmist's command, "On the law of the Lord he will meditate day and night" (Ps 1:2). This was presented as a practice that brought the life of angels down to humans on earth.[112] Eventually, Alexander set off with a company of psalm-singing monks to evangelize the empire's eastern borderland before turning to Constantinople, where his harassment of authorities prompted them to charge him with heresy and drive him out. When Alexander died in the early 430s, his company seemed doomed, exiled far up the Bosphorus under the uncertain direction of an elder named John.

Then, a few years later, they were given land on a promontory much closer to Constantinople, John died, and the ambitious Marcellus (d. 484) took over. According to a hagiography written ca. 484–511,[113] Marcellus came from Apamea (Qallat al-Madiq, Syria), the Roman capital of Second Syria. Born ca. 400 to a wealthy family, he received a classical education at Antioch, after which he resided at Ephesus, copying biblical texts and giving all unneeded earnings to the poor.[114] While living there he not only embraced asceticism but reportedly became so enthusiastic about singing the psalms that he would sneak into monasteries after visiting hours in order to join their all-night vigils. Hearing about Alexander's regimen of sleepless psalmody, he left for Constantinople, only to find Alexander living in exile.[115] Alexander trained him, but soon died. What happened next is hazy: Marcellus left for a while, then returned as a deacon to take over the company's communal affairs until Alexander's successor, John, died; then Marcellus was elected to succeed him as abbot despite allegations of arrogance and opposition that he reportedly addressed by voluntarily assuming the *diakonia* of the monastery's mule keeper for a period.[116] The *Life of Marcellus the Sleepless* is evasive about the details surrounding such institutional politics, but it does record that someone prophesized, in advance of his election, that under Marcellus, "the monastery's glory will fill the entire world, God will receive assiduous service both in it and through it, and word of His kerygma will spread . . . as from some new Jerusalem, drawing many to God."[117]

Clearly the Sleepless Ones were already reviving when they received the land on the promontory called Irenaion (Çubuklu, Turkey), closer to Constantinople on the east side of the Bosphorus. The *Life of Marcellus,* however, claims that their prospects really improved once Marcellus recruited an aristocrat named Pharetius to join their ranks. He was the son of a senator, said to possess "the kind of wealth that made a man preeminent in that great council."[118] Upon enlisting, Pharetius gave the community sufficient means to add a church, multiple dormitories, and other buildings to its compound;[119] equally important, he may have also given it a list of high social contacts. In any case the monastery grew quickly thereafter. By the time Marcellus died, the Acoemetes had the most cosmopolitan monastery of the day, boasting connections in the West, Mesopotamia, and Sassanian Persia, as well as martyrs' relics assembled "from everywhere," even from Persia and Illyria, all reportedly received by the community with great celebration as a gift from God; a hostile source in the sixth century reports that it had at that time about a thousand monks who allegedly passed their time luxuriating in baths.[120] In keeping with Marcellus's earlier interests, the monastery maintained a scriptorium that copied Greek, Latin, and Syriac manuscripts. This produced conciliar *acta,* epistolary collections, and pseudepigrapha (perhaps including the works ascribed to Dionysius the Areopagite).[121] But what made the Sleepless Ones truly famous was their liturgical work, their *opus dei.*[122] The *Life* describes this as "an unceasing regimen of divine hymnody through successions of liturgical performances."[123] It entailed at least four different choirs, each separately comprising Greek-, Latin-, Syriac-, and Coptic-speaking monks. Following practices devised by Alexander, each took a turn singing psalms, making genuflections, and exclaiming the doxological phrase "Glory to God on the highest and peace, goodwill toward men" (Lk 2:14), seventy-seven times in alternating shifts. Performed day and night throughout the week, this created a sensational liturgy that anticipated the so-called *laus perennis* (perpetual prayers of doxology) practiced by monks much later in the medieval West.[124]

The *Life* shows how the enterprising Marcellus turned Alexander's innovation into the monastery's signature product. Under his direction, "this pristine regimen and precise imitation of the unsleeping liturgy of the powers above . . . began to pour forth from Marcellus's tabernacle to the entire world."

> This business got its start in the imperial city. . . . As many as there were in it who, because they valued piety, either were constructing houses of prayer or founding ascetic communities of pious men—all of these received abbots for their flocks, custodians for their sanctuaries, and trained guardians for their brethren from Marcellus. For they believed that from him they would obtain not only ascetic rigor but also holy purity both for the houses and for the men whom they were presenting to God.[125]

Marcellus reportedly rejoiced seeing his Sleepless Ones grafted onto fledgling institutions "all over the world," and kept watch to ensure that all lived up to Acoemete standards.[126] We know that in ca. 460–463 he supplied monks for the church of St. John the Baptist that a former Roman consul named Studius built on his urban estate in southwestern Constantinople. His recruitment of Acoemete monks marked the beginning of the "Studite" monastery that would become so influential in medieval Byzantium. (The shell of its basilica still remains, with traces of its polychrome floor, rows of green columns, and atrium that once opened up to the sky.)[127] Oddly, Marcellus's hagiographer fails to mention this particular monastic colony or any of the others by name. Yet his emphasis on the worldwide diffusion of the Acoemete liturgy and training of many "Greeks, Romans, and barbarians" lends credence to the old supposition that the Western monastery of Saint-Maurice d'Agaune (St. Maurice, Switzerland), built in 515 as a burial complex by Sigismund, first Catholic ruler of the Burgundians, and served by monks who sang liturgies in constant rotation ("une innovation sans exemple en Occident") was another, albeit later, Acoemete franchise.[128]

MONKS, FREEDMEN, AND THE PERENNIAL QUEST
FOR PERPETUAL COMMEMORATION

The *Life of Marcellus the Sleepless* shows that the proliferation of patronal foundations during the fifth century created a demand for elite monks who combined
expert skills in organized, formal prayer with credentials for holiness from a repu-
table institution. Almost by definition, such work precluded other types of employment. That was a problem with the clerical model that Chrysostom proposed for
staffing private churches. Priesthood paid little in this era and was usually a part-
time job; the Korykos tombstones mention priests who moonlighted as potters,
subdeacons who worked as net-makers and cloth-workers, and a lector who ran a
wine shop.[129] Chrysostom suggested that estate priests would "constantly" perform
prayers for their patron in church, but he also envisioned them toiling in the fields
alongside the peasantry, "girded up with their hoe and working like Abraham."[130]
The only emoluments he imagined them receiving were occasional firstfruits and
an annual tithe from the crop.

Serious practitioners of perpetual prayer sought other arrangements. Alexander's disciples seemingly subsisted only on the *karpophoriai* they raised through
their liturgical performances. Likewise, the later monks of Samuel the Mountaineer's monastery high above the Tigris River were "so concerned for perfection in
the divine labors, that they . . . did not plant, but were sustained by the grace of the
faithful," while rival Nestorian monks allegedly seduced the neighboring laity with
the "sweet modulations of their chanting."[131] Marcellus took a different approach:
his monastery seems to have derived enough income from Pharetius's donations
and its scriptorium that he could release some of his monks to perform liturgies
for outside patrons (it is perhaps a sign of the wealth of his establishment that
Marcellus is said to have later dispersed all of his own considerable inheritance as
alms, using none to "purchase an income," as others wanted him to do).[132] Most
foundations, however, depended on securing and receiving predictable incomes
from property-based endowments to support their work.[133] Some may have even
refused to accept such work unless a patron clearly showed he had made arrangements to support them in advance. According to Leontius, when John the
Almsgiver solicited companies of monks to staff the two oratories he built for himself in Alexandria, he promised to take care of all their bodily needs with proceeds
from his properties in Cyprus as long as they took care of his salvation with prayers
from their all-night vigils.[134]

If hagiographers like Leontius could describe these monastic arrangements in
such purely transactional terms, we should expect no less from ordinary laypeople. An explicit exchange of material resources for spiritual services is exactly what
is found in the papyrological record. Foundational documents and monastic charters do not survive for this period. What we have instead are papyri receipts

recording the dispatch to, or arrival at, a monastery of certain amounts of wine, grain, or cash; these items are variously designated as *prosphorai* offerings,[135] as materials sent for a holy *prosphora,* or as *prosphorai* given to fund holy *prosphorai* over an extended period of time.[136] As John Philip Thomas observes, "There was a close connection between *prosphora* donations of this sort and the undertaking of funeral services for the deceased."[137]

Even more illuminating than these receipts are the testamentary documents— that is, the legal wills and codicils specifying formal burial arrangements—that survive from the fifth to the seventh centuries. These set forth the original arrangements that probably lie behind many of the *prosophorai* deliveries recorded by the receipts mentioned above. Some of these wills have survived almost completely intact. Several of them bequeath a portion (and in one case, all) of the testator's property to fund annual *prosphorai* and *agapai* (probably memorial feasts like those prescribed in the *Apostolic Constitutions,* resulting in a distribution of alms). For example, Flavius Pousi of Oxyrhyncus reserved half of his government pension to provide commemorative offerings; his wife received the other half.[138] Flavius Theodosius of Aphrodito, having no children, gave all his immovable property to one monastery to provide for his own annual *prosphora* and its attendant distributions, and then gave all his moveable property to another monastery to provide for the same rituals to be performed in his wife's memory. He also left something for his wife's grandmother, but stipulated that she must not try to claim more, since the rest was needed for the two monasteries to carry out the prescribed activities.[139]

Then there is the extensive will that Flavius Phoebammon, Chief Physician of Antinoe-Antinopolis (Sheikh 'Ibada, Egypt), prepared on November 15, 570. Dictated to a scribe and preserved in full, it runs over three hundred lines, longer than Jacob of Serug's *On the Loaf for the Departed.*[140] Apart from legacies for his hospital, a few friends, and nurses, Phoebammon bequeathed nearly everything else to his children. But he also gave incoming-producing assets to a certain monastery of Apa Jeremiah. These consisted of a tax-free vineyard, "selected from all the vineyard lands that I inherited from my father," as well as irrigation equipment and a boat with riggings. He explained that he was giving these assets, especially the real estate, "for eternal commemoration and intercession for the sake of the atonement of my soul, and for its holy *prosphora* as it departs to God." He was giving it the vineyard according to an "undiminishable" grant that could not "in any way, ever at all" be nullified, so that the monastery could perform his holy—"eternal"—*prosphora*. Its monks were to extract "every sort of income each year" from this grant to ensure that his offering would be carried out every year; they could administer it any way they thought best, as long as they never gave it away. "It is to remain permanent and constant," Phoebammon insists, "in order to service my holy *prosphora,* according to my straight and just decision." But that was not all. Phoebammon also makes the abbot swear to put his bodily remains in the monastery's communal tomb "as a memorial of my lowliness forever." Furthermore, the monastery was to include his name "in the recitation of the catalogue of the blessed who are resting there, during the calling of names of the deceased."[141]

These Egyptian documents show what must have been happening in most places by this time in Early Byzantium. Here we find prosperous lay Christians who, though not as rich as the founders of private monasteries at Jerusalem and Constantinople, similarly wished to secure lasting commemoration, and did so by making arrangements with preexisting local monasteries. These were expressly quid pro quo arrangements that resemble long-term contracts. Evidently, there were different postmortem privileges available, depending on the size of an offering and the degree of ownership or control of a property being ceded to a monastery. Patrons who did not bequeath real estate itself but simply arranged to have offerings delivered annually from its income after their deaths received an annual Eucharist ceremony and *agapē* distribution. Such arrangements were technically known as hypothecations, a form of mortgage in which the family making the endowment retained legal ownership and rights to a property, but allocated a portion or all of its proceeds to a formally designated recipient, such as a church or monastery. Because this legal arrangement kept valuable assets within a family, such "hypothecated" endowments remained popular throughout the era, and according to John Philip Thomas, account for most of the *prosodon* incomes mentioned by our sources in connection to private religious foundations.[142] For obvious reasons, however, most monasteries would have preferred to own and control such income-producing assets entirely themselves. It therefore took complete transfer of land or other valuable assets to get one's name into a monastery's "catalogue of the blessed."[143] Phoebammon arranged this at the Jeremiah monastery by giving it not just the produce of a vineyard but the vineyard itself; Melania too, it will be recalled, endowed her monasteries in Africa (presumably in Jerusalem as well) not only with revenues but with assets like houses and land, giving them actual possession of real estate. But it must be emphasized that evidence for laypeople arranging to give complete ownership of such productive assets, rather than simply the income they produced through hypothecation, was relatively rare in the late Roman East.

These different arrangements had further implications, which are discussed below. But first, the papyri reveal something more. No matter the quantity or nature of the offerings involved, each donor expresses explicit concern that his or her heir might neglect, obstruct, contest, or nullify the arrangements the donor describes. Flavius Pousi inserted a statement that his wife would lose everything if she tried to interfere with any of his testamentary arrangements.[144] Aurelia Maria chose a particular daughter to serve as her executive, bequeathing half of her total estate to this daughter—more than to any of her other children—with the understanding that she would see to it that her annual offerings would actually be performed.[145] Another woman left an allowance to a man named Agathocleus to carry out her *prosphorai* each year, saying that she "trusted this would happen" because of his character.[146] Aurelius Pankab exhorted the priests and monks of a certain monastery to demand "constantly, willingly or unwillingly" from his heirs the grain and wine he had arranged for it to receive as *prosphorai* each year; he urged them to do so, "so that the dead can forever expect the rites of their holy *prosphora* to proceed without interference."[147] A bishop bequeathed all that he possessed to his successor, a monk, to carry out his *prosphorai* and charitable distributions, prohibiting any of his relatives from changing his terms.[148] As for Flavius Phoebammon, Joëlle Beaucamp believes that the emphasis he placed on the irrevocability of his will "reflects a distinct preoccupation to ensure the irrevocability of the dispositions he had made in favor of the monastery." She detects similar concerns in Flavius Theodosius's stipulation against his grandmother taking anything from the monasteries designated in his will.[149]

Jacob had decried a similar negligence among the "wicked heirs" known to his own congregation at Serug. That one's descendants and other surviving beneficiaries could not be trusted to fulfill their commemorative responsibilities was, in fact, an old anxiety. Modern studies of the Roman cult of the dead sometimes give the impression that families always followed through with its commemorative customs and expectations. No doubt many did, but Gabriel Le Bras and Ted Champlin have found another side to the story. Just as happens today, wills in antiquity were often contested after their creators had died, especially if the terms of a will diverted a significant amount of an inheritance to external foundations.[150] But Roman testamentary documents also express concern that designated heirs will not bother to maintain a tomb, provide annual meals, or otherwise live up to a testator's commemorative expectations after a funeral or its first anniversary. "Burial and cult were important to society," Champlin observes, but "memory was what mattered to the individual."[151] Testators therefore took great care in laying out the financing of their tombs, even specifying the minimum that heirs were expected to spend so as to prevent them from skimping on memorial construction or banquet costs. But of greater relevance to our era, these earlier Romans also sought to find more reliable custodians outside their own families, trusting the custodians to maintain their tombs, perform annual meals, and other commemorative acts as well.

Champlin and Le Bas do not discuss later examples, but Christian Romans had just as many reasons to fear their heirs might similarly default on the arrangements set down in their wills. In Early Byzantium, as in earlier times,[152] it was customary to prioritize one's kin ahead of an external beneficiary. Yet this continued to raise the same questions of trust. Angry letters survive in the papyrological record, accusing members of Christian families of not living up to their commemorative responsibilities. One sister wrote to another, "[I] have been told that thou didst omit thy mother's *prosphora* yesterday. God knoweth, if word come to my ears that thou hast omitted thy mother's *prosphora* again, . . . I will take thy items and give them on behalf [of the offering]."[153] The sixth-century preacher Leontius of Constantinople observed how casually ordinary heirs treated their dead after a funeral. "As soon as they move away from the tomb, immediately they lay aside the memory," he remarks in one sermon; "Today you [as heir] . . . promise to adorn and design and build, and on the next day all plans have passed away," he complains in another.[154]

Justinian himself addressed the issue. In 530 he denounced those who not only had failed to make good on delivering the annuities that testators had arranged for religious foundations via hypothecations in their wills, but had even sold the properties that had been hypothecated and set aside to generate those annuity incomes. As a result, "the deceased's perpetual memory [is not being] preserved, on account of which he had bequeathed this annual legacy, but straightway will be obliterated." Justinian demanded that bishops replace such heirs with more reliable executors "who have fear of the Great God and the terrible day of the great and endless Judgment in their mind." He sought to punish whoever alienated properties meant for Christian foundations by fining them double the replacement cost, concluding, "Those who have been burdened by such things should be subject perpetually to the donation of the annual legacies, so that the name and the memory of the deceased and of the legacy should be preserved perpetually."[155] Justinian demanded that if a will provided funds for the construction of an oratory, the heirs must complete its construction within three years, and he ordered secular officials to work with bishops to enforce such measures.[156]

We do not know how Early Byzantine bishops responded to this responsibility. A Persian council held in 585 excommunicated all children who "effaced their parents' memory" by destroying their parents' wills in order to nullify any bequests these made to churches, monasteries, and philanthropic foundations.[157] But to see how individual bishops addressed specific cases, we must turn to Gregory the Great. Twenty-eight of his papal letters refer to the foundation by lay or ecclesiastical benefactors of private monasteries (these far surpass his references to church foundations).[158] Gregory mentions most of these monastic foundations, however, only because their founder's heirs or local clergy had failed to build them or intervened in their funding. "With regard to the founding of monasteries, which different people have ordered to be constructed," Gregory told a Sardinian bishop, "if you see that some on whom these works have been imposed are putting them off with unjust excuses, we want you to put subtle pressure on them according to the laws' instructions, lest the pious wishes of the dead come to nothing."[159] Evidently, it was customary in Italy to endow religious institutions with full ownership of assets rather than hypothecations: bishops were to investigate whether their founders had given enough in advance, usually including one or more farms, vineyards, horses, oxen, cattle, sheep, and pigs.[160] But a major problem was having to prevent bishops and clergy from pilfering such assets themselves. When a church had been built for a monastery, one ploy was to delay its conveyance to the monastery's possession for as long as possible, so that clerics could take whatever offerings might be brought there in the meantime.[161]

Gregory's voluminous *Registrum* amply attests the kind of problem that we probably would find as widespread in the Roman East if we were to discover a similar collection of episcopal correspondence from Early Byzantium. His letters corroborate what we find in the papyri—namely, that many laypeople wanted to establish monasteries or leave them bequests after their deaths, but felt they could not rely on their families or clergy to follow through. Prudent testators therefore did not entrust their memory to kith and kin. As in the earlier Roman Empire, they sought custodians on whose piety they felt they could depend. The group most often chosen in the early empire for this role, as Champlin and others point out, were freedmen and freedwomen—former slaves who, despite being legally manumitted, still remained socially and economically bound to provide expressions of *obsequium* and *pietas* to their former masters.[162] Written wills and memorial inscriptions show testators repeatedly recruiting members of this group to serve as stewards of their memory. Since nothing forced such *liberti* to maintain a former master's monument after his or her death, wealthy testators devised incentives. These included giving them the privilege of living at the monument, of receiving the proceeds from its gardens, and of being interred within the monument itself. The repetition of this arrangement shows that it was believed to work. "The social and economic dependence of freedmen on their patron was a much more certain foundation for the monument and the memory than was the piety of an independent heir," concludes Champlin.[163]

By the sixth century, freed persons no longer appear to have been recruited or appointed in this capacity, at least not in the Christian testamentary record. This was not for lack of *liberti*.[164] It was because Christian monks had emerged as alternative and even preferrable stewards of a patron's memory. Hagiography, of course, emphasized ascetic purity and skills in liturgical prayers, qualifications that would have made them desirable to serve in a Christian memorial foundation. But as with earlier freed persons, lingering bonds of social and economic dependency, caused by their marginal relation to mainstream society and the vulnerabilities this created, must have played a role too.

In other words, monks assumed a structural role for the assurance of postmortem loyalty and remembrance in the later Roman Empire that had previously been assumed by freed persons in the earlier empire, and for the same structural reasons. This overlap was sometimes exact. At the end of his life, when looking for an executor of his will, in which he bequeathed his possessions to the poor of his church, Gregory of Nazianzus passed over all members of his family and designated someone outside of it, who was also named Gregory. Significantly, this Gregory was not only a monk but also one of Gregory's former slaves—that is, one of his freedman.[165] Gerontius explicitly states that Melania and Pinian populated their North African monasteries entirely with freedmen and freedwomen, as we have seen. The *Sayings of the Desert Fathers* includes a story about a slave who was freed by his masters in Alexandria so that he could become a monk at Scetis. Like a good Roman freedman, this monk remained faithful to them and mindful of their interests: each year he returned to wash their feet and bring them earnings from his labors. When given the option to discontinue such work, he protested, affirming that his gratitude for their letting him become a monk was so great that he intended to continue serving them as well as God. Happy to hear this, they sent him back to the desert with all he needed to "make Charity [Feasts] on their behalf," thereby winning enduring fame, we are told, at Scetis.[166] This was truly *obsequium* in the old freedman tradition.

Otherwise, an appreciation for a benefactor's needs, gratitude for his support, and humble respect for authority would have fostered lasting bonds between monks and their patrons, dead or alive. Despite the fact that the Praetorian Prefect Rufinus had died in disgrace, having been executed by imperial decree, monks at his Rufinianae entered his name among the ranks of the blessed, thereby rehabilitating his memory, apparently for no other reason than that he had been their founding patron.[167] Two centuries later, Narses provided "incomes [*prosodoi*] that never fail" for the monks on his suburban estate. When he later died in northern Italy, these monks had his bones shipped back and "consecrated" in their monastery, effectively canonizing him as founder in a ritual attended by Emperor Justin II and Empress Sophia.[168] This, on a grand scale, is essentially what Flavius Phoebammon had sought to obtain by giving the Jeremiah monastery in Egypt just a small piece of real estate. The repetition of references to this arrangement between patrons and monks shows that it was believed to have worked.

MEMORY, SALVATION, AND THE ECONOMICS OF MONASTIC PATRONAGE

According to Cyril of Scythopolis, Sabas, the great Palestinian solitary (439–532), refused to obtain any landed income for his monasteries and lavras in the Judean desert. Instead he let them rely entirely on resources from God, meaning the material *eulogiai, karpophoriai,* and *prosphorai* they periodically received from the faithful. Cyril explains that all previous archimandrites whom patriarchs had appointed to supervise the monks around Jerusalem had soon become overwhelmed by "earthly cares and worldly profits"; therefore, when Sabas and his colleague Theodosius the Cenobiarch were given those same appointments, they resolved to remain "desert monks, without possessions." Cyril emphasizes the contrast that resulted between Sabas and other archimandrites. While the latter asked successive emperors to give them land near their monasteries, Sabas, when offered the same, declined, accepting only a thousand solidi to pass around, telling Justinian, "Those who pray for your Piety do not need such [land-generated] incomes, for their portion and income is the Lord."[169] Indeed, when severe famine ravaged Palestine, "God provided Sabas all he needed without stint," Cyril claims, noting that "it was those monasteries that relied on properties and incomes that fell short, rather than those under his care." But one week not even Sabas's Great Lavra could support all the visitors who came to celebrate the Eucharist. Since Sabas refused to impede the liturgy, he sent his *prosphorarius*—his monastery's "keeper of the offerings"—to sell one of their liturgical vessels in Jerusalem. As a result, thirty mules arrived carrying bread, wine, and cheese that Friday, bringing everything needed to feed all who came for the service.[170] God's offerings and blessings thus proved as reliable as any permanent endowment.

One implication of this story is that Sabas's monastery possessed liturgical vessels sufficiently sumptuous to raise enough money to quickly buy food even during a severe famine. Another is that the monastic world had become divided between those who were determined to subsist on whatever came to them through moveable offerings alone, and those who preferred to possess land and live off the income it produced. Writing in the middle of the sixth century, Cyril presents this not just as a division between solitaries and cenobites, but as a rift between monastic traditionalists who stayed true to their *aktēmosynē* by trusting in God to provide, and all the rest who put their trust in earthly possessions.

Cyril came to writing hagiography having already steeped himself in the classics of Christian ascetic literature. These included the early fifth-century *Ascetic Discourse* by Nilus of Ancyra, an author who censured his monastic contemporaries for "thinking piety was procuring" and accumulating land for entrepreneurial purposes rather than trusting in God and whatever family wealth they had to support their contemplative endeavors. Cyril incorporated phrases from Nilus's treatise into his *Life of Sabas,* and depicted Sabas as precisely the type of monk that Nilus preferred—not a difficult task, since Sabas himself came from a wealthy family and was similarly well connected to the aristocracy.[171] If not seduced by Nilus's snobbery, Cyril must have recognized his point that acquiring productive assets encouraged monks to invest their profits in even more assets, and thus entangled them in a spiral of business preoccupations and anxieties. The *Life of Marcellus* reports that the Acoemetes had wanted Marcellus to do exactly this when he received his own family inheritance, but he successfully resisted.[172]

We can appreciate, however, why other monastic authorities would have been wary of relying solely on the laity to continually provide offerings, even annuities from hypothecated land, rather than owning and controlling income-producing real estate itself. Setting aside for a moment our modern instinct to focus on practical considerations of financial security, we have seen hagiographers repeatedly warn against the ethical issues raised by lay offerings, and their stories reveal how those gifts often exerted their influence: namely, by impressing the memory of their donor upon their recipients. Ascetic saints were often depicted as giving visitors souvenirs (an animal skin, a wicker basket, a fishing net) as a humble "token of remembrance" of themselves,[173] but when laypeople did the same, it is always depicted as being entangled with expectations of reciprocity. A widow in Oxyrhyncus, for example, reportedly sent three measures of oil each year to the monastery of Samuel of Kalamun so that she and her children "might be remembered" (i.e., mentioned in monastic liturgies).[174] An Alexandrian shipowner offered John the Almsgiver all his gold to petition God to protect his son who was sailing to Africa. John complied: after uttering a prayer in the man's presence, he put the gold beneath an altar and spent the entire next night performing a private liturgy "for him who offered it."[175] In another case, a landowner, seeing John sleeping in tattered sheets, took the opportunity to send him a costly quilt, "repeatedly asking that he wrap himself in it, in remembrance of the one who offered it." John at first complied, but upon thinking how bad it would look to be seen wrapped in warmth while others were freezing outside in the cold, he sold it to buy blankets for the poor.[176]

Such examples demonstrate the power of offerings to establish lasting bonds of memory and obligation in Early Byzantine imaginations. This would not surprise anthropologists. As already noted, it has been recognized that gifts which retain the personhood of their donor to the highest degree have the highest probability of forging lasting relationships.[177] This is what we especially find with Christian liturgical offerings. These differed from all blessings and most fruitbearings by being emphatically identified with a donor's name and thus, highly personalized. The only Early Byzantine gift invested with a comparable sense of individual identity and transactional expectation was a gift of alms given for the sake of personal redemption. Significantly, preachers also conceptualized almsgiving as a type of liturgical sacrifice— Chrysostom occasionally presents it as a superior type of liturgical offering, a *prosphora* that Christ in the form of the poor wanted more than costly liturgical objects.[178] Indeed, alms and offerings alike "worked" in part by making their recipients remember their donors. When distributing alms, bishops were instructed to give the name of whoever had donated a sum to the poor so that they could "pray by name on his behalf."[179] The *Life of Macarius of Scetis* depicts a child giving alms at a family funeral so that the poor might "remember his parents."[180] Leontius has another almsgiver, different from the landowner mentioned above, give a beggar an expensive coat to wrap himself in as "a memento of myself."[181] Like the quilt that the landowner offered to John the Almsgiver to wrap himself in, as described above, this alms was literally intended to envelop its recipient with the memory of its donor.

Thus, alms and offerings served as Christian instruments for generating a strong memory. The goal, however, was not just securing lasting memorialization but positive remembrance—to be "remembered for good," as synagogue inscriptions put it.[182] This is what secured redemption. To be remembered in a positive rather than a negative light, Christians had to reconcile themselves with those they had despoiled, ignored, or otherwise aggrieved. Giving just a small gift of alms, preferably in person, could sway the memory of those who sat in judgment for the better. Leontius indicates this by telling a tale about a merciless customs official who lived in Roman North Africa. One day some beggars at Carthage were warming themselves in the winter sun across from a row of mansions. Looking at one mansion after the other, they praised and prayed for each that had shown any of them mercy, but cursed any that had not. On seeing the custom official's mansion and hearing his name, none could recall ever having received anything from him at all. One of the beggars bet with the others that he could extract something from him that very day. Just then, the official returned from a bakery and hit the beggar on the head with a piece of bread. Picking it up, the beggar ran back to the others, saying, "Look what I just received from his own hands." That night the official dreamt that angels and demons were examining his life on a balance sheet. When his deeds were weighed on a scale, it sank toward eternal perdition. Then a tiny piece of bread suddenly appeared— just enough to raise it up. Waking and realizing how much could be done with so little, the official became "excessively merciful" thereafter, selling all he owned, "not even sparing his own body," to give to the poor.[183]

As Shenoute of Atripe remarked in a sermon, people accustomed to having doors shut in their faces tend to be grateful when they find any house that hands out food, "giving thanks to God and to those who had remembered them."[184] For Christians seeking eternal salvation, however, securing positive remembrance from fellow humans was part of the larger project of securing positive remembrance from God himself. The notion that God could be cajoled into positive remembrance may have been encouraged by Jesus's warning that on Judgment Day, those who had treated him kindly in the guise of the poor would alone be saved (Mt 25:34–46). Speculation also arose about God's memory in connection to scriptural imagery regarding books or records that God was said to possess, write, or erase (e.g., Ex 32:32; Ps 68:28, 139:16; Dn 13:1; Col 2:14–15; Phil 4:3; Rv 20:12, 15). Theodoret of Cyrrhus explained that all such imagery symbolized "God's complete, compendious knowledge and imperishable memory,"[185] using the phrase (alēston mnēma) that Gerontius used to convey the goal of Melania's monastic endowments. Of course, authorities denied that such imagery should be taken literally—"God needs no reminders, in human fashion," Pseudo-Dionysius the Areopagite affirmed when discussing church diptychs.[186] Nonetheless, the notion that God could be reminded remained fixed in the imagination. Chrysostom assured listeners that by feeding the poor, they could gain eternal gratitude, "since you will have God, who always remembers and never forgets, in your debt."[187]

Such preaching supported the notion that divine memory could be influenced by petitions of the poor, setting the stage for Leontius's tale about the customs official and beggars of seventh-century Carthage. Monks offered similar assurances, and, indeed, long-term services. Barsanuphius at one point responded to an anxious Christlover who asked him to "pray on his behalf, so that the Lord might remember him in His kingdom" (cf. Lk 23:42). Barsanuphius assured him not to worry, since "Our Lord Jesus Christ . . . has granted me the salvation of your soul and given me the grace of remembering you in His kingdom."[188] As this remarkable exchange shows, Barsanuphius believed that whatever he remembered, Christ remembered; this layperson's salvation was assured due to this monk's confident capacities for memory and prayer.

Barsanuphius was the real deal, but we find similar commemorative dynamics depicted in hagiography. The intercessory prayers that Leontius of Neapolis ascribes to the monk Symeon of Emesa (a.k.a. Symeon the Holy Fool) after his mother died are presented as a series of urgent reminders that Symeon pressed upon God, culminating with one about a *prosphora* she had offered just before her death:

> Do not forget, Master, that she could not be separated from me, even for an hour. . . . Recall, Master who knows all, that although she wished to rejoice in me, I deprived her of myself for your name's sake. Do not forget, O Righteous One, the rending of her innards, which she endured the day I left for you. . . . Do not forget, Lover of Humanity, what sort of pain embraced her heart when she melted, seeing my monastic garb, because her pearl no longer existed, being clothed thus. Recall, Master, that I robbed her of her consolation. . . . And if, being a woman, she sinned in word or deed in this life, forgive her soul on behalf of the sacrifice which she bore and offered to you, Master—namely, me, your unworthy servant.[189]

In this passage Leontius presents Symeon as his mother's ultimate liturgical *prosphora*, persistently reminding God of all the other sacrifices she had made throughout her life before her death. Likewise, according to a seventh-century hagiography of Symeon Stylites the Elder, after Symeon's mother died, her corpse was placed within eyesight of his pillar "so he would remember her when he prayed." As he petitioned God to receive her soul, her corpse is said to have turned to him and smiled.[190]

It is against this imaginative background that we must understand the recruitment and endowment of monks to carry out liturgical commemorations from the fifth century onward. Yet, again, it is also in this light that we must appreciate the ambivalence monks felt toward whatever long-term arrangements, when presented as offerings, were made to support them. Church and imperial law prohibited anything given to a church or monastic institution as an offering (with the exception of liturgical vessels) to be legally alienated. Legally, therefore, they could therefore never be given away as a blessing.[191] Indeed, the more permanent the offering, the more lasting the obligations of service that came with it, without any assurance that the people demanding service deserved such attention. Some monks tried to control this situation by setting their own terms. Theodore of Sykeon reportedly told Emperor Phocas (r. 602–610) and his vicious henchman Bonosus that if they wanted him to "always remember" them in his prayers, then they must amend their ways.[192] This was the same cooperative arrangement that Barsanuphius had proposed when agreeing to bear another monk's sins, presented by Theodore's hagiographer as an effort to speak truth to power.

Theodore actually represents our last recorded Early Byzantine monastic saint. By his day, the ethical and practical problems related to the reliance of monks on the generosity of lay donors would have been clear. As noted above, families in this era were rarely willing to cede complete possession and control over material assets that generated incomes, especially real estate (which, after all, was still the main basis for status among the lay aristocracy). Therefore, monks who failed to procure ownership of material assets had little financial independence, remaining dependent on a patron's heirs to deliver whatever income had been allocated to fund commemorations after his or her death. Of course, an institution built on a patron's estate might be given rights to the ground on which it stood. Yet that placed it even more directly under the control of that patron's family, which might later send bailiffs to ensure that it provided further services, such as baking bread for other estate workers. Monasteries built on private estates in Egypt tended to become, as Roger Rémondon observes, "prisoners of the established order."[193]

The consequences are illustrated by a series of letters written on potsherds by monks imploring their patrons to remember them and send their expected offerings:

> We beg your Lordship to ordain that we be sent the liberality which it is the custom of your illustrious house to bestow on us, so that we may give your Lordship our thanks and, sinners as we are, may send up to heaven our customary prayers for the health of your Lordship and for the prosperity of your illustrious house. (5th century, Oxyrhyncus)[194]

> I prostrate myself before all and embrace your beloved Lordship, witnessing by my soul how often we have sent up prayers to God. . . . I sent to your Affection our brother Abraham with the brothers, so that he might help them with respect to the business of the holy monastery. For we sent him relying on your good soul just as we rely on you yourself, so that he might help them until they collect the small *prosphora* of the holy monastery. (6th–7th century, provenance unknown)[195]

> When thy God-lovingness sent to us, saying, "Send that I may give you the *medimnus* of corn which is for the [*prosphora*]," we sent our son K[allini]kos. Thou didst not give him an *artab* . . . though every day he brought a sack. Do not lose thy predilection for the monastery, for which the angel of the desert monastery will bless thee and they children and thy beasts, and everyone who is with thee. (Date and provenance unknown)[196]

These unknown monks found themselves in a position similar to that of Jacob of Serug, trying to persuade wealthy Christians to live up to their commemorative obligations. Acquiring land and other assets may have brought worldly preoccupations and obligations to provide commemorative services for deceased donors. But at least it brought financial and spiritual independence. Otherwise, for monasteries that did not possess charismatic assets like Sabas, Barsanuphius, and Symeon Stylites to attract an unceasing flow of gifts, the likely consequences were clear. Relying on offerings may have enabled them to perform liturgical work without distractions, but it came at the price of subservience to patrons, and at the risk of becoming utterly forgettable and forgotten.

Epilogue

When Holy Men Walked the Earth

"Oh, child . . . I remember one time before the Persians came, we were going from our cells to the cenobium for the evening prayers on the Lord's day, when one of the brothers went down to this same caper patch, gathered a full basket, and [the next day] gathered the same amount." I said to him, "Why was this, father?" He said, "At that time holy men were walking about and treading the earth, and the earth was blessed. . . . But now evil-doers and murderers dwell upon the earth . . . and the earth is defiled and accursed. So how can the things on it be blessed?"

—ANTONY OF CHOZIBA,[1] *LIFE OF GEORGE OF CHOZIBA*

In the preceding pages, we have seen how Christian philanthropy became articulated in the late Roman East through a repertoire of religious gifts and gift-giving practices from the conversion of Constantine to the Arab conquests. Guided by the insight that any gift must be understood as a "total social fact" based on a society's assumptions of what relationships are worth promoting and prioritizing, I have argued that Christian gift giving in Early Byzantium was shaped not only by religious purposes and concerns but by social expectations, governmental structures, and the rise of professionalism among "those who pray" in the empire's Christian establishment. The variety of religious gift ideals studied here reflects the fact that we have been examining history's first complex and affluent Christian society, in which church and monastic authorities had to negotiate, for the first time, conflicting concerns regarding wealth, salvation, dignity, social order, and social justice. These gift ideals aimed in part to foster "righteous" interactions among groups that otherwise seemed hard to integrate: lay and holy, rich and poor, human and divine. If readers feel better informed about the tensions between Christian ideals and the social, political, and economic developments of this relatively unfamiliar period of late antique history, I will have accomplished part of my job.

After positing that the Christianized version of *philanthrōpia*—an ancient ideal that could be expressed in many ways, as Julian the Apostate observed—imposed an obligation to give material or immaterial aid to all who asked, I showed how church and monastic authorities sought to fulfill this ideal not only by establishing a variety of welfare institutions and institutional priorities but also by promoting five different gift ideals: alms, charity, blessings, fruitbearings, and liturgical offerings. Though closely interrelated, each of these gift ideals became associated with a distinct set of resources, relationships, responsibilities, and purposes. Where possible, I showed how each gained definition over time by contrast against each other, as well as against older, secular gift-giving practices. By explaining these things, I hope to have clarified the early anatomy and evolution of Christian philanthropy. As far as the gifts themselves are concerned, some of their defining and distinguishing characteristics may be summarized as follows.

Regarding material or spiritual substances involved, a gift of alms—that is, of mercy—was considered to be anything kindly given that came from a human-generated surplus resource. By contrast, gifts of charity were self-sacrificial gifts derived from essential resources; blessings were supplemental gifts of divine benevolence derived from any surplus God had bestowed; fruitbearings were gifts of gratitude derived from any God-given human profit; and liturgical offerings were gifts of gratitude given to God for life itself, both present and future, drawn from human-generated resources of any sort. These five gifts can be distinguished as "caritative," "sacerdotal," and "sacrificial" in purpose; yet, due to overlapping facets of their natures, liturgical offerings and fruitbearings could be used to produce material blessings, blessings to produce alms, and alms to produce both charity and liturgical offerings. The circularity of this "system" of giving (though it was never presented in such comprehensive terms) may perhaps reflect the overwhelming emphasis on circulation and flow found in early Christian notions of stewardship.

Regarding the positive social dynamics fostered by such gift giving, gifts of alms, blessings, and fruitbearings all tended to be identified with temporary, intermittent, ad hoc interactions or relationships, while charity and offerings tended to be identified with efforts to establish permanent or long-lasting personal relationships. As for the obligations involved, alms and offerings obliged their recipients to reciprocate, especially with intercessory prayers, either momentarily or over extended periods of time. Charity implied mutual giving and reciprocity at exhaustive levels, selflessly undertaken for the sake of giver and recipient alike. Fruitbearings and offerings expressed reciprocation for benefits already obtained, but implied some expectation of (and therefore, obligation to provide) continuing benefactions. Only material blessings imposed no obligation between givers and recipients, except that they be shared with others. This "divine" facet made them ideal symbols of Christian philanthropy, providential order, and sacred wealth.

We know that the present-giving world of Early Byzantium did not last. In these final pages, let me say something about its trajectory and the possible consequences this had on the Christian gift ideals discussed above.

. . .

The fortunes of the Roman East fell dramatically during the seventh century. In 602 an army revolt in the Balkans led to the sudden execution of Emperor Maurice and his family, ending the long dynastic stability of the Justinianic Age in a single day. The ensuing civil war put a competent usurper, Heraclius, on the throne, but not before it had depleted border defenses so severely that it looked like the Eastern empire would soon have the same fate that the Western empire had suffered two centuries earlier. Shah Khosrow II Parviz launched a series of invasions aimed at complete conquest. His armies sacked Antioch in 610 and, after defeating Heraclius in a major engagement below the Cilician Gates, took Damascus in 613, Jerusalem in 614, and Alexandria in 619, making the entire Near East his own for the next decade. Meanwhile, Avars and Slavs slipped easily into provinces south of the Danube. In 626 they besieged Constantinople together with the Persians, who had trampled over Asia Minor up to Chalcedon, turning its cities into castles and Anatolia into a war zone. Remarkably, Constantinople survived, the Avars collapsed, the Romans rebounded, the Sassanians imploded, Khosrow was executed, and Heraclius celebrated a triumph of messianic proportions in Jerusalem at the end of March 629. But the reversals were not over: in the next ten years Rome lost the Mediterranean Near East again, this time to Arab armies from the south, this time forever.

Monastic eyewitnesses described the disorder wrought by the first conflict, during the Persian conquest of Palestine.[2] The best known among these is Strategius's *On the Fall of Jerusalem* (ca. 630), a detailed account of the slaughter of tens of thousands of Christians and removal of the True Cross as booty to the Sassanian capital. The scale of the slaughter that Strategius describes was shocking, but it was not repeated, since Persia wished to preserve Palestine, Syria, or Egypt intact for its own gain.[3] A more pervasive problem was that of brigandage, as armed gangs took advantage of the absence of Roman troops to rob monasteries and take monks for ransom. This is the situation described by Antiochus, a monk of Saba's Great Lavra. Writing soon after the Persians' withdrawal, and responding to an abbot who had requested epitomes of the Old and New Testaments, having lost all his books while fleeing the "Chaldaean storm" in Asia Minor, Antiochus described how the Great Lavra itself had fallen prey to local bedouins looking for loot:

> Ishmaelites descended upon our Lavra one week before the [Persian] attack upon the holy city, and pillaged all the church's holy vessels. Most of the fathers fled at once, but the more steadfast slaves of Christ remained in the Lavra, not wanting to leave the place. The barbarians, however, seized them and mercilessly beat them for many days, thinking they would find some money among those who know nothing of this world.

Antiochus and the abbot were among those who fled; they returned to find forty-four bodies of their former brethren heaped outside. Despite being well fortified, this desert monastery took a long time to be resettled, he says, due to fears of further attacks.[4]

Such were the changed circumstances that Antony of Choziba meant to describe in the passage from his *Life of George of Choziba* (ca. 631) quoted above.[5] The words he puts in the mouth of his ascetic mentor, George, just before his death at the end of the hagiography, seem like a requiem for the entire Byzantine period of the Mediterranean Near East, when Christianity reigned and monasticism flourished under Roman rule. This was no longer the same Holy Land that the Piacenza Pilgrim had visited at the beginning of this book. Many monasteries besides Saba's Lavra had been pillaged, and some, like the Martyrius Monastery, were permanently abandoned, their monks having fled to more secure locations in western Europe. Nor was such abandonment the only setback. How much Palestinian monasteries suffered from a decline of pilgrims during the occupation is indicated by Antiochus's comment that because the patriarch was rebuilding Jerusalem's chief sanctuaries, "we also [at the Lavra] have good hopes for the future, and in particular that people will come from other regions to worship at the holy places."[6] Antiochus thus acknowledges that it took pilgrims as well as monks to give the Holy Land its accustomed prosperity. In light of his comment, we might rephrase Antony of Choziba's question: Without pilgrims walking the earth, how could it be blessed?

As it turned out, both the monk Antiochus's optimism and the hagiographer Antony's pessimism were prescient. Although our understanding of Christian society under early Islam is still in its infancy,[7] it is clear that the consequences of Muslim rule and of separation from the Roman Empire were decidedly mixed for the regions studied in this book.

On the positive side, there is now consensus that, despite changes on top and the gradual development of discriminatory Islamic institutions and practices, most Christian communities in Syria and Palestine suffered "only short-term dislocations."[8] Like the Persians, the new rulers preferred to leave most of what they had conquered in the hands of tax-producing owners and workers. Conversion to Islam was slow. The process of ruralization that had accelerated throughout the Near East during the Persian wars continued unabated, but that does not seem to have harmed Christian institutions. Christians remained in the majority for at least the next two or three hundred years, during which they continued to refurbish and occasionally even build churches and monasteries. In fact, some institutions flourished under the circumstances. This is evident from Thomas of Marga's ninth-century *Book of the Abbots,* as well as from hagiographies like the *Life of Symeon of the Olives,* which details how an abbot named Symeon (d. 734) used a treasure hoard discovered by his nephew (perhaps left by retreating Roman forces) to purchase twelve thousand olive trees and other productive assets for the Qartmin/Mar Gabriel monastery on Ṭur ʿAbdin, thereby initiating its medieval revival.[9] Indeed, because the Koran occasionally praises Christian monks (e.g., K. 5.85–87), because many Muslims were recent converts from churchgoing families, and because monasteries often provided safe havens from the strictures of early Muslim society, emirs sometimes patronized monasteries just as wealthy Christians had done in the past (and continued to do).[10] The seventh-century *Life of Rabban Hormizd* describes the competition between the Nestorian monastery of Rabban Hormizd and miaphysite monastery of Mar Mattai for the favor of an emir of Mosul. It presents this as a zero-sum game, the prosperity of each community at stake. Lacking Hormizd's sanctity, the miaphysite abbot allegedly sacrificed dogs, cats, and apes each day to an idol in his monastery's church, which had previously helped him "triumph in many ways before kings and governors." After Hormizd stole this "wicked little idol," the abbot sent a loaf of bread through the air to the emir's bedroom door, where demons placed it "as a blessing" while still hot. Thus Hormizd's rival managed to seduce this potential Muslim patron, putting him "under subjection to his bread cake."[11]

Similar situations presumably held elsewhere from the Transjordan to Egypt, where archaeology and papyri show little change until the ninth century. As Antiochus had hoped, pilgrims resumed coming to Palestine, and at least nine monasteries around Jerusalem revived, including the Great Lavra, the Choziba monastery, and those of Euthymius and Theodosius the Cenobiarch. These remained centers of literary production and Chalcedonian leadership; they continued to maintain contact with Constantinople and contributed significantly to its debates over icons.[12] But they never regained the prosperity they had enjoyed during the Justinianic age. Just how low their fortunes had sunk by the ninth century is evident from the Carolingian documents preserved in the so-called Basel Roll. These describe the situation that Frankish envoys found in Jerusalem ca. 808 when they arrived to deliver the "disinterested generosity" that Charlemagne (d. 814) had sent after hearing of the Patriarch's indigence. From the figures they preserve, Michael McCormick estimates that expenditures in the Jerusalem patriarchate had fallen to just a third of their sixth-century total, that bishoprics in the Holy Land had dwindled from around forty to around five or six, that monasteries had gone from sixty-five to a mere nine, and that the number of monks in the region had plummeted "from somewhere in the vicinity of 2,200–3,000 to about 380." More could be found living in Jerusalem than in most medieval cities, but that was partly because it was no longer safe to live out in the Judean desert. Monastic life consolidated around the surviving monasteries, whose hagiographical output now often focused on martyrdoms.[13]

That it was the upstart Western "emperor" Charlemagne and not the Roman emperor in Constantinople who aided the Jerusalem saints in the ninth century is not surprising. Constantinople was in no position to help: the Christian state that had invested so much in the Holy Land during the fourth, fifth, and sixth centuries spent most of the seventh, eighth, and ninth just struggling to survive. Eventually, a reconstituted Roman Empire clawed its way back to a "Middle Byzantine" era of relative prosperity, ca. 843–1204. But it first passed through a long dark age, during which the population of Constantinople fell by perhaps 90 percent of its pre-plague, sixth-century level; repairs were discontinued; literature (including hagiography) stopped being produced; and surrounding monasteries dropped from an estimated 150–200 to an estimated 50.[14] Only two communities are known to have been newly founded in the imperial city before the Middle Byzantine revival, and even fewer churches.[15] Meanwhile, "monastic affairs seem to have drifted into a cloud of ordinariness."[16] Our sources suggest an erosion of discipline and prestige. At some point, a monastic author complained that whereas God wanted humans to give their choicest animals and children as firstfruits, rich Christians were doing the opposite: the best wine, fruit, and clothing they saved for themselves, leaving only scraps for the poor; "as for infants, those who are healthy and well-formed they keep for marriage alliances . . . but those who are sick, one-eyed, lame, and malformed they consecrate to God and send off to monasteries."[17] Monasticism resurged in medieval Byzantium, but, like the rest of the downsized empire, it did so with more restricted horizons and a less cosmopolitan elite.[18]

. . .

What impact did this have on the gift ideals discussed in this book? The last extended treatment to survive from Early Byzantium is found in the *Book on Ascetic Life* and its companion treatise, the *Chapters on Charity*, written by a Palestinian monk known today as Maximus the Confessor (d. 662). After the Persian invasions, Maximus became a hardline leader of opposition to Heraclius's Christological compromises known as monotheletism and monoenergism, adopting a recalcitrant stance that eventually cost him his tongue and a hand.[19] Before engaging in polemics, however, he revealed a combative streak in his *Book on Ascetic Life*. Writing during the Persian occupation, Maximus meant partly to explain why God had abandoned his holy people to "wild devils, and 'a king unjust and most evil beyond the whole world' [Dn 3:32]."[20] The reason was obvious: they had ignored the Gospel's commandments on charity. Instead of imitating God, who, "out of *philanthrōpia*," fought Satan with love rather than hate ("O, what paradoxical warfare!"), or imitating Jesus and his apostles, who "showed compassion for whoever had fallen," Maximus saw monks behave with unforgiving hatred toward each other. Instead of preferring "charity for every human, above all visible things," they preferred "worldly things, above the commandment of charity."[21]

Not unlike Pseudo-Clement's *Homily* discussed in chapter 2, Maximus took this opportunity to explain how it was obligatory for God's exemplars to love even those who might hate and abuse them—something only possible if they committed themselves without compromise to Christian priorities. Such had been the way of Jesus and his disciples, but "since we are lovers of material things . . . we are not only unable to love those who hate us, but even repulse those who love us."[22] To illustrate this further, he composed *Chapters on Charity,* a list of four hundred summations of material drawn from the *Sayings of the Desert Fathers* and related sources. For example:

> He, who does almsgiving in imitation of God, knows no difference between good and evil or just and unjust in regard to needs of the body, but distributes equally to all according to need—even though . . . he prefers the virtuous to the bad.[23]

> Not only by dispensing money is a charitable intention made manifest; no, far more by dispensing God's word, and through physical *diakonia* to others.[24]

> There are four kinds of people concerned about money. . . . Stewards . . . alone get it right: their aim is to never run short when dispensing to each in his need.[25]

> He is a genuine friend who, when . . . accidental afflictions, hardships, and misfortunes befall his neighbor, bears . . . them calmly and without hesitations as though they were his own.[26]

These were principles of Christian philanthropy, distilled from what we have seen developed in Early Byzantium: give to all, even if your recipient does not deserve it; give to each, according to need; express mercy through kind actions as much as through material items; give in such a way that neither your capacity nor your inclination fails; and seek to bear your neighbor's burdens as if they were your own. Maximus made no claim for originality, but he affirmed that these principles were essential not just to Christianity but to the survival of monasticism itself.

· · ·

Needless to say, later church and monastic authorities affirmed *philanthrōpia* and almsgiving to be good works, incumbent on all Christians.[27] Indeed, later Byzantine Romans looked on Early Byzantium as its own classical age, and in particular made John Chrysostom, along with his direct, "Chrysostomic" approach to almsgiving, a central part of its medieval religious culture. I leave it to others, however, to determine in what ways or to what extent such ideals were actually upheld amid the changed circumstances of Middle Byzantium. Judith Herrin senses that philanthropy became marked by "an increase in discrimination against certain types of poor."[28] It would be equally important to investigate whether the concept of philanthropy itself changed. Although I would not expect any of the ideals discussed in this book to completely disappear, I would expect them to recede from prominence or receive different emphasis as new circumstances and priorities took hold.[29]

Certainly, this was true of the gift ideal most distinctive of Early Byzantium and central to this book—namely, blessings. When visiting Mount Athos in the early

1950s, the archaeologist Richard Dawkins was struck by all the material meanings that monks attached to the word *eulogia*. On the one hand, they used it to refer to any extra amount gratuitously thrown into a commercial purchase not out of obligation, but as a gesture of goodwill. They also used it for small gifts asked of visitors upon entrance to a sacred shrine ("almost . . . a decorous ecclesiastical word for a tip"), as well as for food that abbots distributed to monks as an allowance. Dawkins considered all these usages to be idiosyncrasies of Athonite monasticism.[30] This was mainly because he had never heard of this type of Christian gift in any other modern setting, but it was also because he was unaware of all the Early Byzantine precedents for the phenomena he found.

Hagiography bears witness to both the long-term survival and the diminishment of this particular gift ideal over time. Medieval Byzantine hagiographers continue to refer to holy people dispensing *eulogiai* to feed individual poor people, refresh other monks, or satisfy lay visitors, as might be expected from earlier tradition.[31] They also include stock episodes in which monastic supplies miraculously multiply, following the Gospel pericope of the loaves and fishes. Yet two striking differences emerge from the hagiography of cenobitic abbots I have sampled from the ninth to the eleventh century.[32] First of all, none of them depict material blessings as gifts given by God; and second, none depict them as resources used for furnishing aid or hospitality to outsiders.

The eleventh-century Greek *Life of Lazarus*, a pillar saint who founded a monastery on Mt. Galesius (Alamandağ, Turkey) in western Asia Minor, provides a case in point. This lengthy hagiography includes an episode in which small loaves of bread called *eulogiai* suddenly materialize as if by miracle. In this episode, however, the bread loaves in question are solely used for liturgical purposes—that is, for consecration and consumption at Eucharists held in Lazarus's cenobium and its two satellite monasteries. One Sunday, when Lazarus's sacristan realized that the storeroom had only two bread blessings in it, he refused to share them with the cenobium's two dependent monasteries on the grounds that Lazarus's cenobium would not have enough for its own liturgy. The problem was resolved when mules suddenly arrived, bearing multiple bread blessings for all, sent by the bishop of a nearby church.[33] Note that, unlike Early Byzantine examples, this hagiography does not depict such *eulogiai* as God-given gifts sent to reward acts of philanthropic hospitality, or depict them as symbols of a monastery's sacred wealth.

So too elsewhere. The Arab conquests and other changes altered the structures that had shaped the religious gift-giving practices discussed in this book.[34] The loss of the Holy Land meant that the empire had permanently lost the most fertile ground for God-given, material blessings, both as a source of such gifts themselves and as a imaginative model for open-handed Christian giving. But other losses had perhaps more direct impact. Among the features of the late Roman state that permanently disappeared was the imperial *annona*, which ceased after 618. As with so much in dark-age Byzantium, nothing tells us how people reacted to its loss. We have reason to suppose, however, that its discontinuation diminished the ability of churches and affiliated monasteries to serve as openhanded outlets of Christian benefaction—or to even imagine them as such. This traditional amenity had subsidized Christian institutions and helped them give blessings to all. It therefore provided imperial support for the Christian practice of philanthropy on a large scale. After its demise, such institutions might continue to display exemplary levels of generosity. But now that would depend more than ever on their ability to attract patrons, acquire land, or share their essential resources with charitable self-denial.

NOTES

ABBREVIATIONS

The following are abbreviations frequently used for scholarship in the notes and bibliography. Further abbreviations for ancient authors and texts are put beside their names or titles in the bibliography. Abbreviations for biblical texts follow conventions of the Chicago Manual of Style, and abbreviations for papyri and ostraca (e.g., *P.Lond., O.Brit.Mus.Copt.*) follow conventions in John F. Oates et al., *Checklist of Editions of Greek, Latin, Demotic and Coptic Papyri, Ostraca and Tablets*, 5th ed. (Oakville, CT: American Society of Papyrologists, 2001). For all other primary sources, I cite editions and translations by giving the names of their editors or translators and relevant page numbers, or by giving the abbreviation for a series, followed by the number in that series and page numbers. All translations are my own except as indicated.

AB	*Analecta Bollandiana*
ACO	*Acta Conciliorum Oecumenicorum*, ed. E. Schwartz
ACW	Ancient Christian Writers
AnTard	*Antiquité tardive*
AP	*Apophthegmata patrum*
AP C	*Apophthegmata patrum*, Coptic Collection
AP G	*Apophthegmata patrum*, Greek Alphabetical Collection
AP GS	*Apophthegmata patrum*, Greek Systematic Collection
AP L	*Apophthegmata patrum*, Latin Systematic Collection
AP N	*Apophthegmata patrum*, Greek Anonymous Collection
AP S	*Apophthegmata patrum*, Syriac Collection
BAH	Bibliothèque archéologique et historique

BHG	*Bibliotheca hagiographica graeca* (Brussels, 1977)
BMGS	*Byzantine and Modern Greek Studies*
BTS	Byzantine Texts and Studies
BZ	*Byzantinische Zeitschrift*
CCSG	Corpus Christianorum, series graeca
CCSL	Corpus Christianorum, series latina
CI	*Codex Justinianus* (vol. 1 of the *CIC*), ed. P. Krüger
CIC	*Corpus Iuris Civilis*
Const. Ap.	*Apostolic Constitutions*
COr	*Cahiers de l'Orient*
CS	Cistercian Studies
CSCO	Corpus scriptorum christianorum orientalium
CTh	*Codex Theodosianus*, ed. Th. Mommsen and P. M. Meyer
DACL	*Dictionnaire d'archéologie chrétienne et de liturgie*
DHGE	*Dictionnaire d'histoire et de géographie ecclésiastique*
Dig.	*Digesta* (vol. 2 of the *CIC*), ed. Th. Mommsen
DOP	*Dumbarton Oaks Papers*
DSp	*Dictionnaire de spiritualité*
ep., epp.	*epistula, epistulae*
GCS	Die griechischen christlichen Schriftsteller der ersten Jahrhunderte
GOTR	*Greek Orthodox Theological Review*
GRBS	*Greek, Roman, and Byzantine Studies*
HE	*Historia ecclesiastica*
HL	Palladius of Helenopolis, *Historia Lausiaca*
HM	*Historia monachorum in Aegypto*
HR	Theodoret of Cyrrhus, *Historia religiosa*
HTR	*Harvard Theological Review*
IEJ	*Israel Exploration Journal*
JAOS	*Journal of the American Oriental Society*
JbAC	*Jahrbuch für Antike und Christentum*
JECS	*Journal of Early Christian Studies*
JEH	*Journal of Ecclesiastical History*
JJP	*Journal of Juristic Papyrology*
JöB	*Jahrbuch der österreichischen Byzantinistik*
JThS	*Journal of Theological Studies*
l., ll.	line, lines
Lampe	*A Patristic Greek Lexicon*, ed. G. W. H. Lampe
LCL	Loeb Classical Library
LSJ	*A Greek English Lexicon*, 9th ed., ed. H. G. Liddell, R. Scott, and H. S. Jones
LXX	Septuagint
Nov.	*Novellae* (vol. 4 of the *CIC*), ed. Rudolf Schoell and Wilhelm Kroll
NPNF	Nicene and Post-Nicene Fathers
OCA	Orientalia Christiana Analecta
OCP	*Orientalia Christiana Periodica*
Payne Smith	*A Compendious Syriac Dictionary*, ed. J. Payne Smith

PG	Patrologia Graeca
PL	Patrologia Latina
PLRE	*The Prosopography of the Later Roman Empire*, 3 vols., ed. A. H. M. Jones, J. R. Martindale, and J. Morris
PO	Patrologia Orientalis
PTS	Patristische Texte und Studien
r.	regnavit (i.e., chronology of imperial office)
REB	*Revue de Études byzantines*
ROC	*Revue de l'Orient chrétien*
SC	Sources Chrétiennes
sed.	sedit (i.e., chronology of episcopal office)
SH	Subsidia Hagiographica
SM	*Studia monastica*
Sophocles	*Greek Lexicon of the Roman and Byzantine Periods (From BC 146 to AD 1100)*, 2 vols., ed. E. A. Sophocles
SP	*Studia patristica*
SyrD.	Syrian *Didascalia*
TAPA	*Transactions of the American Philological Association*
TCH	Transformation of the Classical Heritage
TM	*Travaux et mémoires*
TLG	Thesaurus Linguae Graecae, University of California, Irvine
TTH	Translated Texts for Historians
TU	Texte und Untersuchungen
VC	*Vigiliae Christianae*
ZPE	*Zeitschrift für Papyrologie und Epigraphik*

PROLOGUE: WHAT IS A CHRISTIAN GIFT?

1. For quantifications, see Caner 2013a: 31–37.

2. Parry 1986: 468. Cf. Mauss 1990.

3. See Parry and Bloch 1989; Laidlaw 1995; Laidlaw 2000; more generally, Testart 2007.

4. Wickham 2010: 256. For scholarship on ancient and medieval gifts in Western Europe, see Algazi, Groebner, and Jussen 2003: esp. 9–27.

5. Parry 1986: 468 proposes that the "arithmetical relationship between alms-offerings and the elimination of sin established by Cyprian" (referring to Bishop Cyprian of Carthage, ca. 200–258) turned Christian almsgiving into something other than disinterested gift giving during the third century.

6. The result was a series of articles, some of which are synthesized in chapter 6 of this book: Caner 2006; Caner 2008; Caner 2013a; and Caner forthcoming-b.

7. Silber 1995a.

8. Silber 2000: 122–24. See also Silber 2002: 299–301; Silber 2007; and Algazi 2003: 12–13, 15.

9. ἐλεημοσύνη, ἀγάπη, εὐλογίαι, καρποφορίαι, and προσφοραί. I focus on Greek not only because it was dominant but because more Greek texts have been edited than Syriac or

Coptic texts, and because the TLG enabled me to collect and analyze them efficiently. I realize that Syriac and Coptic terms are not identical to Greek counterparts (e.g., as noted in chapter 3, the Syriac *zdaqa*, "righteousness," differs in nuance from ἐλεημοσύνη) and that Eastern Christian authors sometimes use different Syriac or Coptic words to translate a Greek word (e.g., Syriac authors occasionally use *ṭaybutā*, "favor" or "grace," instead of *burktā*, "blessing," to translate εὐλογία). The Syriac, Coptic, and Latin translations of φιλανθρωπία in Tit 3:4 and Acts 27:3 and 28:2 are *mraḥmānutā, mntmairome/metmairomi*, and *humanitas*, respectively.

10. Other Christian gift concepts certainly existed: besides χάρις (and cognates like χαρίσματα), there were εὐχαί (vows), εὐχαριστήρια (thank-offerings), *ḥnāna* (literally "pity," frequently applied to medicaments dispensed by holy people), and tithes. I touch on some of these in chapter 6, but not in detail, both because I consider them a species of the broader categories under discussion, and because I have not found them as prominently attested as the others.

11. This is a problem with most scholarship on early Christian philanthropy and almsgiving, including Constantelos 1991; and Finn 2006a. An exception is Davies and Fouracre 2010, but their brief treatment of Western equivalents to gift categories examined here (e.g., Western *evolgiae*) draws different conclusions, perhaps because they analyze a different historical context. Needless to say, Early Byzantine distinctions become more apparent when read in the original language; modern translations rarely render relevant words with consistency or precision.

12. Cf. Wickham 2010: 261: "Why were there so many words for gift, and for giving, in the early Medieval ages? Because gift giving was always . . . potentially ambiguous, with meanings that could be attached and competed over both at the moment of giving and later. The languages of gift, precisely because they cannot be fully decoded, are thus a pointer to the many-facetedness of the practice of gift-giving, in our period as in every other." For further discussion, see Silber 1995a.

13. For imperial laws on gifts, see *CI* 8.53(54)–56(57); *Dig.* 39.5–6; *Nov.* 52.2. See also Anné 1941; Jobert 1977: 84–93; and Borkowski and du Plessis 2005: 205–7. Except where necessary, I do not discuss how Christian gift ideals conformed to these Roman laws or to such legal definitions as *donationes inter vivos* and *donationes mortis causa*. For this aspect, see Papaconstaninou 2012.

14. Thomas 1987: 4 makes a similar observation.

15. For classical terminology, see Jim 2012: 310–37; and Parker 1998: 105–25. For rabbinic terminology, see Novick 2012; and Sorek 2010.

16. For example, Zeisel 1975: 97 describes church offerings as "a symbolic act of clerical authority and lay subservience." But power relations explain only part of the phenomenon. On "fictions of reciprocity" in late antique society, see Grey 2011: 75–84.

INTRODUCTION

1. The quotation is from MacMullen 1988: 126, describing the earlier empire but implying its application to the later empire.

2. To be clear, not all holy people were monks, but all monks were theoretically training to become holy people.

3. Gibbon 1898 (vol. 4): 74, discussed in Chadwick 2017: 278.

4. Herrin 1987: 144.

5. For general background to such rabbinic concerns, Stroumsa 2009; and Schwartz 2010. For post-Temple Jewish practices, Sorek 2010; Novick 2012; and Gardner 2015.

6. On the Antonine Constitution and its effects, Corcoran 2006; and Mathisen 2012.

7. See Payne 2015; and Walker 2006. Of course, contemporary Western societies were also complex, but Gothic and Germanic conquests replaced their imperial superstructure (except for Italy under Theodoric). Booth 2014; Millar 2006; Sarris 2006; Brown 2002; and Brown 1992 also focus more or less exclusively on the Eastern empire and provide important background to my own study.

8. Trombley 1987; for fuller discussion, Patlagean 1977: 158–72. See also Carlà 2016.

9. Jo. Mosch., *prat.* 79 (PG 87[3].2937).

10. Fortunately, the preaching of a few others, like Asterius of Amasea and Leontius of Constantinople, were preserved, probably to serve as models. It should be noted that many important sources, such as Chrysostom's homilies, still lack modern editions and show signs of later interpolation. See Allen, Neil, and Mayer 2009: esp. 38–40. My confidence lies in the aggregate of examples I assemble rather than in any single instance.

11. Although Brown 2012 and I have ostensibly written about the same topic in the same period, readers will find we have produced very different (and happily complementary) studies on Christian wealth. Besides our focusing on different historical circumstances (imperial Roman East vs. post-Roman West), our available sources are different. Whereas Brown is able to focus on people first and abstract ideals second, I have had to work the other way around, especially because many of my sources, unlike his, cannot be securely identified with any particular author, time, or place.

12. I actually make little use of Shenoute's corpus, partly because the relevant issues are explored in exemplary fashion by López 2013.

13. For an introduction, see Efthymiades and Déroche 2011; and Flusin 2011. For hagiography as a historical source, see Barnes 2010; Krueger 2010b; Rapp 2010; and Lifshitz 1994.

14. Cf. Wickham 2010: 241–42: "Narrativization gives us the only semiological context we have for gift-giving, but it is itself part of the 'struggle to control' its meaning. . . . We can usually analyse only this subsequent, competitive negotiation of meaning, not the meaning for the actors. But at least that conveys to us the rhetorical fields inside which gifts and their exchange had meaning, which is not a marginal thing to study. . . . Some of the words do undoubtably cluster in different ways, and this is crucial for the language of gift."

15. Cyril Scyth., *v.Euthym.* 17 (Schwartz, 27); cf. Jo. Mosch., *prat.* 230 (= Nissen 12).

16. By *discourse*, I mean reiterative processes by which ways of thinking about a subject become naturalized and disseminated without maintaining awareness of their historical origins.

17. See Caner, forthcoming-a; cf. the eighth-century Syriac inscription recording "blessed gifts" given to the Mar Jacob Monastery in Tur Abdin (Palmer 1990: 186–87, 206–7).

18. Watts 2010: 115–17, 127–30, 142–52; Dagron 1989: 1080–85; Sijpesteijn 1989: 95–99; Horden 1986; Patlagean 1977: 191–92; Nedungatt 1973; Wipszycka 1970; and Pétridès 1904.

19. Alexandrian *philoponoi* were considered ready to host anti-Chalcedonian monks: Jo. Ruf., *v.Petr.Ib.* 101. For anonymous "Christlovers," *HM* 14.19; Cyril Scyth., *v.Jo.Hesych.* 20 (describing how monks used his parents' house like an inn); Jo. Mosch., *prat.* 13, 39, 60, 73, 75, 196, 201, 216, 224 (= Nissen 5), 225 (Nissen 6), 230 (Nissen 11), 233 (Mioni 2), 236–37 (Mioni 5–6); Leont. Neap. *v.Jo.Eleem.* 23. For Eucharistius and similar exemplars, *AP* G, Eucharistius the Secular 1, John Colobus 40, Or 6; *AP* GS 18.41, 20.2; and Pall., *HL* 52. On Vincomalus, Gratisimus, and Christopher, see Thdr. Lect., *HE* frgs. 384 and 387 (GCS n.F.3.108–9); with *PLRE* 2.519, 1169–70; and Jo. Mosch., *prat.* 234–35 (= Mioni 3–4).

20. On *scholastici* in Isaiah of Gaza's circle, see Chitty 1971: 62–63. On Cosmas and John, Wolska-Conus 1968: 147–51, 254–57, 304–5; and Elweskiöld 2005.

21. For examples, see Rapp 2008; Évieux 1995: 112–18; and Caner 2002: 226.

22. Bars. et Jo., *resp.* 644 (SC 468.70–72); cf. Isid. Pel., *ep.* 1125 (PG 78.985C). For financial support from such people, Camplani 2013: 143–47; and Caner 2021.

23. Call., *v.Hyp.*, prol. 10 (SC 177.70); also Soz., *HE* 6.20, 27; Marc. Diac., *v.Porph.* 11; Rom. Mel., *hymn* 53.

24. Caner 2013a: 32–33.

25. For the sixth century as the earliest era in which we can speak generally of Eastern church or monastic wealth, see Brown 2002: 54; Bagnall 1993: 291–92; and Zeisel 1975: 88–95. For creating or supporting monasteries as a pious act on par with giving to the poor, see Soz., *HE* 9.1.8; with Horn 2004; and Caner 2002: 158–205; also Jo. Eph., *HE* 3.2.28.

26. I quote Kaplan 2020: 342, 360. As Kaplan emphasizes, Early Byzantine sources do not enable us to reconstruct the economies of early monasteries in detail, so I will not pursue the matter extensively here; see Wipszycka 2001; Wipszycka 2009; Wipszycka 2011; Blanke 2019; and Schachner 2006. For donations to Palestinian monasteries, see Binns 1994: 85–91; Patrich 1995: 9, 43, 194–95, 252; and Hirschfeld 1992: 102–4; for Egypt, Gascou 1991: 1639–45; and Wipszycka 1972: 64–92.

27. *CI* 1.3.52.1 (*CIC* 2.35): οὐκ ἂν εἴη δίκαιον . . . πράττειν τὰ πάντων πικρότατα, εὐθὺς δὲ ἱερέα χειροτονεῖσθαι περὶ φιλανθρωπίας τε καὶ ἀκτημοσύνης . . . δόγματα. I adapt De Ste. Croix's translation (see next note), which renders φιλανθρωπία and ἀκτημοσύνη as "benevolence" and "poverty."

28. De Ste. Croix 1981: 474, 493.

29. Jo. Lyd., *De mag.* 3.72.4 (Schamp, 135; trans. Bandy, 315, adapted). On Lydus, see chapter 1, "Christian Gifts in the Late Roman Holy Land."

30. Jo. Lyd., *De mag.* 3.75.3 (138). Cf. Leont. Neap., *v.Jo.Eleem.* 21; and *AP* G Theodore of Pherme 18.

CHAPTER 1. THE PRESENT-GIVING WORLD OF EARLY BYZANTIUM

1. For different assessments, Moorhead 2013; O'Donnell 2008; Kaldellis 2004; Meier 2004; and Mazal 2001. For Justinian's successors, Whitby 1988; and Whitby 2001.

2. Plac., *Itin.* 18, 34, 44 (CCSL 175.138, 145, 153). His *Itinerarium* has two recensions. The *recensio prior* is preferable to the *altera*, whose Carolingian authors tried to clarify passages. See Mian 1972; and Milani 1977: 31–46.

3. Plac., *Itin.*14.

4. Plac., *Itin.* 7–8 (CCSL 175.132–33). Egeria mentions many *mansiones* but only thirty-eight cities; the Pilgrim mentions no *mansiones* but far more cities and counts distances by milestones. Whereas her pilgrimage lasted three years (381–384), his apparently lasted only months: he mentions observing only Epiphany (*Itin.* 11), suggesting he left before Easter (admittedly, the text breaks before finishing). On the sixth-century Holy Land, see Wilken 1992: 173–92.

5. Plac., *Itin.* 2, 5, 33, 46 (CCSL 175.129, 131, 145, 153). Brown 2012 characterizes the meaning of *splendor* in the late antique West as an "éclat, that spoke of the majesty of city and empire in a fully public manner that was intended to leave the onlookers stunned" (27–30).

6. Plac., *Itin.* 2, 3, 5, 8, 45 (CCSL 175.129–33, 152); in 30, he observes that a screen divided Christian and Jewish visitors at Mamre. Samaritans had twice revolted and suffered brutal suppression during the century before the Pilgrim's visit; see Sivan 2008: 107–42.

7. Plac., *Itin.* 39, 45 (CCSL 175.149, 152).

8. Plac., *Itin.* 40 (CCSL 175.149–50). For related sources and commentary, Sivan 2008: 70–77; and Caner 2010.

9. For the possible impact of the little ice age and bubonic plague, see Harper 2017; for the Elusa garbage dump, Bar-Oz et al. 2019. Magness 2003 challenges the consensus that economic and demographic decline occurred in late sixth-century Syria-Palestine; Walmsley 2007 argues that prosperity expanded in the Transjordan into the seventh century. None of this debate applies to East Roman territory in the Balkans, which was largely lost to the Avars and Slavs in the second half of the sixth century.

10. Di Segni 1999: 165; Saradi 2006: 67–93, 406–12; and Wipszycka 2015: 109. For synagogues, Weiss 2019.

11. Avi-Yonah 1953; Armstrong 1967; and Hunt 1982: 128–54. For inscriptions, Kraemer 1958: 15–16; and Sivan 2008: 74–75. Such building also reflected competition for local prestige; see Ruffini 2011.

12. Jones 1964: 406. In 395, the Roman Empire was formally divided (not for the first time) for military, administrative, and fiscal purposes; the Eastern empire also had a separate prefecture for the Balkans. On the system, see Jones 1964: 37–73, 523–606; with Barnish, Lee, and Whitby 2001; Liebeschuetz 2001; Kelly 2004; and Millar 2006.

13. Banaji 2001; and Sarris 2006.

14. On Lydus and his writings, see Kelly 2004: 11–63; and Maas 1992. For estimates on the purchasing power of a solidus, see Jones 1964: 447–48; and Patlagean 1977: 380–96.

15. See Introduction, "The Complementary Virtues of Philanthropy and Asceticism."

16. Jo. Lyd., *De mag.* 3.74.2 (Schamp, 3.137–38): τοῖς ἱερουμένοις πρόσοδον ὀγδοήκοντα χρυσῶν προσγενέσθαι τῷ ἱερῷ εἰς φιλοξενίαν ἐσπούδασεν. On this episode, see Schamp, 3.cxciii–cxcv; and Maas 1992: 78–82. This is a non-hagiographical example of laypeople giving annuities to support church and monastic hospitality, discussed in chapter 5.

17. See Kelly 2004; and Harries 1999; over, for example, MacMullen 1988.

18. Plac., *Itin.* 40–41; cf. Whitby 2001: 92.

19. Plac., *Itin.* 2, 9, 10, 12, 16, 22, 23, 26, 29, 32, 34–38, 46 (CCSL 175.130, 134–37, 141, 143, 145–48). For the role of monks in promoting Palestine as a "holy land," see Wilken 1992:

149–72. For imperially financed forts to protect monks in Palestine and Sinai, Caner 2010: 57, 277–78.

20. On exarchs or comparable appointments, see Patrich 1995: 287–88; and Wipszycka 2007: 341. For introductions to early monasticism in the East, see Filoramo 2010; Rousseau 2001; Patrich 1995; and Chitty 1966. Bolman 2016a; and Hevelone-Harper 2005 are the most comprehensive introductions to a single monastic community. On the identity of early Christian monks as philosophers and their relation to the ancient philosophical heritage, see Rubenson 2012; and Caner 2002: 177–90.

21. On Justinianic monastic legislation, see Granić 1929; and Hasse-Ungeheuer 2016. For its impact, Neary 2017; Lesieur 2011; Parrinello 2006; and de Vogüé 2001: 227–31.

22. On Barsanuphius, see chapter 4. For similar hybrid arrangements, see Jo. Mosch., *prat.* 226; and *Nov.* 133.1.

23. Rousseau 2001: 758–61.

24. Athanasius of Alexandria is especially responsible for the image of early monks as unlearned, having deliberately misrepresented Antony the Great as an illiterate peasant in his *Life of Antony*. See Rubenson 1995; and Rubenson 2013. For levels of monastic education and literacy evinced in Egypt, see Larsen and Rubenson 2018.

25. *v.Dos.* 2–4, 11. On Dositheus, see Flusin 2011: 211; and Hevelone-Harper 2005: 69–72. Jo. Eph., *v.SS.Or.* 51, says he and a friend joined their monastery when fifteen years old. Bars. et Jo., *resp.* 492–502, were written to another former soldier. See also *v.Longini* 36; and Jo. Mosch., *prat.* 20, 23, 25 (cf. 73). Greg. Mag., *reg.* 3.61 and 64 (both dated 593) refer to a law of Emperor Marcian prohibiting soldiers to become monks before their discharge.

26. Patlagean 1977: 144–48, 338–40; Gascou 1991: 1644; Dey 2008; and Laniado 2009: 28.

27. For Constantinople, Hatlie 2007b: 89, 94–95, 109. For Egypt (including Alexandria), Wipszycka 2005. For Jerusalem and environs, Di Segni 2001: 36; Patrich 1995: 8–9, 67; and Hirschfeld 1992: 10. For Roman Arabia (roughly modern Jordan), Millar 2009. For Gaza, Hirschfeld 2004: 67. For Syrian and Asia Minor numbers, Zeisel 1975: 320; with Jo. Eph., *v.SS.Or.* 39. For Korykos, Trombley 1987: 18n11. More generally, Savramis 1962: 54.

28. Plac., *Itin.* 43 (CCSL 175.152); cf. Eg., *Itin.* Y2, *HM* 18.3. On patristic interpretations of Joseph's example and the pyramids, see Holman 2001: 126–32.

29. Plac., *Itin.* 5 (CCSL 175.131).

30. Plac., *Itin.*13–14 (CCSL 175.136–37).

31. Plac., *Itin.* 9, 39, 42 (CCSL 175.133–34, 149, 151); Plac., *Itin.* 3 (130) identifies a stone's *virtutes* as the source of its miracles.

32. Limor 2017: 6, notes how the Pilgrim differs from Egeria in focusing on material blessings. On this focus of sixth-century pilgrimage, see Krueger 2005: 302–5, with photographs.

33. For example, Plac., *Itin.* 39 (CCSL 175.149): "habent in monasterio, unde et benedictionem dant ampullas modicas." Cf. 18, 22, 23, 42 (138, 141, 151).

34. Plac., *Itin.* 4, 11, 17, 22 (CCSL 175.130, 135, 137, 140).

35. Plac., *Itin.* 2, 4, 18, 20 (CCSL 175.129, 130, 138, 139).

36. Plac., *Itin.* 34 (CCSL 175.146): "quas Christiani valabant ... quibus ... offerebat ille Christianissimus, cum quem fui." Wilkinson interprets *quibus* to refer to the ass and lion, but this, though amusing, does not make grammatical or logical sense.

37. See chapter 5, "The Institutional and Lay Provision of Material Blessings." The legend of Mary was circulating in Judea by the 550s, as attested in Cyril Scyth., *v.Cyriac.* 18–19. The best-known version was the *v.Mariae Aegyptiacae* attributed to Sophronius of Jerusalem, on which see Flusin 2004.

38. Georg. Syc., *v.Thdr.Syc.* 104, identifies people who brought food to a monastery from afar in time of famine as Christlovers. Some scholars, however, have assumed that the superlative *Christianissimus* simply meant that the companion was a priest. For interactions between Palestinian monks and lay pilgrims, see Di Segni 2001: 31–36; and chapter 5.

39. Corippus, *Laud. Just.* 2.399–402: "largior inventus patre est, clementior idem." Cameron 1976: 177–78, notes that by *clementia*, Corippus means *philanthrōpia*. On his depiction of the accession and its precedents, MacCormack 1981: 151–56.

40. Corippus, *Laud. Just.* 4.68–73, 145–47, 226 (trans. Cameron, 111, 113, 114). On Kalends celebrations elsewhere, see Kaldellis 2011.

41. Corippus, *Laud. Just.* 4.11–12, 315–16 (trans. Cameron, 110, 116).

42. Theoph., *Chron.* AM 6058 (De Boor, 242); cf. MacMullen 1962: 160–61.

43. MacMullen 1988: 126. For a survey of traditional Roman gift types, see Stuiber 1977. The classic discussion of euergetism is Veyne 1976; with significant refinements in Domingo-Gygax and Zuiderhoek 2021; Zuiderhoek 2009; and Lendon 1997. The distinctiveness of Greco-Roman tradition in contrast with Judaic tradition is brought out by Schwartz 2010. For earlier background, Coffee 2017.

44. Wood 2000.

45. Herrin 2013a. Besides Finn 2006a; Brown 2002; and Patlagean 1977, important contributions include Salzman 2017; and Holman 2001: 31–63.

46. *Nov.* 67, pr. (*CIC* 3.344). On the disjuncture between classicizing descriptions of Early Byzantine cities and their actual Christian appearance, see Saradi 2006. For an interesting discussion of the classicizing portrait of the "Lady of Silto" on the sixth-century basilica church floor at Kissufim, southern Israel, see Britt 2008.

47. Brown 2002: 80; Patlagean 1974; and Caner 2021.

48. Jo. Lyd., *De mag.* 1.20.6–7 (Schamp, 1.2, p.29; trans. Bandy, 90–91, adapted): διῆλθε δὲ ὅμως καὶ ἐπὶ τὴν καθ᾽ ἡμᾶς Ῥώμην ἡ τοιαύτη φιλανθρωπία καὶ τὸ λοιπὸν οὐκ ἔστη, τῶν ἐν ἡμῖν ἐνδόξων ἄχρις ἑαυτῶν τὴν ὑπεροχὴν τῆς τύχης ἐνδεικνυμένων. On the consequences of this development for ancient cities, see Saradi 2006: 168–77; and Smith 2016.

49. Proc. Caes., *Aed.* 2.1.3 (LCL 343.96–97); cf. 1.1.4, 11.1. On imperial benefactions and their emphasis on utility, see Saradi 2006: 60, 159–60, 178–81; on benefactions by governors (an important precursor to activities of bishops), see Haensch 1997: 380–89.

50. On this ceremony, see McCormick 1998: 37–42. On the origin and mechanics of the Constantinopolitan dole, Müller 1993; Durliat 1990; Carrié 1975; and Jones 1964: 696–700. For John of Ephesus's example, Jo. Eph., *HE* 3.2.41.

51. Corippus, *Laud. Just.* 2.195–250.

52. Corippus, *Laud. Just.* 2.245, 4.187–88 (trans. Cameron, 99, 114); see also 2.280–95; 3.160–65, 180–210; 4.230–45, describing the processions and assemblies.

53. See Delmaire 1988; and MacMullen 1962: 164. For the earlier period, Millar 1977: 491–508, and its index of imperial gifts, 642–43. An imperial officer, the Count of the Sacred

Largesses, was appointed to prepare such gifts; the emblem of his office in the *Notitia Dignitatum* is a chest bursting with coins and silverware.

54. See Kelly 2004: 19–20; and Almagro-Gorbea et al. 2000. This is one of nineteen *missoria* depicting ceremonial gift giving: Leader-Newby 2004: 11; and MacCormack 1981: 214–21.

55. *Nov.* 7.2.1 (issued 534; *CIC* 3.53, trans. Miller and Sarris 1.117, adapted).

56. *Dial.* 5.61 (Mazzucchi, 27; TTH 52.157). Already by the early second century, even Tacitus accepted that internal peace required monarchical rule; Harris 2016: 155.

57. Liebeschuetz 2001: 197, see also 280–81, 346–48; Kelly 2004: 145–52; Laniado 2002: 160–61; and MacMullen 1988: 58–104. Of course, hierarchical order was more a wish than reality, and late Roman emperors probably had less power than earlier emperors; see Harris 2016: 292–93.

58. Liebeschuetz 2001: 348; see Jones 1964: 523–24; and De Ste. Croix 1981: 318–19, 483–99; with the observation of Trombley 1987: 18, that clerics often moonlighted in productive professions.

59. *Nov.* 13.1 (issued 535 CE); *Dial.* 5.93, 111, 132, 136, 173. On this civic ideal, see Petit 1955: 220–23, 243–45.

60. Theoph., *Chron.* AM 6058 (de Boor, 242); *v.Sym.Styl.iun.* 206–210 (SH 32.177–79). We do not know if Symeon was rewarded, but twelve years later Theodore of Sykeon prophesied in support of Emperor Maurice (r. 588–602) and received both a silver altar set and roughly four tons of wheat a year for his monastic complex. Georg. Syc., *v.Thdr.Syc.* 54.

61. *Nov.* 7.2.1 (issued 534; *CIC* 3.53, trans. Miller and Sarris 1.117, adapted): πᾶσα ταῖς ἁγιωτάταις ἐκκλησίαις εὐπορία τε καὶ σύστασις ἐκ τῶν παρὰ τῆς βασιλείας φιλοτιμιῶν διηνεκῶς ἐπιδίδοτα. On imperial expectations for priests, see Rapp 2005: 235–73; Moorhead 1994: 118–19; and Jones 1964: 933–37. For monks, Gascou 1976.

62. *Nov.* 6 pr. (issued 534; *CIC* 3.35–36, trans. Miller and Sarris, 1.97–98, adapted).

63. *Nov.* 133.5.1 (issued 539; *CIC* 3.674, trans. Miller and Sarris, 2.886–87, adapted); cf. *CJ* 1.3.34 (issued 529); with Sherk 2004: 172–75; and Rapp 2005: 278–79.

64. Agap., *Cap.* 58. For similar imagery, *HM* prol. 9–10; Thdt., *HE* 26.19; Sev. Ant., *Hom. cath.* 7 (PO 23.90), 61 (8.265), 67 (8.365); and Bars. et Jo., *resp.* 569.

65. *CJ* 1.2.19 and 22 (issued 528 and 529). Legal procedures for making gifts had already been reformed by Constantine. See Jobert 1977: 83–85; and Patlagean 1977: 195. But restrictions were imposed to prevent alienation of property to evade municipal responsibilities; Laniado 2009. For examples of imperial and aristocratic donations to the church after 313, Zeisel 1975: 69–90.

66. On the church *annona*, Brown 2012: 49–52, 333; Brown 2002: 32; Liebeschuetz 2001: 167–68; Wipszycka 1997; Durliat 1990: 354–55, 365–75, 552n155; and Zeisel 1975: 79–81, 178.

67. *Nov.* 7.2.1 (issued 534; *CIC* 3.53, trans. Miller and Sarris 1.117, adapted): εἰς ἁγιωτάτας ἐκκλησίας, ἐφ' ὧν ἄριστον μέτρον ἡ τῶν δωρουμένων καθέστηκεν ἀμετρία.... πᾶσα ταῖς ἁγιωτάταις ἐκκλησίαις εὐπορία τε καὶ σύστασις ἐκ τῶν παρὰ τῆς βασιλείας φιλοτιμιῶν διηνεκῶς ἐπιδίδοτα; and *Nov.* 7.7.8 (*CIC* 3.60): τοιαύτας εἶναι σιτήσεις οὐ μόνον ἐπὶ τῆς βασιλίδος ταύτης πόλεως, ἀλλὰ καὶ ἐπὶ τῆς μεγάλης Ἀλεξανδρείας καὶ ἐπὶ τῆς Θεουπολιτῶν εἶναι μεμαθήκαμεν, ἴσως δὲ τὸ τοιοῦτο καὶ ἐν ἑτέραις τισὶν ἐπαρχίαις εἶναι. See also *CJ* 1.2.17 (issued ca. 491–518); *Nov.* 120.1 (issued 544); and Athanasius of Emesa, *syntagm.* 2.1.1, written in the 570s.

68. Evagr. Schol., *HE* 4.35 (Bidez-Parmentier, 184): τὴν ἐπέτειον χορηγίαν κομιούμενος τῆς κατ᾽ αὐτὸν μονῆς ἐντέτακτο δὲ ἐκ τῆς αὐτόσε ἐκκλησίας; Plac., *Itin.* 35 (CCSL 175.147): "castrum . . . in quo habent. . . . heremitae stipendia." See also Jo. Cass., *Inst.* 4.5; Cyril Scyth., *v.Sab.* 6; Jo. Eph., *HE* 3.2.43; and Jo. Mosch., *prat.* 41, 88.

69. Caner 2002: 206–41.

70. On monks as political constituents, Frend 1972a; and Caner 2021. Jones 1964: 933; and De Ste. Croix 1981: 495–97, uses the phrase "idle mouths" to describe the burden that clerics and monks allegedly imposed.

71. *CJ* 1.2.12 (issued 451).

72. Chrys., *In 2 Thess.* 2.2 (PG 62.475); see also Chrys., *In Gen.* 1.4 (Brottier, SC 433.170); Soc., *HE* 7.17.7; and Marc. Diac., *v.Porph.* 85.

73. Evagr. Schol., *HE* 4.9. For social and political dimensions after Chalcedon, see Menze 2008; Meyendorff 1989; and Frend 1972b.

74. Sev. Ant., *ep.Coll.* 1 1.22 (dated 516–517; Brooks, Syr. 87, trans.78).

75. For Anastasius's effort, Thdr. Petr., *v.Thds.* (Usener 54.1–56.19); also Geront., *v.Mel.gr.* 27; *v. Long.* 30; Ps.-Zach., *Chron.* 3.2, 3.8; Jo. Eph., *HE* 3.1.11; and Jo. Eph., *v.SS.Or.* 36 (PO 18.428–31), and 49 (19.696).

76. Philox., *Rules* 1 (Vööbus, 53). See Menze 2008: 257, 262; Binns 1994: 182, 208; and Flusin 1992: 2.64.

77. Soc., *HE* 7.3; and Jo. Eph., *v.SS.Or.* 5 (PO 17.91).

78. Geront., *v.Mel. gr.* 19, 29; cf. Kelly 2004: 178.

79. Brown 2002: 32.

80. Jo. Nik., *Chron.* 90.54–60.

81. Crone 1991: 21–42. Sassanian Persia represented the great alternative to the Late Roman state, its monotheism, and political structure. For introductions, see Walker 2006; and Payne 2015.

82. It is hard to know if allegations against followers of Eustathius of Sebaste ca. 340–350 reflect authentic views or simply fears of episcopal judges. See Brown 2002: 37; and Fitschen 1998: 27–28.

83. See Harrison 2016: 91–95; Watts 2015: 149–89; De Ste. Croix 1975: 25–26; and Kurbatov 1958.

84. Chrys., *In 1 Cor.* 34.3–4 (PG 61.290–91); cf. Chrys., *In 1 Cor* 26.3 (216); Chrys., *In 2 Thess.* 4.1 (62.486); and Chrys., *salut.* 2.5 (51.204); with Petit 1955: 220; and Mayer 2009: 100–101. This is not to say that Chrysostom did not express provocative ideas, as discussed in, for example, Mitchell 2004.

85. *AP GS* 15.1 (SC 474.284); cf. 7.47; and Bars. et Jo., *resp.* 712, an important expression of deference to laity of high rank, even on doctrinal matters.

86. Dion., Ps.-, *ep.* 8.1, 3 (Heil-Ritter, 176, 181–83). On his concerns, see Rorem 1993: 18–24; and Booth 2014: 27–32.

87. Booth 2014: 7–43; and Hatlie 2007a: 118–27, 133–71.

88. Chrys., *In Eph.* 10.2 (PG 62.78); Chrys., *In 1 Cor.* 30.6–7 (61.253–5); and Greg. Naz., *or.* 14.31 (35.900B).

89. *AP GS* 10.187 (SC 474.132).

90. Jo. Clim., *scal.* 26 (PG 88. 1020–21). On the honorific treatment of monks after death, *v.Pach. boh.* 82.

91. Philox., *ep. de vita mon.* 12 (Graffin, 333); *v.Bars.* 33; *v.Aux.* 14, 18, 60 (PG 114.1388, 1392, 1428); and Greg. Mag., *Dial.* 5.69–71. For legislation prohibiting mocking monks on stage, Longosz 1993; for mockery more generally, Caner 2013b; and Sarris 2011.

92. Zos., *Hist. nov.* 5.23.4 (Paschoud, 3.1.35): τὸ πολὺ μέρος τῆς γῆς ᾠκειώσαντο, προφάσει τοῦ μεταδιδόναι πάντων πτωχοῖς πάντας ὡς εἰπεῖν πτωχοὺς καταστήσαντες. Cf. Martyrius of Antioch, Ps.-, *or.fun.* 6. Zosimus probably used Eunapius of Sardis's lost history written in the late fourth or early fifth century, when monks were seizing temple lands in Syria, as noted in chapter 6.

93. Jo. Eph., *HE* 3.3.37. For annual payments of tribute (*madatâ*) by monasteries to churches, see Sev. Ant., *ep.Coll.1.* 1.4; and the Arabic *v.Pisentii* 15 (PO 22.374–75). Wipszycka 2007 notes that visiting bishops were supposed to give monasteries gifts: "The church thus complied with the same principle of gifts and counter-gifts known to apply in relationships between the emperor and members of the imperial court elite" (336). On resources attributed to Cyril of Alexandria and other bishops, see MacMullen 1988: 165–66; and Zeisel 1975: 82–95, 182, noting that the salaries of bishops in major sees were 1,440 times larger than those in rural sees. For a more comprehensive treatment, see Rapp 2005: 211–19.

94. Schachner 2006: 1.98 notes that much of this monastic land was marginal, fragmented, and not a great loss to local villagers. He dates the acceleration of monastic wealth in Syria, Palestine, and Egypt to ca. 450–550.

95. Zuckerman 2004a: 227–28, revising an earlier estimate that these monasteries owned a third of the land. On the difficulty of assessing total monastic holdings, see Wipszycka 2018: 461–62. From the silence of Justinian's legislation on the matter, Kaplan 2020: 341–45, infers that most monasteries, unlike churches, did not have enough property to cause problems requiring imperial intervention.

96. See Tchalenko 1953: 1.149, 156, 158, 174, 397; Magen 1993; Palmer 1990: 40–72; and López 2013: 47–50; cf. Brenk 2004: 464; and Schroeder 2004.

97. *v.Sin.* 104 (CS 73.72). For the material environment of the White Monastery (which covered a total area of about 77,000 square meters), the occupations of its monks, and its refugee episode, see Blanke 2019: 59–149; López 2013: 47–49, 57–63; and Zeisel 1975: 307–15; for monasteries with smaller monastic or village dependencies, Schachner 2006: 87.

98. Bolman 2016b.

99. Jo. Eph., *HE* 3.3.37, on which see Zeisel 1975: 330–31; quotation from Rousseau 2001: 785–86, referring to Jo. Eph., *v.SS.Or.* 4, 7, 12, 14, 17, 20, 31, 33, 35, 42, 47, 58. For cash at the Euthymius monastery, see Cyril Scyth., *v.Euthym.* 48. Although papyrological evidence is insufficient to reconstruct monastic finances in detail, *P.Oxy* 63.4397 shows that at least one small monastery in sixth-century Egypt could fund two round trips to Constantinople while loaning 130 solidi to a local. See Wipszycka 2011: 169–70.

100. *v.Sym.styl.* 92 (trans. Doran, 169); cf. 56.

101. Wipszycka 1996b: 287. Cf. Goehring 2007: 405: "As the monastic movement became more complex and wealthier, its literary memory fashioned its past as simpler and more austere. As the later basilicas became in fact more ornate, the earlier basilica became in the imagination more primitive."

102. Evagr. Schol., *HE* 2.9, 5.6, 5.16.

103. Bas. Caes., *ep.* 150 (Deferrari, 2.367); on the criterion of "need," see Bas. Caes., *RF* 35; Bas. Caes., *RB* 70; and Bars. et Jo., *resp.* 570, 594; with Newhauser 2000: 23–29. For the early history behind this ascetic issue, see Brown 2016; Caner 2002; and Escolan 1999.

104. See Bagnall 2001; Gould 1987; and more broadly, Wood 2002: 42–63.

105. *Nov.* 5.5 (issued 535). On this and related laws, see Laniado 2009.

106. Leont. Neap., *v.Jo.Eleem.* 23; Cyril. Scyth., and *v.Sab.* 6 (Schwartz, 90); cf. Patrich 1995: 5. This may have been inspired by fees imposed on people entering the clergy, discussed in Zeisel 1975: 256–57.

107. Philox., *Asc.* 8.5 (trans. Kitchen 179–80).

108. First discussed in detail by Déroche 1995: 238–48.

109. Jo. Ruf., *Plerophoriae* 16 (PO 8.32–33). On the prominence of such descriptions in East Syrian ("Nestorian") hagiography, see Villagomez 1998.

110. Thdr. Petr., *v.Thds.* (Usener, 91); cf. Georg. Syc., *v.Thdr.Syc.* 42.

111. *v.Sym.Styl.* 26 (trans. Doran, 116). Cf. Ath., *v.Ant.* 94.1.

112. Hamel 1990: 97–99, 141.

113. De Ste. Croix 1981: 33, 40, 115–33; Wood 2002; Brown 2012: 11–14.

114. Chrys., *In 1 Tim* 12.3 (PG 62.562); Chrys., *In Gen.* 48.5 (53.440–41); with Mitchell 2004: 91–98; see also Anast. Sin., *resp.* 45; and Brown 2010: 315.

115. Cf. Laiou 1996: 439, 457–59 (quoted from 441); with Bas. Caes., *ep.* 22.3; Bas. Caes., *RF* 20.3; Bas. Caes., *RB* 37.1; Chrys., *In Mt.* 57.5, 64.5; and Chrys., *In 2 Cor* 19.4.

116. See Laiou 1996 for this "realist" stance of Chrysostom and the Cappadocian fathers.

117. Jo. Eph., *v.SS.Or.* 31 ("Lives of Elijah and Theodore"; PO 18.577). On the church's acceptance of usury among laypeople in the Early Byzantine era, Laiou 1996: 439–50.

118. See Courtonne 1935: 101–8; Christophe 1964: 82–86, 111–12, 135–39; Viner 1978: 1–45; Avila 1983: 125–50; Gordon 1989: 108–20; Meredith 1998: 95; and Sessa 2012: 63–86. There was more variety than I have suggested here (patristic thought was not monolithic), but the discourse was remarkably uniform. For a helpful survey of classical and Christian ideas regarding private property, see Garnsey 2007.

119. Chrys., *In I Cor.* 3.2 (PG 61.24): Δείκνυσι μὲν γὰρ τοῦ Θεοῦ τὴν φιλανθρωπίαν καὶ ἡ τοῦ κόσμου δεμιουργία. Cf. *Ad Pop.* 7.2 (PG 49.93); *In Gen.* 7.1 (PG 54: 62).

120. Zeisel 1975: 65.

121. Chrys., *In Jo.* 36.1 (PG 59.204); see also Georg. Syc., *v.Thdr.Syc* 127. On "purity" as a requirement for gifts of grace, see Bars. et Jo., *resp.* 59 and 67.

122. For μισθαποδότης θεός and related words, see Dagron and Feissel 1987: 79–80 (no. 35); and Dagron 1998: 84n12. For the early Christian conception of God as a giver who responds with gratitude to human efforts of righteousness, see Leithart 2014. An extravagant example of this view is found in Nilus, Ps.-, *Narr.*, 7.15 (Conca, 51; trans. Caner, 133–34): "God . . . knows how to reward each repayment with a second gift of grace. When a debt is repaid, He receives it back not as a debt, but as if being given a loan. Acknowledging Himself to be indebted for our repayment of the debt, He rewards the debtor's good faith with another gift, giving it as if repaying a loan. He always pays his gifts of grace in advance; He always guarantees Himself to be indebted to those who borrow from His benefits, and reckons it a point of honor to repay them in full, in order that He might forever be the original

source of gracious gifts, repaying such gifts of grace as if He actually owed them. Such is his gift-giving and honor-pursuing nature." Cf. Chrys., *In Rom.* 18.6; and *AP* G Epiphanius 17.

123. Jo. Clim., *scal.* 1 (PG 88.637C; trans. Luibheid and Russell, 77). Cf. *AP* GS 15.128.

124. Jas 1:17: πᾶσα δόσις ἀγαθὴ καὶ πᾶν δώρημα τέλειον ἄνωθέν ἐστιν, καταβαῖνον ἀπὸ τοῦ πατρὸς τῶν φώτων. Discussed in Osteen 2002: 241.

125. Bas. Caes., *hom.6.* 3 (Courtonne, 21): πάντα τὰ τῆς φιλανθρωπίας . . . ὀνόματα. For his river analogy, Bas. Caes., *hom.6.* 5 (29).

126. Greg. Naz., *or.* 14.23 (888A–C): Οὐχ οὗτος, ὃς νῦν πρὸ πάντων καὶ ἀντὶ πάντων αἰτεῖ παρὰ σοῦ τὸ φιλάνθρωπον; Εἶτα οὐκ αἰσχυνόμεθα, εἰ τοσαῦτα παρ' αὐτοῦ . . . μηδὲ ἓν τοῦτο εἰσοίσομεν τῷ Θεῷ, τὸ φιλάνθρωπον;

CHAPTER 2. "GIVE TO ALL WHO ASK OF YOU": THE CHALLENGE OF EARLY BYZANTINE PHILANTHROPY

1. *Nov.* 163 (issued 575; *CIC* 3.749): δικαιοσύνη τε καὶ φιλανθρωπία, ἡ μὲν τὸ ἴσον ἑκάστῳ νέμουσα καὶ τῶν ἀλλοτρίων οὐκ ἐφιεμένη, ἡ δὲ πρὸς ἔλεον τρέχουσα καὶ χρεῶν τοὺς δεομένους ἐλευθεροῦσα δυσκόλως. For historical context of this law, see Miller and Sarris 2018: 1013–17; Whitby 1998: 327–28.

2. *Nov.* 2pr. (issued 535; *CIC* 3.11): τῶν φιλανθρώπων ἡμῶν . . . χρόνων. This law extended inheritance rights to illegitimate children; Justinian says that doing so was philanthropic, adding that Roman law had become more philanthropic after Constantine. For philanthropy as a motif of Justinianic legislation, see Meier 2004: 123–24; Hunger 1964: 143–53; and *Nov.* 89pr (issued 539; *CIC* 3.428).

3. On its connection to petitions for legal clemency, see Humfress 2005: 175; cf. *Nov.* 80.3; Procopius, *Aed.* 1.11.26–27, *HA* 13.1,15.2; and Paul Sil., *Soph.* ll. 40–45.

4. Procopius, *Aed.* 1.2.14–17, 9.13, 11.26–27; 5.3.20, 4.4,15–17; 6.25; 9.4, 22, 27, 34, 35, 38; cf. *Nov.* 120. Paul Sil., *Soph.*, ll. 798–99, says that images of hospitals were woven into the fringe of Justinian's altar cloth in Hagia Sophia. On his foundations, see Klein 2008: 110; Krumpholz 1992; and Thomas 1987: 44–46. Evagr. Schol., *HE* 4.30 claims that he financed them through confiscations, suggesting a connection to the Nika riot.

5. Pall., *Dial.* 17 (SC 341.340): δι' ὑπερβολὴν φιλανθρωπίας ξενοδοχεῖον . . . εἰς ἀνάψυξιν καὶ τῶν ἀρρωστούντων μοναχῶν καὶ τῶν ἐπιχωριαζόντων ξένων. This is the only extant Greek passage that explicitly presents the construction of *xenodocheia* as an expression of the virtue of *philanthrōpia*. The connection is clearly implied in Choric. Gaz., *Laud. Marc.* 1.78 (Foester-Richsteig, 22), however, and the fact that Zach., Ps.-, *HE* 12.7 (Brooks, 217–18) explains the construction of one in Persia to a shah's *mraḥmānutā* (Syriac for *philanthrōpia* in Peshitta Tit 3:4) confirms that they were associated with that ideal in particular. On such institutions see Horden 2012; Serfass 2008; Miller 1990; Miller 1997: 89–117; and Patlagean 1977: 193–96. On their funding, Jones 1964: 901–2. Cyril Scyth., *v.Sab.*73, notes that one in Jerusalem had a hundred beds and an annual revenue of 1,850 solidi. To my knowledge, the only service known to have been offered for free (at least initially) was church-supervised burials, for which taxes from 950 shops were allocated in fourth-century Constantinople. Leont. Neap., *v.Jo.Eleem.* 6, suggests that others were free only during a crisis. Timothy Miller has suggested to me that they operated on a "sliding scale."

6. Brown 2002: 33–35, highlights this nonclassical aspect.

7. Herrin 2013a: 274–89 posits a three-stage evolution, moving from a pre-Constantinian era of non-institutionalized Christian philanthropy, to a post-Constantinian era of church and state partnership culminating with Justinian, to a post-Justinianic era directed mainly by the church. Rapp 2009 discusses pastoral aspects not discussed here.

8. Daley 1999: 434; cf. Constantelos 1991. Christian writers did not apply the term to material benefits to the poor until the fourth century. Pétré 1948: 209–11.

9. *Nov.* 129 (issued 551; *CIC* 3.647). Discussed in Hunger 1963: 14. For late antique examples, see Caner 2018a; as Hunger observes, the usage continued throughout Byzantine history.

10. Agap., *Cap.* 6 (Riedinger, 6): Οὐδὲν οὕτως εὐδόκιμον ἐργάζεται ἄνθρωπον ὡς τὸ δύνασθαι μὲν ἃ βούλεται πράττειν, ἀεὶ δὲ φιλάνθρωπα καὶ βούλεσθαι καὶ πράττειν. Cf. Isid. Pel. *ep.* 2.15 (PG 78.458): Οὐδὲν οὕτω καὶ παρὰ ἀνθρώποις ἔνδοξον . . . ὡς τὸ δύνασθαι μὲν ἃ βούλεται πράττειν, ἀεὶ δὲ φιλάνθρωπα καὶ βούλεσθαι καὶ πράττειν. Isidore's letter, from which Agapetus seems to have drawn this precept (unless it came from a common source), confirms the contrafactual force of Agapetus's μὲν . . . δὲ construction; this nuance is missing from Bell's translation, p.102. On Agapetus's concern for clemency, see Henry 1967: 301–2.

11. Agap., *Cap.* 40 (Riedinger, 52).

12. Agap., *Cap.* 63 (Riedinger, 68). Cf. Agap., *Cap.* 8.

13. Tierney 1959: 363–64; and Dassmann 1998; cf. Augustine, *De doct. Chr.* 1.28.29, *ep.* 262.9.

14. For fuller discussion (taking into account Patlagean 1977: 26–34, the standard treatment), see Caner 2018b: 42–44; and Caner, forthcoming-b. The connection of πτῶχος to a sense of ruin explains the "tendency toward a 'social upgrading'" of late antique recipients of church aid, noted by Brown 2002: 58. In other words, privileging distressed gentlefolk should be seen as evidence of adherence to a basic Christian principle.

15. Origen, *fr. in Ps.* 111.6 (PG 12.1201B): φασὶ δὲ πτωχὸν τὸν ἐκπεσόντα πλούτου· πένητα δὲ τὸν ἐκ πόνου τὰ πρὸς τὸν βίον περιποιούμενον. Bas. Caes., *RB* 262 (PG 31.1260CD): πτωχὸς μέν ἐστιν ὁ ἀπὸ πλούτου κατελθὼν εἰς ἔνδειαν· πένης δὲ ἐξ ἀρχῆς ἐν ἐνδείᾳ ὢν καὶ εὐαρέστως τῷ Κυρίῳ κυβερνήσας τὴν τοιαύτην περίστασιν. Some ancient etymologists maintained erroneously that πτῶχος derived from πίπτω, "I fall" (perf. πέπτωκα). See Ammonius, *adfin.*, no. 387. Rabbis sanctioned a similar privileging of "fallen" people. Hamel 1990: 195–96.

16. For patristic and monastic discussions of this pericope, see Angstenberger 1997.

17. *P.Lond.* 1915, 3–5, in Bell 1972: 73–74: Τοῖ[ς ἐν. . . .]ηφθονει συμφορᾷ παραπεσοῦσιν βοη[θεῖ]ν π[α]ρ[α]γγέλ⟨λ⟩εται ἡμῖν ὁ θεῖος λόγος πᾶσι, μάλιστα τοῖς ἀδελφοῖς ἡμῶν. Bell dates this letter ca. 330–40; Rémondon 1972: 254, believes a Melitian monk wrote it to a monastic priest.

18. *Nov.* 80.4–5 (issued 539 CE); on which see Laniado 2015: 172–256.

19. On Julian's temple reformations, see Elm 2012: 321–24; Smith 1995: 42–44, 110–12; Caltabiano 1991: 264–67; and Athanassadi-Fowden 1981: 41, 181–91.

20. Julian, *ep.* 84, 429A (= Wright, *ep.* 22; LCL 157.66–68), adapted: οὐδὲ ἀποβλέπομεν ὡς μάλιστα τὴν ἀθεότητα συνηύξησεν ἡ περὶ τοὺς ξένους φιλανθρωπία . . . Ξενοδοχεῖα καθ' ἑκάστην πόλιν κατάστησον πυκνά, ἵν' ἀπολαύσωσιν οἱ ξένοι τῆς παρ' ἡμῶν φιλανθρωπίας, οὐ τῶν ἡμετέρων μόνον, ἀλλὰ καὶ τῶν ἄλλων ὅστις ἂν δεηθῇ. οὐ τῶν ἡμετέρων μόνον, ἀλλὰ καὶ τῶν ἄλλων ὅστις ἂν δεηθῇ. . . . Αἰσχρὸν γὰρ εἰ . . . τρέφουσι δὲ οἱ δυσσεβεῖς Γαλιλαῖοι πρὸς τοῖς ἑαυτῶν καὶ τοὺς ἡμετέρους, οἱ δὲ ἡμέτεροι τῆς παρ' ἡμῶν ἐπικουρίας ἐνδεεῖς φαίνοιντο.

21. Horden 2012: 725.

22. Van Nuffelen 2002 argues that *ep.* 84 is a forgery, since it is not transmitted among Julian's works, uses language unattested in his writings, and presents details (including institutional aspects of Christian philanthropy) not found in *ep.* 89b (see next note). Bouffartigue 2005 notes, however, that Julian promises in *ep.* 89b to dispatch more general ordinances for his priests, which conceivably accounts for *ep.* 84.

23. Julian, *ep.* 89b, 289A, 290D–291B (LCL 29.298–304, adapted): ἡ δὲ φιλανθρωπία πολλὴ καὶ παντοία· καὶ τὸ πεφεισμένως κολάζειν ἀνθρώπους ... καὶ τὸ τὰς χρείας ἐπανορθοῦν. Κοινωνητέον οὖν τῶν χρημάτων ἅπασιν ἀνθρώποις, ἀλλὰ τοῖς μὲν ἐπιεικέσιν ἐλευθεριώτερον, τοῖς δὲ ἀπόροις καὶ πένησιν ὅσον ἐπακρέσαι τῇ χρείᾳ· φαίην δ᾽ ἄν, εἰ καὶ παράδοχον εἰπεῖν, ὅτι καὶ τοῖς πολεμίοις ἐσθῆτος καὶ τροφῆς ὅσιον ἂν εἴη μεταδιδόναι· τῷ γὰρ ἀνθρωπίνῳ καὶ οὐ τῷ τρόπῳ δίδομεν. On the date of *ep.* 89b and its relation to *ep.* 89a (= Wright 20), see Caltabiano 1991: 123–26. Note Julian's assertion that philanthropy can be articulated through both material and immaterial gestures (φιλανθρωπία πολλὴ καὶ παντοία).

24. Julian, *ep.* 89b, 289BC, 290C–291D (LCL 29. 298, 304), arguing that humans descended from gods. For this and other classical conceptions of human unity, see Richter 2011: 87–134.

25. Kabiersch 1960: 75, presuming that *ep.* 84 was prior, maintained that Julian's philanthropy could not have derived from classical ideals because *ep.* 84 implies that giving to needy people was only done by Christians.

26. Julian *ep.* 89b, 305BC (LCL 29.336–38): διὰ τῆς λεγομένης παρ᾽ αὐτοῖς ἀγάπης καὶ ὑποδοχῆς καὶ διακονίας τραπεζῶν (ἔστι γὰρ ὥσπερ τὸ ἔργον, οὕτω δὲ καὶ τοὔνομα παρ᾽ αὐτοῖς πολύ). On Constantius's provisions at Constantinople and Antioch see the section in this chapter "Constantine and the Extension of Christian Philanthropy."

27. Julian *ep.* 89b 290D (LCL 29.303): ὅσιον ἂν εἴη.

28. Brown 2002: 77–78; Parkin 2006; Cecchet 2014; and Cecchet 2015 update Hands 1968, all providing correctives to the seminal Bolkestein 1939.

29. Holman 2001: 31–48; and Christ 2012. On Judaic norms, Lieu 2007: 14–15; and Hamel 1990: 218–19.

30. The following is based on Hiltbrunner 1994; De Romilly 1979: 44–47, 127–44; Hunger 1963; Martin 1961; Downey 1955; Bell 1949; Kortenbeutel 1940; and Tromp de Roiter 1932. I am seeking only to demonstrate here that the concessive force of classical tradition was central to Christian tradition as well. I do not believe this point has been sufficiently made before, perhaps because scholars have tended to focus on a presumed correspondence with the Latin notion of *humanitas* rather than *clementia*. True, the Vulgate uses the former to translate φιλανθρωπία in the New Testament. Hunger 1963: 9, notes, however, that it usually corresponds more closely with the latter.

31. Themistius, *or.* 34.25 (Downey-Schenkl-Norman, 2.229), dated ca. 384; see Penella 2000: 38–40. Soz., *HE* 9.5, claims that Hunnic warriors decided to defect to the Romans after hearing of the emperor's *philanthrōpia*.

32. Hunger 1963: 12.

33. Finn 2006a: 216; cf. Kabiersch 1960: 26–49. While noting that Kabiersch's distinction between classical and Christian philanthropy is too schematic, Weimer 1995: 233n178, similarly distinguishes "imperial" clemency from "universal" philanthropic giving.

34. Ps.-Aristotle, *Ath. Pol.* 16.2 (Chambers, 13–14; I underline the emphatic *kai*): φιλάνθρωπος ἦν καὶ πρᾷος <u>καὶ</u> τοῖς ἁμαρτάνουσι συγγνωμονικός, καὶ δὴ <u>καὶ</u> τοῖς ἀ[πό]ροις προεδάνειζε χρήματα ... ὥστε διατρέφεσθαι γεωργοῦντας. Cf. Dion. Hal., *Ant. Rom.* 2.9.3, 3.1.5, 4.10.1 (*aporoi*), 5.22.1, 10.57.4 (*penētes*). In *ep.* 89b Julian merges both discourses, using *penētes* and *aporoi* to describe the poor who received Christian *philanthrōpia*.

35. Diog. Laert., *v.Phil.* 3.98 (Long, 1.159–60, underlining words indicating inclusivity): τὸν ἐντυχόντα <u>πάντα</u> προσαγορεύουσα ... βοηθητικὸς ἢ <u>παντὶ</u> τῷ ἀτυχοῦντι. Lucian, *Timon* 8 (Macleod, 313): φιλανθρωπία καὶ ὁ πρὸς τοὺς δεομένους <u>ἅπαντας</u> οἶκτος. Cf. Philostratus, *Ep. et dial.* 7.1.

36. Themistius, *or.* 1.6 (Schenkl-Downey-Norman, 1.10; trans. Heather-Moncour, 83). Note that Themistius is not saying that a poor person is unlikely to show philanthropy, but that a person who lives a circumscribed existence is unlikely to do so.

37. See Seneca, *Ben.* 4.29.2; and Marcus Aurelius, *Med.* 12.26.1 (cf. Gellius, *Noct.* 9.2; Diog. Laert., *v.Phil.* 5.1.17, 21); with Kabiersch 1960: 32–33, 70–73. On differences between *philanthrōpia* and *humanitas*, see Hunger 1963: 9.

38. Griffin 2003: 102–3, adding that Seneca and others were mainly interested in promoting exchanges among aristocrats.

39. Parkin 2006: 61–66.

40. Konstan 2006: 210, 218; Konstan 2001. However, as noted by Christ 2013: 213–16; and Cecchet 2015: 141–70, Athenian orators intertwined philanthropy with pity and forgiveness, so these ideas must have been closely connected by average listeners.

41. Winslow 1965: 353–54. Among non-Christian authors, Philo alone associates it with *eusebeia*. See Tromp de Roiter 1932: 294–95; and Bolkestein 1939: 427–28.

42. Mt 5:42–48: τῷ αἰτοῦντί σε δός, καὶ τὸν θέλοντα ἀπὸ σοῦ δανίσθαι μὴ ἀποστραφῇς. [43]Ἠκούσατε ὅτι ἐρρέθη, Ἀγαπήσεις τὸν πλησίον σου καὶ μισήσεις τὸν ἐχθρόν σου. [44] ἐγὼ δὲ λέγω ὑμῖν, ἀγαπᾶτε τοὺς ἐχθροὺς ὑμῶν καὶ προσεύχεσθε ὑπὲρ τῶν διωκόντων ὑμᾶς, [45] ὅπως γένησθε υἱοὶ τοῦ πατρὸς ὑμῶν τοῦ ἐν οὐρανοῖς, ὅτι τὸν αὐτοῦ ἀνατέλλει ἐπὶ πονηροὺς καὶ ἀγαθοὺς καὶ βρέχει ἐπὶ δικαίους καὶ ἀδίκους. Cf. Lk 6:30: παντὶ αἰτοῦντί σε δίδου.

43. Hermas, *Pastor* 27.4–6. Cf. Countryman 1980: 107–8; and Harnack 1961: 147–98. Dassmann 1998: 16–18 notes that the *Didache* instructs givers to await worthy recipients. For *agapē* feasts as distributive mechanisms, see Hamman 1968: 153–226.

44. Horden 2012: 723. Also Lieu 2007: 19; Dassmann 1998; Gray 1989: 18–19; Countryman 1980: 123n11; Leclercq 1924: 2749. Lucian, *De mort. Peregrin.* 12 shows that pagan authors regarded care for widows, orphans, and clerics as distinctively Christian, but his description, perhaps informed by apologetic literature, does not imply that Christians helped people outside their community. See Edwards 1989: 95. On Paul's admonitions that Christians show each other charity, see Constantelos 1991: 12–13, but there is no evidence that Paul was referring to non-Christians or that early churches pursued (or sought to fund) any extramural "philanthropic mission."

45. For the setting, see Brown 1988: 124–39; Jakab 2001: 257–92; and Finn 2006a: 187.

46. Clem. Alex., *Quis div. salv.* 31.9 (SC 537.184): Θεοῦ γὰρ ὄντως ἡ τοιαύτη φιλοδωρία. Philo also frequently mentions *philodōria* as an attribute of God.

47. Clem. Alex., *Quis div. salv.* 33.2–6 (SC 537.186–88): πᾶσιν ... τοῖς τοῦ θεοῦ μαθηταῖς ἀπογεγραμμένοις.

48. Clem. Alex., *Quis div. salv.* 36.1 (SC 537.192): τινὲς καὶ τῶν ἐκλεκτῶν ἐκλεκτότεροι. Cf. 30.1 (178) and 31.6–9 (182–84).

49. For the phrase "enrolled disciples," Clem. Alex., *Quis div. salv.* 33.5 (Greek text above, in note 47); in 34.2–3, Clement explains that these would offer donors prayers in return, on which arrangement, see Nardi and Descourtieux 2011: 51–53. By the third century, ascetics were considered a privileged Christian group in Syrian and Mediterranean churches; see, e.g., Athen., *leg. pro Chr.* 33; on Clement's sages, see Brown 1988: 134–39.

50. Clem. Alex., *Quis div. salv.* 19.2–3 (SC 537.148): γνήσιος πτωχὸς καὶ νόθος ἄλλος πτωχὸς καὶ ψευδώνυμος. ὃ μὲν κατὰ πνεῦμα πτωχός, τὸ ἴδιον, ὃ δὲ κατὰ κόσμον, τὸ ἀλλότριον. Cf. 11.3–4 and 17.4. On Clement's distinctions, see Nardi 1983; and Paterson 2016. I do not see that Clement advocates giving to the poor mentioned in 17.4, as others have assumed.

51. *SyrD* 8 (CSCO 401.94, 97; trans. Vööbus, 90, 92) and 18 (407.183; trans. Vööbus 165); for the inference that the strangers came from another community, 12 (CSCO 407.146, 148; trans. Vööbus 132, 134). On this list and the responsibilities it entailed for clerics, Schöllgen 1998: 84–85; Dassmann 1998: 30–36.

52. Clem. Alex., *Quis div. salv.* 1.4, 3.5.

53. Pétré 1948: 208–11 notes that, when used, it almost exclusively refers to God's act of incarnation, ability to forgive, or (especially in Origen) indiscriminate love of humanity. It does not refer to material gifts before the fourth century.

54. *Hom. Clem.* 12.25.3–6 (GCS 42.187).

55. *Hom. Clem.* 12.25.7–8 (GCS 42.187).

56. *Hom. Clem.* 12.26.5 (GCS 42.187): εἰ μὲν οὖν ἡ ἐλεήσασα ξενοδόχος καὶ ἐχθροὺς ἀδικήσαντας ἐλεῶσα εὐεργέτει, φιλάνθρωπος ἂν ἦν. . . . φιλάνθρωπός ἐστιν ὁ καὶ ἐχθροὺς εὐεργετῶν.

57. *Hom. Clem.* 12.26.6–8 (GCS 42.187–88): φιλανθρωπία ἐστὶν ἀρρενόθηλυς, ἧς τὸ θῆλυ μέρος ἐλεημοσύνη λέγεται, τὸ δὲ ἄρρεν αὐτῆς ἀγάπη πρὸς τὸν πλησίον ὠνόμασται· πλησίον δὲ ἀνθρώπῳ ἐστὶν ὁ πᾶς ἄνθρωπος, οὐχ ὅ τις ἄνθρωπος· ἄνθρωπος γάρ ἐστιν καὶ ὁ κακὸς καὶ ἀγαθὸς καὶ ὁ ἐχθρὸς καὶ ὁ φίλος. χρὴ οὖν τὸν φιλανθρωπίαν ἀσκοῦντα μιμητὴν εἶναι τοῦ θεοῦ εὐεργετοῦντα δικαίους καὶ ἀδίκους, ὡς αὐτὸς ὁ θεὸς πᾶσιν ἐν τῷ νῦν κόσμῳ τόν τε ἥλιον καὶ τοὺς ὑετοὺς αὐτοῦ παρέχων. εἰ δὲ θέλεις ἀγαθοὺς μὲν εὐεργετεῖν, κακοὺς δὲ μηκέτι ἢ καὶ κολάζειν, κριτοῦ ἔργον ἐπιχειρεῖς πράττειν, οὐ τὸ τῆς φιλανθρωπίας σπουδάζεις ἔχειν.

58. *Hom. Clem.* 32.4–7 (GCS 42.191): ἀγάπη ἡ πρὸς πάντα ἄνθρωπον τελεία τὸ ἄρρεν μέρος ἐστιν οὖσα τῆς φιλανθρωπίας, τὸ δὲ ἐλεεῖν τὸ θῆλυ μέρος ἐστὶν αὐτῆς. ὅπερ ἐστὶν . . . ἁπαξαπλῶς τὸν ἐν συμφοραῖς ἐλεῆσαι.

59. See Kelley 2006: 1–27; and Bremmer 2010: 6–9. Jones 1982 is an indispensable guide through earlier scholarship.

60. The major exception is van Kooten 2010, who compares it to strands of classical thought but makes different inferences than presented here. Hiltbrunner 1994: 744 mentions it only as a theoretical analysis of "reine philanthropia."

61. Perhaps made known through popular diatribes such as described in Konstan 2006: 216.

62. Acts 27:3: φιλανθρώπως τε ὁ Ἰούλιος τῷ Παύλῳ χρησάμενος ἐπέτρεψεν πρὸς τοὺς φίλους πορευθέντι ἐπιμελείας τυχεῖν. . . . Acts 28:2: βάρβαροι παρεῖχον οὐ τὴν τυχοῦσαν φιλανθρωπίαν ἡμῖν.

63. Ti 3:4: ὅτε δὲ ἡ χρηστότης καὶ ἡ φιλανθρωπία ἐπεφάνη τοῦ σωτῆρος ἡμῶν θεοῦ, οὐκ ἐξ ἔργων τῶν ἐν δικαιοσύνῃ ἃ ἐποιήσαμεν ἡμεῖς ἀλλὰ κατὰ τὸ αὐτοῦ ἔλεος ἔσωσεν. The Peshitta uses *mraḥmānutā* for philanthropy and *raḥmē* for mercy.

64. Of the thirteen times it appears in LXX, ten refer to acts of clemency: 1 Ezr 8:10; Est 8:12l; 2 Macc 4:11, 6:22, 9:27, 13:23, 14:9; 3 Macc 3:15, 18, 20; 4 Macc 5:12. All other references are in Ws 1:6, 7:23, 12:19, each instance listed among attributes of a wise man. For Hellenistic uses of *philanthrōpia*, see Cavallero 2000–2001. Hiltbrunner 1990 proposes that its infrequency in LXX stems from its association with Greek political domination.

65. Brown 2002: 22–25; also Dassmann 1998; and Zeisel 1975: 163–68.

66. *SyrD* 17 (CSCO 407.178 [Syr]): *meskinē mhaymnē* (Vööbus translates as "faithful poor"); and 14 (152/142). Cf. 17 (177/161); 18 (184/166). Such caution is even more pronounced in the fourth-century version of the manual *Const. Ap.* 2.4.3, 3.4.3, 4.4.1. For Alexandria, see Origen, *Comm. in Mt.* 61 (PG 13.1697AC); with Vogt 1993: 196. For Rome, Eus. Caes., *HE* 6.43.11 (SC 41.156): χήρας σὺν θλιβομένοις ὑπὲρ χιλίας πεντακοσίας. Schöllgen 1998: 100 estimates that clerics and their families would have represented six hundred claimants.

67. See *Hom. Clem.* 3.71.5; *SyrD* 18; and Eus. Caes., *HE* 7.22.7, 9.8.14, 10.8.11; with Horden 2012: 724; and Harnack 1961: 171–73.

68. *v.Pach.gr. prim.* 4–5. Dionysius of Alexandria reports that individual Christians helped the sick when others did not during the third-century plague but does not suggest this happened at an institutional level. Eus. Caes., *HE* 7.22.1–11, 23.7–8.

69. Eus. Caes., *HE* 10.8.11, 9.2 (SC 55. 116, 118–19; trans. Williamson, 331, adapted); and Eus. Caes., *v.Const.* 1.9.1, 1.45.3, 4.31.1 (SC 559.188, 246, 492); also 2.20.1.

70. Eus. Caes., *v.Const.* 1.43.1–2 (SC 559.240–42; I underline the emphatic *kai* and the distributive *men... de...*): καὶ τοῖς ἔξωθεν αὐτῷ προσιοῦσι φιλάνθρωπον καὶ εὐεργετικὸν παρέχων ἑαυτόν, τοῖς μὲν ἐπ’ ἀγορᾶς μεταιτοῦσιν οἰκτροῖς τισι καὶ ἀπερριμμένοις οὐ χρημάτων μόνον γε τῆς ἀναγκαίας τροφῆς ἀλλὰ καὶ σκέπης εὐσχήμονος τοῦ σώματος προὐνόει, τοῖς δ’ εὖ μὲν τὰ πρῶτα γεγονόσι βίου δὲ μεταβλῇ δυστυχήσασι δαψιλεστέρας παρεῖχε τὰς χορηγίας.

71. Chrys., *In Mt.* 72.3 (PG 58.666): Αὐτὸ δὲ τὸ μυστήριον πόσου ἐλέου, πόσης φιλανθρωπίας.

72. Brown 2002: 26–33. On the history of the term *xenodocheion* and its relation to other terms, see Kislinger 1984. The terminology never became completely stable or uniform, as observed in Patlagean 1977: 195–96. In Syriac, ’aksenodokā remained the standard loan word for "hospital." For papyrological evidence, see Serfass 2008, including several examples named after donors.

73. Leont. Neap. *v.Jo.Eleem.* 27. For a description of the nasty conditions—fleas, bedbugs, mice, fetid smells—found in one outside Constantinople, see Jo. Eph., *HE* 3.2.5.

74. *Chron. Pascale* 282 and 285 (Dindorf, 535, 545) refer to *xenodocheia* at Antioch and Constantinople in 349 and 360 CE and to gifts made to the latter by Constantius II (r. 337–361). On the Constantinopolitan foundations and their association with Bishop Macedonius (sed. 342–46, 351–360) and a deacon, Marathonius, see Dagron 1970; and Miller 1997: 76–81, who speculates that the Antiochene facility was born out of competition for adherents during the Arian controversy. Brown 2002: 36–38 sees precedent for use of *xenodocheia* to serve the homeless in later sources for Armenia, but whether these illuminate Roman practice is uncertain: see note 112.

75. Bas. Caes., *hom.* 8.8 (PG 31.325A).

76. Greg. Nyss., *In Bas.* 17 (Heil-Cavarnos-Lendle, 124): καὶ τοῖς τῶν Ἰουδαίων παισὶν ἐκ τοῦ ἴσου προθεῖναι τῆς φιλανθρωπίας ταύτης τὴν μετουσίαν. For Basil's soup relief, Greg. Naz., *or.* 43.35–36. Gregory of Nyssa's reference to a Jewish community suggests an inspiration for Basil's choice of soup to handle this crisis. As pointed out by Herrin 2013a: 269, soup has always been a ways to stretch limited resources, but during the second and third centuries, rabbis instituted soup kitchens (*tamhui*) to provide food on a regular (theoretically daily) basis to unprivileged poor people within their communities. See Gardner (2015): 67–83.

77. On the evidence of Aphrahat, see Becker 2002; on synagogue practices, Gardner 2015. Widows and orphans were established as primary Christian constituents by the New Testament in James 1:27.

78. Περὶ Φιλοπτωχίας is the title attested for *or.* 14 in Jerome, *De vir. ill.* 117 (ca. 393) and should be preferred to Περὶ Πτωχοτροφίας, which appears in many manuscripts. No edition has replaced Louvard's in PG 35.857–909. Holman 2001: 143–45 discusses its transmission and probable influence on Gregory of Nyssa's two *de pauperibus amandis* sermons. Those, however, mention *philanthrōpia* only four times; *or.* 14 does twenty-two times.

79. Thus McGuckin 2001: 148–51. For its formal features and place in Gregory's oeuvre, see Daley 1999: 454–58; Meredith 1998: 100–101; and Winslow 1965. The traditional date is based on its presumed relevance to Basil's Basilias.

80. For Gregory's effort to help listeners appreciate suffering, see Wessel 2016: 38–48; for theological aspects, Holman 2001: 143–47.

81. Greg. Naz., *or.* 14.5 (PG 35.864C–865A): Πᾶσι μὲν δὴ πτωχοῖς ἀνοικτέον τὰ σπλάγχνα, καὶ τοῖς καθ' ἡντιναοῦν αἰτίαν κακοπαθοῦσι . . . πάντες γὰρ ὁμοίως ἐλεεινοί. . . . καὶ τούτων αὐτῶν οἱ παρ' ἀξίαν κακοπαθοῦντες, τῶν ἐν ἔθει τοῦ δυστυχεῖν ὄντων ἐλεεινότεροι.

82. Gregory is the earliest Christian author to cast leprosy as "the sacred disease," a designation classical authors had used to describe epilepsy. See Lascartos 1996.

83. Greg. Naz., *or.* 14. 9–10 (PG 35.868C–69C).

84. Greg. Naz., *or.* 14. 14 (PG 35.876A): οἱ κατὰ Θεὸν ἡμῶν ἀδελφοί, κἂν μὴ βούλησθε.

85. For this stewardship excursus, one of the longest in early Christian literature, see Winslow 1965: 357–58; and Coulie 1985: 171–77. McGuckin 2001: 152 notes that Gregory's connection of human greed to the Fall follows Origen.

86. Greg. Naz., *or.* 14. 26 (PG 35.892B): βλέπε μοι τὴν πρώτην ἰσονομίαν, μὴ τὴν τελευταίαν διαίρεσιν.

87. Greg. Naz., *or.* 14. 15–21 (PG 35.876B–887B).

88. Greg. Naz., *or.* 14. 24–26 (PG 35.889A): μιμήσθε ἰσότητα θεοῦ, καὶ οὐδεὶς ἔσται πένης. (889C): Μιμησώμεθα νόμον Θεοῦ τὸν ἀνωτάτω καὶ πρῶτον, ὃς βρέχει μὲν ἐπὶ δικαίους καὶ ἁμαρτωλούς, ἀνατέλλει δὲ πᾶσιν ὁμοίως τὸν ἥλιον. . . . τό τε τῆς φύσεως ὁμότιμον ἰσότητι τῆς δωρεᾶς τιμῶν.

89. Greg. Naz., *or.* 14. 5 (PG 35.864BC).

90. Greg. Naz., *or.* 14. 23 (PG 35.888BC); for this passage, see chapter 1, "The Christian Ideal of Stewardship."

91. Greg. Naz., *or.* 14. 27 (PG 35.892D–893C).

92. Greg. Naz., *or.* 14. 38 (PG 35.908C); cf. 39 (909A).

93. Greg. Naz., *or.* 14. 12 (PG 35.872D–873A).

94. Greg. Naz., *or.* 14. 10 and 11 (PG 35. 869B and 872B). Inhumanity is a recurrent theme; see also Greg. Naz., *or.* 14. 28 (896B).

95. Greg. Naz., *or.* 14. 27 (PG 35.896A).

96. Greg. Naz., *or.* 14. 36 (PG 35.905B).

97. Greg. Naz., *or.* 14. 29-35 (PG 35.896C-904A). Isid. Pel., *ep.*1489 (SC 454.152) explains that lepers were being divinely punished for their parents' sins. See Miller and Nesbitt 2014: 38-40.

98. Greg. Naz., *or.* 14. 6 (PG 35.865AC).

99. Greg. Naz., *or.* 14. 10 (PG 35.869A), 12 (872C).

100. Greg. Naz., *or.* 14. 7 (PG 35.865C); cf. 35 (904A). On this theme, see Holman 2001: 148-53.

101. Greg. Naz., *or.* 14. 12 (PG 35.873A).

102. Greg. Naz., *or.* 14. 15 (PG 35.876BC): οἱ Χριστοῦ μαθηταὶ τοῦ πράου καὶ φιλανθρώπου ... τοῦ δι' ἡμᾶς πτωχεύσαντος τὴν σάρκα ταύτην καὶ τὸ γεῶδες σκῆνος ... ἵνα ἡμεῖς, οἱ τοσοῦτον εὐσπλαγχανίας καὶ συμπαθείας λαβόντες ὑποδείγμα; ... ἐκ τῆς ἴσης ἀσθενείας μαθοῦσα τὸ εὐσεβὲς καὶ φιλάνθρωπον.

103. Greg. Naz., *or.* 14. 8 (PG 35.868B); cf. 18 (880C).

104. Greg. Naz., *or.* 14. 5 (PG 35.865A): οἱ παρ' ἀξίαν κακοπαθοῦντες. 27 (893A): σὺ δὲ πεσόντα μὴ παρίδῃς. This applies to Gregory of Nyssa's sermons as well. See Caner 2018b: 44.

105. Greg. Naz., *or.* 14.1 (PG 36.858D-860A) πτωχοὶ ... ἅπαντες, καὶ τῆς θείας χάριτος ἐπιδεεῖς κἂν ἄλλος ἄλλου προέχειν δοκῇ.

106. Quoted from Rousseau 1994: 139; and Horden 2012: 716-17; for further discussion, see Caner 2018b: 26. Such descriptions are largely inspired by Basil's vague description in *ep.* 94 and Gregory of Nazianzus's panegyrical description in *or.* 43.63.

107. The following summarizes Caner 2018b. Horden 2012: 719 points out that since the Basilias provided overnight medical care, it qualifies to be called a hospital in a modern sense. Yet doing so misleadingly connotes a hospital open to all.

108. Thdt., *HE* 4.16.13 (GCS nF. 5.245): χωρία τὰ κάλλιστα ὧν εἶχεν αὐτόθι τοῖς ὑπ' αὐτοῦ φροντιζομένοις δωρήσασθαι πένησιν, οἳ τὸ σῶμα ἅπαν λελωβημένοι πλείονος ὅτι μάλιστα θεραπείας προσδέονται.

109. As noted in, for example, Gläser 1986. Most (but not all) scholars recognize that the Basilias featured a leprosarium, but virtually all have assumed that it was meant for more than lepers.

110. Greg. Presb., *v.Greg.Naz.* 11 (CCSG 44.154-56): Ὁρῶν ὁ μέγας Βασίλειος τοὺς λωβουμένους ἀδελφοὺς λίαν μὲν ἐλεεινοὺς καὶ συμπαθείας ἀξίους, ἥκιστα δὲ οἰκτειρομένους, καὶ ὡς ἄγος τι καὶ μίασμα καὶ ἀποτρόπαιον τοῖς πολλοῖς ὄντας δι' ἀμαθίαν καὶ μισανθρωπίαν, καὶ εἰς ἔννοιαν τῆς φύσεως ἐλθών, βουλὴν προτίθεται, εὐσεβῆ καὶ τῆς ἐκείνου φιλαδελφίας ἀξίαν. οἴκους παμμεγέθεις ἀναδειμάμενος καὶ προσόδους ἐτησίας τάξας, ἃς ἐκ τῶν εὐπόρων περιεποιήσατο, προτρέψας συνέσεως λόγοις πρὸς τὴν ἐπίδοσιν, πάντας τοὺς ἀσθενεῖς εἰς ταὐτὸν ἤθροισε, φροντιστήρια ταῦτα καλέσας πτωχῶν.

111. Aretaeus, *caus.*, 4.13.19. For fuller discussion, Caner 2018b: 35-38.

112. See Caner 2018b: 19, 46-47. Brown 2002: 36-38 proposes that Basil was inspired by secular imperial initiatives in Armenia, Antioch, and Constantinople. I am not persuaded— on the Armenian evidence, see the criticism implicit in Horden 2012: 722, 725—but perhaps Eustathius himself was inspired by governmental initiatives established near his region?

113. Bas. Caes., *ep.* 94 (Courtonne, 206): οἴκησιν . . . ὑποβεβηκυίας τοῖς θεραπευταῖς τοῦ θείου. cf. Lampe, s.v. θεραπευτής 1 b. Van Dam 1996: 54 notes that the conventional dating of this letter to the early 370s is problematic.

114. Bas. Caes., *In Ps. 33* (PG 29: 361); Bas. Caes., *RB* 204 (PG 31: 1217); and Bas. Caes., *RF* 20 (969–72). Cf. Caner 2018b: 39–40.

115. Greg. Nyss., *In Bas.* 21 (Heil-Cavarnos-Lendle, 127–28): μαρτυρίου σκηνὴν καὶ σωματικῶς μὲν ἐν τῷ προαστείῳ κατεσκευάσατο, τοὺς πτωχοὺς τῷ σώματι πτωχοὺς τῷ πνεύματι διὰ τῆς ἀγαθῆς διδασκαλίας εἶναι ποιήσας. On this passage, see Caner 2018b: 39.

116. Bas. Caes., *ep.* 94 (Courtonne, 206): καταγώγια τοῖς ξένοις οἰκοδομοῦντες, τοῖς τε κατὰ πάροδον ἐπιφοιτῶσι καὶ τοῖς θεραπείας τινὸς διὰ τὴν ἀσθένειαν δεομένοις, καὶ τὴν ἀναγκαίαν τούτοις παραμυθίαν ἐγκαθιστῶντες, τοὺς νοσοκομοῦντας, τοὺς ἰατρεύοντας, τὰ νωτοφόρα, τοὺς παραπέμποντας· τούτοις ἀνάγκη καὶ τέχνας ἔπεσθαι, τάς τε πρὸς τὸ ζῆν ἀναγκαίας . . . οἴκους πάλιν ἑτέρους ταῖς ἐργασίαις ἐπιτηδείους. For the martyrium, see Bas. Caes. *ep.* 174.

117. Others have thought *or.* 14 too long to have been spoken in public, but it is no longer than Gregory's funeral oration for Basil (*or.* 43). Performance at the Basilias would account for references to an ongoing martyr's festival, the sound of lepers' songs outside, and the opportunity to donate bandages or "philosophize" with lepers about their infirmities. Greg. Naz., *or.* 14. 9, 13, 15, 27, and 40 (PG 35: 868C, 873, 876BC, 892D–893C, 909C).

118. Greg. Naz., *or.* 14. 5 (865A).

119. Bas. Caes., *RB* 100, 101 and 302 (PG 31.1152B, 1152D–53A, 1296C); Bas. Caes., *ep.* 105.3. For a comparison to advice of Barsanuphius and John on similar issues, see Caner 2008: 226–29.

120. Asterius, *hom.* 1.10.1–4, a passage that sharply distinguishes between (dishonorable) *penētes* and (honorable) *ptōchoi.*

121. Bas. Caes., *RB* 205 (PG 31: 1217); and esp. Bas. Caes., *In Ps. 33* (PG 29: 361). As the scriptural *ptōchos* par excellence, Lazarus was considered a leper. Holman 2001: 161.

122. Bas. Caes., *In Ps.14 hom.1.6* (PG 29.261C–64B): Ἐπειδὴ γὰρ πολλοὶ ὑπερβαίνοντες τὴν χρῆσιν τῶν ἀναγκαίων . . . ἀναγκαίως παρὰ τοῖς τὴν ἐπιμέλειαν τῶν πτωχῶν πεπιστευμένοις ἡ συγκομιδὴ τῶν χρημάτων ἐγίνετο, ὥστε ἐκεῖθεν ἐπιστημόνως καὶ οἰκονομικῶς ταῖς ἑκάστου χρείαις τὴν διανομὴν τῶν ἀναγκαίων γίνεσθαι.

123. Bas. Caes., *In Ps.14 hom.1.6* (PG 29.261C–64B): ἡ περὶ τὴν θεραπείαν τῶν δεομένων οἰκονομία οὐ παρὰ πάντων ὠφελίμως ἐνεργεῖσθαι δύναται. Τοῖς γὰρ δὴ τὰ θρηνώδη μέλη πρὸς τὴν τῶν γυναικῶν ἀπάτην συντιθεῖσι . . . οὐ πάντως τὸ δαψιλὲς τῆς διακονίας ὠφέλιμον . . . μικρᾷ δόσει χρὴ τὴν τῶν τοιούτων ὑλακὴν ἀπωθεῖσθαι, τὸ δὲ συμπαθὲς καὶ φιλάδελφον ἐπιδεικνυμένους, ἐν τοῖς μεθ᾽ ὑπομονῆς τὴν θλῖψιν φέρειν δεδιδαγμένοις.

124. Monasticism being the main example. See Rousseau 1994; and Sherk 2004.

125. Greg. Naz., *or.* 43.63.1 (Bernardi, 260): Καλὸν φιλανθρωπία καὶ πτωχοτροφία καὶ τὸ τῆς ἀνθρωπίνης ἀσθενείας βοήθημα.

126. For Chrysostom: Martyrius, Ps.-, *or. fun.* 64 (the other references to *philanthrōpia* in this oration do not pertain to Chrysostom). For Rabbula, *Pan. Rabb.* (Overbeck, 203; trans. Doran, 101), highlighting Rabbula's *mraḥmānutā,* mentioned only in relation to his leprosarium.

127. Soc., *HE* 7.25.5–8 (GCS n.F.1.373): Βουλήσῃ δέ που πάντως τοῖς αἰσχυνομένοις τὴν αἴτησιν, ἀλλ᾽ οὐχὶ τοῖς ἐμπορίαν διὰ βίου τὴν γαστέρα προτεθεικόσι. Διδοὺς τοίνυν μηδὲ

θρησκείαν λογίσῃ κατὰ τοῦτο τὸ μέρος, ἑνὸς καὶ μόνου γενόμενος τοῦ τρέφειν τοὺς πεινῶντας, ἀλλὰ μὴ λογιστεύειν τοὺς τὸν ἡμέτερον τρόπον μὴ φρονοῦντας.

128. Philipsborn 1961 is still useful; in general, Miller 1997: 90–95.

129. Finn 2006a: 67–74; for the categorical features of such lists, Roueché 2007; Hermann-Otto 2003; Brown 2002: 65, 78; and Dassmann 1998: 34–38.

130. *Const. Ap.* 3.4.4 (SC 320.126): Δῆλον δὲ ὡς τῷ χρῄζοντι κατὰ ἀλήθειαν.

131. Dassmann 1998: 32–36, though the doctors Basil mentions in *ep.*94 may have served this purpose at the Basilias. For letters of certification, see Council of Antioch, *can.* 7; Council of Chalcedon, *can.* 11; with Second Council of Ephesus, *Acta* (Flemming, 82). For possible papyrus examples, Brown 2002: 65–66; and Schmelz 2002: 256–61.

132. *AP* N 282 and 287 (*ROC* 14.373, 375). See the section in this chapter "'To Each According to Rank.'"

133. Caner, forthcoming-a; Finn 2006a: 35–67.

134. Eus. Caes., *HE* 6.43.11 (SC 41.156): χήρας σὺν θλιβομένοις, which may have been a technical term, taken from Psalms. See *Const. Ap.* 2.25, 27, 28, 31, 32; 3.19; 4.8. Cf. the description of recipients in Clem. Alex., *Quis div. salv.* 34.2 (SC 537.190). Describing the generosity of Epiphanius of Salamis (310–403), Soz., *HE* 7.27.2 (Hansen, 342) glosses "needy people" as "those who had suffered shipwrecks or had otherwise fallen into misfortune,"—that is, *ptōchoi.* The fifth- or sixth-century *Canons of Marutha* 47.9 (Vööbus, 127–28) also focuses on "fallenness," explaining, "If there is a believer upon whom has come the ruin, and he has not squandered his possessions in gluttony [or] drinking . . . everyone shall give something which suffices from his hands . . . and he shall be brought out from the necessity that had come upon him." This seems to refer to debt.

135. Chrys., *In Mt.* 66.3 (PG 58.630): ἐπαρκεῖ καθ' ἑκάστην ἡμέραν χήραις, ὅσαις παρθένοις· καὶ γὰρ εἰς τὸν τῶν τρισχιλίων ἀριθμὸν ὁ κατάλογος αὐτῶν ἔφθασε. Μετὰ τούτων τοῖς τὸ δεσμωτήριον οἰκοῦσι, τοῖς ἐν τῷ ξενοδοχείῳ κάμνουσι, τοῖς ὑγιαίνουσι, τοῖς ἀποδημοῦσι, τοῖς τὰ σώματα λελωβημένοις, τοῖς τῷ θυσιαστηρίῳ προσεδρεύουσι, καὶ τροφῆς καὶ ἐνδυμάτων ἕνεκεν, τοῖς ἁπλῶς προσιοῦσι καθ' ἑκάστην ἡμέραν. Cf. Chrys., *sacer.* 3.16–17.

136. Ephr. Gr., *De pauperum amore.* (Phrantzoles, 137): χήραι, ὀρφανοί, ἀδύνατοι, ἀνάπηροι, χωλοί, τυφλοί, λεπροί, καὶ πάντες οἱ ταῖς θύραις τῶν ἐκκλησιῶν παρακαθεζόμενοι πένητες.

137. Bars. et Jo., *resp.* 831. On asylum for debtors within church perimeters, see Caseau 2003: 67–69; on ecclesiastical asylum and its relation to episcopal poor care more generally, Rapp 2005: 253–60. Jo. Eph., *v.SS.Or.* 21 ("Life of Thomas the Armenian"; PO 17.289), lists "those who had creditors" as recipients of Thomas's alms in addition to monks and the needy and afflicted; Geront., *v.Mel. gr.* 9, says that Melania, besides tending the sick, the poor, and strangers, also paid off the debts of anyone held in prison for that reason. Cf. *Canons of Marutha* 49.7.

138. Ath., Ps.-, *Can. Ath.* 61 (Reidel-Crum, 127), and 80–82 (49–50). Roger Bagnall informs me that an *oipe* was roughly one-tenth of an *artab*, and an *artab* of wheat constituted a month's supply for an individual. Jones 1964: 792. Wipszycka 2015: 29–31 dates this manual to the "first half of the fifth century."

139. Ath., Ps.-, *Can. Ath.* 80 (Reidel-Crum, 49).

140. Ath., Ps.-, *Can. Ath.* 82 (Reidel-Crum, 50).

141. Leont. Neap., *v.Jo.Eleem.* 1 (Festugière-Rydén, 347–48): πτωχοὺς καὶ ἐπαίτας. . . . ἐπέτρεψεν τούτους ἡμέριον διορίζεσθαι ἐκ τοῦ οἰκείου αὐτοῦ διαδότου τὴν ἐπαρκοῦσαν χρείαν αὐτοῖς. This hagiography and its subject and author are discussed in chapter 3.

142. *Pan. Rabb.* (Overbeck, 190, 6; trans. Doran, 89).

143. Martyrius, Ps.-, *or. fun.* 61 (Wallraff, 114; trans. Barnes-Bevan, 74).

144. Chrys., *In 1 Cor.* 21.6–7 (PG 61.179–80); cf. *In Act.* 45.4 (60.319). On his ranking of the church's affluence, *In Mt.* 66.3 (58.630); with Mayer 2009: 91–92; and Brown 2002: 65.

145. Bas. Caes., *ep.* 285, remarks that philanthropic institutions cost more than churches received.

146. Chrys., *Laz. et div.* 2.4 (PG 48.989).

147. Chrys., *Laz. et div.* 1.6, and 6.5 (PG 48.971, 1034). On these sermons, see Cardman 2008. In Chrys., *mut. nom.* (PG 51.152), Lazarus is described as πάντων πτωχότερος ὢν ἐν τῷ κόσμῳ.

148. Chrys., *Laz. et div.* 2.5–6 (PG 48.989–991; trans. Roth, 52–53, adapted):˙Ἐλεημοσύνη διὰ τοῦτο λέγεται, ὅτι καὶ τοῖς ἀναξίοις δίδομεν. . . . Ἀξία γὰρ τοῦ πένητος ἡ χρεία μόνον ἐστί· κἂν ὁστισοῦν μετὰ ταύτης ἔλθῃ πρὸς ἡμᾶς ποτε, μηδὲν περιεργαζώμεθα πλέον οὐ γὰρ τῷ τρόπῳ παρέχομεν, ἀλλὰ τῷ ἀνθρώπῳ· οὐδὲ διὰ τὴν ἀρετὴν αὐτὸν, ἀλλὰ διὰ τὴν συμφορὰν ἐλεῶμεν. . . . Εἰ γὰρ μέλλοιμεν τὴν ἀξίαν ἐπιζητεῖν ἐπὶ τῶν συνδούλων τῶν ἡμετέρων, καὶ ἀκριβολογεῖσθαι, τοῦτο καὶ ὁ Θεὸς ἐφ᾽ ἡμῶν ἐργάσεται· καὶ ζητοῦντες τοὺς ὁμοδούλους ἀπαιτῆσαι εὐθύνας, αὐτοὶ τῆς ἄνωθεν ἐκπεσούμεθα φιλανθρωπίας.

149. Chrys., *In Heb.* 11.10 (PG 63.95); cf. Chrys., *compunct.* 1.4 (47.399); Chrys., *In Mt.* 35.4–5 (57:411); and Chrys., *In Phil.* 1.5 (62.190).

150. Chrys., *In Mt.* 66.3 (PG 58.630).

151. On Chrysostom's critique of civic patronage, see Sandwell 2007: 206; and Natali 1982. I do not want to exaggerate the difference between him and Cappadocians like Gregory of Nazianzus; he also drew on classical tropes to promote almsgiving (see Leyerle 1994) and was ambivalent about beggars (Mayer 2009). But I find nothing in Chrysostom like Basil's classicizing description of Christian almsgiving in *hom.* 6.3, even if Basil goes on to identify it with *philanthrōpia*.

152. Leont. Neap., *v.Jo.Eleem.* 6 (Festugière-Rydén, 351) invokes Lk 6:30 as a rationale for indiscriminate giving (admittedly, during a crisis).

153. Sev. Ant., *ep.Coll.1* 1.8, 17, 35. Justinian bestowed four thousand solidi on a hospice to get it running after an earthquake in Antioch in 526. Jo. Mal., *Chron.* 18.48.

154. Chrys., *In Gal.* 5.2 (PG 61.667). See also Chrys., *In 1 Cor.* 44.5 (61.578); Soc., *HE* 7.25.8; Thdt., *Interp. in ep. Pauli* (PG 82.501); and Finn 2006a: 67.

155. *Const. Ap.* 7.2.7 (SC 336.28); see also Chrys., *In Heb.*10.4 (PG 63.88).

156. Thdr. Petr., *v.Thds.* (Usener, 35, ll.1–19): ἄλλο δὲ τὸ τῶν λειπομένων ἐν τοῖς ἀναγκαίοις, πτωχῶν δὴ τούτων ὀνομαζομένων, ὁμοειδῶν δὲ τῇ φύσει ὄντων ἡμῖν, ὧν ἐποιεῖτο μάλιστα πρόνοιαν ὁ τοῦ δι᾽ ἡμᾶς πτωχεύσαντος. . . . ἑτέρους δὲ πτωχείᾳ καὶ νόσῳ ταλαιπωρουμένους. On the ruins, Weigand 1914; and Hirschfeld 1992: 159–61; on Theodore of Petra, Binns 1994: 44–45; Patrich 1995: 198; and Déroche 2004. This may be the monastery outside Bethlehem mentioned in Plac., *Itin.* 29.

157. Thdr. Petr., *v.Thds.* (Usener, 29, l.17).

158. Thdr. Petr., *v. Thds.* (Usener, 50–51), citing Bas. Caes, *RF,* pr. (PG 31: 889BC); cf. Chitty 1966: 109. Theodosius had previously run a facility in Jerusalem based on Basil's rules. On tradition of kissing lepers, Miller and Nesbitt 2015: 43–44.

159. Thdr. Petr., *v. Thds.* (Usener, 47, ll.4–5 and 85, ll.13–15) describing the gift of estates by a Comes Orientis. Cyril Scyth., *v. Thds.* 3 refers to gifts from a certain Acacius the *illustris*. The monastery's exceptional connections, wealth, and services are discussed in Di Segni 2001.

160. Cyril Scyth., *v. Thds.* 4 (Schwartz 238, ll.26–27): πρὸς τοὺς ξένους καὶ πτωχοὺς δαψιλῆ καὶ ἀπροσωπόληπτον φιλοφροσύνην.

161. Cyril Scyth., *v. Thds.* 3 (Schwartz 238,16); Thdr. Petr., *v. Thds.* 36, ll.9–11; 37, ll.18–22, 38–39, 40–41. The monastery reportedly feasted the entire region on Palm Sundays. Cf. *Test. Iobi* 10; with Rümer and Thissen 1989.

162. Thdr. Petr., *v. Thds.* 34, ll.14–20: ἄλλων μὲν ἄλλως ξενοδοχουμένων, πάντων δὲ ὁμοίως θεραπευομένων· τοῦ γὰρ ἴσου ἅπασιν ἐν ἰσότητι φυλαττομένου πληροῦται ἥ ἀρχαία τῶν ἀποστόλων παράδοσις τὸ "διεδίδοτο ἑκάστῳ καθ᾽ ὅτι ἄν τις χρείαν εἶχεν."

163. Grossman 1998: 287.

164. *v. Pach. gr. prim.* 28 (SH 19.18): κατὰ τὴν ἑκάστου διαφοράν. . . . πρὸς τὴν ἀξίαν ἑκάστου.

165. *AP* N 287 (*ROC* 17.375).

166. *AP* L 13.12 (PL 73.945–46) describes both as poor or needy (*indigentibus*). This is to be preferred to the Greek version in *AP* GS 13.13 (SC 474.238–40), which only lacks an equivalent to *indigentibus* but adds that the woman wearing older clothes was εὐποροῦσα, probably a later gloss. Chrys., *In Heb.* 11.8–9 mentions a beggar who dressed well to deceive people that he came from noble stock.

167. Cf. Leont. Neap., *v. Jo. Eleem.* 6 (Festugière-Rydén, 350–51); Marc. Diac., *v. Porph.* 94 (Grégoire-Kugener, 72–73); and Pontinus, *v. Cypr.* 9; with Brown 2002: 60, for the sliding scale applied by Gregory the Great. On concern for déclassés in the late antique West, Brown 2012: 124, 169, 345, and 467.

168. Bars. et Jo., *resp.* 617, 620–24, 631–34. On the letter collection from which John's correspondence is drawn, see chapter 4, "Gifts of Charity in the Seridos Monastery."

169. Bars. et Jo., *resp.* 630 (SC 468.56–58): Πάντας τοὺς φανερῶς λαμβάνοντας ἔχε ἐν μιᾷ τάξει, εἰ μή τις ἐν αὐτοῖς ἐστιν ἔχων ἀσθένειαν καὶ πάθος, τούτῳ γὰρ δεῖ προσθεῖναι μικρόν. Τοὺς δὲ ἐρυθριῶντας φανερῶς καὶ δημοσίᾳ λαμβάνειν, καὶ τοὺς ἐν ἀσθενείαις κατα κειμένους, ἔχε ἐν ἑτέρᾳ τάξει, παρέχων αὐτοῖς περισσὸν κατὰ τὴν χρείαν αὐτῶν.

170. Bars. et Jo., *resp.* 635 (SC 468.62): ἐν τούτῳ γὰρ δοξάζεται ὁ φιλάνθρωπος Θεός. Cf. 589 (SC 451.786), discussed in chapter 5, "Ascetic Stewardship and the Multiplication of Monastic Blessings."

171. See the sections in this chapter "Preaching Philanthropy in Christian Cappadocia" and "'To Each According to Need.'"

172. Already prominent in fourth-century sermons. See Blowers 2010; and Mayer 2009: 82–83.

173. Jo. Mosch., *prat.* 193 (PG 87.3.3072D–3073A): περιπεσὼν καὶ ἀπὸ μεγάλων γεγονὼς μικρὸς . . . πολὺ ἄνω παρέχων ἐν χρήμασι πολλῷ πλέον κάτω γέγονεν. . . . τῆς ἐσχάτης πτωχείας κατέστηκε σύμβολα. See also Jo. Mosch., *prat.* 37, 189; and Leont. Neap., *v. Jo.*

Eleem. 10, 11, 29. On Moschus and the state of his text, Booth 2014: 90–93; Pattenden 1975; and Chadwick 1974.

174. Isid. Pel., *ep.* 3.140 (PG 78.837): Μὴ καταφρόνει τῶν εὐτελεῖ σχήματι προσιόντων σοι. . . . Εἰ δὲ καὶ ἀφανεῖς εἶεν καὶ ἐξ ἀφανῶν, μηδ' οὕτως ἀποστρέφω, ἀλλ' ὄρεγε, ἐν οἷς ἂν δύναιο χεῖρα· λογιζόμενος ὅτι καὶ ἡ δοκοῦσα δυσγένεια ἀκούσιος ἐστι, καὶ οὐ μεμπτή.

175. Jo. Ruf., *v.Petr. Ib.* 27 (trans. Horn-Phenix, 37); cf. Lib., *or.* 8.3–4; Asterius, *Hom..* 2.1.3, 3.13.3; and Leont. Const., *hom.* 7.13–14.

176. Jo. Eph., *v.SS.Or.* 57 ("Life of Theodore, the Chamberlin and Castrensis"); cf. Jo. Mal., *Chron.* 18.3; and Procop., *HA* 29.24–25.

177. Plin., *ep.* 9.5.1,3; cf. 2.12.5; and Plut., *Mor.* 719bc. On the principle, see Uhlhorn 1883: 767–70; De Ste. Croix 1981: 309, 413–14; Fantham 1973; and Harvey 1965.

178. See Hamel 1990: 70, 100–101, 107n77; Silber 2000; and Gray 2009. Monastic attitudes were analogous to those of earlier rabbis.

179. Rae 1981: 59; see Harrison 2016 for its relevance to Chrysostom.

180. Bars. et Jo., *resp.* 630 (SC 468.62–64); see also *resp.* 681.

181. Pachomius, *prec.* 51 (Veilleux, 153).

182. *v.Aux.* 36 (PG 114:1405B); cf. Rémondon 1972: 255. Inclusivity was a goal of the graded hospitality offered in the earlier empire. See D'Arms 1990: 313, 315.

183. Bars. et Jo., *resp.* 686 (SC 468.122–24): Εἰ δὲ φιλάνθρωπός ἐστιν εἰς πάντας καὶ βρέχει ἐπὶ δικαίους καὶ ἀδίκους, διὰ τί σὺ θέλεις εἶναι ἀπάνθρωπος.

184. Pall., *HL* 66.2 (Bartelink, 278): κατὰ σπλάγχνων χωροῦντος, τὰς αἱρέσεις εἰς ὀρθοδοξίαν μετήνεγκαν. For an even more ambivalent example, see Thdt., *HR* 1.10. Chrys., *In Heb.*11.4 (PG 63.96) warns against giving to priests of unknown affiliation, while Severus of Antioch warns not to provide for hypocrites, possibly Chalcedonians, in *Hom. cath.* 43 (PO 36.91), 64 (8.643), 103 (22.294). Leont. Neap., *v.Jo.Eleem.* 34 espouses philanthropic treatment for slaves. Brown 2002: 62–63 notes the virtual silence regarding slaves, proposing that they were neglected for social and ideological reasons, being perceived not to have destinies that bishops had to protect.

CHAPTER 3. "BEND YOUR HEART TO MERCY": ALMSGIVING AND THE CHRISTIAN ADVOCACY OF SOCIAL COMPASSION

1. Jo. Eph., *HE* 3.2.15 (CSCO 105.76–77; trans. Payne Smith, 114, adapted). On John of Ephesus (a.k.a. John of Asia or Yuhanon of Amida), the Syrian Orthodox author of *Lives of the Eastern Saints* (ca. 569) and *Church History* (ca. 586), see Harvey 1990: 28–42. James of Edessa preserves and attributes to Severus of Antioch fragments of hymns for deaconries asking for purification from sins: Sev. Ant., *hymn.* nos. 314–15 (PO 7.754). If genuine, these would indicate that such organizations already existed at Antioch in the early sixth century.

2. Jo. Eph., *v.SS.Or.* 46 ("Life of Paul of Antioch"; PO 18.673, adapted). Miller 1997: 131 seems to identify this Paul as the anti-Chalcedonian Patriarch Paul II of Antioch (sed. 550–575), but John gives no indication that he was more than a layperson.

3. Jo. Eph., *v.SS.Or.* 45 ("Life of Isaac"; PO 18.671): "mukoko d-meṭṭul ʾaloho w-law ʾa(y) k sniqo šaʿbed napšeh l-tešmešto da-krihe."

4. Magdalino 1990: 184. Miller 1997: 123–30 infers that these had roots in monasticism espoused by Eustathius of Sebaste and Basil of Caesarea, but I see no genetic connection.

5. On their staffing, Miller 1997: 90–93, 118–27; and Haas 1997: 235–38.

6. Jo. Eph., *HE* 3.2.15 (CSCO 105.77; trans. Payne Smith, 115) notes that "in none did he [i.e., Paul] welcome anyone at all of those who adhered to the Council of Chalcedon." Paul's initiative may have been necessary because imperial law (e.g., *CJ* 1.5.10, issued ca. 466–472) forbad heretics to possess ecclesiastical property. Samellas 2002: 260–65 emphasizes sectarian origins, while Horn 2006: 275–99 discusses the general importance of hospitality to the fledgling Miaphysite movement. Magdalino 1990, however, is cautious: Chalcedonian authors refer to deaconries without suggesting that they had sectarian origins (e.g., Daniel of Scete's story of Andronicus and Athanasia).

7. Dan. Scet. *log*.7 ("Andronicus and Athanasia"; Dahlman, 166): τῶν φιλοπτωχείας ἕνεκα. Deaconries featuring washing and bathing appeared in seventh-century Rome, perhaps brought by Eastern monks fleeing invasions. See Herrin 2013a: 282.

8. Jo. Eph., *v.SS.Or.* 46 ("Life of Paul of Antioch"; PO 18.676).

9. Jo. Eph., *v.SS.Or.* 46 (PO 18.672–73); and Jo. Eph., *HE* 3.2.15 (CSCO 105.77), a scriptural passage also cited to promote humility and compassion in Ant. Choz., *v.Geo.Choz.* 9.11.

10. Needless to say, much has been written on early Christian almsgiving. Besides Brown 2002; Brown 2008; and Finn 2006a, see Downs 2008, focusing on almsgiving as atonement from the New Testament to Cyprian; and Rhee 2012, in relation to evolving ecclesiology.

11. Holman 2009 is invaluable. For parallels in Latin authors, see Rhee 2012: 135–37. On the Hebrew concept, Cohen 2005: 5–7; Weinfeld 1995: 25–44; and Hamel 1990: 21.

12. Mauss 1990: 65. Cf. De Ste. Croix 1975: 27.

13. *Const. Ap.* 2.27.6 (SC 320.242), 3.4.2 (329.126). Cf. Bas. Caes., *ep.* 150; Finn 2006a: 107–8, 163; Daley 1999: 449; and Zeisel 1975: 100–101.

14. Chrys., *In Heb.* 32.3 (PG 63.224): Οὐδὲν οὕτω χαρακτηριστικὸν Χριστιανοῦ, ὡς ἐλεημοσύνη· οὐδὲν οὕτω καὶ ἄπιστοι καὶ πάντες θαυμάζουσιν, ὡς ὅταν ἐλεῶμεν.

15. On this older ideal, Harris 2016: 155, 211. Cf. Shaw 1985.

16. Chrys., *In Act.* 14.2 (PG 60.115); Council in Trullo, *can.* 16 (Ohme, 31): οἳ τύπος ἡμῖν κἂν τούτῳ γεγόνασι τῆς περὶ τοὺς δεομένους φιλανθρωπίας τε καὶ σπουδῆς. On *diakonia*, see Collins 1990; and Hamman 1968: 67–83. For its gendered aspect, embodied by Martha in Lk 10:25–38, see Destephen 2012. Implications of servitude are more germane to my discussion.

17. Georg. Alex., *v.Chrys.* 22 (Halkin, 134): ὁ τῆς ἐλεημοσύνης, to be distinguished from ὁ ἐλεήμων, "the Merciful," applied to figures like Count Eusebius of Alexandria (Sev. Ant., *ep.Coll.1* 2.3) and John of Cyprus, Bishop of Alexandria (sed. 610–620; often called, confusingly, "the Almsgiver").

18. Chrys., *In 1 Cor.* 27.1 (PG 61.223–24). Cf. Sandwell 2007: 190–98; Stötzel 1984: 71–122; and Brändle 1979: 125, 151–52.

19. On the prominence of condescension in his social thought, see De Andia 2010: 253–54; Brown 1992: 152–58; Brown 2002: 93–94; and Brändle 1979: 310–18. For its possible difference with Cappadocian outlook, see Harrison 2016: 91–93; cf. Kurbatov 1958.

20. Asterius, *hom*.13.2.2 ("On Repentance"; Datema, 184): διὰ τοῦτο συγκαταβαίνοντες, οὐχ ἵνα ἑαυτοὺς τοῖς κειμένοις συνταπεινώσωμεν, ἀλλ' ἵνα κἀκείνους ὑψώσωμεν. To be clear, Chrysostom's idea that almsgiving promotes humility is occasionally found in other

preaching. In *serm.* 259.5, Augustine advocates giving directly to gain humility; cf. Bas. Caes., *ep.* 43.2.

21. On its significance for Chrysostom, see Brändle 1979; and Gray 1989: 50–53.

22. Jo. Mosch., *prat.* 230 (Nissen, 368): τῇ ὀλιγοψυχίᾳ μου . . . ὡς ἄνθρωπος τουτο ἐλογισάμην. Cf. Leont. Neap., *v.Jo.Eleem.* 7.

23. Jo. Mosch., *prat.* 128 (PG 87[3].2993B).

24. Jo. Eph., *HE* 3.2.16 (CSCO 105.78): "Saggi(')ē kāneš hwo w- 'a(y)k ṭakso d-dayrayuto tāba' hwo lhon . . . w-bah b-dorto hāy meštamloy (h)wot kolah tešmešto d-meskine."

25. Previous studies focus on Italy and Egypt: Giorda 2010; Alciati 2010; Dey 2008; Kahle 1954: 30–40; and Marrou 1940.

26. *v.Sym.Styl.iun.* 27 (SH 32.23–24): Καύχημα μοναχοῦ ποιεῖν ἐλεημοσύνας ἐκ τῶν ἐνόντων . . . τὸ μὴ καταλαλεῖν, συμπάσχειν δὲ τοῖς ἐν θλίψει οὖσιν ἀδελφοῖς . . . πλῦναι πόδας ἀδελφῶν καὶ λέγειν εὐλόγησον . . . ὑπερηφανίαν νικῆσαι καὶ μηδένα ἐπαισχυνθῆναι . . . τὸ ταπεινοῦν ἑαυτὸν καὶ ἔσχατον πάντων εἶναι νομίζειν . . . ἡ εἰς πάντας, ὡς εἰς αὐτὸν τὸν σωτῆρα Χριστόν, μικρούς τε καὶ μεγάλους, πένητάς τε καὶ πλουσίους, ἁγνὴ φιλαδελφία καὶ φιλοξενία καὶ ἀνυπόκριτος διακονία.

27. Lib., *or.* 11.16 (Foerster, 442; trans. Norman, 10); and Amm. Marc., *RG* 22.9.14; cf. Chrys., *stat.* 3.1, 17.2, 49.47. On the city's layout, see Mayer and Allen 2012, which questions the location of the Golden House on the island. For its social, administrative, and cultural structures, Liebeschuetz 1972; Downey 1961; and Petit 1955.

28. Lib., *or.* 7.1–3 (Foerster, 374) perhaps responding to Chrys., *In 1 Cor.* 11.5 (PG 61.94). For Chrysostom's estimate of its economic disparities, *In Mt.* 66.3 (58.630); and Brown 2002: 14. For its population, Liebeschuetz 1972: 92–98; Downey 1961: 582–83; and Petit 1955: 310–11.

29. Chrys., *De eleem.* 1 and 6 (PG 51.261). I assume the homilies discussed here apart from *In Act.*, *In Heb.*, *In Thess.*, and *In Col.* were delivered in Antioch; note the cautions of Mayer 1997; and Mayer 2005: 496–73, 511–12.

30. Maxwell 2006: 65–87; Hartney 2004: 43–47; and Mayer 1997 believe that Chrysostom's audiences represented the full social spectrum, but MacMullen 2009 compellingly argues that metropolitan churches usually served the elite.

31. On these facilities, see Chrys., *In Mt.* 66.3 (PG 58.630); with Downey 1961: 349; and Mayer and Allen 2012: 68–80, 174–82.

32. Chrys., *poenit.* 3.2 (PG 49.294). Poor at church doors, Chrys., *In 1 Cor.* 30.4 (61.265); Chrys., *In 1 Thess.* 11.4 (62.466); Pall., *HL* 68.2. Wash basins, Mayer and Allen 2012: 220–21. For Chrysostom's liturgical use of the poor, see De Andia 2010; and Holman 2001: 60–62. On his view of alms as a means of purification, see chapter 4, "Sins of Excess and Redemptive Almsgiving."

33. Chrys., *In 1 Cor.* 27.5 (PG 61.230–31). Cf. Chrys., *In 1 Cor.* 20.5 (168–69); Brown 2002: 49–54; and Sandwell 2007: 192–93.

34. For differing assessments of Christian rhetoric on the poor, see Brown 1992: 89–103; Finn 2006a: 137–59; Finn 2006b; and Allen, Neil, and Mayer 2009, from which I take the phrase "call to alms" (209).

35. Chrys., *In Mt.* 88.3 (PG 58.779); Chrys., *In 1 Cor.* 30.5 (61.256). Cf. Hartney 2004: 157.

36. Chrys., *In 1 Tim.* 14.3 (PG 62.574): σὺ διακόνησον . . . οἰκείας χερσὶ δός. . . . δίδου διὰ σαυτοῦ· πολλὰ γὰρ ἔστι δι' ἑαυτοῦ ὠφελῆσαι ἐὰν δῷς. . . . 6 (578): Εἰ δὲ πόδας αὐτῶν νίπτειν δεῖ, πολλῷ μᾶλλον καὶ ἐκ χειρὸς ἐπιδιδόναι αὐτοῖς τὰ χρήματα.

37. Chrys., *In 1 Cor.* 21.6 (PG 61.179): ἅπερ ἡμεῖς ὑπὲρ ἐλεημοσύνης λέγομεν, οὐχ ἵνα ἡμῖν προσαγάγῃς λέγομεν, ἀλλ᾽ ἵνα αὐτὸς διὰ σαυτοῦ διακονῇς.

38. Chrys., *In 1 Tim.* 14.2 (PG 62.573). See also Chrys., *In 2 Tim.* 1.4 (62.606); Chrys., *In Act.* 45.3 (60.318).

39. *Sefer Ha-Aggadah* 2.1.79. Cf. Arterbury 2003, 2005: 59–71; Colish 2005: 58–59.

40. Chrys., *In 1 Tim.* 14.2 (PG 62.573): τὸ πλέον τῆς διακονίας καὶ αὐτὸς δι᾽ ἑαυτοῦ ἔπραττε. . . . οὕτω δεῖ φιλοξενίαν ἐπιδείκνυσθαι δι᾽ ἑαυτῶν πάντας πράττοντας ἵνα ἡμεῖς ἁγιαζώμεθα, ἵν᾽αἱ χεῖρες αἱ ἡμέτεραι εὐλογῶνται.

41. Chrys., *In Rom.* 21.3 (PG 60.606): ἱκέτου σχῆμα ἀνέλαβε καὶ οἰκέτου. Chrys., *In Gen.* 41.6 (53.382): ἐν τάξει ὑπηρέτου ἵσταται. . . . ὦ ταπεινοφροσύνης ὑπερβολὴ.

42. In general, Miquel 1995: 811; Greer 1974: 29–34; and Finn 2006a: 161. For Chrysostom, Plassmann 1961: 26–30; cf. Chrys., *In Mt.* 50.3–4 (PG 58.508–509); Chrys., *In Act.* 45.4 (60.320); Chrys., *In Rom.* 22.4 (60.606); Chrys., *In 1 Cor.* 34.6 (61.294–95), 35.5 (303); Chrys., *In 1 Thess.* 10, 11.5 (62.459, 467); Chrys., *In 1 Tim.*14.2 (62.573–74).

43. Chrys., *In Jo.* 16.3 (PG 59.102); Chrys., *In Col.* 1.5–6 (62.306–308).

44. Chrys., *In Rom.* 21.3 (PG 60.606).

45. Chrys., *In Mt.* 35.5 (PG 57.412).

46. Harris 2016: 151. Cf. Fikhman 1973; Fikhman 1974; and Harper 2011.

47. Chrys., *In Col.* 1.4 (PG 62.304); and Chrys., *In 1 Cor.* 40.5 (PG 60.354; cf. the *yassakji* of Ottoman cities); with Finn 2006a: 69; and MacMullen 1988: 62. On late Roman reliefs, Dunbabin 2003.

48. Chrys., *In 1 Thess.* 11.5 (PG 62.467): σὺ δὲ ἴσως ἀπαξιοῖς καὶ ὀφθῆναι, διδοὺς πένησιν, ἢ καὶ προσδιαλεγόμενος; Βαβαὶ τῆς ἀπονοίας καὶ τοῦ τύφου. Cf. Chrys., *In Mt.* 35.5 (57.412); Chrys., *In Rom.* 21.3 (60.607); Chrys., *In 1 Cor.* 27.5 (61.231); with Finn 2006a: 20–21, 69, 100–101.

49. Chrys. *In Mt.* 71.3 (PG 58.665). Cf. Isid. Pel., *epp.* 2.214, 4.41, 4.227 (PG 78: 656BC, 1092CD–1093A, 1321BC); and Leyerle 1994: 34–37.

50. Chrys., *In 2 Cor.* 13.4 (PG 61.495)

51. Chrys., *In Rom.* 21.1 (PG 60.603).

52. Chrys., *In Gen.* 41.5 (PG 53.380).

53. Chrys., *In Gen.* 41.6 (PG 53.382): μεθ᾽ ὅσης τιμῆς, μεθ᾽ ὅσης ταπεινοφροσύνης τὰ τῆς φιλοξενίας ἐπεδείκνυτο· οὐ καθάπερ οἱ πολλοί, κἂν ποιήσωσί ποτέ τι τοιοῦτον, μέγα φρονοῦσι κατὰ τῶν ὑποδεχθέντων, καὶ πολλάκις καὶ ὑπερορῶσιν αὐτῶν διὰ τὴν φθάσασαν εἰς αὐτοὺς θεραπείαν. See also Chrys., *In 1 Tim.* 14.2 (PG 62.573); and Chrys., *In Act.* 45.3 (60.318).

54. Chrys., *In Rom.* 19.8 (PG 60.594).

55. Chrys., *In Rom.* 19.8 (PG 60.594): Κἂν μηδὲν δὲ ἔχῃς, συναλγοῦσαν δὲ ἔχῃς ψυχήν, καὶ τούτου σοι μισθὸς ἀποκείσεται.

56. Chrys., *In dict. Pauli* 3 (PG 51.256); Chrys., *De vid.* 12 (51.332); Chrys., *In Gen.* 41.6 (53.32). Cf. 2 Cor 8:12.

57. Stressed by Wessel 2016.

58. Chrys., *In Rom.* 21.1 (PG 60.601). See also Chrys., *In Gen.* 41.6 (53.382); Chrys., *In Jo.* 65.3 (59.365); Chrys., *In Rom.* 20.3 (60.600); Chrys., *In 2 Thess.* 1.2 (62.470); and Chrys., *In 1 Tim.* 14.2 (62.573).

59. Chrys., *In 1 Tim.*14.3 (PG 62.573): κενοδοξίας ἀπήλλακται . . . καὶ φρόνημα κατασπᾷ.

60. Chrys., *In Jo.* 81.3 (PG 59.442): ὁ διατελῶν ἐν τῷ διδόναι πένησι, ταχέως καὶ ὀργῆς ἀποσήσεται καὶ οὐδὲ μέγα φρονήσει ποτέ. Cf. Chrys., *In Eph.* 18.4 (PG 62.125); and Evagr. Pont., *Th.* 3.

61. Chrys., *In 1 Cor.* 30.4–5 (PG 61.255). Cf. Chrys., *In 1 Thess.* 11.4 (62.467).

62. Chrys., *In Eutropium* 6 (52:279). On this rationale, see Blowers 2010.

63. Chrys., *In 1 Cor.* 32.5 (PG 61.270–71). Chrysostom's emphasis on obtaining humility and compassion through alms is noted by Brändle 1979: 146–47; and Plassmann 1961: 80.

64. Chrys., *In Jo.* 40.4 (PG 59.233): Τί γὰρ ὄφελος . . . ὅταν ἐλεῇ μὲν δαψιλῶς . . . πρὸς ἐπίδειξιν δὲ ἀνθρώπων καὶ φιλοτιμίαν τῶν ὁρώντων; ἢ ὅταν ἐλεῇ μὲν πάσης ἀκριβείας καὶ πρὸς τὸ τῷ Θεῷ δοκοῦν, ἐπαίρηται δὲ αὐτῷ τούτῳ καὶ μέγα φρονῇ.

65. See Becker 2002, noting that Aphrahat differs from later Syrian authorities in focusing on lay rather than episcopal or monastic good works.

66. Becker 2002: 323–26.

67. Pinard 1919: 209. Cf. Angstenberger 1997: 134–42; Rylaarsdam 1999; and Mitchell 2001: 205–12. Georg. Syc., *v.Thdr.Syc.* 31 illustrates that "condescension" is an accurate translation of what early Byzantine Christians understood by *synkatabasis* and is not a modern calque.

68. Chrys., *In Rom.*7.9 (PG 60.454): ὁ τοίνυν βουλόμενος γενέσθαι πλούσιος, γενέσθω πένης, ἵνα γένεται πλούσιος. See also Chrys., *In Mt.* 4.12 (PG 57.53); Chrys., *In Rom.* 15.6 (60.547–548); and Chrys., *In 1 Tit.* 6.1 (62.695). For its relevance to almsgiving, Brändle 1979: 310–18; Brown 2002: 93–94; and De Andia 2010: 253–55.

69. Chrys., *In Heb.* 9.5 (PG 63.82): ἀπὸ ἐλεημοσύνης . . . ταπεινώσωμεν ἑαυτῶν τὰς ψυχάς.

70. Jo. Eph., *v.SS.Or.* 2 ("Life of Zʿura"; PO 17.34). See also *v.SS.Or.* 5 ("Life of Symeon and Sergius"; 17.85); *v.SS.Or.* 34 ("Life of Symeon the Elder"; 18.603); *v.SS.Or.* 55 ("Life of John and Sosiana"; 19.194); *v.SS.Or.* 57 ("Life of Theodore the Castrensis"; 19.202); Cyril Scyth., *v.Cyriac.* 21; and Leont. Neap., *v.Jo.Eleem.* 9.

71. Chrys., *In Mt.* 35.5 (PG 57.412).

72. Agathias, *Hist.* 5.3.7–8, 4–6 (Reydell, 170; trans. Frendo, 140–41, adapted): τάξις τε ἅπασα καὶ αἰδὼς καὶ ἡ τῶν γερῶν μεγαλαυχία . . . ἀνετετάρακτο. . . . οἵ τε ἐλάττονες πρὸς τοὺς ἐν τέλει ἐς ἰσοτιμίαν καθίσταντο.

73. Chrys., *In Mt.* 72.3 (PG 58.671): ἐκεῖ τὸ ὕψος τῆς ταπεινοφροσύνης. . . . ἄνθρωποι γὰρ οἱ μὲν ἀπὸ τῶν ἔξωθεν ἀξιωμάτων, οἱ δὲ καὶ ἀπὸ χρημάτων ὄντες λαμπροί, πάντοθεν ἑαυτοὺς καταστέλλουσιν. . . πάντες τῶν διακονουμένων εἰσι. . . . σύγχυσις· μὴ γένοιτο· ἀλλ' ἡ πρώτη εὐταξία. κἂν γὰρ ᾖ τις μικρός, ὁ μέγας οὐχ ὁρᾷ τοῦτο, ἀλλὰ καὶ ἐκείνου πάλιν καταδεέστερον ἑαυτὸν εἶναι νενόμικε, καὶ ταύτῃ γίνεται μείζων. . . . 72.4 (PG 58.672): πολλὴ παρ' αὐτοῖς ἰσότης· διὸ καὶ εὐκολία πολλὴ τῆς ἀρετῆς.

74. Implied by Leont. Neap., *v.Jo.Eleem.* 23 (Festugière, 374), describing a monk's effort to raise money to put an orphan into a convent. Initiation fees called *apotagai* became common in Middle Byzantium, with consequences discussed in Herman 1941. On the relevance of economic status to anchoretic discourse, see Brakke 2008; and Rubenson 2009.

75. Mark the Monk., *paen.* 3 (SC 445.220–24; trans. Vivian 148–50, adapted).

76. See De Durand 1999: 205; and Vivian 2009: 24–25.

77. Dan. Scet., *Life of Doulas* 11 (Clugnet, 387). For other examples, Dilley 2017: 76–77.

78. Shenoute, *de vita mon.* 1 (Leipoldt, 28). Cf. Brakke 2008: 81–82.

79. *AP* GS 11.79 (SC 474.182).

80. Anast. Sin., *paterika* 29; and *v.Longini* 16. See Wipszycka 2001; Wipszycka 1991; Patrich 1995: 258–66; Palmer 1990: 84; and Kahle 1954: 35–40. Jo. Eph., *v.SS.Or.* 20 (PO 17.280–82) describes three months of menial work followed by three years of penance.

81. Bars. et Jo., *resp.* 360 (SC 450.382–84); Jo. Cassian, *Inst.* 4.7 (Guy, 130): "prima institutione humilitatis ac patientiae"; also Jo. Cassian, *Coll.* 18.14.3. On Cassian's description and purpose, see Goodrich 2007: 53–55, 184–87, 190–205.

82. Cyril Scyth., *v.Jo.Hesych.* 5 (Schwartz, 205): μετὰ πασῆς ταπεινοφροσύνης καὶ προθυμίας ὑπερετῶν. Cf. Cyril Scyth., *v.Cyriac.* 4; *v.Pach. gr. prim.* 28; and Jo. Cassian, *Inst.* 4.7.

83. Cyril Scyth. *v.Cyriac.* 7 lists these seriatim, suggesting they were successive *diakoniai* in Palestinian monasteries. But the list is not exhaustive; some had positions such as camel driver, lamplighter, and deputy to a senior monk. *v.Pach. gr. prim.* 26; and Patrich 1995: 179–94.

84. *Canons of Marutha* 49 (Vööbus, 92): "w-ʿal dayrā nēʾṣpun kol nāš b-dukteh." An irascible monk is denied the rank of steward in *v.Pach. gr. prim.* 42.

85. Lesieur 2011: 17.

86. *v.Pach.boh.* 61 (Veilleux, 81). Cf. Ant. Choz., *v.Geo.Choz.* 2.19.

87. For the estimate, Schachner 2006: 285, with extensive discussion of monastic hospitality at 282–83. For *xenodocheia* and *nosokomeia* (infirmaries) at the Sabas monastery, Patrich 1995: 165–66.

88. Dor. Gaz., *log.* 11.119. Dorotheus is discussed further in this section and in chapter 4, "Gifts of Charity in the Seridos Monastery."

89. Magen 1993.

90. Elter and Hassoune 2004: 364–65. For a survey, see Whiting 2016: 109–10. Henry 2015: 46–47, identifies a structure in the ruins of Symeon's Marvelous Mountain monastery as a hostel, a reference I owe to Dina Boero.

91. *Reg. Sab.* 14 (Kurtz, 170): οἰκονόμους δὲ καὶ δοχειαρίους καὶ εἰς τὰς λοιπὰς διακονίας προτιμᾶσθαι τοὺς Σύους καὶ διαταττόμεθα . . . ὡς ἀνθστικωτέρους ὄντας καὶ δραστικοὺς. For the possible early origins of this eleventh-century text, see Patrich 1995: 256–57.

92. Jo. Cassian, *Inst.* 4.5 (Guy, 128): "nec erubescat pauperibus id est corpori fraternitatis aequari." Cf. *v.Pach. gr. prim.* 24; and Cyril Scyth., *v.Euthym.* 18. In *v.Marc.Acoem* 10, the future abbot is sent to tend a donkey to see if this would insult him; he assumes the duty with "highest humility."

93. Jo. Eph., *HE* 3.2.12 (CSCO 105.74): "koloh ḥšaḥto ṣʿirto d-dayroyuto." In *v.Sym.Styl. iun.*164, an imperial officer condemns pagans to serve in a hospice.

94. *v.Pach. gr. prim.* 24 (SH 19.15): οὔπω γὰρ οἱ νεόφυτοι ἀδελφοὶ ἔφθασαν εἰς τοιαύτην διάθεσιν ὡς ἄλλοις δουλεύειν.

95. Jo. Mosch., *prat.* 230 (Nissen, 369): τινες τῶν ἀδελφῶν ἐσκανδαίζοντο καὶ μάλιστα οἱ τὴν ἕξιν ὄντες ἀπλούστεροι. . . . (371): ἐκτήσατο μεγάλην ταπείνωσιν . . . πρὸς πάντας. Jo. Cassian, *Inst.* 4.4, claims that Egyptian cenobia refused postulants' wealth to avoid such problems.

96. Cyril Scyth., *v.Jo.Hesych.* 5 (Schwartz, 205): μετὰ πασῆς ταπεινοφροσύνης καὶ προθυμίας ὑπερετῶν; 6 (206): μετὰ προθυμίας καὶ χαρᾶς τὴν διακονίαν δεξάμενος πάντας τοὺς πατέρας ταῖς ὑπουργίαις ἐθεράπευεν δουλεύων ἑκαστῷ μετὰ πάσης ταπεοφροσύνης

καὶ ἐπιεικείας. Cf. Cyril Scyth., *v.Cyriac.* 4 (225): πᾶσαν διακονίαν μετὰ προθυμίας ἐκτελῶν. Ant. Choz., *v.Geo.Choz.* 1.1; and Georg. Syc., *v.Thdr.Syc.* 64.

97. Jo. Mosch., *prat.* 24 (PG 87[3].2869). Di Segni 2001: 33, notes that the monastery oversaw a watering hole for pilgrims beside the Jericho-Jerusalem highway.

98. Jo. Eph., *v.SS.Or.* 33 ("Life of Ḥala"; PO 18.592–93, trans. Brooks, adapted).

99. Jo. Clim., *scal.* 26 (PG 88.1032): δαίμων κενοδοξίας πρὸς ἐλεημοσύνην προτρεπόμενος ὥσπερ καὶ φιληδονίας. Ἐὰν ἀμφοτέρων τοίνυν καθαρεύσωμεν, ἐν παντὶ τόπῳ ἐλεεῖν μὴ παυσώμεθα.

100. Derrida 1995: 30; cf. Derrida 1992: 29. This pessimistic view has been criticized by, for example, Silber 2009: 180, 184. But his insight is relevant to monastic communities whose members were supposed to constantly reflect on moral justifications for their actions.

101. Bars. et Jo., *resp.* 252, 253, 324. Cf. *v.Olympias* 4, Pall., *HL* 17.

102. Isaiah Scet., *log.* 5 (trans. Chryssavgis, 73). Cf. Jo. Cassian, *Inst.* 18.7.8; and Bars. et Jo., *resp.* 318, 535.

103. Bars. et Jo., *resp.* 618 (SC 468.40): Ἐπειδὴ περὶ ἐλεημοσύνης ἐστὶ τὸ πρᾶγμα, οὐ πάντες χωροῦσι βαστάξαι. . . . Εἰσὶ γάρ τινες τάσσοντες ἑαυτοὺς εἰς τὴν τοιαύτην διακονίαν. See also Bars. et Jo., *resp.* 620–24, 628, 629.

104. Geront., *v.Mel. gr.* 9 (SC 90.142–44). Melania, Pinian, and their hagiographer Gerontius are discussed in chapter 7.

105. Jo. Ruf., *v.Petr.Ib.* 68 (trans. Horn-Phenix, 99). Cf. *AP* GS 13.6, 14, 18–19; 14.13; *AP* G Or 6.

106. *HM* 1.62–63 (SH 53.34; trans. Price, 62, adapted).

107. Thdr. Petr., *v.Thds.* (Usener, 29).

108. Bars. et Jo., *resp.* 315 (SC 450.310; trans. Chryssavgis, 296, adapted).

109. Bars. et Jo., *resp.* 316 (SC 450.310–12).

110. Bars. et Jo., *resp.* 314 (SC 450.309): εἰς τὸ ἔλεος κλῖνον τὴν καρδίαν σου. . . . Ἐὰν οὖν συμπαθήσῃς, εὑρίσκεις βοήθειαν.

111. On the Zaqqara infirmary, see Crislip 2004: 10. For monastic bathhouses, Detoraki 2004; and Elter and Hassoune 2004: 363–64.

112. Crislip 2004: 137. Cf. Patrich 1995: 184–85; Miller 1985: 118–40; and Rousseau 1985: 125–26.

113. Evagr. Pont., *Th.* 11 (SC 438.188–90; trans. Sinkewicz, 160–61, adapted). Cf. Bars. et Jo., *resp.* 316 (SC 450.312); also Bars. et Jo., *resp.* 56, 57, 101, 108, 109, 250.

114. Crislip 2004: 16, calls them "a special corps of the monastics," but see *v.Pach. gr. prim.* 26.

115. *v.Dos.* 6 (SC 92.130). Sick monks did not necessarily make good patients. Crislip 2005: 91–99; and Crislip 2008: 22–23. On infirmary work as *diakonia*, Crislip 2004: 30; and *v.Marth.* 8 (SH 32.259). Savramis 1962: 25–27, emphasizes the role of sick care in socializing monks.

116. Dor. Gaz., *ep.* 4.189 (SC 92.506): τοὺς ἀσθενεῖς θεράπευε, πρῶτον μὲν ἵνα κτήσῃ ἐκ τούτου συμπάθειαν. Cf. Bas. Caes., *RB* 28 (PG 31.1104A).

117. Cyril Scyth., *v.Euthym.* 33; cf. *AP* G Arsenius 8; and Bars. et Jo., *resp.* 55. For the custom of allowing monks to become solitaries after *diakonia* training, see Patrich 1995: 264–65.

118. Thdr. Petr., *v.Thds.* (Usener, 42). See also Call., *v.Hyp.*12.3; Cyril Scyth., *v.Euthym.* 4; and Cyril Scyth., *v.Sab.* 62.

119. Jo. Eph., *v.SS.Or.* 17 ("Life of a Poor Stranger"; PO 17.250). Alternatively, John emphasizes the cruelty of Chalcedonian monks toward Anti-Chalcedonians imprisoned in their monasteries and hospitals; see Jo. Eph., *HE* 3.1.15, 17, 29, 31; 3.2.9. Hatlie 2007: 127–28, notes the lack of evidence for monastic involvement in philanthropy at Constantinople, but does not adequately distinguish between passive reception of the sick and poor who came to a monastery in search of aid (which he acknowledges did happen) and active outreach to the sick and poor of the sort exemplified by Paul's *diakoniai*.

120. Sev. Ant., *ep.Coll.1* 2.3; Cyril Scyth., *v.Jo.Hesych.* 14; and Jo. Mosch., *prat.* 34, 37, 193; with Brown 1992: 154; and Rapp 2009. Cf. *v.Jo.Jeiun.* 5 on the generosity of the future patriarch John the Faster (sed. 582–595), whom God enabled to dispense so many coins in Constantinople's Bull Square in one day that a beggar pleaded with him for mercy.

121. On Leontius's hagiography and its relation to other hagiographies about John, see Efthymiades and Déroche 2011: 72–76; and Déroche 1995: 238–49.

122. Leont. Neap., *v.Jo.Eleem.* 6 (Festugière-Rydén, 350), 12 (355). On the dream, see Rapp (2004): 129.

123. Booth 2014: 276. On John's background, Rapp 2004. For an attempt to assess realities behind this representation of his philanthropy, Wipszycka 2015: 210–36, 349–63.

124. Leont. Neap., *v.Jo.Eleem.* 40 (Festugière-Rydén, 392): οὐ τοσοῦτον μισθὸν ἔχουσιν οἱ ἐκ φύσεως ὄντες ἐλεήμονες . . . ἀλλ᾽ οἱ βιαζόμενοι τὴν οἰκείαν πρόσθεσιν καὶ καρδίαν ἀπὸ βίας καὶ πόνου τὴν ἀρετὴν κατορθοῦντες.

125. Leont. Neap., *v.Jo.Eleem.* 6, 22 (Festugière-Rydén, 353, 372). On Sarapion, see Pall., *HL* 37; cf. *Man of God of Edessa* (trans. Doran, 23–25).

126. López 2013: 14–17, quote at 43. Cf. Brakke and Crislip 2015: 212–65. López's argument is anticipated in Mitchell 1993, vol. 2: 121.

127. Call., *v.Hyp.* 31 (SC 177.204). On Hypatius's public persona, see Maxwell 2016.

Another notable abbot was Ishāq of Antioch (d. ca. 460). Best known for his *memrā* on a parrot that sang the *Trishagion* in the marketplace (Van Esbroeck 1996), Ishāq was fully engaged with urban life. His monastery on Mt. Silpius was close enough to be kept up all night by Kalends festivities. Isaac Ant., *serm.* 65 ("On the Vigil at Antioch"); Bedjan, 815–82. Four homilies attributed to him deal with almsgiving, including one emphasizing direct giving in Chrysostomic fashion. Isaac Ant., *serm.* 53, Bedjan, 651.1–5, 652.15–18, 653.14–15. Unfortunately, other Ishāqs exist and it is notoriously difficult to ascertain who wrote which homily. In my estimation, *serm.* 53 does not fit the criteria proposed by Bou Mansour 2003 for identifying those of this one. *Serm.* 11, 26, and 28, however, seem to have been written by the same person, and in any case exemplify López's thesis of monastic appropriation of episcopal discourse.

128. Call., *v.Hyp.* 30, 32–33. Shenoute also censured clerics for shortcomings like fraternizing with pagans. See Brakke and Crislip 2015: 91–117, 225–27. A comparable example is Rabbula of Edessa (d. 435), who after ordination remained "in mind . . . a monk." *Pan. Rabb.* (trans. Doran, 85; cf. 77–82, 88–89).

129. *v.Sym.Styl.sen.* 58–59 (trans. Doran 137–38); cf. 40–43. On this episode, see Harvey 1994: 55; cf. *v.Sin.* 33–34; and Jo.Eph., *v.SS.Or.* 53 ("Life of Priscus"; PO 19.180). Symeon's hagiographers do not specify what gifts were involved. They seem to resemble thank offerings (discussed in chapter 6), whence monasteries often derived resources for alms. Cf. *v.Thecl.* 28 (SH 62.280).

130. Isid. Pel., *ep.* 37 (PG 78.205AB). On the incident, see Évieux 1995: 206–12. On building as a facet of urban episcopal duties, Rapp 2005: 220–23.

131. For example, Orig., *comm. in Mt.* 11.9, 16.22; Bas. Caes., *ep.* 92.2; Epiph., *Pan.* 75.2.2; and Jo. Eph., *HE* 3.2.28; cf. Zeisel 1975: 33–49. For this development, see Caner 2021.

132. Zeisel 1975: 116–17, 139–41 argues that churches mixed their funds and therefore suffered fiscal confusion. Edessa's annual church income of seven thousand darics reportedly funded both its clergy and the poor on its dole. *Pan. Rabb.* (trans. Doran, 89).

133. Chrys., *ep.* 217 (PG 52.731). Rabbula reportedly put "trustworthy and truly caring" deacons in charge of his hospital and leprosarium. *Pan. Rabb.* (trans. Doran, 101). It was only due to Euphemia's intervention that hospitals admitted the poor at Amida. Jo. Eph., *v.SS.Or.* 12 ("Lives of Mary and Euphemia"; PO 17.180); cf. Wipszycka 2015: 354.

134. Sev. Ant., *Hom. cath.* 62 (PO 8.283); cf. Finn 2006a: 77–78. See Sev. Ant., *Hom. cath.* 81 (PO 20.368) for a scheme to enroll debtors on the dole so that creditors could receive money given by the church. On administrative preoccupations of Chrysostom and Severus, see Allen and Mayer 2000: 361–93.

135. Jo. Eph., *v.SS.Or.* 12 ("Lives of Mary and Euphemia"; PO 17.180).

136. Bars. et Jo., *resp.* 618–619. Cf. Pall., *HL* 40.1; Geront., *v.Mel. gr.* 27.

137. See Rapp 2005: 274–89; and Allen 2011; also Sev. Ant., *ep.Coll.1* 1.7–8, 13, 43, and 48.

138. On the contrast in social origin, pay, and status, see Zeisel 1975: 229–35; Rapp 2005: 172–202; and Hübner 2005: 183–85. Zeisel 1975: 182–83 calculates that salaries of bishops in major sees were 1,440 times greater than those of rural bishops. Rapp 2005: 103–4 notes the uneasy relations that sometimes arose because of such differences.

139. Jo. Mosch., *prat.* 34, 37, 193. Cf. Jo. Mosch., *prat.* 33; and Booth 2014: 123. For church bureaucracies and clerical numbers, see Jones 1964: 910–12, 932; Zeisel 1975: 214–17; Haas 1997: 215–27.

140. Evagr. Schol., *HE* 3.34 (Whitby, 178). On Severus's preaching and audience, see Allen 1998: 120–21. For the influence of Mt 25:35–40 and Chrysostom, see Alpi 2009: 162–66; and Brown 2002: 109–10. When, however, Severus alludes to Abraham as an exemplar of philanthropy in *Hom. cath.* 67 (PO 8.84), he states only that the church similarly ministered to strangers, without proposing that laypeople follow suit.

141. Leont. Neap., *v.Jo.Eleem.* 5 (Festugière-Rydén, 349). Cf. Joshua, Ps.-, *Chron.* 29. On the *episcopalis audientia*, Rapp 2005: 242–52. Her remark that these courts "worked fast, efficiently and without payment of hefty fees" (248) must be qualified for major sees by Leontius's passage and *v.Alex.Acoem.* 40, alluding to a holy man's suppression of clerical fees collected in (evidently episcopal) courts at Antioch. For the challenges faced by petitioners trying to gain access to imperial officials, as well as the burden of paperwork generated by those who succeeded, see Kelly 2004: 114–45.

142. Leont. Neap., *v.Jo.Eleem.* 7.

143. Leont. Neap., *v.Jo.Eleem.* 29. Cf. Jo. Mosch., *prat.* 193.

144. Leont. Neap., *v.Jo.Eleem.*1, 6, 7, 27 and 37 (Festugière-Rydén, 347, 351, 352, 379, 391), where *diadotes* attack a beggar for insulting John. The term designates a municipal officer in *CTh.* 7.4.28.

145. Sev. Ant., *ep.Coll.1* 1.9 (trans. Brooks, 46). Cf. Leont. Neap., *v.Jo.Eleem.* 1 (Festugière-Rydén, 347): μεταστειλάμενος ... τὸν λεγόμενον ἐπὶ τῆς εἰρήνης and 23 (373): οἱ ἐκκλησιέκδικοι.

146. Sev. Ant., *Hom. cath.* 27 (PO 36.573).

147. *v.Sym.Styl.iun.* 72 (SH 32.62–63): πάθει συγχωρήσει καὶ αὐτὸν ὁ Κύριος . . . περιπεσεῖν, ἵνα γνῷ διὰ τῆς πείρας συμπάσχειν, ὅπερ διὰ τῆς φύσεως οὐκ ἐδιδάχθη. Lucy Parker 2017 plausibly suggests that Domninus incurred Symeon's wrath because he decided to stop funding his constructions on the mountain, which the previous patriarch had supported.

148. In addition to Van den Ven 1962, see Parker 2017; and Déroche 1996, 2004.

149. On the site, see Van den Ven 1962; and Henry 2015.

150. In general, see Allen 1998: 205–6. For editions of three sermons, Van den Ven 1957, who shows that *serm.* 3 is behind *v.Sym.Styl.iun.* 24. Similarly, *v.Sym.Styl.iun.* 27 shows close parallels with *serm.* 21.3. No modern edition for the rest of his corpus exists. For their theological content, see Hester 1990. Symeon also wrote hymns and letters. See Pétridès 1902.

151. Sym. Cion., *serm.* 6.4 (Mai-Cozza-Lupi, 19). On the term *krētores*, see Laniado 2002.

152. Sym. Cion., *serm.* 14.2 (Mai-Cozza-Lupi, 64); cf. *serm.*16.1 (73–74).

153. Sym. Cion., *serm.* 16.4 (Mai-Cozza-Lupi, 77–79).

154. *v.Sym.Styl.iun.* 27 (SH 32.24): Μὴ τῇ κοσμικῇ φαντασίᾳ ἐνυβρίσῃς τὸν ἐν τῇ πενίᾳ τοῦ πένητος περιερχόμενον Χριστὸν καὶ ποῦ κλῖναι τὴν κεφαλὴν μὴ ἔχοντα, καὶ αὐτοῦ εἰσιν οἱ οὐρανοὶ καὶ ἡ γῆ. . . . Διὸ ἐν ἱλαρότητι δέχεσθε τοὺς πλουσίους ὡς τοὺς πένητας, καὶ τοὺς πένητας ὡς τοὺς πλουσίους, πάντα ἄνθρωπον ὡς ἕνα ὁρῶντες. Cf. Isaiah Scet., *log.* 29.

155. See Greatrex and Lieu 1995: 102–111; and Downey 1961: 514–36.

156. Lassus 1977: 62, 77–78; Foss 2000: 25; Sarris 2006: 124.

157. *v.Sym.Styl.iun.* 123 (SH 32.105): διὰ τῆς εἰς τοὺς πένητας ἐλεημοσύνης καὶ εὐχαρίστου διακονίας.

158. Georg. Syc., *v.Theod.Syc.* 120 (SH 48.97). Cf. *v.Sym.Styl.iun.* 161, 168, 221–22; Jo. Eph., *v.SS.Or.* 34 ("Life of Symeon the Scribe"; PO 18.605); and Call., *v.Hyp.* 11.4; with Maxwell 2016; and Patlagean 1977: 194. Some twenty-three imperial officials are recorded as visiting the White Monastery while Shenoute was abbot. See Behlmer 1998; with Zeisel 1975: 319–20.

159. Sym. Cion., *serm.* 21.3 (Mai-Cozza-Lupi, 105): βδελύσεσθαι πᾶσαν ἀρετῆς δύναμιν ἐπὶ ἀδελφικῆς διακονίας, καὶ τὸν μὲν πλούσιον προηγεῖσθαι πείθει διὰ κενοδοξίαν· τοῦ δὲ πτωχοῦ τὸ πρόσωπον καταισχύνει, καὶ τὸ μὲν σῶμα Χριστοῦ ἐπὶ τοῦ πένητος ἀπονοεῖται.

160. Ant. Choz., *v.Geo.Choz* 6 [25] (Houze, 124–25): λάβε τὴν εὐλογίαν ταύτην. . . . ὁ τόπος ὁ ἅγιος οὗτος τῶν πτωχῶν καὶ τῶν ξένων ἐστὶν ἀναπαυστήριον, καὶ οὐ τῶν πλουσίων μόνον ἀπαντητήριον.

CHAPTER 4. "GIVE IT WITH YOUR WHOLE SOUL": FROM ALMS TO CHARITY IN EARLY BYZANTINE MONASTICISM

1. Dor. Gaz., *log.* 14.156 (SC 92.438–40). On Gaza in this era, see Glucker 1987; and Bitton-Ashkelony and Kofsky 2004. On Dorotheus, Hevelone-Harper 2005, but I disagree that he wrote his discourses as abbot of the Seridos monastery in later life. The coexistence of the names Seridos and Dorotheus for seventh-century Gazan monasteries (Jo. Mosch., *prat.* 166; Leont. Neap., *v.Jo.Eleem.* 38) indicates separate places. For his work as a spiritual master, see Stenger 2017.

2. Dor. Gaz., *log.* 14.157 (SC 92.440–42): δι' αὐτὸ τὸ καλόν, συμπάσχοντες ἀλλήλοις ὡς ἰδίοις μέλεσιν, οὕτως θεραπεύοντές τινα ὡς ὅτι ἡμεῖς δι' ἐκείνου θεραπευόμεθα, οὕτως δίδοντες ὡς λαμβάνοντες. Καὶ αὕτη ἐστὶν ἡ ἐν γνώσει ἐλεημοσύνη.

3. Dor. Gaz., *log.* 14.155 (SC 92.436–38): οὐ διά τινα λογισμὸν ἀνθρώπινον, ἀλλὰ δι' αὐτὸ τὸ καλόν, δι' αὐτὴν τὴν συμπάθειαν.

4. Dor. Gaz., *log.* 14.155 (SC 92.442): Οὐδὲ οὕτως ἔχεις; . . . δύνασαι δι' ὑπερσίας ἐλεῆσαι τὸν ἀσθενοῦντα. Οὐ δύνασαι οὐδὲ τοῦτο . . . Ἐλέησον οὖν αὐτὸν διὰ τοῦ λόγου καὶ ἄκουσον τοῦ λέγοντος· Ἀγαθὸν λόγος ὑπὲρ δόμα.

5. Dor. Gaz., *log.* 14.154 (SC 92.432–34): Διὰ γὰρ τοῦ κατὰ μικρὸν μικρὸν βοηθεῖν τῷ πλησίον, ἔρχῃ καὶ εἰς τὸ θέλειν τὸ συμφέρον αὐτῷ ὡς τὸ συμφέρον σοι, καὶ τὴν ὠφέλειαν αὐτοῦ ὡς τὴν ἑαυτόν. Καὶ τοῦτό ἐστι τὸ Ἀγαπήσεις τὸν πλησίον σου ὡς ἑαυτόν. Cf. Dor. Gaz., *log.* 6.77

6. Isaiah Scet., *log.* 15.55 (CSCO 293.295): ἡ ἐν γνώσει ἐλεημοσύνη τίκτει τὸ προορᾶν, καὶ ὁδηγεῖ εἰς τὴν ἀγάπην. Cf. Evagr. Pont., *Exp. in Prov.* (SC 340.104); Ath., Ps.-, *renunt.* (PG 28.1412); and Ath., Ps.-, *v.Syncl.* (discussed in this chapter's section "Sins of Excess and Redemptive Almsgiving"). Pétré 1948: 229–39, explores the relation between *caritas* and *misericordia*/*eleēmosyna*, simply concluding that they were close synonyms.

7. Chrys., *In Act.* 22.4 (PG 60.175): δι' ἧς ἀγάπης τὸ φυτὸν τρέφεται. Οὐδὲν γὰρ οὕτως ἀγάπην τρέφειν εἴωθεν, ὡς τὸ ἐλεήμονα εἶναί τινα.

8. Chrys., *In 1 Cor.* 32.9 (PG 61.271): Διὰ τοῦτο καὶ ἐλεημοσύνη παρὰ τοῦ Θεοῦ νενομοθέτηται. Καὶ γὰρ ἠδύνατο τοὺς πένητας διατρέφειν ὁ Θεὸς καὶ χωρὶς τούτου, ἀλλ' ἵνα ἡμᾶς εἰς τὴν ἀγάπην συνδήσῃ, καὶ ἵνα διαθερμαινώμεθα πρὸς ἀλλήλους, παρ' ἡμῶν αὐτοὺς ἐκέλευσε τρέφεσθαι.

9. Chrys., *In Tit.* 6.3 (PG 62.698): Αὕτη [viz., ἐλεημοσύνη] γὰρ μήτηρ ἀγάπης ἐστὶν, ἀγάπης τῆς τὸν Χριστιανισμὸν χαρακτηριζούσης, τῆς τῶν σημείων ἁπάντων μείζονος, δι' ἧς οἱ μαθηταὶ φαίνονται τοῦ Χριστοῦ. Cf. Chrys., *In Phil.* 4.1 (62.212); also Bas. Caes., *RF* 3.1 (PG 31.917); and *Pan. Rabb.* (trans. Doran, 100): "As soon as his friends hear the sweet name of Rabbula, love of him is inflamed in their hearts. Their compassion bubbles up and they give alms."

10. *Hom. Clem.* 12.26; see chapter 2, "Christian Philanthropy before Constantine."

11. *AP* G Matoes 10 (PG 65.293); with Gould 1993b. The thirteen are *AP* GS 4.102, 13.7 (= *AP* G Poemen 69), 13.14 (= *AP* L 13.13, N 286), 13.15 (= *AP* L 13.15, N 281), 13.16 (= *AP* L 13.14, N 282), 13.18 (= *AP* G Timothy 1), 13.19 (= *AP* G Sarah 7); *AP* N 38, 39, 40, 222; *AP* Or 6; and Poemen 109. Only *AP* GS 13.15 and 16 use ἐλεημοσύνη and ἀγάπη together; in the latter, an almsgiver's reluctance disqualifies his alms as charity.

12. Gould 1993a: 96–97.

13. Brakke 2008: 81–82. The classic study is Goehring 1990.

14. This is one of Guy's additions to the alphabetical collection ("John Colobus 7"; Guy, 24). Guy 1984: 129–30 notes that the *apophthegmata* represent "une source par excellence, difficile à utiliser." Rather than supposing they reflect reality, I treat them as (a more or less consistent) didactic fiction aimed at promoting a certain ascetic logic.

15. See Regnault 1981; Neyt 2004; Larsen 2006; Bitton-Ashkelony and Kofsky 2006; Rubenson 2009; and Rubenson 2012: 499.

16. On Gazan monasticism, see Chitty 1966: 132–40; Bitton-Ashkelony and Kofsky 2006; Chryssavgis 2001; Parrinello 2010.

17. Brown 1988: 233, translating Regnault 1972a: 6.

18. Essential studies: Chitty 1966: 1–45; Guillaumont 1975; Brown 1988: 213–40; Burton-Christie 1993; Gould 1993a; and Brakke 2006: 127–56. Regarding the *AP* cited in this section, the Latin collection (*AP* L) may be prior to the Greek systematic collection (*AP* GS), whereas the Greek alphabetical collection (*AP* G) and Greek anonymous collections (*AP* N) may be earlier than both *AP* L and *AP* GS; the Syriac collection (*AP* S) was compiled in the seventh century. See Gould 1993a: 5–25; and Rubenson 1995: 145–52.

19. *AP* GS 6.1, 6, 8, 14, 16; and *AP* G Arsenius 22. For *autarchia*, *AP* G Agathon 10–12. On the actual economic practices of Egyptian anchorites, see Wipszycka 2018: 492–514.

20. *AP* S 2.1.413 (Budge, 2.237). On fasting in desert tradition, see Shaw 1998.

21. What follows is indebted to Burton-Christie 1993; and Gould 1993a. Cf. Wortley 2013.

22. Burton-Christie 1993: 261. Cf. *AP* GS 14.7, 15.72, 17.31; *AP* G Or 11.

23. *AP* GS 17.7 (SC 498.14).

24. *AP* GS 17.19 (SC 498.22): εὐδοκήσῃ καὶ ὁ λογισμὸς εἰς τὸ διδόμενον. . . . ἐὰν τίς σε αἰτήσῃ πρᾶγμα δὸς αὐτὸ ἀπὸ ὅλης ψυχῆς. Cf. *AP* G Sisoes 31.

25. *AP* GS 17.22 (SC 498.24). In our day, a similar reluctance to accept a gift that seems too much of a sacrifice sometimes arises regarding gifts of organ transplants.

26. *AP* N 347 (*ROC* 17.298).

27. *AP* G Theodore of Pherme 18 (PG 65.308BC). Cf. *AP* G Nistherus 4; and *AP* G Agathon 26. In Ḥenanisho's version (*AP* S 1.9.426), the body was not a leper's but a heretic's body!

28. *AP* GS 17.17 (SC 498.20–22).

29. *AP* GS 5.31 (SC 387.268–70). See also *AP* GS 5.32; 15.39; 17.20, 24, and 29.

30. *AP* GS 10.156 (SC 474.116–18): ἐὰν δῷ αὐτῇ ἀγάπην οὔκ ἐστιν ὡς εἰς τῶν πτωχῶν. . . . οὐχί . . . ὅτι τὸ αἷμα ἕλκει σε μικρόν. Cf. *AP* GS 17.27; and Mt 5:43–44: "Love your enemies and pray for those who persecute you, that you may become sons of your Father in heaven."

31. *AP* GS 17.13 (SC 498.18). Cf. Burton-Christie 1993: 267–82; and Wortley 2013: 730–39.

32. *AP* G Arsenius 11.

33. *AP* GS 12.14 (SC 474.262–64). See also *AP* GS 11.114 and 17.30. On the theme of compassion in the *AP*, see Burton-Christie 1993: 281–84.

34. *AP* G Lot 2 (PG 65.256): βαστάζω μετὰ σοῦ τὸ ἥμισυ τῆς ἁμαρτίας. See also *AP* N 180.

35. Burton-Christie 1993: 282–87; Torrance 2009: 467–68. For its penitential aspects, see Bitton-Ashkelony 1999: 179–94; Bitton-Ashkelony and Kofsky 2006: 63–81, 151–52; and Rapp 2008: 138–44.

36. Neatly illustrated in *AP* N 346; and *AP* GS 17.29.

37. *AP* N 389 (*ROC* 18.143–44).

38. *AP* GS 18.44 (SC 498.94–96): ὀφείλει ἕκαστος τὸ τοῦ πλησίον οἰκειοῦσθαι ὅπως ἂν ἔχῃ, καὶ σχεδὸν ἐνδύσασθαι αὐτὸν μετὰ τοῦ σώματος καὶ ὅλον φορεῖν τὸν ἄνθρωπον καὶ συμπάσχειν αὐτῷ καὶ συγχαίρειν ἐπὶ πᾶσιν καὶ συγκλαίειν αὐτῷ, καὶ ἁπλῶς οὕτω διακεῖσθαι ὅτι τὸ αὐτὸ φορεῖ σῶμα, αὐτὸ πρόσωπον ἔχει καὶ τὴν αὐτὴν ψυχήν, καὶ ὡς ὑπὲρ ἑαυτοῦ θλίβεσθαι εἴ ποτε συμβῇ αὐτῷ θλίψις.

39. *AP* GS 17.30 (SC 498.30). Cf. the allusion to Phil 2:7 in *AP* GS 5.32.

40. *AP* N 6 (*ROC* 12.50): διὰ τῶν σαρκικῶν σου ἐστύλησάς μου τὰ πνευματικά. On the perception of material possessions as a danger in Evagrius's writings, Brakke 2008: 78–82.

41. *AP* G Macarius 30. See also *AP* G Nisterius 4; and *AP* GS 6.21–23.

42. *AP* GS 18.42 (SC 498.92); and *AP* G Arsenius 39. Cf. Jo. Cassian, *Inst.* 3.12. In general, see Donahue 1953; Gorce 1972: 6–91; and Alcock 2000.

43. *AP* G Sisoes 2 (PG 65.392C); and *AP* GS 12.24 (SC 474.224).

44. *AP* GS 13.11 (SC 474.236). For prioritizing charity over fasting, *AP* GS 13.2, 4; 14.7; 17.22, 32.

45. Gould 1993a: 148.

46. *AP* G John Colobus 39 (PG 65: 217A); also *AP* GS 17.2 (SC 498.12). On the relation of this motif to charity and Jesus's "great commandments," Burton-Christie 1993: 264.

47. *AP* G Paphnutius 2 (PG 65.377D).

48. *AP* G Agathon 17 (PG 65.113B): τὸ δοῦναι καὶ λαβεῖν ἀγάπη μοι ἦν· λογιζόμενος ὅτι τὸ κέρδος τοῦ ἀδελφοῦ μου, ἔργον καρποφορίας ἐστίν. On this remark, see Gould 1993a: 94. See also *AP* G Achilles 1; *AP* N 288, 353; *AP* GS 10.23, 37; and *AP* L 17.24. For καρποφορία as "contribution," see chapter 6, introduction.

49. Jo. Mosch., *prat.* 113 (PG 87[3].2977C).

50. For an overview, Wipszycka 2005: 269–86; and Wipszycka 2011: 176–77. On the archaeology, Weidmann 1984: 59–62, focusing on the sixth- and seventh-century structures in a part of Kellia known as Qouçoûr el-Izeila.

51. *AP* GS 17.23. Cf. *AP* G Abraham 1; and Burton-Christie 1993: 261.

52. See Hevelone-Harper 2005: 16–18; Bitton-Ashkelony and Kofsky 2000; and Glucker 1987. Hilarion literally put Tawatha (a.k.a. Thavatha) on the map; otherwise, it is hard to account for its depiction on the Madaba Map. The region may have produced the earliest compilation of *apophthegmata patrum*. Regnault 1981.

53. Bars. et Jo., *resp.* 252 (SC 450.210): χιλιάδες . . . νομισμάτων ἐδίδουν αὐτῷ. The donors were perhaps the Georgian prince Peter the Iberian (d. 488) and his companion, who lived with Isaiah for three years. On Isaiah's community, see Chitty 1971. For the topic of wealth in his teachings, Rubenson 2009. Some local monks kept slaves. Bitton-Ashkelony and Kofsky 2006: 194–96.

54. Identifying John of Beersheba with John of Gaza, following Hevelone-Harper 2005: 32–44.

55. For the military connections, *v.Dos.* 2–3. I estimate the number of monks from descriptions in the letter prefaces (43 cenobites, 12 solitaries). In *log.* 2.34, Dorotheus mentions conversing with the wealthiest man in Gaza, evidently a regular if not fictional acquaintance. For the apparent conformity of the monastery to Justinianic laws, see Lesieur 2011.

56. Hirschfeld 2004: 76–77 believed this site at Umm el-'Amr was the Seridos monastery, but an inscription identifies it with Hilarion. See Elter and Hassoune 2004.

57. Di Segni 2001: 32 calculates that 64 percent of the letters were written to monks (who made up 59 percent of all correspondents), 31 percent to laity (34.8 percent of correspondents), 4.5 percent to clergy (6 percent of correspondents). On Dorotheus's probable editorship, see Hevelone-Harper 2005: 76–77.

58. Bars. et Jo., *resp.* 259, 286, 488.

59. Dor. Gaz., *log.* 4.57 (SC 92.242–44, Wheeler 118). Cf. Lesieur 2011: 18.

60. Bars. et Jo., *resp.* 318. Cf. Torrance 2009.

61. Dor. Gaz., *log.* 4.56 (SC 92.240). Cf. Bars. et Jo., *resp.* 17 (trans. Chryssavgis, 37); and Bitton-Ashkelony and Kofsky 2006: 202–3.

62. Perrone 2004: 148.

63. Stroumsa 2009: 126, citing Isaiah Scet., *log.*1. For discipleship at the monastery, see Hevelone-Harper 2005: 5–6, 32–76; and Bitton-Ashkelony and Kofsky 2006.

64. Emphasized by Parrinello 2010: 139.

65. Bars. et Jo., *resp.* 184.

66. Torrance 2009: 468.

67. Bars. et Jo., *resp.* 579. Cf. Bars. et Jo., *resp.* 483.

68. Bars. et Jo., *resp.* 339 (SC 450.344-46): Ἡ πρὸς τὸν πλησίον ἀγάπη κατὰ πολλοὺς τρόπους φανεροῦται, οὐχὶ ἐν τῷ δοῦναί τι αὐτῷ μόνον. . . . ἐὰν θελήσωμεν τούτῳ τῷ τρόπῳ πληρῶσαι τὸν γραφικὸν λόγον, οὐ μὴ σταθῇ μεθ' ἡμῶν.

69. Bars. et Jo., *resp.* 341 (SC 450.350): Τῶν τελείων γάρ ἐστι τὸ συμπαθῆσαι τῷ πλησίον. Νεωτέρῳ δὲ τὸ συμπαθῆσαι ἄλλῳ χλεύη δαιμόνων ἐστίν. . . . Τὸ συμπαθῆσαι δέ τινι ὡς διὰ τὴν ἀγάπην, οὔπω ἦλθες εἰς τὸ μέτρον τοῦτο.

70. Bars. et Jo., *resp.* 342 (SC 450.352-54): ἄλλη ἐστὶν ἡ ἀγάπη τῶν Πατέρων πρὸς τὰ τέκνα αὐτῶν καὶ ἄλλη ἐστὶν ἡ ἀγάπης τῶν ἀδελφῶν πρὸς τοὺς ἀδελφοὺς αὐτῶν. . . . Ἕκαστος δὲ κατὰ τὸ μέτρον αὐτοῦ ἀγαπᾷ τὸν πλησίον αὐτοῦ. Τὸ μέτρον οὖν τῆς τελείας ἀγάπης ἐστί . . . ἀγαπᾶν καὶ τὸν πλησίον αὐτοῦ ὡς ἑαυτόν. Ἡ δὲ νεότης ὀφείλει φυλάξαι ἐν πᾶσι . . . Τὸ δὲ μέτρον τῆς ἀγάπης αὐτῶν πρὸς ἀλλήλους οὕτως ὀφείλει εἶναι μὴ καταλαλεῖν ἀλλήλων, μὴ μισεῖν, μὴ ἐξουθενεῖν, μὴ ζητεῖν τὰ ἑαυτῶν, μὴ ἀγαπᾶν διὰ τὸ κάλλος τοῦ σώματος ἢ διὰ σωματικὴν εὐεργεσίαν, μὴ καθέζεσθαι μετ' ἀλλήλων χωρὶς ἀνάγκης μεγάλης. . . . Ἕως ὧδέ ἐστι τὸ μέτρον τῆς ἀγάπης τῶν νεωτέρων πρὸς ἀλλήλους.

71. Bars. et Jo., *resp.* 252 indicates that "burden bearer" corresponded to "spiritual master" in this monastery. Cf. Rapp 2005: 72-73; Bitton-Ashkelony 2006: 87-88; and Torrance 2009: 467-69.

72. Bars. et Jo., *resp.* 270 (SC 450.254; trans. Chryssavgis, 113.274, adapted): δεικνύω σοι τὰ μέτρα τῆς ἀγάπης, ὅτι ἀναγκάζει ἑαυτὴν καὶ εἰς τὰ ὑπέρμετρα. . . . βαστάζω, ἀλλ' ἐπὶ τῷ ὅρῳ τούτῳ ἵνα καὶ σὺ βαστάζῃς τὸ φυλάξεσθαί μου τοὺς λόγους καὶ τὰς ἐντολάς.

73. Bars. et Jo., *resp.* 273, 274 (SC 450.258): ἡ πρὸς σὲ ἀπ' ἐμοῦ διαθήκη . . . ἀραβῶνά σοι δέδωκα εἰς σωτηρίαν τῆς ψυχῆς σου. For contractual implications, see Rapp 2008: 137-44.

74. Bars. et Jo., *resp.* 353 (SC 450.374; trans. Chryssavgis, 114.3): Τοῦτο δὲ μάθε ἀδελφέ, ὅτι καθὼς οἶδας, τὴν ψυχήν μου ἡδέως ὑπερτίθημί σου καὶ ἡ δέησίς μου ὑπὲρ σοῦ ἀδιάλειπτός ἐστιν.

75. Bars. et Jo., *resp.* 58. In *resp.* 388, Barsanuphius explains that Jesus did not need cooperation for his prayers to be effective, but the apostles needed cooperation and mutual prayer. On this issue, see especially Bars. et Jo., *resp.* 616.

76. Bars. et Jo., *resp.* 139, 198. For papyrus references to monastic advocates being sent to petition imperial courts, see Urbanik 2009: 229.

77. Bars. et Jo., *resp.* 97, 498. Cf. *AP GS* 10.4. Prescription of prostrations, Bars. et Jo., *resp.* 107, 229. Cf. Bars. et Jo., *resp.* 88, 92, 96, 97, 105, 108, 124, 196, 199, 243, 265, 412, 553; and Torrance 2009.

78. Bars. et Jo., *resp.* 229, 231, 234, 237, 242, 616, which graphically illustrate such reasoning.

79. Bars. et Jo., *resp.* 73 (SC 427.348-50): βαστάζω τὸ ἥμισυ τῶν σῶν ἁμαρτιῶν, συγκοινὸν ἐποιησά σε. Οὐ γὰρ εἶπόν σοι τὸ τρίτον βαστάζω καὶ ἀφῆκά σε περισσότερόν μου βαστάζοντα καὶ βαρούμενον. Καὶ πάλιν ἐξορίζων τὴν φιλαυτίαν εἶπον ὃ εἶπον, καὶ οὐκ εἶπόν σοι τὸ δίμοιρον. . . . οὐκ εἶπον τὸ ὅλον βαστάζω. Τῶν γὰρ τελείων ἐστὶ τοῦτο τῶν γενομένων ἀδελφῶν τοῦ Χριστοῦ τοῦ θήσαντος ὑπὲρ ἡμῶν τὴν ἑαυτοῦ ψυχήν, καὶ ἀγαπήσαντος τοὺς ἀγαπήσαντας ἡμᾶς ἐν τελείᾳ ἀγάπῃ ποιεῖν τοῦτο. . . . Οὐκ κενοδοξῶ . . . συγκοινωνόν σε ποιήσας. Cf. Bars. et Jo., *resp.* 72.

278 NOTES TO PAGES 111–114

80. Bars. et Jo., *resp.* 239 (SC 427.348–50; trans. Chryssavgis, 113.244–45). Cf. Bars. et Jo., *resp.* 104 on the devil's machinations.

81. Bars. et Jo., *resp.* 237 (trans. Chryssavgis, 113.242).

82. Bars. et Jo., *resp.* 68, 104. Cf. 16, 48, 615, 616.

83. Bars. et Jo., *resp.* 73 (SC 427.348–50): Ἐπειδὴ οὖν οὐκ ἐνόησας τί εἶπον σοι ὅτι Βαστάζω τὸ ἥμισυ τῶν σῶν ἁμαρτιῶν, συγκοινωνὸν ἐποίησά σε. Cf. Bars. et Jo., *resp.* 92, 106, 107, 351; and 2 Cor 1:7, which refers to partnership in Christ's sufferings; for the foolishness of "brothers outside," Bars. et Jo., *resp.* 68.

84. On the term ὁμόψυχος, see Bitton-Ashkelony and Kofsky 2006: 148–49; Torrance 2009: 469. Barsanuphius reserves it for the hesychasts John (Bars. et Jo., *resp* 5, 7, 10, 35, 141, 188), Paul (57), Euthymius (64), and Andrew (93, 96, 99, 105). He applies γνησίος ἀδελφός/ γνησίος ἀγαπητός (genuine brother/genuine beloved) only to John (7, 13, 265), Paul (57), and Euthymius (70).

85. Bars. et Jo., *resp.* 71 (SC 426.344): Ζεύξωμεν ἑαυτοὺς ὁμοθυμαδὸν.

86. Bars. et Jo., *resp.* 13, 68, 305.

87. Bars. et Jo., *resp.* 58 (SC 426.248). John acknowledges in 305 (SC 450.296) that Barsanuphius's willingness to show him mercy united them as one:Ἔλεος γὰρ ποιεῖ μετ᾽ ἐμοῦ, τοῦ εἶναι τοὺς δύο ἕν. Cf. Bars. et Jo., *resp.* 55, 57, 58, 68, 69, 72, 74, 75, 77, 79, 86, 353. On such "vicarious lateral penance," see Rapp 2008: 144–47.

88. Bars. et Jo., *resp.* 63 (SC 426.318): διὰ τὴν ἀγάπην καὶ ἕλκε με πρὸς αὐτόν, καὶ διὰ σοῦ σῴζει με τὸν ἐλεεινόν. Cf. Bars. et Jo., *resp.* 56, 65,79, 86. While most of such letters include a request for prayer, only in these does Barsanuphius specify his own need for mercy.

89. Bars. et Jo., *resp.* 97. Cf. Bars. et Jo., *resp.* 91 (SC 427.388): Τὸ οὖν εὑρεῖν ἔλεος, εὐχαῖς ἁγίων εὑρίσκεις; and Bars. et Jo., *resp.* 111. Torrance 2009: 469–71 discusses the paradigm of Christ's charity. On Barsanuphius's exchange with Andrew, see Crislip 2013: 141–65.

90. Bars. et Jo., *resp.* 544. Cf. Bars. et Jo., *resp.* 77, 145, 198, 223, 232, 243, 264, 450, 507.

91. Bars. et Jo., *resp.* 219.

92. Bars. et Jo., *resp.* 65, 70, 72, 101, 420, 464.

93. Dor. Gaz., *log.* 1.25

94. *v.Sym.Styl.iun.* 69 (SH 32.59–60): σπλαγχνισθεὶς ἐδεήθη τοῦ Θεοῦ μετὰ δακρύων ἐλεῆσαι τὸν λαὸν αὐτοῦ. Καὶ εἶπεν αὐτῷ ὁ σωτήρ· "Πολλαί εἰσιν αἰνειῶν αὐτῶν· οὐδὲ γὰρ πλείω μου ἀγαπᾷς αὐτούς." On Symeon's burden bearing, *v.Sym.Styl.iun.* 113, 121.

95. For date and discussion, Efthymiades and Déroche 2011: 46; Brakke 2006: 188–93; and Ampelarga 2002: 21–24.

96. Ath., Ps.-, *v.Syncl.*, ll. 715–35 (Ampelarga 238–40): οὐ γὰρ πρὸς ἕνα ἄνθρωπον ὁ Κύριος τὴν ἀγάπην ἐνετείλατο, ἀλλὰ πρὸς πάντας· οὐκοῦν οὐ δέον ἔχοντά τινα παριδεῖν τοὺς χρῄζοντας· ὑποκλέπτεται γὰρ τῆς ἀγάπης· τὸ μὲν γὰρ πᾶσιν ἐξαρκεῖν ἀδύνατον ἀνθρώπῳ ... Τί οὖν, φησίν; ὁ μὴ ἔχων περὶ ἐλεημοσύνης ἀγωνίζῃ, καὶ αὕτη σοι πρόφασις τοῦ κτήσασθαι γίνεται; κοσμικοῖς τοῦτο προστέτακται· οὐ γὰρ τοσοῦτον πρὸς τὸ τραφῆναι τὸν πένητα ἡ ἐλεημοσύνη ὥρισται, ὅσον διὰ τὴν ἀγάπην· οὐ γάρ τὸν πλούσιον διοικῶν Θεὸς καὶ τὸν πένητα τρέφει· περιττῶς οὖν ἡ ἐλεημοσύνη προσετάγη; μὴ γένοιτο! ἀλλὰ ἀρχὴ τῆς ἀγάπης τοῖς μὴ εἰδόσι γίνεται· ὥσπερ γὰρ ὑπογραμμὸς ἦν ἡ τῆς ἀκροβυστίας περιτομὴ τῆς καρδίας, οὕτως ἡ ἐλεημοσύνη τῆς ἀγάπης διδάσκαλος κατέστη· οἷς οὖν ἡ ἀγάπη ἐκ χάριτος ἐδόθη, περιττὴ ἡ ἐλεημοσύνη. οὐ διαβάλλουσα τὸν ἔλεον ταῦτα λέγω,

ἀλλὰ τῆς ἀκτημοσύνης τὸ καθαρὸν δεικνύουσα μὴ γινέσθω οὖν κώλυσις τὸ ἔλαττον τοῦ μείζονος· ἐν ὀλίγῳ τὸ μικρὸν κατορθώσας, πάντα γὰρ ὑφ'ἓν δέδωκας, πρὸς τὸ μεῖζον τὸ λοιπὸν ἀνάνευσον, τὴν ἀγάπην.

97. Ath., Ps.-, *v.Syncl.*, ll. 737–58 (Ampelarga 240–41): ὁ γὰρ Κύριος δημιουργάσας τὴν οἰκουμένην διπλῆν ἐν ταύτῃ τῶν οἰκητόρων ἔθετο τὴν τάξιν. ... ἐκεῖ φησιν· Ἐργάσῃ τὴν γῆν, καὶ ὧδε· Μὴ μεριμνήσητε περὶ τῆς αὔριον. ... τῇ ψυχῇ ζῶμεν· αὐτῇ τὰς ἀρετὰς ἐπιδείξωμεν· κατὰ διάνοια ἐλεήσωμεν· Μακάριοι γὰρ οἱ ἐλεήμονες τῇ ψυχῇ. This conflates Mt 5:7 ("Blessed are the Merciful," often applied to almsgivers) with Mt 5:3 ("Blessed are the Poor in Spirit," often applied to monks).

98. Bars. et Jo., *resp.* 627 (SC 468.52); *AP* GS 13.6 17–18, 14.13; *AP* G Or 6; Poemen 51; *AP* N 38–40; and Leont. Neap., *v.Sym.* (Festugière-Rydén 61). For the ancient Syrian tradition, exemplified above all by the *Liber graduum*, see Caner 2002: 50–157.

99. *AP* GS 13.14 (SC 498.242): ἐξότε δὲ οὐδὲν λαμβάνω παρὰ σοῦ, περισσεύω καὶ ὁ Θεὸς εὐλογεῖ με ... τοῦτο δὲ μᾶλλον ὠφελεῖ αὐτόν· τοῦ ποιεῖν αὐτὸν ἐκ τοῦ κόπου αὐτοῦ ἐλεημοσύνην καὶ λαμβάνειν εὐχὴν παρὰ τῶν ἁγίων, καὶ οὕτως εὐλογεῖται.

100. Bars. et Jo., *resp.* 77 (SC 427.358). Moschus thought it notable that an anchorite remained a gifted almsgiver *despite* his commitment to voluntary poverty. Jo. Mosch., *prat.* 9 (PG 87[3].2860A). Cf. Ps.-Ath., *v.Syncl.*, ll.149–50: ἡ ἐλεημοσύνη, εἰ καὶ μὴ ἡ κατ' ἐνέργειαν, ἀλλ' οὖν γε ἡ κατὰ πρόθεσιν.

101. Bas. Caes., *RB* 271 (PG 31.1269B): πάντα ταῦτα δηλονότι ὅσα ἐν τῷ ἁρπάζειν καὶ πλεονεκτεῖν ἁμαρτάνομεν, καὶ πονηρευόμεθα ... Ὥστε ὅσα τοιαῦτά ἐστιν ἁμαρτήματα, ἅπερ δύνατον ἀναλῦσαι, καὶ ὑπὲρ ὧν ἔστιν ἀντιδοῦναι πολυπλάσιον, τούτῳ τῷ τρόπῳ καθαρίζεσθαι.

102. Garrison 1993; Anderson 2007; Anderson 2012; Downs 2008. I cannot speculate here whether Basil and John Chrysostom's discussions of redemptive almsgiving might have been influenced by exposure to Jewish or Syrian Christian notions of almsgiving as righteousness, but it seems probable.

103. Chrys., *In Mt.* 61.2 (PG 58.591).

104. Chrys., *In Mt.* 61.3 (PG 58.591–92). On the exploitation of laborers that such passages attest. see De Ste. Croix 1981: 185–86, 198–201.

105. Chrys., *In 1 Thess.* 10.5 (PG 62.460–61).

106. Chrys., *In Jo.* 76.3 (PG 59.413).

107. Newhauser 2000: 38–46, quoted at 41. For an incomplete but useful discussion of Chrysostom's focus on *pleonexia*, see Plassmann 1961: 74–80, 94–96.

108. Chrys., *In Gen.* 16.4 (PG 53.130, Hill 74.213): ἐκεῖνος τὰ ὑπὲρ τὴν ἀξίαν φρονήσας, καὶ τῆς παρασχεθείσης ἀξίας ἐξεβλήθη, καὶ ἐκ τῶν οὐρανῶν εἰς τὴν γῆν κατηνέχθη. On God setting limits on everything, transgressed by excess, see Chrys., *In Eph.* 1.4 (PG 62.22): Καίτοι ὁ Θεὸς διὰ τοῦτο τῇ φύσει μέτρον καὶ ὅριον ἔθηκεν, ἵνα μηδεμίαν ἔχωμεν ἀνάγκην τοῦ τὸν πλοῦτον ἐπιζητεῖν, οἷον ἑνὶ ἱματίῳ ἢ καὶ δευτέρῳ περιβάλλεσθαι τὸ σῶμα ἐκέλευσε, καὶ περιττοῦ οὐ χρεία πρὸς τὴν σκέπην.

109. Chrys., *In Gen.* 16.4 (PG 53.129; trans. Hill, 74.213): οὐκ ἀνασχομένη μεῖναι ἐπὶ τῶν οἰκείων ὅρων. ... παρεσκεύασε μείζονα τῆς οἰκείας ἀξίας φρονῆσαι.

110. Chrys., *In Gen.* 16.1 (PG 53:126).

111. Chrys., *In Gen.* 16.4 (PG 53.130) blames the Fall on Eve's "untimely desire" (ἀκαίρου ἐπιθυμίας ἐκείνης). Chrys., *In Eph.* 18.3 (PG 62.125) claims that Ὁ Κάιν τὸν Θεὸν

ἐπλεονέκτησεν. On Origen's identification of *pleonexia* as Adam's sin, see Newhauser 2000: 12–14. The idea is central to the Syriac *Book of Steps*. Brown 1988: 336–37.

112. Chrys., *In Act.* 51.5 (PG 60.358): τοῦτο γὰρ πλεονεξία, πλέον ἔχειν τοῦ ὡρισμένου. Cf. Chrys., *In Eph.* 13.3 (62.97); and Chrys., *In 2 Tim.* 7.1 (637). Others believed *pleonexia* meant more than greed. Newhauser 2000: 7.

113. Chrys., *In Tit.* 3.3 (PG 62.682): οὐδὲν πλεονεξίας ἀκαθαρτότερον. Cf. Chrys., *In 2 Tim.* 6.3 (635); Chrys., *In Heb.* 25.7–8 (63.176). This understanding of *pleonexia* as imbalance and impurity existed among middle Platonists. Malherbe 1996: 125–26. For Chrysostom's awareness of medical principles, see Plassmann 1961: 22.

114. Chrys., *In Eph.* 18.3 (PG 62.125):Ἵνα γάρ σου τὴν πλεονεξίαν σβέσῃ ὁ Θεὸς, εἰς τοσοῦτον μέτρον τὰ κτίσματα ἐξήγαγε· σὺ δέ ἁρπάζεις. Cf. Chrys., *In 1 Tim.* 17.3 (595).

115. Chrys., *In Jo.* 34.3 (PG 59.197): ἀποστάντας φάρμακα ἐπιθεῖναι τοῖς τραύμασι τὰ ἐναντία τῶν ἁμαρτημάτων. Οἷόν τι λέγω; Ἥρπαγας καὶ ἐπλεονέκτησας; ἀπόστηθι τῆς ἁρπαγῆς καὶ ἐπίθες ἐλεημοσύνην τῷ τραύματι. Cf. Chrys., *In Jo.* 81.3 (59.442); Chrys., *In Rom.* 10.5 (60.480); Chrys., *In 2 Cor.* 19.2 (61.532); Aster., *hom.* 3.3.1, 13.11.3; Isid. Pel., *ep.*1234; and Dor. Gaz., *log.* 11.113, 12.133.

116. Chrys., *In Jo.* 13.14 (PG 59.90–92): μόνον ἂν ἐκ δικαίου κέρδους καὶ πόνων τοιούτων, καὶ πάσης ἦ καθαρὰ πλεονεξίας καὶ καὶ ἁρπαγῆς καὶ βίας. Cf. Chrys., *In 1 Cor* 35.3 (61.299); Chrys., *In Mt.* 41.4 (57.450), 85.3 (58.761); Chrys., *In Jo.* 34.3 (59.197), 73.3 (400), 88.3 (482); Chrys., *In 2 Tim.* 6.3 (62.634).

117. On holiness, Chrys., *In Eph.* 13.2 (PG 62.96): Τὸ δὲ ὅσιον τί ἐστι; Τὸ καθαρὸν, τὸ ὀφειλόμεν. Cf. Chrys., *In Mt.* 74.4 (PG 58.684), presenting self-sufficiency (*autarkeia*) as an antidote to *pleonexia*.

118. Chrys., *In Mt.* 61.2 (PG 58.591): μοναχοὶ οὐδὲ τί ποτέ ἐστιν ἡ πλεονεξία ἴσασιν. Cf. Chrys., *In Mt.* 8.3, 69.3, and 72.4. For his use of monks as exemplars, Brändle 1979: 164–71; and Caner 2002: 169–77.

119. Evagr. Pont., *Fnd.* 8 (PG 40.1260D; trans. Sinkewicz, 9).

120. Bars. et Jo., *resp.* 749 (SC 468.192): Σπούδασον ἐκ τοῦ ἐναντίου μικρόν τι περισσὸν δοῦναι . . . ἵνα φύγῃς τὴν πονηρὰν πλεονεξίαν. Cf. Bars. et Jo., *resp.* 335, 626. In Bars. et Jo., *resp.* 337, humility offsets *pleonexia*.

121. *AP* G Agathon 16 and Pistamon 1. Cf. Isaiah Scet., *log.* 10.53, 11.52–53.

122. *Paralip.* 9.23 (Halkin, 149–50; trans. Veilleux, 47): ἐν ἑαυτῷ τὸ κοσμικὸν φρόνημα . . .Ἡμάρτηκας μεγάλως, τὸ πλέον ἀγαπήσας.

123. *Const. Ap.* 4.6.3, 4.8.3 (SC 329.178 and 184). For date and provenance, see *Const. Ap.* (Metzger, "Introduction," SC 320.54–60).

124. Ps.-Ath., *qu. Ant.* 88 (PG 28: 652).

125. Anast. Sin., *resp.* 44.1–2 (CCSG 59: 97–98): Δεκτὰ ἄρα εἰσιν τῷ Θεῷ τὰ ἀπὸ κλεμμάτων ἢ ἀδικιῶν προσαγόμενα αὐτῷ χρήματα;Ἔστι κλέμματα καὶ ἀδικία· ἄλλο γάρ ἐστι τὸ παράψασθαι ἀπὸ τοῦ ἱεροῦ, καὶ ἕτερον τὸ ἐκ προσόδων γῆς ἢ θαλάττῶν ἀνδρῶν ἀπίστων, καὶ ἄλλο τὸ ἀδικῆσαι γεωρούς καὶ πτωχούς, καὶ ἕτερον τὸ ἐπᾶραι ἀπὸ εὐπόρων πονηρῶν καὶ φιλαργύρων. Πλὴν οὐ τὰ πολλὰ ζητεῖ ὁ Θεός, ἀλλὰ μόνον τὴν πρόθεσιν· εἰ δὲ ὅλως παρὰ τὸ ἀδικῆσαι οὐ δύνασαι, συμφέραι τὰ ἀπὸ κακῶν εἰς καλὰ δαπανηθῆναι καὶ μὴ τὰ ἀπὸ κακῶν εἰς κακόν. Μέντοιγε τὰ ἀπὸ ἀδικίας πτωχῶν καὶ γεωρῶν ὑπάρχοντα ἀπρόσδεκτα τῷ Θεῷ καὶ κεκατηραμένα ὑπάρχουσιν.

126. Chrys., *anom.* 6 (PG 48.754).

127. Chrys., *In 1 Thess.* 10.5 (PG 62.460): καίτοι αὐτά τε ἀποδοῦναι ἐκεῖνα, καὶ ἐκ τῶν οἴκοθεν προσθεῖναι ἕτερα. Chrys., *In Mt.* 52.3 (58.525): Οὐδὲ ... τῷ αὐτῷ μέτρῳ τῆς ἐλεημοσύνης θεραπεῦσαι τὸ ἀπὸ τῆς πλεονεξίας κακόν.

128. Chrys., *In Jo.* 88.3 (PG 59.482); see also Chrys., *In Mt.* 41.4 (57.451).

129. Geront., *v.Mel. gr.* 30 (SC 90.184): τὴν δὲ ἐλεημοσύνην οὕτως κατώρθωσιν, ὡς ἐξ αὐτῆς μόνης ἐλεηθῆναι ἐλπίζουσα. Cf. Anast. Sin., *resp.* 41.4.

130. Georg. Syc., *v.Thdr.Syc.* 25 (SH 48.22): σωφροσύνη καὶ ἁγνείᾳ, ἐλημοσύναις τε καὶ εὐχαῖς ἑαυτὰς ἐκκαθαίρουσαι καὶ σεμνύνουσαι. ... 38 (34): νηστείαις τε καὶ ἐλεημοσύναις καθάρας. ... 147 (115): ἐν νηστείαις, προσευχαῖς, τε καὶ ἐλεημοσύναις αὐτοὺς καθαίρων. Cf. *HM* 14.19, 23.4; *AP* G coll. syst. 13.18, 18.46; Marc. Diac., *v.Porph.* 52; Jo. Eph., *v.SS.Or.* 31; Jo. Mosch., *prat.* 32; and Anast. Sin., *resp.* app.10a.4.

131. Jo. Clim., *scal.* 5 (PG 88.780): δι᾽ ἐλεημοσύνης δέ τινες τρέχουσιν ἐν ἐξόδῳ τὸ ἑαυτῶν κέρδος γνωρίζοντες.

132. Jo. Eph., *v.SS.Or.* 21 ("Life of Thomas the Armenian"; PO 17.287–89).

133. Jo. Eph., *v.SS.Or.* 36 ("Life of Mare the Solitary"; PO 18.635).

134. Jo. Eph., *v.SS.Or.* 44 ("Life of Tribunus the Layman"; PO 18.665).

135. Jo. Eph., *v.SS.Or.* 12 ("Life of Mary and Euphemia"; PO 17.175).

136. Brock and Harvey 1998: 8–9.

137. Camenisch 1981: 3. Cf. Mauss 1990: 10; and Parry 1986: 461.

138. *SyrD.* 17.4.8–10, 18.4.6; noted by Zeisel 1975: 66.

139. *Const. Ap.* 4.6.9–10.3 (SC 329.186): οὐ γὰρ τῇ φύσει φαῦλα τὰ προσφερόμενα, ἀλλὰ τῇ γνώμῃ τῶν προσκομιζόντων αὐτά. For the identification of money derived from prostitution with money from plunder and of both with *pleonexia*, see *Const. Ap.* 3.8.2–3.

140. *v.Pelag. syr.* 39 (Brock and Harvey, 56–57). Cf. *AP* G John of Kellia 1 (PG 65 .233BC).

141. Anast. Sin., *resp.* 41.2–3 (CCSG 59.94–95): δι᾽ ἐλεημοσύνης ἡ ψυχὴ ἀποσμήχεται. ... οὐ γὰρ ἀπαντᾷ μοι θερίσαι ἀλλοτρίας ἀκάνθας ἁμαρτημάτων· εἴθε κἂν τὰς ἑαυτοῦ δυνηθῶ καθαρίσαι. Cf. *AP* GS 17.22 (SC 498.22).

142. *SyrD.* 15 (CSCO 179.164, trans. Vööbus 150).

143. *Const. Ap.* 3.8.2–3 (SC 329.140–42): ὑπὲρ ἑνὸς ἑκάστου τούτων δώσει λόγον τῷ Θεῷ δεχομένη ἀναξίως Θεοῦ. ... Ὁ γὰρ ἀπὸ τοιούτου ἐπιρρήτου ἢ ἀποσυναγώγου δεχόμενος καὶ ὑπὲρ τούτου προσευχόμενος, ἐμμένειν τοῖς κακοῖς τούτῳ προαιρουμένου καὶ θέλοντες μεταμεληθῆναι ποτε, κοινωνεῖ τούτῳ τῇ προσευχῇ καὶ λυπεῖ Χριστὸν τὸν τοὺς ἀδίκους ἀποστρεφόμενον, καὶ οἰκοδομεῖ αὐτοὺς διὰ τῆς ἀναξίου δόσεως καὶ συμμολύνεται αὐτοῖς. On screening such gifts, *Const. Ap.* 3.4.2, 3.8.1.

144. Chrys., *In Jo.* 77.5 (PG 59.420): διὰ τῆς εἰς ἐκείνους ἐλεημοσύνης ἀποδύεσθαι τὰ ἁμαρτήματα. On the comparison to slaves, Chrys., *In Heb.* 11.3 (63.93–94). Cf. Chrys., *In 1 Thess.* 11.3 (62.465).

145. For expectations that alms recipients would provide prayers, Finn 2006a: 179–81. In Greek hagiography of this era I have found monks depicted as alms recipients only in Pall., *HL* 47.7 (given to a female ascetic); Call., *v.Hyp.* 31 (to "poor monks"); Leont. Neap., *v.Jo. Eleem.* 15 (to a gyrovague); and Anast. Sin., *resp.* 41.2–3. For sociological considerations, see Camenisch 1981: 6–10.

146. Jo. Eph., *v.SS.Or.* 12 ("Life of Mary and Euphemia"; PO 17.178–79). Brooks translates as charity the Syriac word *ṭaybutā*, "grace," which Ḥenanisho᾽ regularly uses to translate

agapē in his Syriac version of the apophthegmata, e.g., *AP* S 2.1.387 (Budge, 539–40; = *AP* GS 13.15, *AP* L 13.15, *AP* N 281), and 2.1.388 (Budge, 540; = *AP* GS 5.31, *AP* N 179).

147. *v.Bars.* 83.3–24 (trans. Palmer, 212–14). This hagiography is discussed in chapter 7.

148. Chrys., *In Heb.* 28.9 (PG 63.197): ἐλεημοσύνη γάρ ἐστιν ἡ τῆς χήρας ἐκείνης, ἥτις τὸν βίον αὐτῆς πάντα ἐκένωσεν. Εἰ δὲ οὐ χωρεῖς τοσοῦτον ὅσον ἡ χήρα καταβαλεῖν, ἀλλὰ κἂν τὸ περίσσευμα ὅλον κατάβαλε· ἔχε τὰ ἀρκοῦντα, μὴ τὰ περιττά. Ἀλλ᾽ οὐδείς ἐστιν οὐδὲ τὸ περίσσευμα καταβάλλων. Cf. Chrys., *In Jo.* 60.4 (59.332–3): Ποῖον δὲ ἔλεος μέγα; Ὅταν μὴ ἐκ τοῦ περισσεύματος δῶμεν, ἀλλ᾽ ἐκ τοῦ ὑστερήματος; and Eus. Em., *hom.* 29.20 (Buytaert, 230).

149. Chrys., *In Rom.* 7.7 (PG 60.450).

150. Bars. et Jo., *resp.* 635; cf. 617, 620, 621.

151. Lk 11:41: πλὴν τὰ ἐνόντα δότε ἐλεημοσύνην, καὶ ἰδοὺ πάντα καθαρὰ ὑμῖν ἐστι.

152. *Life of Macarius of Scetis* 9 (trans. Vivian, 122–23). Cf. Pall., *HL* 17.12–13.

153. Leont. Neap., *v.Sym.* 1744A (Festugière-Rydén, 101): πάσῃ σου δυμάμει, εἰ ἔνδεκτον καὶ ὑπὲρ δύναμιν ἀγάπησον τὸν πλησίον σου διὰ τῆς ἐλεημοσύνης. αὕτη γὰρ ἡ ἀρετὴ ὑπὲρ πάσας βοηθεῖ ἡμῖν τότε. See also *v.Marc.Acoem.* 11; Call., *v.Hyp.* 31; *v.Pach. gr. prim.* 39; Jo. Mosch., *prat.* 184; and Leont. Neap., *v.Jo.Eleem.* 1, 22, 23.

154. *AP* GS 10.148; *AP* N 39, 40, 226; with Finn 2006a: 177–79; and Suzuki 2009.

155. Bars. et Jo., *resp.* 111 (SC 427.436). Cf. Bars. et Jo., *resp.* 205, 581.

156. Bars. et Jo., *resp.* 315 (SC 450.308), 845 (468.328); cf. 71, 67, 119.

157. Evagr. Pont., *Pr.* 18 (SC 171.546): ἀναιρετικὴ γὰρ οὐ μόνον χρημάτων ἡ ἀγάπη, ἀλλὰ καὶ αὐτῆς ἡμῶν τῆς προσκαίρου ζωῆς. Cf. Bas. Caes., *hom.* 7.1; Chrys., *In Act.* 11.1; and Jo. Clim., *scal.* 16; with Driscoll 2001: 23–24.

158. Bars. et Jo., *resp.* 9, which I interpret to be related to the question of labor discussed in Bars. et Jo., *resp.* 30, 31, 42. Cf. Hevelone-Harper 2005: 39.

159. *Const. Ap.* 5.1.3, 20.18; Greg. Nyss., *De ben.* 457; Sev. Ant., *Hom. cath.* 105 (PO 25.652); Jo. Eph., *v.SS.Or.* 12 ("Life of Mary and Euphemia"; PO 17.171); and Jo. Mosch., *prat.* 127. Guillaume 1954: 1–70 discusses earlier and Western sources; his discussion, pp.73–129, of Pope Leo's concept of caritas offers parallels to Early Byzantine thought.

160. *AP* GS 13.15 (SC 474.242–44): Ἦν δὲ ὁ γέρων ἐλεήμων, καὶ γενομένου λιμοῦ ἤρξαντό τινες εἰς τὴν θύραν αὐτοῦ ἔρχεσθαι καὶ λαμβάνειν ἀγάπην. Ὁ δὲ γέρων πᾶσι τοῖς ἐρχομένοις παρεῖχε ψωμία.... ἐποίει ἐλεημοσύνην ἐκ τοῦ μέρους αὐτοῦ. Πολλοὶ δὲ συνέτρεχον πρὸς τὸν γέροντα ἀκούοντες ὅτι πᾶσι παρέχει. Ἰδὼν δὲ ὁ Θεὸς τὴν πρόθεσιν αὐτοῦ εὐλόγησε τοὺς ἄρτους καὶ οὐκ ἐξέλιπον.... γενομένης δὲ τῆς εὐθηνίας, ἤρχοντο πάλιν οἱ χρήζοντες λαμβάνειν ἀγάπην. Cf. *AP* G Nistherus 4 (65.308BC).

CHAPTER 5. "WHAT GOD HAS PUT IN YOUR HEART":
DIVINE PATRONAGE, SACRED WEALTH, AND MATERIAL BLESSINGS

This chapter is an augmented version of an article originally published in the Fall 2006 issue of JECS.

1. Cyril Scyth., *v.Euthym.* 17 (Schwartz, 27–28; trans. Price, 22–23): θεία γὰρ εὐλογία τὴν κέλλαν ἐπήρωσεν ἕως ἄνω ... ὁμοίως καὶ ἐπὶ οἴνου καὶ ἐλαίου ἡ αὐτὴ γέγονεν εὐλογία.... καὶ τῷ θείῳ τούτῳ γέροντι τῇ προθυμίᾳ τῆς φιλοξενίας τὴν χορηγίαν τῆς εὐλογίας ἰσόμετρον ἐχαρίσατο.... ὁ σπείρων ἐν εὐλογίαις, ἐπ᾽ εὐλογίαις καὶ θερίσει.... Cf. Cyril

Scyth., *v.Euthym.* 39. The Greek singular was frequently used referring to "blessings" collectively (as here with a definite article, χορηγίαν τῆς εὐλογίας): e.g., Sophron., *v.Mar.Aeg.* 26 (PG 87.3716B); *P.Ness.* III 79, ll. 44, 56, in Kramer 1958: 229–32.

2. Cyril Scyth., *v.Euthym.* 18 (Schwartz, 28): ἀπὸ τοῦ εἰρημένου θαύματος ἤρξατο εὐλογεῖσθαι ἡ λαύρα ἔν τε εἰσόδοις καὶ ἐξόδοις καὶ διαφόροις εἴδεσιν. The community became a large cenobium after Euthymius's death (Cyril Scyth., *v.Euthym.* 43). For its ruins off the ancient highway, see Hirschfeld 1993; and Binns 1994: 80. Theodosius the Cenobiarch and Cyril of Scythopolis both trained in it.

3. See, however, Flusin 1983: 187; Déroche 1995: 238–54; Caner 2008; and López 2016.

4. On such flasks, see Vikan 2010. Though generally correct as far as pilgrims are concerned, his interpretations, like Hahn 1990; and Limor 2017, reduce all *eulogiai* to "souvenirs" or "secondary relics."

5. Caner 2013a: 32–35, quantifies the preponderance of references to *eulogiai* over alms (which predominate in the fourth century) and other gifts in hagiography. My assertion that this is the first explicit example of a "pure" gift in Western tradition is based on its deliberate articulation by Paul in 2 Cor 9:5–12 and the (apparent) absence of a comparable concept in Greco-Roman and Hebrew sources.

6. Chrys., *In Rom.* 30.1 (PG 60.662): Εὐλογίαν γὰρ, ὡς τὰ πολλὰ, τὴν ἐλεημοσύνην εἴωθε λέγειν· ὡς ὅταν λέγῃ, Ὡς εὐλογίαν, μὴ ὡς πλεονεξίαν· καὶ ἔθος δὲ παλαιὸν οὕτως ἦν καλεῖσθαι τὸ πρᾶγμα. Cf. Chrys., *In Cor.* 43.2 (61.370).

7. *P.Ness.* III 79 (Kraemer, 1958: 227–29), which is discussed in the Introduction, "Surviving Sources." I discuss it in light of the modern philanthropic concept of an "unrestricted" gift in Caner forthcoming-a.

8. On *xenia* in an earlier milieu, see Herman 1987. Josephus shows that they were well known in Palestine before Christian times. See Avidov 1998.

9. Greg. Mag., *reg.* 11.37 (601 CE) equates the material *benedictiones* of St. Peter he is sending with *exenia*. Leont. Neap., *v.Jo.Eleem.* 9 (Festugière-Rydén, 355) identifies a *xenion* of 500 gold pounds offered to John the Almsgiver by a widow as both a *eulogia* and a *karpophoria*. Geront., *v.Mel. gr.* 1.11–14 (Gorce, 146–56) describes how Melania the Younger offered luxurious gifts (*kosmai*) as *eulogiai* to the imperial court in Rome to ensure it would let her sell her estates, and at the end of the episode, she calls them a *xenion*. Gerontius's passage is contemporaneous with the notorious letter describing the *benedictiones* Cyril of Alexandria sent to influence the imperial court in the 430s, discussed in this chapter in "Human Avarice and Divine Patronage."

10. Based on early medieval Western sources, Davies and Fouracre 2010: 238, define a *eulogia* as "a gift presented to a guest, or to a highly placed person, often a customary render owed, e.g., by a tenant to a lord or exacted, e.g., by the lord of a church from a priest, or by a priest in return for services." This definition may describe what happened when the ideals a *eulogia* represented were not observed, but it does not adequately reflect the Early Byzantine significance of the term.

11. See note 4 and the section "Human Avarice and Divine Patronage."

12. Limor 2017; Pentcheva 2010: 25–36; Jullien and Jullien 2010: 334–36; Vikan 2010; and Vikan 1984.

13. McCulloh 1976.

14. Sophocles, s.v. εὐλογία 3; Lampe, s.v. εὐλογία E,1–3; and Caseau 2012.

15. See notes 44–45.

16. Lampe, s.v. εὐλογία F,1–3; Drews 1898: 35–36; and Stuiber 1966: 922–27.

17. See notes 62–68.

18. Murtonen 1959; Stuiber 1966: 900–904, 912–13; and Mitchell 1987.

19. LXX, Gn 33:11; Jo 15:19; Jgs 1:15; 1 Sm 25:27; 2 Kgs 5:15. That Murtonen 1959: 173 interprets these OT examples as departure and reconciliation gifts shows how uncertain the passages are for interpretation in either isolation or aggregate. Septuagint translators may have understood such *eulogiai* as Paul later did, but these passages provide no clear evidence of that.

20. Stuiber 1966: 904–5.

21. *Trad. ap.* 26 and 28 (SC 11.102 and 108): "cum cenant, qui adsunt fideles sument de manu episcopi paululum panis antequam frangant proprium panem, quia eulogia est et non eucharistia sicut caro domini. . . . si autem non est episcopus ibi . . . in cena accipiant eulogiam de manu presbyteri. . . . Laicus enim non potest dare eulogium." Unfortunately, this passage has different recensions, all somewhat garbled. See Botte's notes ad loc.; and Hamman 1968: 184–90.

22. Vikan 2010: 13; Taft 1999: 29–30; Galavaris 1970: 109–11; Franz 1960: 1.232–44; Dix 1945: 82–100; Drews 1898: 23–24, 34–35.

23. ἄρτος τῆς εὐλογίας: *A.Th.* 49, 133 and *v.Sym.Styl.iun.*116. Cf. Greg. Tur., *Gloria conf.* 30. Kiljn 1962: 244 proposes that this phrase was inspired by 1 Cor 10:16, "cup of blessing that we bless."

24. 2 Cor 9:5–12: ἀναγκαῖον οὖν ἡγησάμην παρακαλέσαι τοὺς ἀδελφούς, ἵνα προέλθωσιν εἰς ὑμᾶς καὶ προκαταρτίσωσιν τὴν προεπηγγελμένην εὐλογίαν ὑμῶν, ταύτην ἑτοίμην εἶναι οὕτως ὡς εὐλογίαν καὶ μὴ ὡς πλεονεξίαν. [6] Τοῦτο δέ, ὁ σπείρων φειδομένως καὶ θερίσει, καὶ ὁ σπείρων ἐπ᾽ εὐλογίαις ἐπ᾽ εὐλογίαις καὶ θερίσει. [7] ἕκαστος καθὼς προῄρηται τῇ καρδίᾳ, μὴ ἐκ λύπης ἢ ἐξ ἀνάγκης· ἱλαρὸν γὰρ δότην ἀγαπᾷ ὁ θεός. [8] δυνατεῖ δὲ ὁ θεὸς πᾶσαν χάριν περισσεῦσαι εἰς ὑμᾶς, ἵνα ἐν παντὶ πάντοτε πᾶσαν αὐτάρκειαν ἔχοντες περισσεύητε εἰς πᾶν ἔργον ἀγαθόν, [9] καθὼς γέγραπται, "Ἐσκόρπισεν, ἔδωκεν τοῖς πένησιν, ἡ δικαιοσύνη αὐτοῦ μένει εἰς τὸν αἰῶνα." [10] ὁ δὲ ἐπιχορηγῶν σπόρον τῷ σπείροντι καὶ ἄρτον εἰς βρῶσιν χορηγήσει καὶ πληθυνεῖ τὸν σπόρον ὑμῶν καὶ αὐξήσει τὰ γενήματα τῆς δικαιοσύνης ὑμῶν· [11] ἐν παντὶ πλουτιζόμενοι εἰς πᾶσαν ἁπλότητα, ἥτις κατεργάζεται δι᾽ ἡμῶν εὐχαριστίαν τῷ θεῷ. [12] ὅτι ἡ διακονία τῆς λειτουργίας ταύτης οὐ μόνον ἐστὶν προσαναπληροῦσα τὰ ὑστερήματα τῶν ἁγίων, ἀλλὰ καὶ περισσεύουσα διὰ πολλῶν εὐχαριστιῶν τῷ θεῷ.

25. On what this passage might have meant to Paul, see Betz 1985; Georgi 1992; Downs 2008: 131–45. He refers to such "collections for the saints" (κοινωνία . . . εἰς τοὺς πτωχοὺς τῶν ἁγίων) in Rm 15:25–26; 1 Cor 16:1; 2 Cor 8:4; and Gal 2:10. Similar collections are attested in rabbinic sources (e.g., Leviticus Rabba 5:4), but none mention a *eulogia/beraka*.

26. For example, Limor 2010: 7: "Through physical contact with the tomb, the external earth became one with it, and thus a true *eulogia*. . . . One can surmise that [the involvement of church functionaries] also included a verbal blessing, inseparable from the token or from any *eulogia*, as can be deduced from its name." I agree even less with Pentcheva 2010: 29, who writes that sealing/imprinting images on tokens was the "process through which the sacred power [was] imparted to matter."

27. A rare exception is *v.Marc.Acoem.* 21 (Dagron, 303): ὁ δὲ ἄρτον εὐλογήσας δίδωσιν αὐτῷ, where Abbot Marcellus verbally blesses bread before sending it to a patient as a heal-

ing talisman. The general fact that a verbal blessing was not necessary to create a material blessing is evinced by *v.Longini* 14–15 (Tito-Comagnano, 60–61), which depicts a material (bread) blessing and a verbal blessing being given to a departing guest simultaneously: "The gatekeeper [said], 'Here, take some bread as a blessing [and added,] 'The Lord be with you.'... When [Longinus] heard the word 'blessing,' he took the loaves with the blessing." In this case the verbal blessing is directed toward Longinus and not to the bread being given to him as *eulogiai*, indicating that these two types of blessings did not rely on each other. I owe this reference to Ellen Muehlberger.

28. Paul stresses the connection between ἁπλότης, περισσεία, and περίσσευμα in 2 Cor 8:2–14. For their relation to his imagery of inexhaustible resources, Bruck 1944; Georgi 1992: 93–99.

29. Aug., *De op. mon.* 16.18–19; Chrys., *In 2 Cor* 19.3 (PG 61.535).

30. Decisive on this point is Taft 1970; see also Hamman 1967: 251–84; and Wipszycka 1972: 65–68. For the liturgical purpose of such *prosphorai,* see chapter 7, "Lay Offerings and Church Commemorations."

31. For identification of a *eulogia* with fresh bread stamped with a cross, see Sophron., *mir.* 38.3. *Eulogia* stamps (usually 6–8.5 cm), see Galavaris 1970: 117–25; and Caseau 2012: 64–66. *Eulogia* reserves, see Jo. Mosch., *prat.* 25 (PG 87[3]: 2869D–72A), where a liturgical chant over *eulogiai* loaves renders them "consecrated and perfect"; cf. Jo. Ruf., *v.Petr.Ib.* 151; *v.Sin.* 143; and Galavaris 1970: 43–44.

32. The theory goes back at least to Leclercq 1922: 734; followed by Raes 1953: 6–13; Galavaris 1970: 111–14; and Caseau 2012. Theophilus of Alexandria, *can.* 7 (Joannou 2: 269) prescribes a distribution of leftover offerings (προσφερόμενα) to "clerics and faithful brethren," excluding only catechumens. Wipszycka 1972: 102 asserts that this refers to blessed loaves of bread, but the exclusion of catechumens indicates that it pertains to consecrated leftovers. Otherwise, no canon on the subject—*Const. Ap.* 8.31 (380s CE); *Can. Ap.* 4 (4th cent.); Synod of Nantes *can.* 9 (658 CE); Council in Trullo *can.* 28 (692 CE)—mentions a general distribution of blessings to laypeople. (The citations offered by Sophocles, s.v. εὐλογία 5; and Lampe, s.v. εὐλογία E,2, are Middle or Late Byzantine.) Taft 1999: 45n1 cites *v.Matr.Perg.* 38, which describes a general distribution of *eulogiai* at a festival of St. Lawrence. But the word refers there to oil from a saint's relics, the distribution of which is announced in the prior sentence. It is true that Jo. Mon., *v.Eus.Alex.* 3 (PG 86[1].307AB), describes a general distribution of blessed bread during the Easter vigil held in Jerusalem's Anastasis Church, but that was a special event.

33. *Const. Ap.* 8.31.1–3 (SC 336.234): [1] ... περὶ περισσευμάτων. [2] Τὰς περισσευούσας ἐν τοῖς μυστικοῖς εὐλογίας κατὰ γνώμην τοῦ ἐπισκόπου ἢ τῶν πρεσβυτέρων, οἱ διάκονοι διανεμέτωσαν τῷ κλήρῳ, τῷ ἐπισκόπῳ μέρη τέσσαρα, πρεσβυτέρῳ μέρη τρία, διακόνῳ μέρη δύο, τοῖς δὲ ἄλλοις ὑποδιακόνοις ἢ ἀναγνώσταις ἢ ψάλταις ἢ διακονίσσαις, μέρος ἕν. [3] Τοῦτο γὰρ καλὸν καὶ τὴν ἀπόδεκτον ἐνώπιον τοῦ Θεοῦ, ἕκαστον τιμᾶσθαι κατὰ τὴν αὐτοῦ ἀξίαν· ἡ γὰρ Ἐκκλησία οὐκ ἀταξίας, ἀλλ' εὐταξίας ἐστὶ διδασκαλεῖον.

34. It passed into the major Syriac and Arabic collections of church canons. See *La version Arabe des 127 Canons des Apotres, can.* 60 (PO 8: 643–44), where a gloss clarifies that such blessings were items *not* consecrated or used in Eucharist services. Cf. *Can. Ath.* [Arabic recension] 32–33; and *Can. Bas.* 96, which describes dividing *prosphorai* after the service in a room set apart from the laity, without mentioning subsequent redistribution.

35. A letter from Gregory the Great is explicit. Greg. Mag., *reg.* 9.76 (598 CE; CCSL 140.631): "fidelium oblatione collata sunt eulogium condidisse." Cf. Caner 2013a: 34–36.

36. Jones 1960: 90–94; Schöllgen 1990; Schöllgen 1998: 34–100; Schmelz 2002: 203–17; and Hübner 2005: 215–26. None discuss *Const. Ap.* 8.31 or *eulogiai* per se, although Schmelz 2002: 205–6, notes that a 6th- or 7th-century papyrus, *P.Vind.Worp.* 14, records a *eulogia* dispatched to a lector by a priest, after it had been collected by deacons.

37. Sev. Ant., *ep.Coll.1* 1.57 (Brooks, 1: 190, 2: 172): "pulogo haw da-'yodo d-burkathon," which Brooks translates as "distribution of presents." Cf. Jones 1960: 93; and Schmelz 2002: 205–6, referring to *P.Vind.Worp.* 14. Severus's diocese suffered from debt. Sev. Ant., *epp.Coll.1* 1.8, 13, 42, refer to clerics trying to supplement their pay. In general, see Zeisel 1975: 130–54.

38. *Canons of Johannan Bar Qursos, can.* 8 (CSCO 367.148–49, with Latin trans. 368.145).

39. See chapter 1, "Secular Gifts and the Late Roman Imperial Order."

40. Leo, *ep.* 9.2 (444/5 CE), cited in Taft 1999: 27; also Jo. Mosch., *prat.* 243 (= Mioni 12; *OCP* 17.93).

41. Socrates, *HE* 7.12.9 (GCS n.F.1.357): ἀπό τε τῶν ἐκκλησιῶν οὐδὲν ἐδέξατο, πλὴν κατὰ κυριακὴν δύο ἄρτους τῶν εὐλογιῶν.

42. Jo. Mosch. *prat.* 42 (PG 86[3].2896BC): προσφορὰν ἤσθιεν λεπτῶν εἴκοσι.... εὐλογίαν. For ταβλία τῶν πλακουνταρίων at Emesa, Leont. Neap., *v.Sym.* 31 (PG 93.1709A). Sale of bread at church gates is condoned in the 8th-century *Answers of Ja'qōb to Jōhannān 'Esṭūnārā* 16 (CSCO 367.241, with Latin trans. 368.222).

43. Aug., *C. litt. Petil.* 3.16.19 (CSEL 52.177): "eulogias panis simpliciter et hilariter datas." Cf. 2 Cor 9:7, 10–11: "hilarem enim dator diligit deus . . . in omnibus locupletati abundetis in omnem simplicitatem."

44. Eg., *Itin.* 21.3 (SC 296.222): "eulogias . . . sicut est consuetudo monachis dare, his tamen quos libenti animo suscipiunt in monasteriis suis." Cf. Eg., *Itin.* 3.6, 11.1, 15.6.

45. *HM* 1.64, 17.2 (perhaps reflecting Palestinian customs); and Call., *v.Hyp.* 41.13.

46. For example, *v.Nicol.Sion.* 25, 47 (Sevčenko, 48, 78): τὰς τρεῖς εὐλογίας . . . δώσωμεν αὐτῷ τρεῖς εὐλογίας. . . . ; Leont. Neap., *v.Sym.* 49 (PG 93.1729CD): τρεῖς εὐλογίας ζεστάς (probably referring to freshness; see *v.Alex.Acoem.*19); *v.Matr.Perg.* 29; Paul Elus., *v.Thgn.* 2.11.

47. Pall., *HL* 51.1, 71.3; *AP* G Macarius 33 (PG 65.276C); *AP* N 20; *AP* L 13.13 (PL 73.946C); *v.Dan.Styl.* 62 (SH 14.61–62); Dan. Scet., *log.* 6 ("Eulogius the Stonecutter"; Dalman, 156): τρία παξαμάτια; Jo. Ruf., *v.Petr.Ib.* 139 (trans. Horn-Phenix, 205); Jo. Eph., *v.SS.Or.* 12 ("Lives of Mary and Euphemia"; PO 17.178); *v.Sym.Styl.iun.* 123 (SH 32.104); *Life of John the Little*, Sahidic frag. 1 (trans. Vivian, 60–62); Paph., *HM*, fol. 4a (trans. Vivian, 76).

48. *v.Syncl.Jord.* 1 (Flusin-Paramelle, 306): μικρὰς εὐλογίας ἀρτῶν. Sophron., *v.Mar.Aeg.* 26 (PG 87[3].3716B): τρεῖς ἐξ αὐτῶν ἠγόρασα ἄρτους, καὶ τούτους ἔλαβον εὐλογίας ἐφόδιον.

49. The 6th-century Apion estate ordered a monastery to distribute three loaves to each laborer who worked for it during the harvest. Wipszycka 2011: 195. That this was a standard ration for harvesters is also implied by *v.Nicol.Sion.* 47, where it is questioned whether three loaves should be given to a figure on horseback (i.e., the plague) seen wielding a harvest sickle.

50. Shenoute, *can.* 5, trans. and discussed in Layton 2002: 46–47.

51. Pachomius, *Rules* 37–38 (CS 46.151); *v.Pach. gr. prim.* 111 mentions its distribution after a meal. A bread basket was placed beside the refectory door at Dorotheus's monastery. *V.Dos.*11. *Korsenēlion* is a *hapax legomenon*; Jerome translated it as *tragēma*, which Veilleux translates as "sweet," but "treat" may be better. See Lefort 1923; and Battaglia 1989: 121–22,

125–26. Revillout 1900: 174–75 includes a 7th-century monastic rule assigning three loaves per day to a *hebdomarius*, as if in compensation for his work.

52. Rabbula, *Rules for Monks, can.* 8 (Vööbus, 81). Palmer 1990: 89 notes that the *Life of Theoduta of Amid*, fol. 58a.3 presents Theoduta as regularly asking his abbot for "three *knišutē* [discs] of bread" to give to sick people outside their monastery. I thank Andrew Palmer for discussing this passage and an unpublished MS he kindly shared.

53. Bars. et Jo., *resp.* 141 (SC 427.518): ἀπόκρισις τοῦ αὐτοῦ μεγάλου Γεροντος πρὸς τὸν αὐτὸν αἰτήσαντα εὐλογίαν. . . . ᾔτησας ἄρτον λαβεῖν παρὰ τῆς ἐμῆς ἀσθενείας καὶ πέρισσον ἄρτων τῶν τεταγμένων τρίων τὴν ἑβδομάδα οὐκ εἰσῆλθεν εἰς τὸ κοιμητήριόν μου. Cf. Bars. et Jo., *resp.* 44.

54. Sophron., *v.Mar.Aeg.* 27. Cf. Jo. Mosch., *prat.* 41, 42, illustrating the austerity of solitaries who ate just one *eulogia* (and nothing else) per week. *HM* 1.58 (SH 34.32) refers to a cenobium that supplied a desert anchorite with bread *eulogias*. Also Cyril Scyth., *v.Sab.* 6; Jo. Mosch., *prat.* 125; and Plac., *Itin.* 35 (CCSL 175.147). Evelyn-White 1932: 202 notes that a two-loaf ration existed among 4th-century Egyptian anchorites.

55. Battaglia 1989: 84–95, 121, 125; and Hirschfeld 1996. According to Wipszycka 2011: 186–87, the bread baked in Egyptian monasteries averaged 12 cm in diameter, weighing about 150 g.

56. Jo. Mosch., *prat.* 125 (PG 87[3].2988B): λαβὼν ἐκ τοῦ μαργονίου αὐτοῦ μίαν εὐλογίαν . . . λέγει αὐτῷ, Λάβε τὴν εὐλογίαν τῶν Πατέρων. Cf. John of Gaza's reference to εὐλογία Πατέρων in Bars. et Jo., *resp.* 752 (see note 116). Both seem to be talking about something different from the εὐλογία τῆς Ἐκκλησίας mentioned in Jo. Mosch., *prat.* 41 (PG 87[3].2896B).

57. Pachomius, *Rules* 79 (Veilleux, 159).

58. Pall., *HL* 44.3; Besa, *hom.* frag. 11 ("To an Erring Monk") 1.5–7; Dan. Scet., *log.* 11 ("The Falsely Accused Monk"; Clugnet, 388); Jo. Eph., *v.SS.Or.* 58 ("On the History of the Convent of John Urtaya"; PO 18.556). In each case, a thief steals bread to give to others rather than to consume himself. Cf. Rabbula, *Rules for Monks, can.* 36 (Vööbus, 85–86): "No one who lives in a monastery shall give anything from the property of the monastery to his relatives; the opulence of the monastery is a grace of our Lord, and he who gives away and distributes shall be a harm to himself and his relations." Zeisel 1975: 315–16 notes the problem of theft in monasteries.

59. Bars. et Jo., *resp.* 587 and 588 (discussed in the section "Ascetic Stewardship and the Multiplication of Monastic Blessings"). Cf. Isaiah Scet., *log.* 10.52.

60. Leont. Neap., *v.Sym.* 49 (PG 93.1729CD): τρεῖς εὐλογίας . . . ἐκ θεοῦ οὔσας. Cf. Pall., *HL* 71.3; and Binns 1994: 87.

61. *AP* G Isaac the Theban 2 (PG 65.241A). Cf. Donahue 1953: 111–12.

62. Thomas 1987: 95; Hirschfeld 1992: 102–4. By monastic wealth, I mean *surplus* material resources. As Wipszycka 1996a: 185 observes, few monasteries could have subsisted on gifts alone. On this, see also Caner 2008.

63. On donations by pilgrims, Binns 1994: 85–91; Hirschfeld 1992: 271; Gorce 1925: 184–85; Plac., *Itin.* 41, discussed in chapter 1, "Christian Gifts in the Late Roman Holy Land," for a vivid example. On church subsidies, also see chapter 1, p. 24. On "*eulogia* of the church," Jo. Mosch., *prat.* 41 (PG 87[3].2896B): ἀρκούμενος τῇ εὐλογίᾳ τῆς Ἐκκλησίας, apparently referring to something other than the εὐλογία τῶν Πατέρων mentioned in *prat.* 125 (see note 56).

64. Jerome, *ep.* 71.4 (CSEL 54.5): "abundantia tua multorum inopiam sustentavit." Cf. Hunt 1982: 146; with Jerome, *ep.* 120.1; and *Vigil.* 17 (PL 23.365A); *Pan. Rabb.* (Overbeck, 201, 205; Doran, 99–100, 103).

65. Thdr. Petr., *v.Thds.* 27.10–21, 28.9; Jo. Mosch., *prat.* 157; and *v.Syncl.Jord.* 7–8, 15. Cf. Cyril Scyth., *v.Jo.Hesych.* 15.

66. Cyril Scyth., *v.Euthym.* 47 (Schwartz, 68): πολλὴν μὲν προσήνεγκεν εὐλογίαν, ἑτέραν δὲ ὑπέσχατο διδόναι καθ' ἕκαστον ἐνιαυτόν . . . ; *v.Jo.Hesych.* 20 (217): εὐλογίαν τινὰ ἐνιαυσίαν εὐλογίαν. . . . ; Cyril Scyth., *v.Thds.* 3 (238): ἐν χρυσῷ καθ' ἕκαστον ἐνιαυτόν. On monastic annuities, see Thomas 1987: 48, 75.

67. Cyril Scyth., *v.Euthym.* 47 (Schwartz, 68). Cf. Flusin 1983: 187; and chapter 6's introduction (assuming such distributions occurred, like so much else, after the harvest season).

68. *P. Ness.,* III 80 ("Account of Church Offerings"; Kraemer 1958: 234). Of the nine donors, one gave ten *modii,* the others two to six each, totaling thirty-six *modii* (approx. 952 lbs.).

69. Winlock, Crum, and Evelyn-White 1926: 173n13, reports an 8th-century papyrus from an Egyptian monastery that refers to "the blessing [*smou*] left at the gate for the poor that pass by."

70. Bas. Caes., *RB* 219 (PG 31.1228A).

71. Leont. Neap. *v.Jo.Eleem.* 9 (Festugière-Rydén, 355): τὴν εὐλογίαν ἣν ἐνέβαλεν ὁ θεὸς ἐν τῇ καρδίᾳ . . . προσενέγκαι. Cf. Isaiah Scet., *log.* 3 (Chryssavgis-Penkett, 51: "The blessing you received from God . . . whatever you have is not yours, but a gift from God"); Bars. et Jo., *resp.* 570, 682; and *P.KRU* 106 (in Till 1964: 107; trans. MacCoull, 168), an 8th-century papyrus recording sentiments of a layperson named Anna: "God, the good and merciful, opened my heart to cast in this my little mite. . . . God put it into my heart that I should make a donation to this . . . holy monastery."

72. Ant. Choz., *v.Geo.Choz.* 3.11 (Houze, 107): ἔρρει αὐτῷ ἡ εὐλογία ὡς ἐκ πηγῆς τῆς εὐλεγομένης θεοτόκου δαψιλῶς ἐπιχορηγούσης κατὰ τὴν προαίρεσιν αὐτοῦ. Αὐτὸς δὲ ἐπιδαψιλεύετο τῇ προθυμίᾳ, κατὰ δύναμιν καὶ ὑπὲρ δύναμιν λειτουργῶν καὶ διακονῶν τῇ εὐλογημένῃ ἐν τῇ ἐλεημοσύνῃ.

73. Jo. Mosch., *prat.* 61 (PG 87[3].2913C): Συγχώρησόν μοι, Πάτερ· οὐ γάρ εἰμι ἐγὼ ὁ παρέχων, ἀλλ' ἡ Δέσποινά μου ἡ Θεοτόκος, ἡ κἀμὲ καὶ αὐτοὺς τρέφουσα. See also Call., *v.Hyp.* 31.1.1; *v.Pach.boh.* 53; and *v.Alex.Acoem.* 45, which especially illustrates such double determination.

74. Bars. et Jo., *resp.* 570 (SC 451.734–36): ἐὰν οἶδεν ὁ Θεὸς ὅτι χρῄζω καὶ σπείρῃ τινὶ καὶ ἐνέγκῃ μοι, δέχομαι. Cf. Bars. et Jo., *resp.* 682.

75. Theoph., *Chron.* AM 5940 (De Boor, 1:98; trans. Mango-Scott 153–54, adapted): . . . ἀπέστειλαι τὰς ὑπὲρ τῆς χειροτονίας εὐλογίας. Ὁ δὲ Φλαβιανὸς καθαροὺς ἄρτους ἀπέστειλεν εὐλογίας, ὁ δὲ Χρυσάφιος ἀποστρέψας ταύτας ἐδήλωσε χρυσᾶς εὐλογίας ζητεῖν τὸν βασίλεια. On the sources from which this story may have originated, see Theoph., *Chron.* (Mango-Scott, lxxiv–lxxxi).

76. Nestor., *Bazaar* 2.1 ([397–98]; trans. Driver-Hodgson 288–89). For context, see Caner 2002: 222. Cf. *Pan. Rabb.* (Overbeck, 199, 17–27; trans. Doran, 98).

77. Letter of Epiphanius (= Cyril, *ep.* 96; preserved in the acts of the Council of Chalcedon, ACO 1.4.2:223; Collectio Casinensi 293–94): *directae sunt benedictiones dignae eis . . . 34, praesta avaritiae;* 224:28: *eulogiae consuetudinae supplices.* Cf. Cyril Alex., *ep.* 94. On Cyril's efforts, see Nestor., *Bazaar* 2.2 [478–81]; with Batiffol 1911: 247–64; Jones 1964: 346;

and Kelly 2004: 171–75. For a similar attempt by a later patriarch to influence the court with lavish gifts, see Jo. Eph., *HE* 3.5.17.

78. Lampe, s.v. εὐλογία, F.2; and MacMullen 1988: 165–66 ("one more illustration of euphemism that surrounded morally dubious matters"), 271n131.

79. Nestor., *Bazaar* 2.2 [468] makes the extortionary aspect of Theophanes's story clear but blames the emperor for the exactions against Bishop Flavian of Constantinople (sed. 446–449).

80. See Parry 1986; Bloch and Parry 1989. As they explain, the ideal of gift giving has become so disconnected from modern economies that most take the notion of a "pure" gift for granted—despite the pervasive academic opinion, partly rooted in a misreading of Mauss, that no such thing exists. See also Zelizer 1994: 2–3, 77–118.

81. *Const. Ap.* 4.6–8 (expanding *SyrD* 18); *Const. Ap.* 8.32. Cf. Chrys., *In Heb.* 34.2 (PG 63.314A). See chapter 4, "Almsgiving as Purification in Eastern Hagiography."

82. On such *munuscula, commoda, sportulae,* etc., see Jones 1964: 496–99; MacMullen 1988: 122–70; and Kelly 2004: 138–231.

83. MacMullen 1988: 148–67; Krause 1987: 6–72; De Ste. Croix 1981: 492–93; Percival 1969. Cf. Thdt., *HR* 10.3. Zelizer 1994: 80 notes that in 1912, the Society for the Prevention of Useless Giving sought to end a "quasi-compulsory" American custom requiring employees to pool money to buy gifts for their employers at Christmas.

84. Schöllgen 2002: 173–95 focuses on the challenge of patronal gifts and *prosōpolēpsia* in churches of the third-century East. On the *parrhēsia* and impartiality expected of bishops, Rapp 2005: 267–70; and more generally, Van Renswoude 2019.

85. Chrys., *In 1 Cor* 20.6 (PG 61.169). For patronal motives, see Leyerle 1994: 45–46; and Zeisel 1975: 147–51.

86. Barḥadbeshabbā, *HE* 21 (PO 9.526): "b-qurbānē wa b-ṭaybutē." Not preserved elsewhere, this letter should be read as a contemporary complaint against the practices attested in Cyril Alex., *epp.* 94, 96.

87. *v.Matr.Perg.* 32 (*AASS Nov.* 3.805; trans. Featherstone 48–49): δεδωκυῖς δὲ μακαρία εὐλογίας βρεκτάς, οὐδὲν ἠτήσατο παρ' αὐτῆς τὸ σύνολον, καὶ μάλιστα προσδοκώησης τῆς βασιλίσσης ἐξαιτηθῆναι τι παρ' αὐτῆς, καίτοι . . . τῆς μακαρίας καὶ μηδὲν εὐπορούσης. ὠφεληθεῖσα οὖν . . . ἡ Ἀγούστα ὑπερεκπερισσοῦ ἐκ τοῦ μήτε αἰτηθῆναί τι παρ' αὐτῆς μήτε αἰδεσθῆναι τοιαύτας εὐλογίας δοῦναι τῇ βασιλίσσῃ. Cf. Sev. Ant., *ep.Coll.1* 1.16 (Brooks 1:62 / 2:68): "Mark the devout came to give us blessings, and not to receive anything."

88. Jo. Eph., *v.SS.Or.* 23 ("Life of Symeon the Solitary"; PO 17.302): "burkto . . . men mawhabteh d-moran." Cf. *Life of Theoduta of Amid* 2.3.41–3.1–4; and *Life of Matthew the Poor* (Amélineau, 720–23).

89. On the theoretical inalienability of a gift, based on the notion that it carries the spirit of its giver, the classic studies are Mauss 1990; and Weiner 1985; Weiner 1992. See also Miller 2007.

90. Sev. Ant., *ep.Coll.1* 1.48 (Brooks 1:146, 2:132). Cf. Greg. Mag., *reg.*1.64, 5.16, 6.63, 8.32.

91. Geront., *v.Mel. gr.*13; an exquisite case of ambiguity, on which see Kelly 2004: 179–80.

92. Kötting 1950: 403–13; Vikan 1984; and Maraval 1985: 237–41.

93. Hahn 1990: 87, 91, 95n23; Maraval 1985: 240. Ducan-Flowers 1990 notes that silver was occasionally used. What the laity did is another matter. The *Life of Symeon Stylites the Younger* attests that *ptōchoi* who received them sometimes put them up for sale in Antioch.

94. *V.Matr.Perg.* 38 (*AASS Nov.* 3.807): ἐν ταύτῃ οὖν μετὰ πάντων συνέδραμον . . . ἐπὶ τὸ μετασχεῖν τοῦ ἁγίου μῦρον. Καὶ δὴ μετασχοῦσαι, ὡς καὶ πάντες, τῆς εὐλογίας.

95. *V.Thecl.* 28 (SH 62.280). Alternatively, they may have functioned like the little candies modern waiters put with restaurant bills as a "free" parting gift (as it is usually understood), an inexpensive gesture that typically results in recipients leaving a 3.3 percent higher tip. See Strohmetz, Rind, Fisher, and Lynn 2002. For commercial aspects of Early Byzantine shrines, see Déroche 2006; Anderson 2007; Campbell 1988. Dina Boero notes that the pilgrimage shop at Qal'at Sim'an (see Pieri 2009) does not seems to have sold *eulogiai* flasks, but tokens, bracelets, and votive goods. What the laity did with theirs is another matter; *v.Sym.Styl. iun.*163 attests that *ptochoi* sometimes sold them in Antioch.

96. *v.Aux.* 57 (PG 114.1428C): σταυρία μικρὰ . . . διετέλει, καὶ οἱ ἀνιόντες ἐκομίζοντο αὐτὰ εὐλογίας χάριν. On the date and possible origin of this text, see Auzépy 1995: 225.

97. Plac., *Itin.* 6, 39, 42. Cf. Eg., *Itin.* 3.6, 25.6. Krueger 2005: 304–5 discusses the heavily ornamented box of stones, dirt, wood, and cloth brought from Palestine ca. 600, now in the Vatican's Museo Sacro, which admittedly suggests an alternative to what I have argued, since the high value of the humble contents seems to be signaled by its expensive packaging.

98. Hence, sending a poisoned loaf as a *eulogia* became a hagiographical motif for violated trust. For example, Greg. Mag., *Dial.* 3.8; *Life of Rabban Hormizd* 24. Whether or not monastic loaves were connected to a liturgy, they were often stamped. Hirschfeld 1996: 149.

99. Greg. Tur., *h. Franc.* 7.1 (Krusch-Levison, 324): *eulogias gratiam plenissimam ministraret.*

100. Similar to Theophanes's story, Ps.-Zachariah, *Chron.* 5.4, describes how an Alexandrian bishop, having given three *paxamatia* each to the emperor and "great men and lords" of the city, is asked for gold instead. See Zeisel 1975: 262n29. For the use of blessings as gifts in asymmetrical social settings, *v.Pach. gr. prim.* 39; Paul Elus., *v.Thgn.* 2.11; Jo. Ruf., *v.Petr.Ib.* 57; and Georg. Syc., *v.Thdr.Syc.* 166, all depicting clerics or monks presenting *eulogiai* to emperors. Such gifts may have been especially helpful when aristocratic monks had to entertain secular guests of high rank, Cf. Bas. Caes., *RF* 20; Call., *v.Hyp.* 36.7; Greg. Tur., *h. Franc.* 10.16; Bars. et Jo., *resp.* 830 on government officials expecting "gifts of welcome" from the Patriarch of Jerusalem, who complained that he had only "goods of the poor" to give. I suspect that a similar dynamic explains the interactions depicted in Western sources analyzed by Curta 2006: 678–80. Conversely, *v.Mel. lat.* 35.6 (Laurence, 224), mentions that when Melania arrived in Jerusalem, she accepted a pillow "pro magna benedictione, et non propter delicias utebatur," suggesting that a humble gift could be augmented when treated reverently as a blessing.

101. Chrys., *In Heb.* 15.6 (PG 63.138). Cf. Chrys., *In Jo.* 54.4 (59.359); and Bars. et Jo., *resp.* 594, 789.

102. Jo. Eph., *v.SS.Or.* 36 ("Life of Mare the Solitary"; PO 19.632–33; trans. Brooks, adapted). Cf. *AP* G Poemen 10; Thdt., *ep.* 123; Thdt., *HR* 24.9; *Pan. Rabb.* (Overbeck, 184, ll. 14–16); *v.Dan.Styl.* 101; *v.Sym.Styl.iun.* 56, 93, 122–23; Jo. Mosch., *prat.* 13; and Sophron. et Mosch., Ps.-, *v.Jo.Eleem.* 5, II.12–17. For the relation between manual labor and ascetic independence, Bas. Caes., *RB* 304–5, 308; Jo. Cassian, *Coll.* 24.12; and Caner 2002: 200–201. Alternatively, when asked what to do when someone offered something "in hope of getting more" from their monastery, Barsanuphius advised that monks take it only if they needed it, then repay the donor with something equivalent, effectively turning the exchange into a transaction. Bars. et Jo., *resp.* 594 (SC 451.790–92): Ἐάν τις ἐνέγκῃ ἡμῖν πρᾶγμα ἐπ' ἐλπίδι

τοῦ λαβεῖν πλέον, τί ποιήσω. . . . Ἐὰν δὲ χρείαν ἔχῃς, εἰπὲ αὐτῷ ὅτι Ἐὰν λάβω, τὴν τιμὴν δίδωμι. Καὶ σπούδασον δοῦναι αὐτῷ τὰ ἴσα.

103. *AP* G Zeno 2 (PG 65.176C). Cf. *AP* G Achilles 1 (PG 65.124B); *AP* G Theodore of Pherme 26 (193BC); and *Life of Theoduta of Amid*, 2.3.41–45. Since grief (λύπη) was a sin, it was imperative not to cause it in others.

104. For example, Greg. Naz., *or.* 16.18; Symeon Bar-Eupolemos and Bar-Ḥaṭar, *v.Sym. Styl.* 56, MS M53b (trans. Doran, 136, 222–23); and Thdr. Paph., *v.Spyr.* 2–4. See also López 2013: 66, 76, 91; Decker 2009: 80–82; Van Dam 2002: 44–47; Newhauser 2000: 16–17; and Brown 1992: 80–81.

105. *v.Dalm.* 1.2 (Banduri, 2.697D–698A): πάντες οἱ ἐρχόμενοι . . . φέροντες προσφορὰς εἰς τὰς χεῖρας τοῦ ἐν ἁγίοις Δαλματίου ἐδίδουν· προσέφερον δὲ ἐν τῷ χρόνῳ αὐτῶν ἱκανά, αὐτοὶ δὲ μετεδίδουν αὐτὰ εἰς αἰχμαλώτους καὶ εἰς τοὺς ἐρχομένους εἰς τὸ ἅγιον μοναστήριον· ρόγαν ποιούμενοι τὸ καθημέραν ἀπαραλείπτως. . . . ἐπειδὴ οὖν τὸ ὄνομα τοῦ κυρίου Δαλματίου ἐπάγετο εἰς τὸ μοναστήριον ἕως τῆς ἡμέρας ταύτης, ἐν τῷ ἔρχεσθαι τοὺς ἀδελφοὺς ἐν τῷ πυλεῶνι, καὶ αἰτοῦντας λαμβάνειν τὴν παρ' αὐτῶν εὐλογίαν, αὐτοὶ καὶ τὸ ὄνομα ἐπέθηκαν λέγοντες πρὸς ἀλλήλους· ἄγωμεν εἰς τὸν κύριον Δαλμάτιον· καὶ αὐτὸς ἔχει ἐκ τῶν παροχῶν τοῦ θεοῦ θρέψαι ἡμᾶς. . . . πολλὰ γὰρ ὁ θεὸς κατὰ τὰς προαιρέσεις αὐτῶν ἐχορήγει τοῖς ἁγίοις· καὶ αὐτοὶ ἁπλότητι πολλῇ μετεδίδουν αὐτά.

106. On this *vita*, see Dagron 1970: 231n1; and Lenski 2004: 109–10. Its combination of *eulogia, haplotēs,* and *eucharisteia* is reminiscent of 2 Cor 9.

107. *Life of Theoduta of Amid,* 2.3.41–45. For scenarios describing a holy person's deflection of offerings toward others, *v.Aux.* 34 (PG 114.1404); *AP* GS 18.11 (SC 498.52).

108. See chapter 6, "Fruitbearings, Gratitude, and Sacred Vessels," and chapter 7, "Monks, Freedmen, and the Quest for Perpetual Commemoration." Ideally, donors would send such gifts anonymously, as indicated by Geront., *v.Mel. gr.* 38; and *HM* 20.11.

109. *Pan. Rabb.* (Overbeck, 199, 17–27; trans. Doran, 98, adapted). Cf. *AP* G Poimen 104 (PG 65.348B); and Jo. Eph., *v.SS.Or.* 53 ("Life of Priscus"; PO 19.179–80).

110. *v.Bars.* 81.2, 4.

111. *v.Bars.* 104.2–3 (trans. Palmer, 226). Cf. Thdt., *HR* 24.9; and John of Nikiû, *Chron.* 89.14.

112. Bloch and Parry 1989: 23–38, 117–64. Cf. Miller 2007: 18 on how passing gifts on to others depersonalizes them by removing the memory or personhood of their original giver.

113. Thdr. Petr., *v.Thds.* (Usener, 100): ἡ πρὸς τοὺς ξένους τε καὶ πτωχοὺς δαψιλής τε καὶ ἀδιάκριτος φιλοφροσύνη. Cyril Scyth., *v.Thds.* (Schwartz, 238): δαψυλήν τε καὶ ἀπροσπόληπτον φιλοφροσύνην. Cf. Cyril Scyth., *v.Euthym.* 39.

114. *v.Sin.* 33–34. On this text, see note 118.

115. Cf. Zeisel 1975: 273: "When . . . monasteries engaged in extraordinary charitable activities, they created among those whom they assisted a reserve of good will against which they could draw in various ways. Often laymen so assisted offered gifts in return, or became unofficial supporters of the convent and its patron saint."

116. Bars. et Jo., *resp.* 752 (SC 468.195–96): Ἐρώτησις· ἆρα καλόν ἐστι διδόναι εὐλογίαν Πατέρων ἀλλοεθνεῖ ἀνθρώπῳ ἢ πτωχῷ; Ἀπόκρισις· Μὴ διακριθῇς τὴν εὐλογίαν παρασχεῖν πτωχῷ, ἔλεος γάρ ἐστι, μήτε δὲ ἀλλοεθνεῖ, ἡ γὰρ εὐλογία οὐδὲν ἐκ τοῦ ἀλλοεθνοῦς βλάπτεται. Εὐλογεῖ δὲ αὐτὸν μᾶλλον καὶ συμβαίνει διὰ τῆς εὐλογίας τῆς ἐχούσης Θεοῦ δύναμιν, κἀκεῖνον εἰς ἐπίγνωσιν ἀληθείας ἐλθεῖν. The meaning of ἀλλοεθνής is unclear;

my interpretation is based on the biblical understanding of ἐθνής ("gentile") and the contents of the letter. Perrone 1998: 91–92 interprets it as evidence for religious toleration among Palestinian monks.

117. Van den Ven 1962: 127n127, notes, "Le miracle de la multiplication de pains ou des grains de blé est presque banal en les textes hagiographiques." For example, *v.Sym.Styl.* 11; Jo. Ruf., *v.Petr.Ib.* 67; *v.Nicol.Sion.* 45; Jo. Eph., *v.SS.Or.* 35; Thdr. Petr., *v.Thds* (Usener 35–39); Ant. Choz., *v.Geo.Choz.* 8.37; Paul Elus., *v.Thgn.* 22; and Jo. Mosch., *prat.* 28, 85.

118. *v.Sin.* 138–43 (Bell 80–82). This text is a compilation whose extant Coptic and Arabic versions were finalized after the fifth century. See Lubomierski 2006. The Arabic version of this episode (Amélineau 351–52) does not present Paul as offering a blessed loaf, but refers to the multiplication of loaves alone to explain the storeroom's name. López 2013: 46–72, discusses the blessings discourse at Shenoute's monastery.

119. So Bell 1983: 98n25, observes in translating this passage of the *v.Sin.* For other *eulogiai* storerooms, see *v.Nicol.Sion.* 25; Jo. Mosch., *prat.* 25; and Georg. Syc., *v.Thdr.Syc.* 30. *V.Sym.Styl.iun.* 123 (SH 32.104–5) offers a parallel, referring to the multiplication of a monk's three loaves—that is, a ration of blessings.

120. Déroche 1995: 238–54, focusing on Mk 10:29–30, a passage prominent in Leontius of Neapolis's hagiography. Cf. Caner 2006: 329–33.

121. Bars. et Jo., *resp.* 587 (SC 451.784; trans. Chryssavgis, 2.168, adapted): Ἐὰν γὰρ ᾖ κλέπτης, καθὼς εἶπον οἱ Πατέρες, *δότε εὐλογίαν καὶ ἀπολύσατε.* . . . Ἱμάτιον δὲ μηδενὶ δώσητε ὡς ἔτυχεν, ἐὰν μὴ πάνυ ᾖ ἄνθρωπος φοβούμενος τὸν Θεὸν καὶ αἰσχύνηται αἰτῆσαι. Ἐρευνῶντες οὖν τὴν ἀλήθειαν, εἰ ὄντως ἀκτήμων ᾖ καὶ χρῄζων ἐστὶ διὰ τὸν Θεὸν καὶ οὐ δι' ἀσωτίαν, συμπαθήσατε αὐτῷ. For a different letter privileging the shamefaced poor written to a lay correspondent, see Bars. et Jo., *resp.* 630.

122. See chapter 2, "Preaching Philanthropy in Christian Cappadocia."

123. See note 121; and Bars. et Jo., *resp.* 588 (SC 451.786): χρὴ εὐλογίαν διδόναι καὶ ἀπολύειν.

124. Bars. et Jo., *resp.* 589 (SC 451.786): Ἀλλ' ἐὰν ᾖ χρεία τοῦ δοῦναι αὐτῷ μικρὸν περισσόν, δὸς καὶ ἀπόλυσον. For similar advice, see Isaiah Scet., *log.* 3 (Chryssavgis-Penkett, 50–51).

125. The second translation is from Georgi 1992: 96. For the Greek text, see note 24.

126. Cf. Lampe, s.v. περισσός, also περισσεία, περίσσευμα, περισσεύω.

127. Isaiah Scet., *log.* 4 (Chryssavgis-Penkett, 55). Cf. Bars. et Jo., *resp.* 636, 681.

128. Pachomius, *Rules* 38. Cf. *reg. mag.* 23.33–37, 25; and *v.Sym.Styl.iun.* 123.

129. Ant. Choz., *v.Geo.Choz.* 3.12 (Houze, 108). Cf. Ant. Choz., *v.Geo.Choz.* 2.6. See also Jo. Eph., *v.SS.Or.* 8 ("Life of Addai the Chorepiscopus"; PO 17.128); Jo. Eph., *v.SS.Or.* 33 ("Life of Ḥala the Zealous";18.594, 600–601); Cyril Scyth., *v.Sab.* 44; and *AP* G Megethius 3 (PG 65.301A).

130. Thdr. Petr., *v.Thds* (Usener, 38): οὕτως τὴν τῶν λειψάνων περισσείαν ἡλιασθεῖσαν ἐπί τινας διαρκέσαι τούτοις ἡμέρας.

131. *v.Nicol.Sion.*, 56–57 (Sevčenko and Sevčenko, 88–90): περιέσσευσεν ἐξ αὐτῶν εὐλογία πολλή, ὥστε ἀπὸ Καρκάβω ἀγαλλιώμενον τὸν δοῦλον τοῦ θεοῦ Νικόλαον ἀπελθεῖν ἐν τῷ εὐκτηρίῳ οἴκῳ τοῦ ἁγίου Θεοδώρου εἰς Καύσας. κἀκεῖ ἔθυσεν ζυγὴν βοϊδίων, καὶ συγκαλεσάμενος πάντα τὸν ἐκεῖσε λαόν . . . καὶ ἐκ τῆς περισσείας τοῦ ἁγίου Θεοδώρου τῶν εὐλογιῶν ἀπ' ἐκεῖθεν παρεγένετο εἰς τὸν εὐκτήριον οἶκον τοῦ ἁγίου ἀρχαγγέλου εἰς Νέαν Κώμην. . . . καὶ ἐπερίσσευσεν ἡ τοῦ θεοῦ δωρεά. καὶ περίσσευσεν εὐλογία μεγάλη, ὥστε τὸν δοῦλον τοῦ θεοῦ ἐπὶ πλεῖον δοξάζειν τὸν θεόν. καὶ ἀπ' ἐκεῖθεν

κατῆλθεν εἰς τὸ εὐκτήριον τοῦ ἀρχαγγέλου καὶ τοῦ ἁγίου Δημητρίου ἐν τῷ Συμβόλῳ . . . καὶ πληθυνθέντων τῶν ἀναλωμάτων.

132. Jo. Eph., *v.SS.Or.* 35 ("On the Amidene Convents"; PO 18.616).

133. *Reg. mag.* 85.1 (SC 106.384): "cum unaquaeque ars aliquod perfectum superuacuum usibus monasterii uel mittendarum oblagiarum [viz., eulogiarum] abundauerit." *Const. Ap.* 8.31.1 (SC 336.234) explains how to handle liturgical *eulogiai* under the title περὶ περισσευμάτων.

134. Bars. et Jo., *resp.* 487 (SC 451.598) notes that a monk who finds rest in an abandoned cell "will ever bless" him who originally built it, even if it is in need of repairs. I discuss blessings in relation to gleanings in Caner 2008: 239.

135. Georg. Syc., *v.Thdr.Syc.* 30 (SH 48.27–28).

136. Bloch and Parry 1989: 21–23, discussing gifts used to "maintain a static and timeless order."

137. Quoted from the 6th-century Persian Synod of Jésyuhb, *can.* 12 (CSCO 367.159, with Latin trans. 368.418), based on Council of Laodicea *can.* 32 (ca. 364 CE). Cf. the general prohibition of gifts from heretics or non-Christians in Council of Elvira, *can.* 28 (early 4th century), Council of Carthage, *can.* 93 (411 CE). For the ecclesiastical practice of sending *eulogiai,* Drews 1898: 35–36; Stuiber 1966: 925; and Taft 1999: 30–31. For its continuation, see, for example, Jo. Ruf., *v.Petr.Ib.* 139; and *P.Ness.* 50 (7th century). As Drews and Taft point out, Eus. Caes., *HE* 5.24, indicates that early communities sent consecrated eucharist bread for this purpose.

138. *AP* G Arsenius 16 (PG 65.92B): ἀφορίσατέ με τοῦ μὴ δοῦναί μου τὴν εὐλογίαν ἣν ἔπεμψεν ὁ θεὸς τοῖς ἀδελφοῖς, ἣν οὐκ ἤμην ἄξιος λαβεῖν.

139. *Const. Ap.* 8.31.3; see text in note 33.

140. Bas. Caes., *RB* 122; *reg. mag.* 17.8. Ps.-Bas. Caes., *Poen. mon.* (PG 31.1308–13), though much later, suggests possibilities for the earlier period.

141. Bars. et Jo., *resp.* 44 (SC 426.246–48) scolds John for serving three *eulogiai* to a disciple without permission. Though obscure, this letter describes a situation different from *resp.* 141, which involved providing *eulogiai* to unexpected outside visitors. Ben., *reg.* 54 (Fry, 254) prohibits cenobites from exchanging "litteras, eulogias vel quaelibet munuscula" without their abbot's permission.

142. *HM* 1.58–61. On his deathbed, Barsauma verbally blessed each member of his monastery "by rank according to precedence." *V.Bars.* 157.2 (trans. Palmer, 253).

143. Pall., *HL* 25.3 (Bartelink, 136): οὐκ εἰμί σου χείρων, ἵνα σὺ ἐμοὶ εὐλογίαν πέμψῃς. These figs had been sent by an outsider; the lay desire to give such gifts (consisting here, as in *AP* G Arsenius 16, of dried fruit) may explain the "pastry-sellers" (*plakountarioi*) noted at Nitria. Pall., *HL* 7.4.

144. Geront., *v.Mel. gr.* 41 (SC 90.206): καὶ ὑπερεκπερισσοῦ κολληθεῖσαι αὐτῇ ἐσπούδαζον κατὰ πάντα αὐτῆς ὑπακούειν,τὴν ἄμετρον αὐτῆς συμπάθειαν ἐννοοῦσαι. In Geront., *v.Mel. gr.* 38 (198), he says that when visiting anchorites in Egypt, she snuck gold into their cells against their wishes so as to benefit by refreshing holy people.

145. *Pan. Rabb.* (Overbeck 184; trans. Doran 85, adapted). For a similar rule, *v.Bars.* 81.3.

146. See this chapter's section "The Pauline Concept of a Christian Blessing"; with Bobertz 1993; and Schöllgen 2002: 116–27.

147. *Canons of Marutha* 27.1 (Vööbus, 123). Cf. Jo. Eph., *v.SS.Or.* 16 ("Life of Symeon the Mountaineer"; PO 17.242).

148. *Reg. mag.* 76 (SC 106.314; trans. Eberle, 239). Cf. *v.Sym.Styl.* 28.

149. Sev. Ant., *ep.Coll.1* 1.35; Greg. Mag., *reg.* 2.54, 7.9, 9.20, 11.48.

150. Perhaps significantly, this identification is only made where bishops are dealing with seculars. Greg. Mag., *reg.* 11.37 (an interesting case, stating that the small *exenia* he is sending with his letter comes "out of the *benedictiones* of St. Peter"); and Leont. Neap., *v.Jo. Eleem.* 9 (Festugière-Rydén, 355), where John calls the *xenion* a widow gives him both a *karpophoria* and a *eulogia*.

151. Sev. Ant., *ep.Coll.1* 1.7 (Brooks, 1.41/2.45), condemning an attempt by lectors to usurp the role of subdeacons.

152. *Const. Ap.* 8.31.3; see text in note 33. Such distributions follow the principle of "to each according to his due," taken for granted in Leont. Neap., *v.Jo.Eleem.* 6.

153. Thdt., *prov.* 6–7 (PG 83.652A–684D). Cf. Thdt, *Quest. in Lev.* 1.6 (Petruccione, 12). For earlier examples, Viner 1978: 1–45; Zeisel 1975: 65–67.

154. Dan. Scet., *log.* 6 ("Eulogius the Stonecutter"; Dalman, 152): παρακαλεῖν τὸν Θεὸν χορηγῆσαι αὐτῷ περισσὸν ἀνάλωμα, ἵνα ἔχῃ καὶ εὐεργετῇ καὶ ἄλλους πλείονας. . . . ἵνα ἐπιχορήσῃ αὐτῷ εὐλογίαν, ὡς ἂν καὶ ἄλλους πλείονας εὐεργετήσῃ. (160–62): φέρω τὸν Εὐλόγιον εἰς τὴν προτέραν αὐτοῦ τάξιν. . . . κατὰ μικρὸν μικρὸν κατέστησεν αὐτὸν εἰς τὴν προτέραν τάξιν . . . Θαυμάσαι δὲ ἐστι τὴν τοῦ Θεῦ ἀγαθότητα πῶς δι᾽ ὀλίγου ὕψωσε τὸν Εὐλόγιον καὶ πάλιν ἐταπείνωσε τοσοῦτον πρὸς τὸν συμφέρον.

155. Foster 1965. The lack of secure banks in antiquity meant that such windfalls were not too uncommon. See Morrison 1981.

156. Dan. Scet., *log.* 6 ("Eulogius the Stonecutter"; Dalman, 152, 162). Cf. Jo. Mosch., *prat.* 154.

157. *P.Ness.* III 79, 80. On which, see Caner forthcoming-a.

158. Hall 1905: 147, appendix 23. Other examples are Crum 1902: 48–49; Winlock, Crum, and Evelyn-White 1926: 1:173n13; and Schmelz 2002: 205–6.

159. *v.Pach. boh.* 197 (Lefort, 192; trans. Veilleux, 244–45). *V.Pach. gr. prim.* 146 includes everything *except* Horsiesius's reassuring reply. For a similar vignette, see *AP* G Gelasius 5 (PG 65.152), discussed in Bagnall 2001. On the Pachomian accumulation of land, Zeisel 1975: 298–301.

160. *Reg. Hors.* 52–53 (Lefort, 97; trans. Veilleux 216–17).

161. Jo. Mosch., *prat.* 85 (PG 85[3].2941).

162. See "Surviving Sources and Historical Discourses" in the Introduction, and "Providential Order and the Rise of a Religious Aristocracy" in chapter 1.

163. On these developments, see Wipszycka 2001; and Zeisel 1975: 302–3.

164. On these annuities, see the section in this chapter "The Institutional and Lay Provision of Material Blessings." For the "unrestricted gift" category in modern philanthropies, see Caner forthcoming-a.

165. Bas. Caes., *RB* 92 (PG 31.1145C); with Gould 1987. See also Bars. et Jo., *resp.* 254; *v.Sym Styl. iun.* 56, 93.

166. On *prospatheia*, see Bas. Caes., *RF* 5.2; Bas. Caes., *RB* 143, 144; Jo. Cassian, *Coll.* 4.21, 10.14.2, 24.7–12; and Bars. et Jo., *resp.* 774. Jo. Clim., *scal.* 26 (PG 88.1029): εὐσεβῶν μὲν, τὸ

παντὶ αἰτοῦντι διδόναι, εὐσεβεστέρων δὲ καὶ τῷ μὴ αἰτοῦντι. Τὸ δὲ ἀπὸ τοῦ αἴροντος μὴ ἀπαιτεῖν δυναμένους μάλιστα, τάχα τῶν ἀπαθῶν καὶ μόνων ἴδιον καθέστηκεν.

167. Dor. Gaz., *ep.* 3 (SC 92.506): ἐὰν μὴ ὡς ἴδια διοικῇς τὰ πράγματα, ἀλλ᾽ ὡς τῷ Θεῷ ἀνακείμενα. See also Bars. et Jo., *resp.* 317; and *AP* G John the Persian 2 (PG 65.237).

168. Bars. et Jo., *resp.* 338 (SC 450.342–44): ἐὰν εὐχαριστοῦντες τῷ δόντι αὐτὴν Θεῷ καὶ κατακρίνοντες ἑαυτοὺς ὡς ἀναξίους λάβωμεν, ὁ Θεὸς ποιεῖ αὐτὴν εἰς ἁγιασμὸν καὶ εὐλογίαν ... κατακρίνων ἑαυτὸν ὡς ἀνάξιον, καὶ ὠθεῖ ὁ Θεὸς ἀπὸ σοῦ τὴν προσπάθεια, where αὐτὴν refers to food as an example of any necessity. Bas. Caes., *RB* 168 (PG 31: 1193A) similarly recommends reflecting whether one has received something ὑπὲρ τὴν ἀξίαν. For a vivid depiction of this ideal, see Jo. Eph., *v.SS.Or.* 17 ("Life of a Poor Stranger"; PO 18.256).

169. Bas. Caes., *RF* 5.2 (PG 31.921A; trans. Clarke 159), τοῦτο δὲ διὰ παντελοῦς ἀναχωρήσεως καὶ λήθης τῶν παλαιῶν ἐθῶν κατορθοῦται ... οἱονεὶ πρὸς ἕτερον κόσμον διὰ τῆς σχέσεως μεταβαίνοντες.

170. Heussi 1936: 53–54.

171. Pall., *HL* 25.3. Cf. Cyril Scyth., *v.Euthym.* 16; *AP* L 10.16; and Bars. et Jo., *resp.* 316, where refusing outside gifts is advised as a way of alienating oneself to become a monk.

172. *Reg. mag.* 22.2 (SC 106.110).

173. Layton 2005: 31: "Vocabularies or semantic fields ... do not simply point to knowledge of the monastic world. They *are* that world."

174. *v.Matr.Perg.* 30, 35, 43 (*AASS Nov.* 3.805, 806, 809; trans. Featherstone, 48, 51, 57). Also *v.Longini* 14–15; *v.Dan.Styl.* 62; *v.Sym.Styl.iun.* 56, 93, 113, 122–23.

175. Greg. Mag., *Dial.* 3.37 is the only example of the multiplying-loaves motif I have found in Western hagiography of this era.

176. Gascou 1991: 1641–42. See also the discussion in "Surviving Sources and Historical Discourses" section of the Introduction.

177. Cyril Scyth., *v.Euthym.* 50 (Schwartz, 72–74): τοίνυν οἱ καρποφοροῦντες μοναστηρίῳ θεῶι προσφέρουσιν καὶ παρ᾽ αὐτοῦ λαμβάνουσιν τὸν μισθόν.

CHAPTER 6. "YOU ARE THE FIRSTFRUITS OF THE WORLD": MONASTICISM, FRUITBEARINGS, AND PROSPERITY IN THE COUNTRYSIDE

1. Jo. Cassian, *Coll.* 21.1.3 (SC 64.76): "possessores, qui certatim decimas vel primitias frugum suarum ... de suis substantiis offerebant." See also Jo. Cassian, *Coll.* 14.7. On the setting and its historicity, see Sternberg 1988.

2. Jo. Cassian, *Coll.* 21.2 (SC 64.76–77; trans. Ramsey, adapted).

3. Bagnall 1993: 21–22; and Brumfield 1981: 54–55. For offerings of grapes, oil, and grain connected to a harvest, Greg. Naz. *or.* 16.17; Jo. Cassian, *Coll.* 14.7.1–3; *HM* 18.1; *AP* G Benjamin 1.

4. Thdt., *Qu. in Ex.* 54 (Petruccione and Hill, 306–307). For a mosaic possibly depicting firstfruits in connection with the month of May in Scythopolis, see Saller and Bagatti 1949: 101. For Judaic background, Brooks 1983.

5. *v.Bars.* 15.1 (trans. Palmer, 187).

6. See López 2016.

7. *HM* 8.38–41 (SH 53.61–62). Cf. Wipszycka 2001: 182 for a depiction of firstfruits in the Coptic *Questions of Theodore*.

8. *P.Mon.Apoll.* 10 and 13 (7th century), discussed in Clackson 2000: 60–61 and 64, as well as *P.Vindob.K.* 11375 (8th century), discussed in Hasitzka 2001, record the collection during harvest months of Pachon and Mesori of *aparches* to pay monastery taxes. See Clackson 2000: 60–64; Wipszycka 2001; and Wipszycka 2009: 559–61. For the relation between harvests and tax/loan cycles, Bagnall 1993: 22; and Tenger 1993: 230.

9. There seems to have been no equivalent to καρποφορία in Latin, Syriac, or Coptic. It is not used in the Old or New Testament, although cognates καρποφορέω and καρποφόρος appear (LXX Ps 106:34, 148:9; Sg 4:17; Ws 10:7; Hb 2:21; Mt 13:23; Mk 4:20, 28; Lk 8:15; Acts 14:16; Rom 7:4, 5; Col 1:6, 10). For these scriptural passages, the Vulgate uses *fructificare/ fructifer*; the Peshitta *y(h)ab pērē* (and forms of the participle, *praya*); the Sahidic, forms of *tikarpos*; the Boharic, forms of *tioutah*.

10. Thomas 1987: 77–78 discusses καρποφορίαι as "inter vivos *prosphorai*." Though accurate, this obscures their intention. Council in Trullo, *can.*28 (692 CE), cited in chapter 7, "Lay Offerings and Church Commemorations," specifies that firstfruits were to express gratitude for material benefits received, while liturgical offerings did so for life itself. For related classical customs, see Jim 2014: 75–83. For Judaic customs, Herman 1991. For early Christian customs, Dix 1945: 110–23; Zeisel 1975: 67–117; Bradshaw 1993; and Serfass 2002: 6–18.

11. Cyril Alex., *Comm. in Zach.* 4.11.3 (Pusey, 2.499) shows the affinity between καρποφορίας, δεκάτας, ἀπαρχὰς, and εὐχαριστήρια. "Vows" (εὐχαί) were also classed as such: *Const. Ap.* 4.8.1, 8.10.12; Greg. Naz., *or.* 45.33; and Soc. *HE* 7.47.2 For discussion of these "paraliturgical" Christian categories, see Mango 1986: 4–6.

12. Peter of Alexandria, Ps.-, *On Riches* (trans. Pearson and Vivian, 104). For prayers conferring blessings on firstfruits and their donors, see Bradshaw 1993.

13. Isid. Pel., *ep.* 1.317 (PG 78. 365C): Καλῶς τὸν Κύριον τιμᾷς, ἡμῖν τῷ καρπῶν ἀπαρχόμενος, καὶ δεκατῶν τὴν εὐφορίαν τῆς γῆς σου τῷ διδόντι . . . νῦν μὲν τῶν ἐν χρείᾳ σοι φυλάττουσαν τὴν αὐτάρκειαν, μετὰ ταῦτα δὲ τὴν αἰώνιον εὐφροσύνην παρέχουσαν.

14. Jim 2014: 81 proposes calling it a *do-quia-dedisti* ("I give because you gave") transaction.

15. τὰ σά ἐκ τῶν σῶν. See Rajak 2004: 236–38; and Bradshaw 1993: 38. The phrase is inscribed on the Riha (or "Tyler") liturgical chalice in the Dumbarton Oaks collection; for this and other examples, see Mango 1986: 4. Saller and Bagatti 1949: 101, relates Chrysostom's preaching on firstfruits to this formula.

16. Jo. Clim., *scal.* 26 (PG 88.1025): ὁ δὲ ἵνα δώροις τὸν Δεσπότην τιμήσῃ. Cf. Geront., *v.Mel. lat.* 46.2 (Laurence, 244).

17. Lev 2:2–3, 27:26–27; Num 18:8–11; Deut 16:9–10, 26:2; *Didache* 13.1–7; *SyrD.* 9; with Brooks 1983; Herman 1991; and Bradshaw 1993.

18. *Karpophoriai* are distinguished from a church's regular income (*prosodon*) in Cyril Alex., *ep.* 78.2; and the petition against Hiba of Edessa in the Council of Chalcedon *acta* (*ACO* 2.1.3), art. 7–8. Cf. Wipszycka 1972: 64–92; and Wipszycka 2015: 198–208. All were pooled together in the church *ptōchika*. On their receipt, see Finn 2006a: 49–56; Zeisel 1975: 65–70; and Boyd 1946. For epigraphical examples, many of which refer to "vows," see Ševčenko 1992: 46n35.

19. Epiph., *De fide* 6.1 (Kroll-Dummer 3.491): διὰ χειρῶν ἰδίων καρποφοροῦσα καὶ ἑαυτῇ ἐπαρκουμένη τοῖς τε ἀδελφοῖς καὶ ἐνδεομένοις. See also *HM* 18.1; and Soz., *HE* 1.11.6.

20. Cyril Scyth., *v.Sab.* 45 (Schwartz, 136): οἱ οἰκήτορες ἤρχοντο ... πλείστας ψυχικὰς εὐεργεσίας ἀρυόμενοι καὶ καρποφοροῦντες τοῖς κοινοβίοις αὐτοῦ καὶ λαύραις σῖτον καὶ ὄσπρεον. Also *HM* 14.19–20; Thdt., *HR* 10.3; Thdr. Petr., *v.Thds.* (Usener, 80); Cyril Scyth., *v.Euthym.* 9; Ant. Choz., *v.Geo.Choz.* 8; *v.Geras.* 2.2–3.4; *v.Sin.* 166–68; with discussion in Hirschfeld 1992: 102–3.

21. Leont. Neap. *v.Jo.Eleem.* 9 (Festugière-Rydén, 355): τὴν εὐλογίαν ἣν ἐνέβαλεν ὁ θεὸς ἐν τῇ καρδίᾳ ... προσενέγκαι. ... ὡς οὖν ἐδέξατο τὴν καρποφορίαν αὐτῆς ὁ πάπας.

22. *CJ* 1.2.38.2–3 (Krueger, 24–25; trans. Coleman-Norton, 937–38, adapted): ὥστε μηδένα τῶν θεοφιλεστάτων ἐπισκόπων ... ἢ κληρικῶν ἄκοντας τοὺς λαϊκοὺς συνελαύνειν πρὸς τὴν τῶν καρποφοριῶν τῶν ἐν τοῖς τόποις καλουμένων ἀπαρχῶν ἤτοι προσφορῶν ἔκτισιν ὥσπερ τι τέλος ταῦτα μεθοδεύοντας, ἢ καὶ γεωργοῖς. ... ἀφορισμοὺς τούτων ἕνεκα τῶν αἰτιῶν ἢ ἀναθεματισμοὺς τούτοις ἐπάγειν καὶ τῆς τῶν ἁγίων μυστηρίων μεταλήψεως. ... τοῦτο γὰρ παρά τινων πεπονθέναι μεμαθήκαμεν καὶ κώμας ὅλας ἤτοι καὶ ἀγροὺς ... ὑπὸ τοῖς τοιούτοις ἀφορισμοῖς ἤτοι ἀναθεματισμοῖς γενομένους. ... γάρ ἐστι πρόδηλον, ὡς προσήκει μάλιστα ἕκαστον ἐκ τῶν οἰκείων πόνων ἑκόντα τῷ θεῷ καὶ τοῖς ὑπηρετουμένοις αὐτῷ προσφέρειν, ἅπερ ἂν αὐτὸς δοκιμάσοι, οὐ μὴν συνωθεῖσθαι πρὸς τοῦτο καὶ ἀναγκάζεσθαι. ... ἴσως καὶ οὐδὲ τῶν ἐκ τῆς γεωργίας καρπῶν διά τινας συμβαινούσας οἵα εἰκὸς ἀφορίας ἀπολαύοντα. Placed among legislation that predates Justin I, the law is usually ascribed to Anastasius. See Patlagean 1977: 273–76, who views such offerings as an informal church tax on the rural poor. A better analogy may be the fees that secular officials customarily charged for completing services, partly to recoup money they had spent on purchasing their offices (a distinct development under Anastasius I). See Kelly 2004: 215–16.

23. Wipszycka 1972: 66 maintains that such offerings were "morally obligatory, but the quantity with which they were given was left to the discretion of the faithful." For different conclusions, reflecting the contradictory nature of the evidence, see Leclercq 1922: 995–98; and Constable 1964: 9–22. Rabbula, *Rules for Clergy and the Bnay Qyāmā* 6 (Vööbus, 37), forbids clerics to demand honoraria (*gebyātā*), affirming that "the church shall be filled by what each gives according to his own will." On the Council of Mâcon (585 CE), see Constable 1964: 21–22; and Boyd 1946: 159–61. Zeisel 1975: 68 notes that Latin sources rarely mention firstfruits, and Eastern sources rarely mention tithes.

24. *SyrD* 8 (replicated in *Const. Ap.* 2.34–35); Leclercq 1922: 996–97.

25. Nilus, *ep.* 1.129 (PG 79.137C): Ἄτοπον δρᾶν πρᾶγμα δοκεῖς μοι, ἐν τῷ μεταξὺ ὕβρεων καὶ θυμοῦ καταναγκάζειν καρποφορεῖν σοί τινας. Τοῦτο δ᾽ οὐκ ἂν λεχθείη καρποφορία, ἀλλὰ βία, καὶ αἰσχρότης, καὶ ἀκαιρία ἐσχάτη, καὶ τραχύτερόν τι τῶν δημοτίων ἐπιταγμάτων, καὶ βαρυτάτων ἀπαιτημάτων. Ἀλλὰ παῦσαι, παρακαλῶ, τῆς ἀπρεπείας ταύτης, μᾶλλον δὲ σχόλασον ταῖς προσευχαῖς, καὶ τῇ πολλῇ κατὰ ψυχὴν ἡσυχίᾳ, καὶ ὁ Θεὸς διεγείρει τοὺς ἀξίους ὄντας τῆς καλοκαγαθίας προσφέρειν σοι μεθ᾽ ἱκεσίας πᾶσαν χρείαν.

26. For Nilus, Alexander, and this letter, see Caner 2002: 147–48.

27. Council of Gangra, *Ep. syn.* (Joannou, 87): καρποφορίας τε τὰς ἐκκλησιαστικὰς τὰς ἀνέκαθεν διδομένας τῇ ἐκκλησιαστικὰς τὰς ἀνέκαθεν διδομένας τῇ ἐκκλεσίᾳ ἑαυτοῖς ... ὡς ἁγίοις τὰς διαδόσεις ποιούμενοι. On the synod, Caner 2002: 99–100.

28. *Const. Ap.* 2.35.3 (SC 320.258): δώσεις τῷ ἱερεῖ τὰ ὀφειλόμενα αὐτῷ ... ὡς μεσίτῃ Θεοῦ καὶ τῶν δεομένων καθάρσεως καὶ παραιτήσεως. Cf. *Const. Ap.* 7.29.1–3; *Const. Ap.* 8.30.1–2; Ath., Ps.-, *Can. Ath.* 63, 69, 82–83. Hamman 1968: 269 remarks, "The *Apostolic Constitutions* reintroduces the Old Testament prescription of firstfruits by giving it a

theological motivation." Thdt., *Qu. in Lev.* 1.5 (Petruccione-Hill, 13) explains that Christian priests should be given firstfruits "because they offer intercession for our sins."

29. Brown 1995: 63–64, calling such hagiography "a trap prepared for their readers by the disciples of the holy man."

30. Discussed in Caner 2013b: 127–46. On monastic penance and intercession in general, see Rapp 2005: 77–85. On "philosophical" monasticism, Rubenson 2012: 487–512.

31. Pettegrew 2007: 746.

32. For a general overview, Decker 2009. For the Negev, Gutwein 1981. For Syria, Tchalenko 1953: 1.377–438; Tate 1992; Foss 2002: 91–92; Butcher 2003: 135–79; and Baumeister 2011. For Asia Minor, Foss 1991; Niewöhner 2006; Izdebski 2013: 1–31.

33. See Decker 2009: 250; Butcher 2003: 186–89. For a less sanguine view, Bintliff 2014.

34. See Chrys., *In Mt.* 61.3; Thdt., *HR* 10.3; Segal 1955: 119.

35. Jones 1964: 554–57; Rossiter 1989; Tate 1998: 913–41; Butcher 2003: 138; Bagnall 1992: 128–49. For differing assessments of the impact of manors in Egypt, Sarris 2006; Hickey 2007. For the fifth-century West, Brown 2012: 189–97.

36. Dagron 1977; Kaplan 1992: 185–200. For one such semi-urban *komē*, see Mango 2017.

37. López 2013: 1–8, 80–81; Feissel and Kaygusuz 1985. See also Jo. Eph., *v.SS.Or.* 1 ("Life of Habib"; PO 17.8–11); Georg. Syc., *v.Thdr.Syc.* 75–76; and Segal 1955: 118.

38. Decker 2009: 20–44, 69–79; Butcher 2003: 148–49.

39. Robert 1960: 324–25, discussed in Decker 2009: 69–72; and Brown 2016: 63–66.

40. In general, Decker 2009: 51–52; and Schachner 2006: 1–15. With important methodological discussion for Palestine, Fischer 1989; Aviam 2004: 185–90; Bar 2005; Seligman 2011; Ashkenazi 2014; Ashkenazi and Aviam 2013; and Ashkenazi and Aviam 2017. For Asia Minor, Trombley 1985.

41. See Caquot 1958; Millar 2009; and Dagron 1977: 49.

42. Bar 2005: 63.

43. Hull 2008. See also Schachner 2006: 65–68.

44. *Pace* Treadgold 1994: 156: "It seems improbable that as much as 5% of the population of the Later Roman Empire ever saw a holy man." I leave aside the academic question as to whether an average monk would have been considered a holy person.

45. Schachner 2010: 379.

46. *v.Sym.Styl.,* 99 (trans. Doran, 172).

47. Schachner 2006: 72.

48. Brown 2016: 68. For this aspect of early Syrian asceticism, see Escolan 1999; and Caner 2002.

49. Nilus, *De mon. ex.* 6–7, 12 (PG 79.725A–D, 732D); Nilus, *De vol. paup.* 30 (1005BC); Isaac. Ant., *Hymn on Penance* L 414, 37 (Bedjan 1890–97, 1:41), cited in Schachner 2006: 112, 183; with Vööbus 1958: 155; Vööbus 1960: 148–50 (discussing Rabbula).

50. Schachner 2006: 324–38. Cf. Brenk 2004.

51. Schachner 2006: 517–20. Also Tate 1992: 339–40. The Mar Bas/Batabu monastery outside Chalcis is an example of a prestige monastery that may have been supported by bishops. See Sev. Ant., *ep.Coll.2* 10.6; and Canivet 1977: 171.

52. Unpublished *Life of Mar Gabriel,* quoted in Schachner 2006: 96. On literary production in monasteries of the region, see Walker 2010.

53. Ashenkenazi and Aviam 2017: 120.

54. Seligman 2011: 517.

55. Schachner 2006: 112, 310–16; *Canons of Marutha* 54.19, 23, 24; and Jo. Mosch., *prat.* 232. For the colophon, see *v.Sym.Styl.* 135 (trans. Doran, 197). I owe this reference to Dina Boero.

56. Jo. Eph., *v.SS.Or.*7 ("Life of Abraham the Recluse"; PO 17.120). "Gift of honor" translates *ʾiqārā*.

57. *v.Sym.Styl.iun.* 95 (SH 32.74): σοφῇ οἰκονομίᾳ τροπώσομαι, τοῦ καὶ σὲ ἀβαρῇ τοῖς ἀνθρώποις γενέσθαι καὶ τὰ τῆς χρείας ἐν τῷ σῷ τόπῳ εἶναι. 113 (92): ἐργιχείρῳ κοπιῶντες τὸν ἐπιούσιον ἄρτον πορίζεσθε. Cf. *v.Sym.Styl.iun.* 56, 60, 93, 122–23; with Van den Ven, 212*–13*. For a comparable arrangement, see Call., *v.Hyp.* 18.1; and *v.Aux.* 33–34, 51.

58. Thdt., *HR* 10.3 (SC 234.442; trans. Price, 90, adapted): παρήνει τοῖς κατὰ ψυχὴν πόνοις καὶ τοὺς σωματικοὺς συνεισφέρειν ἱδρῶτας· "καὶ γὰρ ἄτοπον τοὺς μὲν ἐν βίῳ στρεφομένους καὶ παιδία καὶ γυναῖκας ταλαιπωρουμένους καὶ πονοῦντας ἀποτρέφειν, καὶ πρὸς τούτοις καὶ φόρους εἰσφέρειν καὶ δασμοὺς ἀπαιτεῖσθαι καὶ τῷ θεῷ προσφέρειν τὰς ἀπαρχὰς καὶ τῶν προσαιτῶν εἰς δύναμιν θεραπεύειν τὴν ἔνδειαν, ἡμᾶς δὲ τὴν ἀναγκαίαν ἐκ τῶν πόνων μὴ πορίζεσθαι χρείαν . . . ἀλλὰ καθῆσθαι εἴσω τὰς χεῖρας ἔχοντας καὶ τὰ τῶν ἀλλοτρίων χειρῶν καρπουμένους.

59. Cyril Scyth., *v.Euthym.* 9 (Schwartz, 18).

60. Jo. Eph., *v.SS.Or.* 17 ("Life of a Poor Stranger"; PO 17.256–57, adapted).

61. Jo. Eph., *v.SS.Or.* 17 ("Life of a Poor Stranger"; PO 17.254): "holen d-ʾeškoryoto mšamšin (h)wow botar tešmeštā w-men holen d-ilpin (h)wow mazmure."

62. For example, Chrys., *In Jo.* 36.2; Thdt., *HR,* prol. 1; Thdr. Petr., *v.Thds.* (Usener 14, 20); Jo. Mosch., *prat.* 153, 171; *v.Sym.Styl.iun.* 124. See Chialà 2017: 37–39.

63. Thdt., *HR* 10.2 (SC 234.440): Πόνοις δὲ πόνους ἐπαύξων. Cf. *HR,* prol. 7; 1.7; 2.16; 3.2, 4–5, 9, 12, 19, 21–22; 4.12; 5.2, 4; 6.5; 8.3; 9.1; 11.3–4; 12.3; 13.3, 18–19; 16.2; 17.1, 5, 7, 11; 18.1, 3; 20.2; 21.1–4, 8, 11, 14, 31; 23.2; 24.1–2, 4–7, 9.

64. Thdt., *HR* 26.22. On Symeon's physical *ponos,* Thdt., *HR* 26.3,6,9,11.

65. See Hunt 2012.

66. Sev. Ant., *ep.Coll.2* 35 (Brooks, 283). Cf. Jo. Eph., *v.SS.Or.* 5 ("Lives of Simeon and Sergius"; PO 17. 87).

67. *HM* 10.26–29 (CS 34.86). See also *HM* 12.16; *v.Pach. boh.* 150; *v.Sin.*102–5; with Cain 2016: 202–4. For documentary evidence of related monastic practices in Egypt, see Frankfurter 2017: 92–100.

68. Jo. Ruf., *v.Petr.Ib.* 36, 137 (trans. Horn-Phenix, 49, 201). Cf. Jerome, *v.Hil.* 25, 27; Bars. et Jo., *resp.* 648.

69. *v.Longini* 12 (trans. Vivian, 15). Cf. *v.Pach. boh.* 54.

70. *v.Sym.Styl.* 135–36 (CS 112.197), amending "Simeon bar Apollo" to "Simeon Bar-Eupolemus," following Boero 2015a: 326. On the *Life* and its variants in general, see Boero 2019. I am indebted to Dina Boero for sharing her work with me. Our understanding of Symeon, his hagiography, and his shrine are put on a solid new footing thanks to her meticulous scholarship.

71. Boero 2015b: 123–41; and Boero 2015a.

72. The Arabic name Qalʿat Simʿān, though apparently medieval, it is appropriate, since its expanse is comparable to Hagia Sophia's in Constantinople. For the probability of imperial involvement and largesse, see Tchalenko 1953: 223–33. Boero 2019: 55–57, notes that

there is no sign that any formal monastic community at the shrine before these constructions arose, nor is Symeon himself presented as a monastic leader.

73. Ὑγία τοῖς κυρίοις αὐτοῦ κέρδος (*IGLS* 2.233–34, no.417), discussed in Boero 2015a:
348. The fairly long lapse between Symeon's death and the construction of the hostel may be
explained by the need to raise sufficient funds.

74. Boero 2015a: 333–34.

75. Cosmas, *Ep. ad Sim.*, ed. Assemani, pp. 394–97 (hereafter cited according to Doran's
translation). For details about the letter, see Boero 2015b: 61–63.

76. Cosmas, *Ep. ad Sim.* = *v.Sym.Styl.* 130 (CS 112.195).

77. Cosmas, *Ep. ad Sim.* = *v.Sym.Styl.* 132 (CS 112.196). That it concludes with a request
that all the people of Panîr say "Amen" suggests that it represents a transcription of a village
meeting.

78. Brown 1971: 90–91.

79. Cosmas, *Ep. ad Sim.* = *v.Sym.Styl.* 130 (trans. Doran, 195–96).

80. *v.Sym.Styl.* 63 (Assemani, 321; trans. Doran, 142); *v.Sym.Styl.* 64 (325; 112.144).

81. For authenticity, contents, and relation to Cosmas's *Letter*, see Boero 2015b: 56–63.

82. Lib., *or.* 30.8–11 (trans. Norman, 109–11). Cf. Zosimus, *Hist. nov.* 5.23.4 (probably
based on a lost history by Eunapius of Sardis, who wrote about developments up to the fifth
century); López 2013: 122–24. On the context of Libanius's speech, see Fowden 1978; Errington 1997; Van Nuffelen 2014; Watts 2015: 204–7. For a survey of pagan temples that once
stood on the Limestone Massif, see Steinsapir 2005.

83. Thus Bar 2005: 60–61. Cf. Schachner 2006: 72–77, 298.

84. Caseau 2001; and Butcher 2003: 378–83, 393–97.

85. Pall., *HL* 66.1 (Butler, 162): τοὺς δὲ καρποὺς τῶν κτημάτων κομιζόμενοι ἐν ἐκκλησίαις
πόλεων καὶ κωμῶν διανέμουσιν.

86. Siegelmann 1974.

87. See Haensch 2006: 53–54; and Donceel-Voûte 1988: 17, 136, 163, 174–77, 133–37, 411–18,
433. For Jewish epigraphical formulas and discourses, Hamel 1990: 174–75; Rajak 2004; and
Satlow 2010.

88. Horden and Purcell 2000: 412.

89. Moffet 1990: 107–8; Horden and Purcell 2000: 418.

90. For an overview, Brown 2016: 17–24; also Lapin 1996; and Siegal 2013: 112–19. For
earlier examples, Wendt 2016—a reference I owe to Reyhan Durmaz, mainly dealing with
urban horoscopes and soothsaying; Nilsson 1961: 27–28.

91. Lucian, *De dea Syria* 28 (Attridge-Oden, 38–39). Cf. Frankfurter 1990.

92. Boero 2013: 60; Council in Trullo, *can.* 65. In general, Trombley 1985a; Trzcionka
2007: 109–10. Underutilized testimony for such "survivals," more detailed than the Council
in Trullo, is the (probably) eighth-century sermons of the fictitious Eusebius of Alexandria:
see MacCoull 1999.

93. See Horden and Purcell 2000: 418; and Nollé 2005: 55–60.

94. See Mitchell 1993: 2.132; and Butcher 2003: 165.

95. Rodgers 1980: 1–4.

96. Peter of Alexandria, Ps.-, *On Riches* 107–10 (trans. Pearson and Vivian, 138–39). Cf.
Grégoire 1922: 124; and Lane Fox 1986: 42–47.

97. Bars. et Jo., *resp.* 684. Cf. Jerome, *v.Hil.* 40; *v.Sym.Styl.* 39, 64, 85; and Georg. Syc., *v.Thdr.Syc.* 36, 43, 52, 101, 141, 145.

98. Horden and Purcell 2000: 406. Cf. Trombley 1985b: 341.

99. On pagan survivals and Christian shamans, Trombley 1985b; and more generally, MacMullen 1997. On such characterizations, see now Frankfurter 2017.

100. Thdt., *HE* 26.11. Symeon lived for thirty-seven years on top of his third or fourth column, which was equipped with a six-foot platform. For details about his life and hagiography, see Doran 1992: 15-66. For ancient portrayals of his asceticism, see Harvey 1988; and Harvey 1998.

101. *v.Sym.Styl.* 3 (CS 112.105).

102. *v.Sym.Styl.* 29 (CS 112.118). For the hermitages, *v.Sym.Styl.* 27-28; cf. *v.Sym.Styl.* 95. The location of Daniel's land and fact that he provided skins for Symeon (95) suggest that it was used for raising goats.

103. Thdt., *HR* 26.12, 14. On Symeon's physical build (he is also said to have been a fast runner), *v.Sym.Styl.* 1 (CS 112.104); *v.Sym.Styl.* 13 (111).

104. *v.Sym.Styl.* 39, 61-64, 70-72, 74-75, 85-88. Individual healings: *v.Sym.Styl.* 33-36, 38, 78-84, 87, 89, 90-91.

105. *v.Sym.Styl.* 74-76 (CS 112.155-58). Cf. Thdt., *HR* 23.19.

106. Soc., *HE* 7.22.

107. Sev. Ant., *hymn* 255.5.4 (PO 7.5.703-704). Cf. Marc. Diac., *v. Porph.* 19-21.

108. Joshua, Ps.-, *Chron.* 36 (Wright, 37).

109. Nathan 1998.

110. *v.Sym.Styl.* 60 (CS 112.139). Cf. the monastic prayers quoted by Chrys., *In Col.* 10.2-3 (PG 62.368).

111. *v.Sym.Styl.* 118 (CS 112.187).

112. *v.Sym.Styl.* 109-110 (Assemani, CS 112.178-79).

113. *v.Sym.Styl.* 43, 45-47, 55 (Assemani, 302-3; CS 112.127-31). Cf. Thdt., *HE* 26.24.

114. *v.Sym.Styl.* 48-54 (CS 112.131-35); *v.Sym.Styl.* 110 (179). Cf. Thdt., *HE* 26.22-23. Magdalino 1981: 55, cites the case of an ascetic "iron-wearer" who established his credentials in twelfth-century Constantinople by smearing a reeking compound of animal livers under his chains and pretended that they were cutting into his flesh, making it ooze and drop away.

115. Jacob of Serug, *On Symeon's Deeds* (Harvey, 22, 26). Cf. Harvey 1993; and Boero 2015a.

116. Brock 1993: 148, 152; Brock 1992: 22-24.

117. Isaiah Scet., *log.* 2 (trans. Chryssavgis, 43); Isaiah Scet., *log.* 25 (197). For similar ideas in Mark the Monk, see Torrance 2013: 105-15. By the seventh century, it was thought that psychological ailments caused by passions "contrary to nature" could be corrected through bouts of prayer and fasting. See Booth 2014: 62-63, 75-76, 85.

118. Isaiah Scet., *log.* 2 (trans. Chryssavgis, 45).

119. Isaiah Scet., *log.* 4 (trans. Chryssavgis, 56).

120. Isaiah Scet., *log.* 25 (trans. Chryssavgis, 199).

121. Dor., *log.*.13.148 (SC 92.418): Αἱ θλίψεις γὰρ κινοῦσι τὸ ἔλεος τοῦ Θεοῦ εἰς τὴν ψυχήν, ὥσπερ οἱ ἄνεμοι κινοῦσι τὴν βροχήν.

122. Flusin 1993: 177–78. Sev. Ant., *Hom. cath.* 55 (PO 4: 72); and Georg. Syc., *v.Thdr.Syc.* 8, 36, 52 emphasize the exceptional purity and acceptability of a monk's prayers.

123. Cyril Scyth., *v.Euthym.* 25 (Schwartz, 38; trans. Price 34–35, adapted): αἱ ἁμαρτίαι ἡμῶν διιστῶσιν ἀνὰ μέσον ἡμῶν καὶ αὐτοῦ.... διὰ τοῦτο ὀργισθεὶς ἐπεισήγαγεν ... τὴν παιδείαν ταύτην, ἵνα δι' αὐτῆς σωφρονισθέντες καὶ διὰ μετανοίας βελτιωθέντες προσέλθωμεν τῷ φόβῳ.

124. Stroumsa 2009: 16–17.

125. Cf. Bas. Caes., *hom.* 8 (PG 31: 108C); with Holman 2001: 78–79; Joshua, Ps.-, *Chron.* 26. On connections to divine philanthropy, Caner 2018a: 9–10. Just., *Nov.* 77.1 states that famines, plagues, and earthquakes were caused by "unnatural" sins. Cf. Horden and Purcell 2000: 300.

126. Council in Trullo, *can.* 43 (Ohme, 42): ὡς οὖν τῆς μοναχικῆς πολιτείας τὴν ἐν μετανοίᾳ ζωὴν στηλογραφούσης ἡμῖν. Cf. Caner 2013b.

127. On ascetic tears, Rapp 2005: 79–81; Hunt 2004; Hausherr 1982; and *AP* G Poemen 119 (PG 114.441A). On penitential ceremonies in monasteries, see Caner 2013b: 134–39.

128. Cyril Scyth., *v.Euthym.* 25 (Schwartz, 39; trans. Price 34–35, adapted): προσέχετε τοίνυν ἀκριβῶς ἑαυτοῖς καὶ δι' ἔργων ἀγαθῶν δοξάσατε τὸν θεὸν τὸν ποιήσαντα εἰς ἡμᾶς πάντας τὸ ἔλεος αὐτοῦ. Cf. Cyril Scyth., *v.Sab.* 67; *v.Nicol.Sion.* 2, 7, 40, 59; and Jo. Eph., *v.SS. Or.* 7 ("Life of Abraham the Recluse"; PO 17.122–23).

129. *v.Sym.Styl.* 45 (CS 112.129); *v.Sym.Styl.* 112 (CS 112.180). Cf. Thdt., *HR* 26.12; and Harvey 1988: 384.

130. For the number, see Schachner 2010: 382. For Egyptian evidence, Wipszycka 2011: 214.

131. Van den Ven 1962: 171*–72*, 201*–202*. Cf. Jo. Eph., *v.SS.Or.* 2 ("Life of Z'ura"; PO 17.32); and Jo. Eph., *v.SS.Or.* 4 ("Life of Abraham and Maro"; 17.89). For similar emphasis on endurance, *v.Dan.Styl.* 82, 98.

132. See Van den Ven 1962: 181*–191*. The younger Symeon is also credited with stopping earthquakes and bringing rain, but his miracles mostly relate to exorcisms and healings, and the purpose of his hagiography seems to have been to promote his sanctuary as a healing shrine. See Déroche 1996: 79–80.

133. For historical aspects, commentary, and translation, see Hahn and Menze 2020. This discussion paraphrases my contribution to that volume.

134. *v.Bars.* 33.1. Cf. *v.Bars.* prol., 4, 46.1–47.2.

135. *v.Bars.* 7.1, 8.1, 10.1–3, 17.2, 20.2, 110.4–7, 113.2 (ʾulṣānē); and *v.Bars.* 83.6, 157.3, 164.2. For constant standing as an ascetic practice, see Palmer 1990: 97–98; and Horn 2020: 56.

136. *v.Bars.* 25.1.

137. *v.Bars.* 75.2–3.

138. *v.Bars.* 9.1.

139. *v.Bars.* 17.3. For these miracles, *v.Bars.* 18, 34–35, 49.1–4, 51.1, 54.2–5, 64–65.

140. *v.Bars.* 54.5 (trans. Palmer, 201).

141. *v.Bars.* 77.3 (trans. Palmer, 210). Cf. *v.Bars.* 67–73, 76–77, 85; *v.Bars.* 49, 88 (purification of springs); *v.Bars.* 87 (defense against hail); *v.Bars.* 28, 58–61, 80–84, 86 (sundry exorcisms and healings).

142. *v.Bars.* 54.4 (trans. Palmer, 201). Cf. *v.Bars.* 51.1.

143. *v.Bars.* 54.1–3 (trans. Palmer 201).

144. I thank Dina Boero for this observation. For the title and its attribution, see Boero 2019: 56–57.

145. See Palmer 1990: 85–86; Horn 2020: 58–68; and Caner 2020: 154–56.

146. Kaplan 1992: 185–280; Mitchell 1993: 2.122–50. For date and hagiographical analysis, see Efthymiades and Déroche 2011: 71–72; and Déroche 2004. For an archaeological survey identifying Sykeon with ruins at the site of Kiliseler, see Brown and Walker 1998.

147. Georg. Syc., *v.Thdr.Syc.* 25 (Baynes, 105). Cf. Georg. Syc., *v.Thdr.Syc.* 18, 42.

148. Georg. Syc., *v.Thdr.Syc.* 35, 43, 46. On the costume, Georg. Syc., *v.Thdr.Syc.* 27. For the initial fast and ordination, Georg. Syc., *v.Thdr.Syc.* 20–21.

149. Georg. Syc., *v.Thdr.Syc.* 27 (trans. Baynes, 108).

150. Georg. Syc., *v.Thdr.Syc.* 50. Cf. 14, 145.

151. Georg. Syc., *v.Thdr.Syc.* 24.

152. Georg. Syc., *v.Thdr.Syc.* 147. Cf. 2, 38, 39, 134, 148, 159.

153. Georg. Syc., *v.Thdr.Syc.* 47–48.

154. For skepticism toward the cult of the saints, and by extension, holy men, see Dal Santo 2012: 205–16.

155. Quoted from Rapp 2005: 81. I thank Claudia Rapp for alerting me to this undated inscription.

156. *AP* C 243 and 247 (Chaîne, 75–77, 147–48). I use the translation in Rapp 2005: 82. On Abba Banes and his cell, see Buschhausen et al. 1991. I am highly skeptical of their dating of Banes to the 4th or 5th century, apparently based on a presumption that these apothegms date from that period. Wipszycka 2015: 353 dates them to the sixth century.

157. Jo. Clim., *scal.* 2 (PG 88.657; trans. Luibheid-Russell, 83).

158. Chrys, *In Jo.* 72.1 (PG 59:389): Μεγάλη τῆς περὶ τοὺς δούλους τοῦ Θεοῦ θεραπείας ἡ ἀνταπόδοσις, καὶ τοὺς καρποὺς ἐντεῦθεν ἡμῖν ἀποδίδωσιν.

159. Georg. Syc., *v.Thdr.Syc.* 87, 109, 120, 128, 142.

160. *v.Dan.Styl.* 3; and Ant. Choz., *v.Geo.Choz.* 8. Cf. *v.Sin.* 166.

161. Georg. Syc., *v.Thdr.Syc.* 52, 101, 103, 144. Cf. *v.Dan.Styl.* 59; Paul Elus., *v.Thgn.*12; Thdr. Petr., *v.Thds.* (Usener, 78); Cyril Scyth., *v.Sab.* 54, 81; and *v.Sym.Styl.iun.* 92.

162. *v.Sym.Styl.* 63 (CS 112.143). Cf. *v.Sym.Styl.* 80, 83, 88. For gifts brought to his monastery, see *v.Sym.Styl.* 58–59 (trans. chapter 3, "Monastic Mediation between the Rich, the Clergy, and the Poor"). For the skin hung in Symeon's enclosure after he helped villagers subdue a lion, *v.Sym.Styl.* 88; cf. *HM* 21.15. One of the ancient reliefs depicting Symeon on his pillar is inscribed, "offered in thanksgiving" (*euchariston . . . prosenegken*): see Mango 1986: 240–41.

163. Bars. et Jo., *resp.* 643. That refusing gifts made their givers sad is noted in *AP* G Zeno 2; and *v.Sym.Styl.* 58 (cf. Pall., *HL* 10).

164. See Camenisch 1981: 6–14; Komter 2004; and Leithart 2014.

165. Jim 2014: 82.

166. Libanius, or. 47.13, noted in Kelly 2004: 165. See also Thdt., *HR* 10.3; Jo. Eph., *v.SS. Or.* 7 ("Life of Abraham the Recluse"; PO 17.120); and López 2013: 80–81.

167. Chrys., *In Gen.*18.4 (PG 53.154): προσήκει καθάπερ Δεσπότῃ ἐκ τῶν οἰκείων κτημάτων προσάγειν τι τῶν γενῶν· οὐκ ἐπειδὴ ὁ Θεὸς τούτων δεῖται, ἀλλ᾽ ἵνα τὴν οἰκείαν εὐγνωμοσύνην ἐπιδείξηται αὐτὸς τῆς τοιαύτης εὐεργεσίας ἀπολαύων. See also Chrys., *In Mt.* 25.4 (PG 57.331).

168. Greg. Naz., *or.* 16.18 (PG 35.957; trans. Browne and Swallow, 253).

169. Joshua, Ps.-, *Chron.* 27 (Wright, 18–19). For a similar scenario, *v.Bars.* 50.

170. Wipszycka 2011: 183.

171. Call., *v.Hyp.* 24.42–43 (SC 177.160): Ὑμεῖς γὰρ ἀπαρχή ἐστε τοῦ κόσμου· ὥσπερ γὰρ γεωργὸς ὅτε ἀλοήσῃ τὸν σῖτον αὐτοῦ προσφέρει ἀπαρχὴν τῷ Κυρίῳ καὶ διὰ τοῦ μικροῦ ὅλον τὸν σῖτον ὁ Κύριος εὐλογεῖ, οὕτως καὶ τὸν κόσμον διὰ τῶν ἁγίων αὐτοῦ ὁ Θεὸς ἐλεεῖ. Cf. Jerome, *ep.* 40.10; and *v.Pach.gr.prim.* 95.

172. Papaconstantinou 2002; also Schroeder 2012.

173. E.g., Cyril Scyth., *v.Thds.* 5 (Schwartz, 240); Pall., *HL* 18.11; Thdt., *HR* 16.4; Call., *v.Hyp.* 12.12–13; *v.Sym.Styl.iun.* 130; Jo. Eph., *v.SS.Or.* 22 ("Lives of Addai and Abraham"; PO 17.299); Isaac the Presbyter, *Life of Samuel of Kalamun* 30; and *Life of Rabban Hormizd* 16.

174. Cyril Scyth., *v.Euthym.* 50 (Schwartz, 73): ἔγνως ἀκριβῶς ὅτι πάντα τὰ ἐν τοῖς μοναστηρίοις ἱερὰ τυγχάνει ὡς ὄντα ἀπὸ καρποφοριῶν; (cf. 72): πάντα τὰ τῶν μοναστηρίων καὶ τῶν λοιπῶν εὐαγῶν οἴκων τῷ θεῷ ἀφιέρωται ὡς ἀπὸ καρποφοριῶν ὄντα.

175. Call., *v.Hyp.* 12.12–13 (SC 177.118–19): Ὅθεν εὐχαριστῶν ὁ Οὐρβίκιος ἦλθε.. προσφέρων καρποφορίαν οὐκ ἐδέχθη. Καὶ λοιπὸν ἠξίου κἂν τὸ μοναστήριον φιλοκαλεῖν, καὶ λαβὼν τεχνίτας συγκαμνόντων καὶ τῶν ἀδελφῶν ἐφιλοκάλησεν τὸν οἶκον τοῦ Θεοῦ, τὸ εὐκτήριον οἰκοδομήσας καὶ ἕτερα κελλία, ὡς γενέσθαι δόξαν Θεοῦ καὶ δύνασθαι πλείονας ἀδελφοὺς κατοικεῖν ἐν αὐτῷ. Urbinus later contributed a communal sepulcher as a *karpophoria* to the monastery. Call., *v.Hyp.* 15.9. Cf. Cyril Scyth., *v.Sab.* 186. As explained in chapter 5, another way of handling an inappropriate offering was to pass it on to the poor, thereby turning it into a blessing. For cases explicitly or implicitly referring to *karpophoriai*, see Jo. Cassian, *Coll.* 21.4.3; Call., *v.Hyp.*18.1; *v.Aux.*12; and *v.Sym.Styl.iun.* 92, 95.

176. Inscriptions show that "paraliturgical" instruments like crosses, patens, chalices, and spoons were common forms of *karpophoriai*. For examples, see chapter 7, "Jacob of Serug's On the Loaf for the Departed." On the distinction between liturgical and paraliturgical uses, see Mango 1986: 4.

177. Ant. Mon., *pand.*120 (PG 89.1808C). Cf. *reg. Hors.* 14.

178. One of the few instances, *HM* 20.11 (SH 53.122), presents it as a "contribution."

179. Geront., *v.Mel. lat.* 46.2 (Laurence, 244). For virtues and prayers as firstfruits, Geront., *v.Mel. gr.* 2.23; Cyril Scyth., *v.Euthym.* 4, 9; Cyril Scyth., *v.Sab.* 13; and Cyril Scyth., *v.Jo.Hesych.* 2.

180. *v.Sym.Styl.iun.* 113 (SH 32.93): ὡς σκεῦος ἅγιον. See Harvey 1998; and Booth 2014: 36–37.

181. Jo. Eph., *v.SS.Or.* 6 ("Life of Paul the Anchorite"; PO 17:118, trans. Brooks, adapted). Cf. Quibell 1912: 55, inscription no. 187.

CHAPTER 7. "IMPERISHABLE REMEMBRANCE IN HEAVEN
AND EARTH": LITURGICAL OFFERINGS AND
THE RISE OF PATRONAL MONASTERIES

1. Geront., *v.Mel. gr.* 21, 22 (SC 90.170–72): εἰ δὲ βούλεσθε ἄληστον ἔχειν μνήμην ἐν οὐρανῷ καὶ ἐπὶ γῆς, δωρήσασθε ἑκάστῳ μοναστηρίῳ καὶ οἰκίαν καὶ πρόσοδον. . . . Ἔκτισαν δὲ καὶ μοναστήρια μεγάλα δύο ἐκεῖσε, παρασχόντες αὐτοῖς αὐτάρκη πρόσοδον. Cf. *v.Mel. lat.* 20.2 (Laurence, 194): "Vultis ergo sempiternam habere memoriam? Per singula monasteria donate et domos et reditus"; and *v.Mel. lat.* 21.4 (194): "donaverunt unicuique monasterio domos, reditus et possessiones." The relation between the Greek and Latin versions of this hagiography is complicated, but they do not represent different recensions, since both

were copied about the same time from a lost Greek original written by Gerontius ca. 439–452. For discussion, see Laurence 2000: 135–41; and Clark 1984: 1–24. However, the Latin version includes details not in the Greek and vice versa. For example, only *v.Mel. lat.* 21.4 and 22.1 describe the size of the estate (as quoted) and use of former slaves to populate the monasteries.

2. Geront., *v.Mel. gr.* 15. On their fortune, Allard 1907: 5–30. On their behavior and historical context, Giardina 1988; Brown 2002: 3–4, 28, 55; Brown 2005a; and Brown 2012: 291–307.

3. Oexle 1976: 77: "ut universa familiarium nostrorum in eo conscripta nomina divino semper conspectui presententur." See also Schreiber 1948; Schmid and Wollasch 1967; Steindorff 1994; McLaughlin 1994; De Jong 1995; Constable 2000; and Magnani Soares-Christen 2003.

4. Papalexandrou 2010: 110. See also Babić 1969; Morris 1984; Morris 1995: 128–36; Thomas 1987: 111–269; and Steindorff 1994: 119–32.

5. Wipszycka 1972: 75–76. Cf. Thomas 1987: 79.

6. Geront., *v.Mel. gr.* 49 (SC 90.220–21): ἐπεθύμησεν μονὴν ἀνδρῶν ἁγίων οἰκοδομῆσαι, ὅπως τὰς νυκτερινάς τε καὶ ἡμερινὰς ψαλμῳδίας ἀδιαλείπτως ἐπιτελοῦσιν . . . ὅπως ἔτι ἐν σαρκὶ ὑπάρχουσα καὶ τὴν ἐκκλησίαν ἀδιαλείπτως λειτουργουμένην θεάσομαι καὶ τὰ ὀστᾶ τῆς ἐμῆς μητρὸς καὶ τοῦ ἐμοῦ κυρίου ἀναπαυόμενα διὰ τῆς αὐτῶν ψαλμῳδίας.

7. Geront., *v.Mel. gr.* 57 (SC 90.240): Κτίσωμεν οὖν ἐνταῦθα σεμνὸν εὐκτήριον, ἵνα μετὰ τὴν ἐμὴν ἐκ τοῦ κόσμου τούτου πρὸς Κύριον ἐκδημίαν ἡ προσφορὰ ὑπὲρ τῆς ἐμῆς ψυχῆς καὶ τῶν ἐμῶν κυρίων ἀδιαλείπτως μέλλει καὶ ἐν τῷ τόπῳ τούτῳ ἐπιτελεῖσθαι. On the location and chronology of Melania's buildings, see Clark 1984: 115–19.

8. Geront., *v.Mel. gr.* 49 (SC 90.222): θεοφιλεῖς καὶ ἁγίους ἄνδρας, ὅτινες φαιδρῶς ἐπετέλουν τὴν λειτουργίαν. Cf. Geront., *v.Mel. gr.* 68.

9. Jo. Ruf., *v.Petr.Ib.* 45 (Horn-Phenix, 60): ḥšaḥtā d-nṭurtā, translated by Horn and Phenix as "watchman," perhaps referring to a building custodian, as found in *v.Marc. Acoem.* 13.

10. Geront., *v.Mel. gr.*, prol., 49; Jo. Ruf., *v.Petr.Ib.* 45. On Gerontius, see Gorce's introduction, SC 90.54–62; for context, Flusin 1996.

11. Clark 1986.

12. Jo. Ruf., *v.Petr.Ib.* 46 (trans. Horn-Phenix, 63). On description of this and other liturgical practices in *v.Mel. gr.* and *lat.*, see Gorce's introduction, SC 90.78–109. Gorce does not observe that Rufus describes Melania as blessed (ṭūbānyītā), a description usually applied to someone who had died. Hence, I infer that John was describing commemorative liturgies.

13. Hillner 2007: 242–43. For the phrase "icing on the cake," see Zuiderhoek 2005. For testamentary evidence from the earlier period, Champlin 1991: 155–68.

14. Jo. Ruf., *v.Petr.Ib.* 39 (trans. Horn-Phenix, 54–55): "For both [monasteries] they set up an endowment ['latā—"income," "harvest"] for the glory and praise of God and for the reception and salvation of the souls of those many [viz., monks] who go there for their salvation." Melania also kept land to supply monasteries. See Pall., *HL* 61.5; with Dunn 2014: 98.

15. This is the usual modern interpretation of Gerontius's passage. For the Latin version of the phrase *alēston mnēma*, see note 1. The complex relationship between the two versions of the *v.Mel.* prevents us from determining which might be closer to the original. In both, Gerontius attributes the advice to all three bishops, not to Augustine alone.

16. Chrys., *De Anna* 4.3 (PG 54.664): πολλὰ πραγματευσάμενοι πολλάκις, ὥστε αὐτῶν ἄληστον γενέσθαι τὴν μνήμην, καὶ τάφους λαμπροὺς οἰκοδομησάμενοι. Cf. Chrys., *In Gen.* 60.2 (54.521).

17. Chrys., *In Ps. 118* (PG 55.682). Cf. Eus. Caes., *HE* 3.4.4; and Eus. Caes., *De mart.* 11.28.

18. Thdt., *Interp. Ps.* 111: 3 (PG 80.1781B): Καὶ ἡ δικαιοσύνη αὐτοῦ μένει εἰς τὸν αἰῶνα τοῦ αἰῶνος." Ἄληστον γὰρ ὁ τῶν ὅλων Θεὸς ἔχει τὴν μνήμην, καὶ ἀείμνηστον αὐτοῦ διαφυλάττει τὸ κλέος. Cf. Thdt., *Interp. Ps.* 139: 16 (1940B).

19. Jerome, *In Hiezech.* 6, 18:5/9 (CCSL 75.238): "publiceque diaconus in ecclesiis recitet offerentium nomina: 'Tantum offert illa, ille tantum pollicitus est'; placentque sibi ad plausum populi." That Jerome was referring to Eastern practices and non-liturgical gifts is inferred by Taft 1991: 38–39; and Constable 2000: 178, supported by the fact that Jerome refers to promises that donors had made for differing sums, which conforms to what we hear about *karpophoriai* contributions, but not about liturgical offerings. On church fundraising, see Caner forthcoming-a.

20. *Can. Ath.* 84 (Riedel-Crum, 51).

21. Probably reflecting donations pooled from a large community, rather than desire for anonymity. Russell 1987: 53–60.

22. As proposed by Russell 1987: 58. For a survey of such Christian prayers and their antecedents, see Di Segni 2017: 63–66. For the church mosaics see Donceel-Voûte 1988: 1.480–81; also Dauphine 1980; and Piccirillo 1993.

23. Choric. Gaz., *Laud.Marc.* 1.11 (Foerster-Richsteig, 5; trans. Litsas, 113–14). For the apse mosaic, Choric. Gaz., *Laud.Marc.* 1.29–31. A fine portrait of a male donor with red hair and black beard standing in *orans* pose has been uncovered near the ceiling of the Red Monastery church. See Bolman 2016b: 16, 24.

24. Yasin 2009: 150. Cf. Yasin 2009: 225–41.

25. Council in Trullo, *can.* 28 (Ohme, 35–36; trans. Percival, 378): εἰς ζωοποίησιν καὶ ἁμαρτιῶν ἄφεσιν .... ἀπαρχὴν ... μεταδιδόναι πρὸς τὴν τοῦ δοτῆρος τῶν καρπῶν εὐχαριστίαν, δι' ὧν τὰ σώματα ἡμῶν ... αὔξει τε καὶ ἐκτρέφεται.

26. *Byzantine Liturgy of St. Basil* (Jasper-Cuming, 120). These prayers and the section in which they appear are missing from the oldest extant manuscript, the 9th-century Barberini version; they come from the somewhat later Grottaferrata G b vii, used by Brightman for his composite edition. On the intercessions, see Taft 1991: 30–35.

27. In general, Taft 1991; and Marinis 2017: 83–99. On the frequency of Eucharists at this time (eventually offered on several days each week), see Taft 1984: 60–66. For reconstruction of the liturgical procedure, Mathews 1971: 155–71.

28. For the *Test. Domini* and its date, see Taft 1991: 39. For the sale of bread for offerings, see chapter 5, "The Institutional and Lay Provision of Material Blessings."

29. *Test. Domini* 1.19 (Ephraem II Rahmani, Syriac 24; Latin 25).

30. *Pace* Rebillard 2009a: 227–29; and Rebillard 2009b: 162–64, that do not discuss the evidence of Gerontius or Jacob of Serug (discussed in this chapter's section "Jacob of Serug's *On the Loaf for the Departed*").

31. Some believed that a name betokened a person's essence. DelCogliano 2010: 190–219.

32. Geront., *v.Mel. gr.* 28 (SC 90.182): ἀνήνεγκα τὸ ὄνομα ἐν τῇ ἁγίᾳ ἀναφορᾷ σὺν τοῖς προτελειωθεῖσιν ἁγίοις–τοῦτο γὰρ ἡμῖν ἔθος ποιεῖν, ἵνα ἐν τῇ ὥρᾳ τῇ φοβερᾷ ἐκείνῃ ὑπὲρ

ἡμῶν πρεσβεύουσιν . . . Ὡς δὲ ἔδωκα αὐτῇ λόγον ἐπὶ τοῦ ἁγίου θυσιαστηρίου μηκέτι αὐτὴν ὀνομάσαι, ἔφη· "Τέως τὸ ἅπαξ τοῦτο, ἐπειδὴ ὠνόμασας αὐτήν, οὐ κοινωνῶ"· οὕτως ἐπίστατο παράβασιν εἶναι τῆς ὀρθοδόξου πίστεως τὸ ὀνομάζειν αἱρετικοὺς ἐν τῇ ἁγίᾳ ἀναφορᾷ. Cf. Geront., v.Mel. lat. 28.2 (Laurence, 206): "Et cum offerrem, niminavi eius nomen inter dormientes, consecrans sanctam oblationem.

Haec enim mihi erat consuetudo in terribili hora illa sanctorum martyrum nomina recitare, ut pro me Dominum postulent, peccatore autem misericordiam consecutos, ut et ipsi pro me intercedant."

33. Taft 1991: 47–58. For the inclusion of names of imperial officials in Constantinople, see Jo. Eph., HE 3.2.11 (Payne Smith, 108).

34. Const. Ap. 8.42 (SC 336: 258–60).

35. Identified as *agapai* in Rabbula, *Rules for Clergy and the Bnay Qyāmā*, can. 8.

36. Const. Ap. 8.41, 43–44. Cf. Velkovska 2001: 30.

37. Chrys., In Phil. 3.5 (PG 62.204): Οὐκ εἰκῇ ταῦτα ἐνομοθετήθη ὑπὸ τῶν ἀποστόλων, τὸ ἐπὶ τῶν φρικτῶν μυστηρίων μνήμην γίνεσθαι τῶν ἀπελθόντων· ἴσασιν αὐτοῖς πολὺ κέρδος γινόμενον, πολλὴν τὴν ὠφέλειαν.

38. Chrys., In Act. 21.5 (PG 60.170): Οὐκ εἰκῇ προσφοραὶ ὑπὲρ τῶν ἀπελθόντων γίνονται, οὐκ εἰκῇ ἱκετηρίαι, οὐκ εἰκῇ ἐλεημοσύναι· ταῦτα πάντα τὸ Πνεῦμα διέταξε. . . . Οὐχ ἁπλῶς ὁ διάκονος βοᾷ· Ὑπὲρ τῶν ἐν Χριστῷ κεκοιμημένων, καὶ τῶν τὰς μνείας ὑπὲρ αὐτῶν ἐπιτελουμένων· οὐχ ὁ διάκονός ἐστιν ὁ ταύτην ἀφιεὶς τὴν φωνήν, ἀλλὰ τὸ Πνεῦμα τὸ ἅγιον.

39. Chrys., In 1 Cor. 41.4–5 (PG 61.361): Οὐ γὰρ ἁπλῶς ταῦτα ἐπινενόηται, οὐδὲ εἰκῇ μνήμην ποιούμεθα τῶν ἀπελθόντων ἐπὶ τῶν θείων μυστηρίων, καὶ ὑπὲρ αὐτῶν πρόσιμεν. . . . Πνεύματος γὰρ διατάξει ταῦτα γίνεται. Βοηθῶμεν τοίνυν αὐτοῖς, καὶ μνείαν ὑπὲρ αὐτῶν ἐπιτελῶμεν. Εἰ γὰρ τοὺς παῖδας τοῦ Ἰὼβ ἐκάθαιρεν ἡ τοῦ πατρὸς θυσία, τί ἀμφιβάλλεις, εἰ καὶ ἡμῶν ὑπὲρ τῶν ἀπελθόντων προσφερόντων γίνεταί τις αὐτοῖς παραμυθία;

40. Sev. Ant., ep.Coll.2 117 (PO 14.284–85). Cf. Can. Bas., can. 31.

41. Chrys., In 1 Cor 41.4 (PG 61.361); and Chrys., In Phil. 3.4 (62.204).

42. Chrys., In 1 Cor. 41.5. Cf. Ntedika 1971: 1–7.

43. Chrys., In Act. 21.5 (PG 60.170): οὕτω καὶ τότε, ἕως ἂν πρόκειται τὰ τῶν μυστηρίων, πᾶσι τιμὴ μεγίστη τὸ μνήμης ἀξιοῦσθαι . . . μετὰ τοῦ θαύματος ἐκείνου εὐκαίρως ὑπομιμνήσκει αὐτὸν τῶν ἡμαρτηκότων.

44. Chrys., In Act. 21.5 (PG 60.171–72) Ταῦτα εἰδότες, ἐπινοῶμεν ὅσας δυνάμεθα παραμυθίας τοῖς ἀπελθοῦσιν, ἀντὶ δακρύων, ἀντὶ θρήνων, ἀντὶ μνημείων, τὰς ἐλεημοσύνας, τὰς εὐχάς, τὰς προσφοράς, ἵνα κἀκεῖνοι καὶ ἡμεῖς τύχωμεν τῶν ἐπηγγελμένων ἀγαθῶν.

45. On the office, see Peachin 1989: 201; and Kelly 2004: 114–85, 235–45.

46. CTh 9.38.3–4, 6–8; Brown 2000: 47–48.

47. Leont. Neap., v.Jo.Eleem. 24 (Festugière-Rydén, 375–76): ἀόκνως καὶ ἀδιστάκτως ἐπιτελεῖν.

48. Greg. Mag., Dial. 4.59.1. On the relation between the two stories, Dal Santo 2012: 132–34, 219. On the Persian prison, Traina 2002. A later version appears in Bede, HE 4.22.

49. Chrys., In Act. 21.4 (PG 60.169): Ἂν οὖν εὐχὰς ὑπὲρ αὐτοῦ ποιῶμεν συνεχεῖς, ἂν ἐλεημοσύνην διδῶμεν· κἂν ἐκεῖνος ἀνάξιος ᾖ, ἡμᾶς ὁ Θεὸς δυσωπήσει.

50. Chrys., In Act. 29.3 (PG 60.218): ἔθος ὁ δεῖνα ἔχει ποιεῖν τὴν ἀνάμνησιν τῆς μητρός, ἢ τῆς γυναικός, ἢ τοῦ παιδίου· τοῦτο ποιεῖ κἄν τε ἀκούῃ, κἄν τε μὴ ἀκούῃ παρ'ἡμῶν, ὑπὸ τῆς συνηθείας καὶ τοῦ συνειδότος ἑλκόμενος. Cf. Sev. Ant., Hom. cath. 71 (PO 12: 67–68).

51. E.g., Brown 2015; Brown 1999; Dal Santo 2012; Constas 2001; Constas 2002; and Kotila 1992.

52. MacMullen 2009: 76–94.

53. Rebillard 2009a: 142–43.

54. Kotila 1992: 72–77; Samellas 2002: 237–39; Constable 2000: 173–77; and Dennis 1996: 250.

55. Rebillard 2009a: 132–41; Rebillard 2009b: 222–25. Cf. Samellas 2002; and Alexiou 1994: 24–35.

56. Dal Santo 2012: 31–73, 116–31; Constas 2010.

57. Dal Santo 2012: 26–63; Kotila 1992: 62–77.

58. Dal Santo 2012: 36. Cf. Epiph., *Pan.* 75.3.5.

59. Rabbula, *Rules for Clergy and the Bnay Qyāmā, can.* 8 (Vööbus, 38); Cyril Alex., *defunct.* (Pusey, 544): ἡμῖν ἀνοσίως τὴν φιλοκερδείαν ἐπιφημίζουσιν οἱ τῶν [ἀγαθῶν] εἰδότες οὐδέν.

60. Harvey 2010: 119. On performative aspects of this homiletic form, see Griffith 2017.

61. Also known as *hom.* 22 of Jacob of Serug. The shorter title may be inferred from coda line 299 (Bedjan-Brock, 550). I use the translation published by the Holy Transfiguration Monastery.

62. Jacob, *hom.* 22, ll. 189–97, 200–204 (trans. Holy Transformation Monastery, 49–50).

63. Jacob, *hom.* 22, l.81. Taft 1991: 53–54 considers it an ordinary anaphora.

64. To describe these offerings, Jacob alternates between the Syriac terms *pristā* (Eucharist loaf), *qṣātā* (liturgical bread fragment, perhaps oblation), and, at the end of the homily, *qūrbānā* (offering, i.e., prosphora). For Greek parallels to this liturgical terminology, see Peterson 1947.

65. Jacob, *hom.* 22, ll. 75–80, 85–88, 253–58 (trans. Holy Transformation Monastery, 44–45 and 52).

66. Jacob, *hom.* 22, ll. 257–60 (trans. Holy Transformation Monastery, 52; cf. ll. 81–82): "She [the Church] gathers them together for the feast of the Body and the Blood, and in spiritual wise they make merry with her."

67. Jacob, *hom.* 22, ll. 101–2 (trans. Holy Transformation Monastery, 45). Taft 1991: 57, is indecisive about whether this reflects the use of diptychs. For the book metaphor, see the section "Memory, Salvation, and the Economics of Monastic Parsonage" in this chapter.

68. Mango 1992: 133.

69. Mango 1986: 1 (discussing the distinction between "liturgical" and "paraliturgical" offerings at pp. 4–6), 4, 75, 88–89; and Ševčenko 1992: 42n.36. Also Zeisel 1975: 70–72; Jalabert and Mouterde 1950; and Jalabert and Mouterde 1959, inscriptions 1234 and 2031. Cf. Evagr. Schol., *HE* 7.20, quoting the inscription on the Persian Shah Khosrow's offering in the church of SS. Sergius and Bacchus.

70. Jo. Eph., *v.SS.Or.* 55 ("Life of John and Sosiana"; PO 19.542). Cf. Pall., *HL* 61.3–4, Geront., *v.Mel. gr.* 19.

71. Jacob, *hom.* 22, ll. 207–208 (trans. Holy Transformation Monastery, 50).

72. Jacob, *hom.* 22, ll. 8, 13–18, 135–39. Cf. Jacob, *hom.* 22, ll. 9–10, 64–67, 121–26, 141–42 (trans. Holy Transformation Monastery, 41–42, 44, 46–47).

73. Jacob, *hom.* 22, ll. 93, 106 (trans. Holy Transformation Monastery, 45–46). In general, Jacob, *hom.* 22, ll. 89–118. For Jacob's position on the soul-sleep debate, see Dal Santo 2012: 244–315; and Guinan 1974.

74. Jacob, *hom.* 22, ll. 165–89.

75. Jacob, *hom.* 22, ll. 209–240, quoted at 229 (trans. Holy Transformation Monastery, 51).

76. Harvey 2010: 120.

77. Jacob, *hom.* 22, ll. 283–86, 293 (trans. Holy Transformation Monastery, 53). In the last eight lines, and only here, Jacob refers to this offering five times as a *qūrbānā*, which the Holy Transformation Monastery translates as *prosphora*.

78. Jacob, *hom.* 22, ll. 267–72, 279–82 (trans. Holy Transformation Monastery, 52–53).

79. Jacob, *hom.* 22, ll. 265–66, 290 (trans. Holy Transformation Monastery, 52–53).

80. Jacob, *hom.* 22, ll. 145–52 (trans. Holy Transformation Monastery, 47).

81. Jacob, *hom.* 22, ll. 123, 157–62 (trans. Holy Transformation Monastery, 46, 48).

82. For Rabbula's actions, see *Pan. Rabb.* (Overbeck, 173, ll. 5–7). For the replacement of old donor inscriptions, Yasin 2017: 108. For the Greco-Roman reluctance to give endowments, Hillner 2007.

83. Chrys., *In Act.* 18.4–5 (PG 60: 147–48).

84. Thanks especially to the example set by Empress Pulcheria (d. 453). So Dagron 1989: 1073.

85. Thomas 1987: 29–32; cf. MacMullen 2009: 20–22. On domestic chapels, Bowes 2015. For epigraphical evidence, Haensch 2006: 51–55.

86. Thomas 1987: 37.

87. Thomas 1987:3, 53–58, 71. Cf. Wood 2006: 10–23.

88. Babić 1969: 67–78 provides a cautious if dated survey. Cf. Mathews 1982; and Saradi 2006: 406–12. For the West, Pietri 2002. For the difficulty of distinguishing their remains, Bavat 2005: 767–68. Gregory the Great's *Registrum* refers to examples in Italy, Sicily, and Sardinia.

89. On the gold expended, Mango 1992: 125–26. In general, Harrison 1989.

90. *Anthol. Gr.* 1.10 (LCL 67.9–11, trans. Paton, adapted). Cf. *Anthol. Gr.* 1.12–17; with Thomas 1987: 23–24.

91. Theoph., *Chron.* (AM 6086), describing Philippicus's Theotokos monastery in Chrysopolis.

92. For churches specifically built for burial purposes, see Thomas 1987: 16–21, 46n46–47; also Greg. Nyss., *v.Macr.* 33–34; *In XL Mart.*1.2; Zach., Ps.-, *Chron.* 8.5; Leont. Neap., *v.Jo. Eleem.* 48; *P.Cairo Masp.* 1.67096; and Mattern 1933: 24. Thomas 1987 does not discuss the burial (or monastic) aspects of these foundations, but Dagron 1989: 1072 notes that their function was usually commemorative. Cf. Babić 1969: 58–61.

93. For monasteries specifically stated to contain lay burials, or burial churches staffed by monks, see Thomas 1987: 16–21, 46n46–47; *v.Dan.Styl.* 64; Cyril Scyth., *v.Euthym.* 6; Cyril Scyth., *v.Abraam.* 2; Jo. Eph., *v.SS.Or.* 54 ("Life of Caesaria the Patrician"; PO 19.537); Leont. Neap., *v.Jo.Eleem.* 48; Palmer 1990: 101; with epigraphical evidence in Goldfus 1997: 1.178–244.

94. For both, see Thomas 1987: 21–22, 46; with Theoph., *Chron.* (AM 6063). See also Jo. Mosch., *prat.* 87. The Second Council of Constantinople, *Acta* 5.48 (trans. Price, 318) mention a monastery on an estate called Pasa outside Tyana.

95. Kötting 1965: 25–34; Samellas 2002: 234. Cf. Mitchell 1993: 2.119–20.

96. Jo. Eph., *v.SS.Or.* 54 ("Life of Caesarea the Patrician"; PO 19.537). Cf. Soz., *HE* 7.26.4; *v.Matr.Perg.* 46; with Pargoire 1899. Pope Gelasius I (d. 496) tried to stop churches from being named after their founders in fifth-century Rome. Taylor 1975: 320. For foundations specifically inscribed or described as *prosphorai*, see *Anthol. Gr.* 1.11 (a church); and Di Segni 1997, inscription nos. 60 (church), 91 (church), 102 (monastery), 106 (monastery).

97. De Jong 1995: 651.

98. Inscription no.1 (Fitzgerald 1939: 13–14): Πρ[οσφορὰ] ὑπὲρ [μν]ήμης κ[αὶ] τελ(ε)ιας ἐν Χ(ριστ)ῷ ἀναπαύσεως Ζωσίμου . . . εὐχ[αῖ]ς τῶν ἁγίων. Di Segni 1995: 313 translates τῶν ἁγίων as "of the saints," without speculating who these might have been.

99. For similar usage in the letters of Barsanuphius and John, see the section in chapter 4, "Gifts of Charity in the Seridos Monastery." Cf. *P.Bala'izah* 190 in Kahle 1954: 620. The two other commemorative inscriptions (nos. 2 and 3 in Fitzgerald 1939: 14), refer the "prayers of the saints."

100. Inscriptions nos. 4–6 refer to Elijah, and no.7 mentions an abbot-priest and his deputy (Fitzgerald 1939: 14–16). It is hard to believe the non-liturgical rooms could have housed many.

101. Rom 1:9–10: ὡς ἀδιαλείπτως μνείαν ὑμῶν ποιοῦμαι πάντοτε ἐπὶ τῶν προσευχῶν μου. Cf. 1 Cor 1:4; Eph 1:16; Phil 1:3–4; Col 1: 3; 1 Thes 1:2–3; 2 Thes 1:3, 11; 2 Tm 1:3; and Phlm 4. On Paul's understanding of "remembering" as an inner engagement with someone from whom one has benefitted, see Georgi 1992: 38–41.

102. *P.Lond.* 1923, 1924, 1926, 1929; *P.Neph.* 10; cf. *P.Misc. inv.* II 98a + I 134a 7. For graffiti, Bachatly 1965.

103. For intercessory aspects of this expression, Rapp 1999: 67–72. On epistolary conventions, Koskenniemi 1956: 134–37, 146–48.

104. As Rapp 1999: 68 notes, these letters present prayer as "the glue" that held correspondents to each other. Cf. Martin 2003: 177–80.

105. Bars. et Jo., *resp.* 17, 27, 121, 189, 353, 513. Cf. Bars. et Jo., *resp.* 87, 249.

106. Bars. et Jo., *resp.* 27 (SC 426.218): Μὴ νομίσῃς, ἀγαπητέ μου, ὅτι εἰς λήθην παρέδωκά σου τὴν μνήμην ἀπὸ τῆς καρδίας μου διὰ τὴν ἀναβολὴν τοῦ γράψαι σοι. . . . καθὼς οὐκ ἐπιλανθάνεται ὁ Θεὸς ἡμῶν τοῦ ἐλεῆσαι τὸν κόσμον, οὐδὲ ἐγὼ τῆς ἀγάπης σου, δεόμενος νύκτα καὶ ἡμέραν τοῦ Θεοῦ ὑπὲρ σωτηρίας τῆς ψυχῆς σου. Cf. *ep.* 233.

107. Bars. et Jo., *resp.* 113 (SC 427.440).

108. Bars. et Jo., *resp.* 573 (SC 451.754): πέπηκταί σου τὸ μνημόσυνον εἰς τὴν ἐμὴν καρδίαν, καὶ πιστεύω ὅτι οὐ γίνεται αὐτοῦ ἐξάλειψις εἰς τὸν αἰῶνα.

109. *P.Neph.* 10 (Kramer, Shelton, and Browne, 67, ll. 13–16; trans. Rapp 1999: 70n25): γιγνώσκω . . . ὅτι ὅσον ἐν μνήμῃ με ἔχεις ἐν ταῖς προσευχες σου οὐκ ἐνκαταλείπει με ὁ δεσπότης θεός. Cf. *P.Neph.* 1, ll. 8–9 (where Nephoros is asked to name the correspondent in his prayers); and *P.Neph.* 4, ll. 3–5, 8–12.

110. Bars. et Jo., *resp.* 249 (SC 450.204): Τὸ δὲ πάντοτε μνημονεύειν αὐτοῦ οὐκ ἔστι σόν, ἀλλὰ τῶν τελείων τῶν δυναμένων εὔχεσθαι ὑπὲρ ἀλλήλων. For a different view, Jo. Clim., *scal.* 28 (PG 88.1136C): μὴ παραιτούμενος, καὶ ὑπὲρ ψυχῆς προσεύχεσθαι, κἂν προσευχὴν μὴ κέκτησαι.

111. Call., *v.Hyp.* 31.13–14 (SC 177.206–208): Εἴ τις οὖν τῶν πάνυ πλουσίων καὶ συνετῶν καὶ τὸν Θεὸν ἀγαπώντων ἐβούλετο μαρτύριον οἰκοδομῆσαι εἰς τοὺς πέριξ τόπους, ηὔχετο ὅπως ἐκ τῶν μαθητῶν Ὑπατίου ποιήσῃ κληρικούς, λέγων ὅτι "Ὄντως ἐκεῖνοι ἐσταυρωμένοι."

Καὶ πολλὰ παρεκάλουν αὐτὸν ἵνα παράσχῃ, καὶ ῥαδίως οὐ παρεῖχεν αὐτοῖς. See also *v.Dan. Styl.* 89; and Cyril Scyth., *v.Euthym.* 30.

112. *v.Alex.Acoem.* 29; and *v.Marc.Acoem.* 4–5. On Alexander and his *vita,* see Caner 2002: 126–57, 249–80; and Caner 2020.

113. For its date, Déroche and Lesieur 2010: 290–91. The hagiography glosses over controversial aspects of Marcellus's career, including participation in Christological disputes. See Dagron 1968: 271–80.

114. *v.Marc. Acoem.* 3. Geront., *v.Mel. gr.* 26, ascribes the same activity to Melania. Interestingly, the three hagiographies (*v.Alex. Acoem., v.Mel., v.Marc. Acoem.*) that describe the creation of liturgical regimens out of biblical references in this era also attribute their invention to classically educated ascetics who were engaged in reading or copying biblical texts.

115. *v.Marc. Acoem.* 4–5 states that when Marcellus arrived, many Bithynians were visiting Alexander, suggesting he was already in exile at Gomon, somewhere in or near Bithynia.

116. *v.Marc. Acoem.* 8–10.

117. *v.Marc. Acoem.* 8 (Dagron, 293): ὡς ἡ δόξα τοῦ μοναστηρίου πᾶσαν ἐμπλήσει τὴν οἰκουμένην καὶ σφόδρα ὁ θεὸς ἐν αὐτῷ καὶ δι᾽ αὐτοῦ θεραπευθήσεται, καὶ ὅτι ὥσπερ ἔκ τινος νέας Ἰερουσαλὴμ ἐκ τοῦ τόπου ἐκείνου πανταχοῦ τῆς οἰκουμένης ὁ λόγος τοῦ κηρύγματος διαδραμεῖται καὶ πολλοὺς ἑλκύσει πρὸς τὸν θεόν.

118. *v.Marc. Acoem.* 2 (Dagron, 296–97): υἱὸς ἀνδρὸς μέγιστον δυνηθέντος ἐν τῇ Ῥωμαίων συγκλήτῳ καὶ πλοῦτον ἔχοντος οἷον εἰκὸς ἄνδρα ἐν τῇ μεγάλῃ βουλῇ πρωτεύοντα. Pharetius is otherwise unknown, but the phrasing suggests his father was a senator in Italy.

119. *v.Marc. Acoem.* 2 (Dagron, 297). In general, Pargoire 1924; and Janin 1975: 13–15. Reyhan Durmaz informs me that a large monastic church and cistern has been excavated in Çubuklu.

120. *v.Marc. Acoem.* 29 (Dagron, 312–13); and Zach., Ps.-, *Chron.* 7.7.

121. The evidence dates from the sixth century, but Dagron 1968: 274–75 notes the affinity to Marcellus's profession at Ephesus. According to Riedinger 1978: 148–53, the Acoemetes specialized in pseudepigrapha. On the monastery more generally, see Hatlie 2007a: 102–8.

122. *v.Marc. Acoem.* 12 (Dagron, 297): τοῦ θεοῦ τὸ ἔργον. Call., *v.Hyp.* 30.3–4 is the earliest attestation of this phrase in a liturgical sense in Greek.

123. *v.Marc. Acoem.* 4–5 (Dagron, 290): ὃς μετὰ ταῦτα ἐν τῷ στόματι τοῦ Πόντου μοναστήριον ἱδρύσας πρῶτος ἔθηκεν τύπον ἀπαύστως ὑμνεῖν τὸν θεὸνπρῶτος ἔθηκεν τύπον ἀπαύστως ὑμνεῖν τὸν θεὸν διαδοχῇ τῶν λειτουργούντων. Here Marcellus's *vita* dates Alexander's invention of his liturgy to his time of exile, but Alexander's *vita* presents it as already perfected in Syria.

124. *v.Alex. Acoem.* 28–30; with Phountoulēs 1963: 49–52. Originally, his program consisted of four choirs of fifty monks each, marshalled by language group (Greek, Latin, Syriac, Coptic). *v.Marc. Acoem.* 8 implies that the monastery featured a similar range of monks under Marcellus.

125. *v.Marc.Acoem.* 13 (Dagron, 297–98): Ἔλαβεν δὲ τὸ πρᾶγμα ἀρχὴν ἐκ τῆς βασιλευούσης πόλεως . . . ὅσοι ἐν αὐτῇ τὴν εὐσέβειαν τιμῶντες ἢ κατεσκευάσαντο οἴκους εὐκτηρίους ἢ συνεστήσαντο ἀνδρῶν εὐλαβῶν ἀσκητήρια, παρὰ Μαρκέλλου ἐλάμβανον καὶ τῆς ποίμνης ἡγεμόνας καὶ τῶν ἱερῶν ἐπιμελητὰς καὶ τῶν ἀδελφῶν τῆς ἐπιστήμης φύλακας. Ἐπίστευον γὰρ ὡς οὐχὶ μόνον τὴν ἀκρίβειαν τῆς ἀσκήσεως, ἀλλὰ καὶ ἁγιασμὸν διὰ Μαρκέλλου πορίζονται τοῖς τε οἴκοις καὶ τοῖς ἀνδράσιν οὓς προσκομίζουσιν τῷ θεῷ.

126. *v.Marc.Acoem.* 14 (Dagron, 298), which also claims that Marcellus viewed this dissemination as a means of spreading God's kerygma, an evangelical motive also attributed to Alexander. See Caner 2002: 130–37. Hatlie 2007a: 106–8 discusses how the Acoemetes differed from other monastic groups in the city. The hagiographer's choice of ἀσκητήρια to describe the patronal institutions they served is intriguing. Usually, it refers to a monastic community (cf. Lampe, s.v. ἀσκητήριον), but Justinian, *Nov.* 59.4.1 (issued 537 CE) applies it to organizations consisting of eight psalm-singing ascetic women and three acolytes that performed at funerals, suggesting a more technical usage related to Christian choirs in the city.

127. Thdr. Lect., *HE* 1.17 (no. 384). Cf. Mango 1978: 120–22. Acoemete monks (if they should be identified as such) were there till Theodore took over in the 8th century. Frazee 1981: 29, 37–38.

128. *v.Marc. Acoem.* 8 (Dagron, 293): ἐκ πάσης γῆς καὶ θαλάττης πλείστους Ἑλλήνων τε καὶ Ῥωμαίων καὶ βαρβάρων ὑποδέξεται καὶ πάντας θεῷ καθιερώσει. Besides the implications of this passage and apparent parallels between liturgical practices at Augane and the Acoemete monastery, the argument is based on the singularity of the Augane practice in the West, its coincidence with the era when the Acoemete monastery was at its height, and the involvement of Avitus of Vienne—who elsewhere shows knowledge of Acoemete activities—in building the relationship between Sigismund and Constantinople. See Leclercq 1907: 857–59 (quote from p. 857); Krüger 1971: 52–67; and Bernard 2006. Rosenwein 2000: 44 challenges this view, partly by claiming that the Acoemetes were "not particularly [known] for their liturgy."

129. See Brown 2002: 29–31; Trombley 1987: 17–18; and Herman 1942: 402–10.

130. Chrys., *In Act.* 18.5 (PG 60.147).

131. Denḥa, *v.Marutae* 2 (PO 3.64–65).

132. *v.Marc. Acoem.* 30 (Dagron, 313): Ἀξιούντων δὲ αὐτὸν τῶν ἀδελφῶν δοῦναί τι καὶ τῷ μοναστηρίῳ καὶ ὠνήσασθαι πρόσοδον. On the technical meaning of the term πρόσοδον, see Thomas 1987: 48. The *Life* gives no details, but significant income probably came from commissions for the production of psalters and other liturgical books to supply institutions staffed with Acoemete monks. On Alexander, see Caner 2002: 150–57.

133. Not all endowments were the same, however. On their variety in this period, see Thomas 1987: 47–53, 75–76.

134. Leont. Neap., *v.Jo.Eleem.* 48 (Festugière-Rydén, 398): συναγαγὼν δύο τάγματα ὁσίων μοναχῶν τάσσει τούτοις τὴν ἅπασαν χρείαν χορηγεῖσθαι ἐκ τῶν προσόντων αὐτῷ χωρίων ἐν τῇ ἐνορίᾳ τῆς αὐτοῦ πόλεως, ποιήσας αὐτοῖς καὶ κελλία καὶ τάξας ἐν τοῖς δυσὶν εὐκτηρίοις τοῖς ἀγχιστεύουσιν ἀλλήλοις ... εἰπὼν τοῖς θεοφιλεστάτοις μοναχοῖς οὕτως· "Αὐτὸς ἐγὼ μετὰ θεὸν τὴν χρείαν τὴν σωματικὴν φροντίζω ὑμῖν, ὑμεῖς δὲ τῆς τοῦ πνεύματός μου φροντίσατε ἐπὶ τούτοις σωτηρίας, ἵνα τὸ λυχνικὸν καὶ ἡ ἐν τῷ μαρτυρίῳ ἐπιτελουμένη ὑφ᾽ ὑμῶν νυκτερινὴ ἀγρυπνία παρὰ θεῷ ἐμοὶ λογίζηται. Cf. Jo. Ruf., *v.Petr.Ib.* 36.

135. *P.Oxy.* 16.1949 (481 CE); *O.Amst* 91 (V–VI), *PSI* 7.786 (581); *P.Oxy.* 16.1898 (587); *P.Oxy.* 16.1993 (VI); and *PSI* 1.89 (605). Thomas 1987: 76–78 interprets these and those in later Coptic wills as *donationes inter vivos* (which he also calls "pious benefactions"). But some may have been sent to provide *mortis causa* donations, since *P.Cair.Masp.* 3.67324 designates as *prosphorai* the materials sent to fund a monastery's annual performance of a donor's liturgical *prosphora*. On legal aspects, see Beaucamp 2001: 7–11.

136. *P.Oxy.* 67.4620 (ca. 475–550 CE); *PSI* 8.953 (6th cent.); *P.Oxy.* 58.3960 (621); Crum 1902, *Coptic Ostraca*, no. 352; and Winlock, Crum, and Evelyn-White 1926, *Epiphanius Monastery*, no. 313. Thomas 1987: 78–80 interprets these and those in later Coptic wills as *donationes mortis causa* ("gifts arranged on approach of death").

137. Thomas 1987: 78, referring to *donationes mortis causa*, on which see Husselman 1957; and Bruck 1926: 302–17.

138. *P.Oxy.* 16.1901. Cf. *P.Koln.* 10.421 (ca. 524–545 CE).

139. *P.Cairo Masp.* 3.67312 (567 CE).

140. *P.Cairo Masp.* 2.67151 (570 CE) (Maspero, 85–101).

141. *P.Cairo Masp.* 2.67151, ll. 101–68 (Maspero, 92–95): καθαρὰν διόλου ạἰώνιọν [ἄ]πτωτον ὑπạρχθῆναι ταύτην ἐν πάσῃ βεβαιώσει καὶ καθαροποιήσει τῷ προειρημένῳ μοναστηρίῳ, εἰς μνημόσυνον αἰώνιον καὶ πρεσβεῖον, ὑπὲρ ἱλασμοῦ ψυχῆς μου καὶ ἁγίας προσφορᾶς, πρὸς Θεὸν ἀπερχομένου. . . . . ὥστε μὴ παντοίας πώπο[τε ἀ]ν[α]τροπῆς τυχεῖν, ἐπὶ πάσης ἀρχῆς καὶ ἐξουσίας καὶ θρόνου κ[αὶ κ]υριότητος ὑφ' ἡλίῳ, καθ' ὅτι ἐπ' ἀγαθῇ καὶ εἰλικρινεῖ προαιρέσει ταύτην ἐχαρισάμην καὶ ἐδωρησάμην τῷ προειρημέ(νῳ) εὐαγεῖ μον(αστηρίῳ) ὑπὲρ ἁγίας μου προσφορᾶς αἰωνίου. . . . τὴν παντοίαν ταύτης πρόσοδον κομίσασθαι καθ' ἔτος ἀπὸ καρπ[ῶν].. καὶ τὴν ταύτης διοίκησιν καθάπερ βούλωνται ἀναθέσθαι εἰς τὴν ἁγίαν μọ(υ) προσφοράν·μέντοι γε αὐτοὺς μὴ δύνασθαι ταύτην πώποτε ἐκποιῆσαι ἢ ἑτέρῳ μεταλλάξαι ἐπὶ τὸν παντελῆ χρόνον, ἀλλ' αὐτὴν ἐπίμονον εἶναι καὶ παραμόνιμον, ἐξυπηρετοῦσαν τῇ ἁγίᾳ μου προσφορᾷ, διὰ τὸ ἐμοὶ οὕτως ὀρθῶς καὶ δικαίως δεδόχθαι. [cf. ll. 183–85.] βούλομαι δὲ καὶ κελεύω. . . . τὸν εὐλαβ(ῆ) καὶ θεοφιλῆ ἡγούμενον τοῦ προειρημένου μον(αστηρίου) Ἄπα Ἱερημίου, κατὰ τῆς ὁμοουσίου Τριάδος ἁγίας καὶ ἀηττήτου, ὑποδέξασθαι τὸ ἐμὸν εἰς δαφὴν. καὶ μνῆμα λείψανον εἰς τὴν εὐαγεστάτην μόνην, εἰς μνείαν τῆς ἐμῆς πάντοτε βραχύτητος, καὶ συναρίθμ[ιον] ὀνομασίαν μου ἐν τῇ τοῦ καταλόγου τῶν μακαρίων ἐκεῖσε πάντων ἀναπαυσαμένων ἐκφ\ρ/άσει ἐνεραδνουμίου γενέσ[θαι].

142. Thomas 1987: 48. Wipszycka 2011: 167–68n13 discusses a 7th-century papyrus attesting the reluctance of heirs to allow a testator to cede family property to a church. Such reluctance may explain why hypothecation appears as a more common method of endowment.

143. An 8th-century Coptic list (*P.Bal.* 306) consisting of three names, each marked "blessed," may be the earliest extant example of such a commemorative monastic record.

144. *P.Oxy.* 17.1901, ll. 42–44.

145. *P.Münch.* 8 (ca. 540 CE); and *P.Lond.* 5. 1857. Cf. Porten 1996: 455–58. Maria refers four times to her *prosphorai*, suggesting they were her paramount concern.

146. *P.Lond.* 3.1308 (ca. 521–522 CE), ll. 8–9 (Salomons, 223).

147. *P.Cairo Masp.* 3.67324 (525–526 CE), ll. 5–7: ἑκόντας καὶ ἄκοντας διὰ παντὸς, πρὸς τῷ ἀκαταγνώστως προβῆναι τὰ τῆς ἁγίας προσφορᾶς εἰς ἀε[ὶ] τοὺς ἀποθανόντας προσδοκεῖν.

148. *P.Lond.* 1.77 (610 CE), ll. 40–47.

149. Beaucamp 2001: 7–9.

150. See Hübner 2014; and Johnson 1985. Wipszycka 2011: 167n11 refers to another sixth- or seventh-century papyrus that records a lay donation of six artabae of wheat "for eternity."

151. Champlin 1991: 175; and Le Bras 1936.

152. Champlin 1991: 89, 104, 107.

153. Crum 1902, *Coptic Texts*, no. 85.

154. Leont. Const., *hom.* 11.27–28, 13.23 (Datema-Allen, 363, 405; trans. 156–57, 165).

155. *CI* 1.3.45.3–15 (issued 530) (Krueger, 2.31–33; trans. Coleman-Norton 3.1074–76).

156. Thomas 1987: 43–44.

157. Synod of Jésuyahb I, *can.* 7 (Chabot, 143–44/405–406). Cf. Finn 2006a: 106–7; and Wipszycka 2015: 351–52.

158. Martyn 2004a: 8–9.

159. Greg. Mag., *reg.* 4.9 (593 CE; CCSL 140.226; trans. adapted from Martyn 1.294).

160. Greg. Mag., *reg.* 9.166, 181, 233; 13.16. Cf. Martyn 2004b.

161. Greg. Mag., *reg.* 3.58; 5.50; 8.32; 9.88, 90, 165, 205. Hillner 2007: 245–47 notes that when earlier Greco-Roman benefactors had set up legacies for their cities or collegia, they tended to distrust local magistrates who had both the motive and the means to divert legacies to other purposes. She reasons that Christian benefactors had similar reservations. This is an important correction to Le Bras 1936: 65–66, who assumes it was church priests (and not monks) who eventually replaced Roman *liberti* in safeguarding testator's wishes. Regarding medieval practice, McLaughlin 1994: 129 notes that while "secular churches might provide prayer, they were not very reliable. . . . In contrast, the reformed monasteries . . . appeared as islands of stability and purity. . . . This view of monastic life as the *vita angelica* was vigorously promoted by the leaders of reformed monasticism, and it seems to have been very influential with the feudal elite."

162. See Champlin 1991: 175–80. Cf. Mouritsen 2011: 146–48; Quadrato 1996; and Waldstein 1986.

163. Champlin 1991: 176–77; with Le Bras 1936: 42–60.

164. On evidence for freedpersons in the later Roman Empire, see Harper 2011: 463–93.

165. Greg. Naz., *exemplum test.* (PG 37.389C). Cf. Van Dam 1995: 128; and Vasileiou 2014. Gregory's will is actually the earliest of any Roman will to survive in its entirety.

166. *AP* G Mios 2 (PG 65.301): ἵνα ποιῇ ὑπὲρ αὐτῶν ἀγάπας. Cf. *AP* GS 15.47.

167. As indicated by Call., *v.Hyp.* 8.4 (SC 177.98): ὁ μακάριος Ῥουφῖνος. See Thomas 1987: 23.

168. Jo. Eph., HE 3.1.39 (CSCO 105.48–49; trans. Payne Smith, 75–76): "w-prosodoi d-lā z'ur 'aqniāh. . . . w-'ettsim(w) bāh b-dayrā . . . samw(hy) bāh w-qadešw(hy)."

169. Cyril Scyth., *v.Sab.* 72 (Schwartz, 175; trans. Price, 185): ὅπου ἐὰν βούλῃ, αἴτησαι πρόσοδον πρὸς τὴν τῶν οἰκούντων χρείαν καὶ παρέξομεν, ἵνα εὔχωνται ὑπὲρ τῆς ἡμῖν ἐμπιστευθείσης πολιτείας. ὁ δὲ εἶπεν· οἱ τῆς ὑμετέρας εὐσεβείας ὑπερευχόμενοι τοιαύτης προσόδου οὐ χρῄζουσιν· ἡ γὰρ μερὶς αὐτῶν καὶ ἡ πρόσοδος ὁ κύριός ἐστιν. Cf. Cyril Scyth., *v.Sab.*18, 30, 31, 36, 37, 45, 51, 55, 56, 58, 72.

170. Cyril Scyth., *v.Sab.* 58 (Schwartz, 159–60; trans. Price, 124, adapted): πρόσοδον τὸ σύνολον περιποιήσασθαι οὐκ ἠνέσχετο, ἀλλὰ πίστει καὶ πεποιθήσει τῇ εἰς θεὸν ἐπερειδόμενος οὐδέποτε κατέπεσεν. Cf. Flusin 1983: 184.

171. Nilus, *De mon. ex.* 7 (PG 79.725D–728A). On Nilus and his treatise, see Caner 2002: 179–87. For its use by Cyril, Flusin 1983: 70–71. Sabas's benefactors included Anicia Juliana. Cyril Scyth., *v.Sab.* 69. On his family wealth and insistence on ἀκτημοσύνη, Cyril Scyth., *v.Sab.*1–2, 9.

172. *v.Marc.Acoem.* 30 (see note 132).

173. *AP* G Achilles 1 (PG 65.124); Pall., *HL* 10.3 (Bartelink, 46); and *Life of Macarius of Alexandria* 2, 21 (trans. Vivian, 142, 158).

174. Isaac the Presbyter, *Life of Samuel of Kalamun* 32 (trans. Alcock, 106).

175. Leont. Neap., *v.Jo.Eleem* 25 (Festugière-Rydén, 376): προσφέρει αὐτῷ ἑπτὰ ἥμισυ λίτρας. . . . ἐποίσεν εὐθέως σύναξιν τελείαν ἐπάνω αὐτοῦ ὑπὲρ τοῦ προσενέγκαντος. See also Jo. Eph., *v.SS.Or.* 55 ("Life of John and Sosiana"; PO 19.542).

176. Leont. Neap., *v.Jo.Eleem* 19 (Festugière-Rydén, 366): παρακαλέσας πολλὰ . . . εἰς τὸ μνημονεύειν, φησίν, τοῦ προσενέγκαντος.

177. See Schwartz 1996: 70. Sigaud 2002; and Weiner 1992: 56–60.

178. Holman 2001: 60–63; and Holman 2010: 46–47. Chrys., *In Hebr.* 11.3 (PG 63.93), conceptualizes both the prayers and alms given by the Roman centurion Cornelius in Acts 10:4 as *prosphorai*.

179. *Const. Ap.* 3.4.2–3 (SC 329.126): Λέγε δὲ αὐτοῖς καί, τίς ὁ δεδωκώς, ἵνα καὶ ἐξ ὀνόματος ὑπὲρ αὐτοῦ προσεύχωνται. Cf. *Const. Ap.* 4.6.7; and Finn 2006a: 180–81.

180. *Life of Macarius of Scetis* 11 (trans. Vivian, 161–62).

181. Leont. Neap., *v.Jo.Eleem.* 21 (Festugière-Rydén, 369): ἵνα σχῇ μου μνημόσυνην ὁ πτῶχος. For a similar locution in *P.KRU* 106 (8th century), see Wilfong 2002: 85–86.

182. Sorek 2010: 72–85.

183. Leont. Neap., *v.Jo.Eleem.* 20 (Festugière-Rydén, 368–69). Leont. Neap., *v.Jo.Eleem.* 21, describes the officer's subsequent exchange of alms for prayers and sale of himself.

184. Shenoute of Atripe, "Michigan 158,20" (trans. Wayne Young, 166). Cf. Jo. Eph., *v.SS. Or.* 12 ("Lives of Mary and Euphemia"; PO 17.174); Jo. Eph., *v.SS.Or.* 21 ("Life of Thomas the Armenian"; 278); Jo. Eph., *v.SS.Or.* 31 ("Lives of Elijah and Theodore"; PO 18.579); Jo. Eph., *v.SS.Or.* 33 ("Life of Ḥala"; 595); Jo. Eph., *v.SS.Or.* 45 ("Life of Isaac"; 670); Isaac the Presbyter, *The Life of Samuel of Kalamun* 2; and Brown 2005b.

185. Thdt., *Interp. Ps.* 139:16 (PG 80.1940B): Βίβλου δὲ νοητέον τὴν πάντα περιέχουσαν τοῦ Θεοῦ γνῶσιν, καὶ τὴν ἄληστον τοῦ Θεοῦ μνήμην. Cf. Thdt., *Interp. Ps.* 111:3 (1781B). On the theme in Greek and Syrian sources, see Koep 1952: 48–68, to which more examples could be added, such as Asterius, *hom.* 4.8.4; Sev. Ant., *hym.* 268.1.1; Leont. Neap., *v.Jo.Eleem.* 18.

186. Dion., Ps.-, *De eccl. hier.* 3.9 (Heil-Ritter, 88–89): μνημοσύνοις ἱεροῖς ἀνατέθεινται τῆς θείας μνήμης οὐκ ἀνθρωπικῶς ἐν τῇ τοῦ μνημονικοῦ φαντασίᾳ δηλουμένης. Cf. Bas. Caes., *Hom. in Ps.* 29 (PG 29.308); Aug., *civ. Dei* 20.15.

187. Chrys., *In Col.*1.3 (PG 62.304): οὐδέποτε ἀπολεῖται ἡ χάρις· τὸν γὰρ πάντοτε μνημονεύοντα Θεόν, καὶ οὐδέποτε ἐπιλανθανόμενον, ἔχεις αὐτὸν ὀφειλέτην. In Chrys., *In Rom.* 17.5 (60.570); and Chrys., *In Hebr.* 11.3 (63.93), he claims that Acts 10:4—"Your prayers and your alms have gone up as a memorial before God" (εἰς μνημόσυνον ἐνώπιον τοῦ Θεοῦ)—means that God listens to prayers of ordinary Christians if and when they listen to the poor who call on them.

188. Bars. et Jo., *resp.* 647 (SC 468.78): Ἄλλος φιλόχριστος ἔπεμψεν αἰτῶν τὸν αὐτὸν μέγαν Γέροντα εὔξασθαι ὑπὲρ αὐτοῦ ἵνα ὁ Κύριος μνησθείη αὐτοῦ ἐν τῇ βασιλείᾳ αὐτοῦ. Ἀπόκρισις· Ἰδοὺ ὁ Κύριος Ἰησοῦς Χριστὸς οὐ κατήσχυνέ μου τὸ πρόσωπον, ἀλλ᾽ ἐχαρίσατό μοι τὴν σωτηρίαν τῆς ψυχῆς σου, καὶ δέδωκέ μοι τὴν χάριν τοῦ μνησθῆναί σου ἐν τῇ βασιλείᾳ αὐτοῦ. Cf. Bars. et Jo., *resp.* 495, 573. McLaughlin 1994: 211 observes, "It is possible of course that prayers . . . were understood not as instruments but simple evocations of the desired end."

189. Leont. Neap., *v.Sym.* 2.140–41 (Festugière-Rydén, 74–75; trans. Krueger, 147, adapted): συγχώρησον τῇ ψυχῇ αὐτῆς ὑπὲρ τῆς θυσίας ἧς ἐγέννησεν καὶ προσήνεγκέν σοι, δέσποτα, ἐμὲ τὸν ἀνάξιον δοῦλόν σου.

190. Anton., *v.Sym.Styl.sen.* 14 (Lietzmann, 1908): 38. Symeon's mother is otherwise unattested, and she was probably inspired in Antonius's 7th-century hagiography by Symeon Stylites the Younger's mother, whose close relation to her son is well attested. See Flusin 1993. I owe this observation and reference to Dina Boero.

191. It is true that Cyril of Scythopolis describes Sabas selling off one of his monastery's liturgical vessels rather than jeopardizing the performance of a Sunday liturgy, but this shows only that the saint understood God's priorities and that Cyril was aware of the law of 544 that sanctioned the sale of liturgical vessels, alone of all offerings, if a pressing need arose. Justinian, *Nov.* 120.10 (issued 544 CE—a reference I owe to Ahmet Ari). As Mango 1992: 123 notes, there was great resistance to any such sale.

192. Georg. Syc., *v.Thdr.Syc.* 133 (Festugière-Rydén, 105): Αἰτοῦντος δὲ αὐτὸν εὔχεσθαι ὑπέρ τε αὐτοῦ καὶ τῆς βασιλείας αὐτοῦ, ἤρξατο παραινεῖν αὐτῷ ὁ τοῦ Χριστοῦ θεράπων ὡς, εἰ θέλοι ἀεὶ μνημονεύεσθαι παρ' αὐτοῦ καὶ ἐνεργεῖν αὐτῷ τὴν εὐχὴν αὐτοῦ, παύσασθαι τῆς ἀνθρωπίνης κατακοπῆς καὶ ἐκχύσεως τῶν αἱμάτων. Cf. *v.Epiphan.* 17 (Dindorf, 19): ἐὰν κρατήσῃς τοὺς ἐμοὺς λόγους, μνημονεύσω σου ὅπου ἂν εἰμι.

193. Rémondon 1972: 269, an exemplary study. Cf. Dagron 1989: 1078.

194. *PSI* 14 1425 (Manfredi, 140): παρακαλοῦμεν αὐτὴν μὴ παριδεῖν ἡμᾶς [-ca.?-]ς [ἀλλὰ [-ca.?-] κε]λεῦσαι προσαπολυθῆναι ἡμῖν ἃ ἐξ ἔθους εὐηργέ[τηκε ὁ [-ca.?-] ἔνδο]ξος ὑμῶν οἶκος ὅπως καὶ κατὰ τοῦτο εὐχαρισ[τῶμεν αὐτῇ. καίπερ ἁμα]ρτωλοί ἐσμεν, τὰς συνήθεις εὐχὰς ἀναπέμψομε(ν) [πρὸς τὸν θεὸν ὑ]πὲρ σωτηρίας αὐτῆς κ(αὶ) συστάσεως παντὸς τοῦ [-ca.?-]ς οἴκου.

195. *SB* 16.12474 (= *P.Vindob. G.* 25887; Sijpesteijn-Worp, 25–26): θαρρουν γὰρ εἰς τὴν ἀγαθὴν ὑμῶν ψυχὴν ὥσπερ σαυτοῖς θαρροῦμεν ὑμῖν ἐπέμψαμεν πρὸς ὑμᾶς ὅπως συνέλθη αὐτοῖς ἄχρι οὗ συνάξουσιν τὴν ὀλίγην προσφορὰν τοῦ εὐαγοῦς μοναστηρί[ου.]

196. *O.Brit.Mus.copt.* I.63.3 (Hall, 87–88). Perhaps also *P.Bal.* 189.

EPILOGUE: WHEN HOLY MEN WALKED THE EARTH

1. Ant. Choz., *v.Geo.Choz.* 9.42 (Houze, 143–44; trans. Vivian, 102, adapted).

2. See especially Flusin 1992; also Wilken 1992: 216–32; and Booth 2014: 90–127.

3. See Sänger 2011; Gariboldi 2009; and Foss 2003.

4. Ant. Mon., *Ep. ad Eust.* (PG 89[1].1424C, 1424C–1425D). I use the translation in Booth 2014: 96. At pp. 95n24 and 204, he dates the letter ca. 630–634 rather than the usual ca. 620. For the event Antiochus describes and related circumstances, see also Patrich 1995: 326–28.

5. I follow Booth's date for Antony's hagiography, but an earlier date is possible. See Olster 1993: 311. On similar descriptions of brigands and brigandage during the Persian and Arab invasions, see Flusin 1991; and Caner 2010: 47–50.

6. Ant. Mon., *Ep. ad Eust.* (PG 89[1]: 1428B). Translation in Booth 2014: 97, mentioning related sources. Olster 1993 argues that Antony wrote to revive pilgrimage to Wadi Qelt.

7. Put on a new footing by Tannous 2018.

8. Walmsley 2007: 321.

9. The ninth century is the terminus for Villagomez 1998; and Schachner 2006, both utilizing Thomas of Marga to study monastic economies in Syria. On the *Life of Symeon of the Olives*, see Tannous 2016. For other sources from Ṭur ʿAbdin, Palmer 1990: 182–90. For

Egypt, see Mikhail 2013; and Sijpesteijn 2010. For the consequences on Egyptian monasticism itself, see Wipszycka 2018: 527–32; and Wipszycka 2008; the latter proposes that declining revenues after the conquest forced the Apollo monastery at Bawit to send out monks to collect the firstfruits expected from farmers of the region.

10. In general, Pahlitzsch 2009; also Tannous 2018: 380–86, 461–71,

11. *Life of Rabban Hormizd* 22–23 (Budge, 2.142–47). Hormizd lived in the sixth or seventh century; though ascribed to his disciple, this hagiography must be much later.

12. Patrich 1995: 328–30, 348–52. For revived pilgrimage, Talbot 2001. For involvement in the iconoclast controversy, Auzépy 2001. On conditions in the Negev and at the Sinai monastery, see Trombley 2014; and Anastasius of Sinai's stories in Caner 2010: 172–95.

13. McCormick 2011: 5–48, 160–62 (quoted from 47). Cf. Binggeli 2018; and Flusin 2010: 215–18.

14. Thus, Hatlie 2007a: 219, 457–72, offering a more optimistic estimate than Charanis 1971: 65–66, which notes that only ten of the ninety-two monasteries Janin counted survived into the tenth century. On the impact of the invasions, see Foss, 1975; and Saradi 2006: 96–97, 349–52. For Constantinople ca. 640–843, Wickham 2009: 255–78; and Izdebski 2013: 228–33.

15. Charanis 1971: 66.

16. Hatlie 2007a: 212–49 (quote from 246).

17. Paul Evergetinos, *Evergetinos* 4.2.5–6 (Langē, 42). Found only in this sixteenth-century collection compiled from an eleventh-century prototype, the apothegm is a pastiche of sixth- and seventh-century stories.

18. See Hatlie 2007a: 446. For introduction to later Byzantine monasticism, see Talbot 2019. For its social history, Morris 1995. For its place in the economy, Kaplan 2020.

19. See Booth 2014: 140–85, 331–42 (quoted from 339).

20. Max., *ascet.* 37 (CCSG 40.91, ll.761–63; trans. Sherwood, 127). I interpret these lines as an allusion to historical circumstance because other seventh-century writers refer to Saracens as demons. See Flusin 1991. The date of the *Liber Asceticus* is, however, uncertain, with suggestions ranging from 626 to later, as discussed by its editor, pp. xviii–xix. See also Booth 2014: 171–73.

21. Max., *ascet.* 7 (CCSG 40.17, ll.119–22; trans. Sherwood, 107); with Max., *ascet.* 12, 17 (40.29, 37, ll.224–25, 320–25; 110, 113). Constantelos 1991: 22 notes that Maximus emphasizes *agapē* as the supreme expression of *philanthrōpia*.

22. Max., *ascet.* 8 (CCSG 40.21, ll.153–57; trans. Sherwood, 108); with Max., *ascet.* 7 and 10 (40.17, 25, ll.110–11, 195).

23. Max., *carit.* 1.24 (Ceresa-Gastaldo, 24).

24. Max., *carit.* 1.26 (Ceresa-Gastaldo, 26)

25. Max., *carit.* 3.19 (Ceresa-Gastaldo, 150 [cf. 149]).

26. Max., *carit.* 3.79 (Ceresa-Gastaldo, 182).

27. For an overview of later Byzantine authors and philanthropic institutions, see Constantelos 1991: 20, 22–24, 98–116; Miller 1997: 3–29; Miller and Nesbitt 2014.

28. Herrin 2013b: 305. Patlagean 1997: 34–35 describes two eleventh- to twelfth-century trends: the monastic subordination of philanthropic activities to liturgical concerns and a general reduction of lay and imperial philanthropy to purely symbolic levels. Dagron 1991 shows that the church transferred responsibility for public burials, instituted by Constantine, to lay confraternities and eventually became restricted to the poorest.

29. Dagron 1998: 85–87; and Savramis 1962: 47 note the importance of a distinction between *psychika* and *leitourgika* in Middle Byzantium. The most prominent new gift ideal—as it seems to have been originally conceived—was the *charistikē*, on which see Thomas 1987: 156–85; and Kaplan 2020: 354.

30. Dawkins 1953: 254–55. For examples in monastic charters, see Thomas and Hero 2000: 1861, s.v. "blessing (*eulogia*)." During the medieval era, *eulogiai* became identified with *antidōra* handed out to lay members of a congregation after a church service; this probably became customary once congregation sizes had shrunk. For discussion of medieval gift giving on Mt. Athos and how monks sought to protect ideals while conforming to law, see Morris 2010.

31. Nicetas, *v.Phil.Mis.* 3C (Ryden, 74–77); Greg. Mon., *v. Lazari* 12, 82.

32. At Alice-Mary Talbot's suggestion, I sampled *vitae* of the cenobitic abbots Eustratius of Agauros, Euthymius the Younger, Evaristus, Irene of Chrysobalaton, John Psichaites, Macarius of Pelekētē, Nicephorus of Medikion, Nicetas of Medikion, Plato of Sakkoudion, and Peter of Atroa. Only the last features a "loaves and fishes" episode (sections 49–50), but it does not involve *eulogiai*. Rosemary Morris informs me that there is no "loaves and fishes" episode in Michael the Monk's *vita* (*vita* B) of Theodore the Studite, which she is editing with Robert Jordan. No doubt an example could be found, but its absence from all of these is striking.

33. Greg. Mon., *v. Lazari* 209 (Delehaye 572; trans. Greenfield 303–304).

34. Efthymiades and Déroche 2011: 79 note that the changed conditions caused a change in the imagery and themes found in Byzantine hagiography.

BIBLIOGRAPHY

PRIMARY WORKS

Acts of Thomas [*A.Th.*]. Greek version: Ed. Maximilian Bonnet and R. A. Lipsius, *Acta Apostolorum Apocrypha* 2.2. Leipzig: Mendelsson, 1903; repr. Hildesheim: Georg Olms, 1959. Trans. Hans J. W. Drijvers in *New Testament Apocrypha*, 2nd. ed., vol. 2. Ed. Edgar Hennecke, Wilhelm Schneemelcher and Robert McWilson. Westminster: John Knox Press, 1992.

Agapetus Diaconus [Agap.]. *Expositio capitum admonitiorum* [*Cap.*]. Ed. Rudolf Riedinger, *Agapetos Diakonos. Der Fürstenspiegel für Kaiser Iustinianos.* Kentron Ereunēs Byzantiou 4. Athens: Hetaireia Philōn tou Laou, 1995. Trans. Peter N. Bell, *Three Political Voices from the Age of Justinian.* TTH 52. Liverpool: Liverpool University Press, 1999.

Agathias. *Historiae* [*Hist.*]. Ed. Rudolf Keydell, *Agathiae Myrinaei historiarum libri quinque.* Corpus Fontium Historiae Byzantinae 2. Berlin: de Gruyter 1967. Trans. Joseph D. Frendo, *Agathias: The Histories.* Corpus fontium historiae byzantinae 2a. Berlin: de Gruyter, 1975.

Ammianus Marcellinus [Amm. Marc.]. *Res Gestae* [*RG*]. Ed. and trans. John C. Rolfe, *Ammianus Marcellinus: History.* 3 vols. LCL 300, 315, 331. Cambridge, MA: Harvard University Press, 1939, 1940, 1950.

Ammonius. *De adfinium vocabularum differentia* [*adfin.*]. Ed. K. Nickau, *Ammonii qui dicitur liber de adfinium vocabulorum differentia.* Leipzig: Teubner, 1966.

Anastasius of Sinai [Anast. Sin.]. *Quaestiones et Responsiones* [*resp.*]. Ed. Marcel Richard and Joseph A. Munitiz, *Anastasii Sinaitae quaestiones et responsiones.* CCSG 59. Turnhout-Leuven: Brepols, 2006.

———. *Tales of the Sinai Fathers* [*paterika*]. Ed. F. Nau, "Le texte grec des récit du moine Anastase sur les saints pères du Sinaï," *Oriens Christianus* 2 (1902): 58–89. Trans. Caner 2010: 172–99. French trans. F. Nau, "Les Récits inédits du moine Anastase: Contribution à l'Histoire du Sinaï au commencement du VIIᵉ siècle," *Revue de l'Institut Catholique de Paris* 1–2 (1902): 1–70.

Answers of Jaʿqōb to Jōḥannān ʿEṣṭūnārā. Ed. and trans. Arthur Vööbus, *The Synodicon in the West Syrian Tradition* CSCO 367/368, Scriptores syri 161–62. Louvain: Secrétariat du CorpusSCO, 1975.

Anthologia Graeca [Anth. Gr.]. Ed. H. Stadtmüller and trans. William R. Paton, *The Greek Anthology*, vol.1. LCL 67. Cambridge, MA: Harvard University Press, 1960.

Antiochus Monachus [Ant. Mon.]. *Epistula ad Eustathium [Ep. ad Eust.]*. PG 89: 1421–28.

———. *Pandecta scripturae sacrae [pand.]*. PG 89: 1428–1849.

Antonius [Anton.]. *Vita Symeonis Stylitis senioris [v.Sym.Styl.sen.]*. Ed. Hans Lietzmann, *Das Leben des heiligen Symeon Stylites*. Texte und Untersuchungen 32.4 Leipzig: Hinrichs, 1908, 20–78. Trans. Robert Doran, *The Lives of Symeon Stylites*. CS 112. Kalamazoo, MI: Cistercian Publications, 1992.

Antony of Choziba [Ant. Choz.]. *Vita Georgii Chozibitae [v.Geo.Choz.]*. Ed. with Latin trans. C. Houze, "Sancti Georgii Chozebitae auctore Antonio eius discipulo," *AB* (1888): 95–144, 336–72. Trans. Timothy Vivian, *Journeying into God: Seven Early Monastic Lives*. Minneapolis: Fortress Press, 1996.

Apophthegmata patrum [AP]. Coptic Collection [C]. Ed. with French trans. M. Chaîne, *Le manuscrit de la version copte en dialect sahidique des "Apophthegmata Patrum."* Bibliothèque d'études coptes 6. Cairo: Institut Français d'archéologie orientale, 1960.

———. Greek Alphabetical Collection [G]. PG 65: 72–440. Trans. Benedicta Ward, *The Sayings of the Desert Fathers*. CS 59. Kalamazoo, MI: Cistercian Publications, 1984.

———. Greek Anonymous Collection [N]. Ed. François Nau, "Histoires des solitaires égyptiens (MS Coislin 126, fol.158f.)," *ROC* 12 (1907): 43–68, 171–81, 393–404; *ROC* 13 (1908): 47–57, 266–83; *ROC* 14 (1909): 357–79; *ROC* 17 (1912): 204–11, 294–301; *ROC* 18 (1913): 137–46. Trans. Columba Stewart, *The World of the Desert Fathers*. Kalamazoo: Cistercian Publications, 1986.

———. Greek Systematic Collection [GS]. Ed. with French trans. Jean-Claude Guy, *Les apophthegmes des pères*, 2 vols. *Collection systématique I–IX*. SC 387. Paris: Édition du Cerf, 1993. *Collection systématique X–XVI*. SC 474: Paris: Édition du Cerf, 2003.

———. Latin Systematic Collection [L]: PL 73: 855–1022. Trans. Owen Chadwick, *Western Asceticism*. Philadelphia: Westminster, 1958, 33–189.

———. Syriac Collection [S]. *Paradisus patrum*. Ed. Paul Bedjan, *Acta martyrum et sanctorum*, vol. 7. Paris: Harassowitz, 1897; repr. Hildesheim: Georg Olms, 1968. Also ed. and trans. Ernest A. Wallis Budge, *The Book of Paradise being the Histories and Sayings of the Monks and Ascetics of the Egyptian Desert by Palladius, Hieronymus and Others. The Syriac Texts, According to the Recension of Anân îshôʿ of Bêth ʿÂbhê, edited with English Translation.* 2 vols. London 1904.

Archive of John. Ed. and trans. Nikolaos Gonis, "Further Letters from the Archive of Apa Ioannes," *Bulletin of the American Society of Papyrologists* 45 (2008): 69–86.

Archive of Nepheros. See *P.Neph.*

Archive of Paphnutius. See *P.Lond.*

Aretaeus. *De causis et signis acutorum et diuturnorum morborum [caus.]*. Ed. Carl Hude, *Corpus medicorum graecorum*, vol. 2.2. Berlin and Leipzig: Teubner, 1958.

Aristotle, Pseudo-. *Athenaion Politeia [Ath. Pol.]*. Ed. Mortimer Chambers, *Aristoteles Athēnaiōn politeia*. Leipzig: Teubner, 1986.

Asterius of Amasea [Aster.]. *Homilies [hom.]*. Ed. Cornelis Datema, *Asterius of Amasea, Homilies I–XIV: Text, Introduction and Notes*. Leiden: Brill, 1970.

Athanasius [Ath.]. *Vita Antonii [v.Ant.]*. Ed. with French trans. G. J. M. Bartelink, *Athanase d'Alexandrie, Vie d'Antoine*. SC 400. Paris: Éditions du Cerf, 2004.

Athanasius of Emesa. *Epitome Syntagmatos [syntagm.]*. Ed. Dieter Simon and Spiros Troianos, *Das Novellensyntagma des Athanasios von Emesa*. Forschungen zur byzantinischen Rechtsgeschichte 16. Frankfurt am Main: Klostermann, 1979.

Athanasius, Pseudo- [Ath., Ps.-]. *Canons*. See *Canons of Athanasius [Can. Ath.]*.

———. *Quaestiones ad Antiochum Ducem [qu. Ant.]*. PG 28: 597–710.

———. *Sermo pro iis qui saeculo renuntiarunt [renunt.]*. PG 28: 1409–20.

———. *Vita Syncleticae [v.Syncl.]*. Ed. Lamprinē G. Ampelarga, *Ho vios tēs Hagias Synklētikēs: Eisagōgē—Kritiko Keimeno—Scholia (The Life of Saint Syncletica: Introduction—Critical Text—Commentary)*. BTS 31. Thessaloniki: Byzantine Research Center, Aristotle University, 2002. Trans. Elizabeth Bryson Bongie, *The Life and Regimen of the Blessed and Holy Teacher, Syncletica*. Toronto: Peregrina, 1995. French trans. Odile Bénédicte Bernard, *Vie de sainte Synclétique*. Spiritualité orientale 9. Bégrolles-en-Mauges: Abbaye de Bellefontaine, 1972.

Athenagoras [Athen.]. *Legatio sive Supplicatio pro Christianis [Leg. pro Chr.]*. Ed. W. R. Schoedel, *Legatio sive Supplicatio pro Christianis*. Oxford: Clarendon Press, 1972.

Augustine of Hippo [Aug.]. *Contra litteras Petiliani [C. litt. Petil.]*. Ed. M. Petschenig, *Contra litteras Petiliani, Epistula ad catholicos de secta Donatistarum, Contra Cresconium*. CSEL 52. Vienna: Garold, 1909.

———. *De civitate Dei [civ. Dei]*. Ed. Christoph Horn, *Augustinus, De civitate dei*. Klassiker auslegen 11. Berlin: Akademie Verlag, 1997.

———. *De opere monachorum [De op. mon.]*. Ed. Joseph Zycha, *S. Aureli Augustini De fide et symbolo*, etc. CSEL 41. Vienna: F. Tempsky, 1900. Trans. Mary Muldowney, in ed. Roy J. Deferrari, *St. Augustine: Treatises on Various Subjects*. Fathers of the Church 16. New York: Fathers of the Church, 1952.

———. *Sermones [serm.]*. PL 38 and 39.

Barhadbeshabbā 'Arbāyā. *Historia ecclesiastica [HE]*, part 2. Ed. with French trans. François Nau, *Le seconde partie de l'Histoire de Barhadbeshabba 'Arbaïa*. PO 9: 501–667. Paris: Firmin Didot, 1913.

Barsanuphius and John of Gaza [Bars. et Jo.]. *Responsiones (resp.)*. Ed. with French trans. François Neyt and Paula de Angelis-Noah, *Barsanuphe et Jean de Gaza: Correspondance [ep.]*. Vol. 1.1: *Aux Solitaires, Lettres 1–71*. SC 426. Paris: Éditions du Cerf, 1997. Vol. 1.2: *Aux Solitaires, Lettres 72–223*. SC 427. Paris: Éditions du Cerf, 1998. Vol. 2.1: *Aux Cénobites, Lettres 224–398*. SC 450. Paris: Éditions du Cerf, 2000. Vol. 2.2: *Aux Cénobites, Lettres 399–616*. SC 451. Paris: Éditions du Cerf, 2001. Vol. 3: *Aux Laïcs et aux Évêques, Lettres 617–848*. SC 468. Paris: Éditions du Cerf, 2002. Trans. John Chryssavgis, *Barsanuphius and John, Letters*, 2 vols. Fathers of the Church 113–14. Washington, DC: Catholic University of America Press, 2006–2007.

Basil of Caesarea [Bas. Caes.]. *Epistulae [ep.]*. Ed. and trans. Roy J. Deferrari and Martin R. P. McGuire, *Saint Basil: The Letters*, 4 vols. LCL 190, 215, 243, 270. Cambridge, MA: Harvard University Press, 1970–1987.

————. *Homilia in illud: Destruam horrea mea* [*hom.6*]. Ed. with French trans. Yves Courtonne, *Saint Basile: Homélies sur la richesse: Édition critique et exégétique.* Paris: Firmin-Didot, 1935, 15–37. Trans. M. F. Toal, *The Sunday Sermons of the Great Fathers,* vol. 3. Chicago: Henry Regnery, 1959.

————. *Homilia in divites* [*hom.7*]. Ed. with French trans. Yves Courtonne, *Saint Basile: Homélies sur la richesse: Édition critique et exégétique.* Paris: Firmin-Didot, 1935.

————. *Homilia dicta tempore famis et siccitatis* [*hom.8*]. PG 31: 304–28. Trans. Holman 2001: 183–92.

————. *Homiliae in Psalmos* 14 [*Hom. in Ps.*]. PG 29: 209–494.

————. *Regulae brevius tractatae* [*RB*]. PG 31: 1080–1305. Trans. W. K. Lowthar Clarke, *The Ascetic Works of Saint Basil.* London: SPCK, 1925.

————. *Regulae fusius tractatae* [*RF*]. PG 31: 889–1025. Trans. W. K. Lowthar Clarke, *The Ascetic Works of Saint Basil.* London: SPCK, 1925.

Benedict of Nursia. *Regulae.* Ed. and trans. Timothy Fry et al., *RB 1980: The Rule of Saint Benedict in Latin and English.* Collegeville, MN: Liturgical Press, 1981.

Besa. *Homilies.* Ed. and trans. K. H. Kuhn, *Letters and Sermons of Besa.* CSCO 157–58, Scriptores coptici 21–22. Louvain: Peeters, 1956.

Byzantine Liturgy of St. Basil. Ed. Stefano Parenti and Elena Velkovska, *L'Eucologio Baberini gr. 336.,* 2nd ed. Rome: Edizioni liturgische, 2000. Trans. R. C. D. Jasper and G. J. Cuming, *Prayers of the Eucharist: Early and Reformed,* 3rd ed. Collegeville, MN: Liturgical Press, 1975.

Callinicus [Call.]. *Vita Hypatii* [*v.Hyp.*]. Ed. with French trans. G. J. M. Bartelink, *Callinicos: Vie d'Hypatios.* SC 177. Paris: Éditions du Cerf, 1971.

Canons of Athanasius [*Can. Ath.*]. Ed. and trans. Wilhelm Riedel and W. E. Crum, *The Canons of Athanasius.* Text and Translation Society 191. Amsterdam: Philo Press, 1973.

Canons of the Apostles [*Can. Ap.*]. German trans. Wilhelm Riedel, *Kirchenrechtsquellen des Patriarchats Alexandrien.* Leipzig: Georg Böhme, 1900.

Canons of Basil. [*Can. Bas.*]. German trans. Wilhelm Riedel, *Kirchenrechtsquellen des Patriarchats Alexandrien.* Leipzig: Georg Böhme, 1900.

Canons of Johannan Bar Qursos. Ed. and trans. Arthur Vööbus, *The Synodicon in the West Syrian Tradition.* CSCO 367–68, Scriptores syri 161–62. Louvain: Secrétariat du CorpusSCO, 1975.

Canons of Marutha. See Marutha of Maypherqaṭ.

Canons of Rabbula. See Rabbula of Edessa.

Cassius Dio. *Historiae Romanae.* Ed. U. P. Boissevain, *Cassii Dionis Cocceiani historiarum Romanarum quae supersunt.* 3 vols. Berlin: Wiedmann, 1895–1901; repr. 1955.

Choricius of Gaza [Choric. Gaz.]. *Laudatio Marciani* [*Laud. Marc.*], 1–2. Ed. Richard Foerster and Eberhard Richtsteig, *Choricii gazaei opera.* Leipzig: Teubner, 1929. Trans. F. K. Litsas, "Choricius of Gaza: An Approach to His Work," PhD diss., University of Chicago, 1980.

Chronicon Pascale [*Chron. Pascale*]. Ed. Ludwig A. Dindorf, *Chronicon paschale.* 2 vols. Corpus scriptorum historiae Byzantinae. Bonn: Weber, 1832. Trans. Michael Whitby and Mary Whitby, *Chronicon Paschale 284–628 AD.* TTH 7. Liverpool: Liverpool University Press, 1989.

Chrysostom [Chrys.], John. See John Chrysostom.

Clement of Alexandria [Clem. Alex.]. *Quis Dives Salvetur [Quis div. salv.]*. Ed. O. Stählin and L. Früchtel, in Carlo Nardi and Patrick Descourtieux, *Clément d'Alexandrie: Quel riche sera sauvé?* SC 536. Paris: Éditions du Cerf, 2011.

Codex Theodosianus [CTh.]. Ed. Theodor Mommsen and P. M. Meyer. *Theodosiani libri xvi cum Constitutionibus Sirmondianis et Leges novellae ad Theodosianum pertinentes.* Berlin: Weidmann, 1954. Trans. Clyde Pharr, *The Theodosian Code and Novels and the Sirmondian Constitutions.* Princeton: Princeton University Press, 1952.

Council in Trullo. *Canones [can.]*. Ed. Heinz Ohme in *Concilium Constantinopolitanum A. 691/2 in Trullo habitum (Concilium Quinisextum).* ACO 2.2.4. Berlin and Boston: De Grutyer, 2013. Trans. Henry R. Percival, *The Seven Ecumenical Councils.* NPNF 2.15. Grand Rapids, MI: Eerdmans, 1988.

Council of Antioch. *Canones.* Ed. Périclès-Pierre Joannou, *Fonti. Fasciolo IX: Discipline générale antique (IVᵉ-IXᵉ).* 1.1: *Les canons des conciles oecuméniques.* Rome: Tipografia Italo-Orientale "S. Nilo," 1962. Trans. Henry R. Percival, *The Seven Ecumenical Councils.* NPNF 2.15. Grand Rapids, MI: Eerdmans, 1988.

Council of Chalcedon, *Acta.* Ed. Eduard Schwartz in *Concilium universale Chalcedonense.* ACO 2.2. Berlin and Leipzig: De Gruyter, 1924–1935. *Canones.* Ed. Périclès-Pierre Joannou, *Fonti. Fasciolo IX: Discipline générale antique (IVᵉ-IXᵉ).* 1.1: *Les canons des conciles oecuméniques.* Rome: Tipografia Italo-Orientale "S. Nilo," 1962. Trans. Richard Price and Michael Gaddis, *The Acts of the Council of Chalcedon.* 3 vols. TTH 45. Liverpool: Liverpool University Press, 2005, 2007.

Council of Constantinople, Second, *Acta.* Ed. Trans. Richard Price, *The Acts of the Council of Constantinople of 553.* TTH 51. Liverpool: Liverpool University Press, 2012.

Council of Ephesus, Second, *Acta.* Ed. Johannes Flemming with German trans. Georg Hoffmann, *Akten der Ephesinischen Synode vom Jahre 449.* Abhandlungen der königlichen Gesellschaft der Wissenschaften zu Göttingen, Phil.-hist. Klasse, NF 15. Berlin: Weidmann, 1917. Trans. S. G. F. Perry, *The Second Synod of Ephesus.* Dartford: Orient Press. 1881.

Council of Gangara. *Epistula synodica [Ep. syn.]*. Ed. Périclès-Pierre Joannou, *Fonti. Fasciolo IX: Discipline générale antique (IVᵉ-IXᵉ).* Vol 1.1: *Les canons des conciles oecuméniques.* Rome: Tipografia Italo-Orientale "S. Nilo," 1962.

Constitutiones Apostolorum [Const. Ap.]. Ed. with French trans. Marcel Metzger, *Les Constitutions apostoliques.* SC 320, 329, 336. Paris: Éditions du Cerf, 1985–1987.

Corippus. *In Laudem Iustini Augusti minoris [Laud. Just.]*. Ed. and trans. Averil Cameron, *Flavius Cresconius Corippus: In Laudem Iustini Augusti minoris libri iv.* London: Athlone Press, 1976.

Corpus iuris civilis [CIC]. Codex Justinianus [CJ]. Ed. Paul Krüger. Berlin: Weidmann, 1963. Trans. S. P. Scott, *The Civil Law, including The Twelve Tables, The Institutes of Gaius, The Rules of Ulpian, The Opinions of Paulus, The Enactments of Justinian, and The Constitutions of Leo.* Vols. 12–14: *Enactments of Justinian: The Code, Books I–VIII.* Vols. 15–17: *Enactments of Justinian: The Code, Books IX–XII; The Novels.* Cincinnati, OH: Central Trust Company, 1932. Trans. Paul R. Coleman-Norton, *Roman State and Christian Church,* 3 vols. London: SPCK, 1966.

———. *Novellae [Nov.]*. Ed. Rudolf Schoell and Wilhelm Kroll. Berlin: Weidmann, 1963. Trans. S. P. Scott, *The Civil Law, including The Twelve Tables, The Institutes of Gaius, The Rules of Ulpian, The Opinions of Paulus, The Enactments of Justinian, and The Constitutions of Leo.* Vols. 15–17: *Enactments of Justinian: The Code, Books IX–XII, The Novels.* Cincinnati, OH: Central Trust Company, 1932. Trans. David J. D. Miller and Peter Sarris, *The Novels of Justinian: A Complete Annotated English Translation.* Cambridge: Cambridge University Press, 2018.

Cosmas of Panîr [Cosmas]. *Epistula Cosmae Presbyteri ad Simeonem Stylitam [Ep. ad Sim.].* Ed. Stefano Evodio Assemani, *Acta sanctorum martyrum orientalium et occidentalium, pars II: Acta S. Simeonis Stylitae.* Rome: Collini, 1748, 394–97. Trans. Robert Doran, *The Lives of Symeon Stylites.* CS 112. Kalamazoo, MI: Cistercian Publications, 1992.

Cyril of Alexandria [Cyril Alex.]. *Adversus eos qui negant offerendum esse pro defunctis [defunct.].* Ed. P. E. Pusey in *Sancti patris nostri Cyrilli archiepiscopi Alexandrini in D. Joannis evangelium,* vol. 3. Oxford: Clarendon Press, 1872, 541–44.

———. *Commentarium in Zachariam [Comm. in Zach.].* Ed. Philip E. Pusey in *Sancti patris nostri Cyrilli archiepiscopi Alexandrini in xii prophetas.* 2 vols. Oxford: Clarendon Press, 1868; repr. Brussels: Culture et Civilization, 1965.

———. *Letter to Domnus [ep. 78].* Ed. P.–P. Joannou, *Fonti. Fascicolo ix. Discipline générale antique (iv–ix s.). Les canons des pères grecs,* vol. 2. Rome: Tipographia Italo-Orientale "S. Nilo," 1962, 276–81.

Cyril of Scythopolis [Cyril Scyth.]. *Vita Euthymii [v.Euthym.], Vita Sabae [v.Sab.], Vita Abraami [v.Abraam.], Vita Joannis Hesychastis [v.Jo.Hesych.], Vita Cyriaci [v.Cyriac.], Vita Theodosii [v.Thds.], Vita Theognii [v.Thgn.].* Ed. Eduard Schwartz, *Kyrillos von Skythopolis.* Leipzig: Hinrichs, 1939. Trans. Richard M. Price, *Cyril of Scythopolis: The Lives of the Monks of Palestine.* CS 114. Kalamazoo, MI: Cistercian Publications.

Daniel of Scetis [Dan. Scet.]. *Life of Doulas.* Ed. Léon Clugnet, "Vie et récits de l'abbé Daniel le Scétiote (VIᵉ siècle)." I. Text grec," *ROC* 5 (1900): 387–91.

———. *Narrationes animae utiles [log.]* Ed. and trans. Britt Dahlman, *Saint Daniel of Sketis: A Group of Hagiographic Texts Edited with Introduction, Translation and Commentary.* Studia Byzantina Upsaliensia 10. Uppsala: University of Uppsala, 2007.

Denḥa, *v.Marutae.* Ed. with French trans. François Nau, *Histoire des divines actions de saint Mar Marouta l'Ancien.* PO 3: 52–96. Paris: Firmin-Didot, 1909.

Dialogue on Political Science [Dial.]. Ed. Carlo Maria Mazzucchi, *Menae patricii cum Thoma referendario, De scientia politica dialogus.* Vita e Pensiero. Milan: Università Cattolica del Sacro Cuore, 1982. Trans. Peter N. Bell, *Three Political Voices from the Age of Justinian: Agapetus, Advice to the Emperor, Dialogue on Political Science,* Paul the Silentiary, *Description of Hagia Sophia.* TTH 52. Liverpool: Liverpool University Press, 2009.

Didache. Ed. with French trans. Willy Rordoff and André Tullier, *La Doctrine des Douze Apôtres (Didachè).* SC 248. Paris: Editions du Cerf, 1978.

Didascalia [SyrD.]. Ed. and trans. Arthur Vööbus, *The Didascalia Apostolorum in Syriac.* 2 vols. CSCO 401–7. Louvain: Secrétariat du CorpusSCO, 1979.

Diogenes Laertius [Diog. Laert.]. *Vitae philosophorum [v.Phil.].* Ed. H. S. Long, *Diogenis Laertii vitae philosophorum.* 2 vols. Oxford: Clarendon Press, 1964.

Dionysius of Halicarnassus [Dion. Hal.]. *Antiquitates Romanae [Ant. Rom.].* Ed. Karl Jacoby, *Dionysii Halicarnasei Antiquitatum Romanarum quae supersunt.* Leipzig: Teubner, 1885–1905.

Dionysius the Areopagite, Pseudo- [Dion., Ps-.]. *De ecclesiastica hierarchia [De eccl. hier.]* and *Epistulae [ep.]* Ed. G. Heil and A. M. Ritter, *Corpus Dionysiacum,* vol. 2: *Pseudo-*

Dionysius Areopagita. De coelesti hierarchia, de ecclesiastica hierarchia, de mystica theologia, epistulae. Patristische Texte und Studien 36. Berlin: De Gruyter, 1991.

Dorotheus of Gaza [Dor. Gaz.]. *Asceticon* [*log.*], *Epistulae* [*ep.*]. Ed. Lucien Regnault and Jacques de Préville, *Dorothée de Gaza: Oeuvres spirituelles.* SC 92. Paris: Éditions du Cerf, 1963. Trans. Eric P. Wheeler, *Dorotheos of Gaza: Discourses and Sayings,* CS 33. Kalamazoo, MI: Cistercian Publications, 1977.

Egeria [Eg.]. *Itinerarium* [*Itin.*]. Ed. with French trans. Pierre Maraval, *Égérie: Journal de Voyage (Itinéraire).* SC 296. Paris: Éditions du Cerf. Trans. John Wilkinson, *Egeria's Travels,* 3rd ed. Warminster: Aris and Phillips, 1999.

Epiphanius of Salamis [Epiph.]. *De fide.* Ed. Karl Kroll, revised Jürgen Dummer. *Epiphanius Werke,* vol. 3. GCS. Berlin: Akademie Verlag, 1985.

———. *Panarion* [*Pan.*]. Ed. Karl Kroll, rev. Jürgen Dummer. *Epiphanius Werke,* vols. 2 and 3. GCS. Berlin: Akademie Verlag, 1980, 1985.

Epitome of the Life of John the Almsgiver. Ed. E. Lappa-Zizicas, "Un épitomé de la Vie de saint Jean l'Aumônier par Jean et Sophronius." *AB* 88 (1970): 265–78.

Ephrem Graecus [Ephr. Gr]. *De pauperum amore (Peri ptōchotrophia).* Ed. K. G. Phrantzoles, *Hosiou Ephraim tou Syrou erga,* vol. 5. Thessalonica: To Perivoli tēs Panagias, 1994, 137–40.

Ephrem of Nisibis. *Memrā de Mensa (Blessing of the Table).* Ed. with French trans. L. Maries, L. Forman and F. Graffin, *L'Orient Syrien* 4 (1959): 73–109, 163–92, 285–98.

Eusebius of Caesarea [Eus. Caes.]. *Commentaria in Psalmos.* PG 23: 71–1396.

———. *De martyribus Palestinae* [*De mart.*]. Ed. Gustave Bardy, *Historie ecclésiastique,* vol. 3. SC 55. Paris: Éditions du Cerf, 1958.

———. *De vita Constantini* [*v.Const.*]. Ed. with French trans. F. Winkelmann in Luce Pietri and Marie-Joseph Rondeau, *Vie de Constantin.* SC 559. Paris: Éditions du Cerf, 2013.

———. *Historia ecclesiastica* [*HE*]. Ed. with French trans. Gustave Bardy (revising a text by Eduard Schwartz), *Eusèbe de Césarée: Histoire ecclésiastique,* 3 vols. SC 31, 41, 55. Paris: Éditions du Cerf, 1952, 1955, 1958. Trans. G. A. Williamson, *Eusebius: The History of the Church from Christ to Constantine.* London: Penguin, 1965.

Eusebius of Emesa [Eus. Em.]. *Sermon 29* ("On Good Works"). Ed. É. M. Buytaert, *Eusèbe d'Émèse. Discours conservés en Latin,* vol. 2: *La collection de Sirmond.* Louvain: Spicilegium Sacrum Lovaniense, 1957, 219–39.

Eustratius of Constantinople. *Vita Eutychii.* Ed. Carl Laga, *Eustratii presbyteri vita Eutychii Patriarchae Constantinopolitani.* Turnhout: Brepols, 1992.

Evagrius of Pontus [Evagr. Pont.]. *Expositio in Proverbia Salomonis* [*Exp. in Prov.*]. Ed. with French trans. P. Géhin, *Évagre le Pontique. Scholies aux Proverbes.* SC 340. Paris: Éditions du Cerf, 1987.

———. *Foundations of the Monastic Life* [*Fnd.*]. PG 40: 1252–64. Trans. Robert E. Sinkewicz, *Evagrius of Pontus: The Greek Ascetic Corpus.* Oxford and New York: Oxford University Press, 2003.

———. *On Thoughts* [*Th.*]. Ed. with French trans. Paul Géhin, Claire Guillaumont, Antoine Guillaumont, *Évagre le Pontique. Sur les Pensées.* SC 438. Paris: Éditions du Cerf, 1998. Trans. Robert E. Sinkewicz, *Evagrius of Pontus: The Greek Ascetic Corpus.* Oxford and New York: Oxford University Press, 2003.

———. *Practicus.* [*Pr.*]. Ed. with French trans. Antoine and Claire Guillaumont; *Évagre le Pontique. Traité pratique ou Le moine.* SC 170,171. Paris: Éditions du Cerf, 1971. Trans.

John Etudes Bamberger, *Evagrius Ponticus: The Praktikos, Chapters on Prayer.* CS 4. Kalamazoo, MI: Cistercian Publications, 1981.

Evagrius Scholasticus [Evagr. Schol.]. *Historia ecclesiastica* [*HE*]. Ed. Joseph Bidez and Léon Parmentier, *The Ecclesiastical History of Evagrius with the Scholia.* London: Methuen, 1898. Trans. Michael Whitby, *The Ecclesiastical History of Evagrius Scholasticus.* TTH 33. Liverpool: Liverpool University Press, 2000.

Evergetinos, Paul. *Evergetinos.* Ed. Matthaios Langē, *Evergetinos, ētoi, Synagōgē tōn theophthongōn rēmatōn kai didaskaliōn tōn theophorōn kai hagiōn paterōn.* 4 vols. Athens: M. Langē, 1983–85.

Firmus of Caesarea [Firm.]. *Epistulae.* Ed. with French trans. M.-A. Valvet-Sebasti and Pierre-Louis Gatier, *Firmus de Césarée: Lettres.* SC 350. Paris: Éditions du Cerf, 1989.

Gellius, Aulus. *Noctes Atticae* [*Noct.*]. Ed. C. Hosius, *Gellii Noctium Atticarum libri xx.* Leipzig: Teubner, 1903.

George of Alexandria [Georg. Alex.]. *v. Iohannis Chrysostomi* [*v.Chrys.*]. Ed. François Halkin, *Douze récits byzantins sur Saint Jean Chrýsostome.* SH 60. Brussels: Société des Bollandistes, 1977, 69–285.

George of Sykeon [Georg. Syc.]. *Vita Theodori Syceotae* [*v.Thdr.Syc.*]. Ed. with French trans. André-Jean Festugière, *Vie de Théodore de Sykéôn.* 2 vols. SH 48. Brussels: Société des Bollandistes, 1970. Trans. (partial) Elizabeth Dawes and Norman H. Baynes, *Three Byzantine Saints: Contemporary Biographies Translated from the Greek.* Crestwood, NY: St. Vladimir's Press, 1996.

Gerontius [Geront.]. *Vita Melaniae Iunioris* [*v.Mel.*]. Greek version [*gr.*]: Ed. Denys Gorce, *Vie de Saint Mélanie.* SC 90. Paris: Éditions du Cerf, 1962. Latin version [*lat.*]: Ed. Patrick Laurence, *La vie latine de Sainte Mélanie.* Studium Biblicum Franciscanum 41. Jerusalem: Franciscan Printing Press, 2000. Trans. Elizabeth Clark, *Life of Melania the Younger: Introduction, Translation, and Commentary.* Studies in Women and Religion 14. New York and Toronto: Edwin Mellen Press, 1984.

Gregory I [Greg. Mag.]. *Dialogorum libri* [*Dial.*]. Ed. Adalbert de Vogüé with French trans. Paul Antin, *Grégoire le Grand: Dialogues.* 3 vols. SC 251, 260, 265. Paris: Éditions du Cerf, 1978–1980. Trans. O. J. Zimmerman, *Saint Gregory the Great: Dialogues.* The Fathers of the Church. Washington, DC: Catholic University of America Press, 1959.

———. *Registrum epistularum* [*reg.*]. Ed. Dag Norberg, *S. Gregorii Magni registrum epistularum.* 2 vols. CCSL 140–140A. Turnhout: Brepols, 1982. Trans. John R. C. Martyn, *The Letters of Gregory the Great.* 3 vols. Medieval Sources in Translation 40. Toronto: Pontifical Institute of Mediaeval Studies, 2004.

Gregory of Caesarea [Greg. Presb.]. *Vita Gregorii Nazianzeni* [*v.Greg.Naz.*]. Ed. Xavier Lequeux, *Gregorii Presbyteri Vita Sancti Gregorii Theologi.* CCSG 44. Turnhout: Brepols, 2001.

Gregory of Nazianzus [Greg. Naz.]. *Exemplum testamenti.* PG 37: 389–96. Trans. Raymond Van Dam, "Self-Representation in the Will of Gregory of Nazianzus." *JThS* n.s. 46 (1995): 143–48.

———. *Oratio* [*or.*] 14. *De pauperibus amandis.* PG 35: 855–910.

———. *Oratio* 16. *In patrem tacentem.* PG 35: 936–64. Trans. Charles Gordon Browne and James Edward Swallow, *Select Orations of Saint Gregory Nazianzen.* NPNF 7. Grand Rapids, MI: Eedermans.

———. *Oratio* 43. *In laudem Basilii.* Ed. Jean Bernardi, *Grégoire de Nazianze: Discours 42–43.* SC 384. Paris: Éditions du Cerf, 1992.

Gregory of Nyssa [Greg. Nyss.]. *De beneficia* [*De ben.*]. Ed. A. van Heck, *Gregorii Nysseni opera*, vol. 9.1. Leiden: Brill, 1967.

———. *De vita Macrinae* [*v.Macr.*]. Ed. with French trans. Pierre Maraval, *Grégoire de Nysse. Vie de sainte Macrine*. SC 178. Paris: Éditions du Cerf, 1971.

———. *Encomium de XL martyribus* 1. PG 46: 749–72.

———. *In Basilium Fratrum* [*In Bas.*]. Ed. Günter Heil, Johannes P. Cavarnos, and Otto Lendle, *Gregorii Nysseni Sermones*, vol. 10.1. Leiden, New York: Brill 1990.

Gregory of Tours [Greg. Tur.]. *Historia Francorum* [*h. Franc.*]. Ed. Bruno Krusch and W. Levison, *Gregorii Turonensis opera* 1. Hannover: Hahn, 1966.

———. *Liber de gloria confessorum* [*Gloria conf.*]. Ed. Bruno Krusch, *Gregorii episcopi Turonensis miracula et opera minora*. Hannover: Hahnsche Buchhandlung, 1885.

Gregory the Monk [Greg. Mon.]. *Vita Lazari in monti Galesio* [*v.Lazari*]. Ed. Hippolyte Delehaye, *Acta Sanctorum (Novembris), Tomus III* (Brussels: Société des Bollandistes, 1910), 508–88. Trans. Richard P. H. Greenfield, *The Life of Lazaros of Mt. Galesion: An Eleventh-Century Pillar Saint*. Byzantine Saints' Lives in Translation 3. Washington, DC: Dumbarton Oaks Research Library, 2000.

Ḥenanishoʿ. *Book of Paradise*. See *Apophthegmata patrum*, Syriac Collection.

Hermas. *Pastor*. Ed. M. Whittaker, *Die apostolischen Väter I. Der Hirt des Hermas*. GCS 48, 2nd ed. Berlin: Akademie Verlag, 1967.

Historia monachorum in Aegypto [*HM*]. Greek version: Ed. André-Jean Festugière, *Historia monachorum in Aegypto*. SH 34. Brussels: Société des Bollandistes, 1961. Trans. Norman Russell, *The Lives of the Desert Fathers*. CS 34. Kalamazoo, MI: Cistercian Publications 1981.

———. Latin version: Ed. Eva Schulz-Flügel, *Tyrannius Rufinus. Historia monachorum sive De vita sanctorum patrum*. PTS 34. Berlin: Walter de Gruyter, 1990. Trans. Norman Russell, *The Lives of the Desert Fathers*. CS 34. Kalamazoo, MI: Cistercian Publications 1981.

Hippolytus of Rome, Pseudo-. *Traditio Apostolica*. Ed. Bernard Botte, *Hippolyte de Rome: La Tradition apostolique d'après les anciennes versions*, 2nd ed. SC 11. Paris: Éditions du Cerf, 1968.

Homilae Clementinae [*Hom. Clem.*]. Ed. Bernard Rehm, *Die Pseudoklementinen I: Homilien*. GCS 42. Berlin: Akademie Verlag, 1953.

Isaac of Antioch [Isaac Ant.]. *Sermons* [*serm.*]. Ed. Paul Bedjan, *Homiliae S. Isaaci Syri Antiocheni*. Leipzig: O. Harrassowitz, 1903. Also ed. Gustav Bickell, *S. Isaaci Antiocheni doctoris Syrorum opera omnia*. 2 vols. Geissen: J. Ricker, 1873–1877.

Isaac the Presbyter. *Life of Samuel of Kalamun*. Ed. and trans. Anthony Alcock, *The Life of Samuel of Kalamun by Isaac the Presbyter*. Warminster: Aris & Phillips, 1983.

Isaiah of Scetis [Isaiah Scet.]. *Asceticon* [*log.*] Ed. with French trans. René Draguet, *Les cinq recensions de l'Ascéticon syriaque d'Abba Isaïe*. Vol.1: *Les témoins et leurs parallèles non-syriaques. Édition des logoi I–XIII*. Vol. 2: *Version des logoi XIV–XXVI avec des parallèles grecs*. CSCO 289–93, Scriptores syri 120–22. Louvain: Secrétariat du CorpusSCO, 1968. Trans. John Chryssavgis and Pachomius Penkett, *Abba Isaiah of Scetis: Ascetic Discourses*. CS 150. Kalamazoo, MI: Cistercian Publications, 2002.

Ishoq of Antioch. See Isaac of Antioch.

Isidore of Pelusium [Isid. Pel.]. *Letters* [*ep.*]. PG 78: 177–1646. Also ed. with French trans. Pierre Évieux and Nicolas Vinel, *Isidore de Péluse: Lettres*. 3 vols. SC 422, 454, 586. Paris: Éditions du Cerf, 1997–2017.

Jacob of Serug [Jacob]. *Homily* [*hom.*] 22 ("On the Loaf for the Departed"). Ed. Paul Bedjan and Sebastian P. Brock in *Homilies of Mar Jacob of Sarug/Homiliae Selectae Mar-Jacobi Sarugensis,* vol. 1. Piscataway, NJ: Gorgias Press, 2006, 535–50. Trans. (prose) R. H. Connolly, *Downside Review* 29 (1910): 260–70. Trans. (verse) Holy Transfiguration Monastery, *The True Vine* 5 (1990): 41–53.

———. *On Symeon's Deeds.* Trans. Susan Ashbrook Harvey, "Jacob of Serug, *Homily on Simeon the Stylite.*" In Vincent L. Wimbush *Ascetic Behavior in Greco-Roman Antiquity,* Minneapolis, MN: Fortress Press, 1990.

Jerome. *Adversus Vigilantium* [*Vigil.*]. Ed. J. L. Feiertag. *Hieronymus: Adversus Vigilantium.* CCSL 79C. Turnhout: Brepols, 2005.

———. *Epistulae.* Ed. Isidor Hilberg and Margit Kamptner. *Sancti Eusebii Hieronymi Epistulae.* 3 vols. CSEL 54-56. Vienna: Österreichischen Akademie der Wissenschaften, 1996.

———. *Liber de viris illustribus* [*De vir. ill.*]. Ed. Ernest Cushing Richardson, *Hieronymus: Liber de viris illustribus.* TU 14. Leipzig: J. C. Hinrichs'sche, 1896.

———. *In Hiezechielem* [*In Hiezech.*]. Ed. Francisci Glorie, *S. Hieronymi Presbyteri Commentariorum in Hiezechielem libri xiv.* CCSL 75. Turnhout: Brepols, 1964.

———. *Vita Hilarionis* [*v.Hil.*]. PL 23: 29–60. Trans. Carolinne White, *Early Christian Lives.* London: Penguin, 1998.

John Cassian [Jo. Cassian]. *Collationes patrum xxvi* [*Coll.*]. Ed. with French trans. E. Pichery, *Jean Cassien: Conférences.* SC 42, 54, 64. Paris: Éditions du Cerf, 1955–1959. Trans. Boniface Ramsay, *John Cassian: The Conferences.* ACW 57. New York: Paulist Press, 1997.

———. *De institutis coenobiorum et de octo principalium vitiorum remediis libri xii* [*Inst.*]. Ed. with French trans. Jean-Claude Guy, *Jean Cassien: Institutions cénobitiques.* SC 109. Paris: Éditions du Cerf, 1965. Trans. Boniface Ramsay, *John Cassian: The Institutes.* ACW 58. New York: Paulist Press, 2000.

John Chrysostom [Chrys.]. *Ad Demetrium monachum de compunctione* [*compunct.*]. PG 47: 393–410.

———. *Ad Stagirium ascetam a daemone vexatum* [*Stag.*]. PG 47: 423–94.

———. *Contra Anomoeos* [*anom.*]. PG 48: 701–812.

———. *De Anna.* PG 54: 631–74.

———. *De eleemosyna homilia* [*De eleem.*]. PG 51: 261–72.

———. *De Lazaro et divite homiliae* [*Laz. et div.*]. PG 48: 963–1054. Trans. C. P. Roth, *St. John Chrysostom: On Wealth and Poverty.* Crestwood NY: St. Vladimir's Seminary Press.

———. *De mutatione nominum homiliae* [*mut. nom.*]. PG 51: 113–55.

———. *De poenitentis homiliae* [*poen.*]. PG 49: 277–350.

———. *De sacerdotio* [*sacer.*]. PG 48: 624–700.

———. *De statuis homiliae.* [*stat.*]. PG 49: 15–222.

———. *Epistulae* [*ep.*]. PG 52: 454–98.

———. *In Acta Apostolorum homiliae* [*In Act.*]. PG 60: 13–384.

———. *In dictum Pauli oportet haereses esse homilia* [*In dict. Pauli*]. PG 51: 251–59.

———. *In Epistulam ad Colossenses homiliae* [*In Col.*]. PG 62: 299–390.

———. *In Epistulas ad Corinthios homiliae* [*In Cor.*]. PG 61: 299–392.

———. *In Epistulam ad Ephesios homiliae* [*In Eph.*]. PG 62: 11–176.

———. *In Epistulam ad Galatas homiliae* [*In Gal.*]. PG 61: 611–80.

———. *In Epistulam ad Hebraeos homiliae* [*In Heb.*]. PG 63: 9–236.

————. *In Epistulam ad Philipenses homiliae* [*In Phil.*]. PG 62: 117–298.

————. *In Epistulam ad Romanos homiliae* [*In Rom.*]. PG 60: 583–680.

————. *In Epistulas ad Thessalonicenses homiliae* [*In Thess.*]. PG 62: 391–500.

————. *In Epistulam 1 ad Timotheum homiliae* [*In 1 Tim.*]. PG 62: 501–98.

————. *In Epistulam 2 ad Timotheum homiliae* [*In 2 Tim.*]. PG 62: 599–662.

————. *In Epistulam ad Titum homiliae* [*In Tit.*]. PG 62: 663–700.

————. *In Genesim homiliae* [*In Gen.*]. PG 53: 23–385, PG 54: 385–630. Also ed. with French trans. Laurence Brottier, *Jean Chrysostome: Sermons sur la Genèse.* SC 433. Paris: Éditions du Cerf, 1998. Trans. Robert C. Hill, *Saint John Chrysostom: Homilies on Genesis.* 3 vols. Fathers of the Church 74, 82, 87. Washington, DC: Catholic University of America, 1985, 1990, 1992.

————. *In illud: Salutate Priscillam et Aquilam homiliae* [*salut.*]. PG 51: 187–208.

————. *In illud: vidua eligatur homilia* [*vid. eligatur*]. PG 51: 321–38.

————. *In Johannem homiliae* [*In Jo.*]. PG 59: 23–482.

————. *In Matthaeum homiliae* [*In Mt.*]. PG 57: 21–472; 58: 473–794.

John Climacus [Jo. Clim.]. *Scala paradise* [*scal.*]. PG 88: 632–1161. Trans. Colm Luibheid and Norman Russell, *John Climacus: The Ladder of Divine Ascent.* Mahwah, NJ: Paulist Press, 1982.

John Lydus [Jo. Lyd.]. *De magistratibus reipublicae Romanae* [*De mag.*]. Ed. Jacques Schamp, *Jean le Lydian: Des Magistratures de l'État Romain.* 3 vols. Paris: Les Belles Lettres, 2006. Trans. Anastasius C. Bandy, *On Powers or The Magistracies of the Roman State (De Magistratibus Reipublicae Romanae).* Lewiston, NY: Edwin Mellen Press.

John Malalas [Jo. Mal.]. *Chronographia* [*Chron.*]. Ed. Ludwig Dindorf, *Ioannis Malalae Chronographia.* Bonn: Weber, 1831. Trans. Elizabeth Jeffreys, Michael Jeffreys and Roger Scott, *The Chronicle of John Malalas.* Byzantina Australiensia 4. Melbourne: Australian Association for Byzantine Studies, 1986.

John the Monk [Jo. Mon.]. *Vita Eusebii Alexandriae* [*v.Eus.Alex.*]. PG 86.1: 297–309.

John Moschus [Jo. Mosch.]. *Pratum spirituale* [*prat.*]. PG 87.3: 2852–3112; Theodor Nissen, "Unbekannte Erzählungen aus dem Pratum Spirituale," *Byzantinische Zeitschrift* 38 (1938): 354–72; Elpidio Mioni, "Il Pratum Spirituale di Giovanni Mosco," *OCP* 17 (1951): 83–94. Trans. John Wortley, *The Spiritual Meadow (Pratum spirituale) by John Moschus.* CS 139. Kalamazoo, MI: Cistercian Publications, 1992.

John of Ephesus [Jo. Eph.]. *Commentarii de beatibus orientalibus* [*v.SS.Or.*]. Ed. and trans. E. W. Brooks, *John of Ephesus: Lives of the Eastern Saints.* PO 17: 1–304 (= *vitae* 1–23). Paris: Firmin-Didot, 1923. PO 18: 513–697 (= *vitae* 24–49). Firmin-Didot, 1924. PO 19: 153–227 (= *vitae* 50–58). Paris: Firmin-Didot, 1926.

————. *Historia ecclesiastica* [*HE*]. Ed. with Latin trans. E. W. Brooks, *Iohannis Ephesini Historiae ecclesiasticae pars tertia,* 2 vols. CSCO 105–6, Scriptores syri 3.3. Louvain: Peeters, 1935–1936. Also trans. R. Payne Smith, *The Third Part of the Ecclesiastical History of John Bishop of Ephesus.* Oxford: Oxford University Press, 1860.

John of Nikiû. *Chronicle* [*Chron.*]. Ed. and trans. R. H. Charles, *The Chronicle of John, Bishop of Nikiu, translated from Zotenberg's Ethiopic Text.* London: Norgate, 1916.

John of Tella. *Canons of Jōḥannān Bar Qursos.* [*canons.*]. Ed. and trans. Arthur Vööbus, *The Synodicon in the West Syrian Tradition* CSCO 367–68, Scriptores syri 161–62. Louvain: Secrétariat du CorpusSCO, 1975.

John Rufus [Jo. Ruf.]. *Life of Peter the Iberian* [*v.Petr.Ib.*]. Ed. and trans. Cornelia B. Horn and Robert R. Phenix Jr., *John Rufus: The Lives of Peter the Iberian, Theodosius of Jerusalem, and the Monk Romanus.* Writings from the Greco-Roman World 24. Atlanta: Society of Biblical Literature, 2008.

———. *Plerophoriae.* Ed. with French trans. François Nau, *Plérophories: Témoignages et révélations contre le Concile de Chalcédon.* PO 8: 1–208. Paris: Firmin-Didot, 1912.

Joshua the Stylite, Pseudo- [Joshua, Ps.-]. *Chronicle* [*Chron.*]. Ed. and trans. William Wright, *The Chronicle of Pseudo-Joshua the Stylite, Composed in Syriac, AD 507.* Cambridge: Cambridge University Press, 1882. Also trans. Frank R. Trombley and John W. Watt, *The Chronicle of Pseudo-Joshua the Stylite.* TTH 32. Liverpool: Liverpool University Press, 2000.

Julian, Emperor. *Epistulae.* Ed. and trans. W. Wright, *The Works of the Emperor Julian,* vols. 2–3. LCL 29, 157. Cambridge, MA: Harvard University Press, 1959, 1980. French trans. J. Bidez, G. Rochefort, and C. Lacombrade, *L'empereur Julien: Œuvres complètes,* vol. 2. Paris: Les Belles Lettres, 2004. Italian trans. and commentary in Caltabiano 1991.

Justinian, Emperor [Just.]. See *Corpus iuris civilis.*

Leontius of Constantinople [Leont. Const.]. *Homilies.* Ed. and trans. Cornelis Datema and Pauline Allen, *Leontii Presbyteri Constantinopolitani homiliae.* CCSG 17. Turnhout: Brepols, 1987. *Leontius, Presbyter of Constantinople: Fourteen Homilies.* Byzantina Australiensa 9. Brisbane: Australian Association for Byzantine Studies, 1991.

Leontius of Neapolis [Leont. Neap.]. *Vita Johannis Eleemosynarii* [*v.Jo.Eleem.*]. Ed. with French trans. André-Jean Festugière and Lennart Rydén, *Léontios de Néapolis: Vie de Syméon le Fou et Vie de Jean de Chypre.* Paris: Geuthner, 1974, 343–409. Trans. (partial) Elizabeth Dawes and Norman H. Baynes, *Three Byzantine Saints: Contemporary Biographies translated from the Greek.* Crestwood, NY: St. Vladimir's Press, 1996.

———. *Vita Symeonis Sali* [*v.Sym.*]. Ed. with French trans. André-Jean Festugière and Lennart Rydén, *Léontios de Néapolis: Vie de Syméon le Fou et Vie de Jean de Chypre.* Paris: Geuthner, 1974, 53–104. Trans. Derek Krueger, *Symeon the Holy Fool: Leontius's Life and the Late Antique City.* TCH 25. Berkeley: University of California Press, 1996.

La version Arabe des 127 Canons des Apôtres. Ed. with French trans. Jean Périer and Augustin Périer. PO 8: 553–710. Paris: Firmin-Didot, 1912.

Libanius [Lib.]. *Epistulae.* Ed. and trans. Albert F. Norman, *Libanius: Autobiography and Selected Letters.* LCL 478, 479. Cambridge: Harvard University Press, 1992.

———. *Oratio* [*or.*] 7. Ed. Richard Foerster, *Libanii opera,* vol. 1.2. Leipzig: Teubner, 1903; repr. Hildesheim: Georg Olms, 1998.

———. *Oratio* [*or.*] 11. Ed. Richard Foerster, *Libanii opera,* vol. 1.2. Leipzig: Teubner, 1903; repr. Hildesheim: Georg Olms, 1998.

———. *Oratio* [*or.*] 30. Ed. Robert Foerster and trans. Albert F. Norman, *Libanius: Selected Orations,* vol. 2. LCL 452. Cambridge: Harvard University Press, 1977.

Life of John the Little. Trans. M. S. Mikhail and Timothy Vivian, "The Life of St. John the Little: An Encomium by Zacharias of Sakha." *Coptic Church Review* 18.1–2 (1997): 17–64.

Life of Longinus [*v.Longini*]. Trans. Timothy Vivian, "Humility and Resistance in Late Antique Egypt: The *Life of Longinus.*" *Coptic Church Review* 20 (1999): 2–30.

Life of Macarius of Alexandria. Trans. Timothy Vivian, *Four Desert Fathers: Pambo, Evagrius, Macarius of Egypt, and Macarius of Alexandria: Coptic Texts Relating to the* Lausiac History *of Palladius.* Crestwood, NY: St. Vladimir's Press, 2004.

Life of Macarius of Scetis. Trans. Timothy Vivian, *Saint Macarius the Spiritbearer: Coptic Texts Relating to Saint Macarius the Great.* Crestwood, NY: St. Vladimir's Press, 2004.

Life of Matthew the Poor. Ed. with French trans. Émile Amélineau, *Monuments pour servir à l'histoire de l'Égypte chrétienne au IVe, V^e, VIe, et VIIe siècles.* Mission Archéologique Française au Caire 4.2. Paris: Leroux, 1895, 707–36.

Life of Pachomius. See *Vita Pachomii.*

Life of Pambo. Ed. Gabriel Bunge and Adalbert de Vogüé, *Quatre ermites égyptiens: d'après les fragments coptes de l'Histoire Lausiaque.* Spiritualité Orientale 60. Bégrolles-en-Mauges: Bellefontaine, 1994. Trans. Timothy Vivian, *Four Desert Fathers: Pambo, Evagrius, Macarius of Egypt, and Macarius of Alexandria: Coptic Texts Relating to the Lausiac History of Palladius.* Crestwood, NY: St. Vladimir's Press, 2004.

Life of Rabban Hormizd. Ed. and trans. Ernest Alfred Wallis Budge, *The Histories of Rabban Hormizd and Rabban Bar-Idta.* 2 vols. London: Luzac, 1902; repr. New York: AMS Press, 1976.

Life of Symeon Stylites the Elder. See Symeon Bar-Eupolemos and Bar-Ḥaṭar.

Life of Theoduta of Amid. Ed. Andrew Palmer, unpublished manuscript.

Lucian. *De dea Syria.* Ed. and trans. Harold W. Attridge and Robert A. Oden, *The Syrian Goddess (De Dea Syria) Attributed to Lucian.* Missoula, MT: Scholar's Press, 1976.

———. *De morte Peregrini [De mort. Peregrin.].* Ed. and trans. A. M. Harmon, *The Works of Lucian.* Vol. 5. LCL 302. Cambridge, MA: Harvard University Press, 1936.

———. *Timon.* Ed. M. D. Macleod, *Luciani opera,* vol. 1. Oxford: Clarendon Press, 1972, 310–36.

The Man of God of Edessa. Ed. with French trans. Arthur Amiaud, *La légende syriaque de Saint Alexis l'homme de Dieu.* Bibliothèque de l'École des Hautes Études, Sciences Philologiques et Historiques 79. Paris: F. Vieweg, 1889. Trans. Robert Doran, *Stewards of the Poor: The Man of God, Rabbula, and Hiba in Fifth-Century Edessa.* CS 208. Kalamazoo, MI: Cistercian Publications, 2006.

Marcus Aurelius. *Meditationes [Med.].* Ed. J. H. Leopold. Oxford: Clarendon Press, 1908.

Mark the Deacon [Marc. Diac.]. *Vita Porphyrii Gazensis [v.Porph.].* Ed. Henri Grégoire and M.-A. Kugener, *Marc le Diacre, Vie de Porphyre, Évêque de Gaza.* Paris: Les Belles Lettres, 1930.

Mark the Monk. *De paenitenia [paen.].* Ed. Georges-Matthieu De Durand, *Marc le Moine: Traités I.* SC 445. Paris: Éditions du Cerf, 1999, 203–59. Trans. Timothy Vivian, *Mark the Monk: Counsels on the Spiritual Life.* PPS 37. Crestwood, NY: St Vladimir's Press, 2009.

Martyrius of Antioch, Pseudo-. *Oratio funebris in laudem sancti Iohannis Chrysostomi [or. fun.].* Ed. M. Wallraff, *Oratio funebris in laudem sancti Iohannis Chrysostomi: Epitaffio attribuito a Martirio di Antiochia (BHG 871, CPG 6517).* Quaderni della Rivista di Bizantinistica 12. Spoleto: Fondazione Centro italiano di studi sull'alto medioevo, 2007. Trans. Timothy D. Barnes and George Bevan, *Funerary Speech for John Chrysostom.* TTH 60. Liverpool: Liverpool University Press, 2013.

Marutha of Mayperqaṭ. *Canones. The So-Called Canons of Marūtā.* Ed. and trans. Arthur Vööbus, *Syriac and Arabic Documents Regarding Legislation Relative to Syrian Asceticism.* PapETSE 11. Stockholm, 1960.

Maximus Confessor [Max.]. *Capitum de caritate quattor centuriae [carit.].* Ed. Aldo Ceresa-Gastaldo, *Massimo Confessore: Capitoli sulla carità.* Verba Seniorum Collana di testi e studi pastristici n.s. 3. Rome: Editrice Studium, 1963. Trans. Polycarp Sherwood, *St.*

Maximus the Confessor: The Ascetic Life, The Four Centuries on Charity. ACW 21. New York and Mahwah, NJ: Newman Press, 1955.

———. *Liber Asceticus* [*ascet.*]. Ed. Peter Van Deun, *Maximi Confessoris Liber Asceticus.* CCSG 40. Turnhout: Brepols, 2000. Trans. Polycarp Sherwood, *St. Maximus the Confessor: The Ascetic Life, The Four Centuries on Charity.* ACW 21. New York and Mahwah, NJ: Newman Press, 1955.

Menander of Laodicaea (Rhetor). *Peri Epideiktikōn.* Ed. and trans. D. A. Russell and N. G. Wilson, *Menander Rhetor.* Oxford: Clarendon Press, 1981.

Nestorius [Nestor.]. *Liber Heraclidis.* Ed. Paul Bedjan, *Nestorius, Le livre de Héraclide de Damas.* Leipzig: O. Harrassowitz, 1910. Trans. G. R. Driver and L. Hodgson, *Nestorius: Bazaar of Heracleides, Newly Translated from the Syriac and Edited with an Introduction* [*Bazaar*]. Oxford: Clarendon Press, 1925.

Nicetas. *Vita Philareti Misericordis* [*v.Phil.Mis.*]. Ed. and trans. Lennart Rydén, *The Life of St Philaretos the Merciful Written by His Grandson Niketas.* Studia Byzantina Upsalensia 8. Uppsala: Uppsala University Library, 2002.

Nilus of Ancyra [Nilus]. *Ad Magnam de voluntaria paupertate* [*De vol. paup.*]. PG 79: 968–1060.

———. *De monastica exercitatione* [*De mon. ex.*]. PG 79: 719–810.

———. *Epistulae* [*ep.*]. PG 79: 81–582.

Nilus, Pseudo- [Nilus, Ps.-]. *Narrationes* [*Narr.*]. Ed. Fabricio Conca, *Nilus Ancyranus Narratio.* Leipzig: Teubner, 1983. Trans. Caner 2010: 84–140.

Novum Testamentum. *The Greek New Testament.* Ed. Kurt Aland, Matthew Black, Carlo Martini, Bruce Metzger, and Allen Wikgren. 3rd ed. Stuttgart: Biblia-Druck, 1983.

O.Amst. Ed. and trans. Roger S. Bagnall, Petra J. Sijpesteijn, and K. A. Worp, *Ostraka in Amsterdam Collections.* Zutphen: Terra, 1976.

O.Brit.Mus.copt. Ed. Harry R. Hall, *Coptic and Greek Texts of the Christian Period from Ostraka, Stelae, etc., in the British Museum.* London: British Museum, 1905.

Origen of Alexandria [Orig.]. *Fragmenta ex commentariis in Mattheum* [*Comm. in Mt.*]. PG 13: 835–1600. Also ed. Erich Klosterman and Ernst Benz, *Origenes* Werke 12.1: *Origenes Matthäuserklärung* 3. GCS 41. Leipzig: Hinrichs, 1941.

———. *Fragmenta in Psalmis* [*fr. in Ps.*]. PG 12: 1053–86. Also ed. René Cadiou, *Commentaires inédits sur les Psaumes.* Paris: Les Belles Lettres, 1936.

P.Bal. Ed. Paul E. Kahle, *Bala'izah: Coptic Texts from Deir El-Bala'izah in Upper Egypt,* 2 vols. Oxford: Oxford University Press, 1954.

P.Cairo Masp. Ed. Jean Maspero, *Papyrus grecs d'époque byzantine, Catalogue général des antiquités égyptiennes du Musée du Caire.* 3 vols. Cairo: Institut Français d'Archeologie Orientale, 1911–16.

P.Köln. Ed. B. Kramer, R. Hübner, and others, *Kölner Papyri.* Opladen: Westdeutscher Verlag, 1976–.

P.Lond. Ed. and trans. Harold Iris Bell, *Jews and Christians in Egypt: The Jewish Troubles in Alexandria and the Athanasian Controversy.* Westport, CT: Greenwood Press, 1972.

P.Misc.inv. II 98a. Ed. and trans. Nikolaos Gonis, "Further Letters from the Archives of Apa Ioannes." *Bulletin of the American Society of Papyrology* 45 (2008): 77–80.

P.Münch. Ed. August Heisenberg, Leopold Wenger and others, *Die Papyri der Bayerischen Staatsbibliothek München.* 3 vols. Stuttgart: Teubner, 1986.

P.Neph. Ed. with German trans. Bärbel Kramer, John C. Shelton, and Gerald M. Browne, *Das Archiv des Nepheros und verwandte Texte.* Vol. 1: *Papyri aus der Trierer und der Heidelberger Papyrussammlung.* Aegyptiaca Treverensia 4. Mainz am Rhein: P. von Zabern, 1987.

P.Ness. III. Ed. and trans. Charles Kraemer, *Excavations at Nessana.* Vol. 3: *Non-Literary Papyri.* Princeton, NJ: Princeton University Press, 1958.

P.Oxy. Ed. and trans. B. P. Grenfell, A. S. Hunt, and others, *The Oxyrhynchus Papyri.* London: Egyptian Exploration Society, 1898–.

Pachomius. *Praecepta et Instituta* [*prec.*]. Trans. Armand Veilleux, *Pachomian Koinonia.* Vol. 3: *Instructions, Letters and Other Writings of Saint Pachomius and His Disciples.* CS 47. Kalamazoo, MI: Cistercian Publications, 1989.

———. *Rules.* Trans. Armand Veilleux, *Pachomian Koinonia.* Vol. 2: *Pachomian Chronicles and Rules.* CS 46. Kalamazoo, MI: Cistercian Publications, 1981.

Palladius [Pall.]. *Dialogus de vita Iohannis Chrysostomi* [*Dial.*]. Ed. with French trans. Anne-Marie Malingrey and Philippe Leclercq, *Palladios: Dialogue sur la vie de Jean Chrysostome.* SC 341, 342. Paris: Éditions du Cerf, 1988. Trans. Robert T. Meyer, *Palladius: Dialogue on the Life of St. John Chrysostom.* ACW 45. New York: Newman Press, 1985.

———. *Historia Lausica* [*HL*]. Ed. G. J. M. Bartelink, *Palladio: La storia Lausiaca.* Vite dei santi 2. Milan: Fondazione Lorenzo Valla, 1974. Trans. Robert T. Mayer, *Palladius: The Lausiac History.* ACW 34. Westminster: Newman Press, 1965.

Panegyric for Rabbula [*Pan. Rabb.*]. Ed. J. J. Overbeck, *S. Ephraemi Syri, Rabulae episcopi Edesseni, Balaei aliorumque Opera selecta.* Oxford: Clarendon Press, 1865. Trans. Robert Doran, *Stewards of the Poor: The Man of God, Rabbula, and Hiba in Fifth-Century Edessa.* CS 208. Kalamazoo, MI: Cistercian Publications, 2006.

Paphnutius [Paph.]. *Historiae monachorum* [*HM*]. Trans. Timothy Vivian, *Paphnutius: Histories of the Monks of Upper Egypt.* CS 140. Kalamazoo, MI: Cistercian Publications, 1993.

Paralipomena [*Paralip.*]. Ed. François Halkin, *Sancti Pachomii vitae graecae.* SH 19. Brussels: Société des Bollandistes, 1932, 122–65. Trans. Armand Veilleux, *Pachomian Koinonia,* vol. 2: *Pachomian Chronicles and Rules.* CS 46; Kalamazoo, MI: Cistercian Publications, 1981.

Paul of Elusa [Paul Elus.]. *Vita Theognii* [*v. Thgn.*]. Ed. J. Van den Gheyn, "Acta Sancti Theogni," *AB* 10 (1892): 73–113. Trans. Timothy Vivian, *Journeying into God: Seven Early Monastic Lives.* Minneapolis: Fortress Press, 1996.

Paul the Silentiary [Paul Sil.]. *Descriptio Sanctae Sophiae* [*Soph.*]. Ed. Claudio De Stefani, *Paulus Silentiarus. Descriptio Sanctae Sophiae; Descriptio Ambonis.* Bibliotheca scriptorum Graecorum et Romanorum Teubneriana 2009. Berlin: De Gruyter, 2011.

Peter of Alexandria, Pseudo-. *On Riches.* Ed. and trans. Birger Pearson and Timothy Vivian, *Two Coptic Homilies Attributed to Saint Peter of Alexandria: On Riches, On the Epiphany.* Rome: C. I. M., 1993.

Philostratus. *Epistulae et dialexeis* [*Ep. et dial.*]. Ed. C. L. Kayser, *Flavii Philostrati opera,* vol. 2. Leipzig: Teubner, 1871; repr. Hildesheim: Olms, 1964.

Philoxenus of Mabbug [Philox.]. *Asceticon* [*Asc.*]. Ed. and trans. Ernst A. Wallis Budge, *The Discourses of Philoxenus, Bishop of Mabbôgh, A.D. 485–519.* 2 vols. London: Asher, 1894. Trans. Robert A. Kitchen, *The Discourses of Philoxenos of Mabbug: A New Translation and Introduction.* CS 235. Kalamazoo, MI: Cistercian Publications, 2013.

————. *Ep. de vita monastica* [*ep. de vita mon.*]. Ed. François Graffin, "La Lettre de Phi-loxène de Mabboug à un supérieur de monastère sur la vie monastique." *L'Orient syrien* 6–7 (1961–1962): 317–52, 455–86, 77–102.

————. *Rules.* Ed. and trans. Arthur Vööbus, *Syriac and Arabic Documents Regarding Legislation Relative to Syrian Asceticism.* PapETSE 11. Stockholm, 1960.

Piacenza Pilgrim [Plac.]. *Itinerarium* [*Itin.*]. Ed. P. Greyer in *Itineraria et alia geographica.* CCSL 175. Turnhout: Brepols, 1965, 129–53 (= Recension I), 158–74 (= Recension II). Also ed. Celestina Milani, *Itinerarium Antonini Placentini: Un viaggio in Terra Sancta del 560–570 d.c.* Pubblicazioni della Università cattolica del Sacro Cuore Scienze filologiche e letteratura 7. Milan: Vita e pensiero, 1977. Trans. John Wilkinson, *Jerusalem Pilgrims Before the Crusades.* 3rd ed. Warminster: Aris & Phillips, 2002.

Procopius of Caesarea [Proc. Caes.]. *Anecdota* [*HA*]. Text and trans. H. B. Dewing, *Procopius: The Anecdota or Secret History.* LCL 290. Cambridge, MA: Harvard University Press, 1935.

————. *De Aedificiis* [*Aed.*]. Text and trans. H. B. Dewing and Glanville Downey, *Procopius: On Buildings.* LCL 343. Cambridge, MA: Harvard University Press, 1940.

Pseudo-Basil of Caesarea [Ps.-Bas. Caes.]. *Poenae in monachos delinquentes* [*Poen. mon.*]. PG 31: 1305–20.

Pseudo-Dionysius the Areopagite. See Dionysius the Areopagite, Pseudo-.

Pseudo-Martyrius of Antioch. See Martyrius of Antioch, Pseudo-.

PSI. Ed. with Italian trans. Girolamo Vitelli and M. Norsa, *Papiri greci e latini.* 14 vols. Pubblicazioni della Società Italiana per la ricerca dei Papiri greci. Florence: G. Vitelli, 1912–1957.

Rabbula of Edessa. *Rules for Monks*; *Rules for Clergy and the Bnay Qyāmā.* Ed. and trans. Arthur Vööbus, *Syriac and Arabic Documents Regarding Legislation Relative to Syrian Asceticism.* PapETSE 11. Stockholm, 1960.

Regula magistri [*reg.mag.*]. Ed. with French trans. Adalbert de Vogüé, *Le Règle du Maître.* SC 105, 106, 107. Paris: Éditions du Cerf, 1964–1965. Trans. Luke Eberle, *The Rule of the Master.* CS 6. Kalamazoo, MI: Cistercian Publications, 1977.

Regulations of Horsiesios [*reg. Hors.*]. Ed. Louis-Théophile Lefort, *Oeuvres de s. Pachôme et ses disciples.* CSCO 159–60, Scriptores coptici 23–24. Louvain: Durbecq, 1956. Trans. Armand Veilleux, *Pachomian Koinonia,* vol. 2: *Pachomian Chronicles and Rules.* CS 46. Kalamazoo, MI: Cistercian Publications 1981.

Rules of Saba [*reg. Sab.*]. Ed. Eduard Kurtz, "Review of A. Dmitrijevskij, *Die Klosterreglen des hl. Sabas.*" *Byzantinische Zeitschrift* 3 (1894): 168–70. Trans. Leah di Segni in Patrich 1995: 274–75.

SB. Ed. Friedrich Preisigke, Friedrich Bilabel, et al., *Sammelbuch griechischer Urkunden aus Aegypten.* 11 vols. Strassburg: Trübner, 1915–1926, Heidelberg, 1931–1955; Wiesbaden: O. Harrassowitz, 1958–.

Seneca the Younger. *De beneficiis* [*Ben.*]. Ed. and trans. John W. Basore, *Seneca: Moral Essays.* Vol. 3: *De Beneficiis.* LCL 310. Cambridge, MA: Harvard University Press, 1935.

Sefer Ha-Aggadah. Ed. Hayim Nahman Bialik and Yehoshua Hana Ravnitzky, *The Book of Legends (Sefer Ha-Aggadah): Legends from the Talmud and Midrash,* trans. William G. Braude. New York: Schocken Books, 1992.

Severus of Antioch [Sev. Ant.]. *Cathedral Homilies* [*Hom. cath.*]. Ed. with French trans. Rubens Duval, *Les Homiliae Cathedrales de Sévère d'Antioche, version syriaque de Jacques d'Édesse* (*Hom. LII à LVII*), PO 4: 7–94. Paris: Firmin-Didot 1906; Maurice Brière, (*Hom. LVII à LXIX*), PO 8: 213–94. Paris: Firmin-Didot 1912; Maurice Brière, (*Hom. LXX à LXXVI*). PO 12: 5–146. Paris: Firmin-Didot, 1919; M.-A. Krugener and Edg. Triffaux, (*Hom. LXXVII*). PO 16: 767–862. Paris: Firmin-Didot, 1922; Maurice Brière, (*Hom. LXXVIII à LXXXIII*). PO 20: 7–163. Paris: Firmin-Didot, 1929; Ignazio Guidi, (*Hom. XCIX à CIII*). PO 22: 207–302. Paris: Firmin-Didot, 1930; Maurice Brière, (*Hom. LXXXIV à XC*). PO 23: 7–165. Paris: Firmin-Didot, 1932; Maurice Brière, (*Hom. XCI à XCVIII*). PO 25: 7–163. Paris: Firmin-Didot, 1943; Maurice Brière, (*Hom. CXIII à CIXX*). PO 26: 265–439. Paris: Firmin-Didot, 1948; Maurice Brière, (*Hom. CXX à CXXV*). PO 29: 74–258. Paris: Firmin-Didot, 1960.

———. *Epistulae, coll.1* [*ep.Coll.1*]. Ed. and trans. E. W. Brooks, *The Sixth Book of the Select Letters of Severus*, 2 vols. London: Williams and Norgate, 1902–1904.

———. *Epistulae, coll.2* [*ep.Coll.2*]. Ed. and trans. E. W. Brooks, *A Collection of Letters of Severus of Antioch from Numerous Syriac Manuscripts*. PO 12: 175–342. Paris: Firmin-Didot, 1919. PO 14: 3–309, Paris: Firmin-Didot, 1920.

———. *Hymns*. Ed. and trans. E. W. Brooks, *The Hymns of Severus of Antioch and Others in the Syriac Version of Paul of Edessa as Revised by James of Edessa*. PO 6: 9–179; 7: 595–802. Paris: Firmin-Didot, 1911.

Shenoute of Atripe. "A Piece of Shenoutiana from the Department of Egyptian Antiquities (EA 71005)." Ed. and trans. Heike Behlmer and Anthony Alcock. *British Museum Occasional Paper* 119. London: British Museum, 1996.

———. *De vita monachorum, i–xxvi* [*De vita mon.*]. Ed. Johannes Leipoldt, trans. Hermann Wiesmann. *Sinuthii Archimandritae vita et opera omnia*, vol. 4. CSCO 73; Scriptores coptici 5. Leuven: Brepols, 1936, repr. 1954.

———. "Michigan 158,20." Ed. and trans. Dwight Wayne Young, *Coptic Manuscripts from the White Monastery: Works of Shenute*. Mitteilungen aus der Papyrussammlung der österreichischen Nationalbibliothek 22. Vienna: Hollinek, 1993.

Socrates Scholasticus [Soc.]. *Historia ecclesiastica* [*HE*]. Ed. Günther Christian Hansen, *Sokrates Kirchengeschichte*. GCS n.F.1. Berlin: Akademie Verlag, 1995. Trans. A. C. Zenos, *The Ecclesiastical History of Socrates*. NPNF 2. 2nd series. Grand Rapids, MI: Eerdmans, 1989.

Sophronius of Jerusalem [Sophron.]. *Miracula* [*mir.*]. Ed. with French trans. Jean Gascou, *Sophrone de Jérusalem: Miracles des saints Cyr et Jean (BHG I 477–479)*. Collections de l'Université Marc-Bloch-Strasbourg. Études d'archéologie et d'histoire ancienne. Paris: De Boccard, 2006.

———. *Vita Mariae Aegyptiacae* [*v.Mar.Aeg.*]. PG 87.3: 3697–3726. Trans. Maria Kouli in Alice-Mary Talbot, ed., *Holy Women of Byzantium: Ten Saints' Lives in English Translation*. Byzantine Saints' Lives in Translation 1. Washington, DC: Dumbarton Oaks Research Library and Collection.

Sophronius of Jerusalem and John Moschus, Pseudo-. [Sophron. et Mosch., Ps.-] *Vita Johannis Eleemosynarii* [*v.Jo.Eleem.*]. Ed. Hippolyte Delehaye, "Une Vie inédite de Saint Jean l'Aumonier." *AB* 45 (1927): 5–74. Trans. Elizabeth Dawes and Norman H. Baynes,

Three Byzantine Saints: Contemporary Biographies Translated from the Greek. Crestwood, NY: St. Vladimir's Press, 1996.

Sozomen Scholasticus [Soz.]. *Historia ecclesiastica* [*HE*]. Ed. Joseph Bidez, rev. Günther Christian Hansen, *Sozomenus Kirchengeschichte*. GCS n.F.4. Berlin: Akademie Verlag, 1995. Trans. Chester D. Hartnaft, *The Ecclesiastical History of Sozomen*. NPNF 2. 2nd series. Grand Rapids, MI: Eerdmans, 1989.

Symeon Bar-Eupolemos and Bar-Ḥaṭar. *Vita Symeonis Stylitae senioris syriaca* (Vatican Syriac MS 160, ff.1–79) [*v.Sym.Styl.*]. Ed. Stefano Evodio Assemani, *Acta sanctorum martyrum orientalium et occidentalium, pars II: Acta S. Simeonis Stylitae*. Rome: Collini, 1748. Trans. Robert Doran, *The Lives of Symeon Stylites*. CS 112. Kalamazoo, MI: Cistercian Publications, 1992.

Symeon Stylites the Younger [Sym. Cion.]. *Homilies*. Ed. with Latin trans. Angelo Mai and Giuseppe Cozza-Lupi, *Novae patrum bibliothecae* 8. Rome: Spithoever, 1871: 1–156.

Synod of Jésuyahb I. Ed. with French trans. Jacques-Baptist Chabot, *Synodicon Orientale ou recueil des synodes nestoriens*. Paris: Imprimerie Nationale, 1902, 130–96, 390–455.

Testamentum Domini nostri Jesu Christi [*Test. Domini*]. Ed. Ignatius Ephraem II Rahmani. Mainz: F. Kirchheim, 1899.

Testamentum Iobi [*Test. Iobi*]. Ed. Sebastian P. Brock, *Testamentum Iobi*. Pseudepigrapha Veteris Testamenti Graece 2. Leiden: Brill 1967.

Themistius. *Orationes* [*or.*]. Ed. Heinrich Schenkl, Granville Downey, and Arthur F. Norman, *Themistii orationes quae supersunt*. 3 vols. Leipzig: Teubner, 1965–1974. Trans. Peter Heather and David Moncur, *Politics, Philosophy, and Empire in the Fourth Century*. TTH 36. Liverpool: Liverpool University Press 2001. (Cf. Penella, *Private Orations of Themistius*, 2000.)

Theodore Lector [Thdr. Lect.]. *Historia ecclesiastica* [*HE*]. Ed. Günther Christian Hansen, *Theodoros Anagnostes Kirchengeschichte*. GCS n.F. 3 Berlin: Akademie Verlag, 1995.

Theodore of Paphos [Thdr. Paph.]. *Vita Spyridonis* [*v.Spyr.*]. Ed. Paul Van den Ven, *La légend de S. Spyridon, Évêque de Trimithonte*. Bibliothèque de Muséon 33. Louvain: Publications universitaires, 1953.

Theodore of Petra [Thdr. Petr.]. *Vita Theodosii coenobiarchae* [*v.Thds.*]. Ed. Hermann Usener, *Der heilige Theodosios. Schriften des Theodoros und Kyrillos*. Leipzig: Teubner, 1890.

Theodoret of Cyrrhus [Thdt.]. *Commentarius in omnes sancti Pauli Epistolas* [*Interp. in ep. Pauli*]. PG 81: 31–878.

———. *De providentia* [*prov.*]. PG 83: 355–774.

———. *Epistulae*. Ed. with French trans. Yvan Azéma. *Théodoret de Cyr: Correspondance*. 4 Vols. SC 40, 98, 111, 429. Paris: Éditions du Cerf, 1976, 1998.

———. *Historia ecclesiastica* [*HE*]. Ed. Léon Parmentier, rev. Günther Christian Hansen, *Theodoret Kirchengeschichte*. GCS n.F.5. Berlin: Akademie Verlag, 1998. Trans. Blomfield Jackson, *The Ecclesiastical History of Theodoret*. NPNF 3. 2nd series. Grand Rapids, MI: Eerdmans, 1979.

———. *Historia religiosa* [*HR*]. Ed. P. Canivet and A. Leroy-Molingen, *Théodoret de Cyr: Histoire des moines de Syrie*. SC 234, 257. Paris: Éditions du Cerf, 1977, 1979. Trans. Richard M. Price, *Theodoret of Cyrrhus: A History of the Monks of Syria*. CS 88. Kalamazoo, MI: Cistercian Publications, 1985.

———. *Interpretatio in Psalmos* [*Interp. Ps.*]. PG 80: 858–1998.

————. *Quaestiones in Exodum*. [*Qu. in Ex.*]. Ed. John F. Petruccione, trans. Robert C. Hill, *Theodoret of Cyrrhus: The Questions on the Octateuch*, vol. 1: *Genesis and Exodus*. Washington, DC: Catholic University of America Press, 2007.

————. *Quaestiones in Leviticum*. [*Qu. in Lev.*] Ed. John F. Petruccione, trans. Robert C. Hill, *Theodoret of Cyrrhus: The Questions on the Octateuch*, vol. 2: *On Leviticus, Numbers, Deuteronomy, Joshua, Judges, and Ruth*. Washington, DC: Catholic University of America Press, 2007.

Theophanes Confessor [Theoph.]. *Chronographia* [*Chron.*]. Ed. Carl de Boor, *Theophanis Chronographia*, 2 vols. Hildesheim: Olms, 1963. Trans. Cyril Mango and R. Scott, *The Chronicle of Theophanes Confessor*. Oxford: Clarendon Press, 1997.

Theophilus of Alexandria. *Canones* [*can.*]. Ed. Périclès-Pierre Joannou, *Fonti. Fasciolo IX: Discipline générale antique (IVᵉ–IXᵉ)*. Vol 1.1. Rome: Tipografia Italo-Orientale "S. Nilo," 1962.

Traditio Apostolorum [*Trad. ap.*]. Ed. with French trans. Bernard Botte, *Hippolyte de Rome: La Tradition apostolique d'apres les anciennes versions*. SC 11b. Paris: Éditions du Cerf, 1984.

Vita Alexandri Acoemeti [*v.Alex.Acoem.*]. Ed. E. de Stoop, *Vie d' Alexandre l' Acémète*, PO 6: 645–704. Trans. Caner 2002: 249–80.

Vita Antonii. See Athanasius of Alexandria.

Vita Auxentii [*v.Aux.*]. PG 114: 1377–1436.

Vita Barsamae [*v.Bars.*]. Trans. Andrew Palmer (based on a new edition in preparation) in Hahn and Menze 2020: 181–262. Synopsis, François Nau, "Résumés de monographies syriaques," *ROC* 18 (1913): 272–76, 379–89; *ROC* 19 (1914): 113–34, 278–79.

Vita Dalmatii [*v.Dalm.*]. Version 1. Ed. Anselmo Banduri, *Imperium orientale, sive Antiquitates Constantinopolitanae in quattuor partes distributae*, vol.2. Paris: J. B. Coignard, 1743, 697–710.

Vita Danielis Stylitae [*v.Dan.Styl.*]. Ed. Hippolyte Delehaye, *Les saints stylites*. SH 14. Brussels: Société des Bollandistes, 1923, 1–94. Trans. Elizabeth Dawes and Norman H. Baynes, *Three Byzantine Saints: Contemporary Biographies Translated from the Greek*. Crestwood, NY: St. Vladimir's Press, 1996.

Vita Dosithei [*v.Dos.*]. Ed. with French trans. Lucien Regnault and Jacques de Préville, *Dorothée de Gaza: Oeuvres spirituelles*. SC 92. Paris: Éditions du Cerf, 1963, 122–44.

Vita Epiphanii [*v.Epiphan.*]. Ed. Wilhelm Dindorf, *Epiphanii episcopi Constantinia opera*, vol. 1. Leipzig: Weigel, 1859, 3–77.

Vita Eusebii Alexandriae. See John the Monk.

Vita Gerasimi [*v.Geras.*]. Ed. Athanasios Papadopoulos-Kérameus, *Analecta Hierosolymitikes Stachyologias*, vol. 4: 175–84. Brussels: Culture et Civilisation, 1891; rpr. 1963.

Vita Joannis Jeiunatoris [*v.Jo.Jeiun.*]. Ed. and trans. Sergey A. Ivanov, "The Life of Patriarch John the Faster as a Historical Source." In Rigo, Trizio, and Despotakis 2018: 221–33.

Vita Isaiae Monachi. Ed. with Latin trans. E. W. Brooks in *Vitae virorum apud Monophysitas celeberrimorum*. CSCO 103, Scriptores syri 7–8. Louvain: Durbecq, 1907.

Vita Longini [*v.Longini*]. See *Life of Longinus*.

Vita Marcelli Acoemeti [*v.Marc.Acoem.*]. Ed. Gilbert Dagron, "La *vie* ancienne de saint Marcel l'Acémète," *AB* 86 (1968): 271–321. French trans. Jean-Marie Baguenard, *Les Moines acémètes: Vies des saints Alexandre, Marcel et Jean Calybite*. Spiritualité orientale 47. Bégrolles-en-Mauges: Abbaye de Bellefontaine, 1988.

Vita Marthae [*v.Marth.*]. Ed. with French trans. Paul Van den Ven, *La vie ancienne de S. Syméon Stylite le jeune (521–592)*, vol. 2. SH 32. Brussels: Société des Bollandistes, 1970, 251–315.

Vita Matronae Pergensis [*v.Matr.Perg.*]. In *Acta Sanctorum (Novembris)*, vol. 3. Brussels: Société des Bollandistes, 1910, 790–813. Trans. Jeffrey Featherstone in Alice-Mary Talbot, ed., *Holy Women of Byzantium. Byzantine Saints' Lives in Translation* 1. Washington, DC: Dumbarton Oaks, 1996.

Vita Melaniae junioris. See Gerontius.

Vita Nicolai Sionitae [*v.Nicol.Sion.*]. Ed. and trans. Ihor Sevčenko and Nancy P. Sevčenko, *The Life of Saint Nicholas of Sion*. Brookline, MA: Hellenic College Press, 1984.

Vita Pachomii [*v.Pach.*]. Bohairic version [*boh.*]: Ed. Louis-Théophile Lefort, *Sancti Pachomii vita bohairice scripta*, CSCO 89, Scriptores coptici 7. Louvain: Durbecq, 1953. Trans. Armand Veilleux, *Pachomian Koinonia*. Vol. 1: *The Life of Saint Pachomius*. CS 45. Kalamazoo, MI: Cistercian Publications, 1978. First Greek version [*gr. prim.*]: Ed. François Halkin, *Sancti Pachomii vitae graecae*. SH 19. Brussels: Société des Bollandistes, 1932, 1–96. Trans. Armand Veilleux, *Pachomian Koinonia*. Vol. 1: *The Life of Saint Pachomius*.

Vita Pelagiae Antiochae [*v.Pelag.*]. Ed. Bernard Flusin, "Les textes grecque," in Pierre Petitmengin, ed. *Pélagie la Pénitente: Métamorphoses d' une légende*, vol 1. Paris: Études Augustiniennes, 1981. Syriac version [*v.Pelag.syr.*]: trans. Sebastian P. Brock and Susan Ashbrook Harvey, *Holy Women of the Syrian Orient*. TCH 13. Berkeley: University of California Press, 1987.

Vita Petri Ib. See John Rufus.

Vita Pisentii [*v.Pisentii*]. Arabic version: Ed. and trans. De Lacy O'Leary, "The Arabic Life of S. Pisentius," PO 22: 315–483. Paris: Firmin-Didot, 1940. Coptic version: Ed. and trans. Ernest Alfred Wallis Budge, "The Life of Bishop Pisentius by John the Elder," in Ernest Alfred Wallis Budge, *Coptic Apocrypha in the Dialect of Upper Egypt*. London: British Museum, 1903, 75–127, 258–321.

Vita Porphyrii Gazensis. See Mark the Deacon.

Vita Rabbulae. See *Panegyric for Rabbula*.

Vita Sinuthii [*v.Sin.*]. Arabic version: Ed. with French trans. Émile Amélineau, "Vie arabe de Schnoude," *Mémoires de la Mission Archéologique Française au Caire*, vol. 4. Paris: Leroux, 1888, 289–478. Bohairic version: Ed. with Latin trans. Johannes Leipoldt, *Sinuthi Archimandritae Vita et Opera Omnia*. CSCO 41, Scriptores coptici 1. Louvain-Paris: Imprimerie orientaliste-Imprimerie Nationale, 1906. Also trans. D. N. Bell, *The Life of Shenoute by Besa*. CS 73. Kalamazoo, MI: Cistercian Publications, 1983.

Vita Symeonis Stylitae [*v.Sym.Styl.*]. See Symeon Bar-Eupolemos and Bar-Ḥaṭar.

Vita Symeonis Stylitae iunioris [*v.Sym.Styl.iun.*]. Ed. with French trans. Paul Van den Ven, *La vie ancienne de S. Syméon Stylite le Jeune (521–592)*, 2 vols. SH 32. Brussels: Société des Bollandistes, 1962.

Vita Syncleticae [*v.Syncl.*]. See Athanasius, Pseudo-.

Vita Syncleticae Jordanis [*v.Syncl.Jord.*]. Ed. Bernard Flusin and Joseph Paramelle, "De Syncletica in Deserto Jordanis (BHG 1318w)." *AB* 100 (1982): 291–317. Trans. Timothy Vivian, *Journeying into God: Seven Monastic Lives*. Minneapolis: Fortress Press, 1996.

Vita Theclae [*v.Thecl.*]. Ed. with French trans. Gilbert Dagron, *Vie et miracles de Sainte Thècle: Texte grec, traduction, et commentaire*. SH 62. Brussels: Société des Bollandistes, 1978.

Trans. Scott F. Johnson in Alice-Mary Talbot, ed., *Miracle Tales from Byzantium*. Dumbarton Oaks Medieval Library 12. Washington, DC: Dumbarton Oaks Research Library, 2012.

Vita Theodorae. Ed. Karl Wessely, *Jahreberichte des Staatsgymnasiums im 17. Bezirke (Hamals)* 13 (1887): 24–44.

Zachariah, Pseudo- [Zach., Ps.-]. *Chronicle* [*Chron.*]. Ed. E. W. Brooks, *Historia ecclesiastica Zachariae Rhetori vulgo adscripta* [*HE*]. 2 vols. CSCO 83–84, Scriptores syri 38–39. Louvain: Durbecq, 1953. Trans. Robert R. Phenix and Cornelia B. Horn, *The Chronicle of Pseudo-Zachariah Rhetor*. TTH 55. Liverpool: Liverpool University Press.

Zosimus [Zos.]. *Historia nova* [*Hist. nov.*]. Ed. with French trans. François Paschoud, *Zosime: Histoire Nouvelle*, 3 vols. Paris: Les Belles Lettres, 1986. Trans. Ronald T. Ridley, *Zosimus: New History*. Canberra: Australian Association for Byzantine Studies, 1982.

SECONDARY SOURCES

Alciati, Roberto. 2010. "Diakono e diaconia nel monachesimo egiziano: La testimonianza di Cassiano." In *Diakonia, "diaconiae," diaconato: semantica e storia nei padri della chiesa.* Studia Ephemeridis Augustinianum 117. Rome: Institutum Augustinianum, 165–75.

Alcock, Anthony. 2000. "The Agape." *VC* 54: 208–9.

Alexiou, Margaret. 1994. *The Ritual Lament in Greek Tradition,* 2nd ed. Cambridge: Cambridge University Press.

Algazi, Gadi. 2003. "Introduction: Doing Things with Gifts." In Algazi, Groebner, and Jussen 2003: 9–27.

Algazi, Gadi, Valentin Groebner, and Bernard Jussen, eds. 2003. *Negotiating the Gift: Pre-Modern Figurations of Exchange.* Veröffentlichungen des Max-Planck-Instituts für Geschichte 188. Göttingen: Vandenhoeck & Ruprecht.

Allard, Paul. 1907. "Une grande fortune romaine au cinquième siècle." *Revue des questions historiques* 81: 5–30.

Alpi, Frédéric. 2004. "Société et vie profane à Antioche sous le Patriacat de Sévère (512–518)." In Bernadette Cabouret, Pierre-Louis Gatier, and Catherine Saliou, eds., *Antioche de Syrie: Histoire, images et traces de la ville antique.* Lyon: De Boccard, 519–42.

———. 2009. *La Route royale: Sévère d'Antioche et les Églises d'Orient (512–518).* 2 vols. Bibliothèque archéologique et historique 188. Beirut: Institut français du Proche-Orient.

Allen, Nigel. 1990. "Hospice to Hospital in the Near East: An Instance of Continuity and Change in Late Antiquity." *Bulletin of the History of Medicine* 64: 446–62.

Allen, Pauline. 1998. "The Sixth-Century Greek Homily: A Re-assessment." In Mary B. Cunningham and Pauline Allen, eds., *Preacher and Audience: Studies in Early Christian and Byzantine Homiletics.* Leiden, Boston, Köln: Brill, 201–26.

———. 2011. "Episcopal Succession in Antioch in the Sixth Century." In Johan Leemans, Peter Van Nuffelen, Shawn W. J. Keough, and Carla Nicolaye, eds. *Episcopal Elections in Late Antiquity.* Arbeiten zur Kirchengeschichte 119. Berlin and Boston: De Gruyter, 23–38.

Allen, Pauline, and Wendy Mayer. 2000. "Through a Bishop's Eyes: Towards a Definition of Pastoral Care in Late Antiquity." *Augustinianum* 20: 345–97.

Allen, Pauline, Bronwen Neil, and Wendy Mayer. 2009. *Preaching Poverty in Late Antiquity: Perceptions and Realities.* Leipzig: Evangelische Verlagsanstalt.

Amélineau, Émile. 1895. *Monuments pour servir à l'histoire de l'Égypte chrétienne aux IVe, V^e, VIe et VIIe siècles*. Mémoires de la Mission archéologique française au Caire 4. Paris: Libraire de la Société Asiatique.

Ammundsen, Darrel, and Gary Ferngren. 1982. "Medicine and Religion: Pre-Christian Antiquity." In Martin E. Marty and Kenneth L. Vaux, eds., *Health/Medicine in the Faith Traditions*. Philadelphia: Fortress Press, 53–92.

Ampelarga, Lamprinē G. 2002. *Ho vios tēs Hagias Synklētikēs: Eisagōgē—Kritiko Keimeno—Scholia (The Life of Saint Syncletica: Introduction—Critical Text—Commentary)*. BTS 31. Thessaloniki: Byzantine Research Center, Aristotle University.

Anderson, Gary A. 2009. *Sin: A History*. New Haven: Yale University Press.

———. 2012. "Redeem Your Sins through Works of Charity." In Robin Darling Young, ed., *To Train His Soul In Books: Syriac Asceticism in Early Christianity*. Washington DC: Catholic University of America Press, 57–65.

Anderson, Mark A. 2012. "Hospitals, Hospices and Shelters for the Poor in Late Antiquity." PhD dissertation, Yale University.

Anderson, William. 2007. "Menas Flasks in the West: Pilgrimage and Trade at the End of Antiquity." *Ancient West & East* 6: 221–43.

Angstenberger, Pius. 1997. *Der reiche und der arme Christus: Die Rezeptionsgeschichte von 2 Kor 8, 9 zwischen dem zweiten und dem sechsten Jahrhundert*. Studien zur Alten Kirchengeschichte 12. Bonn: Borengässer.

Anné, Lucien. 1941. *Les rites des fiançailles et la donation pour cause de mariage sous le Bas Empire*. Louvain: Desclée de Brouwer.

Armstrong, Gregory T. 1967. "Fifth and Sixth Century Church Buildings in the Holy Land." *GOTR* 14: 17–30.

Arterbury, Andrew E. 2003. "Abraham's Hospitality among Jewish and Early Christian Writers: A Tradition History of Gen 18:1–16 and Its Relevance for the Study of the New Testament." *Perspectives in Religious Studies* 30: 359–76.

———. 2005. *Entertaining Angels: Early Christian Hospitality in Its Mediterranean Setting*. New Testament Monographs 8. Sheffield: Sheffield Phoenix.

Ashkenazi, Jakob. 2014. "Holy Man versus Monk–Village and Monastery in the Late Antique Levant: Between Hagiography and Archaeology." *Journal of the Economic and Social History of the Orient* 57: 745–65.

Ashkenazi, Jakob, and Aviam, Mordechai. 2013. "Monasteries, Monks and Villages in Western Galilee in Late Antiquity." *Journal of Late Antiquity* 5: 269–97.

———. 2017. "Monasteries and Villages: Rural Economy and Religious Interdependency in Late Antique Palestine." *VC* 71: 117–33.

Athanassadi-Fowden, Polymnia. 1981. *Julian and Hellenism: An Intellectual Biography*. Oxford: Clarendon Press.

Atkins, Margaret, and Robin Osborne, eds. 2006. *Poverty in the Roman World*. Cambridge: Cambridge University Press.

Aubineau, Michel. 1975. "Zoticos de Constantinople: Nourricier des pauvres et serviteur des lépreux." *AB* 93: 67–108.

Auzépy, Marie-France. 1995. "Les *Vies d'Auxence* et le monachisme 'Auxentien.'" *REB* 53: 205–35.

———. 2001. "Les Sabaïtes et l'iconoclasme." In Patrich 2001: 305–16.

Aviam, Mordechai. 2004. *Jews, Pagans, and Christians in the Galilee: 25 Years of Archaeological Excavation and Surveys, Hellenistic to Byzantine Periods.* Rochester, NY: University of Rochester Press.

Avidov, Avi. 1998. "Peer Solidarity and Communal Loyalty in Roman Judaea." *Journal of Jewish Studies* 49: 264–79.

Avila, Charles. 1983. *Ownership: Early Christian Teaching.* Maryknoll, NY: Orbis.

Avi-Yonah, M. 1953. "The Economics of Byzantine Palestine." *IEJ* 8: 39–51.

Babić, Gordana. 1969. *Les chapelles annexes des églises byzantines: Fonction liturgique et programmes iconographique.* Bibliothèque des Cahiers Archéologique 3. Paris: Éditions Klincksieck.

Bachatly, Charles. 1965. *Le monastère de Phoebammon dans la Thébaïde,* vol. 2: *Graffiti, inscriptions et ostraca.* Cairo: Société d'archéologie copte.

Bagnall, Roger. 1992. "Landholding in Late Roman Egypt: The Distribution of Wealth." *JRS* 82: 128–49.

———. 1993. *Egypt in Late Antiquity.* Princeton, NJ: Princeton University Press.

———. 2001. "Monks and Property: Rhetoric, Law, and Patronage in the *Apophthegmata Patrum* and the Papyri." *GRBS* 42: 7–24.

———, ed. 2007. *Egypt in the Byzantine World, 300–700.* Cambridge: Cambridge University Press.

Banaji, Jairus. 2001. *Agrarian Change in Late Antiquity: Gold, Labour, and Aristocratic Dominance.* Oxford: Oxford University Press.

Bar, Doron. 2005. "Rural Monasticism as a Key Element in the Christianization of Byzantine Palestine." *HTR* 98: 49–65.

Barnes, Timothy D. 2010. *Early Christian Hagiography and Roman History.* Tria Corda: Jenaer Vorlesungen zu Judentum, Antike und Christentum 5. Tübingen: Mohr Siebeck.

Barnish, Sam, A. D. Lee, and Michael Whitby. 2001. "Government and Administration." In Cameron, Ward-Perkins, and Whitby 2001: 164–206.

Bar-Asher Siegal, Michal. 2013. *Early Christian Monastic Literature and the Babylonian Talmud.* Cambridge: Cambridge University Press.

Bar-Oz, Guy, et al. 2019. "Ancient Trash Mounds Unravel Urban Collapse a Century before the End of Byzantine Hegemony in the Southern Levant." *Proceedings of the National Academy of Sciences* 116: 8239–48.

Bartelink, G. J. M. 1971. "Introduction." In Callinicus, *v.Hyp.*: 9–60.

Batiffol, Pierre. 1911. *Études de liturgie et d'archéologie chrétienne.* Paris: Picard.

Battaglia, Emanuela. 1989. *"ARTOS" il lessico della panificazione nei papiri greci.* Milan: Vita e Pensiero.

Baumeister, Peter. 2011. "Some Aspects of the Development of Osrhoene in Late Antiquity." In Ortwin Dally and Christopher Ratté, eds., *Archaeology and the Cities of Asia Minor in Late Antiquity.* Kelsey Museum Publication 6. Ann Arbor, MI: Kelsey Museum of Archaeology, 225–45.

Bavant, Bernard. 2005. "Les églises du Massif Calcaire de Syrie du Nord (VIᵉ–VIIᵉ s.)." *JRA* 18: 757–70.

Bayer, F. W. 1950. "Aussatz." *RAC* 1: 1023–28.

Beagon, Philip. 1990. "Social and Political Aspects of the Career of St. Basil." PhD diss., Oxford University.

Beaucamp, Joëlle. 2001. "La transmission du patrimoine: legislation de Justinien et pratiques observables dans les papyrus." *Subseciva Groningana* 7: 2–7.

Becker, Adam. 2002. "Anti-Judaism and Care for the Poor in Aphrahat's *Demonstration 20*." *JECS* 10: 305–27.

Behlmer, Heike. 1998. "Visitors to Shenoute's Monastery." In Frankfurter 1998: 341–71.

Bell, Harold Idris. 1949. "Philanthropia in the Papyri of the Roman Period." In *Hommages à Joseph Bidez et à Franz Cumont*. Collection Latomus 2. Brussels: Latomus, 31–37.

———. 1972. *Jews and Christians in Egypt: The Jewish Troubles in Alexandria and the Athanasian Controversy*. Westport, CT: Greenwood Press.

Bell, Peter N. 2009. *Three Political Voices from the Age of Justinian*. TTH 52. Liverpool: Liverpool University Press.

Bernard, Philippe. 2006. "La *laus perennis* d'Agaune dans la Gaule de l' antiquité tardive: état des questions et éléments d'un bilan." In Franco Bernabei and Antonio Lovato, eds., *Sine Musica Nulla Disciplina . . .: Studi in onore di Giulio Cattin*. Padua: Il Poligrafo.

Bernardi, Jean. 1968. *La prédication des Pères Cappadociens: Le prédicateur et son auditoire*. Marseille: Sopic.

Betz, Hans Dieter. 1985. *2 Corinthians 8 and 9: A Commentary on Two Administrative Letters of the Apostle Paul*. Philadelphia: Fortress Press.

Binggeli, André. 2018. "La réception de l'hagiographie palestinienne à Byzance après les conquêtes arabes." In Rigo, Trizio, and Despotakis 2018, 265–84.

Binns, John. 1994. *Ascetics and Ambassadors of Christ: The Monasteries of Palestine, 314–631*. Oxford: Clarendon Press.

Bintliff, John. 2014. "Prosperity, Sustainability, and Poverty in the Late Antique World: Mediterranean Case Studies." In Ine Jacobs, ed., *Production and Prosperity in the Theodosian Period*. Interdisciplinary Studies in Ancient Culture and Religion 4. Leuven: Peeter, 319–26.

Bitton-Ashkelony, Brouria. 1999. "Penitence in Late Antique Monastic Literature." In Jan Assman and Guy Stroumsa, eds., *Transformations of the Inner Self in Ancient Religions*. Leiden: Brill, 179–94.

———. 2006. "The Necessity of Penitence, 'Bear One Another's Burdens' (Gal. 6:2)." In Bitton-Ashkelony and Kofsky 2006, 145–56.

Bitton-Ashkelony, Brouria, and Aryeh Kofsky 2000. "Gazan Monasticism in the Fourth–Sixth Centuries: From Anchoritic to Cenobitic." *Proche-Orient Chrétien* 50: 14–62.

———, eds. 2004. *Christian Gaza in Late Antiquity*. Jerusalem Studies in Religion and Culture 3. Leiden: Brill.

———, eds. 2006. *The Monastic School of Gaza*. Supplements to *Vigiliae Christianae* 78. Leiden: Brill.

Bitton-Ashkelony, Brouria, and Derek Krueger, eds. 2017. *Prayer and Worship in Eastern Christianities, 5th to 11th Centuries*. London: Routledge.

Blanke, Louise. 2019. *An Archaeology of Egyptian Monasticism: Settlement, Economy, and Daily Life at the White Monastery Federation*. Yale Egyptological Publications 2. New Haven, CT: Yale Egyptology.

Bloch, Maurice, and Jonathan Parry 1989. "Introduction." In Parry and Bloch 1989, 1–32.

Blowers, Paul M. 2010. "Pity, Empathy, and the Tragic Spectacle of Human Suffering: Exploring the Emotional Culture of Compassion in Late Ancient Christianity." *JECS* 18: 1–27.

Bobertz, Charles A. 1993. "The Role of the Patron in the *Cena Dominica* of Hippolytus' *Apostolic Tradition.*" *JThS* n.s., 44: 170–84.

Bolkestein, Hendrik. 1939. *Wohltätigkeit und Armenpflege im vorchristlichen Altertum: Ein Beitrag zum Problem "Moral und Gesellschaft.*" Utrecht: A. Oosthoek.

Boero, Dina. 2015a. "The Context of Production of the Vatican Manuscript of the Syriac *Life of Symeon the Stylite.*" *Hugoye: Journal of Syriac Studies* 18: 319–59.

———. 2015b. *Symeon and the Making of the Stylite: The Construction of Sanctity in Late Antique Syria.* PhD diss., University of Southern California.

———. 2019. "Making a Manuscript, Making a Cult: Scribal Production of the Syriac *Life of Symeon the Stylite* in Late Antiquity." *DOP* 73: 25–67.

Bolman, Elizabeth S., ed. 2016a. *The Red Monastery Church: Beauty and Asceticism in Upper Egypt.* New Haven, CT: Yale University Press

———. 2016b. "'The Possessions of Our Poverty': Beauty, Wealth and Asceticism in the Shenoute Federation." In Bolman 2016a: 17–26.

Booth, Phil. 2014. *Crisis of Empire: Doctrine and Dissent at the End of Late Antiquity.* TCH 52. Berkeley: University of California Press.

Boojamra, John L. 1975. "Christian Philanthropia: A Study of Justinian's Welfare Policy and the Church." *Byzantina* 8: 345–73.

Borkowski, Andrew J., and Paul J. du Plessis. 2005. *Textbook on Roman Law,* 3rd ed. Oxford: Oxford University Press.

Boud'hors, Anne, James Clackson, Catherine Louis, and Petra Sijpestijn, eds. 2009. *Monastic Estates in Late Antique and Early Islamic Egypt: Ostraca, Papyri and Essays in Memory of Sarah Clackson (P. Clackson).* Cincinnati, OH: American Society of Papyrologists.

Bouffartigue, Jean. 2005. "L'authenticité de la lettre 84 de l'empereur Julien." *Revue de philologie* 79: 231–42.

Bou Mansour, Tanios. 2003. "Une clé pour la distinction des écrits des Isaac d'Antioche." *Ephemerides Theologicae Lovanienses* 79: 365–402.

Bowes, Kim. 2015. "Sixth-Century Individual Rituals: Private Chapels and the Reserved Eucharist." In Éric Rebillard and Jörg Rüpke, eds., *Group Identity and Religious Individuality in Late Antiquity.* Washington, DC: Catholic University of America Press, 54–88.

Boyd, Catherine E. 1946. "The Beginnings of the Tithe in Italy." *Speculum* 21: 158–72.

Bradshaw, Paul F. 1993. "The Offering of the Firstfruits of Creation: An Historical Study." In Ralph McMichael Jr., ed., *Creation and Liturgy: Studies in Honor of H. Boone Porter.* Washington, DC: Pastoral Press, 29–41.

Brakke, David. 2006. *Demons and the Making of the Monk: Spiritual Combat in Early Christianity.* Cambridge, MA: Harvard University Press.

———. 2008. "Care for the Poor, Fear of Poverty, and Love of Money: Evagrius Ponticus on the Monk's Economic Vulnerability." In Holman 2008: 76–87.

Brakke, David, and Crislip, Andrew T. 2015. *Selected Discourses of Shenoute the Great: Community, Theology, and Social Conflict in Late Antique Egypt.* Cambridge: Cambridge University Press.

Brändle, Rudolf. 1979. *Matth. 25,31–46 im Werk des Johannes Chrysostomos: Ein Beitrag zur Auslegungsgeschichte und zur Erforschung der Ethik der griechischen Kirche um die Wende vom 4. zum 5. Jahrhundert.* Beiträge zur Geschichte der biblischen Exegese 22. Tübingen: J. C. B. Mohr.

————. 2008. "This Sweetest Passage: Matthew 25: 31–46 and Assistance to the Poor in the Homilies of John Chrysostom." In Holman 2008: 127–39.

Bremmer, Jan N. 2010. "Pseudo-Clementines: Texts, Dates, Places, Authors and Magic." In Jan N. Bremmer, ed., *The Pseudo-Clementines*. Leuven: Peeters, 1–23.

Brenk, Beat. 2003. *Die Christianisierung der spätrömischen Welt: Stadt, Land, Haus, Kirche und Kloster in frühchristlicher Zeit*. Wiesbaden: Reichert Verlag.

————. 2004. "Monasteries as Rural Settlements: Patron-Dependence or Self-Sufficiency?" In William Bowden, Luke Lavan, and Carlos Machado, eds., *Recent Research on the Late Antique Countryside*. Leiden: Brill, 447–76.

Bridel, Philippe, ed. 1986. *Le site monastique copte des Kellia: Sources historiques et exploration archéologique*. Geneva: Mission suisse d'archéologie copte de l'Université de Genève.

Britt, Karen C. 2008. "Fama et Memoria: Portraits of Female Patrons in Mosaic Pavements of Churches in Byzantine Palestine and Arabia." *Medieval Feminist Forum: A Journal of Gender and Sexuality* 44: 119–43.

Brock, Sebastian P. 1992. *The Luminous Eye: The Spiritual World of Saint Ephrem the Syrian*, 2nd ed. CS 142. Kalamazoo, MI: Cistercian Publications.

————. 1993. "Humanity and the Natural World in Syrian Tradition." *Christian Orient* 14: 145–53.

————. 2011. "Radical Renunciation: The Ideal of *msarrqûtâ*." In Robin Darling Young and Monica J. Blanchard, eds., *To Train His Soul in Books: Syriac Asceticism in Early Christianity*. Washington, DC: Catholic University of America Press, 122–33.

Brock, Sebastian P., and Susan Ashbrook Harvey. 1998. *Holy Women of the Syrian Orient*. TCH 13. Berkeley: University of California Press.

Broc-Schmezer, Catherine. 2006. "De l'aumône faite au pauvre à l'aumône du pauvre: Pauvreté et spiritualité chez Jean Chrysostome." In Pascal-Grégoire Delage, ed., *Les Pères de l'Église et la voix des pauvres: Actes du IIᵉ colloque de La Rochelle, 2-4 septembre 2005*. La Rochelle: Histoire et Culture, 131–48.

Brodman, James. 2009. *Charity and Religion in Medieval Europe*. Washington, DC: Catholic University of America Press.

Brooks, Roger. 1983. *Support for the Poor in the Mishnaic Law of Agriculture: Tractate Peah*. Chico, CA: Scholars Press.

Brooks Headstrom, Darlene L. 2017. *The Monastic Landscape of Late Antique Egypt: An Archaeological Reconstruction*. Cambridge: Cambridge University Press.

Brown, Peter. 1971. "The Rise and Function of the Holy Man in Late Antiquity." *JRS* 61: 80–101; repr. with additional notes in Peter Brown, *Society and the Holy in Late Antiquity*. Berkeley: University of California Press, 1982, 103–52.

————. 1982. "Response." In Robert M. Grant and Irene Lawrence, eds., *The Problem of Miraculous Feedings in the Graeco-Roman world: Protocol of the Forty-Second Colloquy, 14 March 1982*. Berkeley: Center for Hermeneutical Studies in Hellenistic and Modern Culture, 16–24.

————. 1988. *The Body and Society: Men, Women, and Sexual Renunciation in Early Christianity*. New York: Columbia University Press.

————. 1992. *Power and Persuasion in Late Antiquity: Towards a Christian Empire*. Madison: University of Wisconsin Press.

———. 1995. *Authority and the Sacred: Aspects of the Christianisation of the Roman World.* Cambridge: Cambridge University Press.

———. 1999. *"Gloriosus Obitus:* The End of the Ancient Other World." In William E. Klingshirn and Mark Vessey, eds., *The Limits of Ancient Christianity: Essays on Late Antique Thought and Culture in Honor of R. A. Markus.* Ann Arbor: University of Michigan Press, 289–314.

———. 2000. "The Decline of the Empire of God: Amnesty, Penance, and the Afterlife from Late Antiquity to the Middle Ages." In Caroline Walker Bynum and Paul Freedman, eds., *Last Things: Death and the Apocalypse in the Middle Ages.* Philadelphia: University of Pennsylvania Press, 41–59.

———. 2002. *Poverty and Leadership in the Late Roman Empire.* Hanover, NH: University Press of New England.

———. 2005a. "Augustine and a Crisis of Wealth in Late Antiquity." *Augustinian Studies* 36: 5–30.

———. 2005b. "Remembering the Poor and the Aesthetic of Society." *Journal of Interdisciplinary History* 35: 513–22.

———. 2008. "Alms and the Afterlife: A Manichaean View of an Early Christian Practice." In T. Corey Brennan and Harriet I. Flower, eds., *East & West: Papers on Ancient History Presented to Glen W. Bowersock.* Cambridge, MA: Harvard University Press, 145–58.

———. 2010. "Richesses, travail, et les 'pauvres parmi les saints': Ascétisme et monachisme entre la Syrie et l'Égypte, IIIᵉ–Vᵉ siècle ap. J-C." In Hervé Inglebert, Sylvain Destephen, and Bruno Dumézil, eds., *Le problème de la christianisation du monde antique.* Textes, Histoire, et Monument de l'Antiquité au Moyen Age. Paris: Picard, 393–403.

———. 2012. *Through the Eye of a Needle: Wealth, the Fall of Rome, and the Making of Christianity in the West, 350–550 AD.* Princeton: Princeton University Press.

———. 2015. *The Ransom of the Soul: Afterlife and Wealth in Early Western Christianity.* Cambridge, MA: Harvard University Press.

———. 2016. *Treasures in Heaven: The Holy Poor in Early Christianity.* Charlottesville: University of Virginia Press.

Brown, Peter, and Joel Walker. 1998. "Archaeological Reconnaissance in Late Roman Galatia." http://courses.washington.edu/tahirler/reports.html.

Bruck, Eberhard F. 1926. *Totenteil und Seelgerat in griechischen Recht. Eine entwicklungsgeschichtliche Untersuchung zum Verhältnis von Recht und Religion mit Beiträgen zur Geschichte des Eigentums und des Erbrechts.* Münchener Beiträge zur Papyrusforschung und antiken Rechtsgeschichte 9. Munich: O. H. Beck.

———. 1934. "Die Gesinnung de Schenkers bei Johannes Chrysostomus: Bemerkungen zum Verhältnis zwischen theologischer und juristischer Willenlehre." In Peter G. Vallindas, ed., *Mnemosyna Pappulias.* Athens: Pyrsos, 65–83.

———. 1944. "Ethics vs. Law: St. Paul, the Fathers of the Church and the 'Cheerful Giver' in Roman Law." *Traditio* 2: 97–121.

Brumfield, Allaire C. 1981. *The Attic Festivals of Demeter and Their Relation to the Agricultural Year.* Salem, NH: Ayer Company.

Büchler, Bernward. 1980. *Die Armut der Armen: Über den ursprünglichen Sinn der mönchischen Armut.* Munich: Kösel.

Bünting, Ulf, and Vladimir S. Myglan, Fredrik C. Ljungqvist, Michael McCormick, Nicola Di Cosmo, Michael Sigl, Johann Junclaus, Sebastian Wagner, Paul J. Krusic, Jan Esper, Jed O. Kaplan, Michiel A. C. de Vaan, Jürg Luterbacher, Lukas Wacker, Willy Tegel, and Alexander V. Kirdyanov. 2016. "Cooling and Societal Change during the Late Antique Little Ice Age from 536 to around 660 AD." *Nature Geoscience* 9: 231–37.

Burton-Christie, Douglas. 1993. *The Word in the Desert: Scripture and the Quest for Holiness in Early Christian Monasticism*. New York: Oxford University Press.

Buschhausen, Helmut, Jenny Albani, Alexander Dostal, Hermann Harrauer, Ulrike Horak, Fathih Mohammed Khorshid, Barbara Mencarelli, and Hans Plach. 1991. "Die Ausgrabungen von Dair Abu Fana in Oberägypten im Jahr 1989." *Ägypten und Levante/ Egypt and the Levant* 2: 121–46.

Butcher, Kevin. 2003. *Roman Syria and the Near East*. Los Angeles: J. Paul Getty Museum.

Caillet, Jean-Pierre. 1987. "Les dédicaces privées de pavements de mosaïque à la fin de l'Antiquité, Occident européen et monde grec: données socio-économiques." In Xavier Barral i Altet, ed., *Artistes, artisans et production artistique au Moyen Âge. Colloque international de Rennes, Université de Haute-Bretagne, 2-6 mai 1983*. Vol 2: *Commande et travail*. Paris: Picard, 15–38.

———. 2003. "L'évergétisme monumental chrétien dans la Jordanie de la fin de l'Antiquité." In Noël Duval, ed., *Les églises de Jordanie et leurs mosaïques. Acts de la journée d'études, organisée à l'occasion de l'inauguration de l'exposition Mosaïques byzantine de Jordanie au musée de la Civilisation gallo-romaine à Lyon en avril 1989*. Beirut: Institut français du archéologie du Proche-Orient, 297–301.

———. 2012. "L'Évolution de la notion d'évergétisme dans l'Antiquité chrétienne." In Spieser and Yota 2012: 11–24.

Cain, Andrew. 2016. *The Greek Historia Monachorum in Aegypto: Monastic Hagiography in the Late Fourth Century*. Oxford: Oxford University Press.

Caltabiano, Matilde. 1991. *L'epistolario di Giuliano imperatore: saggio storico, traduzione, note e testo*. KOINΩNIA: Collana di studi et testi 14. Naples: M. D'Auria.

Camenisch, Paul F. 1981. "Gift and Gratitude in Ethics." *Journal of Religious Ethics* 9: 1–34.

Cameron, Averil. 1976. "The Early Religious Policies of Justin II." In Derek Baker, ed., *The Orthodox Churches and the West*. Studies in Church History 13. Oxford: Blackwell, 51–67.

Cameron, Averil, Bryan Ward-Perkins, and Michael Whitby, eds. 2001. *The Cambridge Ancient History*, vol. 14: *Late Antiquity: The Empire and Successors, AD 425–600*. Cambridge: Cambridge University Press.

Campbell, Sheila D. 1988. "Armchair Pilgrims: Ampullae from Aphrodisias in Caria." *Mediaeval Studies* 50: 539–45.

Camplani, Alberto. 2013. "The Transmission of the Early Christian Memories in Late Antiquity: The Editorial Activities of Laymen and Philoponoi." In Brouria Bitton-Ashkelony and Lorenzo Perrone, eds. *Between Personal and Institutional Religion: Self, Doctrine and Practice in Late Antique Eastern Christianity*. Cultural Encounters in Late Antiquity and the Middle Ages 15. Turnhout: Brepols, 129–53.

Caner, Daniel. 2002. *Wandering, Begging Monks: Spiritual Authority and the Promotion of Monasticism in Late Antiquity*. TCH 33. Berkeley: University of California Press.

———. 2006. "Towards a Miraculous Economy: Christian Gifts and Material 'Blessings' in Late Antiquity." *JECS* 14: 328–77.

———. 2008. "Wealth, Stewardship, and Charitable 'Blessings' in Early Byzantine Monasticism." In Holman 2008: 221–42.

———. 2009. "Charitable Ministrations (*Diakoniai*), Monasticism, and the Social Aesthetic of Sixth-Century Byzantium." In Frenkel and Lev 2009: 45–74.

———. 2010. *History and Hagiography from the Late Antique Sinai.* TTH 53. Liverpool: Liverpool University Press.

———. 2013a. "Alms, Blessings, Offerings: The Repertoire of Christian Gifts in Early Byzantine Hagiography." In Satlow 2013: 25–44.

———. 2013b. "From the Pillar to the Prison: Penitential Spectacles in Early Byzantine Monasticism." In Blake Leyerle and Robin Darling Young, eds., *Ascetic Culture: Essays in Honor of Philip Rousseau.* Notre Dame, IN: Notre Dame University Press, 127–46.

———. 2018a. "Clemency, a Neglected Aspect of Early Christian Philanthropy." *Religions* 9: 1–22.

———. 2018b. "Not a Hospital but a Leprosarium: Basil's Basilias and an Early Byzantine Notion of the Deserving Poor." *DOP* 72: 25–48.

———. 2020. "Wandering Monks Remembered: Hagiography in the *Lives* of Alexander the Sleepless and Barsauma the Mourner." In Hahn and Menze 2020: 149–70.

———. 2021. "Bishops and the Politics of Lithomania in Early Byzantium." In Domingo-Gygax and Zuiderhoek 2021: 267–96.

———. Forthcoming-a. "Distinguishing Offerings from Blessings in Early Byzantine Monasticism: The Significance of *P.Ness.* III 79." In Louise Blanke and Jennifer Cromwell, eds., *Monastic Economies of Egypt and Palestine.*

———. Forthcoming-b. "*Not All Poverty Is To Be Praised:* Defining the Poor in a Christian Empire." In Filippo Carlà, Lucia Cecchet, and Carlos Machado, eds., *Poverty in the Ancient World.* Oxfordshire: Routledge.

Canivet, Pierre. 1977. *Le monachisme syrien selon Théodoret de Cyr.* Théologie historique 42. Paris: Beauchesne.

Caquot, André. 1958. "Appendix 3: Couvents antiques." In Tchalenko 1958: 63–85.

Cardman, Francine. 2008. "Poverty and Wealth as Theater: John Chrysostom's Homilies on Lazarus and the Rich Man." In Holman 2008: 159–75.

Carlà, Filippo. 2014. "Exchange and the Saints: Gift-giving and the Commerce of Relics." In Carlà and Gori 2014, 403–37.

———. 2016. "Middle Classes in Late Antiquity: an Economic Perspective." In Errietta M. A. Bissa and Federico Santangelo, eds., *Studies on Wealth in the Ancient World.* Bulletin of the Institute of Classical Studies Suppl. 133. London: University of London Institute of Classical Studies, 53–82.

Carlà, Filippo, and Maja Gori, eds. 2014. *Gift Giving and the 'Embedded' Economy in the Ancient World.* Akademiekonferenzen 17. Heidelberg: Universitätsverlag Winter.

Carrié, Jean-Michel. 1975. "Les Distributions alimentaires dans les cités de l'Empire romain tardif." *Mélanges de l'École française de Rome: Antiquité* 87: 995–1101.

———. 2006. "Pratique et idéologie chrétiennes de l'économique (IVᵉ–VIᵉ siècles)." *AnTard* 14: 17–26.

Caseau, Béatrice. 2001. "Πολεμειν λιθοις: La désacralisation des espaces et des objets religieux païens durant l'Antiquité tardive." In Michel Kaplan, ed., *Le sacré et son inscription dans l'espace à Byzance et en Occident.* Byzantina Sorbonensia 18. Paris: Publications de la Sorbonne, 61–123.

———. 2003. "A Case Study for the Transformation of Law in Late Antiquity: The Legal Protection of Churches." In Linda Hall Jones, ed., *Confrontation in Late Antiquity: Imperial Presentation and Regional Adaption.* Cambridge: Orchard Academic, 61–78.

———. 2012. "Autour de l'autel: Le contrôle des donateurs et des donations alimentaires." In Spieser and Yota 2012: 47–73.

Caseau, Béatrice, and Sabine R. Hübner, eds., 2014. *Inheritance, Law and Religions in the Ancient and Mediaeval Worlds.* CNRS Centre de recherche d'histoire et civilisation de Byzance 45. Paris: ACHByz.

Cavallero, Pablo A. 2000–2001. "Philanthropía en los *Nombres divinos* de Pseudo Dionisio." *Byzantion Nea Hellás* 19–20: 130–42.

Cecchet, Lucia. 2014. "Gift-giving to the Poor in the Greek World." In Carlà and Gori 2014: 157–79.

———. 2015. *Poverty in Athenian Public Discourse from the Eve of the Peloponnesian War to the Rise of Macedonia.* Historia-Einzelschriften 239. Stuttgart: Franz Steiner.

Çetin Şahin, Mehmet. 1982. *Die Inschriften von Stratonikeia* 2.1: *Lagina, Stratonikeia und Umgebung.* Inschriften griechischer Städte aus Kleinasien 22.1. Bonn: Habelt.

Chadwick, Henry. 1974. "John Moschus and His Friend Sophronius the Sophist." *JThS* n.s. 25: 41–74.

———. 2017. "Pachomios and the Idea of Sanctity." In William G. Rusch, ed., *Henry Chadwick: Selected Writings.* Grand Rapids, MI: Eerdmans, 277–93.

Champlin, Edward. 1991. *Final Judgments: Duty and Emotion in Roman Wills, 200 B.C.–A.D. 250.* Berkeley: University of California Press.

Charanis, Peter. 1971. "The Monk as an Element of Byzantine Society." *DOP* 25: 61–84.

Chastel, Étienne Louis. 1853. *Études historiques sur l'influence de la charité durant les premiers siècles chrétiens, et considérations sur son rôle dans les sociétés modernes.* Paris: Capelle.

Chialà, Sabino. 2017. "Prayer and Body according to Isaac of Nineveh." In Bitton-Askkelony and Krueger 2017: 34–43.

Chitty, Derwas J. 1966. *The Desert a City: An Introduction to the Study of Egyptian and Palestinian Monasticism under the Christian Empire.* Oxford: Basil Blackwell.

———. 1971. "Abba Isaiah." *JThS* 22: 47–72.

Christ, Matthew R. 2012. *The Limits of Altruism in Democratic Athens.* Cambridge: Cambridge University Press.

———. 2013. "Demosthenes on *PHILANTHRŌPIA* as a Democratic Virtue." *Classical Philology* 108: 202–22.

Christophe, Paul. 1964. *L'Usage chrétien du droit de propriété dans l'écriture et la tradition patristique.* Collection Théologie, Pastorale et Spiritualité 14. Paris: Lethielleux.

Chryssavgis, John. 2001. "Abba Isaiah of Scetis: Aspects of Spiritual Direction." *SP* 35: 30–40.

———. 2006. "Introduction." In John Chryssavgis, trans., *Barsanuphius and John: Letters,* vol 1. Fathers of the Church 113. Washington, DC: Catholic University of America, 1–17.

Clackson, Sarah J. 2000. *Coptic and Greek Texts Related to the Hermopolite Monastery of Apa Apollo.* Oxford: Ashmolean Museum.

Clark, Elizabeth. 1984. See Gerontius.

———. 1986. "Piety, Propaganda, and Politics in the *Life of Melania the Younger*." In Elizabeth Clark, *Ascetic Piety and Women's Faith: Essays on Late Ancient Christianity*. Studies in Women and Religion 20. Lewiston, NY: Mellen Press, 61–94.

Claude, Dietrich. 1969. *Die byzantinische Stadt im 6 Jahrhundert*. Byzantinisches Archiv 13. Munich: Beck.

Coffee, Neil. 2017. *Gift and Gain: How Money Transformed Ancient Rome*. New York: Oxford University Press.

Cohen, Mark. R. 2005. *Poverty and Charity in the Jewish Community of Medieval Egypt*. Princeton, NJ: Princeton University Press.

Coke, Brian. 2005. "Justinian's Constantinople." In Maas 2005: 60–86.

Colish, Marcia L. 2005. *Ambrose's Patriarchs: Ethics for the Common Man*. Notre Dame, IN: Notre Dame University Press.

Collins, John N. 1990. *Diakonia: Re-interpreting the Ancient Sources*. New York: Oxford University Press.

Constable, Giles. 1964. *Monastic Tithes: From Their Origins to the Twelfth Century*. Cambridge: Cambridge University Press.

———. 2000. "The Commemoration of the Dead in the Early Medieval Ages." In J. M. H. Smith, ed., *Early Medieval Rome and the Christian West: Essays in Honour of Donald A. Bullough*. Leiden: Brill, 169–95.

Constantelos, Demetri. 1991. *Byzantine Philanthropy and Social Welfare*. 2nd ed. New Rochelle, NY: Caratzas.

———. 2008. "The Hellenic Background and Nature of Patristic Philanthropy in the Early Byantine Era." In Holman 2008: 187–210.

Constas, Nicholas. 2001. "'To Sleep, Perchance to Dream': The Middle State of Souls in Patristic and Byzantine Literature." *DOP* 55: 92–124.

———. 2002. "An Apology for the Cult of the Saints in Late Antiquity: Eustratius Presbyter of Constantinople, *On the State of Souls After Death*." *JECS* 10: 267–85.

Copeland, Kirsti B. 2004. "The Earthly Monastery and the Transformation of the Heavenly City in Late Antique Egypt." In Ra'anan S. Boustan and Annette Yoshiko Reed, eds., *Heavenly Realms and Earthly Realities in Late Antique Religions*. Cambridge: Cambridge University Press, 142–58.

Corbo, Chiara. 2006. *Paupertas: La legislazione tardoantica (IV–V sec. d. C)*. Naples: Satura.

Corcoran, Simon. 2006. "The Tetrarchy: Policy and Image as Reflected in Imperial Announcements." In Dietrich Boschung and Werner Eck, eds., *Die Tetrarchie: Ein neues Regierungssystem und seine mediale Präesentation*. Wiesbaden: Reichert, 31–62.

Coulie, Bernard. 1985. *Les richesses dans l'oeuvre de S. Grégoire de Nazianze. Étude littéraire et historique*. Publications de l'Institut Orientaliste de Louvain 32. Louvain-la-Neuve: Université Catholique de Louvain.

Countryman, L. William. 1980. *The Rich Christian in the Church of the Early Empire: Contradictions and Accommodations*. New York: Edwin Mellen Press.

Courtonne, Yves. 1935. *Saint Basile: Homélies sur la richesse: Édition critique et exégétique*. Paris: Firmin-Didot.

Crislip, Andrew T. 2005. *From Monastery to Hospital: Christian Monasticism and the Transformation of Health Care in Late Antiquity*. Ann Arbor: University of Michigan Press.

———. 2008. "Care for the Sick in Shenoute's Monasteries." In Gawdat Gabra and Hany N. Takla, eds., *Christianity and Monasticism in Upper Egypt*, vol.1: *Akhmim and Sohag*. Cairo and New York: American University in Cairo Press, 21–30.

———. 2013. *Thorns in the Flesh: Illness and Sanctity in Late Ancient Christianity*. Philadelphia: University of Pennsylvania Press.

———. 2016. "The Red Monastery in Early Byzantine Egypt." In Bolman 2016a: 3–9.

Crone, Patricia. 1991. "Kavād's Heresy and Mazdak's Revolt." *Iran* 29: 21–42.

Crum, Walter Ewing. 1902. *Coptic Ostraca from the Collections of the Egypt Exploration Fund, the Cairo Museum and Others*. London: British Museum.

———. 1926. "Theban Hermits and Their Life." In Winlock, Crum, and Evelyn-White 1926: 125–85.

Curta, Florin. 2006. "Merovingian and Carolingian Gift Giving." *Speculum* 81: 671–99.

Dagron, Gilbert. 1968. "La *vie* ancienne de saint Marcel l'Acémète." *AB* 86: 271–321.

———. 1970. "Les moines et la ville: Le monachisme à Constantinople jusqu'au concile de Chalcédoine (451)." *TM* 4: 229–76.

———. 1977. "Entre village et cité: la bourgade rurale des IVᵉ–VIIᵉ siècles en Orient." *Koinonia* 3: 29–52. Rpr. in *La romanité chrétienne en Orient*. London: Variorum, 1984, VII.

———. 1989. "L'Organisation de la vie religieuse à Constantinople." In Noël Duval, ed., *Actes du XIᵉ congrès international d'archéologie chrétienne Lyon, Vienne, Grenoble, Genève et Aoste (21–28 Septembre 1986)*, vol 2. Rome: École française de Rome et Pontificio Istituto di archeologia cristiana, 1069–85.

———. 1991. "'Ainsi rien n'échappera à la règlementation': État, Église, corporations, confréries: à propos des inhumations à Constantinople (IVᵉ–Xᵉ siècle)." In Vassiliki Kravari, Jacques Lefort, and Cecil Morrison, eds., *Hommes et richesses dans l'empire byzantin, II, VIIIᵉ–XVᵉ*. Réalités Byzantines 3. Paris: P. Lethielleux, 155–82.

———. 1992. "L'Ombre d'un doute: l'hagiographie en question, VIᵉ–XIᵉ siècle." *DOP* 46: 59–68.

———. 1993. "L'Église et la chrétienté byzantine entre les invasions et l'iconoclasme (viiᵉ–début viiiᵉ siècle)." In Jean-Marie Mayeur, Charles Pietri, Luce Pietri, André Vauchez, and Marc Venard, eds., *Histoire du Christianisme des origines à nos jours*, vol.4: *Évêques, Moines et Empereurs (610–1054)*. Paris: Desclée, 9–91.

———. 1998. "Hériter de soi-même." In Joëlle Beaucamp and Gilbert Dagron, eds., *La transmission du patrimoine: Byzance et l'aire méditerranéenne*. Travaux et Mémoires du Centre de Recherche d'Histoire et Civilisation de Byzance 11. Paris: De Boccard, 81–99.

Dagron, Gilbert, and Denis Feissel. 1987. *Inscriptions de Cilicie*. Paris: De Boccard.

Dal Santo, Matthew. 2012. *Debating the Saints' Cult in the Age of Gregory the Great*. Oxford: Oxford University Press.

Daley, Brian E. 1999. "Building a New City: The Cappadocian Fathers and the Rhetoric of Philanthropy." *JECS* 7: 431–61.

D'Arms, John. 1990. "The Roman *Convivium* and the Idea of Equality." In Oswyn Murray, ed., *Sympotica: A Symposium on the Symposium*. New York: Oxford University Press; Oxford: Clarendon Press, 308–20.

Dassmann, Ernst. 1998. "Nächstenliebe unter den Bedingungen der Knappheit: Zum Problem der Prioritäten und Grenzen der Karitas in frühchristlicher Zeit." In Josef Isensee, ed., *Solidarität in Knappheit: Zum Problem der Priorität*. Wissenschaftliche Abhandlungen und Reden zur Philosophie, Politik und Geistesgeschichte 20. Berlin: Duncker and Humblot, 9–40.

Dauphine, Claudine. 1980. "Mosaic Pavements as an Index of Prosperity and Fashion." *Levant* 12: 112–34.

Davies, Wendy, and Paul Fouracre, eds. 2010. *The Languages of Gift in the Early Middle Ages.* Cambridge: Cambridge University Press.

Dawkins, Richard MacGillivray. 1953. "Notes on Life in the Monasteries of Mount Athos." *HTR* 46: 217–31.

De Andia, Ysabel. 2010. "Liturgie, diaconie des pauvres et theologie du corps du Christ chez Saint Jean Chrysostome." In *Diakonia, "diaconiae," diaconato: Semantica e storia nei padri della chiesa.* Studia ephemerides Augustinianum 117. Rome: Institutum Augustinianum, 245–60.

De Durand, Georges-Matthieu. 1999. *Marc le Moine: Traités I.* SC 445. Paris: Éditions du Cerf.

De Jong, Mayke. 1995. "Carolingian Monasticism: The Power of Prayer." In Rosamond McKitterick, ed., *The New Cambridge Medieval History,* vol. 2: *c. 700–c. 900.* Cambridge: Cambridge University Press, 622–53.

De Romilly, Jacqueline. 1979. *La douceur dans la pensée grecque.* Paris: Les Belles Lettres.

De Ste. Croix, Geoffrey E. M. 1975. "Early Christian Attitudes to Poverty and Slavery." *Studies in Church History* 12: 1–38.

———. 1981. *The Class Struggle in the Ancient Greek World.* Ithaca, NY: Cornell University Press.

De Vogüé, Adalbert. 2001. "La Règle de Saint Benoît et la Législation de Justinien." *SM* 43: 227–31.

Decker, Michael. 2009. *Tilling the Hateful Earth: Agricultural Production and Trade in the Late Antique East.* Oxford Studies in Byzantium. Oxford: Oxford University Press.

Dekkers, E. 1980. "Limites sociales et linguistiques de la pastorale liturgique de saint Jean Chrysostome." In Victor Saxer, ed., *Ecclesia orans. Mélanges patristiques offerts au Père Adalbert G. Hamman OFM à l'occasion de ses quarante ans d'enseignement.* Rome: Institutum Patristicum "Augustinianum," 119–29.

DelCogliano, Mark. 2010. *Basil of Caesarea's Anti-Eunomian Theory of Names: Christian Theology and Late-Antique Philosophy in the Fourth-Century Trinitarian Controversy.* Supplements to Vigiliae Christianae 103. Leiden: Brill.

Delmaire, Roland. 1988. "Les largesses impériales et l'émission d'argenterie du IVᵉ au VIᵉ siècle." In François Baratte and Noël Duval, eds., *Argenterie romaine et byzantine.* 2 vols. Paris: De Boccard, 2: 113–22.

Demaitre, Luke. 2007. *Leprosy in Premodern Medicine: A Malady of the Whole Body.* Baltimore: Johns Hopkins University Press.

Dennis, George T. 1996. "Popular Religious Attitudes and Practices in Byzantium." In Robert F. Taft, ed., *The Christian East, its Institutions and its Thought: A Critical Reflection. Papers of the International Scholarly Congress for the 75th Anniversary of the Pontifical Oriental Institute, Rome, 30 May–5 June 1993.* OCA 251. Rome: Pontificio istituto orientale, 245–64.

Déroche, Vincent. 1995. *Études sur Léontios de Néapolis.* Studia Byzantina Upsalensia 3. Uppsala: Alqmvist and Wiksell.

———. 1996. "Quelques interrogations à propos de la *Vie de Syméon Stylite de Jeune.*" *Eranos* 94: 65–83.

————. 2004. "La Forme de l'informe: La Vie de Théodore de Sykéôn et la Vie de Syméon Stylite le Jeune." In Odorico 2004: 367–85.

————. 2006. "Vraiment anargyres? Don et contredon dans les recueils de miracles proto-byzantines." In Beatrix Caseau, J.-C. Cheynet, and Vincent Déroche, eds., Pèlerinages et lieux saints dans l'Antiquité et le Moyen Âge. Mélanges offerts à Pierre Maraval. Paris: Association des Amis du Centre d'histoire et civilisation de Byzance, 153–58.

————. 2010. "Thésaurisation et circulation monétaire chez les moins d'après la littérature édifiante del' Antiquité tardive." In Jean-Claude Cheynet, ed., Mélanges Cécile Morrisson, TM 16. Paris: Association des Amis du Centre d'histoire et civilisation de Byzance, 245–52.

Déroche, Vincent, and Bénédicte Lesieur. 2010. "Notes d'hagiographie byzantine: Daniel le Stylite-Marcel l'Acémète-Hypatios de Rufinianes-Auxentios de Bithynie." AB 128: 283–95.

Derrida, Jacques. 1992. Given Time: I. Counterfeit Money. Trans. Peggy Kamuf. Chicago: University of Chicago Press.

————. 1995. The Gift of Death. Trans. David Wills. Chicago: University of Chicago Press.

Destephen, Sylvain. 2012. "L'Évergétisme aristocratique au féminin dans l'Empire romain d'Orient." In Beatrice Caseau, ed., Les réseaux familiaux: Antiquité tardive et Moyen Âge. Centre de recherche d'histoire et civilisation de Byzance 37. Paris: Association des Amis du Centre d'histoire et civilisation de Byzance, 183–203.

Detoraki, Marina. 2004. "Copie sous dictée et baines monastiques: Deux renseignement propres à la Vie latine de sainte Mélanie la Jeune." JbAC 47: 98–107.

Dey, Hendrik W. 2008. "Diaconiae, Xenodochia, Hospitalia and Monasteries: 'Social Security' and the Meaning of Monasticism in Early Medieval Rome." Early Medieval Europe 16: 398–422.

Dignas, Beate. 2002. Economy of the Sacred in Hellenistic and Roman Asia Minor. Oxford: Clarendon Press; New York: Oxford University Press.

————. 2005. "Sacred Revenues in Roman Hands: The Economic Dimension of Sanctuaries in Western Asia Minor." In Stephen Mitchell and Constantina Katsari, eds., Patterns in the Economy of Roman Asia Minor. Swansea: Classical Press of Wales, 207–24.

Dilley, Paul C. 2017. Monasteries and the Care of Souls in Late Antique Christianity: Cognition and Discipline. Cambridge: Cambridge University Press.

Dimitropoulou, Vassiliki. 2010. "Giving Gifts to God: Aspects of Patronage in Byzantine Art." In Liz James, ed., A Companion to Byzantium. Oxford: Wiley-Blackwell, 161–70.

Dirkse, Saskia. 2014. "Τελωνεῖα: The Tollgates of the Air as an Egyptian Motif in Patristic Sources and Early Byzantine Hagiography." In Panagiotis Roilos, ed., Medieval Greek Story Telling: Fictionality and Narrative in Byzantium. Mainzer Veröffentlichungen zur Byzantinistik 12. Weisbaden: O. Harrassowitz, 41–53.

Di Segni, Leah. 1990. "The Monastery of Martyrius at Ma'ale Adummim (Khirbet el-Murassas): The Inscriptions." In Giovanni Claudio Bottini, Leah Di Segni, and Eugenio Alliata, eds., Christian Archaeology in the Holy Land. New Discoveries: Essays in Honour of Virgilio C. Corbo, OFM. Jerusalem: Franciscan Printing Press, 153–61.

————. 1995. "The Involvement of Local, Municipal and Provincial Authorities in Urban Building in Late Antique Palestine and Arabia." In John H. Humphrey, ed., The Roman and Byzantine Near East: Some Recent Archaeological Research. JRA Supplementary Series 14. Ann Arbor, MI: Cushing–Malloy, 312–32.

——. 1997. *Dated Greek Inscriptions from Palestine from the Roman and Byzantine Periods*, vol. 1: *Text*. PhD diss., Hebrew University of Jerusalem.

——. 1999. "Epigraphic Documentation on Building in the Provinces of *Palaestina* and *Arabia*, 4th–7th C." In John H. Humphrey, ed., *Roman and Byzantine Near East*, vol. 2: *Some Recent Archaeological Research*. JRA Supplementary Series 31. Portsmouth, RI: Journal of Roman Archaeology, 149–78.

——. 2001. "Monks and Society: The Case of Palestine." In Patrich 2001: 31–36.

——. 2017. "Expressions of Prayer in Late Antique Inscriptions in the Provinces of Palaestina and Arabia." In Bitton-Ashkelony and Krueger 2017: 63–88.

Dix, Gregory. 1945. *The Shape of the Liturgy*. Westminster: Dacre.

Domingo-Gygax, Marc, and Arjan Zuiderhoek, eds. 2021. *Benefactors and the Polis: The Public Gift in the Greek Cities from the Homeric World to Late Antiquity*. Cambridge: Cambridge University Press.

Donahue, Cecil. 1953. "The ΑΓΑΠΗ of the Hermits of Scete." *SM* 1: 97–114.

Donceel-Voûte, Pauline. 1988. *Les pavements des églises byzantines de Syrie et du Liban. Décor, archéologie et liturge*. 2 vols. Publications d'histoire de l'art et d'archéologie de l'Université catholique de Louvain 69. Louvain-la-neuve: Département d'archéologie et d'histoire de l'art, Collège Erasme.

Doran, Robert. 1992. "Introduction." In Robert Doran, *The Lives of Symeon Stylites*. CS 112. Kalamazoo, MI: Cistercian Publications, 15–66.

Downey, Glanville. 1955. "Philanthropia in Religion and Statecraft in the Fourth Century after Christ." *Historia* 4: 199–288.

——. 1961. *A History of Antioch in Syria from Seleucus to the Arab Conquest*. Princeton, NJ: Princeton University Press.

Downs, David J. 2008. *The Offering of the Gentiles: Paul's Collection for Jerusalem in Its Chronological, Cultural and Cultic Contexts*. Wissenschaftliche Untersuchungen zum Neuen Testament, n.f. Tübingen: Mohr Siebeck.

Drews, D. 1898. "Zur Geschichte de 'Eulogien' in der alten Kirche." *Zeitschrift für praktische Theologie* 20: 18–39.

Driscoll, Jeremy. 2001. "'Love of Money' in Evagrius Ponticus." *SM* 43: 21–30.

Ducan-Flowers, Maggie. 1990. "A Pilgrim's Ampulla from the Shrine of St. John the Evangelist at Ephesus." In Ousterhout 1990: 125–39.

Duff, P. W. 1926. "The Charitable Foundations of Byzantium." In George Glover Alexander, ed., *Cambridge Legal Essays Written in Honour of and Presented to Doctor Bond, Professor Buckland and Professor Kenney*. Cambridge: W. Heffer and Sons, 83–101.

Dunbabin, Katherine M. D. 2003. "The Waiting Servant in Later Roman Art." *American Journal of Philology* 124: 443–68.

Dunn, Geoffrey D. 2014. "The Poverty of Melania the Younger and Pinianus." *Augustinianum* 54: 93–115.

Dunn, Geoffrey D., David Luckensmeyer, and Lawrence Cross, eds. 2009. *Prayer and Spirituality in the Early Church. Vol. 5: Poverty and Riches*. Alexandria, VA: St. Paul's.

Durliat, Jean. 1990. *De la ville antique à la ville byzantine. Le problème des subsistances*. Collection de l'École française de Rome 136. Rome: Palais Farnèse.

Eastmond, Antony. 1999. "Body vs. Column: The Cults of St Symeon Stylites." In Liz James, ed., *Desire and Denial in Byzantium: Papers from the 31st Spring Symposium of*

Byzantine Studies, University of Sussex, Brighton, March 1997. Aldershot, UK: Ashgate, 87–100.

Edwards, Mark. 1989. "Satire and Verisimilitude: Christianity in Lucian's *Peregrinus.*" *Historia* 38: 89–98.

Efthymiades, Stephanos, ed. 2011a. *The Ashgate Research Companion to Byzantine Hagiography.* Vol. 1: *Periods and Places.* Farnham and Burlington, VT: Ashgate.

———. 2011b. "Hagiography from the 'Dark Age' to the Age of Symeon Metaphrastes (Eighth-Tenth Centuries)." In Efthymiades 2011a: 95–142.

Efthymiades, Stephanos, and Vincent Déroche. 2011. "Greek Hagiography in Late Antiquity (Fourth-Seventh Centuries)." In Efthymiades 2011a: 35–94.

Elm, Susanna. 2012. *Sons of Hellenism, Fathers of the Church: Emperor Julian, Gregory of Nazianzus, and the Vision of Rome.* TCH 49. Berkeley: University of California Press.

Elter, René, and Ayman Hassoune. 2004. "Le monastère de Saint-Hilarion à Umm-el-'Amr (bande de Gaza)." *Comptes rendus des séances de l'Académie des Inscriptions et Belles-Lettres, 148ᵉ année, N. 1, 2004.* Paris: De Boccard, 359–82.

Elweskiöld, Birgitta. 2005. *John Philoponus against Cosmas Indicopleustes: A Christian Controversy on the Structure of the World in Sixth-Century Alexandria.* Lund: Lund University Press.

Errington, R. Malcolm. 1997. "Christian Accounts of the Religious Legislation of Theodosius I." *Klio* 79: 398–443.

Escolan, Phillipe. 1999. *Monachisme et Église. La monachisme syrien du IVᵉ au VIIᵉ siècle: une ministère charismatique.* Théologie historique 109. Paris: Beauchesne.

Evelyn-White, Hugh G. 1932. *The Monasteries of the Wâdi 'N Natrûn.* Part II: *The History of the Monasteries of Nitria and of Scetis.* New York: Metropolitan Museum of Art.

Évieux, Pierre. 1995. *Isidore de Péluse.* Théologie historique 99. Paris: Beachesne.

Fantham, Elaine. 1973. "*Aequabilitas* in Cicero's Political Theory and the Greek Tradition of Proportional Justice." *Classical Quarterly* n.s. 23: 39–66.

Feissel, Denis, and Ismail Kaygusuz. 1985. "Un mandement impériale du VIᵉ siècle dans une inscription d' Hadrianoupolis d' Honoriade." *TM* 9: 397–419.

Ferradou, André. 1896. *Des Biens des monastères à Byzance.* Bordeaux: Cadoret.

Fikhman, Itzhak. 1973. "Sklaven und Sklavenarbeit im spätrömischen Oxyrhynchos." *Jahrbuch für Wirtschaftsgeschichte* 2: 149–206.

———. 1974. "Slaves in Byzantine Oxyrhynchos." In *Akten des XII internationalen Papyrologenkongresses.* Munich: Beck, 117–24.

———. 1997. "Review of R. Bagnall, *Reading Papyri, Writing Ancient History.*" *Scripta Classica Israelica* 16: 279–85.

Filoramo, Giovanni, ed. 2010. *Monachesimo orientale. Un'introduzione.* Storia 40. Brescia: Morcelliana.

Finn, Richard. 2006a. *Almsgiving in the Later Roman Empire (313–450).* New York: Oxford University Press.

———. 2006b. "Portraying the Poor: Descriptions of Poverty in Christian Texts from the Late Roman Empire." In Atkins and Osborne 2006: 130–44.

Fischer, Mosche. 1989. "An Early Byzantine Settlement at Kh. Zikrin." In *Actes du XIe congrès international d' archéologie chrétienne* II. Collection de l'École français de Rome 123. Rome: École français, 1781–1807.

Fitschen, Klaus. 1998. *Messalianismus und Antimessalianismus: Ein Beispiel ostkirchlicher Ketzergeschichte.* Forschungen zur Kirchen-und Dogmengeschichte 71. Göttingen: Vandenhoeck und Ruprecht.

Fitzgerald, Gerald M. 1939. *A Sixth-Century Monastery at Beth-Shan (Scythopolis).* Publications of the Palestine Section of the University Museum, University of Pennsylvania 6. Philadelphia: University of Pennsylvania Press.

Florovsky, Georges. 1975. "St. John Chrysostom: The Prophet of Charity." In *Collected Works.* Vol. 4: *Aspects of Church History.* Belmont, MA: Nordland, 79–88.

Flusin, Bernard. 1983. *Miracle et histoire dans l'oeuvre de Cyrille de Scythopolis.* Paris: Études augustiniennes.

———. 1991. "Démons et sarrasins." *TM* 11: 381–409.

———. 1992. *Saint Anastase le Perse et l'histoire de la Palestine au début du VIIe siècle.* 2 vols. Paris: Éditions du centre national de recherche scientifique.

———. 1993. "Syméon et les philologues, ou la mort du stylite." In Catherine Jolivet-Lévy, Michel Kaplan, and Jean-Pierre Sodini, eds., *Les Saints et leur sanctuaire à Byzance: texts, images et monuments.* Byzantina Sorbonensia 11. Paris: Publications de la Sorbonne, 1–23.

———. 1996. "L'hagiographie palestinienne et la réception du concile de Chalcédoine." In Jan Olaf Rosenqvist, ed., *ΛΕΙΜΩΝ: Studies Presented to L. Rydén on His Sixty-Fifth Birthday.* Uppsala: Uppsala Universitet, 25–47.

———. 2004. "Le serviteur caché ou le saint sans existence." In Odorico 2004: 59–71.

———. 2011. "Palestinian Hagiography (Fourth-Eighth Centuries)." In Efthymiades 2011a: 199–226.

Foss, Clive. 1975. "The Persians in Asia Minor and the End of Antiquity." *English Historical Review* 90: 721–47.

———. 1991. "Cities and Villages of Lycia in the Life of Saint Nicholas of Holy Zion." *GOTR* 36: 303–39.

———. 2000. "Late Antique Antioch." In Christine Kondoleon, ed., *Antioch the Lost City.* Princeton, NJ: Princeton University Press, 23–27.

———. 2002. "Life in City and Country." In Mango 2002: 71–95.

———. 2003. "The Persians in the Roman Near East (602–630 AD)." *Journal of the Asiatic Society* (third series) 13: 149–70.

Foster, George M. 1961. "The Dyadic Contract: A Model for the Social Structure of a Mexican Peasant Village." *American Anthropologist* 63: 1173–92.

———. 1965. "Peasant Society and the Image of the Limited Good." *American Anthropologist* 67: 293–315.

Fowden, Garth. 1978. "Bishops and Temples in the Eastern Roman Empire, AD 320–435." *JThS* 29: 53–78.

Frankfurter, David. 1990. "Stylites and Phallobates: Pillar Religions in Late Antique Syria." *VC* 44: 168–98.

———, ed. 1998. *Pilgrimage and Holy Space in Late Antique Egypt.* Leiden: Brill.

———. 2017. *Christianizing Egypt: Syncretism and Local Worlds in Late Antiquity.* Martin Classical Lectures. Princeton, NJ: Princeton University Press.

Franz, Adoph. 1960. *Die kirchlichen Benediktionen im Mittelalter.* 2 vols. Graz: Akademische Druck und Verlagsanstalt.

Frazee, Charles. 1981. "St. Theodore of Stoudios and Ninth Century Monasticism in Constantinople." *SM* 23: 27–58.

Frend, William Hugh Clifford. 1972a. "The Monks and the Survival of the East Roman Empire in the Fifth Century." *Past and Present* 54: 3–24.

———. 1972b. *The Rise of the Monophysite Movement: Chapters in the History of the Church in the Fifth and Sixth Centuries.* Cambridge: Cambridge University Press.

Frenkel, Miriam, and Yaacov Lev, eds. 2009. *Charity and Giving in Monotheistic Religions.* Studien zur Geschichte und Kultur des islamischen Orients n.F. 22. Berlin: de Gruyter.

Gain, Benoît. 1985. *L'Église de Cappadoce au IVᵉ siècle d'après la correspondance de Basile de Césarée (330–379).* OCA 225. Rome: Pontificium Institutum Orientale.

Galavaris, George. 1970. *Bread and the Liturgy: The Symbolism of Early Christian and Byzantine Bread Stamps.* Madison: University of Wisconsin Press.

Gardner, Gregg E. 2015. *The Origins of Organized Charity in Rabbinic Judaism.* Cambridge: Cambridge University Press.

Gariboldi, Andrea. 2009. "Social Conditions in Egypt under the Sasanian Occupation." *La parole del passato* 64: 312–53.

Garland, Robert. 1995. *The Eye of the Beholder: Deformity and Disability in the Graeco-Roman World.* London: Duckworth.

Garnsey, Peter. 2007. *Thinking about Property: From Antiquity to the Age of Revolution.* Ideas in Context 90. Cambridge: Cambridge University Press.

———. 2010. "Roman Patronage." In Scott McGill, Cristiana Sogno, and Edward Watts, eds., *From the Tetrarchs to the Theodosians: Later Roman History and Culture, 284–450 C.E.* Yale Classical Studies 34. Cambridge: Cambridge University Press, 33–54.

Garnsey, Peter, and Caroline Humfress. 2001. *The Evolution of the Late Antique World.* Cambridge: Orchard Academic.

Garrison, Roman. 1993. *Redemptive Almsgiving in Early Christianity.* Journal for the Study of the New Testament, suppl. 77. Sheffield: Sheffield Academic.

Gascou, Jean. 1976. "*P.Fouad* 87: Les monastères pachômiens et l'état byzantin." *Bulletin de l'Institut français d'archéologie orientale.* 17: 171–90.

———. 1991. "Monasteries, Economic Activities of." In Aziz S. Atiya, ed., *The Coptic Encyclopedia,* vol. 5. New York: MacMillan, 1639–45.

———. 2006. "Un nouveau document sur les confréries chrétiennes." In Anne Boud'hors, Jean Gascou, and Denyse Vaillancourt, eds., *Journées d'études coptes, IX. Onzième journée d'études (Strasbourg, 12–14 juin 2003).* Cahiers de la Bibliothèque copte 14. Paris: De Boccard, 167–77.

Gaudemet, Jean. 1958. *L'Église dans l'Empire romain (IVᵉ–Vᵉ siècles).* Paris: Sirey.

Georgi, Dieter. 1992. *Remembering the Poor: The History of Paul's Collection for Jerusalem.* Nashville: Abington Press.

Geremek, Bronislaw. 1994. *Poverty: A History.* Trans. Agnieszka Kolakowska. Oxford and Cambridge, MA: Blackwell.

Giardina, Andrea. 1988. "Carità eversiva: le donazioni di *Melania* la giovane e gli equilibri della società tardoromana." *Studi storici* 29: 127–42.

Gibbon, Edward (1896–1898) *The History of the Decline and Fall of the Roman Empire,* ed. John B. Bury. 7 vols. London: Methuen.

Giet, Stanislas. 1941. *Les idées et l'action sociales de Saint Basile.* Paris: Gabalda.

Giorda, Maria Chiara. 2010. "La Diaconia: espressioni monastiche di un servizio, nell' egitto protobizantino." In *Diakonia, "diaconiae," diaconato: Semantica e storia nei padri della chiesa*. Studia ephemerides Augustinianum 117. Rome: Institutum Augustinianum, 177–88.

Gläser, P. P. 1986. "Der Lepra-Begriff in der patristischen Literatur." In Christa Habrich and Jörn Hennig Wolf, eds., *Aussatz, Lepra, Hansen-Krankheit: Ein Menschheitsproblem im Wandel*, vol. 2: *Aufsätze*. Kataloge des deutschen medizinhistorischen Museums 1. Ingolstadt: Deutsches Medizinhistorisches Museum, 63–67.

Glucker, Carol A. M. 1987. *The City of Gaza in the Roman and Byzantine Periods*. BAR International Series 325. Oxford: BAR.

Goehring, James E. 1990. "The World Engaged: The Social and Economic World of Early Egyptian Monasticism." In James E. Goering, ed., *Gnosticism and the Early Christian World: In Honor of James M. Robinson*. Sonoma, CA: Polebridge Press, 134–44; rpr. in Goehring 1999, 32–54.

———. 1999. *Ascetics, Society, and the Desert: Studies in Early Egyptian Monasticism*. Harrisburg, PA: Trinity Press.

———. 2007. "Monasticism in Byzantine Egypt: Continuity and Memory." In Bagnall 2007: 390–407.

Goldfus, Haim. 1997. *Tombs and Burials in Churches and Monasteries of Byzantine Palestine (324–628 A.D.)*. 2 vols. PhD diss., Princeton University.

Goodrich, Richard J. 2007. *Contextualizing Cassian: Aristocrats, Asceticism, and Reformation in Fifth-Century Gaul*. Oxford: Oxford University Press.

Gorce, Denys. 1925. *Les Voyages, l'hospitalité et le port des lettres dans le monde chrétien des IVᵉ et Vᵉ siècles*. Paris: A. Picard.

———. 1972. "Die Gastfreundlichkeit der altchristlichen Einsielder und Mönche." *JbAC* 15: 66–91.

Gordon, Barry. 1989. "The Problem of Scarcity and the Christian Fathers: John Chrysostom and Some Contemporaries." *SP* 22: 108–20.

Gottesman, Alex. 2010. "The Beggar and the Clod: The Mythic Notion of Property in Ancient Greece." *TAPA* 140: 287–322.

Gould, Graham E. 1987. "Basil of Caesarea and the Problem of the Wealth of Monasteries." In W. J. Sheils and Diana Wood, eds., *The Church and Wealth: Papers Read at the 1986 Summer Meeting and the 1987 Winter Meeting of the Ecclesiastical History Society*. Oxford: Blackwell, 15–24.

———. 1993a. *The Desert Fathers on Monastic Community*. Oxford: Clarendon Press.

———. 1993b. "Lay Christians, Bishops, and Clergy in the *Apophthegmata Patrum*." *SP* 25: 396–404.

Granić, Branco. 1929. "Die rechtliche Stellung und Organisation der griechischen Klöster nach dem justinianischen Recht." *Byzantinische Zeitschrift* 29: 6–34.

Gray, Alissa M. 2009. "The Formerly Wealthy Poor: From Empathy to Ambivalence in Rabbinic Literature of Late Antiquity." *Association of Jewish Studies Review* 33: 101–33.

Gray, Sherman W. 1989. *The Least of My Brothers: Matthew 25:31–46. A History of Interpretation*. Society of Biblical Literature Dissertation Series 114. Atlanta: Scholars Press.

Greatrex, Geoffrey, and Samuel N. C. Lieu, eds. 2005. *The Roman Eastern Frontier and the Persian Wars. Part II: AD 363–630. A Narrative Sourcebook*. London and New York: Routledge.

Greer, Rowan A. 1974. "Hospitality in the First Five Centuries of the Church." *Monastic Studies* 10: 29–48.

Grégoire, Henri. 1922. *Recueil des inscriptions grecques chrétiennes d'Asie mineure*, vol. 1. Paris: Leroux.

Gremk, Mirko D. 1989. *Diseases in the Ancient World*. Trans. Mireille Muellner and Leonard Muellner. Baltimore: Johns Hopkins University Press.

Grey, Cam. 2011. *Constructing Communities in the Late Roman Countryside*. Cambridge: Cambridge University Press.

Griffin, Miriam. 2003. "*De Beneficiis* and Roman Society." *JRS* 93: 92–113.

Griffith, Sydney H. 2017. "The Poetics of Scriptural Reasoning: Syriac *Mêmrê* at Work." In Markus Vinzent, ed., *SP* 78, vol. 4. Leuven: Peeters, 5–23.

Grossman, Peter. 1998. "The Pilgrimage Center of Abû Mînâ." In Frankfurter 1998: 281–302.

Guillaume, Alexandre. 1954. *Jeûne et charité dans l'église latine, des orignes au XIIe siécle en particuler chez Saint Léon le Grand*. Paris: Laboureur.

Guillaumont, Antoine. 1975. "La conception du désert chez les moines d'Égypte." *Revue de l'histoire des Religions* 188: 3–21.

Guinan, Michael. 1974. "Where Are the Dead? Purgatory and Immediate Retribution in James of Sarug." In Ignatius Ortiz de Urbina, ed., *Symposium Syriacum 1972*. OCA 197. Rome: Pontificium Institutum Orientalium Studiorum, 541–49.

Gutwein, Kenneth C. 1981. *Third Palestine: A Regional Study in Byzantine Urbanization*. Washington, DC: University Press of America.

Guy, Jean-Claude. 1984. *Recherches sur la tradition grecque des Apophthegmata Patrum*. SH 36. Brussels: Société des Bollandistes.

Haas, Christopher. 1997. *Alexandria in Late Antiquity: Topography and Social Conflict*. Baltimore: Johns Hopkins University Press.

Habas, Lihi. 2009. "Donations and Donors as Reflected in the Mosaic Pavements of Transjordan's Churches in the Byzantine and Umayyad Periods." In Katrin Kogman-Appel and Mati Meyer, eds., *Between Judaism and Christianity: Art Historical Essays in Honor of Elisheva (Elizabeth) Revel-Neher*. The Medieval Mediterranean 81. Leiden: Brill 2009, 73–90.

Haensch, Rudolf. 1997. *Capita provinciarum: Statthaltersitze und Provinzialverwaltung in der römischen Kaiserzeit*. Kölner Forschungen 7. Mainz: Philipp von Zabern.

———. 2006. "Le financement de la construction des églises pendant l'Antiquité tardive et l'évergétisme antique." *AnTard* 14: 47–58.

Hahn, Cynthia. 1990. "Loca Sancta Souvenirs: Sealing the Pilgrim's Experience." In Ousterhout 1990: 85–96.

Hahn, Johannes, and Völker Menze, eds. 2020. *The Wandering Holy Man: The Life of Barsauma, Christian Asceticism, and Religious Conflict in Late Antique Palestine*. TCH 60. Oakland: University of California Press.

Haldon, John F., ed. 2009. *A Social History of Byzantium*. London: Wiley-Blackwell.

Hall, Harry R. 1905. *Coptic and Greek Texts of the Christian Period from Ostraka, Stelae, etc., in the British Museum*. London: British Museum.

Hamel, Gildas. 1990. *Poverty and Charity in Roman Palestine, First Three Centuries C.E.* Near Eastern Studies 23. Berkeley: University of California Press.

Hamman, Adalbert Gautier. 1968. *Vie liturgique et vie sociale: Repas des pauvres. Diaconie et diaconat. Agape et repas de charité. Offrande dans l'antiquité chrétienne*. Paris: Desclée.

Hands, Arthur. R. 1968. *Charities and Social Aid in Greece and Rome*. Ithaca, NY: Cornell University Press.

Harl, Kenneth W. 1990. "Sacrifice and Pagan Belief in Fifth- and Sixth-Century Byzantium." *Past and Present* 128: 7–27.

Harnack, Adolf. 1961. *The Mission and Expansion of Christianity in the First Three Centuries*. Trans. James Moffatt. New York: Harper and Brothers.

Harper, Kyle. 2011. *Slavery in the Late Roman World, AD 275–425*. Cambridge: Cambridge University Press.

———. 2017. *The Fate of Rome: Climate, Disease, and the End of an Empire*. Princeton, NJ: Princeton University Press.

Harries, Jill. 1999. *Law and Empire in Late Antiquity*. Cambridge: Cambridge University Press.

Harris, William V. 2016. *Roman Power: A Thousand Years of Empire*. Cambridge: Cambridge University Press.

Harrison, Nonna Verna. 2016. "Greek Patristic Perspectives on the Origins of Social Injustice." In Nonna Verna Harrison and David G. Vigiler, eds., *Suffering and Evil in Early Christian Thought. Holy Cross Studies in Patristic Theology and History*. Grand Rapids, MI: Baker Academic, 81–96.

Harrison, Richard Martin. 1989. *A Temple for Byzantium: The Discovery and Excavation of Anicia Juliana's Palace Church in Istanbul*. London: Harvey Miller.

Hartney, Aideen. 2004. *John Chrysostom and the Transformation of the City*. London: Duckworth.

Harvey, F. David. 1965. "Two Kinds of Equality." *Classica et Mediaevalia* 26: 101–46.

Harvey, Susan Ashbrook. 1988. "The Sense of a Stylite: Perspectives on Symeon Stylites the Elder." *VC* 42: 376–94.

———. 1990. *Asceticism and Society in Crisis: John of Ephesus and The Lives of the Eastern Saints*. TCH 18. Berkeley: University of California Press.

———. 1993. "The Memory and Meaning of a Saint: Two Homilies on Simeon Stylites." *Aram* 5: 219–41.

———. 1994. "The Holy and the Poor: Models from Early Syriac Christianity." In Emily Albu Hanawalt, ed., *Through the Eye of a Needle: Judeo-Christian Roots of Social Welfare*. Kirksville, MO: Thomas Jefferson University Press, 43–66.

———. 1998. "The Stylite's Liturgy: Ritual and Religious Identity in Late Antiquity." *JECS* 6: 523–39.

———. 2006. "Praying Bodies, Bodies at Prayer: Ritual Relations in Early Syriac Christianity." In Wendy Mayer, Pauline Allen, and Lawrence Cross, eds., *Prayer and Spirituality in the Early Church*, vol.4: *The Spiritual Life*. Strathfield: St. Paul's Publications, 149–67.

———. 2010. "To Whom Did Jacob Preach?" In Kiraz 2010: 115–31.

Hasan-Rokem, Galit. 2009. "Did Rabbinic Culture Conceive of the Category of Folk Narrative?" *European Journal of Jewish Studies* 3: 19–55.

Hasitzka, Monika R. M. 2001. "Brief des Klostervorstehers Theodoros die APARCHÊ-Sammlung Betreffend." *JJP* 31: 55–58.

Hasse-Ungeheuer, Alexandra. 2016. *Das Mönchtum in der Religionspolitik Kaiser Justinians I: Die Engel des Himmels und der Stellvertreter Gottes auf Erden*. Millennium-Studien 59. Berlin: De Gruyter.

Hatlie, Peter. 2002. "A Rough-Guide to Byzantine Monasticism in the Early Seventh Century." In Gerrit J. Reinink and Bernard H. Stolte, eds., *The Reign of Heraclius (610–641): Crisis and Confrontation.* Groningen Studies in Cultural Change 2. Leuven: Peeters, 205–26.

———. 2007a. "Byzantine Monastic Rules before the Typikon: From the Sixth to the Eighth Century." In Mullett 2007: 140–81.

———. 2007b. *The Monks and Monasteries of Constantinople, ca. 350–850.* Cambridge: Cambridge University Press.

Hausherr, Iréné. 1982. *Penthos: The Doctrine of Compunction in the Christian East.* Trans. Anselm Hufstader. CS 53. Kalamazoo, MI: Cistercian Publications.

Hénaff, Marcel. 2010. *The Price of Truth: Gift, Money, and Philosophy.* Trans. Jean-Louis Morhange. Stanford, CA: Stanford University Press.

Hendy, Michael F. 1989. "Economy and State in Late Rome and Early Byzantium: An Introduction." *The Economy, Fiscal Administration and Coinage of Byzantium.* Collected Studies 305. Northampton: Variorum Reprints, 1–23.

Henner, Jutta. 2008. "Die anaphorische Interzession für die Verstorbenen nach den frühen Zeugnissen koptischer Liturgie." In Boud'hors et al. 2009: 148–58.

Henry, Ayşe. 2015. "The Pilgrimage Center of St. Symeon the Younger: Designed by Angels, Supervised by a Saint, Constructed by Pilgrims." PhD diss., University of Illinois at Urbana-Champaign.

Henry, Paul. 1967. "A Mirror of Justinian: The *Ekthesis* of Agapetus Diaconus." *GRBS* 8: 281–308.

Henze, Mattias. 1999. *The Madness of King Nebuchadnezzar: The Ancient Near Eastern Origins and Early History of Interpretation of Daniel 4.* Supplements to the Journal for the Study of Judaism 61. Leiden: Brill.

Herman, Emil. 1941. "Die Regelung der Armut in den byzantinischen Klöstern." *OCP* 7: 406–60.

———. 1942. "Die kirchlichen Einkünfte des byzantinischen Niederklerus." *OCP* 8: 402–10.

Herman, Gabriel. 1987. *Ritualised Friendship and the Greek City.* Cambridge: Cambridge University Press.

Herman, Menahem. 1991. *Tithe as Gift: The Institution in the Pentateuch and in Light of Mauss' Prestation Theory.* San Francisco: Mellen Research University Press.

Hermann-Otto, Elisabeth. 2003. "Die 'armen' Alten. Das neue Modell des Christentums?" In Andreas Gutsfeld and Winfried Schmitz, eds., *Altersbilder in der Antike: Am schlimmen Rand des Lebens?* Super alta perennis. Studien zur Wirkung der Klassischen Antike 8. Cologne: Böhlau, 181–208.

Hermes, Raimund. 1996. "Die stadtrömischen Diakonien." *Römische Quartalschrift für christliche Altertumskunde und Kirchengeschichte* 91: 1–120.

Herrin, Judith. 1987. *The Formation of Christendom.* Princeton: Princeton University Press.

———. 2013a. "From Bread and Circuses to Soup and Salvation: The Origins of Byzantine Charity." In Judith Herrin, *Margins and Metropolis: Authority across the Byzantine Empire.* Princeton, NJ: Princeton University Press, 267–98.

———. 2013b. "Ideals of Charity, Realities of Welfare: The Philanthropic Activity of the Byzantine Church." In Judith Herrin, *Margins and Metropolis: Authority across the Byzantine Empire.* Princeton and Oxford: Princeton University Press, 299–311.

Hester, David P. 1990. "The Eschatology of the Sermons of Symeon the Younger the Stylite." *St. Vladimir's Theological Quarterly* 34: 329–42.

Heussi, Karl. 1936. *Der Ursprung des Mönchtums*. Tübingen: Mohr.

Hevelone-Harper, Jennifer L. 2005. *Disciples of the Desert: Monks, Laity, and Spiritual Authority in Sixth-Century Gaza*. Baltimore: Johns Hopkins University Press.

Hickey, Todd. 2007. "Aristocratic Landholding and the Economy of Byzantine Egypt." In Bagnall 2007: 288–308.

Hill, Robert C. 1981. "On Looking Again at *Sunkatabasis*." *Prudentia* 13: 3–11.

Hillner, Julia. 2007. "Families, Patronage and the Titular Churches of Rome, c. 300–c. 600." In Kate Cooper and Julia Hillner, eds., *Religion, Dynasty, and Patronage in Early Christian Rome, 300–900*. Cambridge: Cambridge University Press, 225–61.

Hiltbrunner, Otto. 1990. "Warum wollten sie nicht 'philanthropoi' heissen?" *JbAC* 33: 7–20.

———. 1994. "Humanitas (φιλανθρωπία)." *RAC* 16: 711–52.

Hirschfeld, Yitzar. 1990. "List of the Byzantine Monasteries in the Judean Desert." In Leah di Segni, G. C. Bottini, and E. Alliata, eds., *Christian Archaeology in the Holy Land: Essays in Honour of Virgilio C. Corbo, OFM*. Jerusalem: Franciscan Printing Press, 1–89.

———. 1992. *The Judean Monasteries in the Byzantine Period*. New Haven, CT: Yale University Press.

———. 1993. "Euthymius and His Monastery in the Judean Desert." *Liber Annus* 43: 339–71.

———. 1996. "The Importance of Bread in the Diet of Monks in the Judean Desert." *Byzantion* 66: 143–55.

———. 2004. "The Monasteries of Gaza: An Archaeological Review." In Bitton-Ashkelony and Kofsky 2004: 61–88.

Holman, Susan R. 2000. "The Entitled Poor: Human Rights Language in the Cappadocians." *Pro Ecclesia* 9: 476–89.

———. 2001. *The Hungry Are Dying: Beggars and Bishops in Roman Cappadocia*. New York: Oxford University Press.

———, ed. 2008. *Wealth and Poverty in Early Church and Society*. Holy Cross Studies in Patristic Theology and History. Grand Rapids, MI: Baker Academic.

———. 2009. "Healing the World with Righteousness? The Language of Social Justice in Early Christian Homilies." In Frenkel and Lev 2009: 89–110.

———. 2010. "On the Ground: Realizing an 'Altared' Philoptochia." In Matthew J. Pereira, ed., *Philanthropy and Social Compassion in Eastern Orthodox Tradition*. Papers of the Sophia Institute Annual Academic Conference Dec. 2009. New York: Theotokos Press, 231–49.

———. 2011. "Out of the Fitting Room: Rethinking Patristic Social Texts on 'The Common Good.'" In Johan Leemans, Brian Matz, and Johan Verstraeten, eds., *Reading Patristic Texts on Social Ethics: Issues and Challenges for 21st Century Christian Social Thought*. Washington, DC: Catholic University of America Press, 103–23.

Holum, Kenneth G. 1982. *Theodosian Empresses: Women and Imperial Dominion in Late Antiquity*. TCH 3. Berkeley: University of California Press.

Hombergen, Daniël. 2004. "Le fonti scritturistiche e patristiche dei padri di Gaza." In Sabino Chialà and Lisa Cremaschi, eds. *Il deserto di Gaza: Barsanufio, Giovanni, Doroteo*. XI Convegno Ecumenico Internazionale, Monastero di Bose, 14–16 settembre 2003. Magnano: Qiqajon/Community of Bose, 81–98.

Honigmann, Ernst. 1954. *Le couvent de Barsauma et le patriarcat jacobite d'Antioche et de Syrie*. Louvain: Durbecq.

Horden, Peregrine. 1986. "The Confraternities of Byzantium." In W. J. Sheils and Diane Wood, eds., *Voluntary Religion*. Studies in Church History 23. London: Ecclesiastical History Society, 25–45.

———. 1998. "Introduction." In Peregrine Horden and Richard Smith, eds., *The Locus of Care: Families, Communities, Institutions and the Provision of Welfare since Antiquity*. London and New York: Routledge, 1–18.

———. 2012. "Poverty, Charity, and the Invention of the Hospital." In Johnson 2012: 715–43.

Horden, Peregrine, and Nicholas Purcell. 2000. *The Corrupting Sea: A Study of Mediterranean History*. Oxford: Blackwell.

Horn, Cornelia. 2004. "Empress Eudocia and the Monk Peter the Iberian: Patronage, Pilgrimage, and the Love of a Foster-mother in Fifth-century Palestine." *Byzantinische Forschungen* 28: 197–213.

———. 2006. *Asceticism and Christological Controversy in Fifth-Century Palestine: The Career of Peter the Iberian*. Oxford and New York: Oxford University Press.

———. 2020. "Ascetic History and Rhetoric in the *Life of Barsauma*." In Hahn and Menze 2020: 50–71.

Hübner, Sabine R. 2005. *Der Klerus in der Gesellschaft des spätantiken Kleinasiens*. Altertumswissenschaftliches Kolloquium 15. Munich: Franz Steiner.

———. 2014. "'It is a difficult matter to be wronged by strangers, but to be wronged by kin is worst of all': Inheritance and Conflict in Greco-Roman Egypt." In Caseau and Hübner 2014: 99–108.

Hull, Daniel. 2008. "A Spatial and Morphological Analysis of Monastic Sites in the Northern Limestone Massif, Syria." *Levant* 40: 89–113.

Humfress, Caroline. 2005. "Law and Legal Practice in the Age of Justinian." In Maas 2005: 161–84.

Hunger, Herbert. 1963. "ΦΙΛΑΝΘΡΩΠΙΑ. Eine griechische Wortprägung auf ihrem Wege von Aischylos bis Theodoros Metochites." *Österreichische Akademie der Wissenschaften, Philosophisch-historische Klasse, Anzeiger* 100: 1–20.

———. 1964. *Prooimion-Elemente der Byzantinischen Kaiseridee in den Arengen der Urkunden*. Wiener byzantinische Studien 1. Vienna: Böhlaus.

Hunt, Edward David. 1982. *Holy Land Pilgrimage in the Later Roman Empire, AD 312–460*. Oxford: Clarendon Press.

Hunt, Hannah. 2004. *Joy-Bearing Grief: Tears of Contrition in the Writings of the Early Syrian and Byzantine Fathers*. The Medieval Mediterranean: People, Economies and Cultures, 400–1500, 57. Leiden: Brill.

———. 2012. "'Working the Earth of the Heart': Images of Cultivation and Harvest in Macarius and Ephrem." In Allen Brent and Markus Vinzent, eds., *SP* 52. Leuven: Peeters, 2012, 149–60.

Husselman, Elinor M. 1957. "*Donationes mortis causa* from Tebtunis." *TAPA* 88: 135–54.

Izdebski, Adam. 2013. *A Rural Economy in Transition: Asia Minor from Late Antiquity into the Early Middle Ages*. JJP Suppl. 28. Warsaw: University of Warsaw.

Jakab, Attila. 2001. *Ecclesia Alexandrina. Évolution sociale et institutionnelle du christianisme alexandrin (IIᵉ et IIIᵉ siècles)*. Christianismes anciens 1. Bern: Peter Lang.

Jalabert, Louis, and Mouterde, René. 1950. *Inscriptiones grecques et latines de la Syrie*. Vol. 3: *Région de l'Amanus. Antioche*. Bibliopthèque archéologique et historique 46. Paris: Paul Geuthner.

———. 1959. *Inscriptiones grecques et latines de la Syrie*. Vol. 5: *Émésène*. Bibliopthèque archéologique et historique 66. Paris: Paul Geuthner

Janin, Raymond. 1975. *Les églises et les monastères des grands centres byzantins*. Paris: Institut français d'études byzantines.

Jim, Suk Fong (Theodora). 2012. "Naming a Gift: The Vocabulary and Purpose of Greek Religious Offerings." *GRBS* 52: 310–37.

———. 2014. *Sharing with the Gods: Aparchai and Dekatai in Ancient Greece*. Oxford: Oxford University Press.

Jobert, Philippe J. 1977. *Le Notion de donation: convergences 630–750*. Publications de l'Université de Dijon 49. Paris: Les Belles Lettres.

Jones, Arnold Hugh Martin. 1960. "Church Finance in the Fifth and Sixth Centuries." *JThS* n.s. 11: 84–94.

———. 1964. *The Later Roman Empire 284–602: A Social, Economic and Administrative Survey*. 2 vols. Baltimore: Johns Hopkins University Press.

Jones, F. Stanley. 1982. "The Pseudo-Clementines: A History of Research." *Second Century* 2: 1–33, 63–99.

Jong, Mayke de. 1995. "Carolingian Monasticism: The Power of Prayer." In Rosamond McKitterick, ed., *The New Cambridge Medieval History, vol. 2: c.700–c.900*. Cambridge: Cambridge University Press, 622–53.

Johnson, David. 1985. "Prohibitions and Perpetuities: Family Settlements in Roman Law." *Zeitschrift der Savigny-Stiftung für Rechtsgeschichte* 102: 220–90.

Johnson, Scott F., ed. 2012. *The Oxford Handbook of Late Antiquity*. Oxford and New York: Oxford University Press.

Jullien, Christelle, and Florence Jullien. 2010. "Du ḥnana ou la bénédiction contestée." In Françoise Briquel Chatonnet and Muriel Debie, eds., *Sur les pas des Araméens chrétiens: Mélanges offerts à Alain Dereumaux*. Cahiers d'études syriaques 1. Paris: Paul Geuthner, 333–48.

Kabiersch, Jürgen. 1960. *Untersuchungen zum Begriff der Philanthropia bei dem Kaiser Julian*. Klassisch-philologische Studien 21. Wiesbaden: O. Harrassowitz.

Kahle, Paul E. 1954. *Bala'izah: Coptic Texts from Deir El-Bala'izah in Upper Egypt*, 2 vols. Oxford: Oxford University Press.

Kaldellis, Anthony. 2004. *Procopius of Caesarea: Tyranny, History, and Philosophy at the End of Antiquity*. Philadelphia: University of Pennsylvania Press.

———. 2011. "The Kalends in Byzantium, 400–1200 AD: A New Interpretation." *Archiv für Religiongeschichte* 13: 187–204.

Karayiannis, Anastassios, and Sarah Drakopoulou-Dodd. 1998. "The Greek Christian Fathers." In S. Todd Lowry and Barry Gordon, eds., *Ancient and Medieval Economic Ideas and Concepts of Social Justice*. Leiden: Brill, 163–208.

Kaplan, Michel. 1976. *Les próprietés de la Couronne et de l'Église dans l'Empire byzantin (Vᵉ–VIᵉ siècles)*. Byzantina Sorbonensia 2. Paris: Publications de la Sorbonne.

———. 1992. *Les hommes et la terre à Byzance du VIᵉ au XIᵉ siècle: Propriété et exploitation du sol*. Byzantina Sorbonensia 10. Paris: Publications de la Sorbonne.

————. 2020. "The Economy of Byzantine Monasteries." In Alison I. Beach and Isabelle Cochelin, eds., *The Cambridge History of Medieval Monasticism in the Latin West*, vol 1. Cambridge: Cambridge University Press, 340–62.

Kelley, Nicole. 2006. *Knowledge and Religious Authority in the Pseudo-Clementines: Situating the Recognitions in the Fourth Century.* Wissenschaftliche Untersuchungen zum Neuen Testament 2.213. Tübingen: Mohr Siebeck.

Kelly, Christopher. 2004. *Ruling the Later Roman Empire.* Cambridge, MA: Harvard University Press.

Kiljn, A. F. J. 1962. *The Acts of Thomas: Introduction, Text, Commentary.* Supplements to Novum Testamentum 5. Leiden: Brill.

Kiraz, George A., ed. 2010. *Jacob of Serugh and His Times: Studies in Sixth-Century Syriac Christianity.* Gorgias Eastern Christian Studies 8. Piscataway, NJ: Gorgias Press.

Kirschner, Robert, 1984. "The Vocation of Holiness in Late Antiquity." *VC* 38: 105–24.

Kislinger, Ewald. 1984. "Kaiser Julian und die (Christlichen) Xenodocheia." In Wolfram Hörandner and Johannes Koder, eds., *BYZANTINOΣ: Festschrift für Herbert Hunger zum 70. Geburtstag.* Vienna: Becvar, 171–84.

Klein, Richard. 2008. *Zum Verhältnis von Staat und Kirche in der Spätantike. Studien zu politischen, sozialen und wirtschaftlichen Frage.* Tria Cordia: Jenaer Vorlesungen zu Judentum, Antike und Christentum 3. Tübingen: Mohr Siebeck.

Koep, Leo. 1952. *Das himmlische Buch in Antike und Christentum: Eine religionsgeschichtliche Untersuchung zur altchristlichen Bildesprache.* Theophaneia 8. Bonn: Peter Hanstein.

Kofsky, Aryeh. 2004. "The Byzantine Holy Person: The Case of Barsanuphius and John of Gaza." In Marcel Poorthuis und Joshua Schwartz, eds., *Saints and Role Models in Judaism and Christianity.* Leiden: Brill, 261–85.

Kosiński, Rafał. 2016. *Holiness and Power: Constantinopolitan Holy Men and Authority in the Fifth Century.* Millenium-Studien 57. Berlin: De Gruyter.

Kotsifou, Chrysi. 2012. "Books and Book Production in the Monastic Communities of Byzantine Egypt." In William E. Klingshirn and Linda Safran, eds., *The Early Christian Book.* Washington, DC: Catholic University Press, 48–66.

————. 2014. "Monks as Mediators in Christian Egypt." In James G. Keenan, Joseph G. Manning, and Uri Yiftach-Firanko, eds., *Law and Legal Practice in Egypt from Alexander to the Arab Conquests.* Cambridge: Cambridge University Press, 530–40.

Kloft, Hans. 1970. *Liberalitas Principis. Herkunft und Bedeutung: Studien zur Prinzipatsideologie.* Kölner historische Abhandlungen 18. Cologne and Vienna: Böhlau.

Komter, Aafke Elisabeth. 2004. "Gratitude and Gift Exchange." In Robert A. Emmons and Michael E. McCullough, eds., *The Psychology of Gratitude.* New York: Oxford University Press, 195–212.

Konstan, David. 2001. *Pity Transformed.* London: Duckworth.

————. 2005. "Clemency as a Virtue." *Classical Philology* 100: 337–46.

————. 2006. *The Emotions of the Ancient Greeks: Studies in Aristotle and Classical Literature.* Toronto: University of Toronto Press.

————. 2010. *Before Forgiveness: The Origins of a Moral Idea.* Cambridge: Cambridge University Press.

Kortenbeutel, Heinz. 1940. "Philanthropon." *Pauly-Wissowa Realencyclopädie der classischen Altertumswissenschaft,* Supplementband 7: 1032–34. Stuttgart: J. B. Metzler Verlag.

Koskenniemi, Heikki. 1956. *Studien zur Ideologie und Phraseologie des griechischen Briefes bis 400 n. Chr.* Suomalaisen Tiedeakatemian Toimituksia, 2nd ser., 102.2. Helsinki: Academy of Sciences.

Kotila, Heikki. 1992. *Memoria Mortuorum: Commemoration of the Departed in Augustine.* Rome: Institutum Patristicum Augustinianum.

Kötting, Bernhard. 1950. *Peregrinatio religiosa: Wallfahrten in der Antike und das Pilgerwesen in der alten Kirche.* Münster: Regensberg.

———. 1965. *Der Fruhchristliche Reliquienkult und die Bestattung im Kirchengebaude.* Arbeitsgemeinschaft für Forschung des Landes Nordrhein-Westfalen 123. Wiesbaden: Springer Fachmedien.

Kraeling, Carl H. 1938. *Gerasa: City of the Decapolis.* New Haven, CT: American Schools of Oriental Research.

Kraemer, Charles. 1958. *Excavations at Nessana.* Vol. 3: *Non-Literary Papyri.* Princeton, NJ: Princeton University Press.

Krause, Jens-Uwe. 1987. *Spätantike Patronatsformen im Westen des römischen Reiches.* Vestigia 38. Munich: Bech.

Kreiner, Jamie, and Helmut Reimitz, eds. 2016. *Motions of Late Antiquity: Essays on Religion, Politics, and Society in Honour of Peter Brown.* Cultural Encounters in Late Antiquity and the Middle Ages 20. Turnhout: Brepols.

Krueger, Derek. 1996. *Symeon the Holy Fool: Leontius's* Life *and the Late Antique City.* TCH 25. Berkeley: University of California Press.

———. 2005. "Christian Piety and Practice in the Sixth Century." In Maas 2005: 291–315.

———. 2010a. "The Liturgical Creation of a Christian Past: Identity and Community in Anaphoral Prayers." In Christopher Kelly, Richard Flower, and Michael Stuart Williams, eds., *Unclassical Traditions,* vol. 1: *Alternatives to the Classical Past in Late Antiquity.* Cambridge Classical Journal, suppl. 34. Cambridge: Cambridge University Press, 58–71.

———. 2010b. "Early Byzantine Historiography and Hagiography as Different Modes of Christian Practice." In Arietta Papaconstantinou, ed., *Writing "True Stories": Historians and Hagiographers in the Late Antique and Mediaeval Near East.* Cultural Encounters in Late Antiquity and the Middle Ages 9. Turnhout: Brepols, 13–20.

Krüger, Karl H. 1971. *Königsgrabkirchen der Franken, Angelsachesen und Langobarden bis zur Mitte des 8. Jahrhunderts: Eine historischer Katalog.* Munich: Wilhelm Fink.

Krumpholz, Helmut. 1992. *Über sozialstaatliche Aspekte in der Novellengesetzgebung Justinians.* Bonn: Habelt.

Krupp, Robert A. 1984. *Saint John Chrysostom: A Scripture Index.* Lanham, MD: University Press of America.

Kurbatov, Georgii L. 1958. "Klassavoja suscnost ucenija Ioanna Zlatausta." *Ezegodnik muzeja istorii i religii i ateiznoz* 2: 80–106. Trans. Andrius Valevicius, "The Nature of Class in the Teaching of John Chrysostom." Accessed October 10, 2010. http://www.cecs.acu.edu.au.

Kurke, Leslie. 1999. *Coins, Bodies, Games, and Gold: The Politics of Meaning in Archaic Greece.* Princeton, NJ: Princeton University Press.

Laidlaw, James. 1995. *Riches and Renunciation: Religion, Economy, and Society among the Jains.* Oxford: Clarendon Press.

———. 2000. "A Free Gift Makes No Friends." *Journal of the Royal Anthropological Institute* 6: 616–34.

Laiou, Angeliki. 1996. "The Church, Economic Thought and Economic Practice." In Robert F. Taft, ed., *The Christian East, Its Institutions and Its Thought: A Critical Reflection.* International Scholarly Conference for the 75th Anniversary of the Pontifical Oriental Institute in Rome, 30 May–5 June 1993. OCA 251. Rome: Pontificio Istituto Orientale, 435–64.

———, ed. 2002. *The Economic History of Byzantium from the Seventh through the Fifteenth Century.* 3 vols. Washington, DC: Dumbarton Oaks.

Lamp, G. W. H. 1961–1968. *A Patristic Greek Lexicon.* Oxford: Oxford University Press.

Lane Fox, Robin. 1986. *Pagans and Christians.* Hammondsworth: Viking.

———. 1997. "Power and Possession in the First Monasteries." In H. W. Pleket and A. Verhoogt, eds., *Aspects of the Fourth Century.* Leiden: AGAPE, 68–95.

Laniado, Avshalom. 2002. *Recherches sur les notables municipaux dans l'empire protobyzantin.* Travaux et Mémoires du Centre de Recherche d'histoire et civilisation de Byzance 13. Paris: Association des Amis du Centre d'histoire et civilisation de Byzance.

———. 2009. "The Early Byzantine State and the Christian Ideal of Voluntary Poverty." In Frenkel and Lev 2009: 15–43.

———. 2015. *Ethnos et droit dans le monde protobyzantin, V^e–VIIe siècle: Fédérés, paysans et provinciaux à la lumière d'une scholie juridique de l'époque de Justinien.* École Pratique des Hautes Études, Sciences Historique et Philologiques 3; Hautes Études du monde grécoromain 52. Geneva: Droz.

Lapin, Hayim. 1996. "Rabbis and Public Prayers for Rain in Later Roman Palestine." In Adele Berlin, ed., *Religion and Politics in the Ancient Near East.* College Park: University Press of Maryland, 105–29.

Larsen, Lillian. 2006. "Pedagogical Parallels: Re-Reading the *Apophthegmata Patrum.*" PhD diss., Columbia University.

Larsen, Lillian, and Samuel Rubenson, eds. 2018. *Monastic Education in Late Antiquity: The Transformation of Classical Paideia.* Cambridge: Cambridge University Press.

Lascartos, John G. 1996. "The Second 'Sacred Disease': Earlier Euphemistic Equivalents of 'Hansen's Disease.'" *International Journal of Dermatology* 35: 376–78.

Lassus, Jean. 1947. *Sanctuaires chrétiens de Syrie. Essai sur la genèse, la forme et l'usage liturgique des édifices du culte chrétien en Syrie, du IIIe siècle à la conquête musulmane.* Institut Français d'Archéologie de Beyrouth, Bibliothèque Archéologique et Historique 42. Paris: Geuthner.

———. 1977. "La ville d'Antioche à l'époque romain d'après l'archéologie." *Aufstieg und Niedergang der romischen Welt* 2: 54–102.

Laurence, Patrick. 2000. See Gerontius.

Layton, Bentley. 2002. "Social Structure and Food Consumption in an Early Christian Monastery: The Evidence of Shenoute's *Canons* and the White Monastery Federation A.D. 385–465." *Le Muséon* 115: 25–57.

Leader-Newby, Ruth E. 2004. *Silver and Society in Late Antiquity: Functions and Meanings of Silver Plate in the Fourth to Seventh Centuries.* London: Routledge.

Le Bras, Gabriel. 1936. "Les fondations privées du Haut Empire." In *Studi in onore di Salvatore Riccobono nel XL anno del suo insegnamento* 3. Palermo; rpr. Aalen: Scientia, 1974, 21–68.

Leclercq, Henri. 1907. "Agaune." *DACL* 1.1: 850–71.

——. 1920a. "Diacre." *DACL* 4.1: 738–46.

——. 1920b. "Dîme." *DACL* 4.1: 995–1003.

——. 1922. "Eulogie." *DACL* 5: 733–34.

——. 1924. "Hôpitaux, Hospices, Hôtelleries." *DACL* 6.2: 2748–70.

——. 1945. "Les paradoxes de l'économie monastique." *Economie et Humanisme* 4: 4–36.

Lefort, Louis Th. 1923. "Un mot nouveau: κορσενήλιον/καρσελήνιον." *Le Muséon* 36: 27–31.

Leithart, Peter J. 2014. *Gratitude: An Intellectual History*. Waco, TX: Baylor University Press.

Lendon, Jon E. 1997. *Empire of Honour: The Art of Government in the Roman World*. Oxford: Clarendon Press.

Lenski, Noel. 2004. "Valens and the Monks: Cudgeling and Conscription as a Means of Social Control." *DOP* 58: 93–117.

Leppin, Hartmut. 2009. "Power from Humility: Justinian and the Religious Authority of Monks." In Andrew Cain and Noel Lenski, eds., *The Power of Religion in Late Antiquity*. Farnham: Ashgate, 155–64.

Lesieur, Bénédicte. 2011. "Le monastère de Séridos sou Barsanuphe et Jean de Gaza: Un monastére conforme à la législation impériale et ecclésiastique?" *REB* 69: 5–47.

Levi, Doro. 1947. *Antioch Mosaic Pavements*. 2 vols. Princeton, NJ: Princeton University Press.

Leyerle, Blake. 1994. "John Chrysostom on Almsgiving and the Use of Money." *HTR* 87: 29–47.

Lieberman, Saul. 1946. "Two Lexicographical Notes." *Journal of Biblical Literature* 65: 67–71.

Liebeschuetz, J. H. W. G. 1972. *Antioch: City and Imperial Administration in the Later Roman Empire*. Oxford: Clarendon Press.

——. 2001. *The Decline and Fall of the Roman City*. Oxford: Oxford University Press.

Lieu, Judith. 2007. "Charity in Early Christian Thought and Practice." In Stathakopoulos 2007: 13–20.

Lifshitz, Felice. 1994. "Beyond Positivism and Genre: 'Hagiographical' Texts as Historical Narrative." *Viator* 25: 95–113.

Limor, Ora. 2017. "Earth, Stone, Water, and Oil: Objects of Veneration in Holy Land Travel Narratives." In Renana Bartal, Neta Bodner, and Bianca Kühnel, eds., *Natural Materials of the Holy Land and the Visual Translation of Place, 500–1500*. London and New York: Routledge, 3–18.

Loewenberg, Frank M. 2001. *From Charity to Social Justice: The Emergence of Communal Institutions for the Support of the Poor in Ancient Judaism*. New Brunswick, NJ: Transaction Publishers.

Longosz, Stanley. 1993. "L'antico mimo anticristiano." *SP* 24: 164–68.

López, Ariel G. 2013. *Shenute of Atripe and the Uses of Poverty: Rural Patronage, Religious Conflict and Monasticism in Late Antique Egypt*. TCH 50. Berkeley: University of California Press.

——. 2016. "Life on Schedule: Monks and the Agricultural Cycle in Late Antique Egypt." In Kreiner and Reimitz 2016: 187–208.

Lorenz, Siegfried. 1914. *De progressu notionis ΦΙΛΑΝΘΡΩΠΙΑΣ*. Leipzig: Thomas and Hubert.

Lubomierski, Nina. 2006. "The *Vita Sinuthii* (The Life of Shenoute): Panegyric or Biography?" *SP* 39: 417–21.

———. 2008. "The Coptic Life of Shenoute." In Gawdat Gabra and Hany N. Takla, eds., *Christianity and Monasticism in Upper Egypt*, vol.1: *Akhmim and Sohag*. Cairo: American University in Cairo Press, 91–98.

Maas, Michael. 1992. *John Lydus and the Roman Past: Antiquarianism and Politics in the Age of Justinian*. London and New York: Routledge.

———, ed. 2005. *The Cambridge Companion to the Age of Justinian*. Cambridge: Cambridge University Press.

MacCormack, Sabine G. 1981. *Art and Ceremony in Late Antiquity*. TCH 1. Berkeley: University of California Press.

MacCoull, Leslie S. B. 1993. "The Apa Apollos Monastery of Pharou (Aphrodito) and Its Papyrus Archive." *Le Muséon* 106: 21–63.

———. 1999. "Who was Eusebius of Alexandria?" *Byzantinoslavica* 60: 9–18.

MacMullen, Ramsay. 1962. "The Emperor's Largesses." *Latomus* 21: 159–66.

———. 1988. *Corruption and the Decline of Rome*. New Haven, CT: Yale University Press.

———. 1997. *Christianity and Paganism in the Fourth to Eighth Centuries*. New Haven, CT: Yale University Press.

———. 2009. *The Second Church: Popular Christianity A.D. 200–400*. New Haven, CT: Yale University Press.

Magdalino, Paul. 1981. "The Byzantine Holy Man in the Twelfth Century." In Sergei Hackel, ed., *The Byzantine Saint*. London: Fellowship of St. Albans and St. Sergius, 51–66.

———. 1990. "Church, Bath, and *Diakonia* in Medieval Constantinople." In Morris 1990: 165–88.

Magen, Iszchak. 1993. *The Monastery of Martyrius at Ma'ale Adummim*. Jerusalem: Israel Antiquities Authority.

Magnani Soares-Christen, Eliana. 2003. "Transforming Things and Persons: The Gift *pro anima* in the Eleventh and Twelfth Centuries." In Algazi, Groebner, and Jussen 2003: 269–84.

———. 2009a. "Almsgiving, *Donatio Pro Anima,* and Eucharist Offering in the Early Middle Ages of Western Europe (4th–9th century)." In Frenkel and Lev 2009: 112–21.

———. 2009b. "Du don aux églises au don pour le salut de l'âme en Occident (IVe–XIe siècle): le paradigme eucharistique." In Nicole Bériou, Béatrice Caseau, and Dominique Rigaux, eds., *Pratiques de l'eucharistie dans les Églises d'Orient et d'Occident (Antiquité et Moyen Âge)*, vol. 2: *Les réceptions*. Collection des Études Augustiniennes, Série Moyen Âge et Temps Modernes, 46. Paris: Institut d'Etudes Augustiniennes, 1021–42.

Magness, Jodi. 2003. *The Archaeology of the Early Islamic Settlement in Palestine*. Winona Lake, IN: Eisenbrauns.

Magoulias, Henry. 1971. "The Lives of the Saints as Sources of Data for the History of Commerce in the Byzantine Empire in the VIth and VIIth Centuries." *Kléronomia* 3: 303–30.

Malherbe, Abraham J. 1996. "The Christianization of a Topos (Luke 12:13–34)." *Novum Testamentum* 38: 123–35.

Mango, Cyril. 1978. "The Date of the Studius Basilica at Istanbul." *Byzantine and Modern Greek Studies* 4: 120–22.

———. 1997. "Saints." In Guglielmo Cavallo, ed., *The Byzantines*. Chicago: University of Chicago Press, 255–80.

————, ed. 2002. *The Oxford History of Byzantium*. Oxford and New York: Oxford University Press.

Mango, Marlia M. 1986. *Silver from Early Byzantium: The Kaper Koraon and Related Treasures*. Baltimore, MD: Walters Art Gallery.

————. 1992. "The Monetary Value of Silver Revetments and Objects Belonging to Churches, A.D. 300–700." In Susan A. Boyd and Marlia M. Mango, eds., *Ecclesiastical Silver Plate in Sixth-Century Byzantium*. Washington, DC: Dumbarton Oaks Research Library and Collection, 123–36.

————. 2017. "Androna and the Late Antique Cities of *Oriens*." In Efthymios Rizos, ed., *New Cities in Late Antiquity: Documents and Archaeology*. Bibliothèque de l'Antiquité tardive 35. Turnhout: Brepols, 189–204.

Maraval, Pierre. 1985. *Lieux saints et pèlerinages d'Orient: histoire et géographie des origines à la conquête arabe*. Paris: Éditions du Cerf.

Marinis, Vasileios. 2017. *Death and the Afterlife in Byzantium: The Fate of the Soul in Theology, Liturgy, and Art*. Cambridge: Cambridge University Press.

Marrou, Henri-Irenée. 1940. "L'origine orientale des diaconies romaines." *Mélanges d'archéologie et d'histoire* 57: 92–142.

Martin, Alain. 2003. "'Souviens-toi de moi dans tes saintes prières': Témoins tardifs de la vitalité du datif grec." *ZPE* 144: 177–80.

Martin, Hubert. 1961. "The Concept of Philanthropy in Plutarch's Lives." *American Journal of Philology* 82: 164–75.

Martyn, John R. C. 2004a. "Introduction." In John R. Martyn, *The Letters of Gregory the Great*, vol.1. Medieval Sources in Translation 40. Toronto: Pontical Institute of Mediaeval Studies, 2004, 1–115.

————. 2004b. "Formulae for the Equipment of Monasteries, Convents and Oratories." *Medievalia et Humanistica* n.s. 30: 115–22.

Mathews, Thomas F. 1971. *The Early Churches of Constantinople: Architecture and Liturgy*. University Park: Pennsylvania State University Press.

————. 1982. "'Private' Liturgy in Byzantine Architecture." *Cahiers archéologiques* 30: 125–38.

Mathisen, Ralph W. 2012. "Concepts of Citizenship." In Johnson 2012: 744–63.

Mattern, P. Joseph. 1933. "À travers les villes mortes de Haute Syrie." *Mélanges de l'Université Saint-Joseph* 17: 1–176.

Maxwell, Jaclyn L. 2006. *Christianization and Communication in Late Antiquity: John Chrysostom and His Congregation in Antioch*. Cambridge: Cambridge University Press.

————. 2016. "Social Interactions in a Rural Monastery: Scholars, Peasants, Monks and More in the *Life of Hypatius*." In Kreiner and Reimitz 2016, 89–106.

Mayer, Wendy. 1997. "John Chrysostom and His Audiences. Distinguishing Different Congregations at Antioch and Constantinople." *SP* 31: 70–75.

————. 2005. *The Homilies of St John Chrysostom: Provenance (Reshaping the Foundations)*. OCA 273. Rome: Edizioni Orientalia Christiana.

————. 2008. "Poverty and Generosity to the Poor in the Time of John Chrysostom." In Holman 2008: 140–58.

————. 2009. "John Chrysostom on Poverty." In Allen, Neil, and Mayer 2009: 69–112.

Mayer, Wendy, and Allen, Pauline. 2012. *The Churches of Syrian Antioch (300–638 CE)*. Late Antique History and Religion 5. Leuven: Peeters.

Mauss, Marcel. 1990. *The Gift: The Form and Reason for Exchange in Archaic Societies*. Trans. W. D. Halls. New York: Norton. Originally published as "Essai sur le don. Forme et raison de l'échange dans les sociétés archaïques." *L'Année sociologique* n.s. 1 (1923–1924): 30–186.

Mazal, Otto. 2001. *Justinian I und seine Zeit. Geschichte und Kultur des Byzantinischen Reiches im 6. Jahrhundert*. Cologne and Vienna: Weimar.

McCormick, Michael. 1998. "Bateaux de vie, bateaux de mort: Maladie, commerce, transports annonaires et le passage économique du Bas-empire au Moyen Âge." In *Morfologie sociali e culturali in Europa fra tarda Antichità e alto Medioevo*. Settimane di studio del Centro Italiano di studi sull' alto medioevo 45. Spoleto: Centro Italiano di Studi sull' Alto Medioevo, 35–118.

———. 2011. *Charlemagne's Survey of the Holy Land: Wealth, Personnel, and Buildings of a Mediterranean Church between Antiquity and the Middle Ages*. Dumbarton Oaks Medieval Humanities. Washington, DC: Dumbarton Oaks.

McCulloh, J. M. 1976. "The Cult of Relics in the Letters and 'Dialogues' of Pope Gregory the Great: A Lexicographical Study." *Traditio* 32: 169–84.

McGuckin, John A. 2001. *St. Gregory of Nazianzus: An Intellectual Biography*. New York: St. Vladimir's Seminary Press.

McLaughlin, Megan. 1994. *Consorting with Saints: Prayer for the Dead in Early Medieval France*. Ithaca: Cornell University Press.

Meier, Mischa. 2004. *Das andere Zeitalter Justinians: Kontingenzerfahrung und Kontingenzbewältigung im 6. Jahrhundert n. Chr*. Hypomnemata: Untersuchungen zur Antike und zu ihrem Nachleben 147. Göttingen: Vandenhoeck & Ruprecht.

Menze, Volker. 2008. *Justinian and the Making of the Syrian Orthodox Church*. Oxford: Oxford University Press.

Meredith, Anthony. 1998. "The Three Cappadocians on Beneficence: A Key to Their Audiences." In Mary B. Cunningham and Pauline Allen, eds., *Preacher and Audience: Studies in Early Christian and Byzantine Homiletics*. Leiden: Brill, 89–104.

Metzger, Marcel. 1985. *Les Constitutions apostoliques*, vol. 1. SC 320. Paris: Éditions du Cerf.

Meyendorff, John. 1989. *Imperial Unity and Christian Divisions: The Church 450–680 AD*. Church History 2. Crestwood, NY: St. Vladimir's Seminary Press.

Mian, F. 1972. "'L'Anonimo Piacentino al Sinai." *Vetera Christianorum* 9: 267–301.

Michaels, Axel. 1997. "Gift and Return Gift, Greeting and Return Greeting in India: On a Consequential Footnote by Marcel Mauss." *Numen* 44: 242–69.

Mikhail, Maged S. A. 2014. *From Byzantine to Islamic Egypt: Religion, Identity, and Politics after the Arab Conquest*. London: I. B. Tauris.

Milani, Celestina. 1977. *Itinerarium Antonini Placentini: Un viaggio in Terra Sancta del 560–570 d.c.* Pubblicazioni della Università cattolica del Sacro Cuore Scienze filologiche e letteratura 7. Milan: Vita e pensiero.

Milik, Jósef T. 1961. "La topographie de Jérusalem vers la fin de l'époque byzantine." In *Mélanges offerts au Père René Mouterde pour son 80ᵉ anniversaire*, vol.1. Mélanges de l'Université Saint Joseph 37. Beirut: Impr. Catholique, 127–89.

Millar, Fergus. 1977. *The Emperor in the Roman World (31 B.C–A.D. 337)*. London: Duckworth.

———. 2006. *A Greek Roman Empire: Power and Belief under Theodosius II, 408–450*. Sather Lecture Series 64. Berkeley: University of California Press.

———. 2009. "Christian Monasticism in Roman Arabia at the Birth of Mahomet." *Semitica et Classica* 2: 97–115.

Miller, David J. D., and Sarris, Peter. 2018. See Primary Sources, *Corpus Iuris Civilis: Novellae*.

Miller, Timothy S. 1990. "The Sampson Hospital of Constantinople." *Byzantinische Forschungen* 15: 101–35.

———. 1997. *The Birth of the Hospital in the Byzantine Empire*. 2nd ed. Baltimore: John Hopkins University Press.

Miller, Timothy S., and John W. Nesbitt. 2014. *Walking Corpses: Leprosy in Byzantium and the Medieval West*. Ithaca, NY: Cornell University Press.

Miller, William Ian. 2007. "Is a Gift Forever?" *Representations* 100: 13–22.

Miquel, Pierre. 1995. "Hospitalité." *DSp* 7: 808–31. Paris: Beauchesne.

Mitchell, Christopher Wright. 1987. *The Meaning of BRK "to Bless" in the Old Testament*. Society of Biblical Literature Dissertation Series. Atlanta: Scholars Press.

Mitchell, Margaret M., 2001. "Pauline Accommodation and 'Condescension' (συνκατάβασις): Cor 9: 19–23 and the History of Influence." In Troels Engberg-Pedersen, ed. *Paul beyond the Judaism/Hellenism Divide*. Louisville, KY: Westminster John Knox, 197–214.

———. 2004. "Silver Chamber Pots and Other Goods Which Are Not Good: John Chrysostom's Discourse against Wealth and Possessions." In William Schweiker and Charles Mathewes, eds., *Having: Property and Possession in Religious and Social Life*. Grand Rapids, MI: Eerdmans, 88–121.

Mitchell, Stephen. 1993. *Anatolia: Land, Men and Gods in Asia Minor*. 2 vols. Oxford: Oxford University Press.

Moffet, Alice. 1990. "A Record of Public Buildings and Monuments." In Elizabeth Jeffreys, Brian Coke, and Roger Scott, eds., *Studies in John Malalas*. Byzantina Australiensia 6. Sydney: Australian Association for Byzantine Studies, 87–110.

Monks, George. 1953. "The Church of Alexandria and the City's Economic Life in the Sixth Century." *Speculum* 28: 349–62.

Moorhead, John. 1994. *Justinian*. New York: Longman.

———. 2013. *The Roman Empire Divided, 400–700*. 2nd ed. New York: Pearson.

Morison, Ernest F. 1912. *St. Basil and His Rule: A Study in Early Monasticism*. London: Oxford University Press.

Morris, Rosemary. 1984. "The Byzantine Aristocracy and the Monasteries." In Michael Angold, ed., *The Byzantine Aristocracy IX to XII Centuries*. BAR International Series 221. Oxford: British Archaeological Research Publishing, 112–37.

———, ed. 1990. *Church and People in Byzantium*. Society for the Promotion of Byzantine Studies, Twentieth Spring Symposium of Byzantine Studies, Manchester, 1986. Birmingham: University of Birmingham.

———. 1995. *Monks and Laymen in Byzantium, 843–1118*. Cambridge: Cambridge University Press.

———. 2010. "Reciprocal Gifts on Mount Athos in the Tenth and Eleventh Centuries." In Davies and Fouracre 2010: 171–92.

Morrison, Cécile. 1981. "Le Decouvert des trésores à l'époque byzantine: Théorique et pratique de l' εὕρεσις θησαυροῦ." *TM* 8: 321–43.

Mossakowska-Gaubert, Maria. 2004. "La Verrerie utilisée par des anachorètes: l'ermitage 44 à Naqlun (Fayyoum)." In Mat Immerzeel and Jacques Van de Vliet, eds., *Coptic Studies on the Threshold of a New Millennium. Proceedings of the Seventh International Congress of Coptic Studies, Leiden, August 27–September 2, 2000.* 2 vols. Orientalia Lovaniensia analecta 133. Louvain: Peeters, 2: 1443–69.

Mouritsen, Henrik. 2011. *The Freedman in the Roman World.* Cambridge: Cambridge University Press.

Muehlberger, Ellen. 2013. *Angels in Late Ancient Christianity.* New York: Oxford University Press.

Müller, Andreas E. 1993. "Getreide für Konstantinopel. Überlegungen zu Justinians Edikt XIII als Grundlage für Aussagen zur Einwohnerzahl Konstantinopels im 6. Jahrhundert." *JöB* 43: 1–20.

Mullett, Margaret, ed. 2007. *Founders and Refounders of Byzantine Monasteries.* Belfast Byzantine Texts and Translations 6.3. Belfast: Belfast Byzantine Enterprises, Institute of Byzantine Studies Queen's University Belfast.

Murtonen, A. 1959. "The Use and Meaning of the Words Lebarak and Berakah in the Old Testament." *Vetus Testamentum* 9: 158–77.

Nardi, Carlo. 1983. "Nota a Clemente Alessandrino, *Quis Dives Salvetur* 19, 3." *Prometheus* 9: 105–10.

Nardi, Carlo, and Descourtieux, Patrick. 2011. "Introduction." *Clément du Alexandrie: Quel Riche Sera Sauvé?* SC 537. Paris: Éditions du Cerf, 9–71.

Natali, Alain. 1982. "Église et évergétisme à Antioche à la fin du IVᵉ siècle d'après Jean Chrysostome." *SP* 17: 1176–84.

Nathan, Geoffrey. 1998. "The Rogation Ceremonies of Late Antique Gaul." *Classica et Mediaevalia* 40: 275–304.

Neary, Daniel. 2017. "The Image of Justinianic Orthopraxy in Eastern Monastic Literature." *JECS* 25: 119–47.

Nechaeva, Ekaterina. 2014. *Embassies-Negotiations-Gifts: Systems of East Roman Diplomacy in Late Antiquity.* Geographica Historica 30. Stuttgart: Franz Steiner Verlag.

Nedungatt, George. 1973. "The Covenanters of the Early Syriac-Speaking Church." *OCP* 39: 191–215, 419–44.

Nelson, Janet L. 2010. "Introduction." In Davis and Fouracre 2010: 1–17.

Newhauser, Richard. 2000. *The Early History of Greed: The Sin of Avarice in Early Medieval Thought and Literature.* Cambridge: Cambridge University Press.

Neyt, François. 2004. "La formation au monastère de l'abbé Séridos à Gaza." In Bitton-Ashkelony and Kofsky 2004: 151–63.

Niewöhner, Philipp. 2006. "Aizanoi and Anatolia: Town and Countryside in Late Late Antiquity." *Millennium: Jahrbuch zur Kultur und Geschichte des ersten Jahrtausends n. Chr.* 3: 239–53.

Nilsson, Martin P. 1961. *Greek Folk Religion.* New York: Harper.

Nollé, Johannes. 2005. "Boars, Bears, and Bugs: Farming in Asia Minor and the Protection of Men, Animals, and Crops." In Stephen Mitchell and Constantina Katsari, eds. *Patterns in the Economy of Roman Asia Minor.* Swansea: Classical Press of Wales, 53–82.

Novick, Tzvi. 2012. "Charity and Reciprocity: Structures of Benevolence in Rabbinic Literature." *HTR* 105: 33–52.

Ntedika, Joseph. 1971. *L'Évocation de l'au-delà dans la prière pour les morts: Étude de patristique et de liturgie latines.* Louvain: Nauwelaerts.

O'Donnell, James J. 2008. *The Ruin of the Roman Empire*. New York: Ecco.

Odorico, Paolo, ed., 2004. *Les Vies des Saints à Byzance: Genre littéraire ou biographie historique? Actes du IIᵉ colloque international philologique "EPIMHNEIA," Paris, 6–8 juin 2002. Dossiers byzantins 4*. Paris: Centre d'études byzantines, néo-helléniques et sud-est européennes.

Oexle, Otto Gerhard. 1976. "Memoria und Memorialüberlieferung im früheren Mittelalter." *Fruhmittelalterliche Studien* 10: 70–95.

Olster, David. 1993. "The Construction of a Byzantine Saint: George of Choziba, Holiness, and the Pilgrimage Trade in Seventh-Century Palestine. *GOTR* 38: 309–22.

Oppenheim, Philipp. 1932. *Symbolik und religiöse Wertung des Mönchskleid im christlichen Altertum*. Münster.

Orestano, Riccardo. 1956. "Beni dei monaci e monasteri nella legislazione Giustinianea." In *Studi in onore di Pietro de Francisci*, vol. 3. Milan: Giuffrè, 561–93.

Osteen, Mark. 2002. "Gift or Commodity." In Mark Osteen, ed., *The Question of the Gift: Essays across Disciplines*. Routledge Studies in Anthropology 2. London and New York: Routledge, 229–47.

Ousterhout, Robert. ed. 1990. *The Blessings of Pilgrimage*. Illinois Byzantine Studies 1. Urbana: University of Illinois Press.

Pahlitzsch, Johannes. 2001. "The Concern for Spiritual Salvation and *Memoria* in Islamic Public Endowments in Jerusalem (XII–XVI C.) as Compared to the Concepts of Christendom." In Urbain Vermeulen and Jo Van Steenbergen, eds., *Egypt and Syria in the Fatimid, Ayyubid and Mamluk Eras*, vol. 3. Orientalia Lovaniensia Analecta 102. Leuven: Uitgeverij Peeters, 329–44.

———. 2009. "Christian Pious Foundations as an Element of Continuity between Late Antiquity and Islam." In Frenkel and Lev 2009: 125–52.

Palmer, Andrew. 1990. *Monk and Mason on the Tigris Frontier: The Early History of Ṭur ʿAbdin*. University of Cambridge Oriental Publications 39. Cambridge: Cambridge University Press.

Papaconstantinou, Arietta. 1992. "L'agapae des martyrs: P. Oxy. LVI 3864." *ZPE* 92: 241–42.

———. 2002. "Θεία οἰκονομία. Les actes thébains de donation d'enfants ou la gestion monastique de la pénurie." *Mélanges Gilbert Dagron. TM* 14: 511–26.

———. 2012. "Donation and Negotiation: Formal Gifts to Religious Institutions in Late Antiquity." In Spieser and Yota 2012: 75–95.

Papalexandrou, Amy. 2010. "The Memory Culture of Byzantium." In Liz James, ed., *A Companion to Byzantium*. Oxford: Wiley-Blackwell, 108–22.

Pargoire, Jules. 1899. "Rufinianes." *BZ* 8: 429–77.

———. 1924. "Acémètes." *DACL* 1: 307–21. Paris: Letouzey et Ané.

Parker, Lucy. 2017. "Symeon Stylites the Younger and his Cult in Context: Hagiography and Society in Sixth- to Seventh-Century Byzantium." PhD diss., Oxford University.

Parker, Robert. 1998. "Pleasing Thighs: Reciprocity in Greek Religion." In Christopher Gill, Norman Postlethwaite, and Richard Seaford, eds., *Reciprocity in Ancient Greece*. Oxford: Oxford University Press, 105–25.

Parkin, Anneliese. 2006. "'You Do Him No Service': An Exploration of Pagan Almsgiving." In Atkins and Osborne 2006: 60–82.

Parrinello, Rosa Maria. 2006. "Prima e dopo Giustiniano. Le trasformazioni del monachesimo di Gaza." *Annali di Storia dell'Esegesi* 23: 165–93.

———. 2010. *Comunità monastiche a Gaza da Isaia a Doroteo (secoli IV–VI)*. Temi e Testi 73. Rome: Edizioni di Storia e Letteratura.

Parry, Jonathan. 1986. "*The Gift*, the Indian Gift, and the 'Indian Gift.'" *Man* 21: 453–71.

Parry, Jonathan, and Bloch, Maurice, eds. 1989. *Money and the Morality of Exchange*. Cambridge: Cambridge University Press.

Paterson, Jeremy. 2016. "'The Eye of the Needle': The Morality of Wealth in the Ancient World." In Errietta M. A. Bissa and Federico Santangelo, eds., *Studies on Wealth in the Ancient World*. Bulletin of the Institute of Classical Studies, Suppl. 133. London: University of London Institute of Classical Studies, 93–103.

Patlagean, Évelyne. 1974. "La pauvreté à Byzance et la législation de Justinien: aux originees d'un modèle politique." In Michel Mollat, ed., *Études sur l'histoire de la pauvreté (Moyen Age–XVIᵉ siècle)*. 2 vols. Paris: Publications de la Sorbonne, vol. 1: 59–81.

———. 1977. *Pauvreté économique et pauvreté sociale à Byzance, 4ᵉ–7ᵉ siècles*. Paris: Mouton.

———. 1997. "The Poor." In Guglielmo Cavallo, ed., *The Byzantines*. Chicago: University of Chicago Press, 15–42.

Patrich, Joseph. 1995. *Sabas, Leader of Palestinian Monasticism: A Comparative Study in Eastern Monasticism, Fourth to Seventh Centuries*. Washington, DC: Dumbarton Oaks.

———, ed. 2001. *The Sabaite Heritage in the Orthodox Church from the Fifth Century to the Present*. Orientalia Lovaniensia Analecta 98. Leuven: Peeters.

Pattenden, P. 1975. "The Text of the *Pratum Spirituale*." *JThS* n.s. 26: 38–54.

Payne, Richard E. 2015. *A State of Mixture: Christians, Zoroastrians, and Iranian Political Culture in Late Antiquity*. TCH 56. Berkeley: University of California Press.

Peachin, Michael. 1989. "The Office of the Memory." In Evangelos Chrysos, ed. *Studien zur Geschichte der römischen Spätantike: Festgabe für Professor Johannes Straub*. Athens: Pelasgos-verlag, 168–208.

Penella, Robert J. 2000. *The Private Orations of Themistius*. TCH 29. Berkeley: University of California Press.

Pentcheva, Bissera V. 2010. *The Sensual Icon: Space, Ritual, and the Senses in Byzantium*. College Park: Pennsylvania State University Press.

Percival, John. 1969. "*P.Ital.* 3 and Roman Estate Management." *Latomus* 102: 607–15.

Perrone, Lorenzo. 1998. "Monasticism as a Factor of Religious Interaction in the Holy Land during the Byzantine Period." In Aryeh Kofsky and Guy G. Stroumsa, eds., *Sharing the Sacred: Religious Contacts and Conflicts in the Holy Land, First–Fifteenth Centuries C.E.* Jerusalem: Yad Ishak Ben Zvi, 67–95.

———. 2004. "The Necessity of Advice: Spiritual Direction as a School of Christianity in the Correspondence of Barsanuphius and John of Gaza." In Bitton-Ashkelony and Kofsky 2004: 131–49.

Peterson, E. 1947. "ΜΕΡΙΣ: Hostien-Partikel und Opfer-Anteil." *Ephemerides liturgicae* 61: 1–10.

Petit, Paul. 1955. *Libanius et la vie municipale à Antioche au IVᵉ siècle après J.-C.* Paris: Geuthner.

Petitat, André. 1991. "Les circuits du don: 'kula,' charité et assurances." *Cahiers Internationaux de Sociologie* 90: 49–65.

Pétré, Hélène. 1948. *Caritas: Étude sur la vocabulaire latin de la charité chrétienne*. Louvain: Spicilegium Sacrum Lovaniense.

Pétridès, S. 1902. "Saint Syméon le Nouveau Stylite: Mélode." *Échos d'Orient* 5: 270–74.

———. 1904. "Spoudaei et Philopones." *Échos d'Orient* 7: 341–48.

Pettegrew, David K. 2007. "The Busy Countryside of Late Roman Corinth: Interpreting Ceramic Data Produced by Regional Archaeological Surveys." *Hesperia* 76: 743–84.

Philipsborn, Alexandre. 1961. "Der Fortschritt in der Entwicklung des byzantinische Krankenhauswesens." *BZ* 54: 338–65.

Phountoulēs, Iōannēs M. 1963. *Hē eikositetraōros akoimētos doxologia*. Athens: Papademetriou.

Piccirillo, Michele. 1993. *The Mosaics of Jordan*. Amman: American Center of Oriental Research.

Pieri, Dominique. 2009. "Saint-Syméon-le-stylite (Syrie du Nord): Les bâtiments d'accueil et les boutiques à l'entrée du sanctuaire." *Comptes rendus des séances de l'Académie des Inscriptions et Belles-Lettres* 153: 1393–420.

Pietri, Luce. 2002. "Evergetisme chrétien et fondations privees dans l'Italie de l'Antiquité tardive." In Rita Lizzi Testa and Jean-Michel Carrié, *Humana Sapit: Études d'Antiquité tardive offertes à Lellia Cracco Ruggini*. Turnhout: Brepols, 253–63.

Pinard, Henry. 1919. "Les infiltrations païennes dans l'Ancienne Loi d'après les Pères de l'Église: La thèse de la condescendance." *Recherches de Science Religieuses* 9: 197–221.

Plassmann, Otto. 1961. *Die Almosen bei Johannes Chrysostomus*. Münster: Ashendorff.

Porten, Bezalel. 1996. *The Elephantine Papyri in English: Three Millenia of Cross-cultural Continuity and Change*. Leiden: Brill.

Potter, David. 2011. "Cities in the Eastern Roman Empire from Constantine to Heraclius." In Ortwin Dally and Christopher Ratté, *Archaeology and the Cities of Asia Minor in Late Antiquity*. Kelsey Museum Publication 6. Ann Arbor, MI: Kelsey Museum of Archaeology, 247–60.

Price, Richard. 2004. "Informal Penance in Early Medieval Christendom." In Kate Cooper and Jeremy Gregory, eds., *Retribution, Repentance, and Reconciliation: Papers Read at the 2002 Summer Meeting and the 2003 Winter Meeting of the Ecclesiastical History Society*. Studies in Church History 40. Suffolk: Boydell Press, 29–38.

Puech, Aimé. 1891. *St. Jean Chrysostome et les mœurs de son temps*. Paris: Hachette.

Quadrato, Renato. 1996. *"Beneficium manumissionis e obsequium."* *Index* 24: 341–53.

Quibell, James. E. 1912. *Excavations at Saqqara (1908–09, 1909–10)*. Cairo: Institut Français d'archéologie orientale.

Rae, Douglas. 1981. *Equalities*. Cambridge, MA: Harvard University Press.

Raeder, Hans. 1944. "Kaiser Julian als Philosoph und religiöser Reformator." *Classica et Mediaevalia* 6: 179–93.

Raes, Alphonse. 1953. "L'antidoron." *Proche Orient Chrétien* 3: 6–13.

Rajak, Tessa. 2004. "The Gifts of God at Sardis." In Mark Goodman, ed., *Jews in a Graeco-Roman World*. Oxford: Oxford University Press, 229–39.

Ramelli, Ilaria E. 2016. *Social Justice and the Legitimacy of Slavery. The Role of Philosophical Asceticism from Ancient Judaism to Christianity*. Oxford: Oxford University Press.

Ramsey, Boniface. 1982. "Almsgiving in the Latin Church: The Late Fourth and Early Fifth Centuries." *JThS* 43: 226–59.

Rapp, Claudia. 1999. "'For Next to God, You Are My Salvation': Reflections on the Rise of the Holy Man in Late Antiquity." In James D. Howard-Johnston and Paul A. Hayward, eds., *The Cult of Saints in Late Antiquity and the Middle Ages: Essays on the Contribution of Peter Brown.* Oxford: Oxford University Press, 63–81.

———. 2004. "All in the Family: John the Almsgiver, Nicetas and Heraclius." *Nea Rhome. Rivista di ricerche bizantinistiche* 1: 121–34.

———. 2005. *Holy Bishops in Late Antiquity: The Nature of Christian Leadership in an Age of Transition.* TCH 37. Berkeley: University of California Press.

———. 2008. "Spiritual Guarantors at Penance, Baptism, and Ordination in the Late Antique East." In Abigail Firey, ed., *A New History of Penance.* Brill's Companions to the Christian Tradition 14. Leiden: Brill, 121–48.

———. 2009. "Charity and Piety as Episcopal and Imperial Virtues in Late Antiquity." In Frenkel and Lev 2009: 75–87.

———. 2010. "The Origins of Hagiography and the Literature of Early Monasticism: Purpose and Genre between Tradition and Innovation." In Christopher Kelly, Richard Flower, and Michael Stuart Williams, eds., *Unclassical Traditions,* vol. 1: *Alternatives to the Classical Past in Late Antiquity.* Cambridge Classical Journal, suppl. 34. Cambridge: Cambridge University Press, 119–30.

Rebillard, Éric. 2009a. "The Church, the Living and the Dead." In Rousseau 2009: 220–30.

———. 2009b. *The Care of the Dead in Late Antiquity.* Trans. E. T. Rawlings and J. Routier-Pucci. Cornell Studies in Classical Philology 59. Ithaca, NY: Cornell University Press.

Regnault, Lucien. 1963. "Introduction." In Lucien Regnault and Jacques de Préville, eds., *Dorothée de Gaza: Oeuvres Spirituelles.* SC 92. Paris: Éditions du Cerf, 1–103.

———. 1972a. "Introduction." *Barsanuphe et Jean de Gaza: Correspondance.* Trans. Lucien Regnault, Philippe Lemair, and Bernard Outtier. Sablé-sur-Sarthe: Abbaye de Solesmes.

———. 1972b. "Introduction, *Vie de sainte Synclétique.*" Spiritualité orientale 9. Bégrolles-en-Mauges: Abbaye de Bellefontaine, 7–19.

———. 1981. "Les Apophtegmes des pères en Palestine aux Vᵉ–VIᵉ siècles." *Irénikon* 54: 320–30.

Rémondon, Roger. 1972. "L'Église dans la société égyptienne à l'époque byzantine." *Chronique d'Égypte: Bulletin pêriodique de la Fondation êgptologique reine Êlisabeth* 47: 254–77.

Revillout, Eugène. 1900. "Extraits de la correspondance de St. Pésunthius Évêque de Coptos et de plusiers documents analogues (juridiques ou économiques)." *Revue Egyptologique* 9: 133–77.

Rhee, Helen. 2012. *Loving the Poor, Saving the Rich: Wealth, Poverty, and Early Christian Formation.* Grand Rapids, MI: Baker Academic.

Richter, Daniel S. 2011. *Cosmopolis: Imagining Community in Late Classical Athens and the Early Roman Empire.* Oxford: Oxford University Press.

Rickman, G. E. 1980. "The Grain Trade under the Roman Empire." *Memoires of the American Academy in Rome* 36: 261–75.

Riedinger, Rudolf. 1978. "Akoimeten." *Theologische Realenzyklopädie* 2: 148–53.

Rigo, Antonio, Michele Trizio, and Eleftherios Despotakis, eds. 2018. *Byzantine Hagiography: Texts, Themes, and Projects.* Byzantios: Studies in Byzantine History and Civilization 13. Turnhout: Brepols.

Ritter, Adolph M. 1975. "Christentum und Eigentum bei Klemens von Alexandrien auf dem Hintergrund der frühchristlichen 'Armenfrömmigkeit' und der Ethik der kaiserzeitichen Stoa." *Zeitschrift für Kirchengeschichte* 86: 1–25.

Robert, Louis. 1957. "Une épigramme de Carie." *Revue Philologique* 31: 7–22.

———. 1960. "Épigrammes de Syrie." In Louis Robert, *Hellenica, Recueil d'épigraphie, de numismatique et d'antiquités grecques*, vol. 11–12. Paris: Andrien Maisonneuve, 319–27.

Rodgers, Robert H. 1980. "Hail, Frost, and Pests in the Vineyard: Anatolius of Berytus as a Source for the Nabataean Agriculture." *Journal of the American Oriental Society* 100: 1–11.

Rorem, Paul. 1993. *Pseudo-Dionysius: A Commentary on the Texts and an Introduction to Their Influence.* New York: Oxford University Press.

Rosenwein, Barbara H. 2000. "Perennial Prayer at Agaune." In Sharon Farmer and Barbara H. Rosenwein, eds., *Monks and Nuns, Saints and Outcasts: Religion in Medieval Society. Essays in Honor of Lester K. Little.* Ithaca, NY: Cornell University Press, 37–56.

Rossiter, Jeremy John. 1989. "Roman Villas of the Greek East and the Villa in Gregory of Nyssa *Ep.* 20." *JRA* 2: 101–10.

Roueché, Charlotte. 2007. "Caring for the Elderly: Creating a New Concept and Practice." In Stathakopoulos 2007: 21–35.

Rousseau, Philip. 1985. *Pachomius: The Making of a Community in Fourth-Century Egypt.* TCH 6. Berkeley: University of California Press.

———. 1994. *Basil of Caesarea.* TCH 20. Berkeley: University of California Press.

———. 2001. "Monasticism." In Cameron, Ward-Perkins, and Whitby 2001: 745–80.

———, ed. 2009. *A Companion to Late Antiquity.* London: Wiley-Blackwell.

Rubenson, Samuel. 1995. *The Letters of St. Antony: Monasticism and the Making of a Saint.* Studies in Antiquity and Christianity. Minneapolis: Fortress Press.

———. 2009. "Power and Politics of Poverty in Early Monasticism." In Geoffrey D. Dunn, David Luckensmeyer, and Lawrence Cross, eds., *Prayer and Spirituality in the Early Church*, vol. 5: *Poverty and Riches.* Strathfield, Aus.: St. Paul's Press, 91–110.

———. 2012. "Monasticism and the Philosophical Heritage." In Johnson 2012: 487–512.

———. 2013. "Apologetics of Asceticism: The *Life of Antony* and Its Political Context." In Blake Leyerle and Robin Darling Young, eds., *Ascetic Culture: Essays in Honor of Philip Rousseau.* Notre Dame, IN: Notre Dame University Press, 75–96.

Ruffini, Giovanni. 2011. "Village Life and Family Power in Late Antique Nessana." *TAPA* 141: 201–25.

Rümer, Cornelia, and Thissen, Russell P. 1989. "P. Köln Inv. Nr 3221: Das Testament des Hiob in koptlischer Sprache. Ein Vorbericht." In Michael A. Knibb and Pieter W. van der Horst, eds., *Studies on the Testament of Job.* Society for New Testament Studies 66. Cambridge: Cambridge University Press, 33–45.

Russell, James. 1987. *The Mosaic Inscriptions of Anemurium.* Ergänzungsbände zu dem Tituli Asiae Minoris 13. Vienna: Verlag der Österreichische Akademie der Wissenschaften.

Rylaarsdam, David M. 1999. "The Adaptability of Divine Pedagogy: *Sunkatabasis* in the Theology and Rhetoric of John Chrysostom." PhD diss., University of Notre Dame.

Saller, Sylvester J., and Bellarmino Bagatti. 1949. *The Town of Nebo (Khirbet El-Mekhayyat) with a Brief Survey of Other Ancient Christian Monuments in Transjordan.* Publications of the Studium Biblicum Franciscanum 7. Jerusalem: Franciscan Press.

Salzman, Michele Renee. 2017. "From a Classical to a Christian City: Civic Euergetism and Charity in Late Antique Rome." *Studies in Late Antiquity* 1: 65–85.

Samellas, Antigone. 2002. *Death in the Eastern Mediterranean (50–600 A.D.): An Interpretation.* Studies and Texts in Antiquity and Christianity 12. Tübingen: Mohr Siebeck.

Sandwell, Isabella. 2004. "Christian Self-Definition in the Fourth Century AD: John Chrysostom on Christianity, Imperial Rule, and the City." In Isabella Sandwell and Janet Huskinson, eds., *Culture and Society in Later Roman Antioch: Papers from a Colloquium. London, 15th December 2001.* Oxford: Oxbow Books, 35–58.

———. 2007. *Religious Identity in Late Antiquity: Greeks, Jews, and Christians in Antioch.* Cambridge: Cambridge University Press.

Sänger, Patrick. 2011. "The Administration of Sasanian Egypt: New Masters and Byzantine Continuity." *GRBS* 51: 653–65.

Sansterre, Jean-Marie. 1983. *Les moines grecs et orientaux à Rome aux époques Byzantine et carolingienne (milieu du VIe siècle–fin du IXe siècle).* 2 vols. Mémoires de la Classe des lettres 80. Brussels: Académie royale de Belgique.

Saradi, Hélène G. 2006. *The Byzantine City in the Sixth Century: Literary Images and Historical Reality.* Athens: Society of Messenian Archaeological Studies.

Sarris, Peter. 2006. *Economy and Society in the Age of Justinian.* Cambridge: Cambridge University Press.

———. 2009. "Social Relations and the Land: The Early Period." In Haldon 2009: 92–111.

———. 2011a. *Empires of Faith: The Fall of Rome to the Rise of Islam, 500–700.* Cambridge: Cambridge University Press.

———. 2011b. "Restless Peasants and Scornful Lords: Lay Hostility to Holy Men and the Church in Late Antiquity and the Early Middle Ages." In Peter Sarris, Matthew Dal Santo, and Phil Booth, eds., *An Age of Saints? Power, Conflict and Dissent in Early Medieval Christianity.* Brill's Series on the Early Middle Ages 20. Leiden: Brill, 1–10.

Satlow, Michael L. 2010. "'Fruit and the Fruit of Fruit': Charity and Piety among Jews in Late Antique Palestine." *Jewish Quarterly Review* 100: 244–77.

———, ed. 2013. *The Gift in Antiquity.* Malden, MA and Oxford: Wiley-Blackwell.

Savramis, Demosthenes. 1962. *Zur Sociologie des byzantinischen Mönchtums.* Leiden: Brill.

Schachner, Lukas Amadeus. 2005. "'I Greet You and Thy Brethren. Here are Fifteen Shentasse of Wine'": Wine as a Product in the Early Monasteries of Egypt and the Levant." *Aram* 17: 157–84.

———. 2006. *Economic Production in the Monasteries of Egypt and Oriens, AD 320–800.* 3 vols. DPhil thesis, Oxford University.

———. 2010. "The Archaeology of the Stylite." In David M. Gwynn and Susanne Bangert, eds., *Religious Diversity in Late Antiquity.* Late Antique Archaeology 6. Leiden: Brill, 329–97.

Schmelz, Georg. 2002. *Kirchliche Amtsträger im spätantiken Ägypten nach den Aussagen der griechischen und koptischen Papyri und Ostraka.* Archive für Paypyrusforschung und verwandte Gebiete 13. Munich: K. G. Saur.

Schmid, Karl, and Joachim Wollasch. 1967. "Die Gemeinschaft der Lebenden und Verstorbenen in Zeugnissen des Mittelalters." *Frühmittelälterliche Studien* 1: 365–405.

Schmitt-Pantel, Pauline. 1990. "Évergétisme et mémoire du mort: À propos des fondations de banquets publics dans les cités grecques à l'époque hellénistique et romaine." In Gherardo Gnoli and Jean-Pierre Vernant, eds., *La mort, les morts dans les sociétés anciennes.* Paris: Maison des sciences de l'homme, 177–88.

Schöllgen, Georg. 1990. "Sportulae: Zur Frühgeschichte des Unterhaltsanspruchs der Kleriker." *ZKG* 101: 1–20.

———. 1998. *Die Anfänge der Professionalisierung des Klerus und das kirchliche Amt in der syrischen Didaskalie.* JbAC Ergänzungsband 26. Münster: Aschendorff.

Schreiber, Georg. 1948. "Kirchliches Abgabenwesen an französischen Eigenkirchen aus Anlaß von Ordalien (oblationes campionum, oblationes pugilum, oblationes bellorum, oblationes iudiciorum)." In Georg Schreiber, *Gemeinschaften des Mittelalters: Recht und Verfassung, Kult und Frömmigkeit. Gesammelte Abhandlungen,* vol.1. Münster: Regensberg, 171–81.

Schroeder, Caroline T. 2004. "'A Suitable Abode for Christ': The Church Building as Symbol of Ascetic Renunciation in Early Monasticism." *Church History* 73: 432–521.

———. 2012. "Child Sacrifice in Egyptian Monastic Culture: From Family Renunciation to Jephtha's Lost Daughter." *JECS* 20: 269–302.

Schwartz, Barry. 1996. "The Social Psychology of the Gift." In Aafke E. Komter, ed., *The Gift: An Interdisciplinary Perspective.* Amsterdam: Amsterdam University Press, 69–80.

Schwartz, Seth. 2010. *Were the Jews a Mediterranean Society? Reciprocity and Solidarity in Ancient Judaism.* Princeton, NJ: Princeton University Press.

Scicolone, Stefania. 1982. "Basilio e la sua organizzazione dell'attività assistenziale a Cesarea." *Civiltà classica e cristiana* 3: 353–72.

Segal, Judah B. 1955. "Mesopotamian Communities from Julian to the Rise of Islam." *Proceedings of the British Academy* 41: 109–39.

Seligman, Jon. 2011. *The Rural Hinterland of Jerusalem in the Byzantine Period.* PhD diss., University of Haifa.

Serfass, Adam. 2002. *Church Finances from Constantine to Justinian 312–565 C.E.* PhD diss., Stanford University.

———. 2008. "Wine for Widows: Papyrological Evidence for Christian Charity in Late Antique Egypt." In Holman 2008: 88–102.

Sessa, Kristina M. 2012. *The Formation of Papal Authority in Late Antique Italy: Roman Bishops and the Domestic Sphere.* Cambridge: Cambridge University Press.

Ševčenko, Ihor. 1992. "The Sion Treasure: The Evidence of the Inscriptions." In Susan A. Boyd and Marlia M. Mango, eds., *Ecclesiastical Silver Plate in Sixth-Century Byzantium.* Washington, DC: Dumbarton Oaks Research Library and Collection, 39–56.

Shaw, Brent D. 1985. "The Divine Economy: Stoicism as Ideology." *Latomus* 44: 14–54.

Shaw, Teresa M. 1998. *The Burden of the Flesh: Fasting and Sexuality in Early Christianity.* Minneapolis, MN: Fortress Press.

Sherk, Andrea. 2004. *Renouncing the World Yet Leading the Church: The Monk-Bishop in Late Antiquity.* Cambridge, MA: Harvard University Press.

Siegelmann, A. 1974. "A Mosaic Floor at Caesarea Maritima." *IEJ* 24: 216–21.

Sigaud, Lygia. 2002. "The Vicissitudes of *The Gift.*" *Social Anthropology* 10: 335–58.

Sijpesteijn, Petra J.1989. "New Light on the Philopones." *Aegyptus* 69: 95–99.

———. 2010. "Multilingual Archives and Documents in Post-Conquest Egypt." In Arietta Papaconstantinou, ed., *The Multilingual Experience in Egypt, from the Ptolemies to the Abbāsids.* Farnham and Burlington, VT: Ashgate, 105–24.

Silber, Ilana Friedrich. 1995a. "Gift-giving in the Great Traditions: The Case of Donations to Monasteries in the Medieval West." *Archives Européennes de Sociologie* 36: 209–43.

———. 1995b. *Virtuosity, Charisma, and Social Order: A Comparative Sociological Study of Monasticism in Theravada Buddhism and Medieval Catholicism.* Cambridge: Cambridge University Press.

———. 2000. "Beyond Purity and Danger: Gift-Giving in the Monotheistic Traditions." In Antoon Vandevelde, ed. *Gifts and Interests.* Leuven: Peeters, 115–34.

———. 2002. "Echoes of Sacrifice? Repertoires of Giving in the Great Religions." In Albert I. Baumgarten, ed. *Sacrifice in Religious Experience.* Studies in the History of Religions/ Numen Book Series 93. Leiden: Brill, 291–312.

———. 2004. "Entre Marcel Mauss et Paul Veyne: Pour une sociologie historique comparée du don." *Sociologie et sociétés* 36: 189–205.

———. 2006. "Prologue: Sortilèges et paradoxes du don." *Revue du M.A.U.S.S.* 27: 39–56.

———. 2007. "Registres et répertoires du don: avec mais aussi après Mauss?" In Eliana Magnani, ed., *Don et sciences sociales. Théories et pratiques croisées.* Dijon: Editions de l'Université de Dijon, 123–44.

———. 2009. "Bourdieu's Gift to Gift Theory: An Unacknowledged Trajectory." *Sociological Theory* 27: 173–90.

Sivan, Hagith. 2008. *Palestine in Late Antiquity.* Oxford: Oxford University Press.

Smith, Rowland. 1995. *Julian's Gods: Religion and Philosophy in the Thought and Action of Julian the Apostate.* London and New York: Routledge.

Smith, R.R.R. 2016. "Statue Practice in the Late Roman Empire." In R.R.R. Smith and Bryan Ward-Perkins, eds., *The Last Statues of Antiquity.* Oxford: Oxford University Press, 1–27.

Smyrlis, Kostis. 2006. *La fortune des grands monastères byzantins (fin du Xe–milieu du XIVe siècle).* Paris: Centre d'Histoire et Civilisation de Byzance.

Sodini, Jean-Pierre, Pierre-Marie Blanc, and Dominique Pieri. 2010. "Nouvelles eulogies de Qal'at Sem'an (fouilles 2007–2010)." In Jean-Claude Cheynet, ed., *Mélanges Cécile Morrisson, TM* 16. Paris: Association des Amis du Centre d'Histoire et Civilisation de Byzance, 793–812.

Solignac, Aimé. 1980. "Mémoire." *DSp* 10: 991–1002.

Sorek, Susan. 2010. *Remembered for Good: A Jewish Benefaction System in Ancient Palestine.* The Social World of Biblical Antiquity, Second Series 3. Sheffield: Sheffield Phoenix Press.

Sotinel, Claire. 2006. "Le don chrétien et ses retombées sur l'économie dans l'antiquité tardive." *AnTard* 14: 105–16.

Spieser, Jean-Michel, and Élisabeth Yota, eds. 2012. *Donation et donateurs dans le monde byzantin. Actes du colloque international de l'Université de Fribourg 13–15 mars 2008.* Réalités Byzantines 14. Paris: Desclée de Brouwer.

Stang, Charles. 2010. "Digging Holes and Building Pillars: Simeon Stylites and the Geometry of Ascetic Practice." *HTR* 103: 447–70.

Stathakopoulos, Dionysios, ed. 2007. *The Kindness of Strangers: Charity in the Pre-Modern Mediterranean.* London: Centre for Hellenic Studies.

Steindorff, Ludwig. 1994. *Memoria in Altrußland. Untersuchungen zu den Formen christlicher Totensorge.* Quellen und Studien zur Geschichte des östlichen Europa 38. Stuttgart: Franz Steiner.

Steinsapir, Ann I. 2005. *Rural Sanctuaries in Roman Syria: The Creation of a Sacred Landscape.* BAR International Ser. 1431. Oxford: British Archaeological Reports.

Steinwenter, Artur. 1930. "Die Rechtsstellung der Kirchen und Klöster nach den Papyri." *Zeitschrift der Savigny Stiftung für Rechtsgeschichte. Kanonistische Abteilung* 19: 1–50.

———. 1932. "Byzantinische Mönchstestamente." *Aegyptus* 12: 55–64.

———. 1958. "Aus dem kirchlichen Vermögensrechte der Papyri." *Zeitschrift der Savigny Stiftung für Rechtsgeschichte. Kanonistische Abteilung* 44: 1–34.

Stenger, Jan R. 2017. "What Does It Mean to Call the Monasteries of Gaza a 'School'? A Reassessment of Dorotheus' Intellectual Identity." *VC* 71: 59–84.

Sternberg, Thomas. 1988. "Der vermeintliche Ursprung der westlichen Diakonien in Ägypten und die *Conlationes* des Johannes Cassian." *JbAC* 31: 173–209.

Stolte, Bernard. 2007. "Laws for Founders." In Mullett 2007: 121–39.

Stötzel, Arnold. 1984. *Kirche als 'neue Gesellschaft.' Die humanisierende Wirkung des Christentums nach Johannes Chrysostomus.* Münsterische Beiträge zur Theologie 51. Munich: Aschendorff.

Strohmetz, David B., Bruce Rind, Reed Fisher, and Michael Lynn. 2002. "Sweetening the Till: The Use of Candy to Increase Restaurant Tipping." *Journal of Applied Social Psychology* 32: 300–309.

Stroumsa, Guy G. 2009. *The End of Sacrifice: Religious Transformations in Late Antiquity.* Chicago: Chicago University Press.

Stuiber, Alfred. 1966. "Eulogia." *Reallexikon für Antike und Christentum* 6: 900–928.

———. 1977. "Geschenk." *Reallexikon für Antike und Christentum* 10: 685–703.

Suzuki, Jun. 2009. "A Monk Who Does Not Talk about Love Towards God, and Charity: Reflections on the Evagrian Theory of Love and its Application." In Dunn, Luckensmeyer, and Cross 2009: 177–89.

Taft, Robert F. 1970. "The Origin of the Offertory Procession in the Syro-Byzantine East." *OCP* 36: 73–107.

———. 1984. *Beyond East and West: Problems in Liturgical Understanding.* Washington, DC: Pastoral Press.

———. 1991. *A History of the Liturgy of St. John Chrysostom.* Vol. 4: *The Diptychs.* OCA 238. Rome: Pontificium Institutum Studiorum Orientalium.

———. 1999. "One Bread, One Body: Ritual Symbols of Ecclesial Communion in the Patristic Period." In Douglas Kries and Catherine B. Tkacz, eds., *Nova Doctrina Vetusque: Essays on Early Christianity in Honor of Fredric W. Schlatter, S.J.* American University Studies 7/Theology and Religion 207. New York: P. Lang, 23–50.

Talbot, Alice-Mary. 2001. "Byzantine Pilgrimage to the Holy Land." In Patrich 2001: 97–110.

———. 2010. "Personal Poverty in Byzantine Monasticism: Ideals and Reality." In Jean-Claude Cheynet, ed., *Mélanges Cécile Morrisson, TM* 16. Paris: Association des Amis du Centre d'Histoire et Civilisation de Byzance, 829–42.

———. 2019. *Varieties of Monastic Experience in Byzantium, 800–1453.* Notre Dame, IN: Notre Dame University Press.

Tannous, Jack. 2016. "The *Life* of Symeon of the Olives: A Christian Puzzle from Islamic Syria." In Kreiner and Reimitz 2016: 309–30.

———. 2018. *The Making of the Medieval Middle East: Religion, Society and Simple Believers.* Princeton, NJ: Princeton University Press.

Tarot, Camille. 2008. "Repères pour une histoire de la naissance de la grâce." In Philippe Chanial, ed., *La société vue du don: Manuel de sociologie anti-utilitariste appliquée*. Paris: La Decouverte, 479–97.

Tate, Georges. 1992. *Les campagnes de la Syrie du Nord du IIe au VIIe siècle: un exemple d'expansion démographique et économique à la fin de l'Antiquité*. BAH 133. Paris: Geuthner.

———. 1998. "Expansion d'une société riche et égalitaire: Les paysans de Syrie du nord du IIe au VIIe siècle." *Comptes Rendus de séances de l'Académie des Inscriptions et Belles Lettres*. Paris: Diffusion de Boccard, 913–41.

Taylor, John H. 2001. *Death and the Afterlife in Ancient Egypt*. Chicago: University of Chicago Press.

Taylor, Justin. 1975. "The Early Papacy at Work: Gelasius I (492–6)." *Journal of Religious History* 8: 317–32.

Tchalenko, Georges. 1953–58. *Villages antiques de la Syrie du Nord: Le massif du Bélus a l'époque romaine*, 3 vols. BAH 50. Paris: Geuthner.

Tenger, Bernhard. 1993. *Die Verschuldung im römischen Ägypten (1.-2. Jh. n. Chrs)*. Pharos Studien zur griechisch-römischen Antike 3. St. Katharien: Scripta Mercaturae Verlag.

Testart, Alain. 2007. *Critique du don: Études sur la circulation non marchande*. Paris: Éditions Syllepse.

Thomas, John Philip. 1987. *Private Religious Foundations in the Byzantine Empire*. Washington, DC: Dumbarton Oaks.

———. 2005. "*In Perpetuum*. Social and Political Consequences of Byzantine Patrons' Aspirations for Permanence for their Foundations." In Michael Borgolte, ed., *Stiftungern in Christentum, Judentum und Islam vor der Moderne*. Berlin: De Gruyter Akademie Forschung, 123–35.

Thomas, John Philip, and Angela Constantinides Hero, ed. 2000. *Byzantine Monastic Foundation Documents: A Complete Translation of the Surviving Founders' Typika and Testaments*. Washington D.C.: Dumbarton Oaks.

Tierney, Brian. 1959. "The Decretists and the 'Deserving Poor.'" *Comparative Studies in History and Society* 1: 360–73.

Till, Walter C. 1964. *Die koptischen Rechtsurkunden aus Theben*. Österreichische Akademie der Wissenschaften, Philosophisch-historische Klasse Sitzungsberichte 244. Vienna: Austrian Academy of Science.

Torrance, Alexis. 2009. "Standing in the Breach: The Significance and Function of the Saints in the Letters of Barsanuphius and John of Gaza." *JECS* 17: 459–73.

———. 2013. *Repentence in Late Antiquity: Eastern Asceticism and the Framing of the Christian Life, c.400–650 CE*. New York and Oxford: Oxford University Press.

Traina, Giusto. 2002. "La Forteresse de l'Oubli." *Le Muséon* 115: 399–402.

Treadgold, Warren T. 1994. "Taking Sources on Their Terms and on Ours: Peter Brown's Late Antiquity." *AnTard* 2: 153–59.

Trombley, Frank R. 1985a. "Monastic Foundations in Sixth-Century Anatolia and Their Role in the Social and Economic Life of the Region." In N. M. Vaporis, ed., *Byzantine Saints and Monasteries*. Brookline, MA: Hellenic College Press, 45–59.

———. 1985b. "Paganism in the Greek World at the End of Antiquity: The Case of Anatolia and Greece." *HTR* 78: 327–52.

———. 1987. "Korykos in Cilicia Trachis: The Economy of a Small Coastal City in Late Antiquity (*Saec.* V–VI)—A Précis." *Ancient History Bulletin* 1: 16–23.

———. 2014. "From *Kastron* to *Qaṣr*: Nessana between Byzantium and the Umayyad Caliphate *ca.* 602–689: Demographic and Microeconomic Aspects of Palaestina III in Interregional Perspective." In Elizabeth B. Aitken and John M Dossey, eds., *The Levant: Crossroads of Late Antiquity: History, Religion and Archaeology.* McGill University Monographs in Classical Archaeology and History 22. Leiden: Brill, 181–223.

Tromp de Roiter, S. 1932. "De vocis quae est ΦΙΛΑΝΘΡΩΠΙΑ significatione et usu." *Mnemosyne* 59: 271–306.

Trzcionka, Silke. 2007. *Magic and the Supernatural in Fourth-Century Syria.* London and New York: Routledge.

Tsafrir, Yoram, ed. 1993. *Ancient Churches Revealed.* Jerusalem: Israel Exploration Society.

Uhalde, Kevin. 2012. "Justice and Equality." In Johnson 2012: 764–88.

Uhlhorn, Gerhard. 1883. *Christian Charity in the Ancient Church.* Trans. Sophia Taylor. Edinburgh: Clark.

Urbanik, Jakub. 2009. "*P.Oxy.* LXIII 4397: The Monastery Comes First or Pious Reasons before Earthly Securities." In Boud'hors et al., 2009: 225–35.

Vailhé, Siméon. 1911. "Les philopones d' Oxyrhynque au IVᵉ siècle." *Echos d'Orient* 14: 277–78.

Van Dam, Raymond. 1995. "The Will of Gregory of Nazianzus." *JThS* n.s. 46: 118–48.

———. 1996. "Governors of Cappadocia During the Fourth Century." *Medieval Prosopography* 17: 7–93.

———. 2002. *Kingdom of Snow: Roman Rule and Greek Culture in Cappadocia.* Philadelphia: University of Pennsylvania Press.

Van den Ven, Paul. 1957. "Les Écrits de S. Syméon Stylite le Jeune avec trois semons inédits." *Le Muséon* 70: 1–57.

———. 1962. "Introduction." *La vie ancienne de S. Syméon Stylite le Jeune (521–592),* vol. 1. SH 32. Brussels: Société des Bollandistes, 11*–221*.

Van Esbroeck, Michael. 1996. "The Memra on the Parrot by Isaac of Antioch." *JThS* n.s. 47: 464–76.

Van Kooten, George H. 2010. "Pagan, Jewish, and Christian Philanthropy in Antiquity: A Pseudo-Clementine Keyword in Context." In Jan N. Bremmer, ed., *The Pseudo-Clementines.* Leuven: Peeters, 36–58.

Van Nuffelen, Peter. 2002. "Deux fausses lettres de Julien d'Apostat (La lettre aux juifs, Ep. 51 [Wright], et la lettre à Arsacius, Ep. 84 [Bidez])." *VC* 56: 131–50.

———. 2014. "Not the Last Pagan: Libanius between Elite Rhetoric and Religion." In Lieve Van Hoof, ed., *Libanius: A Critical Introduction.* Cambridge: Cambridge University Press, 293–314.

Van Renswoude, Irene. 2019. *The Rhetoric of Free Speech in Late Antiquity and the Early Middle Ages.* Cambridge: Cambridge University Press.

Van Rompey, Lucas. 2005. "Society and Community in the Christian East." In Maas 2005: 239–66.

Van Straten, F. T. 1981. "Gifts for the Gods." In Hendrik S. Versnel, ed., *Faith, Hope and Worship: Aspects of Religious Mentality in the Ancient World.* Leiden: Brill, 65–104.

Van Uytfanghe, Marc. 1993. "L'hagiographie: Un 'genre' chrétien ou antique tardif?" *AB* 111: 135–88.

Vasey, Vince. 1986. "The Social Ideas of Asterius of Amasea." *Augustinianum* 26: 413–36.

Vasileiou, Fotis. 2014. "For the Poor, the Family, the Friends: Gregory of Nazianzus' Testament in the Context of Early Christian Literature." In Caseau and Hübner 2014: 141–58.

Vecoli, Fabrizio. 2007. *Il sole e il fango. Puro e impuro tra i Padri del deserto.* Centro Alti Studi in Scienze Religiose 5. Rome: Edizioni di Storia e Letteratura.

Velkovska, Elena. 2001. "Funeral Rites according to the Byzantine Liturgical Sources." *DOP* 55: 21–45.

Veyne, Paul. 1976. *Le pain et le cirque: Sociologie historique d'un pluralisme politique.* L'Univers historique. Paris: Seuil.

Viard, Paul. 1969. "Hospitalité." *DSp* 7: 808–831. Paris: Beauchesne.

Vikan, Gary. 1984. "Art, Medicine, and Magic in Early Byzantium." *DOP* 38: 65–86.

———. 2010. *Early Byzantine Pilgrimage Art.* 2nd ed. Dumbarton Oaks Byzantine Collection Publications 3. Washington, DC: Dumbarton Oaks Research Library and Collection.

Villagomez, Cynthia. 1998. *The Fields, Flocks, and Finances of Monks: Economic Life at Nestorian Monasteries, 500–850 CE.* PhD diss., University of California at Los Angeles.

Viner, Jacob. 1978. *Religious Thought and Economic Society: Four Chapters of an Unfinished Work by Jacob Viner,* ed. Jacques Melitz and Donald Winch. Durham, NC: Duke University Press.

Visser, Margaret. 2009. *The Gift of Thanks.* Boston: Houghton Mifflin Harcourt.

Vivian, Timothy. 1999. "Monks, Middle Egypt, and Metanoia: The *Life of Phib* by Papohe the Steward. (Translation and Introduction)." *JECS* 7: 547–71.

———. 2005. "Figures in the Carpet: Macarius the Great, Isaiah of Scetis, Daniel of Scetis and Monastic Spirituality in the Wadi al-Natrun (Scetis) from the Fourth to the Sixth Century." *American Benedictine Review* 56: 2: 117–51.

———. 2009. *Mark the Monk: Counsels on the Spiritual Life.* PPS 37. Crestwood, NY: St. Vladimir's Press.

Vogt, Hermann. 1993. *Origenes: Der Kommentar zum Evangelium nach Matthäus.* Bibliothek der griechischen Literatur 38. Stuttgart: Anton Hiersemann.

Volk, Robert. 1983. *Gesundheitswesen und Wohltätigkeit im Spiegel der byzantinischen Klostertypika.* Miscellanea byzantina monacensia 28. Munich: Institut für Byzantinistik und neugriechische Philologie.

Vööbus, Arthur. 1958. *History of Asceticism in the Syrian Orient,* vol. 1. CSCO 184/Subsidia 14. Louvain: Secrétariat du CorpusSCO.

———. 1960. *History of Asceticism in the Syrian Orient,* vol. 2. CSCO 197/Subsidia 17. Louvain: Secrétariat du CorpusSCO.

Waldstein, Wolfgang. 1986. *Operae Libertorum: Untersuchungen zur Dienstpflicht freigelassener Sklaven.* Stuttgart: Franz Steiner.

Walker, Joel T. 2006. *The Legend of Mar Qardagh: Narrative and Christian Heroism in Late Antique Iraq.* TCH 40. Berkeley: University of California Press.

———. 2010. "Ascetic Literacy: Books and Readers in East Syrian Monastic Tradition." In Henning Börm and Josef Weisehöfer, eds., *Commutatio et Contentio: Studies in the Late Roman, Sasanian and Early Islamic Near East in Memory of Zeev Rubin.* Düsseldorf: Wellem Verlag, 307–45.

Walmsley, Alan. 2007. "Economic Development and the Nature of Settlement in the Towns and Countryside of Syria-Palestine, ca. 565–800." *DOP* 61: 319–59.

Walters, Colin. 1974. *Monastic Archaeology in Egypt*. Modern Egyptology Series. Warminster: Aris and Phillips.

Watts, Edward. 2010. *Riot in Alexandria: Tradition and Group Dynamics in Late Antique Pagan and Christian Communities*. TCH 46. Berkeley: University of California Press.

———. 2015. *The Final Pagan Generation*. TCH 53. Berkeley: University of California Press.

Weidmann, Denis. 1984. "Première image du développementdes Kellia." In Rodolphe Kasser, ed. *Le site monastique des Kellia (Basse-Égypte): Recherches des Années 1981–1983*. Louvain: Éditions Peeters, 59–62.

Weigand, Edmund. 1914. "Das Theodosiosklöster." *Byzantinische Zeitschrift* 23: 167–216.

Weimer, Hans-Ulrich. 1995. *Libanios und Julian. Studien zum Verhältnis von Rhetorik und Politik im vierten Jahrhundert n. Chr.* Vestigia: Beiträge zur Alten Geschichte 46. Munich: Beck.

Weiner, Annette. 1985. "Inalienable Wealth." *American Ethnologist* 12: 210–27.

———. 1992. *Inalienable Possessions: The Paradox of Keeping-While-Giving*. Berkeley: University of California Press.

Weinfeld, Moshe. 1995. *Social Justice in Ancient Israel and the Ancient Near East*. Jerusalem: Magnes Press.

Weiss, Zeev. 2019. "Defining Limits in Times of Shifting Borders: Jewish Life in Fifth-Century Palestine." In Jan W. Drijvers and Noel Lenski, eds., *The Fifth Century: Age of Transformation. Proceedings of the 12th Biennial Shifting Frontiers in Late Antiquity Conference*. Munera: Studi Storici sulla Tarda Antichità 46. Bari: Edipuglia, 105–20.

Wendt, Heidi. 2016. *At the Temple Gates: The Religion of Freelance Experts in the Roman Empire*. New York: Oxford University Press.

Wessel, Susan. 2016. *Passion and Compassion in Early Christianity*. Cambridge: Cambridge University Press.

Whitby, Michael. 1988. *The Emperor Maurice and His Historian: Theophylact Simocatta on Persian and Balkan Warfare*. Oxford: Clarendon Press.

———. 1998. "Evagrius on Emperors and Patriarchs." In Mary Whitby, ed., *The Propaganda of Power: The Role of Panegyric in Late Antiquity*. Mnemosyne 183. Leiden: Brill, 321–44.

———. 2001. "The Successors of Justinian." In Cameron, Ward-Perkins, and Whitby 2001: 86–111.

Whiting, Marlena. 2016. "Monastery Hostels in Late Antique Syria, Palestine, and Transjordan." In Zbigniew T. Fiema, Jaakko Frösén, and Maija Holappa, eds. *Petra—The Mountain of Aaron II: The Nabataean Sanctuary and the Byzantine Monastery*. Helsinki: Societas Scientiarum Fennica, 108–13.

Wickham, Christopher. 2009. *The Inheritance of Rome: Illuminating the Dark Ages, 400–1000*. Penguin History of Europe 2. London: Penguin.

———. 2010. "Conclusion." In Davis and Fouracre 2010: 238–61.

Wilfong, Terry G. 2002. *The Women of Jeme: Lives in a Coptic Town in Late Antique Egypt*. Ann Arbor: University of Michigan Press.

———. 2004. "Christian Monasticism and Pilgrimage in Northern Egypt." In Roger Bagnall and Dominic W. Rathbone, eds., *Egypt from Alexander to the Early Christians: An Archaeological and Historical Guide*. Los Angeles: J. P. Getty Museum, 107–26.

Wilken, Robert L. 1992. *The Land Called Holy: Palestine in Christian History and Thought*. New Haven, CT: Yale University Press.

Winlock, Herbert E., Walter E. Crum, and Evelyn-White, Hugh G., eds. 1926; repr. 1973. *The Monastery of Epiphanius at Thebes*, 2 vols. New York: Arno Press.

Winslow, Donald F. 1965. "Gregory of Nazianzus and Love for the Poor." *Anglican Theological Review* 47: 348–59.

Wipszycka, Ewa. 1970. "Les confréries dans la vie religieuse de l'Égypte chrétienne." In Deborah H. Samuel, ed., *Proceedings of the Twelfth International Congress of Papyrology*. Toronto: Hakkert, 511–25.

———. 1972. *Les ressources et les activités économiques des églises en Égypte du Ve au VIIIe siècle*. Papyrologica Bruxellensia 10. Brussels: Fondation égyptologique Reine Élisabeth.

———. 1991. "Diaconia." In Aziz S. Atiya, ed., *The Coptic Encyclopedia*, vol. 3. New York: MacMillan, 895–97.

———. 1996a. "Contribution à l'étude de l'économies de la congrégation pachômienne." *JJP* 26: 167–210.

———. 1996b. "La monachisme égyptien et les villes." In Ewa Wipszycka, *Études sur le christianisme dans l'Égypte de l' antiquité tardive*. Studia ephemeridis Augustinienne 52. Rome: Institutum Patristicum Augustinianum, 1996, 281–336.

———. 1997. "La sovvenzione constantiniana in favore del clero." *Rendiconti Lincei* 8: 483–98.

———. 2001. "Le Fonctionnement interne des monastères et des laures en Égypte du point de vue économique à propos d'une publication récente de textes coptes de Bawit." *JJP* 31: 169–86.

———. 2002. "L'économie du patriarcat alexandrin à travers les Vies de saint Jean l'Aumônier." In Christian Décobert, ed., *Alexandrie médiévale*, vol. 2. Études Alexandrines 8. Cairo: Institut français d'archéologie orientale, 61–81.

———. 2005. "Le nombre des moines dans les communautés monastiques d'Égypte." *JJP* 35: 265–309.

———. 2007. "The Institutional Church." In Bagnall 2007: 331–49.

———. 2008. "Le monastère d'Apa Apollôs: un cas typique ou un cas exceptionnel?" In Jean-Luc Fournet, ed., *Les archives de Dioscore d'Aphrodité cent ans après leur découverte: Histoire et culture dans l'Égypte byzantine. Actes du colloque de Strasbourg (8–10 décembre 2005)*. Paris: De Boccard, 261–73.

———. 2009. *Moines et communautés monastiques en Egypte, IVe–VIIIe siecles*. JJP Supplement 11. Warsaw: Journal of Juristic Papyrology.

———. 2011. "Resources and Economic Activities of the Egyptian Monastic Communities (4th–8th Century)." *JJP* 41: 159–263.

———. 2015. *The Alexandrian Church: People and Institutions*. JJP Supplement 25. Warsaw: Journal of Juristic Papyrology.

———. 2018. *The Second Gift of the Nile: Monks and Monasticism in Late Antique Egypt*, trans. Damian Jasi´niski. JJP Supplement 33. Warsaw: Journal of Juristic Papyrology.

Witters, D. Willibrord. 1974. "Pauvres et pauvreté dans les coutumiers monastiques du Moyen Age." In M. Mollat, ed., *Études sur l'histoire de la pauvreté*. Paris: Publications de la Sorbonne, 177–217.

Wolska-Conus, W. 1968. *Cosmas Indicopleustès: Topographie chrétienne*, vol. 1. SC 141. Paris: Le Cerf.

Wood, Diana. 2002. *Medieval Economic Thought*. Cambridge: Cambridge University Press.

Wood, Ian. 2000. "The Exchange of Gifts among the Late Antique Aristocracy." In Martín Almagro-Gorbea, José M. Álvaraz Martínez, José M. Blázquez Martínez, and Salvador Rovira, eds., *El disco de Teodosio*. Madrid: Real Academia de la Historia, 301–14.

Wood, Susan. 2006. *The Proprietary Church in the Medieval West*. Oxford: Oxford University Press.

Wortley, John. 2013. "How a Monk Ought to Relate to his Neighbor." *GRBS* 53: 726–41.

Yasin, Ann Marie. 2009. *Saints and Church Spaces in the Late Antique Mediterranean: Architecture, Cult, and Community*. Cambridge: Cambridge University Press.

———. 2017. "Renovation and the Early Byzantine Church: Staging Past and Prayer." In Bitton-Ashkelony and Krueger 2017: 89–115.

Yousif, Pierre. 1979–1980. "Le repas fraternel ou l'agape dans les memre sur la table attributes à saint Ephrem." *Parole de l'Orient* 9: 51–66.

Zeisel, William N. 1975. *An Economic Survey of the Early Byzantine Church*. PhD diss., Rutgers University.

Zelizer, Viviana. 1994. *The Social Meaning of Money*. New York: Basic Books.

Zemon Davis, Natalie. 2000. *The Gift in Sixteenth-Century France*. Madison: University of Wisconsin Press.

Zuckerman, Constantin. 2004a. *Du village à l'empire: Autour du registre fiscal d'Aphroditô (525/526)*. Centre de Recherch d'histoire et civilization de Byzance 16. Paris: Association des amis du Centre d'histoire et civilization de Byzance.

———. 2004b. "Les deux Dioscore d'Afroditè ou les limites de la pétition." In Denis Feissel and Jean Gascou, eds., *La pétition à Byzance*. Paris: Association des amis du Centre d'histoire et civilization de Byzance, 74–92.

Zuiderhoek, Arjan. 2005. "The Icing on the Cake: Benefactors, Economics, and Public Buildings in Roman Asia Minor." In Stephen Mitchell and Constantina Katsari, eds., *Patterns in the Economy of Roman Asia Minor*. Swansea: Classical Press of Wales, 167–86.

Zuiderhoek, Arjan. 2009. *The Politics of Munificence in the Roman Empire: Citizens, Elites, and Benefactors in Asia Minor*. Cambridge: Cambridge University Press.

Founded in 1893,
UNIVERSITY OF CALIFORNIA PRESS
publishes bold, progressive books and journals
on topics in the arts, humanities, social sciences,
and natural sciences—with a focus on social
justice issues—that inspire thought and action
among readers worldwide.

The UC PRESS FOUNDATION
raises funds to uphold the press's vital role
as an independent, nonprofit publisher, and
receives philanthropic support from a wide
range of individuals and institutions—and from
committed readers like you. To learn more, visit
ucpress.edu/supportus.